Innovative Approaches of Data Visualization and Visual Analytics

Mao Lin Huang
University of Technology, Sydney, Australia

Weidong Huang
CSIRO, Australia

A volume in the Advances in Data Mining and Database Management (ADMDM) Book Series

Managing Director:	Lindsay Johnston
Editorial Director:	Joel Gamon
Production Manager:	Jennifer Yoder
Publishing Systems Analyst:	Adrienne Freeland
Development Editor:	Christine Smith
Assistant Acquisitions Editor:	Kayla Wolfe
Typesetter:	Travis Gundrum
Cover Design:	Jason Mull

Published in the United States of America by
Information Science Reference (an imprint of IGI Global)
701 E. Chocolate Avenue
Hershey PA 17033
Tel: 717-533-8845
Fax: 717-533-8661
E-mail: cust@igi-global.com
Web site: http://www.igi-global.com

Library of Congress Cataloging-in-Publication Data

Innovative approaches of data visualization and visual analytics / Mao Lin Huang and Weidong Huang, editors.
    pages cm
  Summary: "This book evaluates the latest trends and developments in force-based data visualization techniques, addressing issues in the design, development, evaluation, and application of algorithms and network topologies"-- Provided by publisher.
  ISBN 978-1-4666-4309-3 (hardcover) -- ISBN 978-1-4666-4310-9 (ebook) -- ISBN 978-1-4666-4311-6 (print & perpetual access) 1. Information visualization. I. Huang, Mao Lin. II. Huang, Weidong, 1968-
  QA76.9.I52I56 2014
  001.4'226--dc23
                                        2013011317

This book is published in the IGI Global book series Advances in Data Mining and Database Management (ADMDM) (ISSN: 2327-1981; eISSN: 2327-199X)

British Cataloguing in Publication Data
A Cataloguing in Publication record for this book is available from the British Library.

Advances in Data Mining and Database Management (ADMDM) Book Series

David Taniar
Monash University, Australia

ISSN: 2327-1981
EISSN: 2327-199X

MISSION

With the large amounts of information available to businesses in today's digital world, there is a need for methods and research on managing and analyzing the information that is collected and stored. IT professionals, software engineers, and business administrators, along with many other researchers and academics, have made the fields of data mining and database management into ones of increasing importance as the digital world expands. The **Advances in Data Mining & Database Management (ADMDM) Book Series** aims to bring together research in both fields in order to become a resource for those involved in either field.

COVERAGE

- Cluster Analysis
- Customer Analytics
- Data Mining
- Data Quality
- Data Warehousing
- Database Security
- Database Testing
- Decision Support Systems
- Enterprise Systems
- Text Mining

IGI Global is currently accepting manuscripts for publication within this series. To submit a proposal for a volume in this series, please contact our Acquisition Editors at Acquisitions@igi-global.com or visit: http://www.igi-global.com/publish/.

Titles in this Series

For a list of additional titles in this series, please visit: www.igi-global.com

DISSEMINATOR OF KNOWLEDGE

www.igi-global.com

701 E. Chocolate Ave., Hershey, PA 17033
Order online at www.igi-global.com or call 717-533-8845 x100
To place a standing order for titles released in this series, contact: cust@igi-global.com
Mon-Fri 8:00 am - 5:00 pm (est) or fax 24 hours a day 717-533-8661

List of Reviewers

Jie Hua, *UTS, Australia*
Mao Lin Huang, *UTS, Australia*
Tony Huang, *CSIRO, Australia*
Tze-Haw Huang, *UTS, Australia*
Christy (Jie) Liang, *UTS, Australia*
Liangfu Lu, *UTS, Australia*
Wen Bo Wang, *UTS, Australia*
Jinson Zhang, *UTS, Australia*

Table of Contents

Detailed Table of Contents

Chapter 1

Heekyoung Jung, University of Cincinnati, USA
Tanyoung Kim, Georgia Institute of Technology, USA
Yang Yang, Dublin City University, Ireland
Luis Carli, University of São Paulo, Brazil
Marco Carnesecchi, Università della Valle d'Aosta, Italy & Università di Siena, Italy
Antonio Rizzo, Università di Siena, Italy
Cathal Gurrin, Dublin City University, Ireland

Data visualization has been one of the major interests among interaction designers thanks to the recent advances of visualization authoring tools. Using such tools including programming languages with Graphics APIs, websites with chart topologies, and open source libraries and component models, interaction designers can more effectively create data visualization harnessing their prototyping skills and aesthetic sensibility. However, there still exist technical and methodological challenges for interaction designers in jumping into the scene. In this article, the authors introduce five case studies of data visualization that highlight different design aspects and issues of the visualization process. The authors also discuss the new roles of designers in this interdisciplinary field and the ways of utilizing, as well as enhancing, visualization tools for the better support of designers.

Chapter 2

Chad A. Steed, Oak Ridge National Laboratory, USA
J. Edward Swan II, Mississippi State University, USA
Patrick J. Fitzpatrick, Mississippi State University, USA
T.J. Jankun-Kelly, Mississippi State University, USA

New approaches that combine the strengths of humans and machines are necessary to equip analysts with the proper tools for exploring today's increasingly complex, multivariate data sets. In this chapter, a visual data mining framework, called the Multidimensional Data eXplorer (MDX), is described that addresses the challenges of today's data by combining automated statistical analytics with a highly interactive parallel coordinates based canvas. In addition to several intuitive interaction capabilities, this framework offers a rich set of graphical statistical indicators, interactive regression analysis, visual correlation mining, automated axis arrangements and filtering, and data classification techniques. This chapter provides a detailed description of the system as well as a discussion of key design aspects and critical feedback from domain experts.

Moonyati Yatid, University of Sydney, Australia
Masahiro Takatsuka, University of Sydney, Australia

The continuously increasing amount of digital information available to computer users has led to the wide use of notification systems. Although these systems could support the management of information, they could also be an interruption to primary work. To minimize this interruption, a number of approaches, which notify the different categorical information, have been introduced. In this work, we focused on understanding the effectiveness of different types of visual cues to effectively represent categorical notification. Five basic visual parameters of motion, colour, shape, motion and spatial were chosen to represent sets of two categories, four categories, six categories and eight categories of information. The effectiveness of these visual cues in assisting users' ability to decode the categorical cues was examined through a series of experimental studies. Findings suggest the superiority of using colour, shape, and spatial cues to represent categorical information. Post experiment questionnaire reveals possible reasons for their efficiency. Spatial memory supports spatial cues while linguistic influence supports the shape/colour cues. The unsuitability of size parameter is possibly due to not being able to measure the cues against something during the encoding process. This makes it difficult to determine how each cue differs from the rest of the cues in the parameter, especially when number of categories increase. As for the motion parameter, encoding the cues took far longer response times, although time taken is consistent across number of categories. The different effects of these basic visual cues suggest the importance of careful design selection to ensure successful visualization.

Keqin Wu, University of Maryland Baltimore County, USA
Song Zhang, Mississippi State University, USA

While uncertainty in scientific data attracts an increasing research interest in the visualization community, two critical issues remain insufficiently studied: (1) visualizing the impact of the uncertainty of a data set on its features and (2) interactively exploring 3D or large 2D data sets with uncertainties. In this chapter, a suite of feature-based techniques is developed to address these issues. First, an interactive visualization tool for exploring scalar data with data-level, contour-level, and topology-level uncertainties is developed. Second, a framework of visualizing feature-level uncertainty is proposed to study the uncertain feature deviations in both scalar and vector data sets. With quantified representation and interactive capability, the proposed feature-based visualizations provide new insights into the uncertainties of both data and their features which otherwise would remain unknown with the visualization of only data uncertainties.

Angela M. Zoss, Duke University, USA

The subject of how visualizations and graphics in general can be understood by their viewers draws on theories from many fields of research. Such theories might address the formal structure of the visualization, the style and graphic design skills of the creator, the task driving the viewer's interaction with the visualization, the type of data being represented, or the skills and experiences of viewer. This chapter focuses on this last question and presents a set of interrelated constructs and viewer traits that contribute to (or interfere with) a viewer's ability to analyze a particular data visualization. The review covers spatial thinking skills, cognitive styles, mental models, and cognitive load in its discussion of theoretical constructs related to graphic comprehension. The review also addresses how these cognitive processes vary by age, sex, and disciplinary background–the most common demographic characteristics studied in relation to graphic comprehension. Together, the constructs and traits contribute to a diverse and nuanced understanding of the viewers of data visualizations.

Chapter 6

With the latest developments in technology, several researchers have integrated other sensorymotor channels in the analysis of scientific datasets. In addition to vision, auditory feedbacks and haptic interactions have been exploited. In this chapter we study how these modalities can contribute to effective analysis processes. Based on psychophysical characteristics of humans the author argues that haptics should be used in order to improve interactions of the user with the dataset to analyze. The author describes a classification that highlights four tasks for which haptics seems to present advantages over vision and audio. Proposed taxonomy is divided into four categories: Select, Locate, Connect and Arrange. Moreover, this work provides a complete view on the contribution of haptics in analysis of scientific datasets.

Chapter 7

Large volumes of heterogeneous data from multiple sources need to be analyzed during the surveillance of large sea, air, and land areas. Timely detection and identification of anomalous behavior or any threat activity is an important objective for enabling homeland security. While it is worth acknowledging that many existing mining applications support identification of anomalous behavior, autonomous anomaly detection systems for area surveillance are rarely used in the real world since these capabilities and applications present two critical challenges: they need to provide adequate user support and they need to involve the user in the underlying detection process. Visualization and interaction play a crucial role in providing adequate user support and involving the user in the detection process. Therefore, this chapter elaborates on the role of visualization and interaction in the anomaly detection process, using the surveillance of sea areas as a case study. After providing a brief description of how operators identify conflict traffic situations and anomalies, the anomaly detection problem is characterized from a data mining point of view, suggesting how operators may enhance the process through visualization and interaction.

Chapter 8

This chapter discusses how various approaches to information visualization can be used to assist users in understanding large digital collections and discovering relationships among the entities involved explicitly or implicitly in their development including people, organizations, and documents. Our main postulate is that visualization schemes, such as fisheye views, starfield displays, or self-organizing maps, when integrated and coupled with semantic layouts of topic areas, can significantly facilitate the analysis and discovery of existing and potential relationships among a wide range of entities. A series of developments illustrates how users play a key role in determining advantages and limitations of information visualization schemes, as well as in finding opportunities for improvement and new application areas.

Highlighting has been known as a basic viewing control mechanism in computer graphics and visualization for guiding users' attention in reading diagrams, images, graphs, and digital texts. Due to the rapid development of theory and practice in information visualization and visual analytics, the role of 'highlighting' in computer graphics has been extended from just acting as a viewing control to being part of an interaction control and a visual recommendation mechanism that is important in modern information visualization and visual analytics. In this chapter, the authors present a brief literature review. They try to assign the word 'highlighting' a contemporary definition and attempt to give a formal summarization and classification of the existing and potential 'highlighting' methods that are to be applied in Information Visualization, Visual Analytics, and Knowledge Visualization. We also propose a new three-layer model of 'highlighting' and discuss the responsibilities of each layer accordingly.

In today's networked economy, contracts are everywhere. Many of them are watertight and legally perfect documents attempting to refer to every conceivable contingency. For people expected to use or comply with them, such contracts are often difficult to read, comprehend, and/or implement. As an alternative to the current predominantly legal and textual approach, the authors propose a user-centered, visualized approach aimed at better usability and easier implementation. Both consumer and commercial contracts should be communicated in simpler and more user-friendly ways, and we believe that visualization can play a fundamental role in achieving this. This chapter introduces the concept of contract visualization and some early examples produced in this novel field. Results obtained in the first year of a five-year research project, carried out in collaboration with a partner company, indicate preliminary confirmation of positive effects in improving contract usability and related user experience through visualization.

This chapter presents an approach to enable non-visualization experts to craft advanced visualizations through the use of natural language as the primary interface. The main challenge in this research is in determining how to translate imprecise verbal queries into effective visualizations. To demonstrate the viability of the concept, the authors developed and evaluated a prototype, Articulate, which allows users to simply ask the computer for questions about their data and have it automatically generate visualizations that answer these questions. The authors discovered that by relieving the user of the burden of learning how to use a complex interface, they enable them to focus on articulating better scientific questions and wasting less time in producing unintended visualizations.

Chapter 12

Although in recent years the Quantified Self (QS) application domain is growing, there are still some palpable fundamental problems that relegate the QS movement in a phase of low maturity. The first is a technological problem, and specifically, a lack of maturity in technologies for the collection, processing, and data visualization. This is accompanied by a perhaps more fundamental problem of deficit, bias, and lack of integration of aspects concerning the human side of the QS idea. The step that the authors tried to make in this chapter is to highlight aspects that could lead to a more robust approach in QS area. This was done, primarily, through a new approach in data visualization and, secondly, through a necessary management of complexity, both in technological terms and, for what concerns the human side of the whole issue, in theoretical terms. The authors have gone a little further stressing how the future directions of research could lead to significant impacts on both individual and social level.

Chapter 13

As geospatial visualizations grow in popularity, their role in human activities is also evolving. While maps have been used to support higher-level cognitive activities such as decision-making, sense making, and knowledge discovery, traditionally their use in such activities has been partial. Nowadays they are being used at various stages of such activities. This trend is simultaneously being accompanied with another shift: a movement from the design and use of data-centered geospatial visualizations to activity-centered visualizations. Data-centered visualizations are primarily focused on representation of data from data layers; activity-centered visualizations, not only represent the data layers, but also focus on users' needs and real-world activities—such as storytelling and comparing data layers with other information. Examples of this shift are being seen in some mashup techniques that deviate from standard data-driven visualization designs. Beyond the discussion of the needed shift, this chapter presents ideas for designing human-activity-centered geospatial visualizations.

Chapter 14

Learning Management Systems (LMS) may use Information Visualization techniques and concepts for presenting their large amounts of data, in order to ease the monitoring and analysis of students learning process problems. Nonetheless, the generally adopted approaches are based on presenting data obtained by predefined database queries only, which does not consider unforeseen situations derived from final user's knowledge about e-learning domain. Therefore, the purpose of this work is to provide a resource for LMS users to define and execute queries related to these unforeseen situations. This resource is a prototype by which users may access a remote LMS database, create their own queries by selecting database attributes they want to analyze, and represent query results by means of automatically selected interactive graphical representations. User evaluations indicate that the approach is appropriate and points out possible enhancements.

Liese Zahabi, Weber State University, USA

In many ways, the promise of the Internet has been overshadowed by a sense of information overload and anxiety for many users. The production and publication of online material has become increasingly accessible and affordable, creating a confusing glut of information users must sift through to locate exactly what they want or need. Even a fundamental Google search can often prove paralyzing. In this chapter, the author examines the points at which design plays a role in the online search process, reconciles those points with the nature of sensemaking and the limitations of working memory, and suggests ways to support users with an information-triage system. The author then describes a speculative online searching prototype that explores these issues and the possibilities for information-triage.

Wei Lai, Swinburne University of Technology, Australia
Weidong Huang, CSIRO ICT Centre, Sydney, Australia

This chapter presents a framework for developing diagram applications. The diagrams refer to those graphs where nodes vary in shape and size used in real world applications, such as flowcharts, UML diagrams, and E-R diagrams. The framework is based on a model the authors developed for diagrams. The model is robust for diagrams and it can represent a wide variety of applications and support the development of powerful application-specific functions. The framework based on this model supports the development of automatic layout techniques for diagrams and the development of the linkage between the graph structure and applications. Automatic layout for diagrams is demonstrated and two case studies for diagram applications are presented.

John McAuley, Trinity College, Ireland
Alex O'Connor, Trinity College, Ireland
Dave Lewis, Trinity College, Ireland

Online communities provide technical support for organisations on a range of products and services. These communities are managed by dedicated online community managers who nurture and help the community grow. While visual analytics are increasingly used to support a range of data-intensive management processes, similar techniques have not been adopted into the community management field. Although relevant tools exist, the majority is developed in the lab, without conducting a domain analysis or eliciting user requirements, or is designed to support more general analytic tasks. In this chapter, the authors describe a case study in which we design, develop, and evaluate a visual analytics application with the help of Symantec's online community management team. The authors suggest that the approach and the resulting application, called Petri, is an important step to promoting online community management as a strategic and data-driven process.

Today, existing graph visualizers are not popular for debugging purposes because they are mostly visualization-oriented, rather than task-oriented, implementing general-purpose graph drawing algorithms. The latter explains why prominent integrated development environments still adopt traditional tree views. The authors introduce a debugging assistant with a visualization technique designed to better fit the actual task of defect detection in runtime object networks, while supporting advanced inspection and configuration features. Its design has been centered on the study of the actual programmer needs in the context of the debugging task, emphasizing: 1.) visualization style inspired by a social networking metaphor enabling easily identify who deploys objects (clients) and whom objects deploy (servers); 2.) inspection features to easily review object contents and associations and to search content patterns (currently regular expressions only); and 3.) interactively configurable levels of information detail, supporting off-line inspection and multiple concurrent views.

Preface

As technologies in storage media continue to advance, the data we need to deal with is becoming increasingly complex and large. Accordingly, making sense of this vast amount of data becomes a challenging issue. Researchers and engineers from a range of application domains and backgrounds are striving to find solutions to meet this challenge. Thanks to recent rapid developments in visualization research and engineering, visual analytics has become a hot topic as well as an active research area that requires an interdisciplinary approach. Visual analytics makes use of powerful human visual system together with other methods and technologies to untangle the complexity of massive data.

The book of *Innovative Approaches of Data Visualization and Visual Analytics* is aimed to present latest developments and trends in data visualization and visual analytics. This book is a timely collection of latest research findings. The chapters of this book are rigorously reviewed and carefully selected to reflect the current state-of-the-art of research in this emerging field. This comprehensive collection will be beneficial to all researchers and professionals working in this promising field. Advanced-level students in science and engineering will also find this book useful as a secondary text or reference.

This book includes 18 chapters that are written by internationally known experts and active researchers. The authors are from a range of disciplines, such as psychology, business, machine learning, human computer interaction, and visualization. These contributions again demonstrate that research in data visualization and visual analytics goes beyond the field of visualization and should benefit from cross-disciplinary cooperation among researchers who have interest in this emerging and increasingly important area. In this book, chapters are grouped into two categories: Foundation and Application, with nine chapters in foundation and nine chapters in application.

Finally we would like to thank all authors who submitted their works for consideration. We also thank our reviewers who worked hard to give their quality feedback within a tight time frame. Last but not least, a big thank-you goes to IGI Global editor Christine Smith for her professional assistance throughout the project.

Weidong Huang
CSIRO ICT Centre, Sydney, Australia

Mao Lin Huang
University of Technology, Sydney, Australia

June 11, 2013

Chapter 1
Aesthetics in Data Visualization:
Case Studies and Design Issues

Heekyoung Jung
University of Cincinnati, USA

Luis Carli
University of São Paulo, Brazil

Tanyoung Kim
Georgia Institute of Technology, USA

Marco Carnesecchi
Università della Valle d'Aosta & Università di Siena, Italy

Yang Yang
Dublin City University, Ireland

Antonio Rizzo
Università di Siena, Italy

Cathal Gurrin
Dublin City University, Ireland

ABSTRACT

Data visualization has been one of the major interests among interaction designers thanks to the recent advances of visualization authoring tools. Using such tools including programming languages with Graphics APIs, websites with chart topologies, and open source libraries and component models, interaction designers can more effectively create data visualization harnessing their prototyping skills and aesthetic sensibility. However, there still exist technical and methodological challenges for interaction designers in jumping into the scene. In this article, the authors introduce five case studies of data visualization that highlight different design aspects and issues of the visualization process. The authors also discuss the new roles of designers in this interdisciplinary field and the ways of utilizing, as well as enhancing, visualization tools for the better support of designers.

DOI: 10.4018/978-1-4666-4309-3.ch001

INTRODUCTION: DATA VISUALIZATION DESIGN

Nowadays we are flooded with data of diverse kinds due to the increasing computational capability and accessibility. Specifically, in addition to public data available on the Internet (e.g., census, demographics, environmental data), data pertaining personal daily activities are now more easily collected, for example, through mobile devices that can log people's running distances and time or their manual record of nutrition consumption. Due to such expanded sources of data, there appear new applications that involve data collection, visualization, exploration, and distribution in daily contexts. These applications do not only display static information but also let users navigate the data in forms of interactive visualizations. This emerging trend has brought both opportunities and challenges to interaction designers to develop new approaches to designing data-based applications.

Conveying information has been one of main functions of graphic and communication design since the analog printing era. The focus of information design is the communicative and aesthetic presentation of structured data as in an example of subway route map. In treating the increasing volumes of unprocessed data accessible either from public media or personal devices, the approaches of information design are now more diverse with the influence of other disciplines (Pousman & Stasko, 2007). Specifically, unlike information design in a traditional and confined manner, data visualization starts with the data that did not proceed through structuring and exist often in large volumes and complicated formats (Manovich, 2010). Thus, data visualization requires designers to obtain diverse knowledge and skill sets in addition to their visual aesthetic senses. The new requirements include human visual perception and cognition, statistics, and computational data mining.

Moreover, as data visualization has been more broadly applied to end-user services, interaction and experiential qualities need to be more critically considered. Those qualities of data application do not only rely on the usability of data perception or task-based navigation but also build up on aesthetics that affords engaging and exploratory data navigation. The latter have been remained as a less investigated area than the former due to the strong disciplinary tradition of data visualization in computer science and cognitive science.

Furthermore, visualizations are presented, used, and shared in diverse contexts from science labs to online journalism sites, to personal mobile devices. This means that data visualization has become a truly interdisciplinary field of research and practice by weaving informatics, programming, graphic design, and even media art (Vande Moere & Purchase, 2011).

In what follows, we overview current design approaches and tools for data visualization, then introduce five case studies for further discussion of design issues, process and tools in regard to aesthetics in data visualization.

CURRENT TOOLS AND PROBLEMS IN AESTHETICS OF DATA VISUALIZATION

In recent years visualization scientists, mostly from computer science, have suggested many visualization-authoring tools with a hope of expanding the creators of visualizations and the contexts of their use. We suppose these tools are largely categorized into three kinds—1.) a standalone programming language and its Integrated Development Environment (IDE) such as Adobe Flash ActionScript (Adobe) and Processing (Processing 2), 2.) online or installation-required programs that provide visualizations of given chart topologies, such as ManyEyes (IBM) and Tableau Public(Tableau, 2013), and 3.) libraries, toolkits or component model architecture integrated with existing programming language, such as d3.js (Bostock, 2012) and gRaphaël.js(Baranovsky) for web documents.

These tools certainly open new spaces in which designers can apply visualization techniques with less effort and can exert their aesthetic expressions. However, throughout the entire process from data acquisition to visualization, there appear challenging aspects for the specific goal—*the aesthetic and interactive qualities* of visualization, and for the specific group of authors—*interaction designers*.

Online tools or visualization applications provide a set of chart templates as a means of presenting complex data into perceivable information. However, the subtle variations of graphic and interactive design attributes are not fully considered in the existing visualization tools, resulting in excluding designers who wants to have the full freedom of aesthetics and expressiveness. Thus, aesthetic consideration is limited to selecting colors or symbols at a later phase of visualization. Visualization libraries, which are provided and shared by altruistic and enthusiastic visualization experts, have expanded interaction designers' job. However, the initial learning curves include the experiences of programming to some extent. Regardless of old-school graphic designers, interaction designers who do not have extensive computer science knowledge may feel difficulty in first facing the libraries and toolkits. The lack of the fundamental knowledge and tactical coding tips in the mother programing language and the library may results in the abandon of aesthetic expression.

In sum, the tools have limitations in aesthetic expression due to either the lack of expressive freedom or the requirements of computer science and programming knowledge. The more significant issue is that the aesthetic concern pertains to the mere surface of visualization, in other words, "making pretty appearance" with the previously processed and well-formatted dataset. We acknowledge that the visually pleasing appearance is a critical aspect of data visualization, especially when it comes to the job of graphic and interaction designers. However we argue that the aesthetic consideration of data visualization goes far beyond that, covering the wider process from the process of *obtaining* and *organizing* data, to *composing* and *narrating* meaningful messages from the given data, and *distributing* the visualizations for the audience's access (Segel & Heer, 2010). In this sense, when we discuss aesthetics of data visualization in this article, it is not only about the look and feel of data representation. Instead, aesthetics should be approached from this holistic perspective. Considering the situations and aesthetics of use is a significant part of the emerging research and practice agendas in interaction and experience design. However, we argue that in the field of data visualization, the concept of aesthetics is still remained as a look of visualization techniques.

Here we introduce the issues of designing visualizations focusing on the aesthetic values throughout the entire process. Unlike general interface design projects, data visualization may not be directly simulated in wireframe forms without a broader picture of how data are actually collected and organized. For example, multiple datasets can be layered in one frame through different modes. In this case, interactive and temporal attributes such as animation and transition become critical aspects, which should result in guiding users' data navigation in easier manners. However, current prototyping approaches are limited in fully supporting such dynamic navigation to some extent. On one hand, designers have used print-based mock-ups of static visualization images; they can produce these with Microsoft Excel, which is limited in demonstrating interactive aspects of data visualization. On the other hand, a programming-b approach can build high fidelity prototypes with interactivity by loading actual data. However, apparently it demands designers too much time and effort to learn a new skillset of coding. Even though designers are willing to learn programming, they often get exhausted in choosing appropriate languages and tools for their particular project; they are initially expected to understand the strengths, shortcomings, and compatibilities of all available tools. Due to these constraints of existing tools and process, interaction designers have not been fully involved in data visualization research and practices although they have much potential to contribute with their *storytelling ability*, *aesthetic sensibility*, and *logical thinking ability*.

CASE STUDIES OF AESTHETICS IN DATA VISUALIZATION

Motivated by the problems and constraints with the current design tools and approaches for data visualization, we propose three issues for designing aesthetic data visualization: data gathering, data representation, and data navigation. Through the discussion of these issues, we hope to explore better ways to utilize and improve visualization tools for designers when they exert their tacit knowledge and aesthetic sensibility. In what follows, we introduce five case studies of design projects in which data visualization plays a core part. Each project is described and analyzed according to the three issues:

- **Data Collection:** How did the designer access and collect the data?
- **Data Representation:** Why did the designer choose the functional forms and the aesthetic styles to represent the collected data?
- **Data Navigation:** How did the designer make the visualizations interactive to navigate the data?

In addition to these issues, we also discuss the process of each case and the tools used in it.

- **Design Process:** In which order did the designer consider and execute the three issues (data collection, representation, and navigation)? How did each step of design process mutually influence with one another?

- **Design Tools:** What visualization tools (libraries or languages) did the designer use? How did the tools influence each step of design process in both positive and negative ways?

Finally, we summarize all case studies by reflecting on challenges and accomplishments from them.

Case Study 1: Visual Representations of Online Banking Transactions

This project is to support online banking customers' financial managements of their income and expenditure through interactive data visualization, which is alternative to typical monthly tabular report. Web-based tools (i.e., JavaScript libraries, Adobe Flash) enable various types of interactive data visualization. This project especially aims to design prototypes of different visual representations—including different layouts, navigation structure and interfaces—according to different customer motivations. The designs of visualizations were evaluated based on real life user scenarios and iteratively refined to a final prototype.

Data Collection and Representation

We first analysed the current visual representations of transaction data offered to customers on the online banking service. It is currently displayed in a table of four columns: 1) date of payment, 2) description of income or expenditure item, 3) amount value and 4) value date. Each row represents a single occurrence of transaction and it is possible to sort their order by clicking on the header of each column. The current online representation allows customers only a little more interaction than paper-based report. In our redesign we focused on exploring more interactive data navigation and manipulation afforded by web technology. In Tufte's words this means letting users understand the data by *having it represented* instead of reading its analysis (Tufte, 2001). To explore possible visual representations we collected income and expenditure reports over the period of a year from around 100 anonymous users of the service who had consented to share their data. Specific research questions include: which type of visualization is most appropriate to different customer profiles? How to support customers reviewing payment history, comparing expenditures in different categories, and eventually managing their income and expenditure from their previous report?

The first prototype was a paper-based sketch (in Figure 1) only with a few changes from the existing table report: 1) income and expenditure are presented in separate columns, 2) the time interval can be specified in input sections and calendar pickers, 3) multiple accounts marked with different colours can be switched by different tabs. The significant change in this version from the tabular report is the separation between income and expenditure and a colour scale to rep-

resent different accounts. Figure 2 shows another representation of the transaction data: there is a spatial and chromatic separation between income and expenditure items. The two sliced segments of the inner circle represent the total amount of income (green) and expenditure (red). User can retrieve details of a selected transaction by clicking each of the outer arcs. The angle of each arc is proportional to the amount of money. This visual form allows comparative representation of single transactions and the overall balance at the same time.

Data Navigation (Embedding Prototypes in Real Life Scenario)

We mapped the sample balance data onto the initial prototypes above, but it was difficult to evaluate actual use in terms of interactive navigation without an activity scenario. Therefore we redesigned the online banking service page with more different visual representations of the sample data (Figure 3). Then we came up with tasks 1) to retrieve a particular payment transaction

Figure 1. The classic balance view

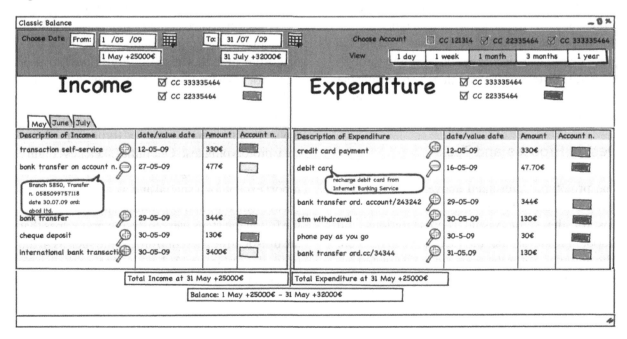

Figure 2. A clockwise view

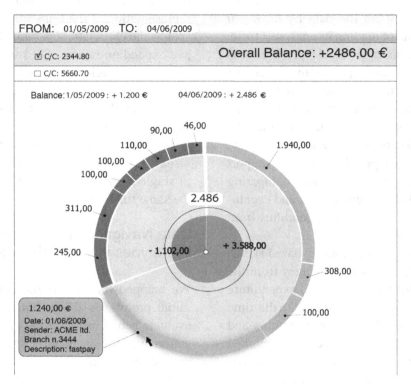

to a fictional travel agency from the report and 2) to make a new payment to the same recipient. The steps for each task consists of accessing the payments archive by choosing one of the visual representations on the main widget. Once the users access the visual report they have to find the particular transaction either by scrolling through the whole history of the month or by querying the name of the agency that received the payment in the search box.

Design Process and Tools

The prototypes presented above were designed using Balsamiq (Balsamiq Studios, 2013) mock-ups for the static visual representations and Adobe Flash for the interactive visualization. The animations for the scenario were created using Actionscript. The choice of graphic-oriented

tool instead of data visualization libraries had an important impact on the project with more freedom of choice in terms of encoding techniques and faster iterations of various visual representations. However, forms and styles of data representation are not only determined by the structure of data or design tools but also closely related to user goals for effective financial management, especially scenario-based iterative process. By using scenario-based process, design concepts and navigation steps were specified through quick and easy prototyping test. Our initial sketches (Figure 1) were barely distinguished from a typical tabular report except for a spatial and a colour separation between income and expenditure items. However, the following steps were to design prototypes that are drastically different from a table such as in the examples in Figures 2, 3 and 4. At first these new visual representations did put users in a situation

Figure 3. The mock-up of the web page of the banking service

where they had to explore the visualization and interpret what the visual elements mean. They then expressed their judgment on the aesthetics of the representation while trying to retrieve information and perform tasks according to given scenarios. After both the most and least similar prototypes to the original table were tested on users, we implemented them into web service in order to test visual representations as a part of the service ecosystem where individual transaction data is collected and retrieved. According to Distributed Cognition theories, the users can benefit from visual elements since external representations allow people to perceive data much faster and to cognitively process longer than they can in their mind internally (Kirsh, 2010). Users' performance in visual search can be more accurate with aesthetically aligned layouts, which is coherent with recent studies (Salimun, Purchase,

Simmons, & Brewster, 2010). These assumptions are confirmed in the test we run on the web service UI. In fact, users preferred a rich and aesthetically attractive visualization (Figure 5) to one that they consider familiar (Figure 1) when the former is more functional than the latter to complete the task they are engaged in.

Case Study 2: Visualization of Weather Changes Over Years in Multiple Cities

This project is the visualization of the weather records over five years in nine cities. To support time-based comparison we came up with a unified viewing mode, which overlays macro patterns of temperature changes from multiple years and still allows the access to details of daily data from the overview (Figure 6).

Figure 4. Comparing two bank accounts

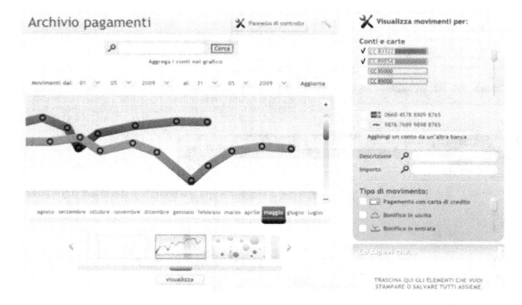

Data Collection: Daily Data of All Years and Hourly Data of the Selected Few Days

We collect the weather records from the Weather Underground (2013) that provides the past five years' hourly-basis temperature data of the major capital cities. A simple URL returns the data that can be saved in CSV file format (Weather Undergound, 2007). Then we made a custom JavaScript to automate the process of accessing, downloading and aggregating the data over the targeting duration and places. Unfortunately, the site blocked this repetitive URL request, so this process was not

Figure 5. Retrieving an expense using search

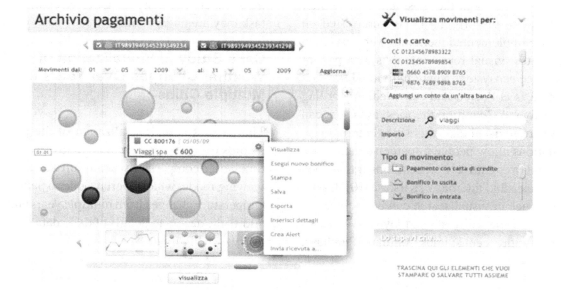

Figure 6. The overview of the weather visualization

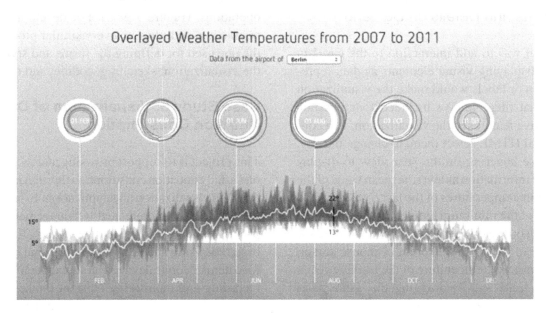

completely automatically performed. Due to this constrains, we had to reconsider the volume of the dataset; finally we decided to collect day-by-day information from 2007 to 2011. Additionally, we collected hour-by-hour information only for six days in each year.

Data Representation: Timeline for Yearly View and Radials for Daily Data

The view of visualization is divided largely into two parts. One part is for the yearly view where the datasets of daily lowest and highest temperature from each year is plotted on one timeline of one year. The five datasets, each of which means a single year, are overlaid on the timeline. The other part is the daily view where the datasets of the six selected days from each year is plotted in a radial form. Each closed curves around the circle represents the hourly temperature change of the day. Same as the overlaid timeline view, the each of five closed curves represent one dataset of a day's hourly temperature change.

In the yearly view timeline, the area between the highest and lowest temperature is filled with a gradient set of colors to provide a sense to scale the differences of temperature in one dataset of one city, as well as within the entire datasets of all cities. The strokes of the radial day view are also painted with the same gradient scheme. Vertical grids that create the divisions between the months are also used to make connections between the yearly view and the daily view above by showing the position of the highlighted date on the yearly timeline. On the Y axis, we set a temperature range and filled it with white with the text of the two temperatures. This area works as a "base zone" of temperature, which helps users investigate the bounds of temperature change. This zone is also displayed as a white circle in each daily view above the year view; the inner bound is set on the minimal temperature, the outer bound on the maximum temperature. In general, our design requirements follow the idea of good "data-ink ratio" on the visualization (Tufte, 2011).

Data Navigation: Switching Datasets and Details on Demand

Our goal was to add interaction to the cases in which displaying visual elements as data representation or labels would make the visualization somewhat illegible. We included four possible interactive features in the visualization: 1) a conventional HTML select menu to change the city, 2) mouse hovering on the year view to display detailed information as text (the mean value of the maximum temperatures of the last five years, and the one of the minimum temperatures), 3) mouse hovering on the five circles of day view to display the time of the day at the point of mouse cursor, and the average temperature of the last five year's pointed time, and 4) dragging the white basis zone in year view, which prompts the change of radius and thickness of the associated circles in the day views.

Design Process and Tools

We started by sketching several possible techniques of data representation with pen and paper. Sketching allowed us envision the visualization forms and the layout. However, hand-drawing sketches are not appropriate to imagine the look when the data are actually populated. Thus, based on the initial forms from the sketches, we started coding and plotted a small portion of real data. We developed this visualization using SVG, JavaScript and the d3.js library (Bostock, Ogievetsky, & Heer 2011). The methods and abstractions that the d3.js provides are easy to use to encode data into graphic elements. We first code the viewing modules separately, which made testing different sizes and positions of the modules easier when we arranged them.

To seek the optimal forms and visually pleasing styles for the visualization, we kept iterating the code with the small parts of the real data. For the cases that we wanted to test various forms, we made the code more parametric, by creating and connecting variables through mathematical operations. (Figure 7 & 8). For developing the interaction we followed a very similar process to the one used for defining the forms and styles of the visualization: sketching, coding, and testing.

Case Study 3: Visualization of Daily Nutrition Consumption

This project is to support browsing and recording one's daily nutrition consumption through interactive data visualization and application. Especially with a focus on mobile health management, this project explored design solutions for small screen based browsing and recording nutritional facts of food items. Mobile devices can support convenient recording and monitoring nutrient intake at any time, which can be critical in health management (Andersson, Rosenqvist, & Sahrawi, 2007). However, there are still challenges in visualizing nutrition entries within a small screen user interface, such as displaying a large amount of data, interactively switching modes of contextual and local data, among others. At the same time, every food consists of various nutrients such as carbohydrates, proteins, and fats, which are hard to be understood, particularly when presented using only numbers. In consideration of these issues, we focused on finding metaphors for cognitive and embodied visual form in order to facilitate small touch screen information visualization and navigation.

Data Visualization

We first surveyed existing mobile and web nutrition management applications to understand specific design issues and the functional requirements in terms of menu structure or interaction modes. Nutrition facts of different foods are hard to be read and kept track of, particularly, when presented as numbers in a table. There is a need for exploring different ways of displaying a large amount of complex information based on the

Figure 7. Some variations developed during the iteration of the year view

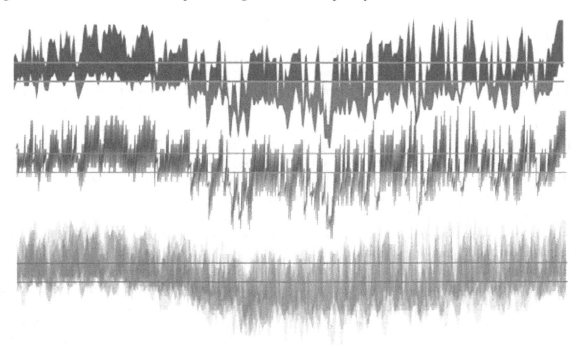

understanding of a person's cognitive processes. Based on the survey of existing applications, we learned that "time" is a pivotal element which people use to record and navigate their daily nutrition consumption. Then we sketched various types of wireframes to visualize nutrition intake over a timeline, for example, in line graphs, bar graphs, bubble charts and pie charts. A set of design requirements are specified below in terms menu structure and navigation of the application:

- Support tracing all food items taken in a day and comparison of nutrition intakes for recommended levels.
- Use food item icons instead of text for quick review and intuitive understanding.
- Provide rich information using preattentive visual elements such as colors and symbols for quick overview.
- Display two modes of information—overall food entries and specific nutrition components for each food, and support dynamic navigation between the modes.

Figure 8. Some variations developed during the iteration of the day view

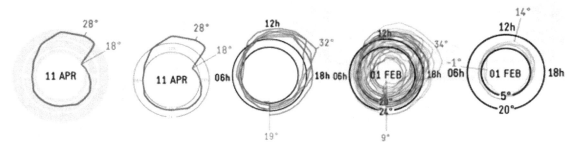

Data Navigation

By analyzing selected applications, we were aware of the lack of motivation to record all food consumed and the cumbersomeness of browsing the data. This means that ease of use or efficiency of use is critical, but at the same time such design criteria are not enough. Some extra values are required to motivate and constantly engage people with a new type of application. Based on the objectives and requirements discussed above, we designed Food Watch, a mobile application for browsing and recording nutritional facts of food items. Food Watch visualizes nutritional composition of different food items (e.g. carbohydrates, proteins, fats) in pictorial elements and pie charts for intuitive perception and navigation of information in a small screen interface. The circular shape in the center of the display was selected with two different metaphors in mind: a wristwatch and a dinner plate (Figure 9).

Specifically, a plate metaphor is considered appropriate not only in terms of its everyday use for serving food, but also in that its image can be applied as display object (Ware, 2000) to embed pie charts of nutrition facts over its round shape. At the same time, the wristwatch metaphor provides a conceptual relation for recording and browsing daily nutrition intake as time-related information with its round shape. In this way, a set of food items can be browsed by turning a graphic plate and food can be dragged onto the plate for selection. Then, daily nutrition intakes can be recorded and browsed over the timeline of a graphic wristwatch in a different mode of interaction.

The interaction of the application consists of the three modes as specified below (Figure 10):

- Set up a user's profile by calculating personal daily nutrition requirements according to one's body factors.
- Browse different foods comparing their nutrition facts to the daily nutrition requirements calculated previously.
- Review all the foods added to the review list and their nutrition facts accumulated in a day.

Figure 9. Food Watch Display Object and Visual Elements

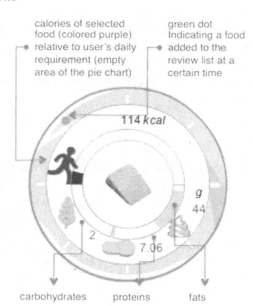

12

Figure 10. Food Watch Interaction: 1) Set Up Profile (top left), 2) Browse Food Items (top right), 3) Select A Food Item (bottom left), and 4) Review Saved Food Items (bottom right)

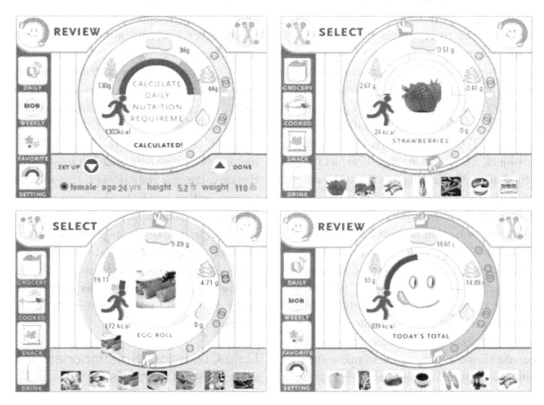

Data Collection

The data was collected after we had made initial decisions on the overall design direction in terms of visualization form, interaction, and layout. The food database is built as a local xml file based on nutrition information collected from USDA Nutrition Data Laboratory (USDA, 2011). By using a local database we more focused on experimenting graphic and interactive design attributes in data visualization instead of real-time database connection. In addition, personal daily nutrition requirements are calculated according to one's body factors based on the formulation provided by WeightLossForAll.com. They are used to simulate a use case of the application by comparing nutrition facts of a selected food item to one's daily nutrition requirements.

Design Process and Tool

This study emphasizes the process of developing a form in order to illustrate how design intention comes into selecting specific shapes for particular aesthetic and functional purposes. The aim of using metaphors of a dinner plate and wristwatch for browsing and selecting food items was to simplify the visualization and navigation of nutrient data within a small touch screen interface. The shapes and functions of two existing physical objects (a dinner plate and a wristwatch), incorporated into a digital form, offer a visual and behavioral analogy for display and navigation of information. In this way a large amount of data is displayed in simple pictorial forms for quick overview of nutrition compositions of different food items while keeping details of data as well.

We used Flash Lite 3.1 (ActionScript 2.0) to simulate interactive visualization. Flash was a good choice to experiment various graphic shapes and symbolic icons to represent data in more familiar and engaging visual forms. However, dynamic data navigation in connection to the local XML database was not intuitive to code with ActionScript especially without expert programming knowledge. Specifically, the challenges are summarized into 1) browsing database by rotating a graphic object, 2) visualizing nutrition facts of a focused food item, 3) selecting food items by drag and drop, and 4) storing their nutrition facts for reviewing total daily consumption. We created so many small functions that had not been planned at the beginning. The overall design process was quite linear by starting from visual sketches, specification of interaction concepts, and building a database. However the implementation was really complicated, not proceeded step by step. We went through multiple sketches of interaction sequence and flowcharts in order to make sense of the relations of functions and variables that are used to store values from database and to draw graphic shapes from them.

Case Study 4: Personal Lifelog Visualization

A variety of life-logging devices with sensing technologies have been created and their applications provide us with the opportunity to track our lives accurately and automatically. In this context, there is a growing interest called the "Quantified Self Movement" driven by technologies that sense numerous aspects of an individual's life in detail. The idea of "quantified self" starts with tracking our daily activities such as location, mood, health factors, sleep patterns, photos, phone calls, and so on. Many technologies support the capturing of lifelogs. For example, ubiquitous smartphones allow us to record our life activities in previously unimaginable detail. These captured logs can be further used to infer interesting and useful insights about people, their communication patterns with others, and their interaction with environments.

However, current tools to manage such rich data archives are still in need of improvement in terms of storing and organizing. Since the captured material are voluminous and mixed in data types, it might be overwhelming and impractical to manually scan the full contents of these lifelogs, which eventually results in lots of "worn memories"—we write once but never read again. Besides, the raw data do not give much insight to users without additional semantic enrichment. Thus, a promising approach is to pre-process raw data to extract and aggregate useful information, and then apply visualization to the large-scale data archives as a means to target users. We argue that lifelog visualization is capable of displaying the sheer quantity of mixed multimedia contents in a meaningful way.

Data Collection: Smartphones with Various Sensors

We developed a lifelogging platform working on Android smartphones. A typical smartphone is equipped with many sensors to capture various sources of data (Table 1). The gathered data is first analyzed in the phone and then uploaded to the central server. At the server we perform additional semantic analysis and enrich the data

Table 1. Available sensors equipped on a user's smartphone

Sensor	Description
Acceleration	Physical movement of the user
GPS	Geographic location
Bluetooth	Social context
Wifi	Indoor location, location cache
Camera	Automatic photo/video capture
Speaker	Environmental sound/noise level

into semantically rich "life streams"; by applying machine learning techniques, we extract semantics from raw sensor log streams; by grouping related sensed logs together, we reconstruct the data and design several use case scenarios. For example, by aggregating the logs from speaker, GPS, and Bluetooth together, we can detect whether test subject is at work or engaged in social activity. In this way, we can extract various semantic contexts that are meaningful to target users. We also run more processor intensive operations with the data such as face detection. Finally, the data were processed into a variety of formats such as JSON, XML, and CSV prior to the representation phase.

Data Representation and Navigation: Three Types of Visual Logs

Sellen and Whittaker (2010) summarized five functions of memory that lifelogs could potentially support, referred to as the 5 Rs: recollecting (recalling a specific piece of information or an experience), reminiscing (reliving past experiences for emotional or sentimental reasons), remembering (supporting memory or tasks such as showing up for appointments), reflecting (facilitating the reflections and reviews on past experiences) and retrieving (revisiting previously encountered digital items or information such as documents, email or web pages). According to these functions of lifelogs, our primary design goal is to support users' self-reflection, sharing, evoking thoughts, and reminiscence. We believe that the form and styles of visualization should be determined by the purpose of uses and context.

Since the data generated from multiple sensor sources are complex, we need a more systematic approach to exploring the match between user needs and data visualization. We first generate three scenarios of different user behaviors and contexts: visual diary, social interaction, and activities review. Then we characterize UI patterns based on these three contexts, and create wireframe and interfaces prototypes. Visual diary use case

scenario help users to support recollecting, remembering, and reminiscing of their past experiences. Social interaction and activities review support more abstract representation of personal lifelogs to facilitate reflecting and retrieving functions.

1. Visual Diary

Sensing devices automatically capture thousands of photos, and many times more sensor readings per day (Kalnikaite, Steve, and Whittaker, 2012). Hence, grouping the sequences of related images into "events" is necessary in order to reduce complexity (Doherty & Smeaton, 2008). The visual design of the visualization is inspired by Squarified treemap pattern (Bruls,1999). Our visualization, called "Visual Diary," provides a summary of user's daily log as photographs, with emphasis on important events (Figure 11). Each grid represents an event and the size of the grid provides an immediate visual cue to the event's importance level. The position of each grid depicts the time sequence. At the same time, users are allowed to drill down (full photo stream and sensor log) inside each event.

2. Social Interaction Radar

For the visualization of social contexts, we utilize the data from three embedded sensors (i.e., Bluetooth, Wi-Fi, and GPS) (Figure 12). With these datasets, we identify the social context of individual users over the course of a year. To support the different features of the multi-dimensional data, we adopted a Coxcomb visualization technique, which helps users to understand the whole and its individual parts simultaneously. This opens up new possibilities for rapid communication of complex constructs. Each concentric circle represents one type of the sensor data. This radar graph has three dimensions: 1) type of sensor, 2) social activity value, 3) time. Scrolling around the circle enables rapid exploration and comparison sensor values between different months.

Figure 11. Interactive visual diary generated for one day, showing event segmentation

Figure 12. Social Interactive Multi-Dimension Radar Graph

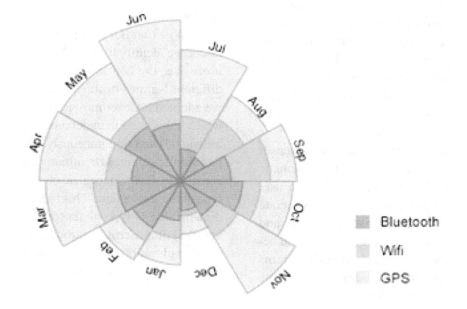

3. Activity Calendar

Activity view allows users to gain a detailed understanding of their physical activities (Figure 13). We calculate the level of physical activity with the data from accelerometer and GPS sensors. We visualize the data in an annual calendar layout, with color-coding to present the activity intensity. A darker color indicates more activity involved in a given day. By investigating the activity pattern over the course of a full year, it is possible to detect a user's extreme days (i.e., the most active or the most quite days).

Design Tool

When choosing the tools for visualization, we had to consider the objectives as well as the time constrains for creating interfaces. Our goal was to analyze the large data archive, and to create dynamic interactive visualizations that are later exhibited on users' web browser. Thus, the accessibility without plug-ins, the compatibility with web standards, and cross-browser support are our main concerns when choosing visualization tools. After the review of available tools, we chose open-source JavaScript-based toolkits—Protovis (Stanford Visual Group, 2010) and d3 (Bostock, 2012). It binds arbitrary data into DOM, and brings data to life using html, CSS, SVG that

appear almost identically on different browsers and platforms. These independent toolkits make it possible to plot data in novel structure with rich user interaction. We also choose jQuery library for more dynamic interactive features. It is lightweight compared to other JavaScript frameworks and uses familiar CSS syntax that designer can learn and use easily. This combination of tools provides designers with powerful approaches to the aesthetic look and interactivity, which also makes the data manipulation customizable. Ultimately they empower designers with the freedom to focus on the aesthetics.

Case Study 5: Visualizations of Mobile Communication Data

This project is to use data visualization as a tool for exploratory data analysis (Shneiderman, 2002) to quickly discover insights for research/design opportunities. Mobile phones can help collect extensive data ranging from personal usage of the phone to inter-personal communication. In addition, due to their pervasive daily use, their various embedded sensors, and ubiquitous wireless technology infrastructure, mobile phones have received increased use as a new kind of research tool. Researchers in this field have primarily used data mining, machine learning, and other quantitative

Figure 13. Yearly activity summary with a calendar view

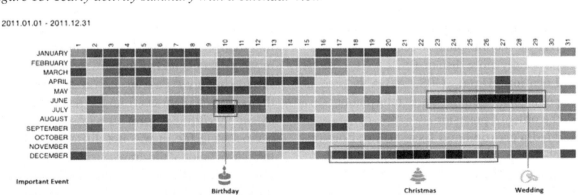

modeling methods, at which interaction designers are not typically trained. Such unmatched skillsets limit designers from being actively involved in data-driven research. In this challenging context, we suggest a new role for interaction designers in which they can apply and enhance their existing skills: designing information visualizations of the available data in a timely manner and deploying them to other researchers during the early phases of data-driven research. Using visualizations as a tool for *exploratory data analysis* (Shneiderman, 2002), researchers can find insights quickly to ground the next phase of research.

Data Collection

In late 2009 for more than one year, over 160 volunteers near Lake Geneva, Switzerland participated in a data collection campaign using mobile phones. We gave study volunteers smart phones equipped with special software that ran in the background and gathered data from embedded sensors continuously when the phone was turned on. The logged data were stored in the mobile phone and automatically uploaded to a database server on a daily basis when a known WLAN access point was detected. The data was subsequently made available to the public through Nokia Mobile Data Challenge (Nokia Research Center, 2012).

We categorize the collected data as follows:

- **Inter-Personal Communication Data:** Voice call logs and text message logs
- **Physical Proximity Data:** The Bluetooth IDs of mobile phones scanned within a physically close distance
- **Location Data:** GPS, WLAN access points, and cell network information (in the order of precision)
- **Media creation and Usage Data:** Logs of photo taking, video shooting, music play, web browsing, alarm setting, etc.

Design Process and Tools (Requirements for Exploratory Data Analysis)

The data set emerging from the mobile phone study was very large and varied. Performing exploratory analysis on this data would require a high degree of flexibility in supporting different subsets of the data extracted from the entire collection. We did not feel that any existing general-purpose visualization systems could provide all the different perspectives we desired on the data. Also, building a custom visualization system for the entire set appeared daunting and could possibly take a long time. Thus, we designed multiple, different interactive visualizations instead of a monolithic visual analytic system. Each visualization focuses on a different aspect of the data collection and is designed to best portray a particular aspect of the dataset. We assumed that the end-users of such visualizations would be researchers who want to explore massive datasets, especially related to mobile communication data, before they begin investigation with other sophisticated data analysis methods.

In designing these visualizations, our priority was to generate flexible datasets that are directly related to researchers' questions and easily modified to their ongoing requests. Initially, we extracted relevant data subsets from a database using simple SQL queries. We stored these data subsets in comma-separated-value formatted separated files to be linked and used in visualizations. To implement the visualizations, we primarily used Java-based Processing. The simple structure of the visualization source files allowed us to easily manage and modify datasets and visual design; we were able to quickly convert data formats, and generate new dimensions or datasets from the linked datasets; by simply editing several lines of source code in a Processing file, it was not difficult to change the size or color of the drawn visual elements. We also reused portions of visualization source code throughout multiple visualizations and modified it as necessary. This highly customized design process would hopefully make the visualizations versatile enough to support analysts' incremental demands during the analysis.

Data Visualization (An Individuals' Daily Life)

Due to space limitations, we select one example exemplifies the micro traits of single participants. This visualization focuses on data about individual participants in order to understand different mobile phone usage patterns depending on different temporal and social contexts. Better understanding the dissimilar lifestyles of individual participants would ground the design of personalized mobile services and applications. For the visualization design, we applied timeline-based visualization because our goal was to best support effective analysis with a minimal learning curve, not to invent new visualization techniques. That said, we believe these visualizations provide innovative designs for the visual analysis of communication and location data.

1. Dataset Datasets: Phone usage, Location, and Bluetooth Readings

Thanks to the wealth of data modalities tracked, the analysis of the data about a single user can inform extensive insights about his or her life. This visualization was created with multiple datasets from multiple users (Figure 14).

- Location data from the high fidelity GPS logs table containing latitude and longitude coordinates: The number of GPS entries is roughly equivalent to the frequency of physical movement.
- Bluetooth readings: Bluetooth detection data show the number of people appearing in a proximate physical distance and the frequency of appearance.
- Mobile phone usage data whose entries were parsed from five different log tables in the server: These tables include voice calls, text messages, web browsing, music play, and photo-shooting.

Figure 14. Integrated visualization of an individual user's phone usage logs (colored squared below x-axis), GPS-based moving status (gray-scale background), and Bluetooth encounters with other people (gray-scale circles above x-axis)

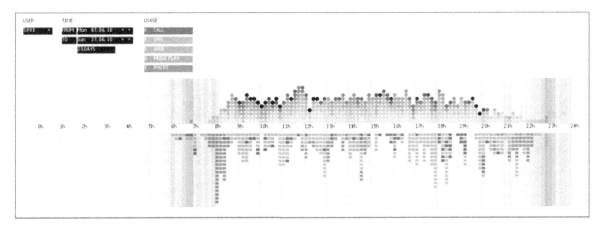

2) Timeline-based Visualization with Multiple Elements

We processed the GPS logs in ten-minute intervals and represent them as the background of the timeline. The presence of more GPS entries results in a darker background. The same time interval is applied to the Bluetooth data, which are represented by the grey-scale dots above the horizontal 24-hour line. The number of dots represents nearby people detected through Bluetooth, and the darkness of each dot is proportional to the frequency of the corresponding person's presence. The squares below the bar are color-coded to represent the five different kinds of phone usage data. We added simple menus to enable analysts to select other participants and to select/de-select the categories of mobile phone usage. We also included a time selector, so they could adjust the time range of the data to any number of days within the sixteen weeks retrieved.

He has many more people using Bluetooth around him during the typical working hours, which might suggest that he is present in an office environment with business colleagues. He also exhibits a rough commuting time range between 6:30 AM to 8 AM. Between 12:10 PM to 12:30 PM, Bluetooth detection is evident by the two darker dots. Based upon consistency of occurrence, we infer that the other participants might be regular lunch friend(s).

Additionally, we examined visualizations of participants who were college students. We observed that students tended to have different patterns in terms of movement and Bluetooth detection (Figure 15). Both students shown did not exhibit a fixed short period of commuting pattern. Instead, they seemed to more randomly move around. One student had two to three mobile phones appear nearby during night time (roughly between 11 PM to 7 AM) (Figure 15-top). One of them might b a roommate, represented as a darkest

Figure 15. Visualization of integrated personal data from two college students

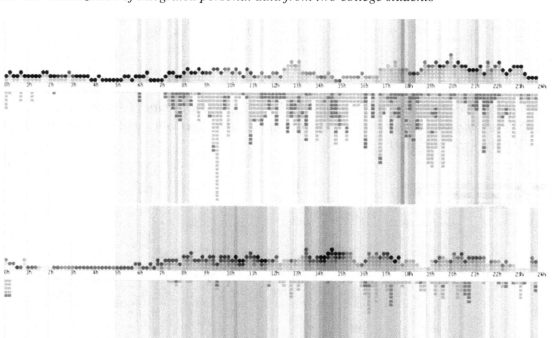

dot, whereas the other dots might represent occasional visitors. The other student did not have a regular peak time in terms of the number of people nearby (Figure 15-bottom). She encountered less people, but was around them more frequently than the office worker (i.e., less number of entire dots, but relatively more dark dots). The mobile usage pattern is also distinguishable; for instance, the students used web browser SMS more than voice calls.

Summary and Reflection

In this chapter we introduced five case studies of data visualization projects. The first project is about visual representation of online bank transactions in order to improve user experience of managing multiple bank accounts and being more aware of their financial status. Traditionally design approaches to scientific visualization have been rather *data-centric* with focus on visual analysis of the data structure. However, with increasing end-user visualization applications, *task-centric* design approach should be more crucially considered in selecting forms of data representation and navigation interfaces that can best afford action-based user goals. The importance of a scenario lies in enabling a clear grasp of the contextual elements and in providing particular interaction paths (Rizzo & Bacigalupo, 2004). In this vein, this study illustrates that paper-based sketches with particular user scenarios can serve as an efficient design medium at early phases of design for quick iterations of initial ideas.

Moreover, as data visualization has been more broadly applied to end-user services, interaction and experiential qualities have become more critical design issues, not only in terms of usability of data perception and task-based navigation but also in terms of attractive and engaging representation and navigation of data. The second and the third case studies are more directly related to aesthetic forms and interface elements of data representation and navigation. In the weather visualization proj-

ect, specific graph shapes, colors, and interfaces were iteratively tested and specified by coding (using d3.js). In the nutrition data application project, the main visual and interaction design directions were determined by metaphors from physical objects, and then simulated in Flash ActionScript. In both cases, programming played a significant role in stimulating design concepts and testing technical constraints in connection to database and interactive navigation. Although programming is still a barrier for many designers, it can provide more logical and consistent visual and interactive styles to multiple parts of a design system over iterative design process. Some common visualization tools and libraries (i.e., Flash ActionScript or d3.js) are efficient to demonstrate new interaction and interface concepts. However one of the big challenges is to manage overall layout and whole sequence of interaction as well as data collection and manipulation of the entire system of visualization applications. It would be really beneficial to create a new design process and tools that can better support designers' systematic thinking and simulation of data ecosystem.

The last two case studies are about exploring new applications of data visualization. Due to increasing data capturing and processing power, we have more challenges as well as opportunities in making sense and use of such voluminous and complex data. The mobile lifelogs project explores different ways of representing personal data for various purposes of raising insights to personal activities and self-reflection. The mobile communication data project focuses on extracting research insights from data by using visualization as a rapid discovery tool for generating insights from large-scale data at an early phase of research. This visualization-based analysis of user-generated data can serve as a new research methodology, which is time-efficient and still people-centric by discovering traits about the people in the data. These approaches envision a new role for visualization with its strength in transforming ideas into visual artifacts in data-driven user research.

CONCLUSION

As discussed in the case studies, this design process is not always linear; when other requests from either users or designer themselves arise, iterations become necessary. Regardless of different design process and tools applied in each case study, they still share general issues to be discussed in terms of *1) data collection, 2) data representation,* and *3) data navigation.*

Data collection is about a whole system in which data is gathered and linked to visualization application. This issue is closely related to both user scenarios of data visualization (in terms of how data is provided, shared, and distributed) and technical challenges (in terms of how to retrieve and link data in proper formats).

Data representation is related to graphic forms through which overall structure of data is represented with its details. There are many standard forms of graphs such as bar chart, line chart, pie chart, etc. Beyond those graph forms, more exploratory forms of graphs are enabled and experimented thanks to advanced computing technology, including network diagram, tag cloud, bubble chart, direct visualization, which shows data as it is like in photo archive, etc. In addition, geographical maps are also frequently used to populate data onto familiar spatial coordinates for simple and efficient data perception. According to the increasing number of various forms of data representation, the criteria to select an efficient but still engaging forms is always a critical design consideration. The selection of an overall representation form proceeds to traditional aesthetic concerns in terms selection of colors, sizes, and layout of graphic shapes, which could be iteratively polished afterwards.

Data navigation, in comparison to data representation, is rather a less investigated aspect than the issue of data representation. There are a few options for standard interactivity including pulling out details-on-demand or browsing data by scrolling, panning, and zooming. While various forms of graphs and interfaces are used to represent data, interactive features to enter and navigate data are relatively limited in terms of diversity with similar interfaces in different applications. It is a great opportunity to explore new types of interactivity to navigate data, at the same time a huge challenge to simulate new interaction ideas with current design tools.

These three design issues—data collection, representation, and navigation—can be considered as significant building blocks that constitute an overall design process of data visualization, not necessarily put in a linear sequence. We expect the identification of the three topical design blocks could support interaction designers flexibly planning out a design process in consideration of iterative simulation and refinement of the connection of the three design issues.

REFERENCES

Adobe. (n.d.). ActionScript technology center. *Adobe Developer Connection.* Retrieved from http://www.adobe.com/devnet/actionscript.html.

Andersson, P., Rosenqvist, C., & Sahrawi, O. (2007). Mobile innovations in healthcare: customer involvement and the co-creation of value. *International Journal of Mobile Communications,* 5(4), 371–388. doi:10.1504/IJMC.2007.012786.

Balsamiq Studios. (2013). *Rapid wireframing tool.* Retrieved from http://www.balsamiq.com/.

Baranovsky, D. (n.d.). *GRaphael-Jevascript library.* Retrieved from http://g.raphaeljs.com/.

Bostock, M. (2012). *Data-driven documents.* Retrieved from http://d3js.org/.

Bostock, M., Ogievetsky, V., & Heer, J. (2011). D³ data-driven documents. *IEEE Transactions on Visualization and Computer Graphics,* 17(12), 2301–2309. doi:10.1109/TVCG.2011.185 PMID:22034350.

Bruls, M., Huizing, K., & Wijk, J. (1999) Squarified treemaps, *In Proceedings of the Joint Eurographics and IEEE TCVG Symposium on Visualization*. New Brunswick, NJ: IEEE Press.

Cross, N. (2011). *Design thinking: Understanding how designers think and work*. Oxford, UK: Berg Publishers.

Doherty, A. R., & Smeaton, A. F. (2008). Automatically segmenting lifelog data into events. In *Proceedings of WIAMIS*. New Brunswick, NJ: IEEE Press.

Goodman, E., Stolterman, E., & Wakkary, R. (2011). Understanding interaction design practice. In *Proceedings of Conference on Human Factors in Computing Systems,* 1061-1070. New York: ACM Press.

IBM. (n.d.). Many eyes. *Software Analytics*. Retrieved from http://www-958.ibm.com/.

Kalnikaite, V., & Whittaker, S. (2012). Recollection: How to design lifelogging tools that help locate the right information. *Human-Computer Interaction: The Agency Perspective Studies in Computational Intelligence*, 329-348. Berlin: Springer. doi:10.1007/978-3-642-25691-2_14.

Kirsh, D. (2010). Thinking with external representations. *AI & Society*, *25*(4), 441–454. doi:10.1007/s00146-010-0272-8.

Löwgren, J., & Stolterman, E. (2004). *Thoughtful Interaction Design: A Design Perspective on Information Technology*. Cambridge, MA: MIT Press.

Manovich, L. (2008). *Introduction to info-aesthetics*. Retrieved from http://goo.gl/NFLvy.

Manovich, L. (2010). *What is visualization?* Retrieved from http://www.datavisualisation.org/2010/11/levmanovichwhat-is-visualization/.

Nokia Research Center. (2012). *Nokia mobile data challenge*. Retrieved from http://research.nokia.com/page/12000.

Pousman, Z., & Stasko, J. T. (2007). Data in everyday life. *IEEE Transactions on Visualization and Computer Graphics*, *13*(6), 1145–1152. doi:10.1109/TVCG.2007.70541 PMID:17968058.

Processing 2. (n.d.). *Processing.org*. Retrieved from http://processing.org/.

Rizzo, A., & Bacigalupo, M. (2004) Scenarios: heuristics for actions. In *Proceedings of XII European Conference on Cognitive Ergonomics*. York, UK: EACE.

Salimun, C., Purchase, H. C., Simmons, D. R., & Brewster, S. (2010). The effect of aesthetically pleasing composition on visual search performance. In *Proceedings of the 6th Nordic Conference on Human-Computer Interaction: Extending Boundaries,* 422–431. New York: ACM Press.

Segel, E., & Heer, J. (2010). Narrative visualization: telling stories with data. *IEEE Transactions on Visualization and Computer Graphics*, *16*(6), 1139–1148. doi:10.1109/TVCG.2010.179 PMID:20975152.

Sellen, A. J., & Whittaker, S. (2010). Beyond total capture: A constructive critique of lifelogging. *Communications of the ACM*, *53*(5), 70–77. doi:10.1145/1735223.1735243.

Shneiderman, B. (2002). Inventing discovery tools: Combining information visualization with data mining. *Information Visualization*, *1*(1), 5–12.

Stanford Visual Group. (2010). Protovis-A graphical approach to visualization. *Protovis*. Retrieved from http://mbostock.github.com/protovis/.

Tableau. (2013). Free data visualization software. *Tableau Public*. Retrieved from http://www.tableausoftware.com/public.

Tufte, E. R. (2001). *The visual display of quantitative information. Visual Explanations, 194–95*. Cockeysville, MD: PR Graphics.

USDA. (2011). Welcome to the USDA national nutrient database for standard reference. *National Agriculture Library*. Retrieved from http://ndb.nal.usda.gov/.

Vande Moere, A., & Purchase, H. (2011). On the role of design in information visualization. *Information Visualization*, *10*(4), 356–371. doi:10.1177/1473871611415996.

Ware, C. (2000). *Information visualization: Perception for design (interactive technologies)*. New York: Morgan Kaufmann.

Weather Underground. (2007). *An example URL of daily weather data of london heathrow airport in 2007*. Retrieved from http://www.wunderground.com/history/airport/EGLL/2007/1/1/CustomHistory.html?dayend=31&monthend=12&yearend=2007&format=1.

Weather Underground. (2013). Welcome to weather underground! *Weather Forecasts & Reports*. Retrieved from http://www.wunderground.com.

Chapter 2
A Visual Analytics Approach for Correlation, Classification, and Regression Analysis

Chad A. Steed
Oak Ridge National Laboratory, USA

J. Edward Swan II
Bagley College of Engineering, Mississippi State University, USA

Patrick J. Fitzpatrick
Northern Gulf Institute, Mississippi State University, USA

T.J. Jankun-Kelly
Bagley College of Engineering, Mississippi State University, USA

ABSTRACT

New approaches that combine the strengths of humans and machines are necessary to equip analysts with the proper tools for exploring today's increasingly complex, multivariate data sets. In this chapter, a visual data mining framework, called the Multidimensional Data eXplorer (MDX), is described that addresses the challenges of today's data by combining automated statistical analytics with a highly interactive parallel coordinates based canvas. In addition to several intuitive interaction capabilities, this framework offers a rich set of graphical statistical indicators, interactive regression analysis, visual correlation mining, automated axis arrangements and filtering, and data classification techniques. This chapter provides a detailed description of the system as well as a discussion of key design aspects and critical feedback from domain experts.

INTRODUCTION

A byproduct of continued technological advances is increasingly complex multivariate data sets, which, in turn, yield information overload when explored with conventional visual analysis techniques. The ability to collect, model, and store information is growing at a much faster rate than our ability to analyze it. However, the transformation of these vast volumes of data into actionable insight is critical in many domains (e.g. climate change, cyber-security, financial analysis). Without the proper techniques, analysts are forced to reduce the problem and discard layers of informa-

DOI: 10.4018/978-1-4666-4309-3.ch002

tion in order to fit the tools. New techniques and approaches are necessary to turn today's flood of information into opportunity.

One of the most promising solutions for the so-called big data challenge lies in the continued development of techniques in the rapidly growing field of visual analytics. Visual analytics, also known as visual data mining, combines interactive visualizations with automated analytics that help the analyst discover and comprehend patterns in complicated, heterogeneous data sets. In general, visual analytics can be described as "the science of analytical reasoning facilitated by interactive visual interfaces" (Thomas, 2005). Visual analytics seeks to combine the strengths of humans with those of machines. While methods from knowledge discovery, statistics, and mathematics drive the automated analytics, human capabilities to perceive, relate, and conclude strengthen the iterative process.

In this chapter, a novel visual data mining framework–called the Multidimensional Data eXplorer (MDX)–is presented that utilizes statistical analysis and data classification techniques in an interactive multivariate representation to improve

knowledge discovery in the complex multivariate data sets that characterize today's data (see Figure 1). In addition to intuitive interaction capabilities, this framework introduces a rich set of graphical statistical indicators, automated regression analysis, visual correlation indicators, optimal axis arrangement techniques, and data classification algorithms. These capabilities are combined into a parallel coordinates based framework for enhanced multivariate visual analysis.

This chapter features an expanded version of MDX that builds on recent efforts in which MDX was applied to tropical cyclone climate studies. In Steed, Fitzpatrick, Jankun-Kelly, Yancey, and Swan II (2009b), the initial version of MDX, which lacked integrated statistical processes, was introduced and the system was demonstrated in a case study with a set of tropical cyclone predictors. Follow-on work by Steed, Fitzpatrick, Swan II, and Jankun-Kelly (2009a) and Steed, Swan II, Jankun-Kelly, Fitzpatrick (2009c) presented an enhanced version of MDX that included statistical analytics and deeper analysis of the previously analyzed tropical cyclone predictors, as well as analysis of a new set of predictors. In the current

Figure 1. The Multidimensional Data eXplorer (MDX) consists of a settings panel (upper left), a data table panel (bottom), and an interactive parallel coordinates panel (upper right)

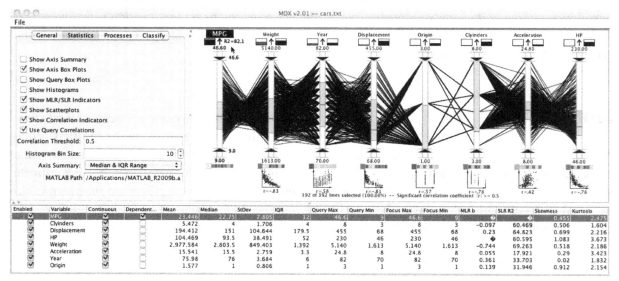

work, the MDX visual data mining and knowledge discovery capabilities are featured. In addition to presenting new features that facilitate visual correlation mining and automated axis arrangements, the new contributions in this work are new data classification capabilities, a novel regression analysis interface that facilitates interactive model development and confirmation, and a detailed description of the visual and automated correlation mining capabilities.

The remainder of this chapter is organized as follows. To begin, a survey of related work is given followed by a description of the cars data set–used in the examples throughout this chapter. Next, the graphical indicators of descriptive statistics are described. Then, a discussion is provided on the interactive correlation analysis indicators and interaction features that are available in the latest version of MDX. Next, the automated correlation analysis algorithms are described and the new automated data classification capabilities are discussed and demonstrated. Then, the details of the enhanced visual regression capabilities are described including the closing of the iterative regression analysis loop. Next, the optimal axis arrangement capabilities are described. Significant findings from the development and use of MDX, visual design criteria, and domain expert feedback are given and, finally, conclusions and future work are discussed.

BACKGROUND

As demonstrated by Wong and Bergeron (1997), there have been many approaches to the visual analysis of multivariate multidimensional data over the years. However, the techniques employed in operational systems are generally constrained to non-interactive, basic graphics using methods developed over a decade ago; and it is questionable whether these methods can cope with the complex data of today. For example, analysts often rely on simple scatter plots and histograms which require several separate plots or layered plots to study multiple attributes in a data set. However, the use of separate plots is not an ideal approach in this type of analysis due to perceptual issues described by Healey, Tateosain, Enns, and Remple (2004) such as the extremely limited memory for information that can be gained from one glance to the next. These issues are illustrated through the so-called change blindness phenomenon (a perceptual issue described by Rensink (2002)) and they are exacerbated when searching for combinations of conditions.

One approach often used by statisticians to overcome this issue is to use the scatterplot matrix (SPLOM), which represents multiple adjacent scatterplots for all the variable comparisons in a single display with a matrix configuration (Wong and Bergeron, 1997); but the SPLOM requires a large amount of screen space and forming multivariate associations is still challenging. Wilkinson, Anand, and Grossman (2006) used statistical measures for organizing both the SPLOM and parallel coordinates plots to guide the viewer through an exploratory analysis of high-dimensional data sets. Although the organization methods improve the analysis, the previously mentioned perceptual issues with SPLOMs remain to some degree. Another alternative is to use layered plots, which condense the information into a single display; but there are significant issues due to layer occlusion and interference as demonstrated by Healey et al. (2004).

The parallel coordinates plot is arguably one of the most popular multivariate visualization techniques and it is the basis of the highly interactive canvas in the MDX framework. The parallel coordinates technique was initially popularized by Inselberg (1985) as a novel approach for representing hyper-dimensional geometries, and later demonstrated in the direct analysis of multivariate relationships in data by Wegman (1990). In general, the technique yields a compact two-dimensional representation of even large multidimensional data sets by representing the N-dimensional data tuple C with coordinates

$(c_1, c_2, \cdots, c_N)$ points on N parallel axes which are joined with a polyline (see Figure 2) whose N vertices are on the X_i-axis for $i = 1, \ldots, N$ and have xy-coordinates $(i - 1, c_i)$ (Inselberg, 2009).

In theory, the number of attributes that can be represented in parallel coordinates is only limited by the horizontal resolution of the display device. But in a practical sense, the axes that are immediately adjacent to one another yield the most obvious information about relationships between attributes in the classical parallel coordinates plot. In order to analyze attributes that are separated by one or more attributes in the plot, intelligent interactions and graphical indicators are required. In light of this limitation, several innovative parallel coordinates extensions that improve interaction and cognition have been described in the visualization research literature since the introduction of the classical technique. For example, Hauser, Ledermann, and Doleisch (2002) described a histogram display, dynamic axis reordering, axis inversion, and some details-on-demand capabilities for parallel coordinates. In addition, Siirtola (2000) presented a rich set of dynamic interaction techniques (e.g., conjunctive

queries) and Johansson, Ljung, Jern, and Cooper (2005) described new line shading schemes for parallel coordinates. Furthermore, several focus+context implementations for parallel coordinates have been introduced by Fua, Ward, and Rundensteiner (1999), Artero, de Oliveira, and Levkowitz (2004), Johansson et al. (2005), and Novotný and Hauser (2006). More recently, Qu et al. (2007) introduced a method for integrating correlation computations into a parallel coordinates display. The MDX system described in the following sections utilizes variants of these extensions to the classical parallel coordinates plot.

The MDX system enhances the classical parallel coordinates axis by providing cues that guide and refine the analyst's exploration of the information space. This approach is akin to the concept of the scented widget described by Willett, Heer, and Agrawala (2007). Scented widgets are graphical user interface components that are augmented with an embedded visualization to enable efficient navigation in the information space of the data items. The concept arises from the information foraging theory described by Pirolli and Card (1999) which models human information gathering to the food foraging activities of animals. In this model, the concept of information scent is identified as the "user perception of the value, cost, or access path of information sources obtained by proximal cues" (Pirolli & Card, 1999).

The scented axis widgets are also assisted by automated data mining processes that reduce the knowledge discovery timelines. In Seo and Shneiderman (2005), a framework is used to explore and comprehend multidimensional data using a powerful rank-by-feature system that guides the user and supports confirmation of discoveries. Recently, Piringer, Berger, and Hauser (2008) expanded this rank-by-feature approach with a specific focus on comparing subsets in high-dimensional data sets. The MDX system is designed to support a similar rank-by-feature framework with subset selection capabilities us-

Figure 2. The polyline in parallel coordinates maps the N-dimensional data tuple C with coordinates $(c_1, c_2, \cdots, c_N)$ with points on N parallel axes, which are joined with a polyline whose N vertices are on the X_i-axis for $i = 1, \ldots, N$

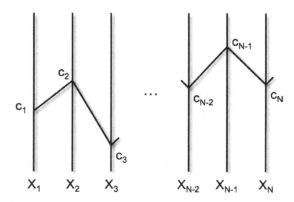

ing stepwise regression, correlation mining, and interactive visual analysis.

CARS DATA SET

The 1983 ASA automobile data set is used throughout the current work to illustrate the MDX capabilities. This popular data set includes 8 variables on 406 different cars and was used in the 1983 ASA Data Exposition. The variables included in this data set are MPG (miles-per-gallon), number of cylinders, engine displacement (cubic inches), horsepower, vehicle weight (lbs.), time to accelerate from 0 to 60 (sec.), model year, and origin of car (1-America, 2-European, and 3-Japanese). The cars data set contains 14 records with null values, which are ignored by MDX reducing the number of records analyzed to 392.

VISUAL DATA MINING AND ANALYSIS TECHNIQUES

In essence, the parallel coordinates panel in MDX (see Figure 1) is a highly interactive canvas that visually presents many multivariate associations in a manner that facilitates multifaceted exploratory data analysis. In addition to providing several fundamental capabilities such as relocatable axes, axis inversion, and details-on-demand, the MDX canvas also provides several novel visual interaction techniques such as axis scaling (focus+context), aerial perspective shading, and dynamic visual queries. These interaction capabilities are described in detail in prior publications of this ongoing research (Steed et al., 2009a, 2009b, 2009c).

In conjunction with these interactive visual query capabilities, MDX provides several data mining techniques that facilitate more rapid, creative, and comprehensive statistical data analysis than conventional systems. As the analyst interacts with the system, several key statistical quantities are calculated on-the-fly and mapped to visual

features within the parallel coordinates display (see Figure 3) to augment the polyline configurations. The statistical indicators guide the analyst in the identification and quantification of the key features and associations in the data set. In addition to graphical indicators of descriptive statistical quantities, the framework offers graphical indicators for correlation measures, tunable data classification methods, regression analysis, an automatic multicollinearity filter, and automatic axis arrangement capabilities. In the remainder of this section, these techniques are presented along with several evaluations of these techniques on the cars data set.

Figure 3. The scented axis widgets in the parallel coordinates display are augmented with graphical indicators of key descriptive statistical quantities, correlation measures, and regression analysis outputs. In this annotated figure, the numbered callouts highlight specific features of the axis widgets which are described in detail in the remainder of this paper

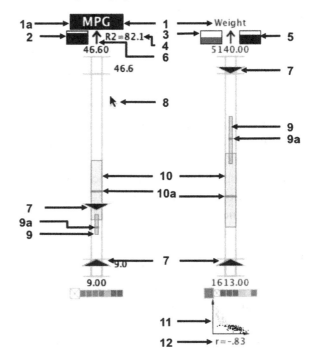

Graphical Indicators of Descriptive Statistics

By providing visual summaries of patterns and general trends in data sets, the graphical statistical indicators in MDX support visual data mining in harmony with the EDA philosophy introduced by Tukey (1977). Each parallel coordinate axis is represented by a scented widget that includes visual representations of several key descriptive statistics. Referring to Figure 3, the median (9a and 10a), InterQuartile Range (IQR) (9 and 10), and frequency information (see Figure 4) are calculated for the data in the focus area of each axis and presented graphically as modified box plots within the interior of the widget. Alternatively, the analyst can switch this display to use the mean and standard deviation range in the box plots.

The wide overall box plot on each axis (see 10 in Figure 3) represents the central tendency and variability for all the axis samples while the more narrow query box plots (see 9 in Figure 3)–drawn over the overall box plots–capture these statistics for only the samples that are selected with the axis query sliders (see 7 in Figure 3). Within the box plots, the thicker horizontal lines (see 9a and 10a in Figure 3) that divide the box vertically represent the median or mean value in the IQR mode or standard deviation range mode, respectively.

The axis query sliders are double-ended and can be manipulated with the mouse cursor to dynamically adjust which lines are highlighted (queried) in the parallel coordinates display. The sliders facilitate the so-called "pinching" query capability described by Inselberg (2009). Lines that are "pinched" between the slider limits for all the axes in the display are rendered in a more prominent manner giving the user the ability to perform rapid Boolean AND selections.

These graphical central tendency and variability indicators provide geometrical shapes that indicate the typical value and how spread out the samples are in the distribution, respectively. For example, in Figure 4 the overall box plots on the

Figure 4. The values on the Acceleration axis are less dispersed than the adjacent Displacement axis. The dispersion of the axes can be perceived visually via a comparison of the overall box plots on each axis. Furthermore, the frequency information, which is displayed as histogram bins shaded according to the number of polylines passing through each bin region, provides a more detailed summary of the dispersiveness of each axis.

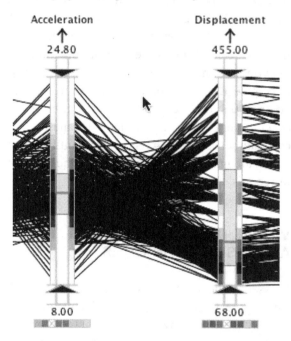

Acceleration axis indicate its values are less dispersed than the adjacent Displacement axis. The dispersiveness of the samples for a particular axis is also shown in more detail in the histogram bins on either side of the axes that encode the frequency information with shading based on the number of polylines that pass through the bin regions. The dispersion of samples for an axis can be a key indicator of the predictability of an attribute. For this reason, these indicators are key elements in such activities as multivariate sensitivity analysis.

The query box plots provide a mechanism to compare subsets of the data with the overall tendencies in the data. In Figure 5, the records with above normal fuel economy are queried using by "pinching" the regions on the MPG

Figure 5. Using the query sliders for the MPG axis, the car records with above normal fuel economy are "pinched" between the sliders to highlight the polylines of interest. The wider box plots characterize the entire set of axis values while the narrow box plots characterize the current subset of "pinched" values In this example, the query shows a single record with good fuel economy and significantly higher engine displacement than the other 94 records that are currently highlighted with the query sliders.

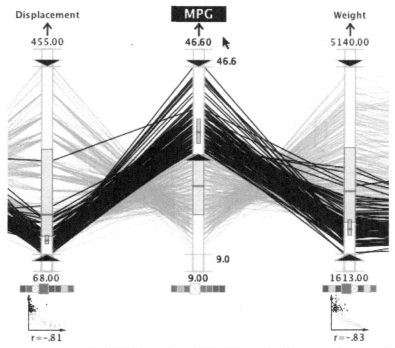

95 of 392 lines selected (24.23%) -- Significant correlation coeff

axis. The query box plots on the Displacement and Weight reveal that the more fuel-efficient car models tend to have lower displacement and weight. This example also highlights a single car record–the queried line connected to the upper range of the Displacement axis box plot–with good fuel economy, but significantly higher engine displacement than the other queried records. Without effective highlighting, such anomalous records can be difficult, at best, to find in a densely packed parallel coordinates display.

On each axis bar interior, the frequency information can also be displayed by representing histogram bins as small rectangles surrounding the axis bar with shades that are indicative of the number of lines that pass through the bin's region (see Figure 4). That is, the darkest bins have the most lines passing through that area of the axis while the lighter bins have less lines. In addition to enabling or disabling the histogram display, the user can also fine tune the frequency display by modifying the histogram bin size in the settings panel.

As an alternative to display each individual record as a polyline in the display, the analyst can modify the display settings to represent the overall central tendency and variability measures using a gray polygon connected between the axes and a blue-gray dashed line, respectively (see Figure 6). The variability polygon is drawn beneath the other polylines in the parallel coordinates display by connecting the IQR or standard deviation range top and bottom limits between the axes. Similarly, the dashed central tendency line is

Figure 6. The user can modify the display settings to enable an axis summary feature and vertical histograms. The axis summary connects the overall central tendency and variability measures with a gray polygon connected between the axes and a blue-gray dashed line. When the data set polylines are not shown, as this figure shows, the summaries and histograms can be combined to explore general trends in large data sets without loss of interactivity.

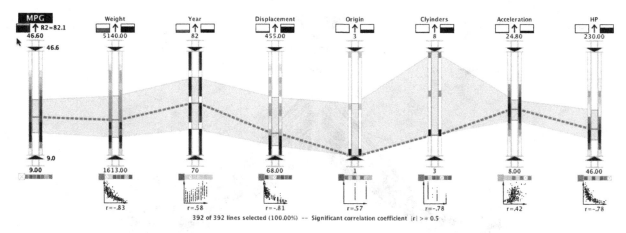

drawn by connecting the median or mean values between the axes. The user can use this feature for quickly summarizing the axes during analysis. For example, if the data set is large enough to reduce interactivity with the individual polylines, the analyst can disable the drawing of all polylines and enable the axis summary to dramatically increase the rendering speed of the system. In addition, the user may enable the display of the frequency indicators to see a more detailed overview of the data. The analyst can then perform all statistical analysis processes, query subsets, and evaluate the descriptive statistics in this summary mode with interactive rendering performance in the display, even with very large data sets. When a detailed plot is desired, the individual polyline rendering can be reactivated in the settings panel.

Visual Correlation Analysis

Correlation mining is an important data mining technique due to its usefulness in identifying underlying dependencies between variables. The correlation mining process attempts to estimate the strength of relationships between pairs of variables to facilitate the prediction of one variable based on what is known about another. The relationship between two variables X and Y can be estimated using a single number, r, that is called the sample correlation coefficient (Walpole & Myers, 1993). MDX uses the Pearson product-moment correlation coefficient to measure the correlation between the axes visible in the parallel coordinates panel. Given a series of n measurements of X and Y written as x_i and y_i where $i = 1, 2, \ldots, n,$ and r is given by Equation 1.

$$r = \frac{n\sum x_i y_i - \left(\sum x_i\right)\left(\sum y_i\right)}{\sqrt{\left[n\sum x_i^2 - \left(\sum x_i\right)^2\right]\left[n\sum y_i^2 - \left(\sum y_i\right)^2\right]}}$$

(1)

For each pair of axes in the display, our system computes r, which results in a correlation matrix. The correlation matrix is a $n \times n$ matrix where each i, j element is equal to the value of r between the i and j variables. As shown in Figure 7, the rows from this correlation matrix are exploded and displayed graphically beneath each axis as a

Figure 7. The graphical correlation indicator blocks that are displayed beneath each axis in the parallel coordinates plot are color-filled representations of the correlation matrix

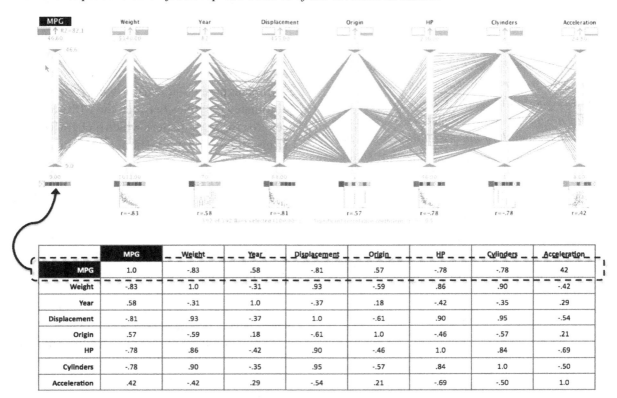

	MPG	Weight	Year	Displacement	Origin	HP	Cylinders	Acceleration
MPG	1.0	-.83	.58	-.81	.57	-.78	-.78	42
Weight	-.83	1.0	-.31	.93	-.59	.86	.90	-.42
Year	.58	-.31	1.0	-.37	.18	-.42	-.35	.29
Displacement	-.81	.93	-.37	1.0	-.61	.90	.95	-.54
Origin	.57	-.59	.18	-.61	1.0	-.46	-.57	.21
HP	-.78	.86	-.42	.90	-.46	1.0	.84	-.69
Cylinders	-.78	.90	-.35	.95	-.57	.84	1.0	-.50
Acceleration	.42	-.42	.29	-.54	.21	-.69	-.50	1.0

series of color-filled blocks. The colors used to fill the blocks are calculated based on the value of r between the axis directly above it and the axis that corresponds to its position in the set of blocks for the particular axis. For example, the first block in the correlation indicators under each axis in Figure 7 represents the correlation strength between the axis above it and the first axis, MPG.

The color of each indicator block is calculated using the color scale shown in Figure 8(b), which results in shades of blue for negative correlations and red for positive correlations. The color scale maps the saturation of the color to the strength of r so that the strongest correlations are displayed more prominently. An axis' r value with itself (the diagonal element) is always equal to one and the corresponding indicator block is shaded white with a gray 'X' symbol (see Figure 8(a)). More-

over, when the absolute value of r is greater than or equal to the user-defined significant correlation threshold, $r_{threshold}$, the block is shaded with the fully saturated color (either red or blue). The current value of $r_{threshold}$ is displayed at the bottom of the parallel coordinates plot (see Figure 6) and this value can be adjusted via the settings panel.

When the mouse cursor (see 8 in Figure 3) hovers over an axis in the parallel coordinates panel–the mouse cursor is hovering over the HP axis in Figure 9–the axis label (see 1 in Figure 3) is enlarged and the correlation coefficient blocks corresponding to it below the other axes are enlarged (see Figure 8(a)). This focus+context effect helps the user to ascertain the correlation of the highlighted axis with all other axes, at a glance. At the same time, the display shows the full correlation matrix for all pairwise combinations of

Figure 8. The correlation indicator blocks that correspond to the diagonal elements are the correlation of the axis with itself–a perfect relationship. In (a), these blocks are shaded white and marked with an 'X' symbol. The enlarged blocks indicate the bivariate correlations between the highlighted axis and the other axes. The color scale in (b) is used to shade the blocks red for positive and blue for negative A saturation scale is applied to encode the strength of the correlations such that correlations above the $r_{threshold}$ value are shaded with the most saturated colors.

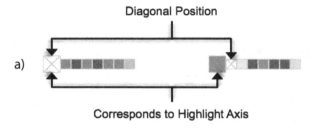

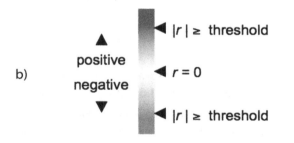

the axes in the display thereby yielding the correlation context.

In addition to graphical representations of r, the system also displays small scatterplots (see 11 in Figure 3) below the axis correlation indicators blocks when an axis is highlighted with the mouse cursor. For example, in Figure 9 the MPG axis is highlighted. These scatterplots are created by plotting the points from the highlighted variable along the y-axis and the variable directly above the scatterplot along the x-axis. Each scatterplot also shows the numerical r value associated with this pair of axes below the scatterplot

(see 12 in Figure 3). The scatterplots in MDX provide a visual mechanism to quickly confirm the type of correlation (positive or negative) as well as the strength of the correlation.

The type of correlation is also visually detectable in the polyline configurations of the parallel coordinates plot. As shown in Figure 9, the parallel coordinates polylines between the MPG and HP axes cross in an 'X' pattern which is characteristic of a negative correlation. The negative correlation is reinforced by the slope in the scatterplot, the color of the correlation indicator blocks, and the r value display. On the other hand, the polylines between the HP and Displacement axes appear more horizontal and parallel to one another, which indicates a positive correlation. Since the visual patterns for the negative correlations tend to dominate the parallel coordinates display, the user can invert an axis by clicking on the arrow beneath each axis label (see 6 in Figure 3).

Unlike the other correlation indicators, the scatterplot is useful for exploring nonlinear relationships between variables. For example, a nonlinear relationship can be observed in a scatterplot even if the correlation coefficient is zero. In Figure 9, a nonlinear relationship is revealed in the scatterplot showing the MPG and HP axes. However, the nonlinearity is not apparent in the parallel coordinate polyline configurations. In Figure 6, the scatterplots beneath the Weight, Displacement, and HP axes reveal nonlinear relationships with the highlighted axis, MPG.

Automated Correlation Analysis

The MDX system provides an automatic multicollinearity filter (see Table 1) to ensure the proper selection of axes in subsequent multiple linear regression analysis. This filter examines the visible axes in the parallel coordinates display for multicollinearity; if any axes are correlated with each other by more than the significant correlation threshold, $r_{threshold}$, one axis is removed from the display (see line 11). The filter removes the axis

Figure 9. The distinct 'X' shaped polyline crossings between the MPG and HP axes are characteristic of strong negative correlations. The more horizontal polylines between the HP and Displacement axes are characteristic of strong positive correlations. Visual correlation mining is facilitated via the parallel coordinate polyline configurations, scatterplots, correlation indicator block colors, and the numeric display of r.

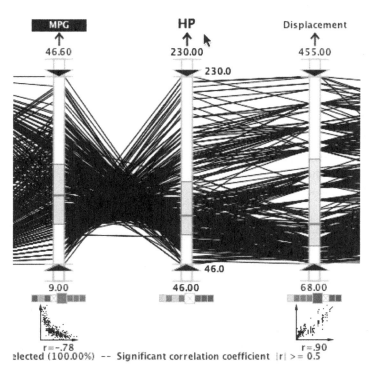

that has a lower *r* with the dependent axis. In this way, the remaining independent axes are truly independent of each other. The analyst can tune the multicollinearity filter by changing the value of $r_{threshold}$.

The user can reduce multicollinearity manually by using the correlation indicators to identify and filter correlated axes using a predetermined threshold; but the filter provides an automatic way to ensure independence and it can be performed at the click of a button. Removing the strongly correlated independent axes will ultimately improve subsequent regression analysis by avoiding over-fitting the data. Although the filtered axes are removed, they can be re-inserted in the display using the checkbox in the Visible

column of the table view (see bottom panel in Figure 1).

Automated Data Classification

Data classification transforms raw data into classes or groups. Data classification can be useful to help discriminate from many differing elements in displays. MDX provides four algorithms from the GeoVista 3 library for classifying the data based on a single attribute (axis): Equal intervals, quantiles, mean-standard deviation, and Jenks' optimal.

With the equal interval classification method, each class occupies an equal interval along the selected classification axis. Although simple to

Algorithm 1. Multicollinearity filter

```
Input: Significant correlation threshold, r_threshold
Input: Array of Axis objects, axes
Input: Single dependent axis, axis_dependent
Output: Truly independent set of axes in display
        // Descending sort by r of each axis with axis_dependent
 1:  axes_sorted ← SORT(axes)
 2:  for Axis object axis ∈ axes_sorted do
 3:     for Axis object axis_compare ∈ axes do
 4:        if axis_compare = axis_dependent then
 5:           continue
 6:        else if axis_compare = axis then
 7:           continue
 8:        else
 9:           r ← CORRELATION(axis, axis_compare)
10:           if r > r_threshold then
11:              remove axis_compare from display
12:           end if
13:        end if
14:     end for
15:  end for
```

compute and easy to interpret, a major disadvantage of the equal intervals approach is that the class limits do not take into consideration the data distribution along the classification axis. The quantile classification method is also simple to compute, but results in the same percentages of observations per class. With the quantiles method, data are rank-ordered with equal numbers of observations placed in each class and the 50th percentile is logically associated with the classes. Like the equal intervals method, the quantiles does not consider how the data are distributed along the classification axis. By contrast, the mean-standard deviation method does consider how the data are distributed along the classification axis; but it only works well for data that are normally distributed. If the data are normally distributed (or near normal), the mean serves as a good dividing point to facilitate a contrast of values above and below it. The Jenks' optimal classification method places similar data values in the same class. Although more difficult to interpret, this optimal classification method is a good choice when the intention is to place

like values in the same class. There are many criteria to consider in selecting the most suitable classification method for a given data set and the reader is referred to the detailed overview of these classification methods and criteria for selecting the "best" method given by Slocum, McMaster, Kessler, and Howard (2009).

Within MDX, the data classification features are controlled by the fields in the Classify tab of the Settings panel (see Figure 10). Within this panel, the analyst can adjust the number of classes that will be produced, the classification algorithm to execute, and the classification axis. When the analyst executes the classification algorithm by clicking on the Classify by Axis button, the system will start the classification algorithm and populate the Classification Classes table in the Classify tab with the information about each class (ID, color, and visibility in the parallel coordinates panel).

In Figure 11(a), the quantile classification method has been applied to the MPG axis to create 4 classes. For the two extreme classes, class 0 captures the most fuel-efficient car models and

Figure 10. MDX features and automated data classification capability that transforms raw data into classes. The data classification settings panel provides the user with control over the class count, classification method, and classification axis. In addition, the panel displays the information about the individual classes in the panel. In this example, the Quantiles classification method was executed on the MPG axis to produce 4 classes.

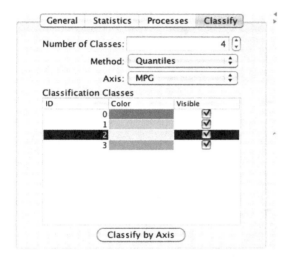

class 3 captures the least fuel-efficient car models. In addition, the two middle classes (classes 1 and 2) capture the cars with average fuel economy.

The checkbox in the Visible column of the class table gives the user control over which polylines are shown in the parallel coordinate plot. Whereas Figure 11(a) shows all the classes, the two middle classes are hidden in Figure 11(b) to facilitate a direct comparison of the extreme upper and lower classes. As a result, only the polylines for class 0 (containing the polylines in the upper range of the MPG axis) and 1 (containing the polylines in the lower range of the MPG axis) are shown. The resulting visual query reveals that the most fuel-efficient car models are those with the lower number of cylinders, displacement, horsepower, and weight. Furthermore, the query also shows that the most fuel-efficient car models are generally slower to accelerate, produced in all

three countries of origin, and are more common in recent year models. Meanwhile, the class containing the least fuel-efficient models has a higher number of cylinders, displacement, horsepower, and weight. As one might expect, acceleration is better in this class. In addition, this class of cars is mostly from the older model years and predominately originate from America (country 1).

The classification capabilities provides an automated way to group similar elements for values on a particular axis and the interaction lets the analyst investigate patterns in class polylines intuitively. The same visual queries facilitated by the classification features can be produced manually using the "pinch" query sliders on the axes. However, the analysis of more than one class of information in a single plot is not possible using the "pinch" query alone. But with the classification method and related interaction capabilities, the user has the ability to rapidly highlight and analyze subsets of the data set in an efficient and iterative manner.

Visual Regression Analysis

Regression analysis is often exploited to identify the most relevant relationships in a particular data set. Such techniques are effective for providing quantitative associations and obtaining an adequate and interpretable description of how a set of predictors affect the dependent variable in a system. In addition to simple linear regression, MDX offers stepwise multiple linear regression with a backwards glance which selects the optimum number of the most important variables using a predefined significance level (Walpole & Myers, 1993).

The MDX MLR analysis includes a normalization procedure so that the y-intercept becomes zero and the importance of a predictor can be assessed by comparing regression coefficients, b_i, between different predictors. Denoting σ as the standard deviation of a variable, y as the dependent

Figure 11. The Quantiles classification method was executed on the MPG axis to produce 4 classes, which are indicated by color in (a). The color legend is shown in Figure 10. The Visible column in the Classification Classes table of the Classify panel gives the user the ability to interactively determine when class polylines are shown in the parallel coordinates plot. This feature provides the ability to perform rapid characterizations and comparisons of a class or a set of classes. In (b), the classes from the upper and lower range of the MPG axis are shown in isolation to reveal the patterns for high and low fuel economy respectively.

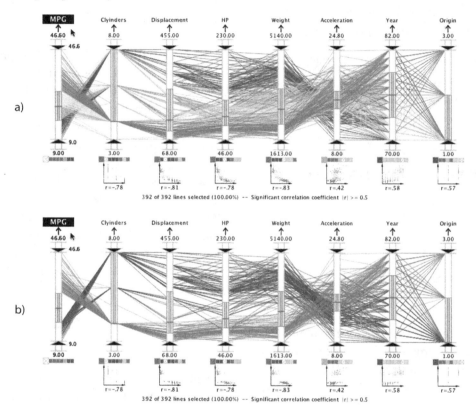

variable, x as a predictor, $\bar{x}$ as the predictor mean, and $\bar{y}$ as the dependent variable mean, a number k of statistically significant predictors are normalized by Equation 2.

$$\frac{\left(y - \bar{y}\right)}{\sigma_y} = \sum_{i=1}^{k} b_i \frac{\left(x_i - \bar{x}_i\right)}{\sigma_i} \qquad (2)$$

The interactive visual analysis features in MDX complement the stepwise regression capabilities by screening and isolating the significant variables in a quantitative fashion. As illustrated in Figure

12, MDX executes a MATLAB process and captures output from the MATLAB regress and stepwisefit commands that perform simple and stepwise regression, respectively. The MATLAB textual output stream is then parsed and relevant statistical information is extracted and represented graphically within the parallel coordinates display.

Referring to 3 in Figure 3, the system graphically encodes b in the parallel coordinates panel using the box that is below the axis label and to the left of the arrow. Like a thermometer, the box is filled from the bottom to the top based on the magnitude of b. The box is colored red if the

Figure 12. MDX features an interactive stepwise multiple regression analysis capability that allows the user to choose or exclude variables, execute the automated analysis, and examine the results in the augmented parallel coordinates display. The regression capability represents an iterative loop designed to reveal the most significant parameters for the chosen dependent axis.

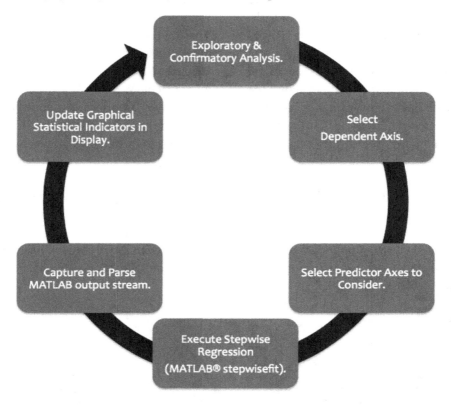

coefficient is positive and blue if it is negative. The box to the right of the arrow, 5 in Figure 3, encodes the r^2 output from the SLR process. In addition to the coefficients, the MLR analysis returns an overall R^2 value, which provides a quantitative indication of how well the model captures the variance between the predictors and the dependent variable. Referring to 2 in Figure 3, the box beneath the dependent variable axis name, 1a in Figure 3, encodes the overall R^2 value from the MLR analysis. The R^2 value is also presented numerically (see 4 in Figure 3).

When these boxes are filled with a light gray 'X', the value is not defined (the SLR or MLR process has not been executed) or, in the case of the MLR analysis, the variable was excluded during the selection process. It is also important to note that the axis corresponding to the dependent variable is indicated by light gray text on a dark gray box for its title (see 1a in Figure 3)–the reverse shading of the other axes.

As shown in Figure 12, the stepwise regression process can be represented as an interactive feedback loop in which the analyst can designate the dependent axis, choose which axes to consider in the regression model, execute the regression analysis via MATLAB, and visually examine the results in the augmented parallel coordinates display. Combining the strengths of automated analytics with human intuition, creativity, and flexibility, this approach provides an effective means to discover the most significant set of predictors.

Figure 13(a) shows the resulting model generated by the MDX stepwise regression analysis for the cars data set using MPG as the dependent axis. In this example, the axes are sorted in descending order based on the resulting value of *b*. In addition to the graphical indicators of *b*, the SLR r^2 graphical indicators convey information about the significance of each variable with respect to the dependent axis. The plot arrangement shows the Weight axis is the most significant axis based on the stepwise regression analysis. Furthermore, the "pinch" sliders are used in this example to highlight the most fuel-efficient records. The high percentage of highly saturated colors in the correlation indicator blocks beneath each axis in Figure 13(a) reveal that several of independent variables are highly correlated with one another. This multicollinearity condition should be addressed prior to the regression process execution. Using the MDX automated multicollinearity filter, all except the Weight, Year, and Acceleration axes are removed from consideration by the next execution of the regression process. In Figure 13(b), the new regression model is shown. In this model, the

Figure 13. With the MPG axis designated as the dependent axis, the regression model shown in (a) was produced by MDX. The high number of highly saturated correlation indicator blocks in this plot indicates the high number of independent variables that are highly correlated with one another. To reduce this condition, the MDX multicollinearity filter is executed and the regression process is repeated. The output of the new regression (b) provides an adequate model with a fewer number of independent variables than the first attempt (a).

a)

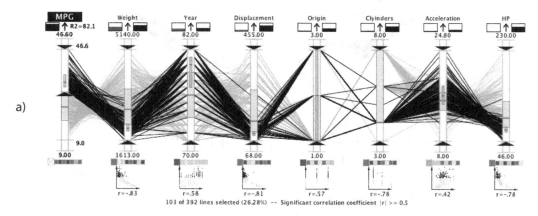

b)

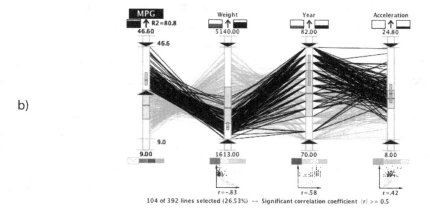

Weight and Year axes were retained but the Acceleration axis was not chosen by the regression process. Although the overall R^2 for the model dropped slightly from the non-filtered version, the new model provides an adequate model with a fewer number of independent variables. Reducing the number of predictors is helpful to exploratory analysis because it simplifies interpretation and it usually means cheaper data collection and analysis.

Furthermore, the small boxplot for the Weight axis in Figure 13(b) reflects the tight clustering of polylines, which are mostly below the median value. These characteristics are indicators that Weight can be used to effectively predict the fuel efficiency of a car. If the lines were mostly dispersed, the small boxplot would be taller and reflect a condition where by the analyst may have difficulty using the predictor to predict the dependent variable. The analyst can continue to utilize the interactive interface to conduct confirmatory analysis of the resulting regression models and, optionally, iterate to produce new regression models.

Optimal Axis Arrangement

In the classic parallel coordinates plot, adjacent axes reveal the most information about one other. The correlation indicators and graphical statistical indicators provide one viable way to reveal information between all axes, simultaneously, regardless of the current axis locations. MDX also provides a set of optimal axis arrangement schemes that automatically arrange the axes in the parallel coordinates panel using one of the following precomputed statistical measures:

- Correlation coefficient (r)
- IQR / standard deviation range
- MLR coefficient (b)
- SLR (r^2) value

This capability facilitates more rapid statistical comparisons between the displayed axes. The analyst can execute the arrangement process using the Process tab in the settings panel or through the pop-up menu that is displayed when the user right clicks in the parallel coordinates panel.

When the axes are sorted by r, one axis is selected initially as the target axis. The axes are then sorted according to the r value of the target axis and the other visible axes. As shown in Figure 14, the axes with negative correlations are arranged to the left of the target axis in ascending order. Similarly, the axes with positive correlations are arranged to the right of the target axis in descending order. The strongest correlations are placed nearest to the target axis while the weakest correlations are placed farthest away. When the axes are sorted in this manner, the analyst can quickly identify the strongest correlations with the target axis and engage in more effective correlation analysis.

The IQR / standard deviation range, b, and r^2 arrangement options all sort the axes in descending order based on the respective statistical measures. The dependent axis is placed at the leftmost position and the other axes are arranged accordingly to the right of it. The IQR / standard deviation range arrangement is useful for examining the dispersion characteristics of each axis. The r^2 arrangement is useful as an alternate method for observing the individual correlation of axes with the dependent axis. The b arrangement (see Figure 13(a)) helps to analyze the stepwise regression model results and quantify the most significant axes for the dependent axis.

Discussion

In traditional data analysis tools, a collection of separate visualization and analysis tools are usually employed. Furthermore, the visualizations are often comprised of static techniques developed more than a decade ago; and it is questionable whether these techniques can meet the demands of today's data. Consequently, the analyst is afforded limited interactivity with the data, thereby hindering the discovery of new hypotheses. By

Figure 14. MDX can automatically arrange the display axes according to the correlation coefficients, r, with a particular axis. In this example, the axes are arranged based on the correlation with the MPG axis. Axes with negative correlations are arranged on the left of the highlighted axis and positively correlated axes are arranged on the right.

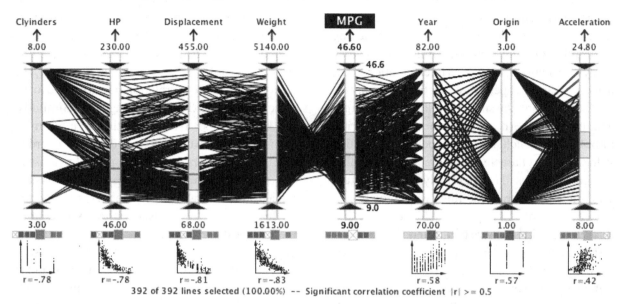

integrating statistical and visualization processes, MDX gives the analyst rapid, visual query capabilities for faster and more creative knowledge discovery. In case studies that utilized MDX to conduct exploratory climate analysis (Steed et al., 2009a, 2009b, 2009c), MDX was compared to more traditional, static systems. Whereas the more traditional process took days to reach conclusions, analysis with MDX required hours. Perhaps the greatest evidence of the promise of the visual analytics approach came during these climate case studies from a weather science expert, Dr. Patrick Fitzpatrick, who, in addition to authoring several articles (Fitzpatrick, 1997) and books (Fitzpatrick, 1999) on hurricane climate studies, is also a co-author of this chapter. Dr. Fitzpatrick indicated that the MDX system facilitated more rapid and comprehensive analysis and validation than traditional static analysis techniques. The utilization of Coordinated Multiple Views (CMV) in MDX helps the viewer conduct more creative exploratory analysis by offering multiple views

of the data where actions in one view are propagated to others according to some visual effect. For example, non-linear relationships are more difficult to discover in parallel coordinates, but straightforward to identify in a scatterplot. On the other hand, the number of variables that can be displayed in a scatterplot is generally restricted to two or three dimensions. Moreover, it is difficult to decipher correlations between axes in all but the extreme cases in the parallel coordinates plot, but the scatterplot is more useful for more subtle cases that are often encountered in real-world data. Having both the parallel coordinates plot and the scatterplots in MDX gives the analyst access to both views in a complementary fashion, which offsets said deficiencies. Furthermore, the inclusion of parallel coordinates plot in new areas such as climate analysis forces the analyst to consider the data in new ways, which often encourages fresh insight.

As discussed in preceding section on Visual Correlation Analysis, extreme negative and positive correlations can be detected by characteristic visual patterns. However, more subtle correlations are not as easily detected and it is impossible to grasp the correlations between all pairs of axes using classical parallel coordinates. With the graphical correlation indicator blocks, the more subtle correlations are conveyed directly using a carefully designed saturation color scale. Also, these correlation indicator blocks capture a holistic overview of all correlations between pairs of axes by exploding the correlation matrix. As Shneiderman (1996) notes, providing an overview helps the analyst build a mental model of how the data covers the attribute space. In turn, the model helps the analyst formulate new queries on the data (Plaisant, Shneiderman, Doan, & Bruns, 1999). These linked views provide the level of interactivity and coordination necessary to cope with today's complex, multivariate data.

A significant amount of time has been devoted to formulating an optimal color scheme and layout for the MDX interface. The color scheme and layout is based upon color design principles from fine art and graphic design (Itten, 1970), as well as empirical perceptual studies (Ware, 2004). For example, muted colors are used in most of the graphical elements reserving the most saturated colors for small portions of the display. This creates a visual balance that is aesthetically pleasing to the viewer. Furthermore, the most vivid colors are placed on the peripheral of the display to further balance the view. The color-coded correlation blocks described in the Section on Visual Correlation Analysis are a good illustration of the significance of a well-planned color design. The saturation scale directs visual attention to the strongest correlations and the blue and red shades cue the analyst to sign of the correlation. When planned intelligently, the overall color scheme of the application will greatly improve the user experience by reducing fatigue and making important relationships stand out to the viewer. The color scheme can also improve the viewer's confidence in the software's capabilities, at least

initially, which is crucial to efficient communication of results.

CONCLUSION AND FUTURE RESEARCH DIRECTIONS

An enhanced version of the MDX framework has been described in this work that offers new visual correlation mining, interactive regression analysis, and interactive, semi-automated data classification. Several illustrations of this new framework have been demonstrated with the popular ASA cars data set to highlight how the approach enhances knowledge discovery in multivariate data sets.

In the future, the MDX system will be expanded to explore additional data sets. The system has already been evaluated with several complex tropical cyclone and oceanographic data sets. In addition to additional climate data sets, new methods for transforming unstructured data into insightful representations within MDX are being investigated now. The MDX system has shown significant promise in several practical evaluations. The results of these evaluations provide compelling evidence that visual analytics solutions can meet the complex challenges of deciphering actionable knowledge from today's increasingly complicated data.

ACKNOWLEDGMENT

This research is sponsored by the U.S. Department of Energy, the U.S. Naval Research Laboratory, the National Oceanographic and Atmospheric Administration (NOAA) with grants NA060AR4600181 and NA050AR4601145, and through the Northern Gulf Institute that is funded by grant NA06OAR4320264. This paper was prepared by the Oak Ridge National Laboratory, P.O. Box 2008, Oak Ridge, Tennessee 37831-6285, managed by UT–Battelle, LLC, for the U.S. Department of Energy, under contract DE- AC05-00OR22725.

The United States Government retains and the publisher, by accepting the article for publication, acknowledges that the United States Government retains a non-exclusive, paid-up, irrevocable, world-wide license to publish or reproduce the published form of this manuscript, or allow others to do so, for United States Government purposes.

REFERENCES

Artero, A. O., de Oliverira, M. C. F., & Levkowitz, H. (2004). Uncovering clusters in crowded parallel coordinates visualization. In *IEEE Symposium on Information Visualization*, 81-88. New Brunswick, NJ: IEEE Press.

Fitzpatrick, P. J. (1997). Understanding and forecasting tropical cyclone intensity change with the Typhoon Intensity Prediction Scheme (TIPS). *Weather and Forecasting*, *12*(4), 826–846. doi:10.1175/1520-0434(1997)012<0826:UAFTCI>2.0.CO;2.

Fitzpatrick, P. J. (1999). *Natural disasters, hurricanes: A reference handbook*. Santa Barbara, CA: ABC-CLIO.

Fua, Y.-H., Ward, M. O., & Rundensteiner, E. A. (1999). Hierarchical parallel coordinates for exploration of large datasets. In *Proceedings of IEEE Visualization*, 43-50. New Brunswick, NJ: IEEE Press.

Hauser, H., Ledermann, F., & Doleisch, H. (2002). Angular brushing of extended parallel coordinates. In *Proceedings of IEEE Symposium on Information Visualization*, 127-130. New Brunswick, NJ: IEEE Press.

Healey, C. G., Tateosian, L., Enns, J. T., & Remple, M. (2004). Perceptually-based brush strokes for non-photorealistic visualization. *ACM Transactions on Graphics*, *23*(1), 64–96. doi:10.1145/966131.966135.

Inselberg, A. (1985). The plane with parallel coordinates. *The Visual Computer*, *1*(4), 69–91. doi:10.1007/BF01898350.

Inselberg, A. (2009). Parallel coordinates: Interactive visualization for high dimensions. InZudilova- Seinstra, E., Adriaansen, T., & Liere, R. (Ed.), *Trends in Interactive Visualization* (49-78). London: Springer-Verlag. doi:10.1007/978-1-84800-269-2_3.

Itten, J. (1970). *The elements of color*. Ravensburg, Germany: Van Nostrand Reinhold Publishing.

Johansson, J., Ljung, P., Jern, M., & Cooper, M. (2005). Revealing structure within clustered parallel coordinates displays. In *IEEE Symposium on Information Visualization*, 125-132. New Brunswick, NJ: IEEE Press.

Novotný, M., & Hauser, H. (2006). Outlier-preserving focus+context visualization in parallel coordinates. *IEEE Transactions on Visualization and Computer Graphics*, *12*(5), 893–900. doi:10.1109/TVCG.2006.170 PMID:17080814.

Piringer, H., Berger, W., & Hauser, H. (2008). Quantifying and comparing features in high-dimensional datasets. In *Proceedings of the International Conference on Information Visualization*, 240-245. New Brunswick, NJ: IEEE Press.

Pirolli, P., & Card, S. K. (1999). Information foraging. *Psychological Review*, *106*(4), 643–675. doi:10.1037/0033-295X.106.4.643.

Plaisant, C., Shneiderman, B., Doan, K., & Bruns, T. (1999). Interface and data architecture for query preview in networked information systems. *ACM Transactions on Information Systems*, *17*(3), 320–341. doi:10.1145/314516.314522.

Qu, H., Chan, W., Xu, A., Chung, K., Lau, K., & Guo, P. (2007). Visual analysis of the air pollution problem in Hong Kong. *IEEE Transactions on Visualization and Computer Graphics*, *13*(6), 1408–1415. doi:10.1109/TVCG.2007.70523 PMID:17968091.

Rensink, R. A. (2002). Change detection. *Annual Review of Psychology*, *53*, 245–577. doi:10.1146/annurev.psych.53.100901.135125 PMID:11752486.

Seo, J., & Shneiderman, B. (2005). A rank-by-feature framework for interactive exploration of multidimensional data. *Information Visualization*, *4*(2), 96–113. doi:10.1057/palgrave.ivs.9500091.

Shneiderman, B. (1996). The eyes have it: A task by data type taxonomy for information visualizations. In *Proceedings of IEEE Symposium on Visual Languages*, 336-343. New Brunswick, NJ: IEEE Press.

Siirtola, H. (2000). Direct manipulation of parallel coordinates. In *Proceedings of the International Conference on Information Visualisation*, 373-378. New Brunswick, NJ: IEEE.

Slocum, T. A., McMaster, R. B., Kessler, F. C., & Howard, H. H. (2009). *Thematic cartography and geovisualization*. Upper Saddle River, NJ: Prentice Hall.

Steed, C. A., Fitzpatrick, P. J., Jankun-Kelly, T. J., Yancey, A. N., & Swan, J. E. II. (2009). An interactive parallel coordinates technique applied to a tropical cyclone climate analysis. *Computers & Geosciences*, *35*(7), 1529–1539. doi:10.1016/j.cageo.2008.11.004.

Steed, C. A., Fitzpatrick, P. J., Swan, J. E. II, & Jankun-Kelly, T. J. (2009). Tropical cyclone trend analysis using enhanced parallel coordinates and statistical analytics. *Cartography and Geographic Information Science*, *36*(3), 251–265. doi:10.1559/152304009788988314.

Steed, C. A., Swan, J. E., II, Jankun-Kelly, T. J., & Fitzpatrick, P. J. (2009). Guided analysis of hurricane trends using statistical processes integrated with interactive parallel coordinates. In *Proceedings of IEEE Symposium on Visual Analytics Science and Technology*, 19-26. New Brunswick, NJ: IEEE Press.

Thomas, J. J., & Cook, K. A. (Eds.). (2005). *Illuminating the path: The research and development agenda for visual analytics*. Los Alamitos, CA: IEEE Press.

Tukey, J. W. (1977). *Exploratory data analysis*. Reading, MA: Addison-Wesley.

Walpole, R. E., & Myers, R. H. (1993). *Probability and statistics for engineers and scientists* (5th ed.). Englewood Cliffs, NJ: Prentice Hall.

Ware, C. (2004). *Information visualization: Perception for design* (2nd ed.). New York: Morgan Kaufmann.

Wegman, E. J. (1990). Hyperdimensional data analysis using parallel coordinates. *Journal of the American Statistical Association*, *85*(411), 664–675. doi:10.1080/01621459.1990.10474926.

Wilkinson, L., Anand, A., & Grossman, R. (2006). High-dimensional visual analytics: Interactive exploration guided by pairwise views of point distributions. *IEEE Transactions on Visualization and Computer Graphics*, *12*(6), 1366–1372. doi:10.1109/TVCG.2006.94 PMID:17073361.

Willett, W., Heer, J., & Agrawala, M. (2007). Scented widgets: Improving navigation cues with embedded visualizations. *IEEE Transactions on Visualization and Computer Graphics*, *13*(6), 1129–1136. doi:10.1109/TVCG.2007.70589 PMID:17968056.

Wong, P. C., & Bergeron, R. D. (1997). 30 years of multidimensional multivariate visualization. InNielson, , Müller, , & Hagen, (Eds.) *Scientific Visualization-Overviews, Methodologies, and Techniques*, (3-33). New Brunswick, NJ: IEEE Computer Society Press.

Chapter 3
Understanding Spatial and Non-Spatial Cues in Representing Categorical Information

Moonyati Yatid
University of Sydney, Australia

Masahiro Takatsuka
University of Sydney, Australia

ABSTRACT

The continuously increasing amount of digital information available to computer users has led to the wide use of notification systems. Although these systems could support the management of information, they could also be an interruption to primary work. To minimize this interruption, a number of approaches, which notify the different categorical information, have been introduced. In this work, we focused on understanding the effectiveness of different types of visual cues to effectively represent categorical notification. Five basic visual parameters of motion, colour, shape, motion and spatial were chosen to represent sets of two categories, four categories, six categories and eight categories of information. The effectiveness of these visual cues in assisting users' ability to decode the categorical cues was examined through a series of experimental studies. Findings suggest the superiority of using colour, shape, and spatial cues to represent categorical information. Post experiment questionnaire reveals possible reasons for their efficiency. Spatial memory supports spatial cues while linguistic influence supports the shape/colour cues. The unsuitability of size parameter is possibly due to not being able to measure the cues against something during the encoding process. This makes it difficult to determine how each cue differs from the rest of the cues in the parameter, especially when number of categories increase. As for the motion parameter, encoding the cues took far longer response times, although time taken is consistent across number of categories. The different effects of these basic visual cues suggest the importance of careful design selection to ensure successful visualization.

DOI: 10.4018/978-1-4666-4309-3.ch003

INTRODUCTION

Notification systems have been widely used in recent years in order to provide the necessary awareness for users. This includes informing on the activities of other users, shared documents that have been created, new emails that have been received and many more. In other words, notification systems could be used to provide various types of information sources by a variety of user interface designs. The most common selections to represent these notifications are visual, auditory and combination of both dimensions.

The effects of visual designs on user's attention have been investigated by many (Hoffman, 2008; Khan, 2005). In these studies, design properties such as colours, luminance, shapes and so forth were investigated to understand which design is most suitable to direct user's attention towards targeted items. Others might be more interested in the effect of design towards user's ability to carry out dual activities, of both primary task and keeping aware of information from notification systems(Maglio, 2000; McCrickard, Catrambone, Chewar, & Stasko, 2003). In those studies, authors investigated the effects of several types of moving texts that delivers information. The direction of the texts as well as the frequency of the movement was among the parameters of interests.

In this study, we are interested to find the effects of different visual properties on user's ability to recognize the meanings they represent. We believe that this study would be useful in designing categorical notification systems. Categorical notification system means that there exist several categories within the system in order to provide users with more information of the new notification. For instance, in managing emails, users could categorize them into groups depending on sender. Thus, when a new email arrives, the notification system will automatically indicate which category that email is grouped into. This allows users to easily decide whether the notification should be attended to immediately or not. Thus, unwanted interruptions could be avoided.

BACKGROUND

1. Notification Systems and Design Consideration

The fast and dynamic exchange of information in today's workplace means that users' management of that information is highly critical. Thus, notification systems have been widely used to provide appropriate support in that matter. Using various visualization approaches, these systems keep users aware of current happenings. Ideally, notification systems should be able to notify users the availability of new and valuable information in an efficient way and be attended to at least a certain degree(McCrickard, Czerwinski, & Bartram, 2003). It is essential that it is not disruptive to primary tasks, while being salient enough to grab user attention when it is highly needed.

Various visual designs have been proposed in order to create appropriate notification systems. Systems could represent various types of data, new email, availability of colleagues, stock prices and many more. These variations also mean that design selections could be data and domain specific. For instance, a majority of notification systems that alert users on new emails use 'badge' to represent information. A numerical number in a 'badge'-like visual icon indicates how many new pieces of information have arrived and also how many have not been attended to. Other examples include the use of different types of moving texts to represent stock prices, and different colours to represent the availability of colleagues.

The designs of notification systems are not limited to visual cues that represent information. Visual and auditory cues have also been evaluated to provide awareness on risky situations in dark rooms(Kanai, 2008). An auditory based prototype system named AudioAura has been developed to provide awareness on people's physical actions within a workplace, such as location of a fellow colleague (Baer, 1998). The design of those auditory cues manipulating different sound effects, music, voice, or a combination of those cues was investigated to explore issues such as privacy and work practice. It has been suggested that application of auditory cues could also be useful in dual-task scenarios. For instance, simultaneously carrying out item search assisted by auditory cues is easier than purely visual cues, when users are walking, as he/she needs to pay attention to the surroundings(Yu, 2010). This means that when a user carries out other tasks that require visual attention, it is an advantage to apply audio cues so that the visual modality is not burdened. Other modalities such as tactile and olfactory have also been investigated (Bodnar, 2004; Chan, 2008), although they have not been a popular choice in notification systems.

In a workplace environment that requires users to have constant interaction with displays, visual cues are most appropriate due to user attention that is already on the display. Furthermore, visual cues could support individual awareness without being interruptive to other colleagues. Investigations on different effects of visual cues such as ability to attract attention(Bartram, 2003; Hoffman, 2008; Khan, 2005) and ability to provide information without being interruptive (Maglio, 2000; McCrickard, Catrambone, Chewar, & Stasko, 2003) suggest the design trade-off of each visual cue. Therefore, it is important to employ suitable design based on users' aims, to ensure a successful notification system. Taxonomy of notification systems has identified four design questions that need to be known before a system could be built (Pousman, 2006). There are the information capacity, notification level, representational fidelity and ecstatic emphasis. While 'Information Capacity' involves the amount of information sources a system represents, 'Notification Level' means the degree of interruption given to users. 'Representational fidelity' describes how the data is encoded, and 'Aesthetic Emphasis' describes the relative importance of aesthetics used in the system. In another study, the costs and benefits of design selection is discussed. In order to compare design selections (McCrickard & Chewar,

2003). Authors discussed three key points that should be considered when making design selections, comprehension, reaction and interruption. 'Comprehension' is when information obtained could be stored for future use. 'Reaction' is when response is made after information has been received. 'Interruption' involves the reallocation of attention from primary task. For instance, when the goal of a notification system is to provide low interruption, high reaction and low comprehension, small sized and in-placed moving texts could be implemented.

2. Notification and Interruption

In designing notification systems, the effects of interruption should not be taken lightly. The degree of interruptions caused by notification systems should be selected based on the importance of the information sources. When importance is low and only general awareness of new information needs to be provided, calm and peripheral interfaces could be applied. On the other hand, salient type of notification that attracts user attention is needed when new information needs to be addressed instantly. However, when user goals and system design do not match, notifications could possibly be interruptive to users' primary task. Interruption is costly, especially to fast and stimulus driven main tasks (Czerwinski, 2000).

Past studies have suggested that interruption could be controlled by exploiting interruption lag(Andrews, 2009; Trafton, 2003). Interruption lag is when there exists an interval in between an alert and actually attending to that alert. This interval allows users to make better preparation on current task so that resuming to it later could be easier. Another approach to limit interruption is by varying the frequency of notification. Interestingly, it has been suggested that frequent interruptions allow users to resume back to primary task faster than infrequent interruptions(Monk, 2004). It is possible that the rapid switching of tasks force users to adopt a strategy that involves actively rehearsing their suspended goals during interruption. In another study, McFarlane has identified and compared four primary methods of coordinating user's interruption(McFarlane, 2002). According to the investigation, user interface that supports the negotiation of interruption is the best solution, compared to other methods of immediate, mediated and scheduled interruptions. It has been suggested that a user's characteristic, whether a polychromic user of a monochromic user, influences how he or she perceives the interruption level and the preference to rapidly attend to them or not (Huang, 2007). However, the differences in user characteristics do not influence user's ability to divide his or her attention in a dual-task paradigm rapidly.

One of the ways to control interruption level caused by overflowing notifications is to categorize the information represented by those notifications. Categorization could be made based on who the sender is, the importance of the notification, the contents and many more. Therefore, users not only are aware that something new has happened, but also given some extra information about the situation. This allows users to prioritize his or her current task, or whether it is worth attending to the newly arrived information. Categorical notifications could be represented by cues of various interface designs, and these representations are usually learned in the beginning of using those systems. It is essential to understand the effect of those representations towards human behaviours, and how a careful design selection has to be made in order to suit them with user goals.

3. Categorical Notifications

As discussed earlier, categorizing information in notification systems could provide extra information that guides user's decision-making process. Based on this extra information, users are able to make better judgment whether to attend to notification immediately or later. For instance, pieces of information could be categorized into 'family'

and 'colleagues' in emails to narrow down the sender. Then, if a user is notified that a new email has arrived, attendance to it could be made based on its relative importance with the current task.

A notification system called Scope (Dantzich, 2002), visualizes multiple information based on various design properties. Multiple information sources such as emails, appointments and alerts are displayed on a circular radar-like design, where the more urgent a notification is, the more centrally it is placed. Different shapes, colours, brightness, and animated cues were also employed to indicate other specific meanings (Figure 1). This allows users to observe items in a low-effort way. However, as there are many properties visualized in the system, the identification of the meanings of those items may be difficult. For instance, the original design of scope shows issues in the colour selection of cues that did not contrast well with the background. Also, too many information presented (thus too many visual cues) questions the value of information and their necessity. If a system becomes too complex to be used, it is possible that it might infer more interruption to users, as they need longer time to encode information.

The use of notification system that unifies multiple information using basic visual cues could be described with commercial system like Dockstar (Ecamm, 2013). Dockstar allows users to control the visual representation used based on their preference. Each cue is located within a different area of an icon, and they could be modified by users' preferred colour, shape and size (Figure 2). Dockstar supports the monitoring of different email accounts simultaneously, as each account is represented by a notification cue.

ENCODING VISUAL PARAMETERS

The categorization of information is commonly represented by texts. However, there have been suggestions that graphical user interfaces could support faster user response and higher user

Figure 1. Scope's original design (left) and refined design (right)

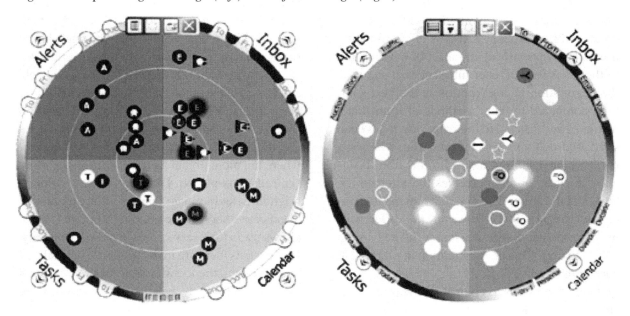

preference compared to text-based interfaces in a variety of tasks (Davis, 1992; Rauterberg, 1992; Staggers, 2000). Furthermore, if textual information could be substituted by graphical elements, less screen space is needed. This is especially useful for mobile devices as display size is more limited compared to desktop computers.

Therefore, the investigations carried out in this study aim to attain other visual parameters that could support the same goal. While the fundamental of visualization with regards to visual parameters and data types have been studied (such as Jaques Bertin's Semiology of Graphics[Bertin, 1983]), we believe that it would be valuable to investigate the relationships between basic visual parameters and human's categorization capability. To construct visual cues optimally we first break down the types of cues into spatial and non-spatial cues. Non-spatial cues consist of colour, shape, motion and size conditions that represent information. User's abilities 1) to differentiate each cue from the others within the same condition

Figure 2. The examples of design selection in Dockstar

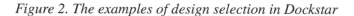

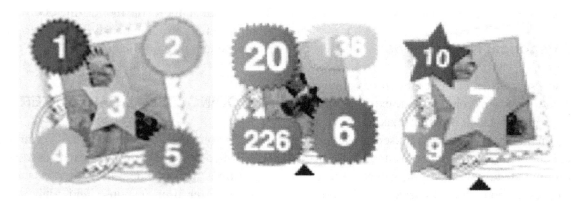

and 2) to encode the information they represent were tested. The correlations between cue and memory, as well as cue and differentiation ability are discussed as follows,

Cue and Memory

We first lay out the importance of memory in the management of information sources associated with visual cues. Past works have suggested a strong relation between memory and spatial information. The method of loci, for instance, is a well-known mnemonic associating spatial relationships to establish, order and recollect memorial content (Yates, 1966). The benefits of spatial memory has been explored in many contexts such as keeping track of rapidly changing information (Hess, 1999) and guiding interrupted users in task resumptions (Ratwani, 2008).

It has also been suggested that spatial location is memorized automatically (Andrade, 1993). That means that difficulty of tasks and the amount of attention given on the memory task have no effect upon spatial memory performance. The memory for colour and size however, are by no means automatic. Memory could be improved by instructions to attend to those colour and size (of text) conditions, however the consequences are that the memory performance decline for the semantic aspects of studied texts (Light, 1974). These differences contribute to the different affect or influence they bring towards other memorization tasks. For instance, as location is not modulated by learning instructions to be memorized, it does not benefit from effortful processing. Effective meaning of texts leads to better memory for spatial information regardless of whether the spatial information is learnt on purpose or incidentally (D'Argembeau & Van der Linden, 2004). In contrast, the effect of those texts only influence memory for colour when the colours are learnt incidentally together with the texts (D'Argembeau & Van der Linden, 2004).

Cue and Differentiation Ability

Differentiating cues or codes is one of the general guideline in the use of coding systems (McCormick, 1982). User performance in cue recognition is superior when the cues employed are easily differentiated (e.g. [Arend, 1987]). It is difficult to do relative comparison for non-spatial cues because users need to compare them in their memory. The ability to recognize the spatial cues however, allow a user to have attribute space on the screen and not just in one's head. Differentiating task may be most difficult when different sizes of cues are involved. As there is a limit to the suitable sizes of cues to be employed (in interface design), there would be very small difference between each one of them as more categories are represented. Different sized cues may be hard to be differentiated, especially when there is nothing to measure them against. Thus, recognizing the different representations of different sized cues could be very difficult.

EXPERIMENTS

Based on these past studies, we carried out an experiment to compare the effectiveness of visual cues to represent pieces of information in a categorical notification system. We believe that each visual parameter would influence user behaviours differently. Therefore, it is worth understanding the correlation between the characteristics of visual cue and user behaviours, so that appropriate design selections could be made.

Five basic visual cues of spatial, colour, shape, size and motion cues are tested. Investigations focus on two aspects, 1) Users' ability to identify separate categories and 2) Users' ability to differentiate visual cues. The impact of individual cues on these capabilities was tested through measuring the user's task performance. We refrained from employing such experiment where the user receives various notifications as they go about other activities, because the response time would then be contaminated with the time taken for users to first notice the cues. We were interested in the situation that users need to extract some pieces of information from visual cues. Since user's goal is to identify categories and differentiate visual cues, we hypothesize that,

H1-1: Spatial cues allow user to more easily identify categories and differentiate cues

H1-2: The use of colour and shape in visual cue yields better identification/differentiation performance than the use of size and motion

Subjects

The study is a within-subjects experiment and we recruited 15 people as subjects. There were 8 females and 7 males, all aged between 21 to 37 years old participating in the experiment. They were all university students in the Information Technology department. None of the participants reported themselves as colour-blind.

Interface

Subjects were required to learn and to make associations between categorical information and visual attributes of location, colour, shape, size and motion. All cues are coloured red, except for the different colour variations in testing the colour

parameter. Other than the cues in the size condition, all cues are sized is 32x32 pixel, which is an accepted icon size typically integrated in websites or toolbars. Each cue represents a number, which vary in different sets and materials. There are 4 sets of each visual parameter in every material, comprises the sets of 2-categories, 4-categories, 6-categories and 8-categories. We employed 3 different materials with different cue sequence and cue choices among the subjects to avoid any potential bias. The following describes the interfaces involved in Task 1, which comprise of 5 different visual parameters, and Task 2, which serves as a distraction.

1. Spatial

Four arrangements of 2x1, 2x2, 2x3 and 2x4 grid designs were tested to represent the effect of spatial cues. Figure 3 shows the arrangement of cues for the 2-categories, 4-categories, 6-categories and 8-categories sets. In the experiment, one of the cues will be outlined in black indicating the targeted cue.

2. Colour

We chose 8 basic colours, which are dark blue, orange, light green, red, yellow, purple, dark green and light blue to test the colour parameter (Figure 4). While in the sets of 8-categories all these cues were investigated to represent different

Figure 3. (from left to right) Grid arrangement for 2-categories, 4-categories, 6-categories and 8-categories of spatial cues

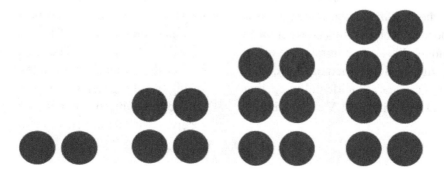

Figure 4. Basic colours used to represent information

categories. In other sets only a few of these cues were tested. The selection of colours used in those sets of 2-categories, 4-categories and 6-categories were randomized.

3. Shape

We employed 8 common shapes, diamond, triangle, square, hexagon, circle, heart, teardrop and cross, to represent the shape parameter as shown in Figure 5. Similar to the colour parameter, only the 8-categories sets will test all of these cues. The selection of colours used in those sets of 2-categories, 4-categories and 6-categories were randomized.

4. Size

The smallest size we employed was 16x16 pixel and the biggest size was 32x32 pixel. As the cue representations are aimed to be used in software interfaces, these sizes are the common icon/cue size employed by software designers. The size for the smallest and biggest cues are fixed, while the others are sized in between those two, according to the number of cue categories presented, as shown in Figure 6.

5. Motion

We employed 4 motion types and 2 motion frequencies to make up 8 cues to test the motion parameter. Blink, flicker (fade), grow and shrink type of motions moved with a fast and slow frequency, moving every 0.5 seconds and 2 seconds respectively. The grow motions increase size to 150% and the shrink motions decrease size to 50%. The cues are illustrated in Figure 7. While all of these motion cues are tested in the 8-categories sets, the cues tested in the 2-categories, 4-categories and 6-categories sets were randomly selected.

Distraction Task

For the distraction task we chose a simple game, which requires participants to spot the differences, occurred in two similar pictures (Figure 8). The slides contained this task were timed for 40 seconds and participants needed to find as many differences as they could in this duration. This is to make sure information in the learning phase is stored in the long-term memory, not just temporarily as the short-term memory. Human's short-term memory fades away very quickly, and after 7 seconds, half of the information has been forgotten(Card, 1983).

Figure 5. Shape cues used to represent information

Figure 6. Different sizes used to represent different categories, top-bottom row: 2-categories, 4-categories, 6-categories and 8-categories

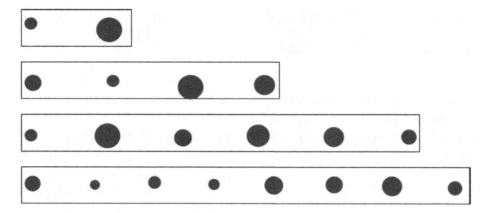

Procedure

Before starting the experiment, participants were given a brief introduction to the study and the task they had to perform. Experimenter guided them through 2 sets of practice to familiarize the participants on the procedure of the experiment. The duration of the experiment varies on individual performance but took approximately 45 minutes to be carried out including survey.

In the beginning of each set, participants learnt the characteristics of the cues and the information (number) they represent. There were two, four, six, and eight items tested for each parameter. For instance, as shown in Figure 9, subjects learnt colour cues for 4 items. Participants had no time limit in the learning phase but could not review the cues again once they had ended it. Following the learning phase, participants performed a distraction task. This phase consists of a fixed 40 seconds

task of comparing two similar pictures and spotting their differences. The purpose of employing the distraction task before the cue categorization task is to ensure information memorized is not just stored temporarily. After the distraction task ends, participants were shown using the mouse clicking the cue they had learnt, one by one. Each cue is presented at the centre of the interface (screen) and accompanied by two questions, one asking which number they represent, and the second question asks if the cue is identical with the one in previous slide (Figure 10). Participants need to click on the button indicating the correct answer. Bear in mind that motor control (moving cursor to target) was involved in target selection. The cue sequences were generated randomly. After the end of each set, participants went through the learning phase again. The same procedure is repeated for different visual parameters and different amount of cue items. No same visual parameter was tested

Figure 7. Different motion types used to represent information, from left: blink, flicker, shrink, and grow

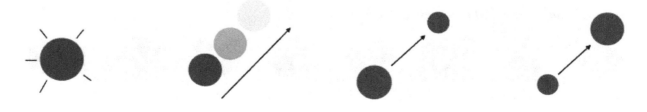

Figure 8. Example of distraction task(Spot The Difference, 2013)

sequentially. There were 4 cues tested in the sets of 2 items, 6 cues tested in the sets of 4 items, 8 cues tested in the sets of 6 items and 10 cues tested in the sets of 8 items. The same cue may appear more than once in each set.

RESULT

The dependent measures in this experiment are users' response time, accuracy, learning time and their differentiation ability. Response time (Table 1) is measured from the time the cue was presented to the time user click on a button, indicating an answer had been chosen. The data is visualized in Figure 11. Accuracy of data is measured from the amount of correct answers chosen (Table 2), and the data is visualized in Figure 12. The time participants took to learn the cues is defined from the moment cues were visible to participants until they clicked on a button to change the slide, and the data recorded as displayed in Table 3. Lastly, to prove the cues we employed were able to be distinguished from one another, participants were asked in every slide if the cues they see differ from the previous ones. We also recorded the accuracy of this answer (Table 4).

The standard deviation of response time in motion 8-categories set is high (see Table 1), and based on z-score we found one outlier (z-score

Figure 9. Four items of different colours representing different categories

Figure 10. Cue being presented one by one, accompanied by two questions

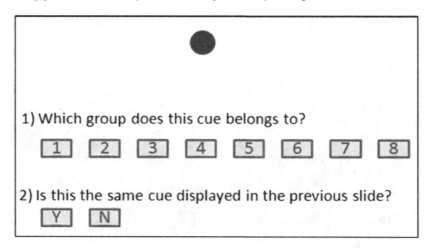

3.59) which is then corrected. This is visualized in Figure 9. We then ran two-way ANalyses Of VAriance (ANOVA) to compare participants' response times in different number of items and visual parameters. There was a significant effect of visual parameters on user response time, F(2.23, 31.21)=19.92, p<0.001. Pairwise comparisons revealed that response time is significantly different between size and location (p<0.05), size and colour (p<0.01), size and shape (p<0.01), motion and location (p<0.001), motion and colour (p<0.01) as well as motion and shape (p<0.001). The mean and standard deviation of those visual

parameters could be referred in Table 1. The was also a significant effect of number of categories towards response time, F(3, 42)=24.83, p<0.001. Pairwise comparisons revealed significant difference between 2-categories and 6-categories (p<0.001), 2-categories and 8-categories (p<0.001), 4-categories and 6-categories (p<0.05) as well as 4-categories and 8-categories (p<0.001). The mean and standard deviation of those visual parameters could be referred in Table 1. The was also a significant interaction between visual parameters and number of categories, F (12, 168)=3.652, p<0.001. This indicates that the effect of visual parameters on user's response time depends on the number of categories employed.

The superiority of visual parameters could be observed through user's accuracy, response time and learning time. Another factor that could determine its superiority is stability across users. Consider two different visual parameters, A and B that has the same user response time. However, the standard deviation in condition A is much higher than condition B, indicating data points that are spread out over a large range of values. This means that the stability of condition A is lower than B, and that different user might response to it differently, some good and some bad. In order to understand deeper the visual parameters we

Table 1. Response times of visual parameters and number of categories

	Location	Colour	Shape	Size	Motion
2	M=2317 SD=1090	M=2195 SD=1306	M=1713 SD=896	M=2431 SD=1130	M=2950 SD=1395
4	M=2065 SD=538	M=2083 SD=450	M=2341 SD=679	M=3603 SD=1105	M=4066 SD=2000
6	M=2862 SD=726	M=2543 SD=559	M=2954 SD=828	M=4826 SD=2023	M=5113 SD=2146
8	M=3076 SD=902	M=4014 SD=1474	M=2721 SD=1170	M=3739 SD=1727	M=9792 SD=16777 Corrected: M=5743 SD=2106
Ave	M=2580 SD=915	M=2709 SD=1284	M=2433 SD=1006	M=3650 SD=1733	M=4468 SD=2169

Figure 11. Response times of visual parameters and number of categories (ms)

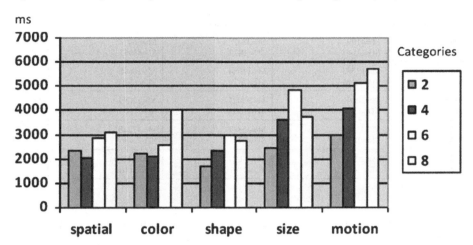

are investigating, we also investigate their stability across users. The methodology is described as follows,

As seen in Figure 12, a triangle could be created in each data distribution. The horizontal axis indicates the standard deviation of data while the vertical axis indicates the mean of data. Therefore, tan θ= mean/sd. The bigger value of θ indicates a smaller ratio between mean and standard deviation, which suggests that data points are very close to mean. This shows the stability of data across different users. The area of triangle could also be calculated, reflecting the correlation between mean and standard deviation. When mean and standard deviation are both small in value, a small area of

triangle could be obtained. Similarly, when mean and standard deviation are of big values, a large area of triangle will be obtained. Based on these two values (area of triangle and θ) we visualize the response times of visual parameters investigated in Figure 13. A data value that falls on the right and bottom area of the graph (high θ value, small triangle area) indicates overall superiority, where both SD and mean are small. While the horizontal axis indicates the distribution of data, the vertical axis indicates mean value. Different

Table 2. Accuracy of visual parameters and number of categories

	Spatial	Colour	Shape	Size	Motion
2	M=0.93 SD=0.26	M=0.93 SD=0.26	M=1.0 SD=0	M=0.93 SD=0.26	M=0.93 SD=0.26
4	M=0.99 SD=0.04	M=0.91 SD=0.18	M=0.97 SD=0.09	M=0.63 SD=0.32	M=0.84 SD=0.24
6	M=0.85 SD=0.28	M=0.93 SD=0.14	M=0.84 SD=0.26	M=0.52 SD=0.25	M=0.76 SD=0.35
8	M=0.91 SD=0.16	M=0.77 SD=0.31	M=0.89 SD=0.22	M=0.31 SD=0.23	M=0.59 SD=0.30
Ave	M=0.92 SD=0.21	M=0.89 SD=0.23	M=0.92 SD=0.18	M=0.6 SD=0.34	M=0.78 SD=0.31

Figure 12. Relationship of θ and M/SD in each data distribution

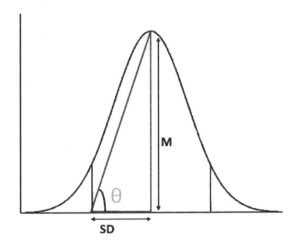

Table 3. User's learning time of visual parameters and number of items

	Spatial	Colour	Shape	Size	Motion
2	M=3204 SD=1634	M=4199 SD=2144	M=3837 SD=1872	M=5647 SD=3957	M=8548 SD=2323
4	M=4919 SD=3411	M=12583 SD=7848	M=13634 SD=5678	M=18090 SD=12295	M=30515 SD=9819
6	M=10364 SD=6586	M=20596 SD=12113	M=33021 SD=13656	M=32699 SD=21061	M=62676 SD=27623
8	M=24524 SD=13046	M=45857 SD=35728	M=45817 SD=24453	M=37248 SD=24709	M=85389 SD=53609
Ave	M=10753 SD=11201	M=20809 SD=245001	M=24077 SD=21610	M=23421 SD=21160	M=46782 SD=42063

visual parameters are indicated by different colour of data points, while the bigger points indicate the average of each parameter. The lines connecting those points are visualized to assist in tracking progression from lower number of categories to the higher.

To interpret the Figure 13, the 4-categories and 6-categories sets of location, colour and shape cues show overall superior performance where stability across different users are high and low mean values. In contrast, cues in the motion parameter show the higher mean values with low stability across users, regardless of number of cues.

Findings of user accuracy across different visual parameters and number of categories (Table 2) suggest different user performance especially when involving larger amount of items categories. Figure 14 visualizes this data. We then apply statistical analysis for a deeper understanding of their correlations. Logistic regression applied on accuracy show a statistically significant effect of visual variables ($p<0.000$) and effect of number of items ($p<0.000$) towards accuracy. Analyses also indicate significant difference between location (reference) and colour ($p<0.05$), size ($p<0.000$), motion ($p<0.000$). We also found a negative value of coefficient B (-0.328) when analysing the effects of number of categories on accuracy, indicating that accuracy is greater with lesser number of categories.

Similar to finding stability of visual parameter based on user response time, we plotted the same graph based on user accuracy (Figure 15). The number of categories is inserted on each point accordingly. Bigger points indicate the mean of data. Based on the mean data points, superior results, which is the stability of visual parameter

Table 4. User's differentiation ability across visual parameters and number of categories

	Spatial	Colour	Shape	Size	Motion
2	M=0.92 SD=0.12	M=0.97 SD=0.09	M=0.97 SD=0.09	M=1.0 SD=0	M=0.95 SD=0.1
4	M=0.93 SD=0.1	M=0.99 SD=0.04	M=1.0 SD=0.0	M=0.96 SD=0.08	M=0.86 SD=0.22
6	M=0.98 SD=0.06	M=0.99 SD=0.03	M=0.98 SD=0.04	M=0.94 SD=0.06	M=0.95 SD=0.08
8	M=0.99 SD=0.04	M=0.99 SD=0.04	M=0.99 SD=0.03	M=0.97 SD=0.06	M=0.97 SD=0.08
Ave	M=0.96 SD=0.09	M=0.98 SD=0.05	M=0.99 SD=0.05	M=0.97 SD=0.06	M=0.93 SD=0.14

Figure 13. Comparing the stability of visual parameters across users (response time)

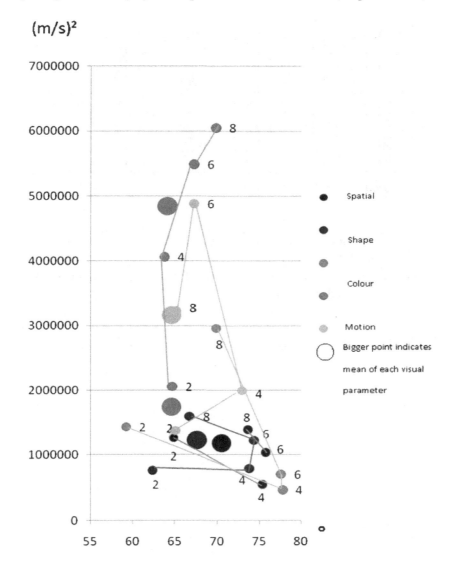

across users as well as higher accuracy in user performance, are shown by shape, location and colour, compared to size and motion parameters.

We also ran two-way ANalyses Of VAriance (ANOVA) to compare the learning time participants took, comparing the number of categories and visual parameters. Findings indicate significant effect of visual parameters on user response time, $F(4, 56)=30.76$, $p<0.001$. Pairwise comparisons revealed significant difference between

location and other visual parameters, with colour ($p<0.05$), shape ($p<0.001$), size ($p<0.01$) and motion ($p<0.001$). Participants took significantly longer time to learn the motion cues compared to other cues, with colour ($p<0.001$), shape ($p<0.001$) and size ($p<0.01$). The data could be referred in Table 3. There was also a significant effect of number of categories towards learning time, $F(1.18, 16.55)=47.31$, $p<0.001$. Participants took significantly shorter time to learn the cues

Figure 14. Accuracy of visual parameters and number of categories

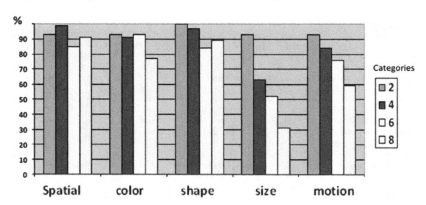

in 2-categories compared to 4-categories, 6-categories and 8-categories (p<0.001). They also took significantly shorter time to learn 4-items cues compared to 6-categories and 8-categories (p<0.001). 6-categories cues were significantly different to learn compared to 8-categories cues (p<0.01). Data is visualized in Figure 16.

Figure 15. Comparing the stability of visual parameters across users (Accuracy)

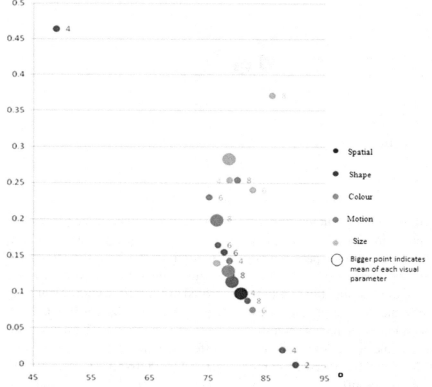

Figure 16. Learning time of visual parameters and number of categories

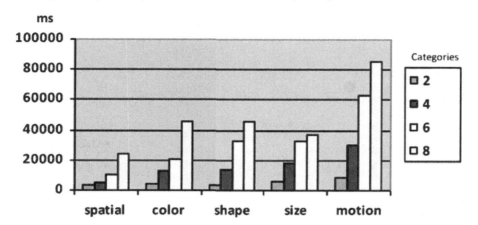

There was also a significant interaction between visual parameters and number of categories, F (3.41, 47.69)=5.77, p<0.001. This indicates that the effect of visual parameters on user's learning time depends on the number of items used. We ran contrasts analyses and compared all item size to their baseline (2-categories) and all visual parameters to their baseline (location). These revealed significant interactions when comparing location and colour parameters for 2-categories compared to 4-categories (F (1, 14)=19.27,p<0.001), 2-categories to 6-categores (F (1, 14)=17.17, p<0.001), and 2-categories to 8-categories, F (1, 14)= 4.64, p<0.05. There is also significant interaction when comparing location and shape parameters for 2-categories compared to 4-categories (F(1, 14)=32.93, p<0.001), 2-categories compared to 6-categories, F(1,14)= 48.69, p<0.001) and 2-categories to 8-categories, F(1,14)= 14.87, p<0.01). When comparing location and size parameters, again significant interaction is found for 2-categories compared to 4-categories, F(1, 14)= 17.2, p<0.01) and between 2-categories and 6-categories, F(1,14)=13.68, p<0.01). Lastly, significant interactions were revealed when comparing location and motion for 2-categories compared with 4-categories (F(1,14)=52. 83, p<0.001), 2-categories com-

pared to 4-categories (F (1,14)=41.37, p<0.001) and 2-categories compared to 8-categories F(1,14)=17.9, p<0.001.

We also show the stability of parameter when users are learning cues, which is visualized in Figure 17. Based on this graph, on average, the stability of motion, shape and size cues are higher than spatial and colour cues (Mean data for each visual parameter is shown with a bigger icon). However, users took the least time to learn cues in the location condition compared to other parameters, and longest time in the motion parameter

In order to make sure that each cue we employed could be differentiated with the rest, participants were asked whether each cue they were viewing (during the experiment) were the same with the previously seen cue. The data collected is shown in Table 4. We ran logistic regression as the data was binary, and findings revealed no significant effects of visual variables or number of categories. Subjects generally had no trouble to differentiate the cues against one other cue at each time. We visualize the interaction between visual parameters and number of categories in Figure 18.

Participants were also required to evaluate the visual cues based on 3 questions. The evaluation was tested on the 5-point Likert scale, where rating '1' indicates 'strongly disagree' and '5' indi-

Figure 17. Comparing the stability of visual parameters across users (learning time)

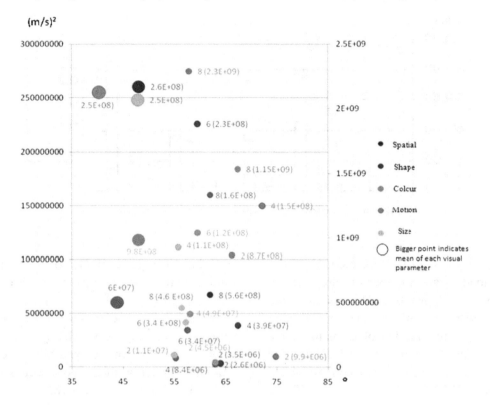

Figure 18. Differentiation ability across different parameters and number of categories

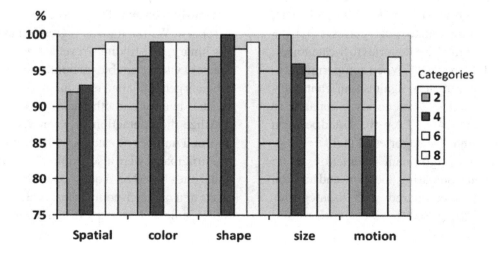

cates 'strongly agree'. They were also required to provide appropriate comments for their ratings. The questions and results based on Kruskal-Wallis Mann-Whitney tests are as follows:

- **Q1:** It was easy to learn/memorize the group (number) each cue represents.
  - Mean rank for location, colour, shape, size and motion cues are 50.77, 52.17, 48.60, 12.80 and 25.67 respectively ($p<0.001$). Post hoc analyses reveal significant differences between location A (reference) and size ($p<0.001$) as well as with motion ($p<0.001$) but not with other perimeters.
- **Q2:** It was easy to recall the group (number) each cue represents even after distraction.
  - Mean rank for location, colour, shape, size and motion cues are 51.67, 50.33, 45.93, 16.70 and 25.37 respectively ($p<0.001$). Post hoc analyses reveal significant differences between location A (reference) and size ($p<0.001$) as well as with motion ($p<0.001$) but not with other perimeters.
- **Q3:** It was easy to differentiate each cue to the rest.
  - Mean rank for location, colour, shape, size and motion cues are 48.77, 48.60, 50.17, 15.33 and 27.13 respectively ($p<0.001$). Post hoc analyses reveal significant differences between location A (reference) and size ($p<0.001$) as well as with motion ($p<0.001$) but not with other perimeters.

Based on the questionnaire results we found that most participants relied on mnemonics to aid the learning phase. A majority stated it was easier to learn and recall cues in the location condition, but faced difficulties to differentiate sizes as they were not able to compare the cues with something. A few participants found that motions get drasti-

cally harder to recognize when there are more cues present, as they get more complicated. A few participants also revealed that reproducing recall was more difficult when there were two tones of the same colour in the set of cues. In order to learn the non-spatial cues, some of the participants revealed that linguistic associations were made. However, they were only successful in the colour and shape cues. These names were then linked to make a 'story', and producing recall was much easier. However, as size and motion cues could not be named, learning and retrieving these cues becomes difficult.

DISCUSSION

Due to the fact that spatial cues could automatically support memory (Andrade, 1993) and better differentiation of cues as they are physically visible on screen, we have predicted superior user performance of spatial cues compared to other non-spatial attributes. However, findings suggest that colour and shape cues are equally as efficient as spatial cues, while motion and size cues show constant weakness.

While accuracy and response times are similar for spatial, colour, and shape cues, learning time for spatial cues was significantly shorter. Findings from questionnaires provided some understanding of these differences. It seems that learning spatial and non-spatial cues were supported by different techniques and processes. While spatial cues are supported by spatial memory, colour, and shape cues were learnt based on linguistic associations of cues and the meaning they represent. Thus, naming the cues was a major element that supports the learning process. Linguistic influence on human behaviours is not something new, as was explored by psychologists in the past. Whorf has reasoned that people could only think about the things their language could describe(1940). His ideas were developed by comparing several language structures and the behaviours and world views of the people who speak those languages. Based on Whorf's view, studies have shown that linguistic associations do support colour memory in both short-term and long-term tasks (1940). The effect of giving names to discriminate stimuli was also stressed in Miller's suggestions as to make patterns less similar (1948).

We had also observed poor user performance in the size and motion parameters. As the variation of cue size employed is limited, as to meet the standard size of cues typically designed, the differentiation of cues becomes very difficult. Although the differentiation task we employed showed that subjects were able to discriminate each cue to another cue at a time, it is possible that difficulties actually lies in judging how much each cue differs to the rest of the cues in the condition. This becomes more challenging as the difference between cues become smaller, or in other words, larger number of cues to be aware of. To overcome this problem, certain visual cues could be added to support measurement so that size differences could be properly judged. Motion cues not only require the most time to learn, but also to be identified. This could be explained that the presentation of each motion cue to complete one cycle requires longer time to be observed compared to static cues. Furthermore, in this study we employed motion cues with two characteristics, type of movement and frequency, which may require more mental effort. As response time towards motion cues are significantly longer then the static cues, it is unsuitable to be applied in this context as it would be too long or too much that is required to be distracted from users' main task in real-life scenarios.

Interaction between visual cues and number of categories were found to influence user performance in their accuracy, response times and learning time. This indicates that user's response differently towards number of items depending on the visual cue used. When the stability of visual parameters across users was evaluated, shorter response time was shown in the 4-categories and 6-categories sets. It is possible that users took longer to response in the 2-categories and 8-categories due to confusion and information overload. However, compared to colour/shape cues, this effect is not very obvious in the spatial condition, suggesting a superior effect of spatial cues. As suggested in past studies, there is a strong correlation between location and human memory, called spatial memory (Andrade, 1993; D'Argembeau & Van der Linden, 2004; Hess, 1999; Ratwani, 2008; Yates, 1966). Thus, this might be support retrieval of information. The stability of visual cues was also investigated for user's accuracy in the experiment as well as their learning time. The mean accuracy shows that location, shape and colour cues not only provide higher accuracy but also more stable across different users, compared to size and motion cues. Furthermore, the most stable cues involve smaller amount of cue categories represented by the shape and location cues, while the least stable ones involve bigger amount of cue categories represented by size and motion cues. Due to these differences, the application of size and motion cues should be avoided in the representation of categorical notification as user ability to accurately response to those cues varies. The stability of cues was also demonstrated in user's learning time. Findings suggest that the learning time is faster for some users but slower for some. Meanwhile, the learning time for motion, shape and size cues seem to be more stable across users. In other words, all users took approximately similar duration to learn the motion, shape and size cues.

Findings from our experiments demonstrate that categorical information could be supported by non-textual notifications, with little learning time. Designers should employ spatial cues to represent categorical information, and while colour/shape cues occupy less space, the selection of those cues is crucial. As there may be possibilities that users code and encode colour/shape cues by linguistic associations, designers need to consider user's ability to discriminate the cues and that any similarity could contribute to confusion and failure of the design interface. Furthermore, it is important that the number of cues or categories displayed in a system is controlled. In order to prevent cognitive overload.

CONCLUSION

The relationship between visual cues and users' ability to recognize categories in a notification system was investigated. Findings suggest overall superiority of spatial, colour, and shape cues compared to motion and size cues. However, the shorter learning time and less effect of number of categories towards the spatial cues suggest that they are memorized and retrieved differently from colour and shape cues. Overall findings suggest careful design considerations involving 1) types of visual cues, and 2) number of categories represented by those cues. In order to develop successful categorical notification systems.

REFERENCES

Andrade, J., & Meudell, P. (1993). Is spatial information encoded automatically in memory? *The Quarterly Journal of Experimental Psychology Section A: Human Experimental Psychology, 46*(2), 365–375. doi:10.1080/14640749308401051 PMID:8316640.

Andrews, A. E., Ratwani, R. M., & Trafton, J. G. (2009). The effect of alert type to an interruption on primary task resumptions. In *Proceedings of HFES*. Boulder, CO: Westview Press.

Arend, A., Muthig, K., & Wandmacher, J. (1987). Evidence for global feature superiority in menu selection by icons. *Behaviour & Information Technology, 6*(4), 411–426. doi:10.1080/01449298708901853.

Baer, M., & Ellis, J. B. (1998). Designing audio aura. In *Proceedings of CHI*. New York: ACM Press.

Bartram, L., Ware, C., & Calvert, T. (2003). Moticons: Detection, distraction, and task. *International Journal of Human-Computer Studies, 58*(5), 515–545. doi:10.1016/S1071-5819(03)00021-1.

Bertin, J. (1983). *Semiology of graphics: Diagrams, networks, maps*. Milwaukee, WI: ESRI Press.

Bodnar, A., Corbett, R., & Nekrasovski, D. (2004). AROMA: Ambient awareness through olfaction in messaging application. In *Proceedings of ICMI*. New York: ACM Press.

Card, S. K., Moran, T. P., & Newell, A. (1983). *The psychology of human-computer interaction*. Hillsdale, NJ: Lawrence Erlbaum.

Chan, A., MacLean, K., & McGrenere, J. (2008). Designing haptic icons to support collaborative turn-taking. *International Journal of Human-Computer Studies, 66*, 333–355. doi:10.1016/j.ijhcs.2007.11.002.

Czerwinski, M., Cutrell, E., & Horvitz, E. (2000). *Instant messaging and interruption: Influence of task type on performance*. In *Proceedings of OZCHI*. New York: ACM Press.

D'Argembeau, A., & Van der Linden, M. (2004). *Influence of affective meaning on memory for contextual information*. Washington, DC: American Psychological Association. doi:10.1037/1528-3542.4.2.173.

Dantzich, M. V., Robbins, D., Horvitz, E., & Czerwinski, M. (2002). *Scope: Providing awareness of multiple notifications at a glance*. In *Proceedings of AVI*. New York: ACM Press.

Davis, S., & Bostrom, R. (1992). An experimental investigation of the roles of the computer interface and individual characteristics in the learning of computer systems. *International Journal of Human-Computer Interaction*, 4(2), 143–172. doi:10.1080/10447319209526033.

Ecamm. (2013). Supercharge your mail dock icon. *DockStar*. Retrieved from www.ecamm.com/mac/dockstar.

Hess, S. M., Detweiler, M. C., & Ellis, R. D. (1999). The utility of display space in keeping track of rapidly changing information. *Human Factors*, 41(2), 257–281. doi:10.1518/001872099779591187.

Hoffman, R., Baudisch, P., & Weld, D. S. (2008). Evaluating visual cues for window switching on large screens. In *Proceedings of CHI*. New York: ACM Press.

Huang, D., Rau, P. P., Su, H., Tu, N., & Zhao, C. (2007). Effects of time orientation on design of notification systems. *Human-Computer Interaction*, 4550, 835–843.

Kanai, H., Tsuruma, G., Nakada, T., & Kunifuji, S. (2008). Notification of dangerous situation for elderly people using visual cues. In *Proceedings of IUI*. New York: ACM Press.

Khan, A., Matejka, J., Fitzmaurice, G., & Kurtenbach, G. (2005). *Spotlight: Directing users' attention on large displays*. In *Proceedings of CHI*. New York: ACM Press.

Light, L. L., & Berger, D. E. (1974). Memory for modality: Within-modality discrimination is not automatic. *Journal of Experimental Psychology*, 103(5), 854–860. doi:10.1037/h0037404.

Maglio, P. P., & Campbell, C. S. (2000). Tradeoffs in displaying peripheral information. In *Proceedings of CHI*. New York: ACM Press.

McCormick, E. J., & Sanders, M. S. (1982). *Human factors in engineering and design*. New York: Mcgraw-Hill.

McCrickard, D. S., Catrambone, R., Chewar, C. M., & Stasko, J. T. (2003). Establishing tradeoffs that leverage attention for utility:empirically evaluating information display in notification systems. *International Journal of Human-Computer Studies*, 58, 547–582. doi:10.1016/S1071-5819(03)00022-3.

McCrickard, D. S., & Chewar, C. M. (2003). Attuning notification design to user goals and attention costs. *Communications of the ACM*, 46(3), 67–72. doi:10.1145/636772.636800.

McCrickard, D. S., Czerwinski, M., & Bartram, L. (2003). Introduction: Design and evaluation of notification user interfaces. *International Journal of Human-Computer Studies*, 58, 509–514. doi:10.1016/S1071-5819(03)00025-9.

McFarlane, D. C. (2002). Comparison of four primary methods for coordinating the interruption of people in human-computer interaction. *Human-Computer Interaction*, 17, 63–139. doi:10.1207/S15327051HCI1701_2.

Miller, N. E. (1948). Theory and experiment relating psychoanalytic displacement to simulus-response generalization. *Journal of Abnormal and Social Psychology*, 43, 155–178. doi:10.1037/h0056728.

Monk, C. A. (2004). The effect of frequent and infrequent interruptions on primary task resumption. *Human Factors*, 48(3), 295–299. doi:10.1177/154193120404800304.

Pousman, Z., & Stasko, J. (2006). A taxonomy of ambient information systems: Four patterns of design. In *Proceedings of AVI*. New York: ACM Press.

Ratwani, R. M., & Trafton, J. G. (2008). Spatial memory guides task resumption. *Visual Cognition*, *16*(8), 1001–1010. doi:10.1080/13506280802025791.

Rauterberg, M. (1992). An empirical comparison of menu-selection (CUI) and desktop (GUI) computer progrmas carried out by beginners and experts. *Behaviour & Information Technology*, *11*, 227–236. doi:10.1080/01449299208924341.

Spot The Difference. (2013). Retrieved from Spotthedifference.com.

Staggers, N., & Kobus, D. (2000). Comparing response time, errors, and satisfaction between tex-based and graphical user interfaces during nursing order tasks. *Journal of the American Medical Informatics Association*, *7*, 164–176. doi:10.1136/jamia.2000.0070164 PMID:10730600.

Trafton, J. G., Altmann, E. M., Brock, D. P., & Mintz, F. E. (2003). Preparing to resume an interrupted task: Effects of prospecting goal encoding and restrospective rehearsal. *International Journal of Human-Computer Studies*, *58*, 583–603. doi:10.1016/S1071-5819(03)00023-5.

Whorf, B. L. (1940). Science and linguistics. *Technology Review*, *42*(6), 229–231, 247–248.

Yates, I. A. (1966). *The Art of memory*. Chicago: University of Chicago Press.

Yu, Y., & Liu, Z. (2010). *Improving the performance and usability for visual menu interface on mobile computers*. In *Proceedings of AVI*. New York: ACM Press.

KEY TERMS AND DEFINITIONS

Categorical Information: We define categorical information as the grouping of several pieces of information, whose category can be defined to identify which category each piece of information belong to. It does not have any information about ordering and distance among those pieces of information.

Non-Spatial Cues: Non-spatial cues refer to cues that do not have a fixed attribute space and not defined by their location within the screen or each other. Instead, they are defined by other characteristics such as colour, size, shape and motion.

Notification System: Notification system is a tool used to deliver new information to keep users aware of current happenings. These information pieces could be represented by cues of various user interface dimensions including visual, auditory and haptic.

Spatial Cues: Spatial cues refer to cues that have fixed attribute space on the screen. They are defined by their location within the screen and each other.

Chapter 4
Feature–Based Uncertainty Visualization

Keqin Wu
University of Maryland Baltimore County, USA

Song Zhang
Mississippi State University, USA

ABSTRACT

While uncertainty in scientific data attracts an increasing research interest in the visualization community, two critical issues remain insufficiently studied: (1) visualizing the impact of the uncertainty of a data set on its features and (2) interactively exploring 3D or large 2D data sets with uncertainties. In this chapter, a suite of feature-based techniques is developed to address these issues. First, an interactive visualization tool for exploring scalar data with data-level, contour-level, and topology-level uncertainties is developed. Second, a framework of visualizing feature-level uncertainty is proposed to study the uncertain feature deviations in both scalar and vector data sets. With quantified representation and interactive capability, the proposed feature-based visualizations provide new insights into the uncertainties of both data and their features which otherwise would remain unknown with the visualization of only data uncertainties.

1. INTRODUCTION

Uncertainty is a common and crucial issue in scientific data. The goal of uncertainty visualization is to provide users with visualizations that incorporate uncertainty information to aid data analysis and decision making. However, it is challenging to quantify uncertainties appropriately and to visualize uncertainties effectively without affecting the visualization effect of the underlying data information.

Uncertainty in scientific data can be broadly defined as statistical variations, spread, errors, differences, minimum maximum range values,

DOI: 10.4018/978-1-4666-4309-3.ch004

etc. (Pang, Wittenbrink, & Lodha, 1997) This broad definition covers most, if not all, of the possible types and sources of uncertainty related to numerical values of the data. In this chapter, however, we investigate the uncertain positional deviations of the features such as extrema, sinks, sources, contours, and contour trees in the data. These feature-related uncertainties are referred to as feature-level uncertainty while the uncertainties related to the uncertain numerical values of the data are referred to as data-level uncertainty. Visualizing feature-level uncertainty reveals the potentially significant impacts of the data-level uncertainty, which in turn helps people gain new insights into data-level uncertainty itself. Therefore, investigating the uncertainty information on both data-level and feature-level provides users a more comprehensive view of the uncertainties in their data.

Many uncertainty visualizations encode data-level uncertainty information into different graphics primitives such as color, glyph, and texture, which are attached to surfaces or embedded in volumes (Brodlie, Osorio, & Lopes, 2012; Pang et al., 1997). Those methods. In essence, give global insight into the data by differentiating the area of high uncertainty from that of low uncertainty, however, the impact of the uncertainty on the important features of the data is hard to assess in such visualizations. Meanwhile, uncertainty visualizations may be subject to cluttered display, occlusion, or information overload due to the large amount of information and interference between the data and its uncertainty. We believe that one promising direction to cope with this challenge is to allow users to explore data interactively and to provide informative clues about where to look.

In this chapter, while our uncertainty representation can be adapted to different uncertainty models, we measure the uncertainty according to the differences between the data values, critical points, contours, or contour trees of different ensemble members. Our objectives are (1) to bring awareness to the existence of feature-level uncertainties, (2) to suggest metrics for measuring feature-level uncertainty, and (3) to design an interactive tool for exploring 3D and large 2D data sets with uncertainty.

In what follows, we first discuss related work, issues, and challenges of uncertainty visualization in section 2, then explain in detail in section 3 and 4 our methods: (1) an interactive contour tree-based visualization for exploratory visualization of 2D and 3D scalar data with uncertainty information and (2) a framework for visualizing feature-level uncertainty based on feature tracking in both scalar and vector fields. Lastly, we conclude this chapter and discuss future directions.

2. BACKGROUND

We discuss issues, challenges, and the related work of uncertainty visualization in this section.

2.1. The Gap between Data-level Uncertainty and Feature-level Uncertainty

Knowing the uncertainty concerning features is important for decision making. Many uncertainty visualizations based on statistical metrics merely measure uncertainty on the data-level—the uncertainty concerning the numerical values of the data and introduced in data acquisition and processing. While these techniques achieved decent visualization results, they do not provide users enough insight into how much uncertainty exists for the features in the data. For example, the uncertainty of the ocean temperature data may result in the uncertain deviation of the center of an important warm eddy. The uncertainty of the hurricane wind data may cause the uncertain location of a hurricane eye. This kind of uncertainty is neglected by many current methods but needs to be quantified and visualized so viewers are aware of it.

In scientific data, the difference between a known correct datum and an estimate is among the uncertainties most frequently investigated. To compare data-level uncertainty and feature-level uncertainty, we investigate two data sets. The first data set is a slice of a simulated hurricane Lili wind field (Figure 1a). The second data set is created by adding random noise to the first dataset. For a wind vector, its data-level uncertainty is represented as both angular difference and magnitude difference between vectors of the two fields. Figure 1c shows the arrow glyphs (Wittenbrink, Pang, & Lodha, 1996) for visualizing the uncertainty of vector fields with the angular uncertainty presented as the span of each arrow glyph and magnitude uncertainty as the two winglets around an arrow head. For details about designing arrow glyphs for vector field uncertainty, please refer to (Wittenbrink et al., 1996).

As shown in Figure 1c, with the uncertainty glyphs, users may notice that the area around the hurricane eye (the major vertex in the middle) exhibits high data-level uncertainty which raises a question: does it affect the location of hurricane eye? Only an explicit comparison between the hurricane eyes in the two fields will answer this question. We therefore extract topologies of the two fields as shown in Figure 1d. The sink point (in black) inside the hurricane eye noticeably shifts northwest (indicated by a red arrow) from the original vector field to the new one (in gray). Another question is, is there anything hidden in the relatively low uncertainty area indicated by the small arrow glyphs? A quick look at the Figure 1d reveals that the upper corner vortex significantly shifts its position (indicated by a red arrow) though it is located at the region with relatively low data-level uncertainty.

This example illustrates that merely investigating the data-level uncertainty may not tell the whole story about the data and that the feature-level uncertainty is an indispensable part of uncertainty

Figure 1. An uncertain vector field and its uncertain feature locations

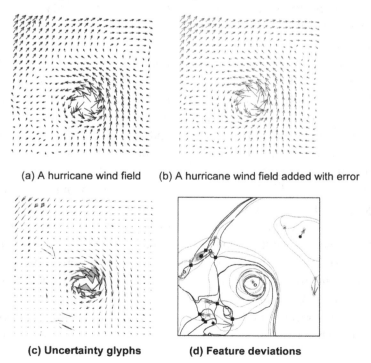

(a) A hurricane wind field   (b) A hurricane wind field added with error

(c) Uncertainty glyphs   **(d) Feature deviations**

that cannot be neglected. Moreover, visualizing uncertainty of features, instead of that of the data, may provide a succinct and meaningful representation of the uncertainty and thus give a better interpretation of the data.

2.2. Challenges of Visualizing Uncertainty

Representing uncertainty in 3D or large 2D data sets could encounter severe issues such as cluttered displays, information overload, and occlusions. Many uncertainty visualizations place glyphs that encode uncertainty within the visualization of the data. For instance, Sanyal et al. (2010) visualized data-level uncertainties via circular or ribbon-like glyphs over a color-mapped image of the data. Despite their effectiveness in revealing uncertainty information accurately at glyph locations, due to the overlaps between the data and uncertainty glyphs, the number of the glyphs has to be limited and information loss for both the data and uncertainty is unavoidable. Other techniques which overlay or embed uncertainty representation in the data visualization face similar issues.

Meanwhile, interaction with the visualization of 3D or large 2D data sets could encounter issues such as geometry bandwidth bottleneck, depth perception, occlusion, and inefficiency in 3D object selection. These issues are inherent in interactive visualizations, and may be intensified in the integrated visualization of a 3D dataset or large 2D data set and its uncertainty because there is simply more information to show in such visualizations.

2.3. Feature-Based Uncertainty Visualization

In feature-based visualization, features are abstracted from the original data and can be visualized efficiently and independently of the data. We believe that the feature-based uncertainty

visualization becomes desirable when the size and complexity of the uncertainty information increase.

Several features interest us the most. Critical points such as sinks, sources, maxima, and minima are representative of topological features that carry significant physical meaning of a scalar or vector data set (Helman & Hesselink, 1989; Keqin, Zhanping, Song, & Moorhead, 2010). Contours, including 2D iso-lines and 3D iso-surfaces, are features frequently investigated for exploring data with uncertainty (Grigoryan & Rheingans, 2004; Sanyal et al., 2010). A contour tree stores the nesting relationships of the contours of a scalar field. It is a popular visualization tool for revealing the topology of contours (Hamish Carr, Snoeyink, & Axen, 2003), generating seed set for accelerated contour extraction (Hamish Carr & Snoeyink, 2003), and providing users an interface to select individual contours (Bajaj, Pascucci, & Schikore, 1997).

Several methods have been developed to address the uncertainty of the size, position, and shape of contours (Grigoryan & Rheingans, 2004; Pfaffelmoser, Reitinger, & Westermann, 2011; Rhodes, Laramee, Bergeron, & Sparr, 2003). Rendering contours from all ensembles in a single image, known as spaghetti plots (Diggle, Heagerty, Liang, & Zeger, 2002), is a conventional technique used by meteorologists for observing uncertainty in their simulations. Pang et al. (Pang et al., 1997) presented fat surfaces that use two surfaces to enclose the volume in which the true but unknown surface lies. Pauly et al. (Pauly, Mitra, & Guibas, 2004) quantified and visualized the uncertainty introduced in the reconstructions of surfaces from point cloud data. Pfaffelmoser et al. (Pfaffelmoser et al., 2011) presented a method for visualizing the positional variability around a mean ISO-surface using direct volume rendering. A method to compute and visualize the positional uncertainty of contours in uncertain input data has been suggested by Pöthkow and Hege (Pöthkow &

Hege, 2011). Assuming certain probability density functions, they modeled a discretely sampled uncertain scalar field by a discrete random field.

Among uncertainty methods, only a few are proposed to address the topological features. Otto et al. studied the uncertain topological segmentation of a vector field by introducing the probability density that a particle starting from a given location will converge to a considered source or sink (Otto, Germer, Hege, & Theisel, 2010). The uncertainty related to the topology structure of a scalar field, is barely studied.

2.4. Visual Encoding of Uncertainty

Several efforts have been made to identify potential visual attributes for uncertainty visualization. MacEachren suggested the use of hue, saturation, and intensity for representing uncertainty on maps (1992). Hengl and Toomanian (2006) showed how color mixing and pixel mixing can be used to visualize uncertainty in soil science applications. Davis and Keller (1997) suggested value, color, and texture for representing uncertainty on static maps. Djurcilov, Kima, Lermusiaxb, and Pang (2002) used opacity deviations and noise effects to provide qualitative measures for the uncertainty in volume rendering. Sanyal, Zhang, Bhattacharya, Amburn, and Morrehead (2009) conducted a user study to compare the effectiveness of four uncertainty representations: traditional error bars, scaled size of glyphs, color-mapping on glyphs, and color-mapping of uncertainty on the data surface. In their experiments, scaled sphere and color mapped sphere perform better than traditional error bars and color-mapped surfaces. Later, they proposed graduated glyphs and ribbons to encode uncertainty information of weather simulations (Sanyal et al., 2010).

While the uncertainty visualization is application-dependent in many cases, two visualization schemes are widely used: using intuitive metaphors, such as blurry and fuzzy effects (Cedilnik & Rheingans, 2000; Djurcilova et al., 2002;

Grigoryan & Rheingans, 2004), which naturally implies the existence of uncertainty, and using quantitative glyphs (Sanyal et al., 2010; Schmidt et al., 2004), which shows quantified uncertainty information explicitly. Both schemes have their own tradeoffs. In quantitative glyphs the uncertainty information has to be shown in a discrete way. By using uncertainty metaphors, people get less quantified information about uncertainty since they cannot tell levels of blur or fuzziness apart accurately (Kosara et al., 2002). To reveal uncertainty accurately, uncertainty glyph is preferred to uncertainty metaphors.

3. AN INTERACTIVE FEATURE-BASED VISUALIZATION OF SCALAR FIELD UNCERTAINTY

In this section, we analyze uncertainty-related information on three levels: on data-level, we study the uncertainty of the data, on contour-level, we quantify the positional variation of the contours, and on topology-level, we reveal the variability of the contour trees.

The core of this method is the use of contour trees as a tool to represent uncertainty and to select contours accordingly. First, a planar contour tree layout which suppresses the branch crossing and integrates with tree view interaction is developed for a flexible navigation between levels of detail for contours of 3D or large 2D data sets. Second, we attach uncertainty information to the planar layout of a simplified contour tree to avoid the visual cluttering and occlusion of viewing uncertainty within volume data or complicated 2D data. We call the scalar field obtained by averaging the values from all the ensemble members at each data point the ensemble mean and the contour tree of the ensemble mean the mean contour tree. We show the data-level uncertainty by displaying the difference between each ensemble member and the ensemble mean at each data point or along a contour. For contour-level uncertainty, given a contour in the ensemble mean, we compute the mean and variance of the differences between this contour in the mean field and its corresponding contours in all the ensemble members. For topology-level uncertainty, we map the contour trees of all the ensemble members to the mean contour tree and show their discrepancy to indicate uncertainty.

This section is structured as follows. Section 3.1 provides the definition, simplification, layout, and tree view graph design of contour trees. The visualization of three levels of uncertainties is discussed in section 3.2. Section 3.3 introduces the interface design. Section 3.4 demonstrates and discusses application results.

3.1. Contour Tree Layout and Tree View Graph Design

We visualize uncertainty and variability information through contour trees. The layout of a contour tree becomes an issue when the size and complexity of the contour tree increase (Heine, Schneider, Carr, & Scheuermann, 2011). To explore data with uncertainty efficiently, a preferred contour tree layout is the one that is two-dimensional, shows hierarchy and height information intuitively, suppresses branch self-intersections, allows for a fast

navigation through different levels of simplification, and allows displaying uncertainty information. To meet these requirements, we propose a planar contour tree layout which is integrated with the tree view graph interaction.

3.1.1. Contour Tree

The contour tree is a loop-free Reeb graph (Tierny, Gyulassy, Simon, & Pascucci, 2009) that tracks the evolution of contours. Each leaf node is a minimum or maximum, each interior node is a saddle, each edge represents a set of adjacent contours with iso-values between the values of its two ends. There is a one-to-one mapping from a point in the contour tree (at a node or in an edge) to a contour of the scalar field. A contour tree example is shown in Figure 2. More detailed information about contour and contour tree can be found in (Carr, 2004).

3.1.2. Contour Tree Simplification

Simplification is introduced to deal with the contour trees that are too large or complicated to be studied or displayed directly (Hamish Carr, Snoeyink, & Panne, 2004; Pascucci, Cole-

Figure 2. The contour tree and contours of a 3D scalar field Each horizontal line cuts exactly an edge of the tree for every contour at the corresponding iso-value Color is used to indicate the correspondence between a line and its corresponding contours

McLaughlin, & Scorzelli, 2004). Contour tree simplification facilitates a high level overview of a scalar field. Particularly, a simplified contour tree attached with uncertainty glyphs reduces the workload in viewing 3D data or complicated 2D data with uncertainty.

Usually, a contour tree simplification is conducted by successively removing branches that have a leaf node (extremum) and an inner node (saddle) (Hamish Carr et al., 2004; Takahashi, Takeshima, & Fujishiro, 2004). Figure 3 shows a top-down simplification (Wu & Zhang, 2013) by repeatedly assembling the longest branches on a current contour tree. The black numbers 0, 1,..., 4, indicate the order of assembling the branches. As shown in this example, the order of assembling the branches suggests a balanced hierarchy. The shorter branches are found at lower hierarchies and higher branches are located at higher hierarchies so that the more simplified contour tree always catches the more significant features. Each branch rooted at an interior node, other than the two ends of the branch, is a child branch. A branch which has child branches is called the parent branch of its child branches. The sub-tree which consists of all the edges and nodes along a branch and its descendants is called the sub-tree of the branch.

Figure 3. Contour tree hierarchy built based on a top-down contour tree simplification

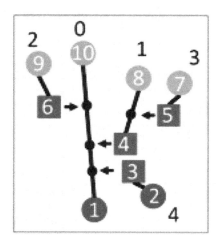

3.1.3. A Rectangular Contour Tree Layout

The key to prevent unnecessary self-intersections is to recursively assigning a vertical slot to a branch so that its child branches are contained entirely within the slot.

To be more specific, a branch B is assigned a vertical slot R, and each child branch b_i of B is assigned a disjoint portion of R—a smaller vertical slot R_i within R. Nodes are positioned on the y-axis according to their function values. To emphasize the hierarchy, a branch is rendered in the middle, and its child branches are spread out to its left and right sides. The longest branch is drawn as a vertical line segment in the middle of the display. All the other branches have L shapes that connect extremum to their paired saddles to prevent them from crossing the slots of their siblings. An example is shown in Figure 4d and e. The rectangular display of the same tree reduces the number of crossings from three to one since the layout design rules out the case where a child branch intersects with its parent or siblings. Some self-intersections are unavoidable due to the strangulation cases where a downward branch appears as a child of an upward branch, or vice versa. A space-saving solution is given in Figure 4c which takes less horizontal space than the tree layout in Figure 4b. For a given parent branch, we separated it into three parts vertically: from high to low, upward branch zone where all the child branches are upward, mixed branch zone where child branches are either upward or downward, downward branch zone where all the child branches are downward. In the mixed branch zone, the upward branches take one side while the downward branch takes the other. In the upward branch or downward branch zone, the child branches stretch outward from the parent branch on both left and right sides without overlapping each other.

Figure 4. Strategies to reduce self-intersections (a) An unguided placement of child branches with multiple branch crossings (b) Placing upward child branches and downward child branches on the different sides (c) Placing upward child branches and downward child branches on the different sides only in the mixed branch zone (d) A 2D layout of a contour tree with 3 branch crossing (e) The rectangular display of the contour tree in d

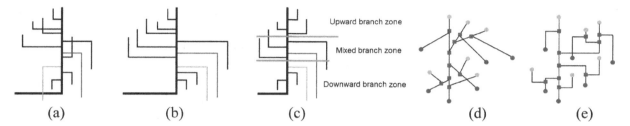

(a)　　　　　(b)　　　　　(c)　　　　　(d)　　　　(e)

3.1.4. Tree View Interaction Design

A typical tree view graph displays a hierarchy of items by indenting child items beneath their parents. In treeview representations, the interactions are directly embedded: the user can collapse (or expand) a particular sub-tree to hide (or show) the items in it.

An example of data exploration through tree view interaction is given in Figure 5. The data is a vorticity magnitude field of a simulated flow with vortices. A click on an inner node of the original contour tree (Figure 5a right) results in hiding or showing the sub-tree rooted at the node. The persistence – indicated as the vertical length of a branch –serves as an importance indicator for users to select contours. An interactively simplified contour tree is shown in Figure 5b. The roots of the collapsed sub-trees are marked with plus mark icons. For each branch of a contour tree, a single contour of the branch is extracted. A contour in the scalar field is represented by a point in the tree (indicated by a horizontal line segment in the same color with the contour). The selected contours are representative contours that give an overview of the whole scalar field. The more a contour tree is simplified, the higher level overview is obtained.

Figure 5. Tree view Interaction (a) A contour tree and a 2D scalar field from which this tree was constructed with contours selected for every branch of it (b) An interactively simplified contour tree after clicking on several nodes and contours selected for every branch of it

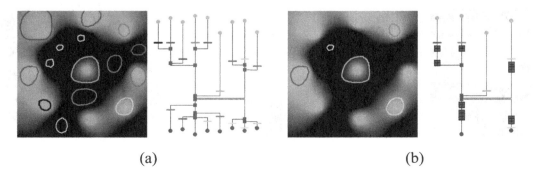

(a)　　　　　　　　　　　　　　　(b)

3.2. Contour Tree-Based Uncertainty Visualization

This section discusses uncertainty metrics for the data-level uncertainty and contour-level uncertainty and their visualization representations. The uncertainty or variability information is attached to the new planar contour tree display to give a high-level overview of uncertainty and to allow a quick and accurate selection of contours with different levels of uncertainty.

3.2.1. Data-Level Uncertainty

The data-level uncertainty measures how uncertain the numerical values of the data are. Uncertainty measures, such as standard deviation, inter-quartile range, and the confidence intervals, fall into this category. As discussed in section 2.2, techniques which overlay or embed uncertainty representation in the underlining data visualization face perception and interaction issues. We therefore propose an alternative visualization that attaches uncertainty glyphs to a contour tree rather than integrating them with data visualization directly.

We adapted graduated glyphs (Sanyal et al., 2010) to visualize data-level uncertainty. A circular glyph encodes the deviation of all ensemble members from the ensemble mean at a data point. A graduated ribbon is constructed by interpolating between circular glyphs placed along an iso-line in the data image. A glyph that has a dense core with a faint periphery indicates that ensemble members have a few outliers and mostly agree. A mostly dark glyph indicates that large differences exist among individual members. The size of a glyph indicates the variability of a location with respect to other locations on the grid. For more details on graduated glyphs, we refer the reader to (Sanyal et al., 2010).

We use graduated glyphs to show uncertainty at each data point. Figure 6 shows a 2D 9×9 uncertain scalar dataset which is a down-sampled sub-region of the data in Figure 5. In Figure 6a, the mean field of eight members is color-mapped and overlaid with uncertainty glyphs at each data point. Likewise, as shown in Figure 6b, the glyph of a data point is attached to its corresponding location in the contour tree. Figure 6c illustrates a segment of a graduated ribbon along a branch. As shown in Figure 6b and d, while a graduated

Figure 6. Data-level uncertainty representation based on the contour tree (a) Graduated circular uncertainty glyphs on an uncertain scalar field (b) A contour tree with circular graduated uncertainty glyphs (c) A segment of a graduated ribbon on a branch (black) constructed by overlaying thinner ribbons successively (d) Contour tree attached with average data-level uncertainty along each contour and four sets of corresponding contours are shown after clicking on four locations (indicated by colored line segments) in the contour tree

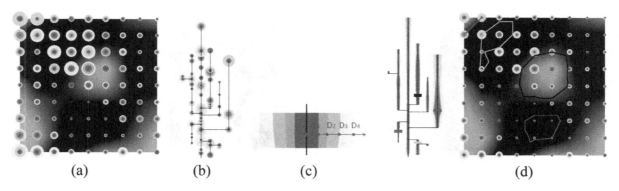

(a)   (b)   (c)   (d)

circle illustrates the data-level uncertainty at a data point, the graduated ribbon provides continuous uncertainty representation along individual contours with less clutter. Therefore, we prefer ribbon-like graduated glyphs over circular graduated glyphs for representing data-level uncertainty along contours.

3.2.2. Contour-Level Uncertainty

In this chapter, contour-level uncertainty measures the variation in the position of a contour. In a spaghetti plot, the most unstable contours and the places where the contours are extremely diverse among individual ensemble members are interesting to users (Sanyal et al., 2010). However, the users' estimates tend to be inaccurate due to the randomness of the contour size, shape and length. Additionally, it is hard to look into such uncertainty in a large data set. Precise and automatic contour variability measurement is needed to assist the exploration of the large uncertain data. We introduce the concept of contour variability which quantifies how diverse a contour is within multiple ensemble members to address this need.

To measure the variability of a contour, we first identify corresponding contours in different ensemble members. Then, we calculate the differences between them and use the mean and variance of the differences to represent the positional variation among contours.

3.2.2.1. Contour Correspondence and Difference

For a contour in one ensemble member, there may be more than one contour in another ensemble member with the same iso-value with it, or it may be missing in some ensemble members. Spatial overlap is frequently used as a similarity measure to match features in different datasets under an assumption that these features only have small spatially deviation (Schneider, Wiebel, Carr, Hlawitschka, & Scheuermann, 2008; Sohn & Chandrajit, 2006). For instance, the correspondence between two contours can be measured by the degree of contour overlap as discussed by Sohn and Bajaj (Sohn & Chandrajit, 2006) when they computed correspondence information of contours in time-varying scalar fields.

The non-overlapped area $A(C, C_i)$ between the two corresponding contours C and C_i decides the difference between the two contours. Given a contour C in the ensemble mean, we search in ensemble member i for the contour $C_i (i = 1, \ldots, k)$ who shares the same iso-value with C and has the best correspondence with C. The best matched contours, if found, are considered the same contours which appear in different ensemble members. Figure 7 gives an example. In Figure 7a, there are three contours (in blue, gray, and brown) in ensemble i with different correspondence degrees with contour C (in red). With the largest overlap

Figure 7. Contour difference measured by non-overlapped areas (a) Three contours in ensemble member i share a domain with contour C (in red) in the ensemble mean (b), (c), and (d) Non-overlapped areas (filled with gray) of different contours

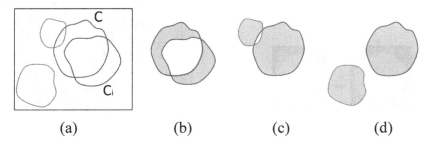

| (a) | (b) | (c) | (d) |

degree with C, the blue contour is identified as the corresponding contour of C in ensemble member i. Figure 7b, c and d illustrate the non-overlapping area in different cases. To reduce bias towards long or short contours, larger or smaller iso-surfaces, we normalize the non-overlapping area with the contour length (or iso-surface area in 3D case) of C:

$$difference\left(C, C_i\right) = A(C, C_i) \,/\, size(C),$$

where $size(C)$ is the contour length (or iso-surface area in 3D case) of C.

3.2.2.2. Contour-Level Uncertainty Metrics and Visualization

We calculate the mean and variance of the differences to the mean to help a user select contours according to the quantified contour variability information. Given a contour C in the ensemble mean, let its corresponding contours of k individual ensemble members be $C_i (i = 1, \ldots, k)$. C_i is the contour with the same iso-value that is matched with C. The average difference among the corresponding contours is:

$$mean = \frac{\sum difference\left(C, C_i\right)}{k}.$$

The variance of difference among contours is:

$$va = \frac{\sum (difference\left(C, C_i\right) - mean)^2}{k - 1}.$$

If an ensemble member does not have a matched contour for C, its contribution is set to a large value, the maximum non-overlapping area found between C and all the matched contours C_i.

The contour variability along a contour can be shown at the corresponding location in the contour tree. Figure 8 illustrates the glyph design to encode the contour variability. Before visualization, both variability statistics are normalized to a range between 0 and a unit width. As discussed in section 3.2.1, ribbon-like glyph is preferred over circular glyph to prevent visual cluttering, we resample the varying contour variability along each branch and use linear interpolation to produce a ribbon-like glyph along each branch. For each branch, two ribbons are attached. The blue one is for the mean difference, while the green one is for the variance. The varying width of each ribbon

Figure 8. Visualization of contour variability based on contour tree (a) A circular glyph for contour variability is produced by combining two circular glyphs for mean and variance of differences between corresponding contours in different ensemble members and the ensemble mean (b) The ribbons attached to the contour tree (left) indicate the variability of corresponding contours in the data (right) Three sets of corresponding contours are shown after clicking on three locations (indicated by arrows) in the contour tree

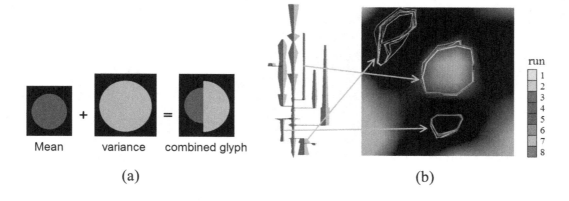

Mean   variance   combined glyph

(a)

(b)

indicates the varying magnitude of each variability measurement for the contours along the branch.

3.2.3. Topology-Level Uncertainty

The uncertainty within the data impact not only the values or the contour positions locally, but also the global pattern of the data which is described by the topology of the data. Visualizing the uncertainty concerning the topology among the ensemble members provides new perspective on the global impact of uncertainty. In this chapter, the topology-level uncertainty is defined as the variation in the height and number of branches in the contour tree of an uncertain scalar field.

The idea is to map the branches between the contour tree of different ensemble members and the contour tree of the ensemble mean and to overlay the mapped branches. A set of matched branches are assigned with a same x-axis value but keep their original y-axis values so that an overlap of the branches on x-axis indicates their correspondence while the disagreements between the branches on y-axis indicate their discrepancy in iso-value. A branch of mean contour tree may not find a matched branch in some ensemble members. The number of matched branches is encoded with the width of the branch. A thicker branch is more certain than a thinner one.

3.2.3.1. Branch Correspondence

We measure the correspondence degree between two branches as the spatial overlap between their contour regions. A contour region of a branch is defined as the region covered by all the contours within the sub-tree of the branch.

Given a branch B in the mean contour tree, we search in ensemble member i for its best matched branch. The best matched branches, if found, are considered the same branches which appear in different ensemble members. We do not need to search all the branches of the contour tree in ensemble member i for the branch with largest

overlap with B. The contour tree hierarchy and branch orientation help us limit the number of branches to compare. (1) The matched branch must be found among the child branches of the matched branch of its parent due to the nesting relationship between child and parent branches. (2) A downward branch does not match an upward branch, or vice versa.

Figure 9 illustrates the branch correspondences detected according to the spatial overlaps of contour regions. The contours and contour trees of two scalar fields in Figure 9a and b share a same spatial domain. In Figure 9a, the sub-tree of the middle branch (1, 10) is the whole contour tree. The sub-tree of branch (0.5, 10.5) is the whole contour tree in Figure 9b. Both branches share the whole data domain and hence are the best matched branches of each other. For the rest branches, the correspondence indicated by overlaps between their contour regions: branch (2, 3) → branch (1.8, 3.3), branch (6, 9) → branch (6.5, 9.6), branch (4, 8) →branch(4.2, 8.3), and branch(5, 7) → branch(5.4, 7.1). For example, branch (4, 8) matches branch (4.2, 8.3) since they have the largest overlaps. Branch (5.4, 7.1) matches branch (5, 7) even when branch (4, 8) has larger overlap with it since branch (4, 8) is mapped to its parent branch (4.2, 8.3). Figure 9c shows the matched branch in the same x-axis location.

3.2.3.2. Topology-Level Uncertainty Visualization via Contour Tree Mapping

We map the contour tree of each ensemble member to the mean contour tree hierarchically. In the resulting visualization, the contour trees of different ensemble members are rendered beneath the mean contour tree in different colors. The x-axis locations of the matched branches are aligned. The number of unmatched branches for a branch in the mean contour tree is encoded as the width of the branch.

As shown in Figure 10, the mapped contour trees indicate how uncertain the iso-value ranges

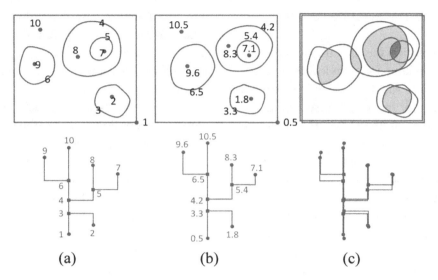

Figure 9. Branch correspondence indicated by contour region overlaps. The nodes and contours are numbered by their iso-values (a) and (b) show contour trees of two data fields and the corresponding contour regions of the tree branches (c) The matched branches are indicated by the shared x-axis locations

of individual branches are and how uncertain the number of branches is. The places where branches of the contour trees disagree with each other indicate the uncertain iso-value ranges of different contour regions segmented by branches. The overall blurring or clearness of the display indicates the overall high or low uncertainty. The thickness of a branch indicates the number of matched branches found in the ensemble members. For example, a

thin branch (indicated by the green arrow) is found in the lower right corner of the tree. It represents an uncertain contour region (or minimum) which only appear in a few ensemble members. As shown in Figure 10, only two contours (in blue and green) from ensemble members 4 and 7 are shown after clicking on the branch. On the contrary, the two sets of contours selected from the middle locations of two thick branches (indicated by red

Figure 10. Topology-level uncertainty visualization. Three sets of contours are shown after clicking on three locations (indicated by arrows) in the contour tree

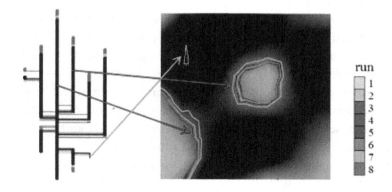

and blue arrows) include corresponding contours from all the ensemble members. Accordingly, the topology-level uncertainty provides users a quick and high level overview of how much uncertainty there is in the topology of contours.

3.3. User Interface Design

The contour tree provides an intuitive interface for exploring uncertainty. Figure 11 shows the interface designed to enable efficient browsing, manipulation, and quantitative analysis of uncertain scalar data fields. The top-left area shows a 2D or 3D visualization of a data set, including iso-lines and color-mapped image for 2D data, or iso-surfaces and volume rendering for 3D data. It provides interactions such as rotation and zooming. The top-right area shows a 2D display of the contour tree of the mean data field. It allows interactive contour tree simplification and contour selection. The three bottom areas show

the data-level uncertainty, contour variability, and topology variability of the data based on contour trees. They allow similar interactions as the top-right contour tree display area. Once a data set is imported with the pre-computed uncertainty and variability information, the tool shows the color-mapped data (volume rendered for 3D data) in the data display area. The contours (iso-lines or iso-surfaces) are also rendered in the data display area and updated accordingly as a user clicks on one contour tree or changes the iso-value by sliding on the vertical bar in the top-right contour tree display area.

Users may simplify the contour tree in two ways. (1) Use a horizontal bar under the contour tree display to control the current number of branches in the contour tree. As a user drags the slider from right to left, branches are removed from the contour tree according to the order stored in the pre-computed simplification sequence. (2)

Figure 11. The user interface Top-left: data display area shows iso-surfaces of the mean field of five brains chosen from the simplified mean contour tree on the top right: Top-right: contour tree display area shows a simplified contour tree; Bottom: display areas for data-level uncertainty, contour-level uncertainty, and topology-level uncertainty shown on simplified contour trees

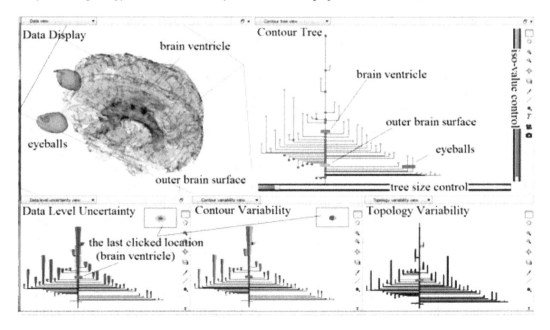

Directly right-click on the inner nodes of the contour tree to prune or extend sub-trees.

Users may select contours to display in two ways. (1) Display multiple contours of the mean field with selected iso-values by clicking on the contour tree of the top-right area. A selected contour is shown in the same distinct color with a point placed at the clicked location. (2) Display a set of corresponding contours (spaghetti plots) with the same iso-value in different ensemble members in the data display area by double-clicking on a location in one of the three contour trees in the bottom. Contours from different ensemble members are shown in different colors.

3.4. Application and Discussion

In this section, we apply the new uncertainty visualization to a simulated weather data set (135×135×30) and a medical volumetric data set (128×128×71).

The first experiment demonstrates an effective application of the new uncertainty visualization on the simulated data from Weather Research and Forecasting (WRF) model runs. The members of numerical weather prediction ensembles are individual simulations with either slightly perturbed initial conditions or different model parameterizations. Scientists use the average ensemble output as a forecast and utilize spaghetti plots to analyze the spread of the ensemble members. In our application, water-vapor mixing ratio data from eight simulation runs of the 1993 Super storm are used. Figure 12a shows the original contour tree (1734 critical points and 867 branches) and all the contours with the iso-value indicated by the red horizontal line connecting the slider of the vertical bar. Uncertainty information is shown in the simplified contour tree in Figure 12c. A few thin branches appear at its bottom region indicating the uncertain contour region (or minima) in the data. Figure 12b shows the volume rendering of the average data with circular uncertainty glyphs whose sizes vary according to the level of data-level un-

certainty. Figure 12d shows a set of corresponding contours with high data-level uncertainty while Figure 12e shows a set of corresponding contours with high contour variability. Circular graduated glyphs indicating the magnitude of the data-level uncertainty and contour variability are shown at the bottom. The color bar on the right indicates the correspondence between the iso-surfaces and simulation runs.

The second application is to visualize non-weighted diffusion images. We apply our method to study the variation between the brain images from five subjects after affine registration to one particular data set chosen at random using FLIRT (Jenkinson & Smith, 2001). Contour trees had been introduced to explore brain data in previous literature (Hamish Carr & Snoeyink, 2003). The between-subject variation in brain anatomy is closely related to the uncertainty study of brain imaging (Eickhoff et al., 2009). The mean field of the brains contains 2143 critical points and 1071 branches in the original contour tree. Figure 13a shows the integrated visualization of both data and uncertainty glyphs. Variability information is shown in the simplified contour tree in Figure 13b. Brain outer surfaces and ventricle surfaces are selected from two points (indicated in red and yellow) in the contour trees. As shown in Figure 13a, the inner part of the brain area exhibit higher data value along with higher data-level uncertainty. This is reflected in the generally thicker graduated ribbons observed in the upper region of the left tree in Figure 13b. Meanwhile, contours corresponding to the upper region of the trees have higher contour variability and higher topology variability, indicating the impact of the data-level uncertainty on the contours and contour trees. The inner features such as brain ventricles exhibit higher variability than the brain outer surfaces based on the quantified uncertainty and variability information shown on the corresponding location in the contour trees. The interactive visualization supports the exploration of variability information that is hidden in the

Figure 12. Exploration of weather ensemble simulation with contour tree based visualization: (a) Original contour tree; (b) Volume rendering with uncertainty glyphs; (c) Left to right: data-level uncertainty, contour variability, and topology variability shown in the simplified contour tree; (d) A set of contours (corresponding to the red points in the contour trees) with high data-level uncertainty indicated by the large graduated circle; (e) A set of contours (corresponding to the yellow points in the contour trees) with high contour variability indicated by the large glyph for contour variability

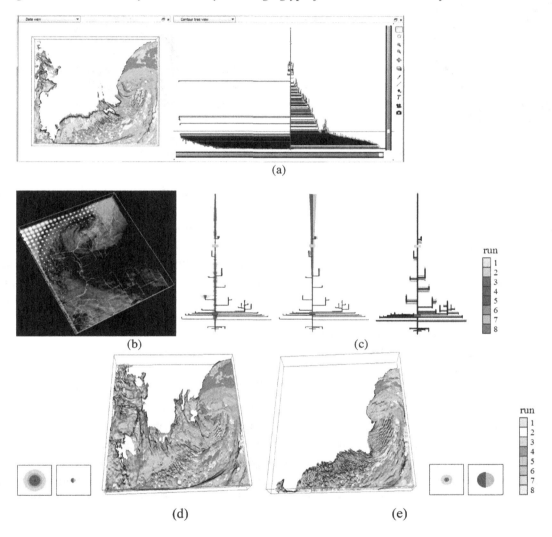

conventional view for selected anatomical structures.

As shown in the above examples, the new contour tree based visualization provides a combined exploration of both the data and the uncertainty. Users are allowed to look into three levels of uncertainty in the data. With the planar contour tree layout, users are allowed to explore data hierarchically and investigate the contours with certain uncertainty or variability more precisely and efficiently. Volume rendering with circular uncertainty glyphs (Figure 12d and Figure 13a) are provided for a comparison purpose. With 3D glyphs placed within the volumetric data, the

Figure 13. Brain data with uncertainty (a) Volume rendering with circular uncertainty glyphs (b) Left to right: data-level uncertainty, contour-level uncertainty, and topology-level uncertainty shown in a simplified contour tree (c) Corresponding contours of the same iso-value in different brain data. Five overlapped brain outer surfaces corresponding to the yellow points in the contour trees and five overlapped ventricle surfaces corresponding to the red points in the contour trees

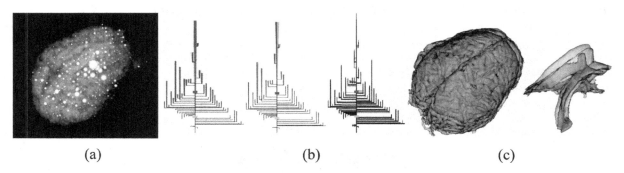

(a)   (b)   (c)

details of the data are noticeably blocked by the glyphs while the glyphs are overlapped with each other or appear to be blurred or buried in a 3D scene. Accordingly, the new visualization method provides an alternative which shows both data and uncertainty clearly.

4. A FEATURE-BASED FRAMEWORK FOR VISUALIZING VECTOR FIELD UNCERTAINTY

In this section, we present a framework to visualize feature-level uncertainties in vector fields. In many cases, locations of features matter more than the data-level uncertainty. For instance, the locations of warm eddies are important in ocean fishery, and the locations of hurricane eyes or the peaks in pressure field are important in weather analysis. Two features are considered the same feature at in different data sets if they share the same tracking path (Tricoche, 2002) or the biggest similarity (Sohn & Chandrajit, 2006). We evaluate the uncertainty related to features by measuring the deviation of those feature pairs in different data sets. The features currently studied by us are vector field critical points. They are intuitive features closely related to physical features (Garth

& Tricoche, 2005). Scalar fields can be analyzed through their gradient fields.

This section is organized as follows. Section 4.1 gives the method framework. Section 4.2, 4.3, and 4.4 discuss feature extraction, uncertainty measurement, and uncertainty glyph design respectively. Section 4.5 demonstrates and discusses application results.

4.1 Method Pipeline

The impact of uncertainty on the features is quantified as feature-level uncertainty which is measured by feature deviation Figure 14). The feature deviation is obtained through a three-step procedure—feature identification, feature mapping, and uncertainty representation. Given a set of data members (e.g. multiple simulation runs) this method first identifies the features within all the data members and the mean field given by averaging all the members. Second, feature tracking is implemented to map the features of each data member to that of the mean field. The mapped features are then assumed to have the same feature with slight position deviation in each of the individual data members. Finally, the feature-level uncertainties are expressed as the deviations of the features.

Figure 14. The pipeline for feature-level uncertainty visualization

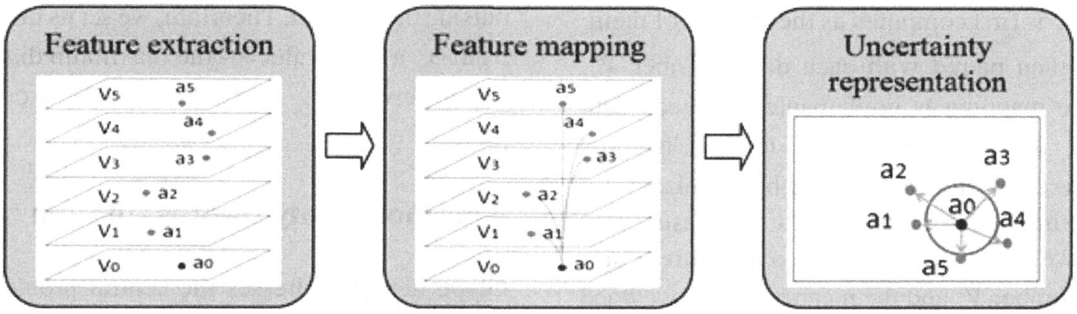

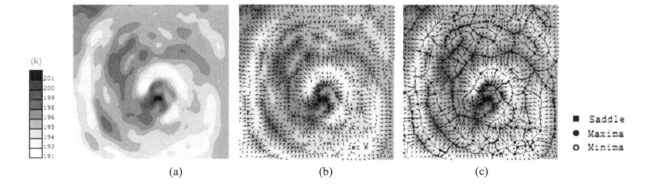

4.2. Feature Extraction

Topology consists of critical points, periodic orbits, and separatrices. It characterizes a flow in that the relatively uniform flow behaviour in each topological region can be deduced from its boundary. The computation of critical points in a vector field can be found in (Helman & Hesselink, 1989). For a scalar field, its gradient field can be used to extract critical points so that the features of scalar fields and vector fields are analyzed in the same way. A vector field V can be constructed out of scalar field f using the gradient operator $\nabla : V = \nabla f = (\partial f / \partial x, \partial f / \partial y)$. The maxima of f appear as sinks and minima appear as sources in its gradient field V. Figure 15 illustrates an example of the critical points extracted from the gradient field of a temperature field.

4.3. Feature-Level Uncertainty Metric Based on Feature Mapping

Feature Flow Field (FFF) (Theisel & Seidel, 2003) is adopted to couple critical points of different fields by tracing streamlines within it. The concept of FFF has been successfully applied to tracking critical points (Theisel, Weinkauf, Hege, & Seidel, 2005), extracting Galilean invariant vortex core lines (Sahner, Weinkauf, & Hege, 2005), simplification (Theisel, Rössl, & Seidel, 2003a), and comparison (Theisel, Rössl, & Seidel, 2003b). In this chapter, it is used to identify the same feature that appears in different data members at different positions. The uncertainty of this feature is then expressed as the deviation between all of its counterparts in different data members.

Figure 15. Topology extracted from the gradient field of a temperature field: (a) Color-mapped temperature; (b) Gradient field represented with arrows; (c) Gradient field with extracted vector topology

Given k data members $V_i, (i = 1, ..., k)$, a mean field V_0 is first computed as the average of them. V_0 is then paired with each data member V_i. Feature mapping is implemented for each data pair V_0 and V_i. With the FFF method, features of different vector fields could be correlated.

Figure 16 demonstrates how to measure feature-level uncertainty related to a feature. For a data member V_1 and the mean field V_0, we trace a streamline from a critical point a_0 in V_0 until it reaches a critical point a_1 in V_1. After tracing critical points between all the pairs, the feature-level uncertainty is measured by the distances between $a_i (i = 1, ..., k)$ and a_0. Figure 16a illustrates the feature mapping between a pair of data. Figure 16b shows a straightforward representation of the uncertainties related to individual features by arrows. Given a data member $V_n (1 \leq n \leq k)$, it is possible that the streamline starting from a_0 reaches the boundary of the FFF or ends at V_0 instead of reaching a critical point in V_n. In these cases, we assume that the mapped critical point a_n for a_0 in this data member exists outside the domain. Therefore, we set its distance from a_0 a large value — the maximum distance found between a_0 and all the mapped critical points a_i.

4.4. Uncertainty Representation

Glyph design addresses the central problem of how uncertainty information is processed into knowledge. For the detected deviations of a critical point, a quantitative glyph is designed to indicate uncertainty level related to the critical point. The new uncertainty glyph is inspired by both graduated circular glyph (Sanyal et al., 2010) and elliptical glyph (Walsum, Post, Silver, & Post, 1996).

4.4.1. Elliptical Glyph

A glyph that can be used at different levels is the elliptical glyph (Walsum et al., 1996). It depicts the covariance between multiple real-valued random variables X_i. In probability theory and

Figure 16. Feature-level uncertainty measurement (a) Feature deviations detected by tracing critical points within FFF between a data member V_1 and the mean field V_0 (b) Feature-level uncertainty measured by the deviations (indicated by arrows) of features (indicated by dots) in all the data members $V_n (n = 1, ..., k)$ from the features in the mean data field V_0

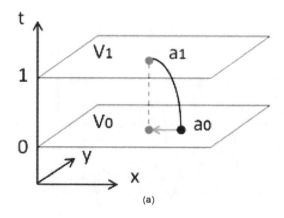

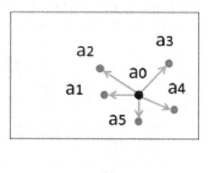

(a)   (b)

statistics, covariance measures how much two variables change together. The covariance matrix $\sum$ generalizes the notion of variance to multiple dimensions.

$$\sum_{i,j} = Cov(X_i, X_j) = E[(X_i - E(X_i))(X_j - E(X_j))]$$

where $E(X_i)$ is the expected value of X_i, and the ellipse axis length is $\lambda = eig(\sum)$. Ellipse axis directions are given by $d = eigvec(\sum)$. An elliptical glyph can be applied to visualize tensors, but can also show a simplified representation of the spatial distribution of a set of 2D or 3D data (Sadarjoen & Post, 2000).

4.4.2. Graduated Elliptical Glyph

Before using the graduated ellipse, we considered using arrows to indicate the uncertainty by showing directions and distances of individual deviations. Nevertheless, it is found that arrows, though showing the deviations in an authentic way, could cause severe information overload when the number of ensemble runs increases. Contrarily, the graduated ellipse possesses the elliptical glyph's ability to depict the overall deviation of a feature and the graduated glyph's intuitive way to depict inner deviation of individual ensemble members. When placed across an image, the overall size and orientation of the glyphs indicate the variability of features while the very shape of and color distribution within an individual glyph give a quick statistical summary of uncertain deviations of a feature.

Let $a_0\ (x_0, y_0)$ be a critical point in the mean data field V_0. Its counter-parts in data members V_i are $a_i\ (x_i, y_i)\ (i = 1, ..., k)$. A graduated elliptical glyph consists of k nested ellipses and is placed at the location of a_0. The nested ellipses share the same orientation and axis ratio. The rendering of each nested ellipse is as follows:

First, assign an ellipse E with axes A and B computed according to the relative locations of a_i towards a_0, $(x_i - x_0, y_i - y_0)$. Let variable X be $x_i - x_0$, and Y be $y_i - y_0$. The lengths and directions of A and B are given by $eig(\sum(X, Y))$ and $eigvec(\sum(X, Y))$, respectively. $\sum(X, Y)$ is the Covariance Matrix of X and Y. Second, nested ellipses are produced by fitting them into ellipse E. Sort a_i according to its distance from a_0, $d_i = \sqrt{(x_i - x_0)^2 + (y_i - y_0)^2}$. In descending order. Let the biggest distance among d_i be D. Each nested ellipse is given axis lengths $|A| \times d_i\ /\ D$ and $|B| \times d_i\ /\ D$. Finally, in a way similar to producing a graduated circular glyph (Sanyal, et al., 2010), assign saturation level s_i for the ith glyph as $s_i = (i - 1)\ /\ (k - 1)$ and overlay the ellipse so that the smaller one is over the larger one.

Figure 17 gives a comparison between using a simple ellipse, arrows, graduated circular glyph, and graduated elliptical glyph for feature-level uncertainty. The individual features $a_i, (i = 1, ..., k)$ (which are not displayed in a final visualization) are shown as well to better illustrate the design concept of each glyph. The simple ellipse (Figure 17a) only characterizes the overall deviation of a feature. Arrows (Figure 17b) indicate the exact locations of all the deviated features while inviting visual clutters when k increases. The graduated circular glyph (Figure 17c) shows the individual deviation of a feature but no direction information is revealed. However, the graduated elliptical glyph (Figure 17d) summarizes overall and individual distribution of a feature in a succinct way. Figure 18 shows a set of graduated ellipse with varying color distributions, sizes, axis length ratios, and orientations.

Figure 17. Feature-level uncertainty glyph design (a) Ellipse (b) Arrows (c) Graduated circular glyph (d) Graduated ellipse

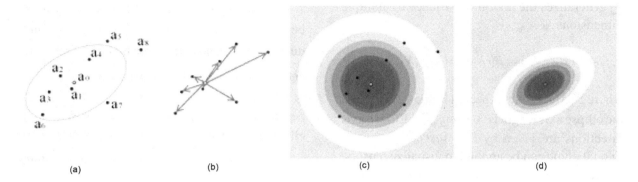

(a)   (b)   (c)   (d)

4.5. Application and Discussion

The method is applied to a 2D vector dataset. The first dataset includes 5 simulated hurricane wind fields (Figure 19). The uncertainty glyphs are placed in critical point locations. The results demonstrate how much features are affected by the uncertainty within the data. Through mapping and comparing the critical points between different ensemble members, the shifts between critical points become perceivable. The graduated elliptical glyphs effectively indicate the magnitude and

Figure 18. Graduated ellipses with varying orientation, saturation distribution, size, and axis length ratio. B / A 8 data members are used

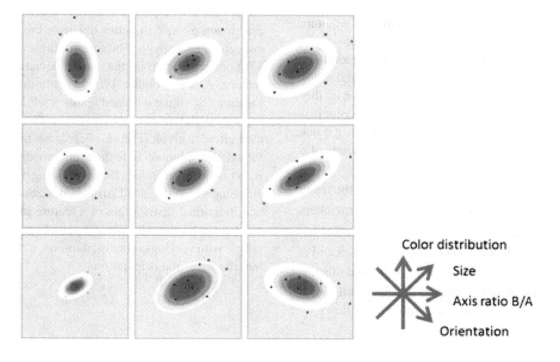

overall orientation of the uncertain deviations of vortices. The uncertain position of the hurricane eye reflects the impact of the uncertainty directly. A side-by-side display of different component data or the visualization of the data-level uncertainty may not give viewers such insight.

Although the result of this feature-level uncertainty visualization is positive, there are a few limitations and areas that need further study. Most notably, more features could be considered in the future. Second, other feature-mapping methods may be included depending on the feature type since the current feature-mapping method, FFF, mainly tracks topological features.

5. CONCLUSION

This chapter has conducted an in-depth investigation of feature-level uncertainties and suggested a promising direction of future uncertainty studies in exploiting topology tools. The presented feature-based techniques alleviate the inherent perception issues such as clutter and occlusion in uncertainty visualizations in 3D or large 2D scenes. The incorporation of the feature-level uncertainties into visualization provides insights into the reliability of the extracted features which otherwise would remain unknown with the visualization of only data-level uncertainty. In addition, the novel use of contour trees provides an effective solution for interacting with 3D or large 2D data sets with uncertainty.

There are many possible directions in which one could extend this work. (1) Extend the developed feature-based uncertainty visualization framework to study uncertainty in various fields. (2) Improve the interactive uncertainty visualization based on user feedbacks. (3) Investigate more metrics to measure uncertainty or variability and apply our methods to address different types of uncertainty models. (4) The possibilities inherent in topology tools are not exhausted yet. For example, the possibility of using Morse-Smale complex (Smale, 1961) for uncertainty study has not been investigated. Therefore, we will continue the current work in utilizing topology tools to visualize uncertainty.

Figure 19. Feature-level uncertainty of a hurricane wind field (a) Feature tracking within FFF of two vector fields V_1 and V_2 (b) Uncertain location of hurricane eye and vortices in a hurricane wind field (5 ensemble members)

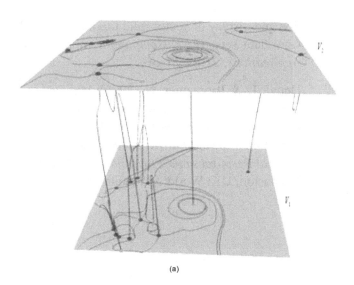

(a)

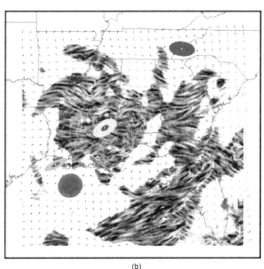

(b)

REFERENCES

Bajaj, C. L., Pascucci, V., & Schikore, D. R. (1997). The contour spectrum. In *Proceedings of Visualization '97*. New Brunswick, NJ: IEEE Press.

Brodlie, K., Osorio, R. A., & Lopes, A. (2012). A review of uncertainty in data visualization. In Dill, J, Earnshaw, R, Kasik, D, Vince, J, & Wong, P. C. (Eds.), *Expanding the Frontiers of Visual Analytics and Visualization* (81-109). Berlin: Springer. doi:10.1007/978-1-4471-2804-5_6.

Carr, H. (2004). *Topological Manipulation of Isosurfaces*. (PhD Thesis). Vancouver, BC, Canada, University of British Columbia.

Carr, H., & Snoeyink, J. (2003). *Path seeds and flexible isosurfaces using topology for exploratory visualization*. In *Proceedings of the Symposium on Data Visualisation*. New Brunswick, NJ: IEEE Press.

Carr, H., Snoeyink, J., & Axen, U. (2003). Computing contour trees in all dimensions. *Computational. Geometry. Theory & Applications*, *24*(2), 75–94.

Carr, H., Snoeyink, J., & Panne, M. V. D. (2004). Simplifying flexible isosurfaces using local geometric measures. In *Proceedings of Visualization '04*. New Brunswick, NJ: IEEE Press. doi:10.1109/VISUAL.2004.96.

Cedilnik, A., & Rheingans, P. (2000). Procedural annotation of uncertain information. In *Proceedings of Visualization '04*. New Brunswick, NJ: IEEE.

Davis, T. J., & Keller, C. P. (1997). Modeling and visualizing multiple spatial uncertainties. *Computers & Geosciences*, *23*(4), 397–408. doi:10.1016/S0098-3004(97)00012-5.

Diggle, P., Heagerty, P., Liang, K.-Y., & Zeger, S. (2002). *Analysis of longitudinal data*. New York: Oxford University Press.

Djurcilova, S., Kima, K., Lermusiauxb, P., & Pang, A. (2002). Visualizing scalar volumetric data with uncertainty. *Computers & Graphics*, *26*(2), 239–248. doi:10.1016/S0097-8493(02)00055-9.

Eickhoff, S. B., Laird, A. R., Grefkes, C., Wang, L. E., Zilles, K., & Fox, P. T. (2009). Coordinate-based activation likelihood estimation meta-analysis of neuroimaging data: A random-effects approach based on empirical estimates of spatial uncertainty. *Human Brain Mapping*, *30*(9), 2907–2926. doi:10.1002/hbm.20718 PMID:19172646.

Garth, C., & Tricoche, X. (2005). Topology- and feature-based flow visualization: Methods and applications. In *Proceedings of the SIAM Conference on Geometric Design and Computing*. New York: ACM Press.

Grigoryan, G., & Rheingans, P. (2004). Point-based probabilistic surfaces to show surface uncertainty. *IEEE Transactions on Visualization and Computer Graphics*, *10*(5), 564–573. doi:10.1109/TVCG.2004.30 PMID:15794138.

Heine, C., Schneider, D., Carr, H., & Scheuermann, G. (2011). Drawing Contour trees in the plane. *IEEE Transactions on Visualization and Computer Graphics*, *17*(11), 1599–1611. doi:10.1109/TVCG.2010.270 PMID:21173451.

Helman, J., & Hesselink, L. (1989). Representation and display of vector field topology in fluid flow data sets. *IEEE Computer Graphics and Applications*, *22*(8), 27–36.

Hengl, T., & Toomanian, N. (2006). Maps are not what they seem: Representing uncertainty in soil-property maps. In *Proceedings of 7th International Symposium on Spatial Accuracy Assessment in Natural Resources and Environmental Sciences*. Edgbaston, UK: World Academic Press.

Jenkinson, M., & Smith, S. (2001). A global optimisation method for robust affine registration of brain images. *Medical Image Analysis*, *5*(2), 143–156. doi:10.1016/S1361-8415(01)00036-6 PMID:11516708.

Keqin, W., Zhanping, L., Song, Z., & Moorhead, R. J. (2010). Topology-aware evenly spaced streamline placement. *IEEE Transactions on Visualization and Computer Graphics*, *16*(5), 791–801. doi:10.1109/TVCG.2009.206 PMID:20616394.

Kosara, R., Miksch, S., Hauser, H., Schrammel, J., Giller, V., & Tscheligi, M. (2002). *Useful Properties of Semantic Depth of Field for Better F+C Visualization*. In *Proceedings of the Symposium on Data Visualisation*. New Brunswick, NJ: IEEE Press.

MacEachren, A. M. (1992). Visualizing uncertain information. *Cartographic Perspective*, *13*(3), 10–19.

Otto, M., Germer, T., Hege, H.-C., & Theisel, H. (2010). Uncertain 2D vector field topology. *Computer Graphics Forum*, *2*(29), 347–356. doi:10.1111/j.1467-8659.2009.01604.x.

Pang, A., Wittenbrink, C., & Lodha, S. (1997). Approaches to uncertainty visualization. *The Visual Computer*, *13*(8), 370–390. doi:10.1007/s003710050111.

Pascucci, V., Cole-McLaughlin, K., & Scorzelli, G. (2004). Multi–resolution computation and presentation of contour tree. In *Proceedings of the IASTED Conference on Visualization, Imaging, and Image*. Calgary, AB: ACTA Press.

Pauly, M., Mitra, N. J., & Guibas, L. (2004). Uncertainty and variability in point cloud surface data. In *Proceedings of Eurographics Symposium on Point-Based Graphics*. New Brunswick, NJ: IEEE Press.

Pfaffelmoser, T., Reitinger, M., & Westermann, R. (2011). Visualizing the positional and geometrical variability of isosurfaces in uncertain scalar fields. In *Proceedings of Eurographics/IEEE Symposium on Visualization*. New Brunswick, NJ: IEEE Press.

Pöthkow, K., & Hege, H.-C. (2011). Positional uncertainty of isocontours: Condition analysis and probabilistic measures. *IEEE Transactions on Visualization and Computer Graphics*, *17*(10), 1393–1406. doi:10.1109/TVCG.2010.247 PMID:21041883.

Rhodes, P. J., Laramee, R. S., Bergeron, R. D., & Sparr, T. M. (2003). Uncertainty visualization methods in isosurface rendering. In *Proceedings of Eurographics*. New Brunswick, NJ: IEEE Press.

Sadarjoen, I. A., & Post, F. H. (2000). Detection, quantification, and tracking of vortices using streamline geometry. *Computers & Graphics*, *24*(3), 333–341. doi:10.1016/S0097-8493(00)00029-7.

Sahner, J., Weinkauf, T., & Hege, H.-C. (2005). Galilean invariant extraction and iconic representation of vortex core lines. In *Proceedings of EuroVis*. New Brunswick, NJ: IEEE Press.

Sanyal, J., Zhang, S., Bhattacharya, G., Amburn, P., & Moorhead, R. (2009). A user study to compare four uncertainty visualization methods for 1D and 2D datasets. *IEEE Transactions on Visualization and Computer Graphics*, *15*(6), 1209–1218. doi:10.1109/TVCG.2009.114 PMID:19834191.

Sanyal, J., Zhang, S., Dyer, J., Mercer, A., Amburn, P., & Moorhead, R. J. (2010). Noodles: A tool for visualization of numerical weather model ensemble uncertainty. *IEEE Transactions on Visualization and Computer Graphics*, *16*(6), 1421–1430. doi:10.1109/TVCG.2010.181 PMID:20975183.

Schmidt, G. S., Chen, S.-L., Bryden, A. N., Livingston, M. A., Osborn, B. R., & Rosenblum, L. J. (2004). Multidimensional visual representations for underwater environmental uncertainty. *IEEE Computer Graphics and Applications*, *24*(5), 56–65. doi:10.1109/MCG.2004.35 PMID:15628101.

Schneider, D., Wiebel, A., Carr, H., Hlawitschka, M., & Scheuermann, G. (2008). Interactive comparison of scalar fields based on largest contours with applications to flow visualization. *IEEE Transactions on Visualization and Computer Graphics*, *14*(6), 1475–1482. doi:10.1109/TVCG.2008.143 PMID:18988999.

Smale, S. (1961). On gradient dynamical systems. *The Annals of Mathematics*, *71*(1), 199–206. doi:10.2307/1970311.

Sohn, B. S., & Chandrajit, B. (2006). Time-varying contour topology. *IEEE Transactions on Visualization and Computer Graphics*, *12*(1), 14–25. doi:10.1109/TVCG.2006.16 PMID:16382604.

Takahashi, S., Takeshima, Y., & Fujishiro, I. (2004). Topological volume skeletonization and its application to transfer function design. *Graphical Models*, *66*(1), 24–49. doi:10.1016/j.gmod.2003.08.002.

Theisel, H., Rössl, C., & Seidel, H.-P. (2003a). Combining topological simplification and topology preserving compression for 2D vector fields. In *Proceedings of Pacific Graphics*. New Brunswick, NJ: IEEE Press. doi:10.1109/PCCGA.2003.1238287.

Theisel, H., Rössl, C., & Seidel, H.-P. (2003b). Using feature flow fields for topological comparison of vector fields. In *Proceedings of Vision, Modeling, and Visualization*. New Brunswick, NJ: IEEE Press.

Theisel, H., & Seidel, H.-P. (2003). Feature flow fields. In *Proceedings of Data Visualization*. New Brunswick, NJ: IEEE Press.

Theisel, H., Weinkauf, T., Hege, H.-C., & Seidel, H.-P. (2005). Topological methods for 2D time-dependent vector fields based on stream lines and path lines. *IEEE Transactions on Visualization and Computer Graphics*, *11*(4), 383–394. doi:10.1109/TVCG.2005.68 PMID:16138549.

Tierny, J., Gyulassy, A., Simon, E., & Pascucci, V. (2009). Loop surgery for volumetric meshes: Reeb graphs reduced to contour trees. *IEEE Transactions on Visualization and Computer Graphics*, *15*(6), 1177–1184. doi:10.1109/TVCG.2009.163 PMID:19834187.

Tricoche, X. (2002). *Vector and Tensor Field Topology Simplification, Tracking and Visualization*. (Dissertation). Kaiserslautern, Germany, University of Kaiserslautern.

Walsum, T. V., Post, F. H., Silver, D., & Post, F. J. (1996). Feature extraction and iconic visualization. *IEEE Transactions on Visualization and Computer Graphics*, *2*(2), 111–119. doi:10.1109/2945.506223.

Wittenbrink, C., Pang, A., & Lodha, S. (1996). Glyphs for visualizing uncertainty in vector fields. *IEEE Transactions on Visualization and Computer Graphics*, *2*(3), 266–279. doi:10.1109/2945.537309.

Wu, K., & Zhang, S. (2013). A contour tree based visualization for exploring data with uncertainty. *International Journal for Uncertainty Quantification*, *3*(3), 203–223. doi:10.1615/Int.J.UncertaintyQuantification.2012003956.

KEY TERMS AND DEFINITIONS

Ensembles: Multiple predictions from an ensemble of model runs with slightly different initial conditions and/or slightly different versions of models. Forecasters use ensembles to improve the accuracy of the forecast by averaging the various forecasts.

Feature: Phenomena, structures, or objects of interest in a dataset. The definitions of features depend on specific applications and users. The examples of topological features in a scalar field are Morse-Smale complex, Reeb-graph, and contour tree. Generally, vector field topology consists of critical points, periodic orbits, and separatrices.

Feature-Based Visualization: A type of visualization which visualizes features extracted from the original and usually large data set.

Uncertainty: The opposite of certainty, having limited knowledge to exactly describe an existing state and the future outcome, etc. Uncertainty in scientific data can be broadly defined as statistical variations, spread, errors, differences, and minimum maximum range values, etc.

Chapter 5
Cognitive Processes and Traits Related to Graphic Comprehension

Angela M. Zoss
Duke University, USA

ABSTRACT

The subject of how visualizations and graphics in general can be understood by their viewers draws on theories from many fields of research. Such theories might address the formal structure of the visualization, the style and graphic design skills of the creator, the task driving the viewer's interaction with the visualization, the type of data being represented, or the skills and experiences of viewer. This chapter focuses on this last question and presents a set of interrelated constructs and viewer traits that contribute to (or interfere with) a viewer's ability to analyze a particular data visualization. The review covers spatial thinking skills, cognitive styles, mental models, and cognitive load in its discussion of theoretical constructs related to graphic comprehension. The review also addresses how these cognitive processes vary by age, sex, and disciplinary background–the most common demographic characteristics studied in relation to graphic comprehension. Together, the constructs and traits contribute to a diverse and nuanced understanding of the viewers of data visualizations.

INTRODUCTION

With the rise of big data initiatives in academia, industry, and the public sector, the need for rapid and reliable pattern and trend analysis that can be easily communicated to a broad audience has created a growing demand for data visualization.

Data visualization as a practice is thus becoming increasingly global, being conducted by and distributed to increasingly diverse stakeholder groups. Users of visualizations may engage in a variety of tasks related to the visualization, including both low-level tasks like data foraging and high-level tasks like problem-solving and

DOI: 10.4018/978-1-4666-4309-3.ch005

composing (Card, Mackinlay, & Shneiderman, 1999), but the success of user interactions with visualizations is dependent on a variety of factors.

Small-scale studies of individual visualizations or common visualization types have established user success at interpreting specific structural devices or artifacts (see work by Fabrikant and colleagues–e.g., [Fabrikant, Montello, Ruocco, & Middleton, 2004]) or selecting appropriate interaction strategies (Molitor, Ballstaedt, & Mandl, 1989), commonly using response rate and accuracy as evaluation metrics (Lam, Bertini, Isenberg, Plaisant, & Carpendale, 2012). These studies, however, are often designed to evaluate a specific graphic or a limited set of visualization properties. With the rise of visual analytics and the broadening of the audiences for visualizations, a detailed examination of the interaction between an individual's skills and success at a full complement of visualization interpretation tasks is crucial to the development of appropriate and successful data visualizations and visual analytics systems.

This chapter will synthesize theoretical work that focuses on the viewer and the cognitive processes and traits that have been found to be relevant to the comprehension and interpretation of visualizations or, more broadly, graphics. We focus on the user/viewer of data visualizations and visual analytic systems to the exclusion of the visualizations and systems themselves; this focus allows us to identify research outside of the fields of data visualization and visual analytics that nonetheless have bearing on the interpretation process.

THEORIES OF COGNITION RELATED TO GRAPHIC COMPREHENSION

Graphic comprehension is at its heart a process of sense making. Low-level perceptual processes interact with higher-level attentional, associative, and interpretational processes to influence what people see and understand. The following section omits the cognitive processes with broader applicability and focuses instead on a series of specific constructs developed and tested to explain some component of graphic comprehension. Research on spatial thinking skills helps to categorize independent sets of skills necessary for different types of graphic comprehension tasks, from mental rotation of objects to maintaining vivid imagery. Mental models research applies across those spatial skills to describe how individuals interacting with an expectable external system gain experience and expertise, which they use to guide future interactions. Finally, cognitive load theory addresses the context surrounding the visualization system, building of the individual's experiences to predict what sorts of modes of communication are likely to be helpful or confusing.

Categories of Spatial Thinking Skills

A major theoretical area related to graphic comprehension is that of spatial thinking. Research within the field of spatial thinking forms a foundation upon which graphic perception can be structured. The visual encodings and reference systems used by graphics and diagrams to represent data in a manner that can be interpreted depends heavily on the skills developed during interactions with the visible world around us. Spatial thinking as a construct incorporates many other, related concepts, including spatial literacy, spatial intelligence, mental maps, and so forth. Research on spatial thinking describes the general types of spatial reasoning competencies people can acquire as they develop (e.g., spatial perception, mental rotation) and provides a broader framework within which more specified theories of graphic perception can be placed.

Spatial thinking, though foundational to a variety of interpretive tasks, is not an undifferentiated pool of tasks and abilities. Linn and Petersen (1985) conducted a meta-analysis of spatial ability research and identified the following three categories of spatial ability: spatial perception, mental rotation, and spatial visualization. Spatial perception relates to the orientation of an individual's body in physical space. Mental rotation is the ability to manipulate two- or three-dimensional objects in mental space, correctly associating one view of the object with a view of the object after it has been rotated along one or more axes. Spatial visualization is a name for a variety of spatial ability tasks that require "multistep manipulations of spatially presented information" (Linn & Petersen, 1985). Spatial visualization can be thought of as a form of problem solving, and as is typical of problem solving, a correct solution can often be found via multiple methods (Downs & DeSouza, 2006); in the case of spatial visualization, tasks may incorporate spatial perception or mental rotation processes, among others.

Skills in the various types of spatial thinking have been found vary across individuals, however, helping us to further explore the relative independence of these skills. One attempt to identify independent spatial thinking skills comes from the literature on intellectual and cognitive styles. Though empirical evidence in its support is sparse, there is a commonly-held belief that learners have differing *intellectual styles* and that matching a learner's intellectual style to different teaching strategies will improve learning outcomes (Mayer, 2011a; Newcombe & Stieff, 2012). Within the umbrella term of intellectual styles there are the related terms of *cognitive*, *learning*, and *thinking* styles (Evans & Cools, 2011). Of particular interest to the study of graphic comprehension is the body of research on cognitive styles, which are often seen as more fixed and stable modes of processing within an individual than learning and thinking styles (ibid).

Within the cognitive styles literature is a long-standing discussion of visuospatial processing. Factor analysis of tests of both general intelligence and specific types of intelligences has identified powerful visual components to intelligence that emerge in response to visuospatial questions included in those tests (Blazhenkova &

Kozhevnikov, 2010). Early acknowledgments of spatial intelligence and a visuospatial cognitive style postulated a bipolar interaction between verbal abilities and visual abilities (Blazhenkova & Kozhevnikov, 2009; Blazhenkova, Becker, & Kozhevnikov, 2011), but further elucidation of the nature of spatial intelligence and its relation to identified cognitive processes suggests that there are actually three, largely-independent dimensions to this cognitive style: verbal, visual-object, and visual-spatial (Blajenkova, Kozhevnikov, & Motes, 2006; Blazhenkova & Kozhevnikov, 2009, 2010; Blazhenkova et al., 2011; Kozhevnikov, Blazhenkova, & Becker, 2010; Kozhevnikov, Hegarty, & Mayer, 2002; Kozhevnikov, Kosslyn, & Shephard, 2005). This three-dimension model is known as the Object-Spatial-Verbal (OSV) cognitive style model.

Many of the tasks and tests related to spatial thinking (e.g., mental rotation, paper folding tests) have been strongly associated with the visual-spatial dimension of the Object-Spatial-Verbal (OSV) cognitive style model. Skills that are specifically visual-spatial include processing images sequentially and representing images schematically and in terms of object locations and spatial relationships (Blazhenkova & Kozhevnikov, 2009). Visual-object skills, however, had largely been ignored by intelligence tests and cognitive style researchers until the recent body of work by Kozhevnikov, Blazhenkova, and colleagues (Blazhenkova & Kozhevnikov, 2010). Visual-object skills include processing images holistically and maintaining vivid imagery with little conscious effort (ibid). Evidence suggests that visual-object tasks and functions are processed by a separate cognitive system than those associated with visual-spatial tasks (Kozhevnikov et al., 2010).

The independence of visual-object and visual-spatial skills, however, may not be the only notable distinction in spatial thinking skills. Another proposed independence separates visual-spatial skills like mental rotation and other "intraobject" skills from navigation, perspective taking, and other "interobject" skills (Newcombe, Uttal, & Sauter, in press). This additional division is supported by behavioral, linguistic, functional, and neurological evidence (ibid). While navigation has been largely absent from studies of individual differences, extensive theory in the development of navigation skills may soon lead to appropriate measures of these skills, enabling the further differentiation of visual-object, intraobject, and interobject components of spatial thinking.

Relevant for the study of graphic comprehension is an understanding of the tradeoff between the various spatial thinking systems. In the earlier bipolar verbal-visual model, it was assumed that increasing skills on the visual dimension of the cognitive style would diminish skills on the verbal dimension. The structure of the OSV cognitive style model presented verbal, visual-object, and visual-spatial skills as largely independent, allowing for the possibility that individuals can, in fact, have high (or low) achievement in all three types of intelligence at the same time. During the development of the self-report instrument that measures OSV cognitive style abilities–the *Object-Spatial Imagery and Verbal Questionnaire* (OSIVQ)–the researchers found that, among a sample of 625 college students and professionals, about 11% scored above average on all three dimensions and about 10% scored below average on all three dimensions (Blazhenkova & Kozhevnikov, 2009). The independence of these dimensions is consistent with findings that, just as mental rotation has been seen to improve with practice among those with initially low performance on this task (Lohman & Nichols, 1990), performance on one or more of the spatial thinking dimensions may be improved with training and experience (Newcombe & Stieff, 2012).

Gaining Domain Expertise

The development of this expertise in a particular spatial thinking task represents another potential focus area for research on graphic comprehension.

As is true for other cognitive processes, the primary mechanism by which individuals gain expertise in graphic comprehension is by repeated practice of the skills. This expertise results in several differences between novice users of data visualizations and expert user. One suggested difference is that the overlearning of particular tasks or stimuli will reduce cognitive load in those or related tasks by allowing automatic process of portions of the task or stimuli (Downs & DeSouza, 2006). (Cognitive load will be addressed more specifically in the following section.) Experts also gain knowledge of meaningful (domain-specific) patterns in stimuli, allowing them to chunk perceptual information and solve problems more effectively. Finally, experts more easily interpret functional information in visual representations, beyond the simple spatial structures that are identified by novices. "While a novice can understand the spatial structure of a bicycle pump or heart from a diagram, only those with some expertise can grasp the functional and causal relations among the parts" (Downs & DeSouza, 2006).

One proposed description of the process of gaining domain expertise is the development of mental models. As a theoretical construct describing cognitive processes related to the simulation or prediction of external mechanisms (Howard, 1995; Hutchins, 2002; Johnson-Laird, 1983; Mantovani, 1996; Norman, 1983; Payne, 2003; Rumelhart, 1984), mental models are widely studied by researchers in many fields, including psychology, cognitive science, human-computer interaction, and information visualization. As such, the mental models construct has undergone redefinition and reification for many decades by these various communities. Recent literature commonly identifies two camps of mental models researchers: those who approach mental models "literally" and those who approach them "figuratively" (Rips, 1986).

A literal approach to mental models uses the term to refer to the structure of the mental model, or how representations are actually constructed and stored, and is epitomized by the early work of Johnson-Laird (1983). "A mental model is the representation of a limited area of reality in a format which permits the internal simulation of external processes, so that conclusions can be drawn and predictions made" (Molitor, Ballstaedt, & Mandl, 1989). This literal mental model might also be called an internal representation (Liu & Stasko, 2010) and is hypothesized to be a detailed representation, analogous to some real-world system or object, held in working memory and serving as an input to mental operations or simulations.

The construct of mental models has been adapted from this foundational psychology literature to the Human-Computer Interaction (HCI) and visualization domains in an attempt better to understand how individuals structure interactions with systems that have semantic organization and, often, dynamic components (Payne, 2003). A secondary, more "figurative" definition of mental models thus emerged and took hold in HCI and similar fields. The alternative use of mental models is a more simplified theory of how a system (whether it be mechanical, behavioral, social, etc.) is organized or will react to perturbations. This definition is less concerned with the structure of mental representations but instead focuses on the content of the representations, emphasizing "the role that world knowledge or domain-specific knowledge plays in cognitive activities like problem solving or comprehension" (Rips, 1986).

Instead of presuming the existence of detailed mental representations, figurative mental models research tends to treat mental models as a set of assumptions about the components and organization of a system that guide the strategies a user uses to approach interactions with the system. The construct presumes that users, rather than being able to store and operate on a detailed representation of a specific system, have a sort of sketch of how the system is organized that is based both on interactions with previous systems and on feedback from the current system. This sketch influences (but does not necessarily solely determines) the strategies a user adopts when working with or interpreting the system.

This transition from literal to figurative mirrors a similar transition in the history of Artificial Intelligence research, where early assumptions about literal representation, or "image-like replicas" (Ekbia, 2008) also gave way to logicist approaches assuming figurative, "word-like" (ibid) representations. The transition also responds to criticisms of the literal approach, which suffers from empirical studies that suggest that individuals find it very difficult to run mental simulations that accurately predict the outcome of external mechanistic processes (Rips, 1986). Because of the tight coupling between HCI and visualization research, the remainder of this discussion will focus on the figurative approach to mental models.

Norman's (1983) summary of the figurative mental models research in HCI introduces helpful terms for the ensuing discussion. Norman describes users' mental models as often inaccurate, and he relates how these inaccuracies can prompt either inefficient or at times incorrect responses to an interactive system. He also defines conceptual model, which is an expert's mental model that can be used as a benchmark for how the user's mental model should be structured, and system image, which encapsulates the interface, feedback, and documentation available to guide the user toward an appropriate mental model.

Mental models research is compelling for interaction and visualization researchers for a variety of reasons, including the need to explain and predict problematic interactions and the goal of improving system design to better reflect the needs and expectations of users. It has intuitive strength in that researchers are able to see patterns of interaction strategies across systems and can associate erroneous strategies with erroneous assumptions about the system. Because the construct can be summarized as the expectations people hold for interactions, mental models also have logical connections to empirical findings showing that expectations based on prior experience affect not only conscious decision-making behavior but also low-level perceptual processes (Mantovani, 1996; Rumelhart, 1984).

Researchers take two predominant approaches to operationalizing mental models. One category of empirical research uses open-ended questions to elicit from users verbal or pictorial representations of thought processes, which are then coded by experts as associated with a particular mental model. Another category of empirical research uses expert assessments of possible mental models as the inspiration for closed-ended questions, and user performance in terms of accuracy, response time, or recall is interpreted as indicative of a particular mental model.

The operationalizations developed and adopted in an attempt to capture the user's mental models themselves typically involve open-ended questions that ask users to describe either their problem-solving strategies for particular tasks or their organizational schemes for tasks or conceptual areas. Interview-based or talk aloud procedures are often employed to gather these data (e.g., Tullio, Dey, Chalecki, & Fogarty, 2007), but verbal representations may also be collected in written form (e.g., Greene & Azevedo, 2007). A recent trend toward graphical representations (Carpenter, Fortune, Delugach, Etzkorn, Utley, Farrington, & Virani, 2008) and sketches (e.g., Denham, 1993; Kerr, 1990; Rieh, Yang, Yakel, & Markey, 2010; Qian, Yang, & Gong, 2011; Zhang, 2008) attempts to address concerns that users may have difficulty verbalizing their own problem-solving strategies. After either verbal or graphical representations are collected from users, domain experts can code the representations as indicative of different mental models that may be more or less appropriate for the task.

The other major approach to mental models research involves instruments with closed-ended questions that have been designed to differentiate between different mental models in a particular domain. An example of a domain that has been very active in mental models research is the study of computer programming, and the mental models of novice programmers are frequently tested using accuracy/success rate on closed-ended questions (e.g., Dehnadi, Bornat, & Adams, 2009; Götschi, Sanders, & Galpin, 2003; Kahney, 1983; Ma, Ferguson, Roper, & Wood, 2007). A related technique involves the logging of a user's actions (including timing and errors or inefficiencies) while using an interactive system (e.g., Waern, 1990). In addition to typical measures of accuracy and reaction time, closed-ended questions can be used after a delay to measure recall of model-related information (Coulson, Shayo, Olfman, & Rohm, 2003).

Either open- or closed-ended instruments that measure mental models can be incorporated into larger research design to test different phenomena. For example, measures can be employed in a within-subjects, pre-test/post-test research design to measure changes in mental models over time. Another technique designed to improve mental models is to test the interaction between different types of instructional or priming materials and measures of mental models (e.g., Fein, Olson, & Olson, 1993; Ziemkiewicz & Kosara, 2008). A final manipulation that can be made to the research design to extend mental models research is to test both a learned task and a slight variation of that task to measure the transfer of a learned mental model to new domain (e.g., Clegg, Gardner, Williams, & Kolodner, 2006).

As powerfully intuitive as the construct is, however, there are two criticisms of mental models that bear review for visualization research. The first addresses flaws in the operationalizations described above. The second relates to the goal of applying mental models research to the design of interactive systems.

The first criticism of mental models questions whether the construct is actually being tested by current studies or if, instead, other theoretical constructs might better explain the results of these studies. For example, there are alternative theories of cognition, including propositions, networks, and production rules, that have been proposed and studied by psychologists for many decades and that each offer explanations of the empirical findings of (especially "literal") mental models research (Nardi & Zarmer, 1990; Rips, 1986). Many of the criticisms levied at literal mental models are doubly true for the figurative approach to mental models, however. The HCI community addressing mental models is even more likely to conflate success of performance with the existence of an identified mental model and not take into account propositional or production-rule explanations. Other similar criticisms relate to specific methodologies, such as the need to take into account differences of skill in verbalizing (Zhang, 2008).

The second relevant criticism of mental models has to do with the application of mental models research to the design of interfaces or visualizations. A common motivation for mental models research is the idea that knowing the users' existing mental models (particularly for a work task) allows a designer to correctly construct a system or visualization to best suit the user's needs. As Young (1981) suggests, "the appropriateness of a design is to be judged in terms of the match (i.e. mapping) between the Task and the Actions needed to perform it," a sentiment which focuses the work of designing an interface on identifying the users' primary tasks and then matching those tasks to actions that need to be taken in such a way as to optimize the interaction for those primary tasks. Norman (1983) despairs for perfect mental models, but he does nonetheless admonish designers to "develop systems and instructional materials that aid users to develop more coherent, useable mental models," highlighting the role of the system image in the development and activation of an appropriate mental model.

A criticism of this approach appears in Nardi and Zarmer (1990):

To see the interface as a mechanism for translating thoughts is to completely miss the interaction between the user and the user interface, and the way in which the user interface itself can stimulate

and initiate cognitive activity. Like other cognitive artifacts...a good user interface helps to organize and direct cognition - it is not a passive receptacle for thoughts emanating from an internal model, but plays an active role in the problem solving process. (Nardi & Zarmer, 1990)

This reminder from Nardi and Zarmer of the co-construction of activity urges designers of systems to avoid expecting "noiseless" transmission of information, perfect comprehension of interfaces. The data visualization is only one component of a larger problem solving process. Espousing a design agenda that presumes that noiseless transmission of information is possible risks trivializing both the role of the artifact and the agency of the user, which may prevent designers from benefiting from what is understood about the complexity of the socio-technical environment.

The construct of mental models, as a description of how a user stores information about and interprets environmental stimuli, has been studied in relation to both information visualization and interaction (e.g., Liu & Stasko, 2010; Nardi & Zarmer, 1990). The full system of graphic comprehension, however, includes not only the skills and expertise of the user as they relate to a particular graphic, but also the context in which the user encounters the graphic.

Graphics in Context

Certain temporary states–the context in which individuals attempt to make sense of graphics–may also have an impact on the ability to comprehend graphics. Many studies use the concept of cognitive load to identify conditions under which users will experience impairments to their ability to effectively process stimuli or complete operations. Cognitive load becomes particularly relevant to graphic perception when dealing with graphics in multimodal environments (Huang, Eades, & Hong, 2009; Mayer, 2002, 2011b; Mayer &

Moreno, 1998, 2003; Mayer, Heiser, & Lonn, 2001; Moreno & Mayer, 1999; Pastore, 2009). Research on cognitive load addresses the cognitive mechanisms that regulate executive function and working memory.

Cognitive load theory is often applied to multimodal instructional environments in an attempt to understand how additional modes of communication (e.g., adding visuals to text) improve or impede comprehension of the instructional content (Mayer, 2002; Mayer & Moreno, 1998, 2003; Mayer, Heiser, & Lonn, 2001; Moreno & Mayer, 1999; Pastore, 2009). Cognitive load can affect three types of cognitive processing in multimodal instructional environments (Mayer & Moreno, 2003). Cognitive load during *essential processing* happens when the load is caused by making sense of the presented material. Cognitive load can also occur during *incidental processing*, when a cognitive process that is not essential but is primed by the learning task increases the load on the learner. Finally, cognitive load can be the result of *representational holding*, or "cognitive processes aimed at holding a mental representation in working memory over a period of time" (Mayer & Moreno, 2003).

Mayer and colleagues have identified many situations that increased cognitive load and have proposed solutions to situations that may result in the various categories of cognitive load (Mayer & Moreno, 2003). For example, essential processing demands have been hypothesized to result in increased cognitive load if a learner is being asked to process both text and visual information, which both employ visuospatial working memory during the organization phase of cognition (ibid). The proposed method of reducing cognitive load for this situation is to transfer verbal information to the audio channel–with or without moderate time compression (Pastore, 2009)–resulting in improved performance on the instructional task (Mayer, 2002; Mayer & Moreno, 1998, 2003; Moreno & Mayer, 1999). Other situations of in-

creased cognitive load include: situations where the pace of instructional content exceeds the learner's pace for selecting, organizing, and integrating the content fully (i.e., essential processing demands in both visual and audio channels exceed capacity); situations where instructional material includes superfluous, high-arousal information (i.e., incidental processing competes with essential processing to exceed capacity); situations where instructional materials are designed in a confusing way, either by including redundant information or by misaligning visual content (where, again, incidental processing is competing with essential processing); and situations where working memory in one or both channels is being used to maintain some mental representation and is unable to meet the essential processing demands of the instructional task (Mayer & Moreno, 2003). For many of these types of cognitive load, suggested solutions involve redesigning the instructional materials, but several are also reduced when learners gain additional experience in certain types of processing (ibid).

Regardless of the presence of multiple modes of communication, users have more generally been found to have less success completing spatial tasks in situations of low automaticity (Downs & DeSouza, 2006). Automaticity is a response to overlearning; when a stimulus is encountered repeatedly, associated materials are recalled more automatically than those of novel stimuli. In terms of spatial thinking, an automatically-processed spatial visualization type (e.g., a bar chart) may successfully accompany the learning of new content because it does not increase cognitive load (i.e., it does not tax working memory). On the other hand, "[i]f the content and form of the map or graph are relatively unfamiliar, then too much working memory capacity is required to process both the unfamiliar form and the intended content of the representation" (Downs & DeSouza, 2006), and the visualization type may inhibit learning.

INDIVIDUAL TRAITS THAT INTERACT WITH GRAPHIC COMPREHENSION

Each of the constructs described above can be explored in connected with additional traits of individuals. Empirical evidence of systematic–but not intractable–differences allow us to make some predictions about how different groups of viewers may vary on comprehension measures. More than that, however, the study of the relationships between traits and cognitive processes provides us with additional resources for overcoming these differences and improving graphic comprehension for all groups of viewers.

Age

Age is one of the most frequently studied traits that interact with graphic perception (Blazhenkova et al., 2011; Downs & DeSouza, 2006; Kirsch & Jungeblut, 1986; Kozhevnikov et al., 2010; Lohman & Nichols, 1990). Research on several cognition theories highlight the ways that (particularly childhood) development relates to graphic perception. This section highlights how experience in spatial and spatialized environments and the transitions from child to adult and novice to expert relate to changes in perceptual strategies.

The interaction between age and cognitive process related to graphic comprehension is somewhat conflated with specific experiences in particular domains. The section on disciplinary background below focuses more directly on differences that have been observed across individuals with specific training in different disciplinary traditions, for example. As individuals age, they experience different types of stimuli and training situations at varying times and in varying contexts, but some generalities and regularities can be described to summarize the types of expertise individuals typically develop over time.

Basic skills related to spatial thinking are acquired gradually over the course of development. Early developmental theories ranging from a Piagetian assumption of a "blank slate" to later "nativist" proposals of core knowledge areas available from birth have been tempered and blended in a neoconstructivist perspective called *adaptive combination* (Newcombe, Uttal, & Sauter, in press). This perspective asserts that infants have a strong starting point for spatial development but continue to progress over time in response to interactions with the environment and symbolic systems, though at a pace more rapid than originally theorized by Piaget.

Preschool-aged children typically acquire skills in topological differentiation (*in, on, next to, between, open,* and *closed*; e.g., distinguishing a U from a circle) (Downs & DeSouza, 2006). During this developmental phase, however, children can make location-based judgments based on both relative, categorical information (e.g., relation to a landmark, containment within a region) and also more precise, metric information (measurable distances) in a manner similar to that used by adults. Additionally, "well before they enter preschool, children have mastered basic spatial relations in physical space, understanding…how to effect skilled movements in space" (Downs & DeSouza, 2006).

The onset of visual-spatial skills like mental rotation likely happens as early as the age of 4 to 5 years, and with appropriate training and testing may be undertaken by much younger infants (Newcombe, Uttal, & Sauter, in press). Such skills have been shown to increase rapidly from ages 10 to 14 (Blazhenkova et al., 2011)–though the increase is perhaps limited to students interested in science (Kozhevnikov et al., 2010)–and to improve rapidly with practice (Lohman & Nichols, 1990). Visual-object and verbal abilities have been found to increase sharply in early childhood and either remain stable or continue to increase slightly with age (Blazhenkova et al., 2011). Skills that are learned at one point in development, however, may decline without maintenance. Performance on visual-spatial tasks begins to decline around age 16 (Blazhenkova et al., 2011).

Over the early elementary school years, individuals continue to acquire additional spatial skills and strategies. Two categories of skills frequently studied are those involving projective and Euclidean concepts (Downs & DeSouza, 2006). Projective concepts include the ability to use point of view to predict the shape of the shadows cast by rotating objects or of cross-sections of 3D objects, as well as the successful use of alternate frames of reference to resolve such conflicts as misaligned "you-are-here" maps. Euclidean concepts are those that utilize concepts like Cartesian coordinate systems to represent spatial problems. Students also gradually develop skills in distinguishing shapes that differ in characteristics other than the topological relations mentioned earlier (e.g., a square from a trapezoid).

Related to the effects of age are the effects of education, regardless of any disciplinary specialization. An early attempt by the National Assessment of Education Progress to catalog literacy skills of young adults from ages 21 to 25 (Kirsch & Jungeblut, 1986) includes a type of literacy called "document literacy" – "the knowledge and skills required to locate and use information contained in job applications or payroll forms, bus schedules, maps, tables, indexes, and so forth." The document literacy tasks from the assessment instrument exhibit varying levels of difficulty, based on the number of features or categories of information required by the task or included as distractors in the document.

While at least 96% of all groups–varied by number of years of education–achieve document literacy at the lowest level (involving tasks like signing one's name on the social security card), proficiency drops rapidly for shorter-duration education groups as complexity increases. For tasks like locating data in a table and on a street map using two features, only 84% of all participants achieved proficiency, including only 31.5% of participants with zero to eight years of education and 83.4% of high school graduates. Increasing the number of features and the differences between question and document phrases, only 50% of high school graduates achieve proficiency at the next level of complexity. Less than 11% of high school graduates successfully completed the most complex task involving a match of six features to a bus schedule.

Skills in reading documents of all kinds, including those with spatial information displays, tend to increase over the course of aging and education to early adulthood, at least, but proficiency levels can vary dramatically depending on task complexity or other individual factors. As discussed in the earlier section on categories of spatial thinking skills, disparities in performance across individuals at different ages can often be reduced with appropriate training and testing (Newcombe & Stieff, 2012). Knowing the typical skill levels for particular age groups, however, may lead to improved design of visualizations, assessment materials, or instructional texts.

Sex

Differences across sexes have been identified in studies relating to many spatial thinking tasks. Though discussion of the mechanisms behind sex differences is outside the scope of this review, it has often been shown that these differences may be reduced to insignificance with training and practice in the skills of concern, suggesting that the differences are not biological in nature (Newcombe & Stieff, 2012). Without additional training, however, the following skills are regularly found to interact with the sex of the participant. Male participants tend to perform better on spatial perception and visual-spatial tasks–especially those involving mental rotation (Vandenberg & Kuse, 1978). Female participants, however, have been found to perform better on visual-object tasks and tasks that involve memory for spatial location (Blajenkova et al., 2006; Blazhenkova & Kozhevnikov, 2009, 2010; Blazhenkova et al., 2011; Downs & DeSouza, 2006). Different strategies may also exist without affecting performance. For example, women more frequently make reference to landmarks, whereas men more frequently use cardinal directions (Downs & DeSouza, 2006). Studies typically do not find an interaction between sex and verbal abilities (Blazhenkova & Kozhevnikov, 2009, 2010; Blazhenkova et al., 2011).

Disciplinary Background

Many studies of graphic perception have used disciplinary background to explore variation across individuals (Blazhenkova & Kozhevnikov, 2010; Burnett & Lane, 1980; Isaac & Marks, 1994). Training in sciences, arts, and even physiological fields relates to differences in graphic perception skills and has been used to identify experts in certain tasks related to data visualization and visual analytics. The causality of the relationship between visual skills and training in certain disciplines is not yet clear; it may be that early development of certain skills influences the pursuit of related disciplines, that the choice of discipline puts an individual through training that improves certain skills, or that some more complicated interaction between skills and training occurs. The early onset of both visual skills and individual differences in performance suggests that success with certain spatial skills may precede a related interest in Science, Technology, Engineering, and Mathematics (STEM) careers (Newcombe, Uttal, & Sauter, in press).

Traditional mental rotation studies identified a link between that spatial reasoning task and individuals with training in mathematics and sciences. Less attention, however, has been paid to the visual skills that are well developed by individuals with training in visual arts and design (i.e., visual-object skills). These two groups of disciplines with known relations to visual abilities were thus used for ecological validity testing for the OSV model (Blazhenkova & Kozhevnikov, 2010). As expected, visual-spatial abilities were shown to be highly developed in individuals with training in sciences and mathematics. Additionally, after two years of college instruction, these abilities also improved to a greater degree among this population than among students with other specializations (Burnett & Lane, 1980). Visual-object abilities have conversely been shown to be highly developed in individuals pursuing visual arts and design (Blajenkova et al., 2006; Blazhenkova & Kozhevnikov, 2009, 2010). High vividness of imagery has likewise been found in physical education students, elite athletes, air traffic controllers, and pilots (Isaac & Marks, 1994). Furthermore, disciplinary specializations are found to exhibit stronger interactions with visual-object and visual-spatial abilities than gender (Blajenkova et al., 2006; Blazhenkova & Kozhevnikov, 2009, 2010).

Other Related Traits and States

Though the research is often done with a different purpose in mind or in a limited capacity, the following studies provide evidence of other traits and skills that interact with graphic comprehension and suggest additional avenues of research that would help form a more complete understanding of individual differences in this area.

Handedness, both of study participants and of their immediate family members, has been suggested as an indication of brain organization, and in some studies, presence of Familial Sinistrality (FS) interacts with sex, spatial experience, or specialization to improve performance on mental rotation tasks (Casey, Winner, Brabeck, & Sullivan, 1990).

Another trait of note may be trait curiosity. One study (Risko, Anderson, Lanthier, & Kingstone, 2012) found that for users viewing images while using an eye tracking system, trait curiosity was correlated to one eye movement measure (number of regions visited). If trait curiosity is related to the number of regions the eyes attend to in an image, there may be implications for how viewers explore novel graphics, particularly in a "free-viewing" setting where no task has been assigned.

Insofar as poor movement control (clumsiness) might be considered a trait (or, perhaps, a condition), clumsy children have been found in one study to have weaker abilities in imagery and movement vividness, perhaps owing to the need for accurate images for negotiation of spatial environments (Isaac & Marks, 1994).

Finally, in terms of state factors for graphic comprehension, mood (slight positive or negative affect) may well play a role in visual processing. Two studies by (Gasper & Clore, 2002) examined how affect related to visual memory and global-local processing of visual stimuli. In each study, positive affect was shown to correlate with global (holistic) processing of visual stimuli, including more accurate reproduction of an image from memory and attentional focus on global (composite) structures within an image. Negative affect had the reverse effect, reducing ability to reproduce an image from memory and focusing attention on component parts of an image. While the authors refer to these results using a "global vs. local frame" context, the nature of the tasks used to measure global and local processing make the results comparable to those of visual abilities studies. The implication would be that positive affect has some relationship to visual-object ability and negative affect to visual-spatial ability, a sentiment that may be echoed by the findings of Blazhenkova and Kozhevnikov (2010) that associate visual-object ability with emotion. Further research on emotion and the OSV model and a comparison between global-local measures and standard object-spatial measures would help to clarify the relationships between these areas of study.

CONCLUSION

Individuals employ many skills and strategies that influence how graph comprehension processes are carried out. This chapter has provided a review of several theories of cognition and individual traits that have been shown to be relevant for individuals engaged in the perception of graphics. Many of the constructs and traits presented, however, are still in their early stages of empirical study. The precise nature of the relationship between visual-object, visual-spatial, and navigation skills has not yet been identified. Likewise, the types of training necessary to reduce differences across age, sex, and disciplinary groups will need extensive investigation and, perhaps, customization for different data visualization forms and visual analytics systems.

Because of the rapidly widening audience for relatively new and specialized visualization types, the common practice of designing visualizations based on the understanding of expert users or the limited scope of a single task environment may contribute to a suboptimal interpretation environment for users. The processes related to graphic comprehension range from the most fundamental perceptual processes to the most complex socio-technical evaluations, and viewers not only interact with the constructed image but also operate within a broader task context. A particularly complicated focus for research, graphic comprehension is also a high stakes topic, potentially influencing both the growth of interest in STEM careers and also the ability of STEM research to reach a broad, public audience. Evidence confirms that it is unwise to be complacent about graphic comprehension; significant differences do exists between different groups of viewers, and those differences can cascade through many layers of cognitive processing. The design of data visualization and visual analytics systems must reflect our growing understanding of both the skills of users and also their capacity for improvement in those skills, given well-designed training and systems.

REFERENCES

Blajenkova, O., Kozhevnikov, M., & Motes, M. A. (2006). Object-spatial imagery: A new self-report imagery questionnaire. *Applied Cognitive Psychology*, *20*(2), 239–263. doi:10.1002/acp.1182.

Blazhenkova, O., Becker, M., & Kozhevnikov, M. (2011). Object–spatial imagery and verbal cognitive styles in children and adolescents: Developmental trajectories in relation to ability. *Learning and Individual Differences*, *21*(3), 281–287. doi:10.1016/j.lindif.2010.11.012.

Blazhenkova, O., & Kozhevnikov, M. (2009). The new object-spatial-verbal cognitive style model: Theory and measurement. *Applied Cognitive Psychology*, *23*(5), 638–663. doi:10.1002/acp.1473.

Blazhenkova, O., & Kozhevnikov, M. (2010). Visual-object ability: A new dimension of non-verbal intelligence. *Cognition*, *117*(3), 276–301. doi:10.1016/j.cognition.2010.08.021 PMID:20887982.

Burnett, S. A., & Lane, D. M. (1980). Effects of academic instruction on spatial visualization. *Intelligence*, *4*(3), 233–242. doi:10.1016/0160-2896(80)90021-5.

Card, S., Mackinlay, J. D., & Shneiderman, B. (1999). *Readings in information visualization: Using vision to think*. San Francisco: Morgan Kaufmann Publishers.

Carpenter, S., Fortune, J. L., Delugach, H. S., Etzkorn, L. H., Utley, D. R., Farrington, P. A., & Virani, S. (2008). Studying team shared mental models. In P. J. Ågerfalk, H. Delugach, & M. Lind (Eds.), *Proceedings of the 3rd International Conference on the Pragmatic Web: Innovating the Interactive Society, Uppsala, Sweden* (41-48). New York: ACM.

Casey, M. B., Winner, E., Brabeck, M., & Sullivan, K. (1990). Visual-spatial abilities in art, maths, and science majors: Effects of sex, family handedness, and spatial experience. In Gilhooly, K. J., Keane, M. T. G., Logie, R. H., & Erdos, G. (Eds.), *Lines of Thinking: On the Psychology of Thought* (Vol. 2, pp. 275–294). West Sussex, UK: John Wiley & Sons Ltd..

Clegg, T., Gardner, C., Williams, O., & Kolodner, J. (2006). Promoting learning in informal learning environments. In *Proceedings of the 7th International Conference on Learning Sciences*, 92-98. Bloomington, IN: International Society of the Learning Sciences.

Coulson, T., Shayo, C., Olfman, L., & Rohm, C. E. T. (2003). ERP training strategies: Conceptual training and the formation of accurate mental models. In *Proceedings of the 2003 SIGMIS Conference on Computer Personnel Research*, 87-97. Philadelphia, PA: ACM.

Dehnadi, S., Bornat, R., & Adams, R. (2009). *Meta-analysis of the effect of consistency on success in early learning of programming*. Paper presented at Psychology Programming Interested Group (PPIG) Annual Workshop. Retrieved from http://www.ppig.org/papers/21st-dehnadi.pdf.

Denham, P. (1993). Nine- to fourteen-year-old children's conception of computers using drawings. *Behaviour & Information Technology*, *12*(6), 346–358. doi:10.1080/01449299308924399.

Downs, R., & DeSouza, A. (Eds.). (2006). *Learning to think spatially: GIS as a support system in the K-12 curriculum*. Washington, D.C.: National Academies Press.

Ekbia, H. R. (2008). *Artificial dreams: The quest for non-biological intelligence*. New York: Cambridge University Press. doi:10.1017/CBO9780511802126.

Evans, C., & Cools, E. (2011). Applying styles research to educational practice. *Learning and Individual Differences*, *21*(3), 249–254. doi:10.1016/j.lindif.2010.11.009.

Fabrikant, S. I., Montello, D. R., Ruocco, M., & Middleton, R. S. (2004). The distance-similarity metaphor in network-display spatializations. *Cartography and Geographic Information Science*, *31*(4), 237–252. doi:10.1559/1523040042742402.

Fein, R. M., Olson, G. M., & Olson, J. S. (1993). A mental model can help with learning to operate a complex device. InAshlund, S, Mullet, K, Henderson, A, Hollnagel, E, & White, T (Eds.), *INTERACT '93 and CHI '93 Conference Companion on Human Factors in Computing Systems* (157-158). Amsterdam: ACM Press. doi:10.1145/259964.260170.

Gasper, K., & Clore, G. L. (2002). Attending to the big picture: Mood and global versus local processing of visual information. *Psychological Science*, *13*(1), 34–40. doi:10.1111/1467-9280.00406 PMID:11892776.

Götschi, T., Sanders, I., & Galpin, V. (2003). Mental models of recursion. In *Proceedings of the 34th SIGCSE Technical Symposium on Computer Science Education* (346-350). Reno, NV: ACM Press.

Greene, J. A., & Azevedo, R. (2007). Adolescents' use of self-regulatory processes and their relation to qualitative mental model shifts while using hypermedia. *Journal of Educational Computing Research*, *36*(2), 125–148. doi:10.2190/G7M1-2734-3JRR-8033.

Howard, R. W. (1995). *Learning and memory: Major ideas, principles, issues, and applications*. Westport, CT: Praeger.

Huang, W., Eades, P., & Hong, S.-H. (2009). Measuring effectiveness of graph visualizations: A cognitive load perspective. *Information Visualization*, *8*(3), 139–152. doi:10.1057/ivs.2009.10.

Hutchins, E. (2002). *Cognition in the wild*. Cambridge, MA: MIT Press.

Isaac, A. R., & Marks, D. F. (1994). Individual differences in mental imagery experience: Developmental changes and specialization. *The British Journal of Psychology*, *85*(4), 479–500. doi:10.1111/j.2044-8295.1994.tb02536.x PMID:7812670.

Johnson-Laird, P. N. (1983). *Mental models: Towards a cognitive science of language, inference, and consciousness*. Cambridge, MA: Harvard University Press.

Kahney, H. (1983). What do novice programmers know about recursion. In A. Janda (Ed.), *CHI '83: Proceedings of the SIGCHI Conference on Human Factors in Computing Systems* (235-239). Boston: ACM.

Kerr, S. T. (1990). Wayfinding in an electronic database: The relative importance of navigational cues vs. mental models. *Information Processing & Management*, *26*(4), 511–523. doi:10.1016/0306-4573(90)90071-9.

Kirsch, I. S., & Jungeblut, A. (1986). *Literacy: Profiles of america's young adults*. Princeton, NJ: Educational Testing Service.

Kozhevnikov, M., Blazhenkova, O., & Becker, M. (2010). Trade-off in object versus spatial visualization abilities: Restriction in the development of visual-processing resources. *Psychonomic Bulletin & Review*, *17*(1), 29–35. doi:10.3758/PBR.17.1.29 PMID:20081157.

Kozhevnikov, M., Hegarty, M., & Mayer, R. E. (2002). Revising the visualizer-verbalizer dimension: Evidence for two types of visualizers. *Cognition and Instruction*, *20*(1), 47–77. doi:10.1207/S1532690XCI2001_3.

Kozhevnikov, M., Kosslyn, S., & Shephard, J. (2005). Spatial versus object visualizers: A new characterization of visual cognitive style. *Memory & Cognition, 33*(4), 710–726. doi:10.3758/BF03195337 PMID:16248335.

Lam, H., Bertini, E., Isenberg, P., Plaisant, C., & Carpendale, S. (2012). Empirical studies in information visualization: Seven scenarios. *IEEE Transactions on Visualization and Computer Graphics, 18*(9), 1520–1536. doi:10.1109/TVCG.2011.279 PMID:22144529.

Linn, M. C., & Petersen, A. C. (1985). Emergence and characterization of sex differences in spatial ability: A meta-analysis. *Child Development, 56*(6), 1479–1498. doi:10.2307/1130467 PMID:4075870.

Liu, Z., & Stasko, J. T. (2010). Mental models, visual reasoning and interaction in Information Visualization: A top-down perspective. *IEEE Transactions on Visualization and Computer Graphics, 16*(6), 999–1008. doi:10.1109/TVCG.2010.177 PMID:20975137.

Lohman, D. F., & Nichols, P. D. (1990). Training spatial abilities: Effects of practice on rotation and synthesis tasks. *Learning and Individual Differences, 2*(1), 67–93. doi:10.1016/1041-6080(90)90017-B.

Ma, L., Ferguson, J., Roper, M., & Wood, M. (2007). Investigating the viability of mental models held by novice programmers. In *Proceedings of the 38th SIGCSE Technical Symposium on Computer Science Education* (499-503).Covington, KY: ACM.

Mantovani, G. (1996). Social context in HCI: A new framework for mental models, cooperation, and communication. *Cognitive Science, 20*(2), 237–269. doi:10.1207/s15516709cog2002_3.

Mayer, R. E. (2002). Multimedia learning. *Psychology of Learning and Motivation, 41*, 85–139. doi:10.1016/S0079-7421(02)80005-6.

Mayer, R. E. (2011a). Does styles research have useful implications for educational practice? *Learning and Individual Differences, 21*(3), 319–320. doi:10.1016/j.lindif.2010.11.016.

Mayer, R. E. (2011b). Applying the science of learning to multimedia instruction. In Mestre, J. P., & Ross, B. H. (Eds.), *The Psychology of Learning and Motivation* (*Vol. 55*, pp. 77–108). Amsterdam: Elsevier. doi:10.1016/B978-0-12-387691-1.00003-X.

Mayer, R. E., Heiser, J., & Lonn, S. (2001). Cognitive constraints on multimedia learning: When presenting more material results in less understanding. *Journal of Educational Psychology, 93*(1), 187–198. doi:10.1037/0022-0663.93.1.187.

Mayer, R. E., & Moreno, R. (1998). *A cognitive theory of multimedia learning: Implications for design principles*. Paper presented at the CHI-98 Workshop on Hyped-Media to Hyper-Media, Los Angeles, CA.

Mayer, R. E., & Moreno, R. (2003). Nine ways to reduce cognitive load in multimedia learning. *Educational Psychologist, 38*(1), 43–52. doi:10.1207/S15326985EP3801_6.

Molitor, S., Ballstaedt, S.-P., & Mandl, H. (1989). Problems in knowledge acquisition from text and pictures. InMandl, H, J. R, , & Levin, (Eds.), *Advances in Psychology, volume 58: Knowledge Acquisition from Text and Pictures* (3-35). Amsterdam: North-Holland. doi:10.1016/S0166-4115(08)62145-7.

Moreno, R., & Mayer, R. E. (1999). Cognitive principles of multimedia learning: The role of modality and contiguity. *Journal of Educational Psychology, 91*(2), 358–368. doi:10.1037/0022-0663.91.2.358.

Nardi, B. A., & Zarmer, C. L. (1990). *Beyond models and metaphors: Visual formalisms in user interface design*. Palo Alto, CA: Hewlett-Packard Laboratories.

Newcombe, N. S., & Stieff, M. (2012). Six myths about spatial thinking. *International Journal of Science Education*, *34*(6), 955–971. doi:10.1080 /09500693.2011.588728.

Newcombe, N. S., Uttal, D. H., & Sauter, M. (in press). Spatial development. In Zelazo, P. (Ed.), *Oxford Handbook of Developmental Psychology*. New York: Oxford University Press. doi:10.1037/ e537272012-075.

Norman, D. A. (1983). Some observations on mental models. InGentner, D, & Stevens, A. L. (Eds.), *Mental Models* (7-14). Hillsdale, NJ: Lawrence Erlbaum Associates.

Pastore, R. S. (2009). The effects of diagrams and time-compressed instruction on learning and learners' perceptions of cognitive load. *Educational Technology Research and Development*, *58*(5), 485–505. doi:10.1007/s11423-009-9145-6.

Payne, S. J. (2003). Users' mental models: The very ideas. InCarroll, J. M. (Ed.), *HCI models, theories, and frameworks: Toward a multidisciplinary science* (135-156). San Francisco: Morgan Kaufmann Publishers. doi:10.1016/ B978-155860808-5/50006-X.

Qian, X., Yang, Y., & Gong, Y. (2011). The art of metaphor: A method for interface design based on mental models. In *Proceedings of the 10th International Conference on Virtual Reality Continuum and Its Applications in Industry* (171-178). Hong Kong: ACM.

Rieh, S. Y., Yang, J. Y., Yakel, E., & Markey, K. (2010). Conceptualizing institutional repositories: Using co-discovery to uncover mental models. In *Proceedings of the Third Symposium on Information Interaction in Context*, 165-174. New York: ACM.

Rips, L. J. (1986). Mental muddles. InBrand, M, & Harnish, R. M. (Eds.), *The Representation of Knowledge and Belief* (258-286). Tucson, AZ: The University of Arizona Press.

Risko, E. F., Anderson, N. C., Lanthier, S., & Kingstone, A. (2012). Curious eyes: Individual differences in personality predict eye movement behavior in scene-viewing. *Cognition*, *122*(1), 86–90. doi:10.1016/j.cognition.2011.08.014 PMID:21983424.

Rumelhart, D. E. (1984). Schemata and the Cognitive System. In Wyer, R. S. Jr, & Srull, T. K. (Eds.), *Handbook of Social Cognition* (*Vol. 1*, pp. 161–188). Hillsdale, NJ: Lawrence Erlbaum Associates.

Tullio, J., Dey, A. K., Chalecki, J., & Fogarty, J. (2007). How it works: A field study of non-technical users interacting with an intelligent system. In *Proceedings of the SIGCHI Conference on Human Factors in Computing Systems*, 31-40. San Jose, CA: ACM.

Vandenberg, S. G., & Kuse, A. R. (1978). Mental rotations, A group test of three-dimensional spatial visualizations. *Perceptual and Motor Skills*, *47*(2), 599–604. doi:10.2466/pms.1978.47.2.599 PMID:724398.

Waern, Y. (1990). *Cognitive aspects of computer supported tasks*. New York, NY: John Wiley & Sons, Inc..

Young, R. M. (1981). The machine inside the machine: Users' models of pocket calculators. *International Journal of Man-Machine Studies*, *15*(1), 51–85. doi:10.1016/S0020-7373(81)80023-5.

Zhang, Y. (2008). The influence of mental models on undergraduate students' searching behavior on the web. *Information Processing & Management*, *44*(3), 1330–1345. doi:10.1016/j. ipm.2007.09.002.

Ziemkiewicz, C., & Kosara, R. (2008). The shaping of information by visual metaphors. *IEEE Transactions on Visualization and Computer Graphics*, *14*(6), 1269–1276. doi:10.1109/ TVCG.2008.171 PMID:18988973.

KEY TERMS AND DEFINITIONS

(Data) Visualization: The term visualization can refer both to the process by which data are visualized and to the graphic that results from that process. In this literature review, the latter use is predominant. Though often used interchangeably with graphic as described above, visualization is used when a more constrained concept is appropriate and when the theories or methodologies involved are strongly tied to the Data Visualization field.

Comprehension: For the purposes of this review, comprehension refers to the process by which an individual makes sense of a graphic. Individuals may bring many experiences, skills, and strategies to bear in the process of comprehension, including the individual's exposure to prior images or related systems of analysis or notation, the individual's assumptions about the image's designer and his/her intentions, the individual's understanding of the content area related to the image, the individual's cultural background, etc. Comprehension is acknowledged to be an active co-construction of meaning between an individual, an image, a social context, and a task environment.

Graphic: Typically used in noun form (e.g., "graphic comprehension"), this term refers to a constructed image or visual representation in general. It is used somewhat interchangeably with visualization throughout this literature review because the review often covers literature that extends to graphics in general. The adjective form is typically graphical (e.g., "graphical devices").

Trait: In the context of psychology processes, traits are persistent characteristics of individuals (e.g., sex, handedness), rather than transient or malleable states (e.g., fatigue, inexperience).

Viewer: The viewer is an individual who is interacting with a particular visualization or graphic.

Chapter 6
Virtual Reality Technologies (Visual, Haptics, and Audio) in Large Datasets Analysis

Bob-Antoine J. Menelas
University of Quebec at Chicoutimi, Canada

ABSTRACT

With the latest developments in technology, several researchers have integrated other sensorymotor channels in the analysis of scientific datasets. In addition to vision, auditory feedbacks and haptic interactions have been exploited. In this chapter we study how these modalities can contribute to effective analysis processes. Based on psychophysical characteristics of humans the author argues that haptics should be used in order to improve interactions of the user with the dataset to analyze. The author describes a classification that highlights four tasks for which haptics seems to present advantages over vision and audio. Proposed taxonomy is divided into four categories: Select, Locate, Connect and Arrange. Moreover, this work provides a complete view on the contribution of haptics in analysis of scientific datasets.

INTRODUCTION

Analysis of scientific datasets typically involves a set of techniques that aims to transform the raw data into representations understandable by a human user. Following the acquisition of the data starts the analysis process that spans into two distinct stages: transformation and representation.

Raw data are generally defined by a set of points that samples the physical space of the studied phenomenon. Mainly two types of transformations, geometric or topological, can occur on these raw data. They aim to change the sampling or to extract a subset in order to take advantages of algorithms that may offer adequate representations. For example, translations, rota-

DOI: 10.4018/978-1-4666-4309-3.ch006

tions, or zooming can change the structure of the sampling grid. Other transformations can *a contrario* change the topology of the grid. This can result in converting an irregular grid into a regular grid. Other topological transformations may only affect the sampling of a regular grid (for instance, changing a 3D rectilinear grid to a 3D hexagonal one). Following the data transformation, rendering algorithms are applied in order to provide representations interpretable by a user.

It has been demonstrated that human beings carry remarkable capacities for detection and recognition of patterns by the mean of the visual channel. Based on this, the first works concerning analysis of numerical data triggered interest for exploitation of our visual abilities. Consequently, the process was called visualization. Gershon et al. (1998) and later Zhu et al. (2004) define visualization as a link between the human eye and computers; it helps to identify patterns and extract knowledge from large datasets. Therefore, data should be presented in a way to be easily understandable. According to Ware (2000), visualization aims to build a mental representation, an intellectual understanding of analyzed process or data. Generally, visualization refers to all the resources aiming at reducing the cognitive effort in acquiring knowledge via the visual channel.

Since vision cannot be considered as a predominant sense for human, it is justified to ask whether other modalities, mainly haptic or audio, may play an important role in analysis of large datasets. In fact in the everyday life, humans do not only rely on vision to analyze their surrounding environment since they are rather multimodal. The purpose of this chapter is to discuss the role of not only visual but also haptic and audio in the analysis of scientific datasets. Therefore, this chapter will focus on the use of different sensorimotor modalities in the analysis of scientific datasets.

POTENTIAL OF VR TECHNOLOGIES FOR ANALYSIS OF LARGE DATASETS

First, visualization applications range from non-interactive to command-driven systems. In such systems, commands are sent, processed and then comes the result. However, the need to interact with the system has emerged quickly. For example, one would like to zoom, rotate or filter the data. At this point starts the fusion, the interleaving between the query and the result via an iterative process. From there, data analysis is not only guided by the need for effective presentation of data: there are two main components that are the *presentation* and *interaction*.

At this point, Shneiderman (1996) identifies four main steps for the implementation of effective interaction process: *Overview first, zoom, filter, then details-on-demand*. Recently, Yi et al. (2007) have suggested that the interaction process can be supported through seven types of interaction based on users' intent while interacting with the system. For several researchers of the field, as part of the Human Computer Interaction (HCI) domain, interactive visualization aims at offering a direct and bidirectional communication between people (users) and the visualization system. Bryson (1996) stated *that the goal is to create the effect of interacting with things, not with pictures of things*. This approach establishes a clear difference between the user and the system: "the user interacts with the system".

Virtual Reality (VR) based-processes adopt a completely different approach in trying to go beyond a simple process of communication between a user and a computer system. The aim is rather to bring the user at the center of the analysis process. In fact, this issue plays a major role in VR technologies that aim at the immersion and presence of the user in a virtual environment. *Immersion* refers to a state of consciousness where the perception of physical reality surrounding the subject is reduced or lost in favor of a totally captivating often artificial environment, one says that the subject is then *present* in this artificial world.

As aarious researchers, we define Virtual Reality as a scientific domain that allows one or more human users to perceive and interact in an immersive, pseudo-natural and in real time with a digital environment called Virtual Environment (VE). This EV can be a copy of reality, but also a simulation of some of its aspects, a symbolic representation of a concept or a phenomenon, or a totally imaginary world (Bideau et al, 2004). Burdea and Coiffet (1994) noted that VR technologies require multisensory interactions and real time rendering in a VE. In the context of the VR-based analysis of large datasets, Loftin et al. (2004) define VR as the use of computer technologies to obtain multisensory rendering and interactions in real time with data, allowing one or more users to occupy, to navigate and to manipulate a computer-generated environment.

By combining all these points of view in the context of analyzing large datasets, for us it seems that VR technologies offer human users the mean to exploit capabilities of their sensorimotor channels (visual, haptics, audio) to pseudo-naturally perceive and interact with the dataset that they want to analyze. Thus, it appears that by the mean of multimodal rendering, VR technologies can allow the improvement of the two main components of user-based analysis of datasets that are *representation* and *interaction*. Moreover, it has been demonstrated that human-like interactions with a computer machine do increase the user efficiency, effectiveness and satisfaction; knowing that multimodality supports human-like interaction, like many others, we support the idea that *multimodal interactions are expected to increase the level of computing accessibility for many categories of users*, (Fikkert et al., 2007; Oviat & Cohen, 2000).

As emphasized by Griffith et al., (2005) having a dataset in a virtual immersive environment creates much better sensory responses to the user when compared to standard visualization systems. One of the primary advantages of using VR for the analysis of large datasets is to improve visual perception. Indeed, it has been shown that an active stereoscopic rendering helps at improving depth perception for distances below 30 meters (Nesbitt, 2003). In addition, the use of display screens, which may have more than seven meters in size, let the user to access a greater amount of information. In the same way, having CAVE-like setups allows the user to perform self-centered movements. Unlike workstations-based situations, the user is able to move, to turn around the object of study in order to benefit from several points of view. LaViola et al., (2009) emphasized that such interactions may be smoother and more efficient (requires less cognitive effort) than those achieved via standard interfaces (keyboard or mouse). Finally, one notes that already in 1996 Bryson (1996) had stated the hypothesis that real-time and intuitive capabilities of VR-based interactions could be exploited for a quick scan of large datasets. He has suggested that the direct manipulation of volume elements is expected to arrive with a more efficient analysis. However, we notice that this possibility is still not established. Recently, Laramee & Kosara, (2007) have stated that a lot of work is still needed in order to arrive with more intuitive interaction methods. Similarly, Zudilova et al. (2008) have highlighted that one of the main obstacles in this area is related to the fact that interfaces that seemed to be intuitive for developers did often proved unnatural for end users. This raises the question of how to get to intuitive interactions.

Knowing that multimodality represents a key factor of VR systems, the way each modality intervenes in an analysis process will be studied in next sections.

ROLE OF EACH MODALITY IN A MULTIMODAL ANALYSIS PROCESS

As most researchers, we agree that modality is directly linked to human senses. We define modality as the form of exchange that can take place between a user and a numerical system. As opposed to a unimodal condition where only one form of communication is possible, several forms of communication are available in a multimodal rendering.

When compared to unimodal rendering, the design of a multimodal rendering requires additional conditions due to interactions that may exist between the various channels. Indeed, it requires that exploitation of different modalities does not oppose one another. Furthermore, it is also desirable that each modality contributes to the achievement of a common goal. Based on such observations, it appears that: *i)* each modality should be exploited for a specific task *ii)* combination of modalities should also address specific tasks. One may note that this conclusion gathers the two points of view generally seen about multimodal rendering.

In the first point of view, multimodality appears as an aggregate of various unimodal rendering having each one its specific characteristics: the Modal Specific Theory proposed in (Friedes, 1974). When analyzing the three main sensory-motor channels of humans, it is obvious that each channel has its own advantages and disadvantages. These differences are not only related to the type of stimuli, but are also due to their spatial, temporal and frequency specificities. Friedes (1974) explains this by the fact that each sensory channel has a unique way of processing information. Because of that, each channel is rather particularly efficient for specific tasks. Visual dominates the perception of spatial information; audio is specialized for temporal processing (Vézien et al., 2009) whereas haptics is particularly adept at sensing movement (Nesbitt, 2000). Based on this, Nesbitt assumes that the perception of information can be

provided via three types of metaphors: *spatial*, *temporal* and *direct*. *Spatial metaphors* inform on size, position and structure of objects in space. *Direct metaphors* are associated with the perception of the intrinsic properties of objects (color, volume, hardness, etc.). *Temporal metaphors* reflect temporal changes of the object occurring over time. Then, he associates the three rendering sensory modes (visual, haptics and audio) to the three metaphors defined above. By doing so, he defines the *M-S Taxonomy*, dedicated to multisensory perception, based on a set of nine cases as shown in Table 1. Hence, the design of a multimodal rendering can be seen as the design of appropriated metaphors that could convey information (spatial, direct, or temporal) through a modality (visual, auditory, or haptics). One of the main advantages of this approach is that it provides a clear distinction between the three modalities. Hence, this approach may help to satisfy the first requirement (defined at *i*).

In the second point of view, multimodality appears as the result of the combination of several unimodal rendering. The mapping of information into interactive multimodal interfaces has been studied in (Bernsen, 1993). Bowman et al. (2004) define multimodality as the combination of multiple input modalities aiming to provide the user with a richer set of interactions compared to traditional unimodal interface. As input interactions, they state that the combination of input

Table 1. Representation of the nine classes of the MS-Taxonomy (Nesbit, 2000)

Rendering Modes			
	Visual	**Haptics**	**Auditory**
Spatial	spatial visual metaphor	spatial haptic metaphor	spatial auditory metaphor
Direct	direct visual metaphor	direct haptic metaphor	direct auditory metaphor
Temporal	temporal visual metaphor	temporal haptic metaphor	temporal auditory metaphor

modalities can be divided into six basic types: *complementarity*, *redundancy*, *equivalence*, *specialization*, *concurrency* and *transfer*. For Fikkert et al. (2007), this combination aspect appears as the goal of the multimodal system: *The goal of a multimodal system is, or should be, to integrate complementary modalities in order to combine the strengths of various modalities and overcome their individual weaknesses* (Fikkert et al, 2007). As in the first point of view, one may note that such an observation is particularly adapted to the second requirements (defined at *ii*).

Here, in order to meet the two requirements, these two approaches will be combined. First, the way each modality can contribute to the achievement of a better analysis will be studied. Second, the add value of associating modalities will be analyzed. Regarding the first step, we share the point of view of many researchers that have demonstrated that vision dominates the perception of spatial information whereas audio suits well the perception of temporal information. Hence, we understand that vision and audio should respectively be exploited for presentation of spatial and temporal properties of information. Regarding the haptic modality, the visuo-haptic association and main physiological characteristics of haptic perception will be analyzed, in the following paragraphs, in order to detect how it may contribute to a better analysis of scientific datasets.

HOW CAN HAPTICS CONTRIBUTE TO EFFECTIVE ANALYSIS OF SCIENTIFIC DATASETS

The word haptics comes from the Greek *haptesthai* and means to touch. It is nonetheless used to refer force feedback (based on muscles and joints) and tactile feedback (based on the skin) (Burdea, 1996). In a more general way, it also provides information on proprioception, namely the perception of the relative position of the body parts. Another feature that makes haptic interactions particularly interesting is that they are the only modality that allows sensorimotor interaction. The haptic modality provides a direct access to information related to the nature of objects. It gives information about their weight, hardness or their texture. Over the past two decades, many studies have suggested that one could use haptics to interpret numerical data (haptization). As in visualization, two main approaches are identified: *haptization of information* and *haptization of scientific data*.

Haptization of information concerns the use of haptic feedbacks to access abstract information via the haptic channel instead of the visual one (Menelas & Otis, 2012). This approach proposes alternatives to visual rendering so that people having visual disabilities can also access information. Here, only the analysis of scientific datasets is considered; hence, the *haptization of information* will not be addressed. For more information regarding *haptization of information*, one may refer to a recent state of the art presented in (Paneels & Roberts, 2009).

Haptization of scientific datasets focuses on data resulting from simulations of phenomena closely related to geometry. Knowing that haptics is generally associated with another channel (often visual), it seems more appropriate to talk about *analysis of scientific datasets*. The analysis of scientific datasets is not intended to replace scientific visualization, but rather aims to exploit various sensorimotor channels of human in order to arrive with more effective analysis of complex datasets.

Added Value of the Visual/ Haptic Combination in Analysis of Scientific Datasets

In the analysis of scientific datasets, the addition of haptics offers an interfacing far richer than just the visual rendering and more diverse means of communication between the user and the digital environment. In doing so it allows:

- **To Unload the Visual Channel:** In such a case, the haptic feedback helps in replacing the visual channel in the communication between a user and a digital environment. For example, Persson et al. emphasize that the use of haptics for transmitting physico-chemical forces of intermolecular bonds allows presenting more information to the user without risking overloading the visual channel (Persson et al., 2007).

- **To Strengthen the Visual Feedback:** This situation happens when haptics help at emphasizing information already available via the visual channel. Particularly in teleoperation field, works of Basdogan et al. (1998) have showed that the addition of haptic feedback reinforces the sense of presence of users in the remote environment. Similarly, in analyzing medical data, it may be interesting to perceive via the touch sense differences in hardness or temperature between different internal organs (Lundin et al., 2002).

- **To Supplement the Visual Feedback:** In this case, the haptic modality gives access to information that is hardly or not perceptible visually. For example, Lawrence et al. (2000) have used haptics to alert users of the presence of a secondary shock (contained in a bigger one), even if it is not visible.

Beyond relative contributions of its association with the visual channel, haptics has features that seem likely to bring something special to the analysis of scientific datasets. In the next subsection, psychophysical characteristics of haptics will be analyzed in order to point out how they can contribute to better analysis processes.

Psychophysical Characteristics of the Haptic Perception

In everyday life, humans use their senses to perform specific tasks to explore and analyze their environment. Thus, MacLean recalls that touch implies a stronger emotional feeling that vision: *it particularly allows initiation or completion of a task, check the status of an object, or connect physically and/or emotionally with others* (MacLean, 2000). These observations emphasize the necessity to properly use the haptics. In the same way, in analysis of scientific datasets, despite resource constraints (at current state of the technology, haptic interfaces do not exploit one's full potential for tactilo-kinestesic perception [Kahol et al., 2006]), it seems essential for humans to use haptics according to human physiological characteristics. In what follows we briefly point out those that have retained our attention.

As seen previously, *representation* and *interaction* are two major components that can contribute to an effective visualization process. This section aims at analyzing whether physiological characteristics of human could, or not, indicate that haptics presents an advantage over other modalities for improving one or both of these two visualization components.

Regarding the characteristics of haptics, we find that:

- **The Visual Channel Seems to Predominate for Presentation of Information:** For example, von der Heyde et al. have shown that the evaluation of an object's weight could be biased by the visual feedback. With an experiment, they observed that subjects always estimated heavier larger objects, although they were the same weight (von der Heyde et al., 1998). More generally, Welch et al. showed that visual feedbacks dominate the other channels in the spatial perception (Welch et al., 1980). Finally, work led on the pseudo-haptic underlines that a visual feedback can influence the perception of information presented via the haptic channel. As an example, one may cite (Lecuyer et al., 2000) which use a visual feedback to generate a haptic sensation.

- **Haptics is Not Adapted to Memorization or to Recalling:** Despite the fact that haptics is very powerful in discrimination, it should be stressed that it is hardly suited to identification or memorization. As mentioned by MacLean, when sliding our finger on a polished surface, one can easily, thanks to successive comparisons, detect an invisible scratch, but it is much more difficult to remember or to identify a given one (MacLean, 2000).

- **Haptic Perception is Tightly Linked to the Concept of Interaction:** Various studies have evidenced that the perception of information, presented via the haptic channel, requires a specific type of movement named *Exploration Procedure (EP)* (Lederman & Klatzky, 1987; Klatzky & Lederman, 1995). Indeed, the evaluation of a weight requires different vertical movements, while lateral ones are better suited for the perception of a texture. Apart from the perception of a temperature, these EP explain that the perception of information presented via the haptic channel requires and/or involves an interaction.

These observations on physiological characteristics of humans related to haptics suggest that this modality would be more adapted for interaction tasks rather than for the presentation of information. Indeed, haptics does not offer any considerable advantage when compared to visual presentation. In addition, when presenting information through the haptic channel, one would have to face great difficulties to achieve identification as well as memorization of a given haptic feedback. Therefore, we infer that the addition of haptics in analysis process is expected to be optimal if it aims at facilitating and/or improving interaction with the data.

Moreover, the analysis of the add value of the visual/haptic association suggests that haptic interactions can have positive impact on presentation of information. Indeed, haptics can unload, strengthen or supplement the visual feedback. In what follows a taxonomy that aims at identifying how haptics should be used is described in order to improve user's interactions in analysis of scientific datasets. By doing so, methods that can help improving the presentation of information in analysis of scientific datasets will be emphasized.

VISUAL, AUDITORY, AND HAPTIC MODALITIES IN INTERACTION WITH SCIENTIFIC DATASETS

In analyzing work that has, over the past two decades, used vision, audio and haptics in the analysis of scientific datasets, we have defined four interaction techniques that may help at classifying the methods dedicated to analysis of scientific datasets. These interaction techniques are related to four basic tasks: "Select, Locate, Connect and Arrange". For each category besides a description, we also present the visual, auditory and haptic methods that fall within that group.

Select

Selection is a key component in the interaction with virtual environments. Selection allows the user to choose the object of interest among several others. It is a mandatory step in haptic interactions. Contrary to vision or hearing, haptic interactions are direct manipulations (Okamura & Cutkosky, 2001). A selection is hence required for any haptic interaction; it represents the virtual counterpart of the physical contact. In haptic enhanced selection processes, a virtual magnet is frequently simulated at the position of the target of interest.

Due to the attractive force, approach toward the point of interest is facilitated and accelerated and the precision of selection is improved. Selection is particularly important in analysis of scientific datasets since it lets the user designate an entity of the dataset that he would like to analyze in detail. The following paragraphs summarize cases where one or more targets (selectable objects) are present in the scene.

Single Target

Regarding single target acquisition, various works have clearly highlighted the benefits of adding force feedback to a purely visual system. In such a condition, a virtual magnet is frequently simulated at the position of the target of interest in order to attract the haptic device. The attraction force can either be constant or function of distance to the target. Evaluations of Keuning (2003) indicate that stronger attractive forces tend to increase accuracy of users.

It was shown in (Hasser et al., 1998) that haptic feedback can improve the speed of task completion. Similar results were observed by Dennerlein & Yang (1999). Their study focused on the add value of an attractive feedback in a point-and-click task. Fifteen adult subjects performed this task 520 times with and without the attractive effect. During this experiment, trajectories imposed to the subjects were random and varied both in terms of direction and distance. Results have firstly shown that the addition of attractive feedback increased the speed of execution, while the time required for the task achievement was significantly reduced (objective assessment). On the other hand, the perception of fatigue and discomfort, measured through a questionnaire (subjective evaluation), were also lowered with the addition of this type of haptic feedback.

In the same way, (Oakley et al., 2000) have used a phantom desktop device for the interaction with a conventional graphic user interface in order to reduce error rate. The experiment aimed at comparing the effects of four types of haptic feedbacks on the usability of a selection task. While the addition of force feedback did not seem to offer an improvement in terms of execution speed of the task, results clearly showed a significant reduction of the number of mistakes.

More recently, Vanacken et al. emphasized that a multisensory rendering was generally preferred by users (subjective opinion) and in many cases it could also accelerate the execution speed of selection tasks (Vanacken et al., 2006). These results were confirmed by Kim and Kwon who examined the impact of a haptic and/or auditory grid in enhancing recognition of ambiguous visual depth cues for position selection in a 3D virtual environment (Kim & Kwon, 2007). During this assessment, four conditions were tested (visual only, grid haptic, sound grid, audio-haptic grid). Results showed that the haptic/auditory grid offered best results. In particular, the errors along the depth axis decreased significantly (nearly by half).

In the same way, Picinali et al. examined whether users were able to integrate information from several sensorimotor channels (haptic and audio) in order to achieve the localization and the selection of single target in a 3D space (Menelas, Picinalli et al., 2009; Picinalli et al., 2010). Realized experiment showed, firstly that an attractive force feedback can easily guide users toward the target. On the other hand, even though the audio channel has a real potential for localization tasks, users have much preferred to use the haptic feedback.

Multiple Targets

Before reviewing works in this area, a brief analysis of difficulties arising from this situation is appropriate. Let us consider Figure 1, by assigning attractive properties to these four targets, the haptic device will be attracted by all targets at the same time. Suppose we want to select the target T_1, with such a situation we are not only attracted by T_1, but also by the three other targets (T_2, T_3 and

Figure 1. Representation of a situation containing multiple targets

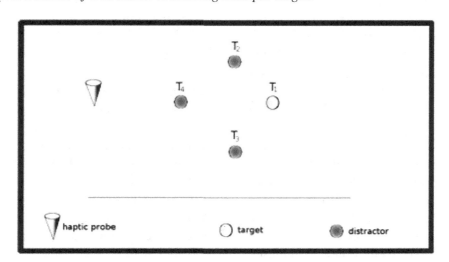

T_4). This situation can be quite disturbing since it will lead to a deviation from the trajectory to the target T_1 because of unwanted attractions from T_2, T_3 and T_4 (distractors).

The few studies conducted in the context of environments with multiple targets have led to somewhat contradictory results regarding the addition of haptic feedback. While some tend to say that the haptic feedback is to banish in such an environment, others point out that a correct setting of the attractive force significantly limits the impact of distractors. The main works of this area are summarized below.

Recently, Vanacken et al. (2009) have investigated a multimodal feedback system for target acquisition in dense environments. Tested system haptic as well as auditory feedbacks were exploited to inform the user about the existence of a target in their immediate vicinity. No directional information was provided to the user by the mean of the haptic or the audio channel, evaluations of such a multimodal system did not show any significant improvement of the results when compared to a purely visual system.

A typical situation that involves multiple targets is in interactions with graphical menu interfaces. Evaluations of Dennerlein et al. (2001) in a point-and-click task showed that performances were better with the addition of force feedback even with distracting force fields; however, they noted that speed tended to decrease with the addition of distracters. On the other hand, Wall et al. (2002) highlighted that in the presence of multiple distracters, adding force feedback (a virtual magnet) to a 3D stereoscopic virtual rendering improved subject's accuracy, but did not improve the time taken to reach the target. These results were confirmed by Cockburn and Brewster, (2005) who examined the impact of three types of interactions (audio, vibrotactile and pseudo-haptic) for a task of target selections in a Graphical User Interface (GUI). The auditory interaction was ensured via audio icons (earcones [Brewster et al., 1995]), while the pseudo-haptic feedback was rendered via the dynamic modification of the display control/ratio of the cursor in vicinity of a target. These authors showed in an initial study that all modes of interaction (particularly the pseudo-haptic) tend to decrease the time required for the task completion in the case where the targets were relatively small and isolated. On the other hand, in a second study regarding the selection in a GUI menu, they stress that the addition of these haptic feedbacks could significantly penalize the interaction performances due to the impact of distractors located in the immediate vicinity of the desired target. In the same way, Hwang et al. (2003) have investigated the impact of multiple haptic distracters on the performance of motion-impaired users. Their studies showed that positioning the distracters along the route of the target was detrimental to performance.

In contrast, Oakley et al. (2002) highlighted benefits of an adjusted haptic condition relatively to both visual-only and visual/haptic conditions. In the adjusted condition, in order to decrease the impact of distracters, which are in fact non-desired attracters; their attractive effects are decreased whenever they do not seem to interest the user. Their results indicate that target selection errors are reduced to the same level as in the haptic condition, while speed is not compromised when compared to the visual condition. These results are confirmed in (Menelas et al., 2010), where purely audio haptic feedbacks are proposed for an acquisition task in a multi-target context in a 3D virtual environment. Their study shows that the haptic adjusted condition is relevant for haptic enhanced selection in multi-target context, and also points out the potential offered by audio-haptic rendering for reducing load of the visual channel in selection tasks.

Synthesis

Through this category, the work dealing with the use of haptics in the selection process is reviewed. Situations involving a single target and those where several targets are presented are analyzed. In spite of results, which at first glance appear to be contradictory, detailed analyses have shown that haptics can offer valuable helps in a selection process. It is known that, in analysis of scientific datasets, it may be important to select an entity of interest, typically in order to launch a more detailed analysis (zoom; study the physical characteristics and more). Therefore, we advocate the use of haptic in order to increase the speed of

task completion, improve the accuracy and also to reduce the fatigue that such a task can generate.

Locate

This category gathers haptic techniques that are exploited to spatially and/or temporally locate an entity of interest in a dataset. In the haptic enhanced localization, haptics is generally used in order to direct the user toward an entity of interest. In analysis of scientific datasets, this type of interaction counts: the location of areas containing high values, strong currents, as well as the tracking of shock waves, extrema and critical points.

Location of Regions Containing High Values

The location of areas containing high values of a given field (Φ), necessitates the *velocity mapping*. The field value is directly mapped onto to the speed of the haptic device (see Equation 1 [Iwata et al., 1993; Pao & Lawrence, 1998]). While moving in the data volume, the user perceives a viscosity feedback proportional to the field value at the position of the haptic effector. Hence, regions where data values are large appear more viscous to the user. Aviles et al. (1999) and later Van Reimersdahl et al. (2003) reveal that this metaphor is very useful for rapidly scanning a volume in order to identify regions containing high values. Withal, since the generated feedback is directly proportional the speed of the user, this method can be applied for the analysis of a specific point (Aviles at al., 1999; Palmerieus et al., 2007). The force feedback perceived by the user being by definition directly proportional to the speed of haptic device, knowing that the analysis of a specific point requires a very low speed, the force feedback coming from this situation is hence almost null regardless of the field value at the explored point.

$$\vec{F} = \left| \vec{\varphi} \right| \cdot \vec{V}$$

$$(1)$$

Location of Strong Flows and Vortices

To locate strong flows by mean of haptics, the value of the vector field row Φ is, at each point of the dataset, proportionally (α) conveyed to the user as a force feedback that corresponds to the magnitude and the direction of the local vector, (see Equation 2) (Durbeck et al., 1998).

$$\vec{F} = \alpha \cdot \vec{\varphi} \tag{2}$$

While exploring the flow dataset, the haptic feedback is analogous to the feeling produced when one puts his finger into a flow. Vectors act upon his fingertip, dragging it in the same direction as the local flow field. If the user does not oppose the movement, his hand describes the trajectory of a fluid particle. Yannier et al. (2008) have recently used this method in the analysis of a wind dataset.

Shock Waves Location

Use of haptics for detecting and locating shock waves in the analysis of CFD datasets has been proposed in (Lawrence et al., 2000). Shock waves are characterized by a high gradient, to detect them a haptic feedback proportional to the gradient value at the probe position is sent to the user. In doing so, the user can be alerted on the presence of any secondary shock (even invisible) contained in the main one. This method allows free motion in regions having low gradients ($\rho < \epsilon$: F=0). Within the shock region, the forces applied to the user result in behavior similar to a ball on a hill. The shock surface can only be penetrated from the low-density side ($\rho < \epsilon$) by pushing against the rendered force, hence allowing users to easily understand regions representing high and low density without cluttering the visual display with additional data.

Extrema Location

In the analysis of scientific datasets, it is frequently interesting to locate maxima and minima of a given field. The first use of haptics to this end is the *Topography metaphor* (Pao & Lawrence, 1998). To distinguish maxima and minima of a scalar field, the values are rendered as a surface elevation. Reimersdahl et al. (2003) emphasized that the disadvantage of this method is the lack of information concerning the sign of analyzed scalars. To this end, they rendered positive values by elevations and negative ones with concavities in the virtual surface. A second method related to such detections is the *pseudo-gravity*. At each point of the space, it associates a virtual mass proportional to the value of the field. As a result, with this method: the user's hand is drawn to the highest values of the field.

Critical Points Location

Another method, which can be classified in the same category, was recently presented in (Menelas, Ammi et al., 2009). In this approach, the haptic interaction is restricted to a local environment surrounding the probe position. The haptic as well as the visual feedback are used to translate information related to the activated local environment. For instance, the vibration capabilities of a 6 Degree of Freedom (DoF) device are exploited in order to provide information about the local area explored. Critical points located in the immediate environment of the users are rendered visually by colored spheres and haptically through a sinusoidal vibration. The experiments show that vibration feedbacks reinforce the visual feedback and facilitate the build of a mental map of the analyzed flow field. Instead of an automatic process where points would be discovered at once, the user may at his convenience and on the basis of his expertise, direct the search for critical points to areas of interest. At the same time, the participant can create a mental map of the analyzed flow.

Synthesis

In this category, the use of haptics in the localization of entities or physical properties is discussed. Several cases of study, regarding the CFD domain, have been described. Results shown that haptics plays an important role in user-centered localization processes. In particular, it may complement or reinforce the visual feedback. Moreover, considering that the localization process seems not to require the development of complex strategies (as compared to way finding); we believe that the use of haptic localization process could help at reducing the cognitive load of users during the analysis of scientific datasets. Nevertheless, at current state of the literature much more experimental studies, involving expert users, are still needed.

Connect

This category has a set of techniques that allow the tracking of structures of interest. In some domains, structures located within the datasets (isosurface, streamlines, etc.) may sometimes be very relevant for the understanding of the studied phenomenon. Thanks to the addition of haptic feedbacks, users can easily follow a structure and at the same time, if necessary, can access some local information (value of a field at the explored position) of this structure. With the addition of haptic feedback, the user has an additional channel that may help reinforcing the visual feedback and accessing a greater amount of data (mainly to local information). This category counts work related to *haptic rendering of flow lines* and *haptic rendering of isosurfaces*.

Haptic Rendering of Lines

Haptic rendering of lines has been notably investigated in Fluid Dynamics. These lines are the flowlines (streamlines or pathlines). In this group are denoted:

Torque Nulling: Produce a torque proportional the field magnitude at the end effector position whenever the probe is not aligned with the vector field (Pao & Lawrence, 1998).

Transverse Damping: Facilitates the following up of a streamline by applying on one hand a large viscosity in directions transverse to the field direction and, on the other hand, some forces in the field direction proportional to field magnitude (Pao et al., 1998).

Relative Drag: Lets the user perceive a feedback proportional to the difference between the field value vector and his velocity. If the user does not oppose the force, his hand traces out a streamlines (Pao et al., 1998). In addition to directional information, this method is particularly useful when the haptic device is approaching or receding from the user. Indeed with this method, the depth variations of the flow may be perceived via the kinaesthetic sense. One has to note that such variations are generally hard to perceive through the visual feedback (van Reimersdahl et al, 2003).

Relative Turnaround: To control the movement of the haptic device along a line, the following metaphor is employed. Turning the stylus clockwise results in a movement in direction of the flow, turning it counter clockwise will inverse that direction (van Reimersdahl et al, 2003).

Feature Shift: Haptically conveys the spatial distance between two similar lines, this method renders forces to display the spatial shift. In the proposed method, the haptic device automatically describes one of the lines while being dragging into the direction of the temporarily equivalent point on the other line. The attraction force translates the spatial length between the two points (van Reimersdahl et al, 2003).

Other works of this group have been presented in (Ikits et al., 2003). Their approach relies on haptic constraints to restrict the movement of the user in certain directions by proposing a set of rules defining the movement of the proxy. As an example, to guide the user in a vector field, the proxy is locked along a streamline. More recently,

Menelas has exploited an attractive feedback in order to assist a user in the following of a flowline while displaying visually values associated with another field of the explored area (Menelas, 2012).

Haptic Surface Rendering

In medical imaging, isosurfaces are same density regions of a three-dimensional scanner. They may serve for the visualization of internal organs or bones. In fluid mechanics, they offer great opportunities for the study of characteristics contained within a given phenomenon. Haptic rendering methods of isosurfaces are divided into two main categories: "Intermediate representation" and "Direct rendering".

1. Intermediate Representation

Traditional approaches of surface rendering aims at extracting a polygonal approximation of the isosurface using voxel data. Algorithms such as *Marching Cubes* (Lorensen et al., 1987) or *Marching Tetrahedral* (Nielson et al., 1997) are commonly used for the calculation of this intermediate representation. Once this geometrical information is known, haptic feedback is simulated thanks to a collision detection algorithm coupled to a classical penalty based method (Mark et al., 1996). With a penalty method the haptic feedback is rendered by a spring model:

$$\vec{F} = -K \cdot \vec{X},$$ more penetration into the virtual

surface $\vec{X}$, results in a larger force feedback. As noted by many authors, using a surface representation provides a stable force feedback. However, because of the computation time required for the surface estimation, such methods do not allow real time changes.

To overcome this limitation, Galean et al. (1991) and later, Korner et al. (1999) have opted for local use of the *Marching Cubes* algorithm. With this method, only voxel data situated in the vicinity of the haptic probe is used to calculate the local surface. With this optimization, real time updating is possible since the surface is generated on the fly. However, there is a direct relation between the computation time and the data count. This tends to restrict the application of such method to non-complex data.

To face this second difficulty, Adachi et al. (1995) have proposed the use of another intermediate representation. In their approach, the local surface is approximated by the mean of a virtual plane (see Figure 2). In order to assume a very fast haptic loop independently to the amount of data, this method updates the virtual plane at a low frequency while maintaining a high update rate for haptic loop. Mark et al. (1996) and later, Chen et al. (2000) have illustrated this model with a haptic rendering method for isosurface without any explicit isosurface extraction (i-e: without any complete polygonal representation).

To express the hardness of objects (internal organs or bones) in the medical imaging domain, Lundin et al. (Lundin et al., 2002) have adapted the proxy method (Ruspuni et al., 1997), defined for the surface representation, to volumic datasets. In the proposed approach, the motion of the proxy is controlled by several rules related to the nature (hard, soft) of the data surrounding its position. Low-density regions offer less resistance to the movement of the user. The proxy is indeed able to move more rapidly in such part of the data volume. Thus, the haptic feedback produced with this method does not only render the presence of a virtual isosurface but also provides some relevant information related to the nature this surface. Because of that information, this method is in some cases listed as a 3D rendering method. When using this method, a user can easily distinguish bones from skin or muscles. However, since the proxy is constrained by the local gradient, one has to note that within high gradient data, this virtual surface does not approximate the isosurface.

Figure 2. Approximation of an isosurface with a virtual plan

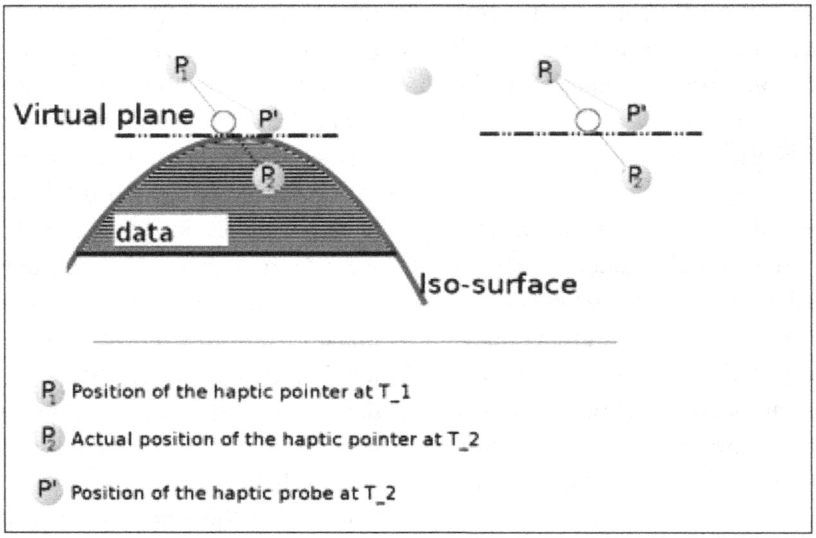

2. Direct Rendering

A well-known method for direct haptic rendering of isosurfaces has been exposed in (Avila & Sobierajski 1996). The proposed method targets the haptic rendering of an isosurface without any intermediate representation. To simulate the touch of the virtual surface, the force feedback is directly approximated as a difference in the field value. Because of this direct computation (approximation), this method offers a very fast haptic loop. On the other hand, due to this approximation, some unwanted vibrations are observed in regions presenting high frequency data (Fauvet et al., 2007). Indeed in such regions, the strong variations of the field are directly conveyed to the force feedback. These changes represent the vibrations perceived by users. To address this issue, an improvement of this approach has been proposed in (Menelas, Fauvet et al., 2008). A more generic approach was then described in (Menelas, Ammi et al., 2008). In this new solution, rays issued from the probe position are launched in multiple directions (cartesian ones were used in the implemented version) in order to compute the position where the haptic probe would situate if

it was not constrained to move on the isosurface. Thereafter the computation of this position, the virtual touch of the isosurface is simulated by the mean of a penalty-based method.

Synthesis

In this category the work addressing the rendering via the touch sense of structures of interest was analyzed. Haptic rendering of flowline and iso-surfaces have been discussed.

Arrange

This category lists techniques where haptics helps to assist users in the spatial arrangement of the elements to be analyzed. The haptic feedback is used to guide the gesture of the user according to some relevant information hidden within the dataset. Such methods have been successfully employed to overcome limitations of traditional docking algorithms. The haptic feedback allows translation of physical and chemical properties of elements to the user involved into the docking process. Through the haptic guidance, a greater amount of information is transmitted to the user without risking the overload of the visual channel. Hou and Sourina noted that the use of hapticovisual molecular-docking systems lets the user to manually explore the conformational molecular space in order to find an optimal conformation faster (Hou & Sourina, 2011).

In (LaiYuen et al., 2005), to assist users in the visualization, manipulation and assembly of molecules in a virtual environment the intermolecular forces were haptically rendered through a 5 DoF haptic device. In such a system, the feasibility in terms of energy and geometry of a ligand to dock or assemble is directly perceived through the haptic channel. The haptic modality is thus used to enlarge the bandwidth between the user and the system. In the same way, in (Persson et al., 2007) a chemical force feedback system has been developed in order to offer a tool that can help students understand the docking protein process. In a semi-immersive environment with stereo graphics, users were able to manipulate the ligand while feeling force feedbacks resulting from the docking process. Experiments point out that the proposed system improves learning speed as well as the understanding of docking processes in terms of the forces involved. In (Ferey et al., 2008), the haptic enhanced reconfiguration capabilities are extended by the means of a bi-manual system. Two proteins are simultaneously handled. While one is manipulated with a tracked 3D mouse, the other is attached to a 6 DoF haptic device that conveys electrostatic and hydrophobic interactions.

DISCUSSION

This work aimed at studying the role of each modality in analysis of scientific datasets. Considering that most researches do agree on the role of visual and audio, this work has focused on exploitation of haptics. After analyzing human sensory characteristics and specifities of the visual/haptic association, we have concluded that to achieve effective analysis processes, it was necessary to use

haptics for facilitating interaction with the datasets, since it should also promote presentation of data through other modalities (visual and auditory). In the previous section, we detailed various tasks where haptics seemed to present advantages over other channels through a four-category taxonomy. This section aims at discussing this taxonomy.

To assess the proposed classification, we refer to the evaluation grid proposed in (Beaudoin-Lafond, 2004) while adapting it to our situation. Three criteria are selected: 1.) *the descriptive power:* the ability to describe a significant range of existing methods; 2.) *the evaluative power:* the ability to help assess multiple existing methods; and 3.) *the generative power:* the ability to help the introduction of effective new methods in the analysis process.

Descriptive Power

For each category in the presented taxonomy, all the literature methods that can be classified into it, is listed. In doing so, over 45 methods were reviewed. Although these numbers may seem limited, it is important to emphasize that the use of haptics in analysis of scientific datasets is not so common. In this regard, it is expect that this taxonomy covered most of the existing methods described in the literature.

Evaluative Power

Evaluation refers to the worth and significance of something using criteria against a set of standards. Speaking about evaluation is equivalent to asking the question about the existence of criteria that defines whether a method is more or less suitable for an effective analysis process. Given a method belonging to the proposed classification, seeing that our taxonomy is oriented toward four well-defined tasks, this method is assessable according to the objective of its category. To evaluate a method, one just has to assess whether it offers or not 1) an efficient selection or 2) an efficient location or 3) efficient link (connect) or 4) an efficient arrangement. Since most of these tasks were widely studied in recent years, it may be said that this taxonomy provides a valuable *evaluative power*. Indeed, for a selection, one can assess the time required for achievement of the selection task and the selection accuracy. For a link, one may assess the following-up accuracy and perception of users.

Generative Power

Unlike data-centric taxonomies (Shneiderman, 1996) or those based on low-level actions (Amar et al., 2005), proposed taxonomy is based on high-level actions that are well-known in the world of human computer interaction. In this sense, this classification aims at fulfilling the needs of end users. Hence, two tracks that can lead to the development of new methods are considered.

1. Since the goal of each category is clearly defined, it is believed that this will promote the development of new methods. Indeed, having stated the goal (selection, link, location or arrangement) is the first step towards the development of new methods. Thereafter it will take, depending on user requirements, to design the method that lets to achieve the task.
2. Since identified tasks refer to end-users goals, we argue that developers will be eager to apply existing haptic methods to new areas. However, to take into account the specificities of any new domain, new methods should likely be created. This is what was observed with the haptic rendering of isosurfaces: methods that suited medical data showed some instability with the data from CFD simulation (Fauvet, 2007). To address this problem, a new method, has been proposed (Menelas, Ammi et al., 2008).

Finally, in addition to these three assessment criteria, we would like to emphasize that despite the fact that this taxonomy has been developed from the desire to improve the interaction component of the analysis process, it also includes methods that target the achievement of better data presentation. Throughout the description of each category, different methods that can actually improve the presentation of data were outlined. For the selection group, the work of Menelas et al. (2010) has demonstrated that audio-haptic rendering may be exploited to unload the visual channel for selection a given target in 3D environments containing several others. In the case of localization, Lawrence et al. (2000) highlighted that the proposed haptic interaction could supplement the visual feedback. Similarly in the connect group, Lundin et al. (2002) by controlling the movement of the proxy, come to convey properties related to medical datasets. In arrangement tasks, since it can convey additional information without risking overloading the visual channel, used haptic feedbacks appear as a mean that let to enlarge the bandwidth between a user and the system (Persson et al., 2007).

In the light of these last observations; this taxonomy reminds the interdependence that exists between interaction and presentation components of visualization processes. This analysis is in line with Yi et al. (2007) who recently concluded that these two components are in a symbiotic relationship.

CONCLUSION

In this chapter, the role of VR technologies (visual, haptics and audio) in analysis of scientific datasets was discussed. First, it was identified that interaction and presentation are the two main components of visualization systems. Having observed that multimodality represents the key component of VR systems that may be exploited in analysis of large datasets, two criteria that should be addressed in designing multimodal systems were stated. Thereafter, the manner in which each modality and how combination of several modalities could be exploited in order to arrive with effective analysis processes was analyzed. By doing this, based on physiological characteristics of humans, it was pointed out that haptic interactions should be used in order to improve the interactions of the user. From this, a taxonomy based on interaction tasks where haptics seems to have advantages when compared to other channels was detailed. Identified task are: *Select, Locate, Connect,* and *Arrange.* Throughout the description of this categorization, a detailed survey of methods of the literature was provided. Finally the descriptive, the evaluative and the generative power of the proposed taxonomy have been discussed.

REFERENCES

Adachi, Y., Kumano, T., & Ogino, K. (1995). Intermediate representation for stiff virtual objects. In *Proceedings of IEEE Virtual Reality Conference,* 203-210). New Brunswick, NJ: IEEE Press.

Amar, R., Eagan, J., & Stasko, J. (2005). Low-level components of analytic activity in information visualization. In *Proceedings of IEEE Symposium on Information Visualization,* 111-117. New Brunswick, NJ: IEEE Press.

Avila, R., & Sobierajski, L. (1996). A haptic interaction method for volume visualization. In *Proceedings of IEEE Symposium on Information Visualization '96,* 197-204. New Brunswick, NJ: IEEE Press.

Aviles, W., & Ranta, J. (1999). Haptic interaction with geoscientific data. In *Proceedings of the Fourth PHANTOM Users Group Workshop,* 78-81. Cambridge, MA: MIT Press.

Basdogan, C., Ho, C., Slater, M., & Srinivasa, M. (1998). The role of haptic communication in shared virtual environments. In *Proceedings of the Fourth PHANTOM Users Group Workshop.* Cambridge, MA: MIT Press.

Beaudouin-Lafon, M. (2004). Designing interaction, not interfaces. In: *Proceedings of AVI '04 The Working Conference on Advanced Visual Interfaces,* 15-22. New York: ACM Press.

Bernsen, N. O. (1993). Modality theory: Supporting multimodal interface design. In *Proceedings of ERCIM Workshop on Multimodal Human-Computer Interaction.* Cambridge, MA: MIT Press.

Bideau, B., Multon, F., Kulpa, R., Fradet, L., Arnaldi, B., & Delamarche, P. (2004). Virtual reality, a new tool to investigate anticipation skills: Application to goalkeeper and handball thrower duel. *Neuroscience Letters, 372*(1-2). PMID:15531100.

Bowman, D., Kruijff, E., LaViola, J., & Poupyrev, I. (2004). *3D user interfaces: Theory and practice.* Upper Saddle River, NJ: Addison-Wesley.

Brewster, S. A. (1995). The development of a sonically-enhanced widget set. In *Proceedings of EWHCI'95 International Centre for Scientific and Technical Information,* 126-129. Moscow: MIT Press.

Bryson, S. (1996). Virtual reality in scientific visualization. *Communications of the ACM, 39*(5), 62–71. doi:10.1145/229459.229467.

Burdea, G., & Coiffet, P. (1994). *Virtual reality technology.* New York: John Wiley & Sons, Inc..

Chen, K. W., Heng, P. A., & H., S. (2000). Direct haptic rendering of isosurface by intermediate representation. In *Proceedings of ACM Symposium on Virtual Reality Software and Technology VRST,* 188-194. New York: ACM Press.

Cockburn, A., & Brewster, S. A. (2005). Multimodal feedback for the acquisition of small targets. *Ergonomics*, *48*(9), 1129–1150. doi:10.1080/00140130500197260 PMID:16251152.

Dennerlein, J., & Yang, M. C. (1999). Perceived musculoskeletal loading during use of a force-feedback computer mouse. In *Proceedings of Human Factors and Ergonomics Conference*. Thousand Oaks, CA: Sage Publishers.

Dennerlein, J., & Yang, M. C. (2001). Haptic force feedback devices for the office computer: Performance and musculoskeletal loading issues. *Human Factors*, *43*(2), 278–286. doi:10.1518/001872001775900850 PMID:11592668.

Durbeck, L. J., Macias, N. J., Weinstein, D. M., Johnson, C. R., & Hollerbach, J. M. (1998). Scirun haptic display for scientific visualization. In *Proceedings of Third Phantom Users Group Workshop*. Cambridge, MA: MIT Press.

Fauvet, N., Ammi, M., & Bourdot, P. (2007). Experiments of haptic perception techniques for computational fluid dynamics. In *Proceedings of International Conference on Cyberworlds CW '07*, 322-329. New Brunswick, NJ: IEEE Press.

Ferey, N., Bouyer, G., Martin, C., Bourdot, P., Nelson, J., & Burkhardt, J. M. (2008). User needs analysis to design a 3d multimodal protein-docking interface. In *Proceedings of IEEE Symposium on 3D User Interfaces 3DUI*, 125-132. New Brunswick, NJ: IEEE Press.

Fikkert, W., D'Ambros, M., Bierz, T., & Jankun-Kelly, T. (2007). Interacting with visualizations. Human-Centered Visualization Environments (77-162). Berlin: Springer. doi:doi:10.1007/978-3-540-71949-6_3 doi:10.1007/978-3-540-71949-6_3.

Friedes, D. (1974). Human information processing and sensory modality: Cross-modal functions, information complexity, memory, and deficit. *Psychological Bulletin*, *81*(5), 284–310. doi:10.1037/h0036331 PMID:4608609.

Galyean, T. A., & Hughes, J. F. (1991). Sculpting: An interactive volumetric modeling technique. In *Proceedings of the 18th Annual Conference on Computer Graphics and Interactive Techniques*, 267-274. New York: ACM Press.

Gershon, N., Eick, S. G., & Card, S. (1998). Design: Information visualization. *Interactions (New York, N.Y.)*, *5*, 9–15. doi:10.1145/274430.274432.

Griffith, E. J., Post, F. H., Koutek, M., Heus, T., & Jonker, H. J. J. (2005). Feature tracking in VR for cumulus cloud life-cycle studies. In Kjems & Blach (Eds.), Virtual Environments 2005 (121–128). Natick, MA: A K Peters.

Hasser, C., & Goldenberg, A. (1998). User performance in a GUI pointing task with a low-cost force-feedback computer mouse. In *Proceedings of Seventh Annual Symposium on Haptic Interfaces, International Mechanical Engineering Congress, and Exposition*. Anaheim, CA: IEEE Press.

Hou, X., & Sourina, O. (2011). Six degree-of-freedom haptic rendering for biomolecular docking. In Gavrilova, M., Tan, C., Sourin, A., & Sourina, O. (Eds.), *Transactions on Computational Science XII* (*Vol. 6670*, pp. 98–117). Lecture Notes in Computer Science Berlin: Springer. doi:10.1007/978-3-642-22336-5_6.

Hwang, F., Keates, S., Langdon, P., & Clarkson, P. J. (2003). Multiple haptic targets for motion-impaired computer users. In *Proceedings of the SIGCHI Conference on Human Factors in Computing Systems*, 41-48. New York: ACM Press.

Ikits, M., Brederson, J., Hansen, C., & Johnson, C. (2003). A constraint-based technique for haptic volume exploration. [New Brunswick, NJ: IEEE Press.]. *Proceedings of IEEE Visualization VIS, 2003*, 263–269.

Iwata, H., & Noma, H. (1993). Volume haptization. In *Proceedings of IEEE Symposium on Research Frontiers in Virtual Reality,* 16-23. New Brunswick, NJ: IEEE Press.

Kahol, K., Tripathi, P., Mcdaniel, T., Bratton, L., & Panchanathan, S. (2006). Modeling context in haptic perception, rendering, and visualization. *ACM Transactions on Multimedia Computing, Communications, and Applications*, 2(3), 219–240. doi:10.1145/1152149.1152153.

Keuning, H. (2003). *Augmented Force Feedback to Facilitate Target Acquisition in Human-Computer Interaction.* (Ph.D. thesis). Eindhoven, The Netherlands, University of Eindhoven.

Kim, S. C., & Kwon, D. S. (2007). Haptic and sound grid for enhanced positioning in a 3D virtual environment. In *Proceedings of Second International Workshop of Haptic and Audio Interaction Design*, 98-109. Seoul, South Korea: HAID Press.

Klatzky, R., & Lederman, S. (1995). Identifying objects from a haptic glance. *Perception & Psychophysics*, *57*, 1111–1123. doi:10.3758/BF03208368 PMID:8539087.

Korner, O., Schill, M., Wagner, C., Bender, H. J., & Mnner, R. (1999). Haptic volume rendering with an intermediate local representation. In *Proceedings of the 1st International Workshop on the Haptic Devices in Medical Applications,* 79-84. Cambridge, MA: MIT Press.

Lai-Yuen, S. K., & Lee, Y. S. (2005). Computer-aided molecular design (CAMD) with force-torque feedback. In *Proceedings of the Ninth International Conference on Computer Aided Design and Computer Graphics,* 199-204. New Brunswick, NJ: IEEE Press.

Laramee, R. S., & Kosara, R. (2007). Human-centered visualization environments: Future challenges and unsolved problems. In A. Kerren, A. Ebert, & J. Meyer (Eds.), Human-Centered Visualization, Lecture Notes in Computer Science, Tutorial Volume 4417 (231–254). Berlin: Springer Verlag.

LaViola, J. J. Prabhat, Forsberg, A. S., Laidlaw, D. H., & van Dam, A. (2009). Trends in interactive visualization. In E. Zudilova-Seinstra (Ed.), Virtual Reality-Based Interactive Scientific Visualization Environments (317-328). London: Springer-Verlag.

Lawrence, D., Lee, C., Pao, L., & Novoselov, R. (2000). Shock and vortex visualization using a combined visual/haptic interface. [New Brunswick, NJ: IEEE Press.]. *Proceedings of Visualization*, *2000*, 131–137.

Lecuyer, A., Coquillart, S., Kheddar, A., Richard, P., & Coiffet, P. (2000). Pseudo-haptic feedback: Can isometric input devices simulate force feedback? In *Proceedings of the IEEE Virtual Reality 2000 Conference*, 83-90. New Brunswick, NJ: IEEE Press.

Lederman, S. J., & Klatzky, R. L. (1987). Hand movements: A window into haptic object recognition. *Cognitive Psychology*, *19*(3), 342–368. doi:10.1016/0010-0285(87)90008-9 PMID:3608405.

Loftin, R. B., Chen, J., & Rosenblum, L. (2004). Visualization using virtual reality. InHansen, C, & Johnson, C (Eds.),*Visualization Handbook* (479-489). Amsterdam: Elsevier.

Lorensen, W. E., & Cline, H. E. (1987). Marching cubes: A high resolution 3d surface construction algorithm. In *Proceedings of the 14th Annual Conference on Computer Graphics and Interactive Techniques*,163-169. New York: ACM Press.

Lundin, K., Ynnerman, A., & Gudmundsson, B. (2002). Proxybased haptic feedback from volumetric density data. In *Proceedings of the Eurohaptic Conference,* 104-109. Edinburgh, UK: University of Edinburgh Press.

MacLean, K. E. (2000). Designing with haptic feedback. In *Proceedings of IEEE International Conference on Robotics and Automation,* 783-788. New Brunswick, NJ: IEEE Press.

Mark, W., Randolph, S., Finch, M., Verth, J. V., & Taylor, R. M. (1996). Adding force feedback to graphics systems: Issues and solutions. In *Proceedings of Computer Graphics,* 447-452. Amsterdam: IOS Press. doi:10.1145/237170.237284.

Menelas, B., Ammi, M., & Bourdot, P. (2008). A flexible method for haptic rendering of isosurface from volumetric data. In *Proceedings of the 6th International EuroHaptics Conference on Haptics.* Berlin Springer-Verlag.

Menelas, B., Ammi, M., Pastur, L., & Bourdot, P. (2009). Haptical exploration of an unsteady flow. In *Symposium on Haptic Interfaces for Virtual Environment and Teleoperator Systems EuroHaptics Conference World Haptics,* 232-237. Berlin: Springer.

Menelas, B., Fauvet, N., Ammi, M., & Bourdot, P. (2008). Direct haptic rendering for large datasets with high gradients. In *Proceedings of the 2008 Ambi-Sys Workshop on Haptic User Interfaces in Ambient Media Systems,* 1-9. New Brunswick, NJ: IEEE Press.

Menelas, B., Picinali, L., Katz, B. F. G., & Bourdot, P. (2010). Audio haptic feedbacks for an acquisition task in a multitarget context. In *Proceedings of IEEE Symposium on 3D User Interface,* 51-54. New Brunswick, NJ: IEEE Press.

Menelas, B., Picinali, L., Katz, B. F. G., Bourdot, P., & Ammi, M. (2009). Haptic audio guidance for target selection in a virtual environment. In *Proceedings of 4th International Haptic and Auditory Interaction Design Workshop,* 1-2. HAID.

Menelas, B.-A. J. & Otis, J.-D., M. (2012) Design of a serious game for learning vibrotactile messages. In Proceedings of *International Workshop on Haptic Audio Visual Environments and Games, 124-129.* New Brunswick, NJ: IEEE Press.

Menelas, B.-A. J. (2012). Interactive analysis of cavity-flows in a virtual environment. In *ACM 28th Spring Conference on Computer Graphics,* 1-6). New York, ACM Press.

Nesbitt, K. (2003). *Designing Multi-Sensory Displays for Abstract Data.* (Ph.D. thesis). Sydney, Australia, University of Sydney.

Nielson, G. M., & Franke, R. (1997). Computing the separating surface for segmented data. In *Proceedings of the 8th Conference on Visualization,* 229-233. Los Alamitos, CA: IEEE Press.

Oakley, I., Adams, A., Brewster, S., & Gray, P. (2002). Guidelines for the design of haptic widgets. In *Proceedings of British Computer Society Conference on Human-Computer Interaction,* 195-212. HCIRN Press.

Oakley, I., McGee, M. R., Brewster, S., & Gray, P. (2000). Putting the feel in 'look and feel'. In *Proceedings of SIGCHI Conference on Human Factors in Computing Systems,* 415-422. New York: ACM Press.

Okamura, A. M., & Cutkosky, M. R. (2001). Feature detection for haptic exploration with robotic fingers. *The International Journal of Robotics Research, 20*(12), 925–938. doi:10.1177/02783640122068191.

Oviatt, S. L., & Cohen, P. R. (2000). Multimodal interfaces that process what comes naturally. *Communications of the ACM, 43*(3), 45–50. doi:10.1145/330534.330538.

Palmerius, K. L. (2007). Direct Volume Haptics for Visualization. (Ph.D. Thesis). Linkoping, Sweden, Linkoping University.

Paneels, S., & Roberts, J. C. (2009). Review of designs for haptic data visualization. *IEEE Transactions on Haptics, 3*(2), 119–137. doi:10.1109/TOH.2009.44.

Pao, L. Y., & Lawrence, D. A. (1998). Synergistic visual/haptic computer interfaces. In *Proceedings of Japan/USA/Vietnam Workshop on Research and Education in Systems, Computation, and Control Engineering,* 155-162. New York: CRC Press.

Persson, P., Cooper, M., Tibell, L., Ainsworth, S., Ynnerman, A., & Jonsson, B. H. (2007). Designing and evaluating a haptic system for biomolecular education. In *Proceedings of IEEE Virtual Reality Conference,* 171-178. New Brunswick, NJ: IEEE Press.

Picinali, L., Menelas, B., Katz, B. F. G., & Bourdot, P. (2010). Evaluation of a haptic/audio system for 3D targeting tasks. In *Proceedings of 128th Convention of the Audio Engineering Society.* New York: AES Press.

Ruspini, D. C., Kolarov, K., & Khatib, O. (1997). The haptic display of complex graphical environments. In *Proceedings of the 24th Annual Conference on Computer Graphics and Interactive Techniques,* 345-352. New York: ACM Press.

Shneiderman, B. (1996). The eyes have it: A task by data type taxonomy for information visualizations. In *Proceedings of IEEE Symposium on Visual Languages,* 336-343. New Brunswick, NJ: IEEE Press.

van Reimersdahl, T., Bley, F., Kuhlen, T., & Bischof, C. H. (2003). Haptic rendering techniques for the interactive exploration of CFD datasets in virtual environments. In *Proceedings of the Workshop on Virtual Environments, 39,* 241-246. New Brunswick, NJ: IEEE Press.

Vanacken, L., Grossman, T., & Coninx, K. (2009). Multimodal selection techniques for dense and occluded 3D virtual environments. *International Journal of Human-Computer Studies, 67*(3), 237–255. doi:10.1016/j.ijhcs.2008.09.001.

Vanacken, L., Raymaekers, C., & Coninx, K. (2006). Evaluating the influence of multimodal feedback on egocentric selection metaphors in virtual environments. In *Proceedings of First International Workshop on Haptic and Audio Interaction Design,* 12-23. HAID Press.

Vézien, J.-M., Ménélas, B., Nelson, J., Picinali, L., Bourdot, P., & Lusseyran, F. et al. (2009). Multisensory VR exploration for computer fluid dynamics in the CoRSAIRe project. *Virtual Reality (Waltham Cross), 13*(4), 257–271. doi:10.1007/s10055-009-0134-1.

von der Heyde, M., & Hager-Ross, C. (1998). Psychophysical experiments in a complex virtual environment. In *Proceedings of the Third PHANTOM Users Group Workshop.* Cambridge, MA: MIT.

Wall, S. A., Paynter, K., Shillito, A. M., Wright, M., & Scali, S. (2002). The effect of haptic feedback and stereo graphics in a 3D target acquisition. In *Proceedings of Eurohaptics,* 23-29. Edinburgh, UK: IEEE Press.

Ware, C. (2000). *Information visualization: Perception for design.* San Francisco: Morgan Kaufmann Publishers Inc..

Welch, R. B., & Warren, D. H. (1980). Immediate perceptual response to intersensory discrepancy. *Psychological Bulletin, 88*(3), 638–667. doi:10.1037/0033-2909.88.3.638 PMID:7003641.

Yannier, N., Basdogan, C., Tasiran, S., & Sen, O. (2008). Using haptics to convey cause-and-effect relations in climate visualization. *IEEE Transaction on Haptics*, *1*(2), 130–141. doi:10.1109/TOH.2008.16.

Yi, J. S., ah Kang, Y, Stasko, J, & Jacko, J. (2007). Toward a deeper understanding of the role of interaction in information visualization. *IEEE Transactions on Visualization and Computer Graphics*, *13*(6), 1224–1231. doi:10.1109/TVCG.2007.70515 PMID:17968068.

Zhu, B., & Chen, H. (2008). *Information visualization for decision making. Handbook on Decision Support Systems*. Heidelber, Germany: Springer-Verlag.

Zudilova-Seinstra, E., Adriaansen, T., & Liere, R. v. (2008). *Trends in Interactive visualization: State-of-the-art survey*. New York: Springer Publishing Inc..

KEY TERMS AND DEFINITIONS

Haptics: Haptics is linked to the sense of touch. Nevertheless, the haptic modality refers not only to tactile perception but also to a complex system based on the muscles and joints: it plays a major role in propricoception. In a non-exhaustive manner, it informs on texture, weight of objects as well as their hardness and shape.

Modality: A modality is directly linked to a human sense. We define modality as the form of exchange that can take place between a user and a numerical system. We thus define the visual, the haptic or the audio modality.

Multimodality: As opposed to a unimodal condition where only one form of communication is possible, several forms of communication are available in a multimodal rendering. When compared to unimodal rendering, the design of a multimodal rendering requires additional conditions due to interactions that may exist between the various channels. Indeed, it requires that exploitation of different modalities does not oppose one another. Furthermore, it is also desirable that each modality contributes to the achievement of a common goal.

Multimodal Analysis: As opposed to standard analysis processes of large datasets where only the visual capabilities of human are exploited, in a multimodal analysis several modalities (visual, haptics and or audio) are exploited in order to provide the user with a richer and more natural interface with the data.

Chapter 7
The Importance of Visualization and Interaction in the Anomaly Detection Process

Maria Riveiro
Informatics Research Centre, University of Skövde, Skövde, Sweden

ABSTRACT

Large volumes of heterogeneous data from multiple sources need to be analyzed during the surveillance of large sea, air, and land areas. Timely detection and identification of anomalous behavior or any threat activity is an important objective for enabling homeland security. While it is worth acknowledging that many existing mining applications support identification of anomalous behavior, autonomous anomaly detection systems for area surveillance are rarely used in the real world since these capabilities and applications present two critical challenges: they need to provide adequate user support and they need to involve the user in the underlying detection process. Visualization and interaction play a crucial role in providing adequate user support and involving the user in the detection process. Therefore, this chapter elaborates on the role of visualization and interaction in the anomaly detection process, using the surveillance of sea areas as a case study. After providing a brief description of how operators identify conflict traffic situations and anomalies, the anomaly detection problem is characterized from a data mining point of view, suggesting how operators may enhance the process through visualization and interaction.

DOI: 10.4018/978-1-4666-4309-3.ch007

INTRODUCTION

Exploring, analyzing and making decisions based on vast amounts data are complex tasks that are carried out in a daily basis. People, both in their business and private lives, walk the path from data to decision using diverse means of support. While purely automatic or purely visual analysis methods are used and continued to be developed, the complex nature of many real-world problems makes it indispensable to include humans in the data analysis process.

Automatic analysis methods cannot be applied on ill-defined problems. Furthermore, some real-world problems require dynamic adaptation of the analysis solution, which is very difficult to be handled by automatic means (Keim et al., 2009). Visual analysis methods exploit human creativity, knowledge, intuition and experience to solve problems at hand. While visualization approaches generally give very good results for small data sets, they fail when the required data for solving the problem is too large to be captured by a human analyst (Keim et al., 2009).

The surveillance of large sea areas normally requires the analysis of huge volumes of heterogeneous, multidimensional and dynamic data, in order to improve vessel traffic safety, efficiency and protect the environment (Kharchenko & Vasylyev, 2002). Human operators may be overwhelmed by the data, by the traditional manual methods of data analysis or by other factors, like time pressure, high stress, inconsistencies or the imperfect and uncertain nature of the information. In order to support the operator while monitoring large sea areas, the identification of anomalous behavior or situations that might need further investigation may reduce operator's cognitive load.

While it is worth acknowledging that many existing mining applications support identification of anomalous behavior, autonomous anomaly detection systems for area surveillance are rarely used in real world settings. We claim that anomaly detection systems present, among others, two key challenges: they need to provide adequate user support and they need to involve the user in the underlying detection process. Although these aspects cannot be considered independently, they present distinctive characteristics and demand different solutions. The first challenge concerns the necessity of providing adequate user support during the whole detection and identification of anomalous behavior process, allowing a true discourse with the information. This issue includes deepen our understanding of the human analytical and decision making processes. Due to the fact that anomaly detection is a complex and not a well-defined problem, user involvement is needed. The second challenge involves the study of adequate ways of interacting and visualizing the underlying data mining layers. Human expert knowledge is very valuable in these cases, as it can be used to guide the anomaly detection process, for example, reducing the search space, updating knowledge expert rules or refining normal models derived from the data. We believe that the visualization of the data and the data mining process, as well as the availability of interaction techniques play a crucial role in such involvement.

Thus, this chapter aims to: (1) review anomaly detection methods used in the maritime domain, with specific emphasis on the challenges they present from a user's perspective, (2) discuss the role that visualization and interaction plays in the anomaly detection process, (3) identify leverage points where the use of visualization and interaction could make a positive difference, and (4) present examples of how some of the challenges encountered have been tackled in current research carried out at our research center.

The remainder of the chapter is structured as follows: the following section briefly explores the use of visualization and interaction in data mining. The role of visualization and interaction in maritime anomaly detection is discussed afterwards. Then, a review of relevant anomaly detection approaches applied to the maritime anomaly detection problem is presented. Based on field work carried out at various maritime control centers, we provide a brief description of how maritime operators monitor traffic. Enhancements of the anomaly detection process using visualization/interaction and examples are introduced thereafter. Finally, conclusions are outlined.

THE ROLE OF VISUALIZATION AND INTERACTION IN DATA MINING

Data Mining (DM) is defined as the process of identifying or discovering useful and as yet undiscovered knowledge from the real-world data (Hand et al., 2001). Data mining is often placed in the broader context of Knowledge Discovery in Databases (KDD). KDD is an iterative process consisting of data preparation and cleaning, hypothesis generation (data mining is used basically in this phase) and interpretation and analysis. The CRISP-DM (CRoss Industry Standard Process for Data Mining) model (Shearer, 2000) describes the data mining process in general, specifying the following phases and tasks: (1) business understanding (determine business objectives, situation assessment, determine data mining goal, produce project plan), (2) data understanding (collect initial data, describe data, explore data, verify data quality), (3) data preparation (data set description, select data, clean data, construct data, integrate data, format data), (4) modeling (select modeling technique, generate test design, build model, asses model), (5) evaluation (evaluate results, review process, determine next steps) and (6) deployment (plan deployment, plan monitoring and maintenance, produce final report). Here, the CRISP-DM is used as a framework to describe the anomaly detection process. Other descriptions of the data mining process can be found in the literature, such as the model presented by Harrison-John (1997), which describes the data mining process as a cyclic process of seven stages: problem definition, data extraction, data cleansing, data engineering, mining algorithm application

and analysis of results, where the emphasis is on the data selection and parameter selection tasks.

The integration of DM and information visualization techniques has received a lot of attention in recent years, since automatic data mining approaches only work well for well-defined and specific problems (Kerren et al., 2007). Numerous authors (e.g. Keim [2002] and Fayyad et al. [2002]) recognize the need to tightly include the human in the exploration process.

Visualization can contribute to the data mining process in three ways: it can represent the results of complex computational algorithms, it can depict the data mining process and it can be used to discover complex patterns which cannot be detected automatically but by the powerful human visual system (visual data mining). Visual data mining focuses on integrating the user in the knowledge discovery process using effective and efficient visualization techniques and interaction capabilities. A classification of visual data mining methods regarding data type, visualization technique and the interaction/distortion technique can be found in Keim (2002). Additionally, significant examples of the use of data mining and data visualization can be found in Fayyad et al. (2002). In Meneses and Grinstein (2001), the authors present a description of the data mining process incorporating visualization as a component. Visualization allows users and analysts to interact with several entities involved in the data mining cycle.

Interaction is a core component of the analysis and knowledge discovery process. Users can interact with the data in many different ways (Fayyad et al., 2002): selecting sources of data, browsing, querying, sampling, selecting graphical representations, and so forth. But users may also interact with the underlying data mining process, selecting input parameters, selecting algorithms, validating models, modifying thresholds, and so forth. Nevertheless, examples of interactions between users and entities that are part of any data mining process are not common in the literature.

THE ROLE OF VISUALIZATION AND INTERACTION IN ANOMALY DETECTION

Anomaly detection methods have been used in multiple areas, like network security, video surveillance, human activity monitoring, etc. The majority of published work on anomaly detection focuses on the technological aspects: new and combinations of methods, additional improvements of existing methods, reduction of false alarms, correlations among alarms, etc. Publications regarding the use of anomaly detection methods in real environments or human factors studies regarding anomaly detection are scarce. Even if interaction, usability, cognitive task analysis or acceptability are not normally matters within anomaly detection research, visualization has received more attention.

The majority of the examples regarding the use of visualization to enhance anomaly detection are published in the area of network security. Even though an exhaustive review on the use of visualization for network security is out of the scope of this chapter, we outline here some examples where visualization has been used for enhancing the anomaly detection process.

Axelsson (2005) addresses the problem of false alarms within intrusion detection and proposes four different visualization approaches to aid the operator to correctly identify false (and true) alarms. Likewise, Mansmann (2008) devotes his dissertation to the use of visualization for monitoring, detecting and interpreting security threats. New scalable visualization metaphors for detailed analysis of large network time series are presented: a hierarchical map of the IP address space, graph-based approaches for tracking behavioral changes of hosts and higher-level network entities and the application of Self Organizing Maps (SOMs) to analyze both structured network protocol data and unstructured information, e.g., textual context of email messages. Other examples of novel visualization approaches for network traffic that support intrusion detection are presented in Onut et al. (2004), Teoh et al. (2004), Muelder et al. (2005), Livnat et al. (2005), and Cai and de M. Franco (2009).

Onut et al. (2004) present two types of graphical views for information extracted at the network layer: services behavior view (behavior of the internal/external hosts with respect to a certain set of services) and category view (hosts are sorted with respect to a particular relevant attribute, like number of IPs used). In Teoh et al. (2004), the authors describe an integration of visual and automated data mining methods for discovering and investigating anomalies in Internet routing. The analysis tool presents different components that complement each other, where visualization and interaction are key to support user involvement. Muelder et al. (2005) employ visualization to detect scans interactively, while Livnat et al. (2005) suggest a novel paradigm for visual correlation of network alerts from disparate logs, that facilitates and promotes situational awareness in complex network environments. This approach is based on the notion that an alert must possess three attributes, namely, what, when, and where. Cai and de M. Franco (2009) exploit both interaction and visualization to reveal real-time network anomalous events. Glyphs are defined with multiple network attributes and clustered with a recursive optimization algorithm for dimensional reduction. The user's visual latency time is incorporated into the recursive process so that it updates the display and the optimization model according to a human-based delay factor.

Despite the extensive number of examples of the application of visualization to anomaly detection in network security, few examples exist outside this domain. An exception is the work presented in Iwata and Saito (2004), where a new anomaly detection method that visualizes data in 2- or 3-dimensional space based on the probabilities of belonging to each component of the model and the probability of not belonging to any component, anomaly, is proposed. For evaluation purposes, the method is applied to an artificial time series.

ANOMALY DETECTION METHODS FOR MARITIME TRAFFIC

It is hard to clarify what exactly anomaly detection means. Anomaly is a many-sided concept and it is normally associated with terms like abnormal, unusual, irregular, rare, deviation, strange, illegal, threat, atypical, inconsistent, etc. Many data mining techniques analyze data in order to find behavioral anomalies. Behavioral anomalies are defined as deviations from the normal behavior. Here, an anomaly is defined from a user (operator or organization) point of view, as events or situations that need to be detected and identified (see Riveiro et al. [2009] for a detailed discussion). A classification and examples of sea traffic anomalies from operators and practitioners point of view is provided in Roy (2008).

Most of the published work regarding anomaly detection, as previously shown, relates to intrusion detection applications for network traffic. Algorithms used in the detection of intrusions/attacks are traditionally classified in three main groups (Patcha & Park, 2007): anomaly (referring only to data-driven approaches), signature or hybrid. Systems based on anomaly detection schemes (data-driven approaches) look for abnormalities in the traffic, assuming that something that is abnormal is probably suspicious. Such detectors are based on what constitutes normal behavior and what percentage of the activity we want or are allowed/willing to flag as abnormal. Signature-based approaches look for predefined patterns in the data. Hybrid approaches combine data and knowledge driven approaches.

In the civil security domain, anomaly detection is not as mature as it is the network security arena. To the best of our knowledge, anomaly detection and behavioral analysis approaches applied to sea surveillance have not been covered in previously published anomaly detection reviews and, in particular, no review includes any analysis regarding human factors.

This section presents a review of anomaly detection approaches for sea surveillance. The objective is to analyze where human involvement is needed and how visualization and interaction might facilitate anomaly detection. The classification and description of each method includes information regarding: (1) detection method (data or knowledge driven), (2) nature of data analyzed, and (3) usage frequency (real-time continuous monitoring or periodic analysis). Moreover, for each method, we provide a brief description of its fundamentals and analyze the following aspects (if they apply): (1) input parameters, (2) normal model and rule set, (3) a description of the detection process, (4) output, and (5) explanation of the detections.

Data-Driven Anomaly Detection

In this category, approaches used within maritime anomaly detection can be classified as statistical (parametric and non-parametric) and machine learning based (e.g. Bayesian networks, neural networks or clustering techniques).

Statistical Parametric

Kraiman et al. (2002) present an anomaly detector processor, which exploits multisensor tracking and surveillance data to identify interesting events. The authors demonstrate the detector within a Vessel Traffic Service (VTS) environment, using input data regarding vessel type, speed, location, report time and heading, as well as environmental information such as tides, wind speed and direction (nonetheless, examples shown in the article are limited to position and speed values). The detection approach is a statistical parametric method, based on a combination of SOMs and Gaussian Mixture Models (GMM). The parameters of the

Gaussian distributions (mean and covariance matrices) can be estimated from the available training data using SOMs. Each node of the grid is characterized by an N-dimensional Gaussian probability function, where the means are given by the final values of the nodes and the variances are given by the dispersion of the training data around each node. Therefore, the baseline profile or normal model is a multidimensional likelihood function that it is used to estimate the probability value of a new observation. Over the likelihood, Bayes' rule is applied to calculate the probability value of obtaining such observation. In order to do so, the user must introduce the percentage of the training data that is anomalous (an important input parameter).

The detector based on this approach presents a Graphical User Interface (GUI) to facilitate operator interaction. Even if the functionality of the GUI is not described in Kraiman et al. (2002), the following input parameters can be determined: attributes used during the training phase, weight of the attributes, characteristics of the SOM (number of nodes and training radius), percentage of training data that is anomalous, threshold for reported anomalies and width of the temporal window for cumulative probability calculation. The output consists of a plot of cumulative probability of anomaly versus time and a characterization of the anomaly, explanation (showing in percent how the different attributes have contributed to the anomaly). Anomalous vessels are displayed in red over the geographical area. The detector was trained over one week of traffic data, but no information regarding the performance of the detector is given.

The method described in Laxhammar (2008) is similar to Kraiman et al.'s approach, but in this case the normal model representing vessel behavior is built using a combination of a greedy version of the Expectation-Maximization (EM) algorithm and GMM. Here, EM is used to estimate the parameters, mean and covariance, needed to combine the Gaussian distributions. Since the classical EM algorithm is very sensitive to initialization (it may converge to a local optimal solution different from the global) a greedy version is proposed. Instead of starting randomly, the greedy EM builds the optimal mixture model adding new components one at a time (support for such initialization and components weights are input parameters). Another input parameter is the maximum number of mixture components. The method is tested over real maritime traffic data from Swedish waters, where position, speed and course are considered. Latitude and longitude are discretized. One week of data was used for training and one week for validation (EM requires a validation set during training).

Statistical Non-Parametric

Ristic et al. (2008) present a statistical non-parametric analysis of vessel motion patterns, in ports and waterways, using Automatic Identification System (AIS) data. The detection is carried out using adaptive Kernel Density Estimation (KDE). The variables used are position (two dimensions) and velocity (two dimensions). The suggested solution assumes that the AIS data has been pre-processed and patterns have been extracted (these patterns constitute the baseline used during the detection process).

The normal model is, thus, a collection of motion patterns extracted from historical AIS data. The necessary input parameters (even if they are not specifically pointed out in the paper) are type of kernel ('normal' is usually the default value), smoothing parameter (bandwidth of the kernel-smoothing window) and threshold value. Threshold determines the probability value of an alarm, establishing the border between two hypotheses (normal, H0, or abnormal vessel behavior, H1). The output is the outcome of the classification (H0 or H1).

The existing publications concerning this method do not contain information regarding how to create the normal model or baseline. It is problematic to define motion patters, since there are multiple origins, destinations and connections paths in maritime traffic data. Moreover, non-parametric methods like KDE require large amounts of representative data of normal behavior, compared to traditional parameterized approaches.

Clustering and Outlier Detection

Vessel motion baseline profiles can also be built considering trajectories. Similar vessel trajectories are grouped thereby modeling regular traffic routes. Deviations from such routes are considered anomalous (Euclidean distances between clusters and trajectories may be used as metrics). An example application in the maritime domain is the work presented in Dahlbom and Niklasson (2007). The authors focus on the use of a trajectory clustering algorithm over maritime traffic in order to create normal sea lanes, not on the problem of detecting anomalies. Simulated radar readings of vessel traffic along the southern coast of Sweden are used in the experiments. The authors discuss the problems the clustering algorithm presents regarding matching incoming trajectories to clusters. The authors argue that prefix matching is not suitable for coastal surveillance and propose the use of splines.

Rhodes' research group (BAE Systems) has extensively studied the problem of learning normal vessel motion patterns (see Rhodes et al. (2005); Bomberger et al. (2006); Rhodes et al. (2007a)). The presented approaches are applied to harbor areas and both simulated and real AIS data are analyzed. Position (latitude and longitude) and velocity (course and speed) are considered. The discretization of both features (position and velocity) is necessary. The system takes real-time tracking information and uses continuous on-the-fly learning that enables concurrent recognition of patterns of current motion states. In Rhodes et al. (2005), the learning approach combines an unsupervised clustering algorithm (Fuzzy ARTMAP neural network) and a supervised mapping and labeling algorithm. Extensions of this approach can be found in Bomberger et al. (2006); Rhodes et al. (2007a). Even if the authors claim that operator intervention is not necessary, they agree that operators or analysts can help teaching the model via simple point and click actions, increasing the speed and performance of the learning phase.

Bayesian Inference

A Bayesian Network (BN) is a graphical model that encodes probabilistic relationships among variables of interest (Patcha & Park, 2007). The graphical model conveys information regarding causal relations and interdependencies between variables. A BN is a suitable approach to anomaly detection, since it can be used when there is a need to combine prior knowledge with data (Patcha & Park, 2007). Moreover, due to their transparency, human domain experts are able to validate and improve BNs.

An example of the application of BN to the maritime anomaly detection problem is provided in Johansson and Falkman (2007). Synthetic data is used during the experimental phase (simulated radar readings). The variables used are *x, y, heading, speed, Δheading, Δspeed and vesseltype*. The feature space is discretized. The BN represents the underlying probability distribution of the data, assuming that we can construct such representation. Based on the data, first the structure of the graph is built and then the conditional probabilities are estimated. Two important input parameters are, as in other approaches, the size of the window (number of most recent samples) that averages the probability value over time and the threshold used to flag an alarm (balance between the detection rate, recall, and the precision, false positives). The normal model is thus the BN built from data and the output is a joint probability value *P(x, y, heading, speed, Δspeed, Δheading, vesseltype)*. When anomalous behavior is detected using this approach, no further information or explanation is provided, meaning that no feature or group of features are suggested as rationale behind alarms.

Knowledge-Driven Anomaly Detection

The majority of the few anomaly detection capabilities implemented in real maritime control centers are rule (signature or misuse) based systems. Such systems allow operators to create simple rules that will trigger an alarm (e.g. IF <vessel in shallow waters> TEHN <danger of grounding>).

Initial steps to more elaborate anomalous situation detector, i.e. combinations of events over time is presented in Edlund et al. (2006). Based on an agent framework and using an ontology geared toward sea surveillance, the authors described a rule-based situation assessment system that analyzes situations developing over time. Rules are created by experts using the rule editor agent. In order to create new rules, experts select known objects from a list, choose their relation (approaching, leaving, inharborarea) and connect them in time. The ontology is based on a previously published core ontology for situation awareness. No user interaction with the ontology is supported. The rule editor GUI and the detector, reasoner agent, are under development.

Hybrid Approaches

Hybrid approaches to anomaly detection combine both data-driven and knowledge-based methods, overcoming some of the drawbacks of each particular method (high false alarm rate in the data-driven case and the possibility of detecting only known patterns in the knowledge-based case). An example of a compound approach to the maritime anomaly detection problem is the detector implemented in *SeeCoast* (Seibert et al., 2006). The detector applies rule-based and learning-based pattern recognition algorithms to alert illegal, threatening and anomalous vessel activities. SeeCoast extends the detection capability of the learning-based pattern module described

above (see Bomberger et al. (2006); Rhodes et al. (2007a,b)) using a rule-based track activity analysis. The rule-based component implements a three-stage approach to rule-building and matching: domain modeling, pattern definition and pattern matching. In the domain modeling stage, an ontology is built describing the data sources and the attributes of data reports (e.g., fused tracks as a data type, with velocity as a data field). In the pattern definition stage, operators use a GUI to create patterns based on the ontology (e.g. <any track whose location is within a restricted area>). A GUI allows operators to script patterns, walking the operator through a series of selections and questions that use information about the data environment to simplify the process. Operators can also create patterns from templates that only require specification of key inputs. In the pattern matching stage, operators select a set of patterns to be monitored for and the system then generates alerts for matching instances. A snapshot of the flagged vessel assists the operator deciding on further actions (offering thus, explanation capabilities).

SeeCoast is a complex and powerful port security and monitoring system that besides the anomalous detector module includes video processing to detect, classify and track vessels; multi-sensor track correlation of video track data with radar and AIS tracks; ship size classification, display enhancements for improved situational awareness and forensic analysis.

HOW DO EXPERTS MONITOR MARITIME TRAFFIC?

In maritime transportation, traffic control is carried out by both coastal and port Vessel Traffic Services (VTS), whose centers aim to improve vessel traffic safety and efficiency, safeguard human life at sea, as well as protect the maritime environment, adjacent shore areas, work sites, and offshore installations from the possible adverse effects of marine traffic. Three maritime control centers were visited during our field work. Such centers offer their services 365 days/year and 24 hours/day. The essential sources of data used for monitoring maritime traffic are radar data, Automatic Identification System (AIS) messages, VHF radio, Closed Circuit TV cameras (CCTV), harbor planning and administrative information, data bases with historical information about the vessels, telephone and fax, and meteo/hydro equipment (weather reports and marine currents information). The VTS operators interviewed have lengthy maritime and seagoing experience and receive education in accordance with the International Association of Marine Aids to Navigation and Lighthouse Authorities guidelines.

VTS operators use various surveillance systems. The systems are customized for each center and display real-time radar and AIS data (sometimes referred to as 'common operating maritime picture') that serve as a basis for carrying out main tasks such as monitoring and information services. The visualization and interaction capabilities of the systems used are quite limited. The main visualization consists of a geographical map where vessels are displayed using different icons and colors. Speed vectors and navigational information are displayed over the background map. Other graphical representations are not provided (no abstract representations, links between entities, or 3D visualizations are available). Selection and zooming in/out are provided as interaction methods. The systems used at the VTS centers allow some manual identification of anomalies. For example, the operators can make queries that show all the vessels exceeding a certain speed value or crossing a particular borderline. These functionalities, which may be considered anomaly detectors, are rarely used, since they must be carried out manually (operators stated that they are time consuming procedures) and do not cover many of the situations the operators are interested in detecting (see Figure 1).

Figure 1. VTS Gothenburg, Sweden The figures depict two working areas in the control room, illustrating environment, tools, and systems used

VTS operators need the timely identification of possible traffic-conflict situations emerging in the surveyed area, and respond appropriately. Examples of such situations are vessel collisions and groundings in the port and entrance areas. Moreover, personnel interviewed in these centers would appreciate support in detecting vessels navigating through restricted zones, vessels not following the established sea lanes, vessels not following the normal route with regard to the reported destination, cargo of special interest, vessels carrying dangerous gods sailing close to passenger ships or protected areas, vessels with a history of being involved in illegal activities, suspicious flag or port, fishing or recreational craft approaching traffic separation zones, etc.

Despite slight differences among the three visited centers, the actual process of finding anomalous behavior and conflict situations can be summarized in five stages: (1) overview (monitor and explore): continuous control of the traffic in real-time, using radar, VHF radio, and AIS information; (2) if something is unusual or unfamiliar (operators normally base their judgment on their experience), detailed information must be obtained, like zooming into the area and starting VHF radio communication with vessel of interest; (3) waiting time: operators usually wait a reasonable period of time, observing how the situation develops. At this stage, operators might listen to VHF radio communications among vessels, to increase their understanding of the situation; (4) more detail (focus): if the situation has not become normal, they intensify the dialog with the vessel of interest or try to obtain more data using, for example, additional information stored in data bases; (5) taking action: if they believe that an incident has occurred, they take action, alerting other organizations and reporting the situation.

This basic pattern, or loop, describes the typical overall process. Operators move back and forth between these stages, for example, between stage

3 (waiting time) and 4 (more detail). The stages vary in length and some stages include several sub-loops.

USING VISUALIZATION AND INTERACTION IN ANOMALY DETECTION

Considering the insights gained during our visits to maritime control centers and the review presented in one of the previous sections, the anomaly detection process can be divided in: on-line and off-line processing (see Figure 2). On-line processing refers to the analysis in real-time of the incoming data, whereas the off-line processing refers to the establishment or normal models from (training) data and rules that are used during the on-line detection process. Both processes resemble typical data mining cycles and are, obviously, interconnected.

Figure 2. Using visualization and interaction to support user involvement in the anomaly detection process

We argue that visualization and interaction is key to improving anomaly detection performance in general, and in particular, visualization and interaction are key to perform an adequate analysis of the data, construct understandable normal models, update and validate such models and create useful and comprehensible output, that can not only generate suitable responses from operators but also improve the whole anomaly detection process. Figure 2 points where visualization and interaction could make a positive difference.

Data Visualization

Data visualization supports the understanding of the data and the interaction between the analyst/operator and the dataset during the preprocessing phase. There is a wide variety of techniques to visualize both low and multidimensional datasets (e.g. pixel-based techniques, scatter-plots, parallel coordinates, geometric projections and icon-based methods). Keim (2002) reviews and provides a classification of visualizations based on the data type to be visualized, the visualization technique and the interaction and distortion technique.

In order to select appropriate visualization techniques, it should be taken into account the spatial and temporal nature of the information in the maritime domain. An interesting example of the visualization of vessel tracks is the work presented in Willems et al. (2009). Analyzing AIS data, the authors present an overlay map that show where sea lanes, anchoring zones or slow moving vessels are located.

The visualization of the data may also support the analyst while cleaning, selecting and transforming the data. A common problematic phase that influences the detector performance in many of the anomaly detection methods reviewed (see Laxhammar (2008); Bomberger et al. (2006)) is the discretization and normalization of the feature space. Proper representations of the data regarding how the discretization affects the construction of the baseline behavior and how samples are distributed over the feature space are needed. Moreover, other aspects that should be considered in this case are, for example, how to represent inconsistencies in the data, uncertainty, quality, reliability, etc.

Parameter Visualization

Parameter visualization supports the interaction between the analyst/operator and the process of selecting, tuning and optimizing input values to the on-line and off-line processes involved. Parameter selection and tuning requires the exploration of several alternatives (Meneses & Grinstein, 2001) and it is a complex optimization problem.

Statistical anomaly detection methods require the selection and tuning of multiple parameters (e.g. learning rates, type of kernel function, smoothing values and number of Gaussian mixtures). The reviewed approaches do not make clear the correlation between domain features and parameter setting values, and parameters seem to be selected in a more or less ad hoc manner. One arduous task in all the reviewed anomaly detection methods is tuning the anomaly threshold. The threshold value balances the detection rate (recall) and the number of false positives or false alarms (precision). Another delicate matter is the selection of the sliding window size that averages probability/likelihood values that are compared to the threshold. If the window size is too small, the system will be sensitive to data or sensor error, while a too large value may hide anomalies.

Visualization and interaction can be used to understand the parameter selection and tuning optimization process for a particular dataset, providing comprehensible views of the impact that these steps have in the final detection stages. Unfortunately, the visualization of parameter selection and tuning processes has been mainly overlooked by the anomaly detection research community (an exception is the work presented in Meneses and Grinstein [2001]).

Model Visualization

Model visualization supports the comprehension and interaction with normal models and rules embedded in the system. Such visual representations may support the creation, validation and update phases. The analyst/operator may be able to compare models, communicate them to colleagues and evaluate if they match his/her understanding of the world.

The representation of normal models built from data has hardly received any attention by the research community. An exception is Rheingans and desJardins (2000), where the authors describe a set of visualization methods that help users to understand and analyze the behavior of learned models (the article focuses on classification tasks using BN).

Knowledge-based approaches normally use a set of rules that represent situations that are of interest to an analyst/operator (unlike data-driven approaches, these signatures represent the 'anomalous' behavior). Visual and interactive representations of rules provide a natural way of understand, create, validate, update and prune them. In opposition to the lack of proposals regarding visualizations of induced models, extensive work has been done on the representation of rules (most of the publications refer to signatures extracted from large data sets). For example, a framework for mining and analyzing large rule sets through visualization is presented in Bruzzese and Davino (2008). During our review on knowledge-based approaches, another important matter related to the creation of rules that may benefit from the use of visualization and interaction is the necessity of constructing proper ontologies that represent objects, concepts, events and relationships (see Seibert et al. (2006)).

Detection Visualization

Detection visualization supports the understanding of the whole process, from data to alarms.

This process is a continuous hypothesis generation and testing cycle that involves all the aspects previously seen. An example of the visualization of the detection process can be seen in Kraiman et al. (2002). The GUI shows data, probability values vs. time, alarms and explanations.

Outcome Visualization

Outcome visualization refers to the representation of triggered alarms. Visual representations of alarms should support their analysis, in order to find, for example, correlations among them. Monitoring generated alarms is normally a challenging activity. In our visits to maritime centers, operators have highlighted the necessity of keeping interactive lists of alarms (ordered by importance). Operator response to the generated alerts (acknowledgment/rejection) may be used as a teaching signal to the detector, refining thus, its performance.

Explanations

Jensen et al. (1995) claim that decision support systems should have features for explaining how they have come up with their recommendations in order to support the decision maker as well as increase his/her confidence in the system. The ability of explaining the reasoning behind an alarm is of great importance in order for an operator to fully accept the advice the system provides. Despite this fact, the amount of research devoted to this subject is relatively sparse and most of the reviewed work does not tackle this issue. One of the reasons is that it might be difficult to point out which features have triggered the alarm or it might be difficult to construct or communicate the evidence. For example, the outcome of data-driven statistical approaches is normally a probability value per observation that represents P(features considered). It might not be possible to point out which feature or features are the cause of the alarm. In this case, we need additional methods that investigate further the outcomes generated.

Limitations

A relevant aspect that we have not discussed during the analysis of the anomaly detection process is the different users and roles that might use the anomaly detection capability. The daily operator (that monitors on-line traffic) might not be able to create or update normal models or rules, due to time constraints, policies or lack of background knowledge. On the other hand, analysts may be able to maintain and configure the system regarding their off-line workings, selection and tuning of parameters, update models, thresholds, etc.

EXAMPLES

In this section we illustrate some of the aspects discussed in the previous section with examples from our own research within the maritime domain. The objective of this section is to demonstrate how visualization can enhance the anomaly detection process, focusing on some of the steps of the process presented above.

The first example illustrates how parameter and model visualization can support the selection of methods that match the problem. Figure 3 (inspired by the study presented in Laxhammar et al. (2009))

shows how two different anomaly detection approaches model two parallel vessel trajectories. The left peak is calculated using GMM and the right peak is calculated using KDE. The GMM peak is unimodal, hiding the separation between the parallel sea lanes while the bimodal KDE satisfactorily captures the separation between them. Hence, we may conclude that KDE method models more accurate the vessel trajectories analyzed.

The second example concerns model visualization. Figure 4 presents a visualization of normal vessel behavioral models built from real AIS data. In order to build such model, we have used a statistical method that combines SOM and GMM. The biggest challenge we have faced while trying to represent the normal model was the fact that we would need an eight-dimensional space to represent such probability density function (we use eight vessel features: position, speed, course over ground, heading, length, width and draught). We projected the probability function over a 2 dimensional map. High values of probability are represented in red, while blue represents lower probability values. These visualizations allow comprehension of normal vessel behavior built from data, supporting validation and improvement of such models.

The last example, Figure 5, shows how explanations can be visualized using trees. In this case, BNs are used to find anomalous vessels hidden in AIS data. In order to generate comprehensible

Figure 3. Two parallel vessel trajectories and their model estimations using GMM and KDE probability density functions. A full comparison between these two methods can be read in Laxhammar et al. (2009)

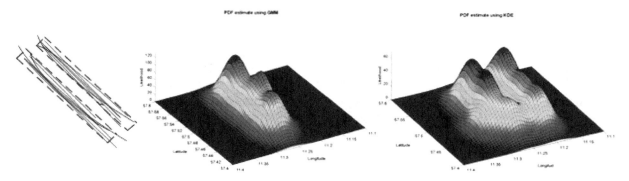

Figure 4. Visualizations of normal behavioral models for cargo (left), tanker (middle) and passenger (right) vessels. The models are calculated using a combination of SOMs and GMMs from real AIS data along the Swedish west coast. The following features are considered: position, speed, course over ground, heading, length, width and draught. The probability values are projected over a geographical map (Google Earth).

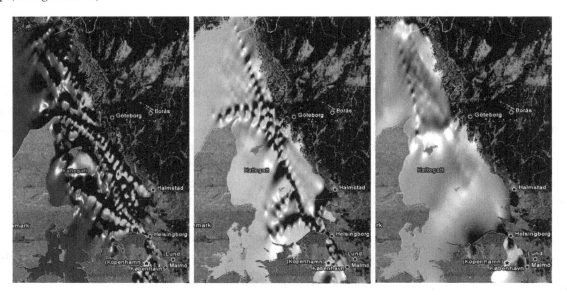

Figure 5. Explanation visualization: A Conditional Explanation Tree (CET) explains the inference made by a BN

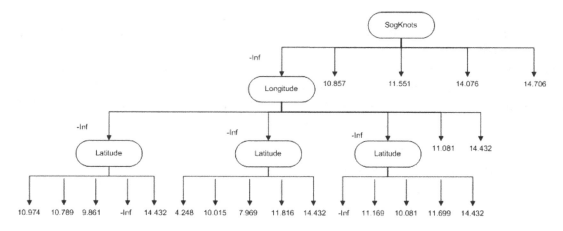

explanations from BNs outcomes, we have tested two algorithms, Explanation Tree and Causal Explanation Tree. The tree in Figure 5 shows which of the features are selected as best causes of anomaly when the BN pointed a vessel as suspicious (in this particular case, the abnormal- ity hidden is a vessel speeding in a slow moving area). More details on the application of these algorithms can be found in Helldin and Riveiro (2009).

CONCLUSION

Current anomaly detection capabilities and tools provide very limited possibilities to incorporate any expert knowledge or any user input at all. In our opinion, designers and developers underestimate the benefits of human involvement in the anomaly detection process. The necessity of such involvement can be seen from two perspectives. Firstly, anomaly detection systems for sea surveillance are not used autonomously in the real world. We need to provide adequate support for human decision makers, making transparent and trustworthy the anomaly detection process. Secondly, since the anomaly detection problem is hard to solve in an automatic manner (it normally generates high number of false alarms due to its complexity), we need to include expert knowledge in the loop in order to improve detector's performance.

Based on a review of anomaly detection methods applied to maritime traffic data, this chapter examines the anomaly detection process, highlighting where visualization and interaction can be used to support human involvement, thus, enhancing the process. The analysis presented here may inform the design of future anomaly detection systems when fully automatic approaches are not viable and human participation is needed. We would like to facilitate the design of interfaces that support human involvement and are properly integrated in the overall KDD process. The feedback that analyst/operator can provide to these processes can hardly be obtained by other means.

REFERENCES

Axelsson, S. (2005). *Understanding Intrusion Detection Through Visualization*. (Ph.D. thesis). Goteborg, Sweden: Chalmers University of Technology.

Bomberger, N., Rhodes, B., Seibert, M., & Waxman, A. (2006). Associative learning of vessel motion patterns for maritime situation awareness. In *Proceedings of 9th International Conference on Information Fusion*. New Brunswick, NJ: IEEE Press.

Bruzzese, D., & Davino, C. (2008). Visual mining of association rules. In *Visual Data Mining* (103–122). Berlin: Springer-Verlag. doi:10.1007/978-3-540-71080-6_8.

Cai, Y. & de M. Franco, R. (2009). Interactive visualization of network anomalous events. In: *Computational Science, 5544*, 450–459. Berlin: Springer.

Dahlbom, A., & Niklasson, L. (2007). Trajectory clustering for coastal surveillance. In *Proceedings of the 10th International Conference on Information Fusion*. QC, Canada: IEEE Press.

Demšar, U. 2006. *Data Mining of Geospatial Data: Combining Visual and Automatic Methods*. (Ph.D. thesis). Stockholm, Royal Institute of Technology (KTH).

Edlund, J., Gronkvist, M., Lingvall, A., & Sviestins, E. (2006). Rule-based situation assessment for sea surveillance. In *Proceedings of SPIE Conference on Multisensor, Multisource Information Fusion: Architectures, Algorithms and Applications, 624,* 1–11. Bellingham, WA: SPIE Press.

Fayyad, U., Grinstein, G., & Wierse, A. (Eds.). (2002). *Information visualization in data mining and knowledge discovery*. San Francisco: Morgan Kaufmann Publishers Inc..

Hand, D. J., Mannila, H., & Smyth, P. (2001). *Principles of data mining. Adaptive computation and machine learning*. Cambridge, MA: The MIT Press.

Harrison-John, G. (1997). *Enhancements to the Data Mining Process*. (Ph.D. thesis). Stanford, CA, Stanford University.

Helldin, T., & Riveiro, M. (2009). Explanation methods for bayesian networks: review and application to a maritime scenario. In: *3rd Annual Skövde Workshop on Information Fusion Topic,* 11–16. New Brunswick, NJ: IEEE Press.

Iwata, T., & Saito, K. (2004). Visualization of anomaly using mixture model. In *Knowledge-Based Intelligent Information and Engineering System,* 624–631. Berlin: Springer. doi:10.1007/978-3-540-30133-2_82.

Jensen, F., Aldenryd, S., & Jensen, K. (1995). Sensitivity analysis in bayesian networks. In *Symbolic and Quantitative Approaches to Reasoning and Uncertainty,* 243–250. Berlin: Springer. doi:10.1007/3-540-60112-0_28.

Johansson, F., & Falkman, G. (2007). Detection of vessel anomalies–A bayesian network approach. In *Proceedings of the 3rd International Conference on Intelligent Sensors, Sensor Networks, and Information Processing.* New Brunswick, NJ: IEEE Press.

Keim, D. (2002). Information visualization and visual data mining. *IEEE Transactions on Visualization and Computer Graphics, 7*(1), 1–8. doi:10.1109/2945.981847.

Keim, D. A., Mansmann, F., & Thomas, J. (2009). Visual analytics: How much visualization and how much analytics. *SIGKDD Explorations, 11*(2).

Kerren, A., Stasko, J., Fekete, J.-D., & North, C. (2007). Workshop report: Information visualization–human-centered issues in visual representation, interaction, and evaluation. *Information Visualization, 6,* 189–196.

Kharchenko, V., & Vasylyev, V. (2002). Application of the intellectual decision making system for vessel traffic control. In *Proceedings of 14th International Conference on Microwaves, Radar, and Wireless Communications, 2,* 639–642. New Brunswick, NJ: IEEE Press.

Kraiman, J. B., Arouh, S. L., & Webb, M. L. (2002). Automated anomaly detection processor. In Sisti & Trevisani (Eds.), *Proceedings of SPIE: Enabling Technologies for Simulation Science VI* (128–137). Bellingham, WA: SPIE Press.

Laxhammar, R. (2008). Anomaly detection for sea surveillance. In *Proceedings of the 11th International Conference on Information Fusion,* 47–54. Cologne, Germany: IEEE Press.

Laxhammar, R., Falkman, G., & Sviestins, E. (2009). Anomaly detection in sea traffic-A comparison of the gaussian mixture model and the kernel density estimator. In *Proceedings of the 12th International Conference on Information Fusion,* 756–763. New Brunswick, NJ: IEEE Press.

Livnat, Y., Agutter, J., Moon, S., Erbacher, R. F., & Foresti, S. (2005). A visual paradigm for network intrusion detection. In *Proceedings of the 2005 IEEE Workshop on Information Assurance and Security,* 92–99. New Brunswick, NJ: IEEE Press.

Mansmann, F. (2008). *Visual Analysis of Network Traffic: Interactive Monitoring, Detection, and Interpretation of Security Threats.* (Ph.D. thesis). Konstanz, Germany, Universität Konstanz.

Meneses, C. J., & Grinstein, G. G. (2001). Visualization for enhancing the data mining process. [Bellingham, WA: SPIE Press.]. *Proceedings of the Society for Photo-Instrumentation Engineers, 4384,* 126–137. doi:10.1117/12.421066.

Muelder, C., Ma, K.-L., & Bartoletti, T. (2005). Interactive visualization for network and port scan detection. In *Proceedings of 2005 Recent Advances in Intrusion Detection,* 1–20. New Brunswick, NJ: IEEE Press.

Onut, I. V., Zhu, B., & Ghorbani, A. A. (2004). A novel visualization technique for network anomaly detection. In *Proceedings of the 2nd Annual Conference on Privacy, Security, and Trust,* 167–174. New York: ACM Press.

Patcha, A., & Park, J.-M. (2007). An overview of anomaly detection techniques: Existing solutions and latest technological trends. *Computer Networks*, *51*(12), 3448–3470. doi:10.1016/j.comnet.2007.02.001.

Rheingans, P., & desJardins, M. (2000). Visualizing high-dimensional predictive model quality. [New Brunswick, NJ: IEEE Press.]. *Proceedings of IEEE Visualization*, *2000*, 493–496.

Rhodes, B., Bomberger, N., Seibert, M., & Waxman, A. (2005). Maritime situation monitoring and awareness using learning mechanisms. *Military Communications Conference, 1,* 646–652. New Brunswick, NJ: IEEE Press.

Rhodes, B., Bomberger, N., & Zandipour, M. (2007a). Probabilistic associative learning of vessel motion patterns at multiple spatial scales for maritime situation awareness. In: *10ᵗʰ International Conference on Information Fusion*, 1–8.

Rhodes, B. J., Bomberger, N. A., Zandipour, M., Waxman, A. M., & Seibert, M. (2007b). Cognitively-inspired motion pattern learning & analysis algorithms for higher-level fusion and automated scene understanding. In *Military Communications Conference (MILCOM 2007)*, 1–6. New Brunswick, NJ: IEEE Press.

Ristic, B., Scala, B. L., Morelande, M., & Gordon, N. (2008). Statistical analysis of motion patterns in AIS data: Anomaly detection and motion prediction. In *Proceedings of 11ᵗʰ International Conference of Information Fusion*. New Brunswick, NJ: IEEE Press.

Riveiro, M., Falkman, G., & Ziemke, T. (2008). Improving maritime anomaly detection and situation awareness through interactive visualization. In *Proceedings of 11th International Conference on Information Fusion*, 47–54. New Brunswick, NJ: IEEE Press.

Riveiro, M., Falkman, G., Ziemke, T., & Kronhamn, T. (2009). Reasoning about anomalies: A study of the analytical process of detecting and identifying anomalous behavior in maritime traffic data. InTolone, , & Ribarsky, (Eds.), *SPIE Defense, Security, and Sensing. Visual Analytics for Homeland Defense and Security. Volume 7346.* Orlando, FL: SPIE Press.

Roy, J. (2008). Anomaly detection in the maritime domain. In *Proceedings of SPIE, Volume 6945, 69450W* 1–14. Bellingham, WA: SPIE Press.

Seibert, M., Rhodes, B. J., Bomberger, N. A., Beane, P. O., Sroka, J. J., et al., & Tillson, R. (2006). SeeCoast port surveillance. In *Proceedings of SPIE, Volume 6204: Photonics for Port and Harbor Security II.* Orlando, FL: SPIE Press.

Shearer, C. (2000). The CRISP-DM model: The new blueprint for data mining. *Journal of Data Warehousing*, *5*(4), 13–22.

Teoh, S. T., Zhang, K., Tseng, S., Ma, K., & Wu, S. F. (2004). Combining visual and automated data mining for near-realtime anomaly detection and analysis in BGP. In *Proceedings of the 2004 ACM Workshop on Visualization and Data Mining for Computer Security*, 35–44. New York: ACM Press.

Thomas, J., & Cook, K. (Eds.). (2005). *Illuminating the Path: The Research and Development Agenda for Visual Analytics.* Los Alametos, CA: IEEE Computer Society.

Willems, N., Wetering, H. V. D., & Wijk, J. J. V. (2009). Visualization of vessel movements. *Computer Graphics Forum*, *28*(3), 959–966. doi:10.1111/j.1467-8659.2009.01440.x.

KEY TERMS AND DEFINITIONS

Anomaly Detection: Process of discovering anomalies in a data set. Such process normally compares the data of interest with a simplified description or model of the normality in order to find mismatches.

Anomaly: In this chapter an anomaly is defined from a user (operator or organization) point of view, as exceptional objects, events or situations that need to be detected and identified. We define the term anomalous as a property, meaning "not conforming to what might be expected because of the class or type to which it belongs or the laws that govern its existence, in a given situation or context".

Behavioral Anomaly: An anomaly that implies a deviation from the normal behavior.

Predictive Data Mining: Class or type of data mining processes used to predict some response of interest. Predictive data mining is employed to identify a model or a set of models from the data that can be used to predict, for example, the value of a particular attribute (Demšar, 2006). Statistical analysis, classification, and decision trees techniques are used to produce such outcomes. Predictive data mining techniques are used for anomaly detection.

Visual Analytics: Analytical reasoning supported by highly interactive visual interfaces (Thomas and Cook, 2005). Visual analytics strives to facilitate the analytical reasoning process by creating software that maximizes the human capacity to perceive, understand, and reason about complex, dynamic data and situations.

Chapter 8
Understanding Collections and Their Implicit Structures through Information Visualization

J. Alfredo Sánchez
Universidad de las Américas Puebla, Mexico

ABSTRACT

This chapter discusses how various approaches to information visualization can be used to assist users in understanding large digital collections and discovering relationships among the entities involved explicitly or implicitly in their development including people, organizations, and documents. Our main postulate is that visualization schemes, such as fisheye views, starfield displays, or self-organizing maps, when integrated and coupled with semantic layouts of topic areas, can significantly facilitate the analysis and discovery of existing and potential relationships among a wide range of entities. A series of developments illustrates how users play a key role in determining advantages and limitations of information visualization schemes, as well as in finding opportunities for improvement and new application areas.

INTRODUCTION

Myriad relationships exist among people, objects, and practically among any entities or concepts. Many new connections are being created every instant and are somehow represented in the digital realm. Thus, for example, contact lists are being extended in social networks, hyperlinks are being created between web pages, and documents are being written that cite various sources. These are examples of explicit relationships that are forged by users or authors. Also, there are a very large number of relationships that may not be evident, and that only exist by virtue of the characteristics of entities, their activities, location or other attributes. Thus, for instance, friends of friends in a

DOI: 10.4018/978-1-4666-4309-3.ch008

social network are indirectly related, users from the same geographical area could be grouped together, papers on the same topic or written by authors from the same institutions or countries can also be considered to be connected in some implicit way.

In order to deal with the volume, complexity and dynamism of this expanding information universe, it has become crucial for people to understand how large collections of digital entities are organized and how their elements are inter-related. Relationships determine structures that can be of interest for various users or perspectives. For example, books grouped according to their publisher may be of interest for booksellers and for librarians, but not necessarily for library patrons, who may be interested in hierarchical, general-to-specific views of the books' subjects. Similarly, roads that connect towns on a map and their travel times may be of interest for tourists, but manufacturers planning product distribution or government officials making budgetary or tax decisions may be more interested in various demographic layers and groupings of the same geographical locations.

Information visualization schemes play a key role in providing graphical representations of large collections and of the relationships among their elements. These visualization schemes, coupled with appropriate control mechanisms for parameters such as scale, attributes on display, or evolution over time, have an enormous potential to become user interfaces that will help users understand not only the attributes of large number of digital objects and their explicit inter-relationships, but also the implicit structures that result from considering multiple perspectives and implicit relationships. In this chapter, we focus on such information visualization schemes. In particular, we discuss the design and applications of user interfaces we have developed for supporting user activities that rely on the analysis and comprehension of very large data sets.

The main emphasis of the chapter is on the potential of three existing techniques for information visualization, namely *starfield displays*, *fisheye views,* and *self-organizing maps*, to help users in detecting and understanding relationships and structures among elements of large collections that are defined implicitly in terms of a number of relevant attributes. Though these techniques were originally devised or applied to the visualization of large collections and explicit relationships, we have worked on adaptations and applications for visualizing implicit relationships and structures.

The chapter is organized as follows: The following section introduces basic concepts and summarizes related work in areas such as applications and advances in starfield visualizations, fisheye views and graphical representation of ontologies, digital repositories, and collaboration networks. The next section discusses our work that focuses on the visualization of digital collections, our experiences with actual users, and the evolution from the use of basic starfields to their enhancement with the introduction of fisheye views. This will provide the basis for the core section on our current work, which integrates starfield visualizations, fisheye views, and lightweight ontologies, as well as its applications to visualizing collaboration networks. Observations from actual use of this integrated visualization scheme are presented and discussed. We then discuss the broader implications of our approach and our findings, and close the chapter by providing conclusions that can be derived from our work.

BACKGROUND

In this section we provide some basic definitions of the concepts involved in the chapter and we also review related work. We first refer to one of the structures we aim to visualize, namely collaboration networks. We also provide some background on ontologies, a notion we have used to classify and organize items to be visualized. Then we describe three major visualization mechanisms we have relied on for supporting collection understanding: starfields, fisheye views and self-organizing maps. Finally, we provide an overview of recent work being conducted in the area of visualization of abstractions and large document collections.

Structures

Collaboration networks are structures that represent interconnected groups of people who work together at various coupling levels. In academic settings, some collaboration networks can easily be determined from the lists of authors of publications held by a digital collection. Other, more implicit structures, on the other hand, can be hidden and can only be suggested as potential networks among authors of documents by inferring relationships from their metadata. Relationships in collaboration networks may vary in strength, as they may result from direct, evident connections (such as co-authorship) or from indirect ties determined, for example, by semantic overlaps in the subjects of their documents in a collection.

In the context of information systems, the literature presents varying definitions of *ontologies*. One that is generally accepted establishes that an ontology is an explicit specification of a conceptualization (Gruber, 1993). This definition has been extended by suggesting that the conceptualization must be shared (Borst, 1997). Lightweight and heavyweight ontologies are distinguished according to the degree of formality involved in their encoding (Lassila & McGuinness, 2001). Both for grouping items and for representing them in visualization interfaces, we have limited our work to the use of lightweight ontologies. These range from enumerations of terms to graphs or taxonomies of concepts with well-defined relationships among them, which provide a representation of an information space. The term lightweight indicates that the construction of ontologies does not involve

domain experts. It also refers to tree-like structures where each node label is a language-independent propositional formula (Giunchiglia, Marchese, & Zaihrayeu, 2007).

Base Visualization Mechanisms

Though our initial explorations in the realm of information visualization focused on the advantages of three-dimensional representations (Amavizca, Sánchez, & Abascal, 1999; Proal, Sánchez, & Fernández, 2000), we soon adopted an approach that relies on simplified two-dimensional graphics that are enhanced by direct manipulation components. This combination of interface elements ensures control by the user to delimit information areas, filter needed or unwanted entities based on their attributes, and select specific information units.

One key representation we introduced in our research is that of a *starfield* (Ahlberg & Shneiderman, 1994) A starfield is a grid-based visualization method that highlights the intersections of two axes on a plane. Each axis typically is used to represent an attribute of the objects being displayed. Thus, for example, we can use the horizontal axis to refer to the subjects of publications held by digital collections, use the vertical axis to refer to authors of publications, and highlight their intersection if there is at least one publication on a given subject written by a given author.

As we experimented with starfield visualizations, initially of metadata associated with large physical collections (Silva, Sanchez, Proal, & Rebollar, 2003), we have been able to observe how users benefit from their potential, but also to obtain first-hand evidence of their shortcomings (Sánchez, Twidale, Nichols, & Silva, 2005). Keeping users oriented as they visualize starfield-based representations has been one of the challenges we decided to address in subsequent research. Thus, as we moved from visualizing physical, centralized collections to vast digital, distributed repositories, we also set out to investigate how fisheye views (Furnas, 1986, 1999, 2006) could be coupled with starfields to provide users with a focus-plus-context mechanism to prevent disorientation.

Fisheye views are the basis for a technique that allows users to explore in detail an area of interest while maintaining its context. The name refers to the distortion effect created around non-important elements while those that are important are magnified. Our research shows that coupling starfields with fisheye views represents an important evolution of basic starfields (Sánchez, Quintana, & Razo, 2007). By observing users, we also found that examining sub-areas of a starfield visualization did not always result in meaningful partitions, as most of our data orderings had been chronological or alphabetical. Clearly, more semantical groupings of attributes on both axes of the starfield were needed.

We have found that one technique that naturally exposes implicit relationships is that of Self-Organizing Maps (SOM). A Self-Organizing Map (SOM), or Kohonen map, is a neural network that competes by means of mutual lateral interaction (Kohonen, 1990). A SOM consist of neurons organized in a low-dimensional grid (typically two dimensions). Each neuron is represented by an n-dimensional weight vector (also known as prototype vector, codebook vector). The main difference between a self-organized network and a conventional one is that correct output cannot be defined *a priori*, therefore a SOM utilizes an unsupervised learning algorithm. A SOM consists of two neuron layers: the input layer (input vector) and the output layer (lattice). The algorithm used in a SOM classifies entities in collections (thesis, papers, etc.) by using their attributes or metadata (input vector for each document), and updates a map (lattice of neurons) so that each neuron represents a set of similar documents based on their characteristics. SOM-based visualization has become an important technique for our ongoing work in the area of collection understanding, a concept discussed in the following section.

Related Work

Proposals for visualizing complex networks have taken various forms (Herman, Melancon, & Marshall, 2000), the most popular of which have been based on the notion of nodes that are linked by edges. Node-link visualizations have been used in many different contexts. There are even US patent applications for registering implemented methods for handling node-link representations, such as the system proposed by (Yakowenko & Matange, 2004) for displaying nodes wherein the nodes have a hierarchical context. Positional information associated with multiple nodes is used to generate a display for the nodes in response to a change in focal position. The generated node display maintains hierarchical contextual information about the nodes.

Similarly, visualization schemes are being used to study the structure of social networks. A social network is a collection of people, each of whom is acquainted with some subset of the others (Barabasi, 2010). Research on this particular structure has been supported by graph-oriented techniques (Yang, Asur, Parthasarathy, & Mehta, 2008) and analysis tools (Smith et al., 2009). However, tools that combine exploration, statistics and visualization techniques have not been proposed. SocialAction (Perer & Shneiderman, 2008) is a tool designed for finding relationships among people by using data sets, and for analyzing the structure of the resulting graph. Based on a similar approach, a system called CrimeNet Explorer (Xu & Chen, 2005) supports police agencies in the exploration of criminal networks and in understanding their complex structure by using a graph representation.

A user interface for visualizing collaboration networks must be able to represent entities, relationships, item groupings and their instances, collaboration groups and various properties of these groups. Ontological representations offer helpful means for organizing relationships and suggesting potential collaboration networks.

However, visualization of ontologies is not an easy task due mainly to volume, complexity and diversity of representation mechanisms. There have been many approaches for tackling this problem. Katifori, Halatsis, Lepouras, Vassilakis, and Giannopoulou (2007) report a very thorough survey of existing ontology visualization methods.

In order to create a visualization method adapted to the detection and visualization of potential collaboration networks to work on specific areas, we surveyed the area and characterized existing methods. Reported works were selected considering some of the criteria established by the classic framework for categorizing visualization methods (Shneiderman, 1996).We included the task topology (overview, zoom, filter, details-on-demand, viewing relationships, history) and other characteristics such as meta-data, 2D or 3D visualization, grouping (on a criteria or using an ontology) and context. Those tasks were used as evaluation dimensions applied to the context of collaboration networks visualization. Details of our survey can be found in (Ramos, Sánchez, & Hernández-Bolaños, 2010).

We observed that most existing approaches make it possible for the user to obtain a general overview of a data set and to view relationships among items, at least within a close perimeter. Other popular functions include the ability to zoom in and out of selected areas, as well as to obtain details of required items. We found it interesting that 2D visualizations remain popular. Even though some 3D representations have been attempted (as in [Yang, Asur, Parthasarathy, & Mehta, 2008]), the simplicity of 2D, both for the user and the developer, has generally outperformed the complexity that 3D brings about. Only few methods allow users to filter items dynamically or to group them semantically. Even fewer offer functionality either to maintain the context while exploring specific areas or to provide access to previously viewed scenarios.

Maintaining context is particularly important when visualizing collaboration networks, hence our decision to focus on features that make this possible. Also, grouping techniques, overview and zoom functionality, as well as context preservation and displaying relationships between entities were considered key features for a model oriented to the discovery and exploration of collaboration networks.

Information visualization has a great potential for assisting users understand what large collections of objects are about. *Collection understanding* has been suggested as an alternative to Information Retrieval (IR), which focuses on finding specific objects in collections by providing "terms," commonly thought of as values of metadata fields. Collection understanding promotes an exploratory approach by providing users with a general sense of collections (Chang et al., 2004). In order to accomplish this goal, collection understanding relies on visualization and filtering mechanisms. This notion has motivated work that produces collages from collections of images (Cunningham & Bennett, 2008; Chang et al., 2004), or uses tags and filters (Girgensohn, Shipman, Turner, & Wilcox, 2010) or explores the use of map-based visualizations (Buchel, 2011). We currently are working on producing visual representations of large, distributed collections based on hierarchical clusters that are produced by applying the notion of self-organizing maps.

DISCOVERING IMPLICIT STRUCTURES FOR UNDERSTANDING COLLECTIONS

Many digital collections are held in institutional repositories and digital libraries that make their contents available through metadata servers. In order to provide access to those collections, applications are needed that collect those metadata in response to specific queries from users. This is performed by a process referred to as harvesting, which contacts various collections and produces a unified view of metadata. If individual collections can be difficult to comprehend by the user, composite collections that result from metadata harvesting may be even more difficult to handle conceptually by users of all types. Visualization mechanisms can be of significant help for providing perspective and interfaces for exploring large and complex collections. However, making metadata available for generating meaningful and useful visual representations is not trivial, as discussed next.

From Disperse Collections to Visualizing Meaningful Structures

In order for data from multiple collections to be available for visualization, several stages need to be completed. These stages should allow objects in diverse collections to be organized, their hidden relationships to be revealed and their implicit structured to be discovered. We propose four general stages for this process: Harvesting, normalization, inference and visualization, as illustrated in Figure 1:

- **Harvesting:** Standard protocols for harvesting and uniform metadata descriptions are necessary for facilitating the process of gathering data from heterogeneous sourc-

es. We have focused most of our efforts to utilizing collections that comply with the Protocol for Metadata Harvesting of the Open Archives Initiative (OAI-PMH version 2.0). OAI-PMH requires that data providers comply at least with the Dublin Core (DC) metadata standard. Prior to looking for implicit relationships in data, we harvest metadata that is exposed by distributed collections and we build an intermediate virtual repository with relevant metadata.

- **Normalization:** Though digital libraries do represent valuable information, data coming from heterogeneous sources needs to undergo significant pre-processing so mining or inference can be performed with some level of effectiveness. Since OAI collections adhere to the Dublin Core (DC) metadata standard, uniformity is expected at least for naming attributes. However, DC is quite flexible and the usage of its elements typically differs from collection to collection. Even within the same collection, uniformity for key attributes such as author or institution names cannot be taken for granted. Thus, a normalization process examines metadata that results from the preceding harvesting stage and produces a version of the intermediate repository that contains uniform metadata.

Figure 1. Stages from metadata collecting to visualization

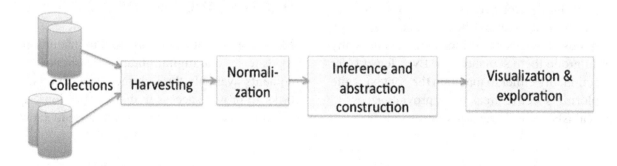

- **Inference:** In this stage, normalized metadata is processed so as to produce representations that can be visualized meaningfully. For example, lightweight ontologies can be constructed to represent the classification of the topics and subtopics found in the collections, neural networks may be used to generate thematic clusters, and hierarchies can be generated that represent the affiliation of authors to their institutions and the countries to which each institution belongs. More importantly for collaboration networks, a representation can be produced for the potential relationships among authors of publications as determined from the collections harvested to assemble an intermediate repository.

- **Visualization:** Finally, graphical representations of the inferred data are produced and made accessible to users so they can visually detect potential relationships and explore the suggested collaboration networks, clusters or other groupings.

Exposing implicit structures and relationships is the result of both the inference and visualization stages. Much of what can be inferred regarding hidden structures can only be perceived by the user if appropriate visualization mechanisms are available. But user interface controls for adjusting and filtering what is being displayed can significantly enhance the potential of information visualization means for discovering additional relationships.

Harvesting has become a stable process particularly for OAI-compliant collections. Normalization efforts require significant human intervention both for reaching agreements on how metadata standards should be used and for adapting non-compliant legacy metadata to newly defined standards. Though these are important tasks, they are not discussed with more depth, as our emphasis in this chapter in on the use of visualization mechanisms. However, given the close connection between our visualization approaches (discussed in the following section) with inference mechanisms, we do discuss the latter with some additional detail.

Inference and Ontology Construction

We take advantage of our previous work on lightweight ontologies for organizing collections of objects so they fall into one of various levels of topics and subtopics. Particularly for OAI collections, we have adapted the *Frequent Itemset-based Hierarchical Clustering* (FIHC) algorithm (Fung, Wang, & Ester, 2003) as the basis for a semi-automatic method for constructing lightweight ontologies of metadata records. Since we have focused on the classification of metadata records, Dublin Core attributes play an important role in this process. In particular, we have used the title, description and subject for each document in the collections. We have applied our method to specific participating collections and the resulting lightweight ontologies have been used as one of the main inputs for our visualization technique. Details of the construction of lightweight ontologies, which are referred to as "ontologies of records", can be found in (Sánchez, Medina, Starostenko, Benitez, & Domínguez, 2012).

VISUALIZATION APPROACHES FOR COLLECTION UNDERSTANDING

We have progressed through various stages in our quest to face the challenge of facilitating access and user comprehension of large digital collections and their explicit or implicit underlying structures. Though our initial explorations focused on the advantages of three-dimensional representations, particularly for navigating through explicit taxonomic classifications (Amavizca, Sánchez, & Abascal, 1999; Proal, Sánchez, & Fernández, 2000), we soon adopted an approach that relied on simplified two-dimensional graphics enhanced by direct manipulation components. This combination of interface elements ensures control by the user to delimit information areas, to filter needed or unwanted entities based on their attributes, and to select specific information units.

Using Starfields for Discovering Patterns

One of our early efforts took advantage of the concepts and tools of Visual Information Seeking (VIS), in which the user is presented, in a two-dimensional depiction, with multi-dimensional overviews of information spaces. Various filters may be applied to this information space by manipulating graphical sliders to zoom in and out of areas of interest until relevant data elements are found (Ahlberg, Williamson, & Shneiderman, 1992; Ahlberg & Shneiderman, 1994). VIS has been considered a promising approach to address issues in the design of interfaces for large repositories and to deal with information overload. However, it had been demonstrated only with relatively small collections of a few thousand items, which

made it possible to keep entire collections in main memory and perform recalculations and rendering in real time as the user manipulated sliders and filters in an interactive fashion. Vast digital libraries, however, comprise collections that may include hundreds of thousands, millions or even more items. We developed EVA2D, a visualization environment that implemented and extended the notion of VIS to facilitate the exploration of large collections comprised by digital libraries. Its main interface components, as applied to a collection of over 192,000 library records, are illustrated in Figure 2.

As observed in the figure, EVA2D presents the now classic scatter plot used in starfields, and also adds functionality to modify the user's perspective by changing the main attributes on display. In the figure, book categories are plotted against their publishers, but the axes may alternatively refer to attributes such as publication year, author name, or place of publication. Interface controls included a magnifying glass (see top right) and filtering sliders (right panel) that allow users to

Figure 2. The EVA2D visualization interface

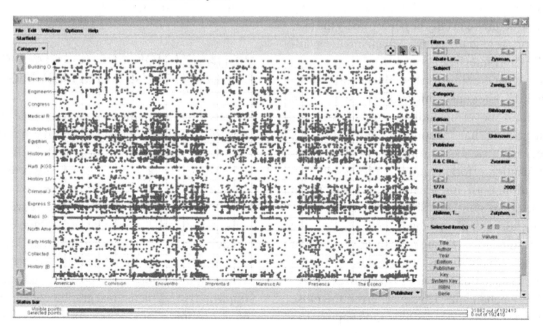

include or eliminate from the display value ranges for any of the collection's attributes. Details of items on display can be viewed on demand (bottom right corner) by clicking on their visual representations.

In order to deal with scale issues, EVA2D introduced four main features: (1) pre-computation of graphical data, which significantly reduced rendering time; (2) simultaneous bi-dimensional selection or direct zooming, which made it possible for users to visually select and work with subcollections; (3) precision filtering mechanisms, based on zoom bars (a variation of a scroll bar), which allows for refinement of the data in the starfield display according to values of additional attributes, and (4) quasi-immediate feedback, which implies that only the initial and final positions for zoom bars are recalculated and rendered. Implementation and experimental details regarding this work are reported in (Silva, Sánchez, Proal, & Rebollar, 2003).

For the purpose of exploring the ways in which EVA2D could support collection understanding, we conducted user studies that produced interesting results in terms of the interpretations given to the starfields. The evolution of collections over time or the abundance or scarcity of items in general subject areas were very easy to grasp for most users. But as users experimented with zooming and filtering functionality, they were able to spot patterns that helped them discover the emphases of collections. For example, some patterns made them conjecture whether a given collection supported specific curricula. More details on our experiments with EVA2D are reported in (Sánchez, Twidale, Nichols, & Silva, 2005).

Providing Help to Make the Most of Starfields

Also based on our user studies, shortcomings of our basic application of starfields became evident. Functionality suggested by users included visual cues to indicate various aspects of items

in the collections being visualized, more accurate filtering options, and improved responsiveness to prevent confusing action sequences with interface components. One problem we observed was the need for users to maintain the context as they zoomed into areas of their interest. They sometimes became disoriented and were not able to easily determine their location with respect to the entire collection. In the next stage of our development, we addressed these issues.

StarFish is a visualization interface that continues to use starfields as its base representation for collections, but also incorporates fisheye viewing functionality. When the user selects a region of the starfield, a magnifying effect is applied to that region, whereas the rest of the starfield is scaled down. In essence, the entire object collection is permanently available on the interface, but a sub-area is shown in detail and its elements can be selected and viewed with further detail. Switching to a different area can be easily accomplished by clicking on its scaled down representation. We developed an operational prototype for this interface on top of a number of heterogeneous collections that make up the Open Network of Digital Libraries (ONeDL, or RABiD, after its initials in Spanish, http://www.rabid.org.mx). Digital theses, journal papers and ancient books are the main document types provided by member institutions of RABiD. Descriptors for documents in these distributed collections are exposed through metadata servers and collected via the OAI-PMH protocol described earlier.

Figure 3 illustrates the main components of the StarFish visualization interface. Noticeably, small, colored icons are used to represent collection items. The shape of each icon indicates the type of document, whereas colors are associated with institutions that provided the documents. Filtering functionality (on top of the starfield in this figure) allows users to easily include or exclude documents of specific types or provided by a given institution. By clicking on one of the grid regions, users can magnify its contents, obtain metadata

Figure 3. The StarFish visualization interface

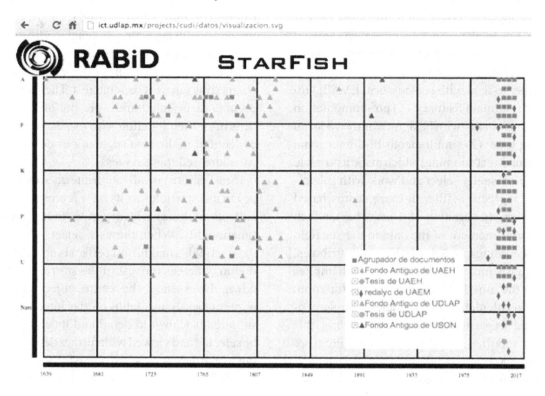

or even the actual documents, whereas the rest of the regions become smaller but remain available for selection. StarFish has been effective both for providing a uniform overview of heterogeneous collections and for facilitating exploration and close examination of documents that are related regardless of their provider. Further information on StarFish can be found in (Sánchez, Quintana, & Razo, 2007).

Discovering Relationships and Collaboration Networks

For the next stage in our search for means to assist users in understanding collections, we focused on the discovery of implicit relationships among collection items and, more specifically, relationships among authors of documents that may result in potential collaboration networks. Implicitly, digital collections can provide access

to knowledge regarding the contents and structure of their documents, as well as the communities of authors, institutions and users of all available information elements.

Finding collaboration networks can be helpful in many areas for at least three main reasons: (1) Researchers may be interested in learning about the global community that is producing scientific advances in their area; (2) Researchers need to find potential partners with similar or complementary interests so as to assemble multi-disciplinary, multi-institutional or multi-national teams required for funding opportunities; and (3) Funding agencies may want to become familiar with existing or potential collaboration networks so as to make sure calls for proposals will find appropriate audiences as well as to validate proposed research groups.

We have successfully applied the process illustrated in Figure 1 for harvesting collections and inferring relationships. In what follows, we discuss two approaches we have explored for visualizing and exploring such relationships so users are able to discover potential collaboration networks.

Egocentric Node-Link Visualizations

As noted earlier, node-link visualizations have been used frequently to represent relationships such as those occurring in social networks. Though generally very intuitive, node-link graphical representations do not scale well. For very large collections of documents, which are common in current settings, the number of relationships rapidly becomes unwieldy and a graphical representation of that complex web of nodes and links becomes impractical.

The feedback we received from user studies with low fidelity prototypes of node-link visualizations indicated this was the most natural representation for collaboration networks. Thus, we decided to tackle scale issues by presenting users with a so-called egocentric representation that shows, at its center, a person or institution for whom a collaboration network is needed, and on its periphery, people or institutions with various degrees of relatedness or collaboration potential. The collaboration potential between authors or institutions is estimated in terms of factors such as co-authorship and overlapping subjects of interest as derived from their publications and is part of the inference and abstraction construction process described earlier.

Even for a single author or institution, the number of potential collaborators can be unmanageably large. We thus have designed various graphical interface components that are used to easily filter out irrelevant relationships, as illustrated in Figure 4. First, the size and color of nodes are related to the strength of their relationship with the entity at the center of the display. Three sizes and colors are used according to thresholds defined experimentally for the estimated relatedness values. Colors can be selected by the user from palettes shown

on the top right area of the interface. Second, the thickness and colors of links or edges are also related to the strength of the estimated relatedness among potential collaborators of the author or institutions at the center of the display. Finally, sliders at the top can be used to filter potential collaborators depending on the strength of their relatedness with respect with the entity at the center or among themselves. Text fields on the top left corner of the interface allow users to search the specific entity that will be placed at the center of the visualization.

User studies in which this visualization has been used have produced encouraging results. We designed exploration tasks for researchers in various domain areas and they were able to delimit nodes and links rapidly and suggest potential relationships and collaboration networks that would not have been evident solely from accessing publications in the underlying collections. Detailed results from user studies have been reported in (Hernández-Bolaños, 2010).

Discovering Collaboration Networks on Starfields

Whereas node-link visualizations have some advantages, an important drawback for collection understanding is that they do not facilitate maintaining the context for the user to have access to a general, clear overview of the entire set of relationships at any given time. We decided to explore alternative interfaces for collaboration networks on our previous experience, particularly with EVA2D and StarFish. We considered that starfields should provide a compact graphical representation that would include all possible relationships. Also, StarFish was a useful evolution of basic starfields but still posed the need for more semantic grouping of attributes on both axes, as generally the horizontal axis presented chronologically ordered data, whereas the vertical axis presented attributes that were ordered alpha-

Figure 4. An egocentric node-link visualization of collaboration networks

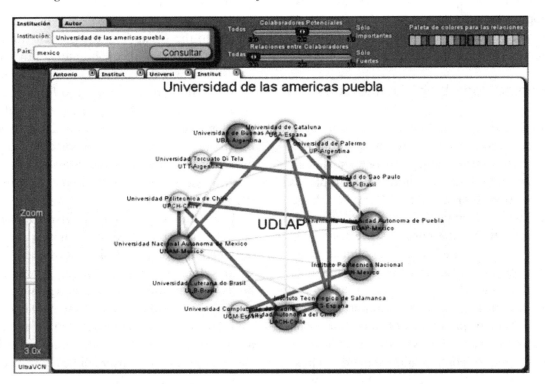

betically. Particularly in the latter case, selecting sub-areas did not result in meaningful partitions.

Our next development, which we termed *OntoStarFish*, results from two key changes to the StarFish base scheme: Adding semantics to starfield axes, and introducing fisheye views through multiple lenses that allow for examination of several regions of the starfield simultaneously.

Figure 5 provides a graphical explanation of the concepts involved in the design of OntoStarFish. In contrast with the original starfields, in which axes display linearly a set of possible values for an attribute, *ontological axes* in OntoStarFish are not flat with respect to semantic groupings of attribute values. Instead, we can display attribute values that may be expanded or collapsed at various levels of abstraction, as selected by the user, corresponding to specializations or generalizations represented by the lightweight ontologies derived from the collections.

With the introduction of what we refer to as ontological axes, it becomes possible to explore countries, institutions and researchers, and look at the relationships each of these elements may have with a general or particular research subject, all simultaneously on the same display. As shown in Figure 5, the horizontal axis is used to display an ontological arrangement of subjects, which are derived from collections, whereas the vertical axis is used to display the countries, institutions or names of the authors of the publications. In ontological terms, subjects on the X-axis participate in "is-a" relationships, whereas people and places on the Y-axis play a role in "belongs-to" relationships. In both cases, it is the user who should decide the level of detail to be displayed. A dot (or a *star*) on the starfield indicates there are documents in the underlying collections on a given subject (or sub-subject), which have been authored in a particular country, at a given institution or by a specific author.

Figure 5. OntoStarFish elements: Ontological axes and multiple fisheye lenses

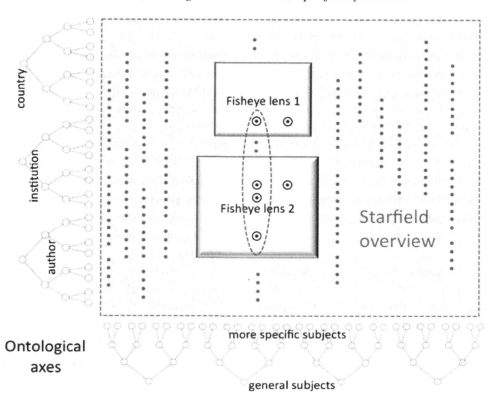

When using the OntoStarFish interface for exploring relationships, the levels of abstraction may vary even on the same axis. In a likely scenario, a user may need to visualize dots that refer to publications authored by specific researchers (author level) at, say, the University of Valparaíso (institution level) in Chile (country level) on a subtopic such as "Fisheries Science", which may be classified under the more general topic of "Marine Biology." The same user should be able to explore, on a different area of the interface, dots that also indicate publications about "Fisheries science" but authored, say, in Argentina (displaying only the country level). Yet another area of the interface may show whether Brazil (at the country level) has work published in the general subject of "Ecology". Users should be able to expand or collapse any section of the ontological axes depending on their interests, and the starfield should be updated accordingly.

One advantage of fisheye views is that they allow for the exploration of details in a starfield while keeping the user oriented in the overall view of the collections. After observing users who performed tasks with low fidelity prototypes, we realized that a single fisheye view would not be sufficient for a thorough exploration and detection of relationships. The new ontological structure suggests that various collaboration networks can be displayed simultaneously, but they may not be evident, as the large number of relationships can hide them. A single fisheye lens may draw attention to relationships in a particular area, but those that are not contiguous still would remain out of sight. As illustrated in Figure 5, we introduced multiple fisheye lenses the user can move around to display details of various regions of the starfield. When two fisheye lenses are positioned in a way that they overlap vertically (as shown in the figure), potential collaboration networks at any level (researchers, countries or institutions that work on related subjects) correspond to coinciding columns in multiple fisheye views. This is exemplified in Figure 5 by the dots within the dashed ellipse. When the lenses overlap horizontally, they can be regarded as referring to potential collaboration networks within the same country or institution (on different subjects). Users should also be able to adjust the size of fisheye lenses so as to dynamically delimit areas of interest. We elaborate on how collaboration networks can be detected next, as we describe a prototypical implementation of OntoStarFish and provide further details of its user interface.

In order to demonstrate how the concepts involved in the design of OntoStarFish, we have implemented an operational prototype, which also takes advantage of the distributed collections provided by the RABiD initiative mentioned earlier. In what follows, we describe the resulting visualization through the use of scenarios that illustrate how OntoStarFish can be used to reveal collaboration networks. We have applied inference methods to find implicit relationships in test collections that involve nearly 120,000 documents about a large number of subjects. Participant data providers include institutions based in six countries from Latin America and Spain.

Finding the Locations of Related Researchers

OntoStarFish can be used to explore existing relationships and determine the affiliation of researchers who work on given subjects. Consider the scenario depicted by Figure 3, in which three fisheye lenses are placed over the starfield. The reddish dots on top of the "Agriculture" label indicate that five out of the six countries listed on the vertical axis have some published work on that subject. When the cursor is placed the cursor over a dot at the intersection of a country and the general subject of "Agriculture", a legend appears next to the cursor indicating the number of researchers in that country (nine in this example) who are potential collaborators in that field.

Each of the graphical elements in OntoStarFish is clickable. When the user clicks on a dot within a lens a the level displayed on Figure 6, both the corresponding country and general subject are expanded, as illustrated in Figure 7. This same effect could have been accomplished by clicking separately on the corresponding axis labels. On the vertical axis, acronyms for all universities or institutions in the country are displayed, whereas on the horizontal axis sub-subjects, such as Agronomy and Aquaculture, are displayed. The starfield is

Figure 6. Visualization at the country and general subject levels

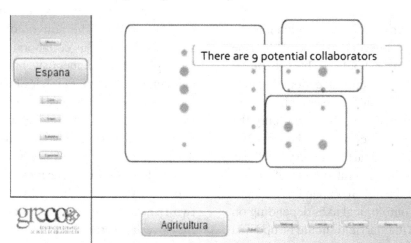

Figure 7. Visualization of relationships at the levels of institution and specific subjects

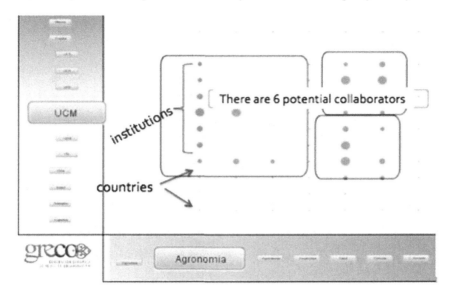

updated accordingly so as to make it possible to visualize relationships at that deeper level. It is worth noting that when an item is expanded on any axis, the others are collapsed but remain on the display to maintain context.

Three main interface components help users in coping with the increase of information on the starfield that results from expanding ontological elements into its sub-categories: Fisheye views, ontological layouts and color coding. Fisheye lenses allow users to explore specific areas by magnifying their contents as they are moved around the display. Ontological arrangement on both axes guarantee that items displayed contiguously also are semantically related. Each subject level is displayed on a different color. As highlighted by arrows and labels on top of the interface in Figure 7, blue dots help distinguish the new institution-subject relationships from the already existing country-subject relationships.

It is interesting to note that the starfield at this point displays universities within Spain that might have common interests and therefore could be in a position to collaborate, but also the countries with which potential collaboration networks could

be established. By moving the lenses around the starfield these relationships may become more evident. In Figure 7, the user has clicked on the blue dot that indicates that the institution labeled UCM (actually "Universidad Complutense de Madrid") has authors who publish in the area of Agronomy, and a legend next to the cursor indicates six authors fall into that category. If the exploration continues and the user clicks on this relationship, both elements are expanded again, as illustrated in Figure 8 (one of the fisheye lenses also has been resized to include as many relationships as possible).

Figure 8 shows, on the vertical axis, all researchers within UCM, whereas more specific subjects within Agronomy are displayed on the horizontal axis. Relationships between authors and subjects are now indicated by green dots, which coexist on the display with blue and reddish dots that refer to institutions and countries, respectively. In this example, the relationship between an author named "Abad" and the specific subject of "Agrarian Policy" has been highlighted. As noted by the labels placed on top of the interface, relationships at all three levels of the

Figure 8. Visualization at the author level and more specific subjects

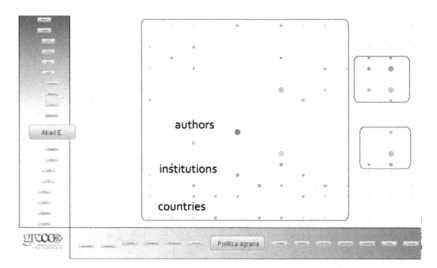

vertical axis coexist on a single display, each colored differently: authors (green), institutions (blue) and countries (reddish). The starfield thus shows, by interpreting the same column, that the university (UCM) does not have other researchers who have published on the subject being examined, as there are no other green dots on the column, but the blue dot below the main author-subject relationship indicates there is one other university in the same country (Spain) who also has published on the subject, and that there are potential collaborators in two other countries (reddish dots on both ends of the column). It can also be noted that rows of the starfield provide helpful information as they indicate all subjects of interest for a given author, institution or country. This may be particularly helpful when collaborators are needed for multi-disciplinary projects.

Using Multiple Fisheye Lenses to Explore Relationships

Should we want to learn about potential collaborators for the researcher "Abad" in the two countries shown as red dots displayed in Figure 8, we would have to click on each of them to find the corresponding institutions and then on the

blue dots to list the researchers. Given that their countries are on both ends of the vertical axis, if we used only one fisheye lens it would become difficult for the user to highlight the relationships of interest, as too many dots would be covered by one lens, and many relationships that are not relevant for the collaboration network would be included in the fisheye view.

The introduction of multiple fisheye lenses addresses these issues, as shown in Figure 9. In this case, the vertical axis includes items for institutions in three countries and researchers in only one university in each country. Fisheye lenses have been placed on green dots that form a column on top of the subject of interest (Agrarian Policy), thus allowing the relationships that are not contiguous to become evident for the user. The user may decide to add or remove fisheye lenses depending on the task at hand and the complexity of the starfield.

Evaluation of OntoStarFish

OntoStarFish has been evaluated at various stages of its development. Formative evaluation based on the observation of two groups of users motivated various adjustments to the user interface and pro-

Figure 9. Using multiple fisheye views for exploring non-contiguous areas

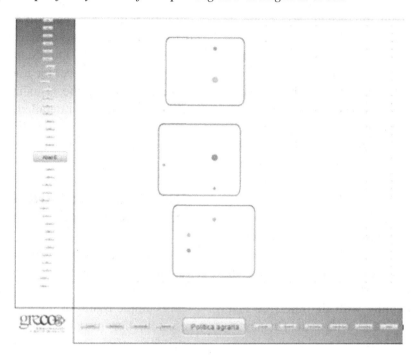

duced the version of the prototype discussed in this paper. We designed a series of tasks related to the characteristics and goals of OntoStarFish, particularly for determining its effectiveness for detecting collaboration networks. Overall, 28 users have been observed while using OntoStarFish in sessions lasting from 30 to 45 minutes. Participants have included university faculty and students with varying backgrounds including business, education, information technologies, industrial engineering and environmental engineering. Sessions were recorded and post-test questionnaires were applied to obtain explicit feedback.

The OntoStarFish visualization interface is very specialized and is far from conventional. Still, users provided positive feedback on its helpfulness for exploring collaboration networks. They were able to find potential collaborations in other institutions and other countries. Semantic grouping of data on the axes, which is a key feature, also was positively evaluated. Users were eager to explore the functionality afforded by clickable elements and expanded and collapsed data on the axes and the starfields at will. Some users even suggested applications for social networks in general and for managing relationships in business and enterprise settings.

We also obtained interesting feedback from open questions in post-test questionnaires. The most important aspect noted by users had to do with the use of multiple fisheyes. Users liked the possibility of exploring different areas on the same starfield and having access to different collaboration groups through multiple lenses. Also, the resizing capability feature of each fisheye was very useful for exploring larger (or smaller) areas of interest over the starfield. We also have observed that users rely on multiple fisheye views to explore several areas of the starfield. Typically, when they have located an area of interest they leave a fisheye lens fixed and start using another one to explore related data, especially when the axes have been expanded to a great level of detail.

The use of colors (red for countries, blue for institutions and green for researchers) made it easy to determine not only the ontological level users are exploring but also to focus on the kinds of groups users wanted to explore. Another important feature commented as positive was the indentation on each axis which helped users in maintaining their focus on the elements they were exploring. Zooming into the various levels of the subject ontology also contributed to find potential collaboration networks.

As for areas of improvement, users raised two main issues. They thought that the starfield-based representation of relationships was not always clear and that some training would be needed before researchers can use OntoStarFish comfortably. In spite of this, we observed that even novice users became familiar rapidly with the interface and were able to perform tasks with some fluency in less than fifteen minutes.

Based on feedback from users and further experimentation, we have produced an improved version of the OntoStarFish interface. Salient enhancements include: (1) a navigation bar to constantly provide contextual information regarding the levels dealt with on the vertical and horizontal axes, as well as on the number of potential collaborators to be displayed if the user clicks on a given dot on the starfield; (2) handy buttons for easily adding or removing fisheye lenses while exploring starfields; and (3) status messages to avoid frustration from clicking and not seeing instant results when the system is recalculating the starfield. Additionally, in the new version of the interface, dots resulting from expanding an ontological level remain highlighted even if the cursor moves to explore a different area. Users suggested this in order to provide visual clues that reduce disorientation or confusion when multiple actions are performed on the interface.

OntoStarFish highlights the importance of the representation mechanism used to support the visualization of collaboration networks, which is but one aspect of collection understanding.

Metadata associated with documents in digital collections does not generally exhibit any evident pattern that describes such networks. The levels of detail provided by OntoStarFish seem to offer several advantages over the traditional node-link scheme, including the visualization of complex network structures, a detailed view of potential collaborative groups, and the visualization of multiple collaboration networks at the same time.

ONGOING WORK AND FUTURE RESEARCH DIRECTIONS

We plan to continue working on two-dimensional visual representations for supporting collection understanding. Our OntoStarFish interface leaves ample room for improvement and further research. For instance, users put forward the need for options for visualizing documents from which relationships are inferred, as researchers find it important to learn about the reasons why potential collaborations are suggested on specific areas. This implies adding new features to the interface, such as a document previewing at the last level of the subject ontology. Performance also is a very important feature of visualization methods. We also are considering the exploration of the alternative applications for OntoStarFish suggested by our users.

Also, we recently started working with a network of institutional repositories that will hold and disseminate the scientific production of a large number of universities. As part of our contribution to the network, we are developing visualization interfaces to assist users in understanding what the repositories are about by providing graphical representations of the collections. Our goal is to provide a visualization mechanism that will represent the subjects in the collections as a map in which regions are charted so their color and shape denote documents grouped according to thematic similarities. The map metaphor has shown significant promise in our initial studies with potential users. In the resulting visualization, map regions displayed with the same color refer to documents about very similar subjects. The shape of the regions is defined in such a way that they get as close as possible to other groups of documents. Some map regions may actually result in disjoint areas of the same color so as to reflect similarities with other thematic areas. In order to obtain meaningful groupings, our graphical representation is tightly coupled with the classification mechanism, which is based on the notion of Self-Organizing Maps (SOM), described earlier.

In order to maintain the number of groups manageable even for very large collections, thresholds are being defined so maps comprise only a relatively small number of groups. This implies that the SOM technique is applied successively, producing naturally a hierarchy of maps that can be used directly for navigation purposes. This hierarchy of maps is illustrated in Figure 10. Starting from the upper left corner, collections are visualized as a map that consists of ten regions, which actually refer to seven general groups of documents, since two of the groups are divided into two and three regions of the same color, respectively. Users will be able to select a region from the map, which will take them to a more specific grouping, and so on until actual documents are displayed. For the sake of illustration, the figure shows only three maps at the second level and one at the third level of detail.

Figure 10. Distributed collections visualized as a hierarchy of maps

One additional feature that will be explored with SOM-based visualization is a timeline slider that will be placed at the bottom of the interface. This will provide users with further analysis tools, as they will be able to understand how a collection or a number of collections have evolved over time. Based on our current low-fidelity prototype, Figure 11 depicts the state of collections at three points in time. User studies indicate this should be an intuitive means for visually keeping track of the emergence, growth, decrease and generally the evolution of the subjects or any attributes related to documents (or other objects) held by digital collections. We expect to release a working prototype for this visualization during the first half of 2013.

CONCLUSION

This chapter has discussed the potential of information visualization techniques for supporting collection understanding, a notion that promotes an exploratory approach and provides users with a general sense of digital collections. We have emphasized the role of visual representations as means to assist the user in discovering patterns and structures that occur implicitly in collections. Through a series of developments, we have demonstrated how two-dimensional visualization techniques, such as starfields, fisheye views and self-organizing maps can be used to provide uniform interfaces for heterogeneous collections and to reveal hidden patterns, implicit structures and relationships, including potential collaboration networks. Throughout the process, we have relied on user studies to inform all our design decisions.

Although significant progress has been made, much work needs to be done in order to provide users with more intuitive, meaningful and responsive visualization interfaces that will help them understand the ever-growing digital collections at hand. Information visualization will continue to play a key role in this quest, but it will also be important to take advantage of new developments in natural user interfaces, including multi-touch interactive surfaces and gestural interfaces. We plan to work on versions of our visualization interfaces for these environments, which also should be produced by working closely with end users.

ACKNOWLEDGMENT

The concepts discussed in this chapter as well as the implementation and evaluation of prototype software that demonstrates their potential are the result of the collaboration of various generations of talented members of the Laboratory of Interactive and Cooperative Technologies at the Universidad de las Américas Puebla. Special recognition goes to Federico Hernández Bolaños, Nilda Galán,

Figure 11. Evolution of collections over time

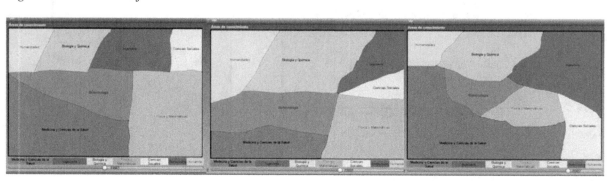

Ernesto Gutiérrez, María Auxilio Medina, Carlos Proal, Alfredo Ramos, Antonio Razo, Christian Rebollar, and Guadalupe Quintana. Yenny Méndez was instrumental in producing the final version of this document. Support for our projects has been provided by our home institution (UDLAP) as well as by Conacyt and the University Corporation for the Advancement of the Internet (CUDI) through its Program for Advanced Applications.

REFERENCES

Ahlberg, C., & Shneiderman, B. (1994). Visual information seeking: Tight coupling of dynamic query filters with starfield displays. In *Proceedings of the SIGCHI Conference on Human Factors in Computing Systems*, 313–317. Boston, MA: ACM Press. doi:10.1145/191666.191775.

Ahlberg, C., Williamson, C., & Shneiderman, B. (1992). Dynamic queries for information exploration. In *Proceedings of the SIGCHI Conference on Human Factors in Computing Systems*, 619–626. New York: ACM Press. doi:10.1145/142750.143054.

Amavizca, M., Sánchez, J., & Abascal, R. (1999). 3DTree: Visualization of large and complex information spaces in the floristic digital library. In *Proceedings of the Workshop on Computer Mediated Interaction, 2nd Mexican International Conference on Computer Science*. Pachuca, México: ACM Press.

Barabasi, A.-L. (2010). *Bursts: The hidden pattern behind everything we do*. Retrieved from http://dl.acm.org/citation.cfm?id=1941887.

Borst, W. (1997). *Construction of Engineering Ontologies for Knowledge Sharing and Reuse*. (Dissertation). Enschede, The Netherlands, University of Twente.

Buchel, O. (2011). Designing map-based visualizations for collection understanding. In *Proceeding of the 11th Annual International ACM/IEEE Joint Conference on Digital Libraries*. New York: ACM Press. doi:10.1145/1998076.1998169.

Chang, M., Leggett, J. J., Furuta, R., Kerne, A., Williams, J. P., Burns, S. A., & Bias, R. G. (2004). Collection understanding. In *Proceedings of the 4th ACM/IEEE-CS Joint Conference on Digital Libraries*, 334–342. New York: ACM. doi:10.1145/996350.996426.

Cunningham, S. J., & Bennett, E. (2008). Understanding collection understanding with collage. In *Proceedings of the 11th International Conference on Asian Digital Libraries: Universal and Ubiquitous Access to Information*, 367–370. Berlin: Springer-Verlag. doi:10.1007/978-3-540-89533-6_46.

Fung, B. C. M., Wang, K., & Ester, M. (2003). *Hierarchical document clustering. Encyclopedia of Data Warehousing and Mining*. Hershey, PA: IGI Global.

Girgensohn, A., Shipman, F., Turner, T., & Wilcox, L. (2010). Flexible access to photo libraries via time, place, tags, and visual features. In *Proceedings of the 10th Annual Joint Conference on Digital Libraries*, 187–196. New York: ACM. doi:10.1145/1816123.1816151.

Giunchiglia, F., Marchese, M., & Zaihrayeu, I. (2007). Encoding classifications into lightweight ontologies. *Journal on Data Semantics VIII, 4380*(4380), 57–81. Retrieved from http://dx.doi.org/10.1007/978-3-540-70664-9_3.

Gruber, T. R. (1993). A translation approach to portable ontology specifications. In H. Burkhardt & B. Smith (Eds.) Knowledge Creation Diffusion Utilization, 5, 199–220. doi:doi:10.1006/knac.1993.1008. doi:10.1006/knac.1993.1008.

Herman, I., Melancon, G., & Marshall, M. S. (2000). Graph visualization and navigation in information visualization: A survey. *IEEE Transactions on Visualization and Computer Graphics, 6*(1), 24–43. doi:10.1109/2945.841119.

Hernández-Bolaños, F. (2010). *UltraVCN: Uso de filtros y características gráficas para la visualización de redes de colaboración.* (Unpublished B.Sc. Thesis). Puebla, Mexico, Universidad de las Américas.

Katifori, A., Halatsis, C., Lepouras, G., Vassilakis, C., & Giannopoulou, E. (2007). Ontology visualization methods-A survey. *ACM Computing Surveys, 39*(4), 10. doi:10.1145/1287620.1287621.

Kohonen, T. (1990). The self-organizing map. *Proceedings of the IEEE, 78*(9), 1464–1480. doi:10.1109/5.58325.

Lassila, O., & McGuinness, D. (2001). The role of frame-based representation on the semantic web. *Linköping Electronic Articles in Computer and Information Science, 6*(5), 2001. Retrieved from http://www.ksl.stanford.edu/KSL_Abstracts/KSL-01-02.html.

Perer, A., & Shneiderman, B. (2008). Integrating statistics and visualization: Case studies of gaining clarity during exploratory data analysis. In M. Burnett, M. F. Costabile, T. Catarci, B. DeRuyter, D. Tan, M. Czerwinski, & A. Lund (Eds.), Human-Computer Interaction (265–274). Florence, Italy: ACM Press. doi:doi:10.1145/1357054.1357101. doi:10.1145/1357054.1357101.

Proal, C., Sánchez, J. A., & Fernández, L. (2000). UVA: 3D representations for visualizing digital collections. In *Proceedings of the Third International Conference on Visual Computing*, 185–192. Mexico City: IEEE Press. Retrieved from http://ict.udlap.mx/pubs/UVA2000.pdf.

Ramos, A., Sánchez, J. A., & Hernández-Bolaños, F. (2010). OntoStarFish: Visualization of collaboration networks using starfields, ontologies, and fisheye views. In *Proceedings of the 3rd Mexican Workshop on Human Computer Interaction*, 44–53. San Luis Potosí, México: Universidad Politécnica de San Luis Potosí. Retrieved from http://dl.acm.org/citation.cfm?id=1978702.1978713.

Sánchez, J. A., Medina, M., Starostenko, O., Benitez, A., & Domínguez, E. (2012). Organizing open archives via lightweight ontologies to facilitate the use of heterogeneous collections. In *Proceedings of ASLIB, 64*, 46–66. New York: Emerald Press. doi:10.1108/00012531211196701

Sánchez, J. A., Quintana, M., & Razo, A. (2007). Star-fish: Starfields+ fisheye visualization and its application to federated digital libraries. In *Proceedings of the 3rd Latin American Conference on Human-Computer Interaction*. Rio de Janeiro, Brazil: HCIR Press. Retrieved from http://clihc.org/2007/papers/StarFish_ID38_longpaper.pdf.

Sánchez, J. A., Twidale, M. B., Nichols, D. M., & Silva, N. N. (2005). Experiences with starfield visualizations for analysis of library collections. In *Proceedings of the Conference on Visualization and Data Analysis, 5669*, 215–225. San Jose, CA: SPIE Press.

Shneiderman, B. (1996). The eyes have it: A Task by data type taxonomy for information visualizations. In *Proceedings of the 1996 IEEE Symposium on Visual Languages*, 336–343. Washington, DC: IEEE Press. Retrieved from http://ieeexplore.ieee.org/xpls/abs_all.jsp?arnumber=545307.

Silva, N. N., Sanchez, J. A., Proal, C., & Rebollar, C. (2003). Visual exploration of large collections in digital libraries. In *Proceedings of the Latin American Conference on Human-Computer Interaction*, 147–157. New York: ACM Press. Retrieved from http://portal.acm.org/citation.cfm?id=944519.944535.

Smith, M. A., Shneiderman, B., Milic-Frayling, N., Mendes Rodrigues, E., Barash, V., Dunne, C., & Capone, T. (2009). Analyzing (social media) networks with NodeXL. In D. Hansen, B. Shneiderman, M. Smith, & R. Ackland (Eds.), *Proceedings of the Fourth International Conference on Communities and Technologies-CT 09* (255–264). New York: ACM Press. doi:10.1145/1556460.1556497.

Xu, J. J., & Chen, H. (2005). CrimeNet explorer: A framework for criminal network knowledge discovery. *ACM Transactions on Information Systems*, *23*(2), 201–226. doi:10.1145/1059981.1059984.

Yakowenko, J., & Matange, S. (2004). Computer-implemented system and method for handling node-link representations. *U. S. Patent No. 7587409*. Retrieved from http://www.patents.com/us-7587409.html.

Yang, X., Asur, S., Parthasarathy, S., & Mehta, S. (2008). A visual-analytic toolkit for dynamic interaction graphs. In *Proceeding of the 14th ACM SIGKDD International Conference on Knowledge Discovery and Data Mining*. Las Vegas, NV: ACM Press. doi:10.1145/1401890.1402011.

ADDITIONAL READING

Ahn, J.-W., Taieb-Maimon, M., Sopan, A., Plaisant, C., & Shneiderman, B. (2011). Temporal visualization of social network dynamics: prototypes for nation of neighbors. In *Proceedings of the 4th International Conference on Social Computing, Behavioral-Cultural Modeling, and Prediction*, 309–316. Berlin: Springer-Verlag. Retrieved from http://dl.acm.org/citation.cfm?id=1964698.1964741.

Andronis, C., Sharma, A., Virvilis, V., Deftereos, S., & Persidis, A. (2011). Literature mining, ontologies, and information visualization for drug repurposing. *Briefings in Bioinformatics*, *12*(4), 357–368. Retrieved from http://www.ncbi.nlm.nih.gov/pubmed/21712342 doi:10.1093/bib/bbr005 PMID:21712342.

Card, S. K., Mackinlay, J. D., & Shneiderman, B. (1999). Readings in information visualization: Using vision to think. In S. K. Card, J. D. Mackinlay, & B. Shneiderman (Eds.), *Information Display* (686). New York: Morgan Kaufmann. Retrieved from http://portal.acm.org/citation.cfm?id=300679.

Dörk, M., Carpendale, S., & Williamson, C. (2012). Fluid views: A zoomable search environment. In *Proceedings of the International Working Conference on Advanced Visual Interfaces*, 233–240. New York: ACM. doi:10.1145/2254556.2254599.

Elmqvist, N., & Fekete, J.-D. (2010). Hierarchical aggregation for information visualization: Overview, techniques, and design guidelines. *IEEE Transactions on Visualization and Computer Graphics*, *16*(3), 439–454. doi:10.1109/TVCG.2009.84 PMID:20224139.

Gleicher, M., Albers, D., Walker, R., Jusufi, I., Hansen, C. D., & Roberts, J. C. (2011). Visual comparison for information visualization. *Information Visualization*, *10*(4), 289–309. doi:10.1177/1473871611416549.

Graham, M., & Kennedy, J. (2010). A survey of multiple tree visualisation. *Information Visualization*, *9*(4), 235–252. doi:10.1057/ivs.2009.29.

Grammel, L., Tory, M., & Storey, M.-A. (2010). How Information visualization novices construct visualizations. *IEEE Transactions on Visualization and Computer Graphics*, *16*(6), 943–952. doi:10.1109/TVCG.2010.164 PMID:20975131.

Heer, J., & Shneiderman, B. (2012). Interactive dynamics for visual analysis. *Communications of the ACM, 55*(4), 45–54. doi:10.1145/2133806.2133821.

Keim, D. A., Mansmann, F., & Thomas, J. (2010). Visual analytics: how much visualization and how much analytics? *SIGKDD Exploration Newsletter, 11*(2), 5–8. doi:10.1145/1809400.1809403.

Kielman, J., Thomas, J., & May, R. (2009). Foundations and frontiers in visual analytics. *Information Visualization, 8*(4), 239–246. doi:10.1057/ivs.2009.25.

Liu, Z., & Stasko, J. (2010). Mental models, visual reasoning, and interaction in information visualization: A top-down perspective. *IEEE Transactions on Visualization and Computer Graphics, 16*(6), 999–1008. doi:10.1109/TVCG.2010.177 PMID:20975137.

Lovejoy, M., Vesna, V., & Paul, C. (2011). *Context providers: Conditions of meaning in media arts.* Bristol, UK: Intellect Ltd..

Meiguins, B. S., Do Carmo, R. M. C., Almeida, L., Gonçalves, A. S., Pinheiro, S. C. V., De Brito Garcia, M., & Godinho, P. I. A. (2006). Multidimensional information visualization using augmented reality. In *Proceedings of the 2006 ACM international conference on Virtual reality continuum and its applications*, 391–394. New York: ACM. doi:10.1145/1128923.1128996.

Newman, M. E. J. (2000). The structure of scientific collaboration networks. In *Proceedings of the National Academy of Sciences of the United States of America.* Washington DC: National Academy of the Sciences. Retrieved from http://arxiv.org/abs/cond-mat/0007214.

Padia, K., AlNoamany, Y., & Weigle, M. C. (2012). Visualizing digital collections at archive-it. In *Proceedings of the 12th ACM/IEEE-CS Joint Conference on Digital Libraries*, 15–18. New York: ACM. doi:10.1145/2232817.2232821.

Segel, E., & Heer, J. (2010). Narrative visualization: Telling stories with data. *IEEE Transactions on Visualization and Computer Graphics, 16*(6), 1139–1148. doi:10.1109/TVCG.2010.179 PMID:20975152.

Shneiderman, B. (2001). Inventing discovery tools: Combining Information visualization with data mining. In *Proceedings of the 4th International Conference on Discovery Science*, 17–28. London, UK: Springer-Verlag. Retrieved from http://dl.acm.org/citation.cfm?id=647858.738688.

Small, H. (1999). Visualizing science by citation mapping. *Journal of the American Society for Information Science American Society for Information Science, 50*(9), 799–813. doi:10.1002/(SICI)1097-4571(1999)50:9<799::AID-ASI9>3.0.CO;2-G.

Spence, R. (2007). *Information visualization: Design for interaction* (2nd ed.). Upper Saddle River, NJ: Prentice-Hall, Inc..

Stasko, J. (2000). An evaluation of space-filling information visualizations for depicting hierarchical structures. *International Journal of Human-Computer Studies, 53*(5), 663–694. doi:10.1006/ijhc.2000.0420.

Steele, J., & Iliinsky, N. (2010). *Beautiful Visualization: Looking at Data through the Eyes of Experts* (1st ed.). Sebastapol, CA: O'Reilly Media, Inc..

Tufte, E. (1990). *Envisioning information.* Cheshire, CT: Graphics Press.

Tufte, E. R. (1986). *The visual display of quantitative information.* Cheshire, CT: Graphics Press.

Tufte, E. R. (2001). *The visual display of quantitative information* (p. 200). Cockeysville, MD: Graphics PR.

Ward, M., Grinstein, G., & Keim, D. (2010). *Interactive data visualization: Foundations, techniques, and applications.* Natick, MA: A. K. Peters, Ltd..

KEY TERMS AND DEFINITIONS

Collaboration Networks: Structures that represent interconnected groups of people who work together at various coupling levels.

Collection Understanding: A technique intended to cope with the complexity of large digital collections that promotes an exploratory approach of repositories by providing users with a general sense of their contents.

Egocentric Network Visualization: A visual representation of a network that shows, at its center, a node of interest, and on its periphery, nodes with various degrees of relatedness.

Fisheye View: A visualization technique that allows users to explore in detail an area of interest while maintaining its context. Its name refers to the distortion effect created around non-important elements while those that are important are magnified.

Low-Fidelity Prototype: A low-cost, simplified representation of a design or concept, typically rendered on physical materials, used to gather user feedback at early stages of design.

Ontology: An explicit shared specification of a conceptualization. Lightweight and heavyweight ontologies can be distinguished according to the degree of formality involved in their encoding.

Starfield: A grid-based visualization method that highlights the intersections of two axes on a plane. Each axis typically is used to represent an attribute of the items being displayed.

Chapter 9
Highlighting in Visual Data Analytics

Mao Lin Huang
University of Technology, Sydney, Australia

Jie Liang
University of Technology, Sydney, Australia

Weidong Huang
CSIRO ICT Centre, Sydney, Australia

ABSTRACT

Highlighting has been known as a basic viewing control mechanism in computer graphics and visualization for guiding users' attention in reading diagrams, images, graphs, and digital texts. Due to the rapid development of theory and practice in information visualization and visual analytics, the role of 'highlighting' in computer graphics has been extended from just acting as a viewing control to being part of an interaction control and a visual recommendation mechanism that is important in modern information visualization and visual analytics. In this chapter, the authors present a brief literature review. They try to assign the word 'highlighting' a contemporary definition and attempt to give a formal summarization and classification of the existing and potential 'highlighting' methods that are to be applied in Information Visualization, Visual Analytics, and Knowledge Visualization. We also propose a new three-layer model of 'highlighting' and discuss the responsibilities of each layer accordingly.

1. INTRODUCTION

Highlighting scheme has been widely applied in real-world applications. Highlighting is a very popular method in computer graphics. It is commonly used to guide users' attention and to reduce the human cognitive effort in reading graphical pictures. As a new applied discipline of computer graphics, Information Visualization has inherited this method as one of the major mechanisms for the viewing control. However, as the result of rapid development in visual computing, highlighting

DOI: 10.4018/978-1-4666-4309-3.ch009

has expanded its role in the traditional computer graphics and formed its specific meaning and functionalities in Information Visualization and Visual Analytics.

Nevertheless, existing understanding of highlighting has stopped its potential functionality and performance in visual analytics. Upon that, inevitably, there are many implementation problems existing in current practices. This research is aimed to raise the attention and emphasis on Highlighting. Highlighting seems to have a simple concept but is more complicated and useful than what we usually think. To address these challenges, we redefine highlighting and refine the theory of highlighting in information visualization and try to distinguish it as a new mechanism of reducing human cognition process for visual analytics. Therefore, we have made an attempt to provide a formal summarization, classification and to further explore evaluation of the existing Highlighting approaches and techniques to date so that its usefulness can be maximized in Information Visualization (Huang & Liang, 2010). We describe the results of this attempt in more detail in this chapter.

2. THE CONTEMPORARY DEFINITION OF HIGHLIGHTING

Highlighting was considered as one of the most common terms in computer graphics. However, the literature shows that there is little agreement on the understanding of highlighting. In non-professional fields, the interpretation of highlighting is either limited to the specific scope of color and lighting, as self evidence of its name, or broadened to be the process of emphasizing information. In the research field, there is also a debate on the definition of highlighting which varies from one domain to another.

Specifically in the domain of information visualization, Becker and Cleveland in 1987 described highlighting as brushing special color to paint the object; in 1999, Liston et al. illustrated highlighting as the process of emphasizing related sets of information, through visual annotation, within a view or across multiple views; in 2003, MacEachren et al. referred highlighting as the indication method by using transient visual effects; in 2004, Seo and Shneiderman suggested the term highlighting for the visual link across multiple views; in 2005, Ware and Borrow further defined it as an effective way with pre-attentive visual cues. Recently, Ware and Borrow discussed highlighting methods from static to dynamic approaches (2004). Nevertheless, these definitions all confined highlighting as the basic techniques for viewing only. Hence, it also implies that the understanding of highlighting in the literature of visualization still remains in the lower level as a viewing control mechanism.

However, the need in processing and understanding large and complex datasets means that further development in visual computing should go beyond the current capacity of visualization tools for exploiting the meaningful information and maximizing the human's ability of interpreting. To response to these challenges, this chapter attempts to establish the highlighting as an essential component of visual computing to offer services for visual navigation and visual analytics.

To put forward the research of highlighting for visual analytics, the first step is to re-define the highlighting. Highlighting naturally is planted in visual thinking and visual communication. Only appropriate definition of highlighting will help researchers and practitioners would be able to design appropriate visualizations for users to extract meaningful information out of the visual processing. However, there are challenges in defining highlighting. The limitation of highlighting definition has obstructed extending scope of highlighting and the understanding of terminology for both non-professional and professional fields. Hence, the primary goal of this research should be to re-define and extend highlighting, and to deliberate the changing role of highlighting from assisting view, to higher functionalities.

Therefore, we defined highlighting in three layers that each have different responsibilities and purposes:

- In traditional view-based visualization, highlighting acts as a viewing control to attract user's attention into a portion of the visualization.
- In interactive visualization, highlighting functions as a navigation control mechanism to guide users progressively reach the final target by visual interactions.
- In knowledge visualization and visual analytics, highlighting is further applied as part of artificial intelligence process to provide users with a set of graphical recommendations for the decision making.

It is worth noting that our new definition has gone beyond the limitation of traditional understanding of highlighting and moved on to the capability of speeding visual thinking and accelerating decision making performance. This profound change is intended not only to expand the boundary and fulfill the theory of highlighting, but also advance the potential development of highlighting in the future.

Therefore, the specific objectives of this study are to refine and extend highlighting, and also to elaborate on the changing roles of highlighting from merely assisting with viewing, to interacting with information, participating directly in cognitive processes and finally facilitating with decision making.

3. THE CONCEPTUAL MODEL OF HIGHLIGHTING

As an independent component of visual computing, highlighting should fundamentally be able to direct a new way to overcome the problem of information overload and reduce the process of human cognition, and at the same time meet challenges of collaborative analysis tasks. The new conceptual model we proposed consists of three layers (see Figure 1 for more details). As can been seen from this figure, the lowest layer is viewing control that is to solve the information overloading problem. The middle layer is interaction control that aims to ease the cognitive process for information seekers. The top layer is visual recommendation that mainly targets for decision makers in collaborative analysis tasks.

3.1. Viewing Control for Information Overloading Problem

The main reason why it is used for visualization is that the highlighting method has the potential to help address information overloading and complexity of information. Due to continuous updating of the data, the visual representation of the data often generates visual clutters that add extra cognition overheads in viewing and understanding the

Figure 1. Conceptual model of highlighting (Huang & Liang, 2010)

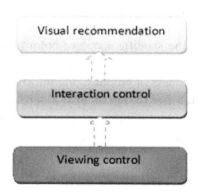

information. Accordingly, the analysis processes have become increasingly time-consuming and complicated. Highlighting as a simple technique aims to reduce confusion, to minimize the learning curve and to increase accuracy and efficiency of humans understanding the information.

3.2. Interaction Control for Information Retrieval

When used for interactive visualization, highlighting has the capability to guide the information seeking process. Users may have difficulties in finding target or useful information since this usually involves extensive and recursive cognitive thinking. In these cases, highlighting should provide mechanisms allowing users to follow the right path and progressively reach their interested information in the most appropriate and comprehensive manner.

3.3. Visual Recommendation for Decision Making

Evaluating options and making decisions are common in visual analytics and knowledge visualization. In these situations, highlighting may be used to attract decision makers' attention to a small portion of highly relevant information and knowledge that is directly beneficial for their decision making. This will help decision makes to spend their valuable time wisely and efficiently, without being distracted to and spending time and effort in reading less or non-relevant information and knowledge.

It is true that often analysts and decision makers are different people in commercial or research communities. Therefore, it is possible that a solution to refining highlighting in one area may not be applicable in another and a new solution is required for collaborative decision making processes.

4. THE ELEMENTS OF HIGHLIGHTING

In this section, we discuss the basic elements of highlighting, from which we can implement a variety of highlighting methods. The following table gives a summarization on the elements that have or can potentially be used to design highlighting (Table 1). The elements of Highlighting is able to utilize are Size, Shape, Lighting, Motion and Presentation (Figure 2).

Table 1. The elements of highlighting (Huang & Liang, 2010)

Differentiation	visual variables	series logic
Differentiation in size	Area of object or view increase or decrease	Large/Medium/Small
Differentiation in shape	2D or 3D geometric shapes regular/irregular	Shape transformation
Differentiation in lighting	Intensity	Light /medium /heavy
	Frequency or wavelength	weak/strong
Differentiation in motion	speed, acceleration, displacement, and time	motionless/relevant motion/absolute motion
Differentiation in presentation	style-based	Abstract/details
	Line-based	focus/outlier/boundary

Figure 2. Illustrations of Differentiation in graphic elements (Huang & Liang, 2010) (a) Color (b) Light contrast (c) Transparency (d) Size (e) Shape (f) Presentation

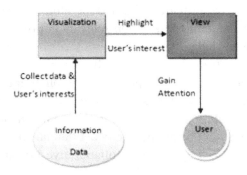

As can be seen from Table 1, the "Differentiation" is essentially the key to classify and implement highlighting. For example, differentiation can be made in lighting, shape, size, motion and presentation. These elements of highlighting can be used either individually or in combination. The mechanisms of such usage can be defined below according to Robinson (2009):

Single Mechanism

In this mechanism, one highlighting method is applied upon one data object at a time. This mechanism uses a simple binary "on or off" method that is common in most visualization software.

Categorical Mechanism

Highlighting methods are applied categorically to define and classify the data objects. This highlighting method could follow a classification that has been applied to a dataset to modify the highlighting method's visual intensity accordingly. If an analyst would like to show the details of for example, the results of a clustering, or wants to reveal some uncertain properties of data and statistical significance in the visualization, this categorical mechanism can also be meaningful to apply.

Compound Mechanism

When single or categorical mechanism is not suitable or fails to adequately reduce visual complexity, this mechanism may come handy and it applies multiple highlighting methods together for the data objects, based on user's interest or specific visual requirements of the visualization. Compound highlighting may facilitate quick interpretation, using multiple elements of highlighting. Compound highlighting may be either conjunctive (same combination of highlighting methods in each view) or disjunctive (different combinations of highlighting methods in each view). Conjunctive compound combines same highlighting methods in each view, while disjunctive compound can select different combinations of highlighting methods in each view. Typical conjunction combines motion, and color.

Continuity Mechanism

This highlighting method is applied along a gradient from one value to another. This mechanism will facilitate to clarify visual transition, in below cases. First, most data attributes are changing dynamically in a continuous scale in real time application. Second, the analysts are interested to monitor the change between the data object to a target.

5. THE CLASSIFICATION OF HIGHLIGHTING

5.1. Viewing Control Layer

Viewing control process is based on pre-defined algorithms. As shown in Figure 3, the visualization defines the parts of the picture that the user is interested in and highlights the corresponding portions of the view to attract user's attention. In this layer of the highlighting, most data properties are commonly used to implement the highlighting,

Figure 3. The framework of viewing control (Huang & Liang, 2010)

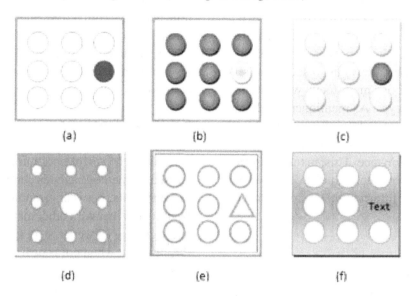

such as color, light, size, shape etc. We discuss these in more detail in what follows.

5.1.1. Differentiation in Lighting

As mentioned earlier, basic highlighting function can enhance visual features and be applied in real world applications with an efficient outcome. That is actively guiding the user's attention to the intended area of the visualization. These features are typically perceived by humans quickly and effectively (e.g. color, light, or transparency).

In general, the differentiation in lighting can be operated into one, two, three or even multiple dimensions visualizations based on different applications. Parallel coordinate visualization has successfully uses highlighting to control the viewing. It displays the focused poly-lines within a thin region. Alternatively, color and light highlighting are used to select data in specific scope of dimensions (Siirtola & KJ, 2006). XmdvTool (Martin & Ward, 1995) created by Martin and Ward progressed the function to highlight a series of data of high dimensions in a "brushed tunnel". Siirtola and Raiha further advanced this solution

in a new version of parallel coordinate explorer interface (Siirtola & KJ, 2006). They rearranged data into multiple layers of highlighting by adopting differentiation in lighting.

5.1.1.1. Color

For the purpose of highlighting, a range of color groups can be displayed by a different range of spectrum. The color difference and level of de-saturation can be used to distinguish between the highlighted objects, depending on the extent to which the required details of views should be revealed in specific visualization environment. For example, in the case of growth matrix in financial data visualization(Keim et. al, 2006), by using color and color de-saturation highlighting techniques, it becomes possible to show the performance of a fund in all time intervals over a time period of 14 years (about 11.000 intervals).

To give a further example, studies have shown that different color highlighting methods can lead to different information seeking behaviors of humans (Huang et al, 2009; Huang & Huang 2010). For example, in finding shortest paths between two nodes, the user will need to look for the target nodes first if these two nodes are not highlighted. On the contrary, the user could start the path search straightaway without having to locate where the two nodes are first. This is because humans have periphery vision that allows us to see what is in the surrounding of our main focus without having to moving our eyes. As mentioned by Huang (2013), these different highlighting strategies lead to different eye movement patterns, thus different levels of task performance. This, in turn, requires different visualization techniques to use in order to support effective information visualization and visual analytics.

5.1.1.2. Contrast

Contrast also can be used to visually separate highlighted objects from background information. Modification relies on measurements or ranking to control either how sharp certain objects appear, or how much blur should apply to background information to make the highlighted objects appear more obvious. In geo-visualization, it is sometime called "Depth of field highlighting" (Robinson, 2009).For example, visualization tool of Kosara et al. adopted Semantic Depth Of Field (SDOF) method (2001) and their user studies have proved its usefulness.

5.1.1.3. Transparency

Transparency can be used as a transient highlighting technique to dissolve the context around the object of interests. The alpha level of objects can be set to render the focused object in the display, but this potential method has not been evaluated. The previous work of context and focus visualization by Huang and Nguyen (Nguyen & Huang, 2004), has proved that if transparency level is carefully selected, it can be designed to guide users in navigation as a highlighting method. While the background of structure fades, the view of "Applets" sub-structure is standing out of the whole data structure and the size of the focus view is also enlarged in the space filling presen-

tation. Nguyen & Huang's work in layering and transparency (Nguyen & Huang, 2004) provides initial reference for further implementation, but it is still a challenge to determine the appropriate level of transparency for displays that have been colored with light-to-dark color schemes.

5.1.2. Differentiation in Size

As another powerful option for highlighting, the size-based method has been common in emphasizing difference between graphical objects. It can be used together with other methods such as color and lighting. However, it is specially applied to the situation when color or lighting based methods fail to deliver the ideal outcome, especially for color-blinds who have troubles to distinguish color and light. For example, in visualizing a social network using a node-link diagram, we can use size to represent important. Nodes with large sizes mean that they are more important. To visualize a scientific citation network, we can use size to represent times a paper is cited by other papers. The larger the node, the more times the paper is cited.

Taking the example of text annotation, the color and light variation seems to be the simplest solution for the presentation of overlapping digital annotation from different authors, but only under the strict restriction of Authors' number. To improve the performance of the digital library query system, digital annotation (Nichols et al., 2000; Bouthors & Dedieu, 1999) and visualizing shared highlighting (Villarroel et. al, 2006), have been used in text documents and make recommendations for recommender systems. The proposed annotation Highlighting is strived to be able to compare annotation from different users and also to achieve the relevance levels which are calculated from the number of coincidence of highlighted fragments. Most work stopped in using highlighting with color and light variation. In order to achieve visualizing annotation shared and comparison mode, Villarroel et al. made notable improvement and jump out of single color style, and attempted several color groups and color contrast. However, beyond three authors, the visual annotation presentation would look like a confusing color palette with mixture of different color fragments, as overlap of annotation creates more color entries. We could hardly identify or compare the annotations from different authors in digital applications (Villarroel et. al, 2006). It is inappropriate to exclusively reply on only one property for shared annotation. In this situation, the shape of text annotation is likely another indicator to go beyond three authors for annotation comparison visualization.

5.1.3. Differentiation in Shape

Similarly, shape can be a potential method applied into existing practices as well. The Gestalt research and Geon Theory has shown that humans have a tendency to seek out the object's edges and they can quickly detect when one shape is different from another. Taking email visual organization as an instance, in order to expand details of email indicators, Bernald Kerr successfully adopt color highlighting of different scheme and finally move on to the indicator of shape (Kerr, 2003). In attribute highlighting, Kerr naturally used color de-saturation to rate the importance of emails, and employed different shapes of circle, solid circle, hollow circle to present the importance of people, to be distinguished from other attributes using light differentiation.

5.1.4. Differentiation in Presentation

5.1.4.1. Style

This method was initially used in geo-visualization (Robinson & Center, 2006). The idea of style reduction or addition is to separate and highlight different data objects in geo-visualizations. This method works especially well with visual representations that are designed with multiple graphical elements. We may change styles of some visual objects by changing, adding, deleting colors, sizes or labels of them, or other graphical elements so that the objects of the interest can stand out. To give an example, we can image a complex social network whose actors have multiple attributions such as age, gender and religion. If our task in consideration is related to age only, they we can simply remove other irrelevant attributes in the visualization without having to removing the actors completely.

5.1.4.2. Line

The line-based highlighting method is mostly used for indicating relationship between positions of data or objects, a direction path from one object to another. For example, leader lines and contouring lines (Robinson & Center, 2006) adopted from map design, also give differentiation for the object in relation to it neighborhood. Line based highlighting can also be drawn in variations of color, width, and stroke style. For example, in a single view of treemaps visualization, analysts usually have to identify several related objects, which may spread over the display.

5.1.4.3. Contouring

Contouring is also inspired by map design. This method outlines data objects and brings the effect that outlined objects are "higher" than non-contoured neighbors (Robinson & Center, 2006). In MEgraph system prototyped by Ware et al., company nodes were colored to categorize into different sectors. When users click on an object or objects, the contour of the selected node will be outlined with bright white. However, the contouring method has not yet much been adopted in prior work as a highlighting style yet.

5.2. Interaction Control Layer

In interaction control, the highlighting is applied in navigation process that guides users to progressively refine their focus views to reach the final

Figure 4. The framework of Interaction Control (Huang & Liang, 2010)

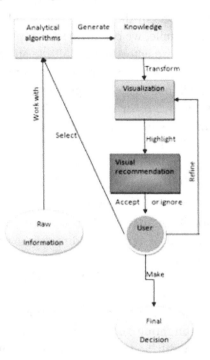

target view. The navigation process may also be the process of data retrieval (see Figure 4). This highlighting layer may apply most elements differentiation, particularly in size of display area.

5.2.1. Differentiation in Size of Display Area

Most view-based highlighting takes advantage of differentiation in size and shape to provide focus and background information based on what level of details of the information should be revealed as required by users. With the support of available information, users may modify view transformation, browse and switch the data by different granularity with highlighting indications.

5.2.1.1. One View

As a special case of one view, information is often highlighted by showing only a part of it. In partially view highlighting, drilling-down + semantic

zooming is a method that adopts differentiation of size and shape. This method is the most commonly used interactive navigation technique. For example, fisheye + zooming (Shi et al., 2005), power finger, and view distortion. This navigation scheme is quick and simple and has been widely established in the current operation systems, web researching and many common applications. Ben Bederson, director of the Human-Computer Interaction Lab, from University of Maryland created Fisheye Menus (Bederson, 2000) with size differentiation highlighting, for the application of linear lists. The interactive Map of Washington D.C., also applies this primary highlighting technique in order to increase size of the station "Metro centre" and transform the shape into the fish eye in the navigation.

5.2.1.2. Two Views

In coordinated views, Focus and context view is another existing method relying on element of size and shape. It provides users with a detailed view of a focused sub-graph and overall graph to maintain user orientation. Typical techniques in focus + context navigation scheme include sunburst (Stasko & Zhang, 2000), and information slices (Andrew & Heidegger, 1998).

5.2.1.3. Different Views

Merging views has also been used for highlighting. This method is adopted from "overlay" Technique in construction planning (Liston et al., 2000). This new highlighting method takes the views from different team members and integrates them into one view. To review the project, the team could focus on comparing and evaluating what is the important information on this one "merged" view. This method implements following types of overlaying actions, overlaying document to document of same type, objects to document of same type and document to document of different type and objects to document of different type by certain mechanisms.

5.2.1.4. Multiple Views

The usage of multiple views for visual highlighting has been largely unexplored in research. We have proposed a visualization method with Multi-context views. In this method, visualization with chains of full history is employed to be one of highlighting techniques in multiple views. It increases the context of an entity collection step by step and integrates the presentation of structure with the presentation of context. It was shown that multi-context view Visualization has successfully solved the conflict between the goal of providing structure and the goal of visualization detail context (Huang, Liang & Nguyen, 2009). Referring to the historical times from multiple context views, and enlarged focus views, analysts could match this significant event to the suspected trading patterns which had frequently occurred in history. As a further benefit of doing this, analysts might be able to identify the actual plans and predict the next action accordingly.

5.3. Differentiation in Motion

Motion based highlighting methods are relatively less popular compared to other main-stream ones. But they are gradually gaining popularity among researcher and professionals in recent years due to the facts that real world data are often dynamic and change all the time and that the technologies are increasingly accessible for realization of motion effects. For example, Microsoft PowerPoint elicits the method of motion highlighting in its customization of presentation slides. It has four categories, object by entrance, by exit, by emphasis, and by motion path. The entrance and exit highlighting includes show and hide function and other dynamic effects. The emphasis positioning may include spin, arrow, circular, jolt, radiating and flash or combination (Ware & Bobrow, 2004). For example, in our previous work of trading network visualization (Huang, Liang, & Nguyen, 2009), a flashing circle highlighting over a suspected focus can be further implemented to identify a suspected behavior of domination of the stock price.

In Visual thinking with an interactive diagram, Ware (Ware et al., 2008) suggested and evaluated three motion highlighting methods, Circular motion, jolt motion and crawl motion. In Circular motion, all of the nodes and links in the connected sub-graph move with a circular motion around center position, with an amplitude of approximately 2 mm and frequency of 1 Hz. Nodes and links in the selected sub-graph in Jolt motion, move in pulse using the function $ampl = 0.5\sin(8.0\pi t)/(60t \times t + 0.5)$ cm. In Crawl motion, the selected links show smoothly animated sawtooth pattern radiating from the selected node. The evaluation shows that in larger application with more than 300 objects, the exploration of diagram can't be discerned without highlighting.

In the motion path highlighting, the object may move in straight-line or along curve according to certain shapes. Bartram's usability study (Bartram & Ware, 2002) proved that motion highlighting is much more effective than color or shape change in signaling a change to a data glyph presented on the screen. He also further supported his assumption that motion highlighting technique is promising solution for separating a group of objects enabling a rapid visual search on the groups.

5.4. Presentation in Interaction

Differentiation in presentation can also be extended to interaction control. In real world systems, it is common to display multiple views in one platform. Analysts may constantly switch between different views, from context or variable to source file. It is normally time-consuming process. During interaction, visual link can be implemented to maintain mental navigation. The links can connect data in separate views and show relationships between them. Steinberger et al.'s technique in 2011 makes visual links standout from the surrounding base representation. They evaluation shows the technique increases the visibility of the links and minimizes the occlusion of important information (Steinberger et al., 2011).

5.4.1. Shapes in Interaction

Differentiation in shape has also used interaction control. Most of the existing Treemaps algorithms are based on axis-aligned rectangles. Hence, limiting Treemaps visualization to vertical-and-horizontal rectangles blocks the utilization of human capability in object recognition, due to the same fixed angles of the shapes in the tree visualization. Variations of angles and/or shaped nodes positively direct a way to achieve better graph perception and insight generation for focus recognition and change tracking. For example, embedding distinctive shapes in traditional rectangular Treemaps in certain division within visualization can highlight anomalies.

A new space-filling visualization method has been created which we call Angular Treemaps (Liang et al., 2012). This version of treemap is capable of laying out large relational structures whose visualization can be varied to highlight important substructures. This is achieved by using a specifically developed angular partitioning algorithm. This algorithm produces the variation and helps users to locate and identify importance of a specific piece of information or focus of interests. This technique is flexible and can be either used based on user's preference manually or applied by supporting automated analysis.

Angular treemaps can be utilized in visual representation of massive datasets in order to emphasis places of interest set by users, during the process of interaction. For example, it can highlight one focus, two focuses, or more on either the same level or different levels. In addition, angular treemaps are able to employ with multiple partition angles, to emphasis the data structure. For example, with angular treemaps, when the level of visualization goes deeper, the rotation angle decreases. This creates a sense of level change, thus being suitable for users to maintain the awareness of structure tracking (Liang et al., 2013).

5.5. Visual Recommendation

In knowledge visualization and visual analytics the role of highlighting can be further extended as part of the knowledge discovery process to provide users with a set of graphical recommendations for their decision making. In knowledge discovery, a large volume of the raw data is pre-processed by analytical algorithms, such as data mining or feature selection algorithms. These algorithms are generated by domain experts or statistical methods based on empirical or mathematical theories and are usually applied to process the data at the background. The resulting knowledge of the analysis is used for facilitating the decision making process.

However, in many cases, the textual or tabular representations of the knowledge are hard to be understood by decision makers, especially the relational structures among knowledge. Therefore, the modern visualization technologies allow decision makers to take advantages of human vision to visually interpret the knowledge. However, for a particular decision maker, he or she may only need a specific segment of the knowledge, rather than a complete set of knowledge displayed in the visualization for the decision making. Therefore, we "highlight" particular segments of the knowledge in the visualization as visual recommendations, which we believe are the most beneficial for a particular decision making process. In the process, users have choices to either accept or ignore the visual suggestions. When visual results are unsatisfied, users are allowed to refine the visualization with different highlighting mechanism. Consequently, this visual recommendation process can be iterative (See Figure 5). In brief, visual recommendation could not only suggest a shortcut for user to reach the knowledge he or she pursue for decision making, but also enhance the knowledge discovery experience for users.

Figure 5. The framework of visual recommendation (Huang & Liang, 2010)

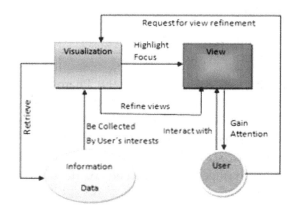

However, prior works mainly focused on traditional highlighting. In existing research, there is insufficient guidance for visual recommendation. Below are two rare cases which are potentially used in knowledge visualization.

5.5.1. Case One

Visual thesaurus (ThinkMap, 2008) powered by think map uses intelligence to suggest the words relating to or synonyms in a given language. Color, size and shape are used for the purpose of highlighting so that the viewing process can be facilitated. Rollover motion highlighting is also employed along with "back and forward" button, which allows users to interact and navigate in the maps of words. To assist learning the knowledge in thesaurus, the visual recommendation process is utilized. This mechanism highlights the words or the meaning of them based on system's definition of the term. As a result of this, users are enabled to act with suggestions made by the system. In this way, users can either narrow or broaden the meaning of term based on his or her own understanding and discover the knowledge. For example, if the user would like to look up the word "highlighting", then the think map could highlight suggestions within the thesaurus. In suc-

cession, the user clicked on one of the suggestions. Then the think map centralized and magnified the word "spotlight" and displayed another series of suggestions.

5.5.2. Case Two

In most situations, overloaded information hidden in complex data set visualized by traditional treemaps could exceed human cognitive ability to process. The Angular Treemap approach offers flexibility to generate different layouts when needed for emphasizing interests of focus in the hierarchy. Angular treemaps can not only be applied to emphasize difference but also highlight similarity. (Liang et al., 2012) For instance, two rotated folders attract our attention. We realized that two folders have similar layouts and same colored file types. We opened the dataset following the directory indicated by angular treemaps. We found that they are almost duplicates with slight difference. In this example, similar structure or even same structure of files contained in two rectangles with different aspect ratios are easily neglected. Angular treemaps successfully prevented the overlook (Liang et al., 2012).

6. CONCLUSION

We believe that the extension of the term of 'highlighting' has not been completed yet. It will be continuously refined and extended with the growth of the data volume and advances of new technologies in information visualization and visual analytics. Most designers have not yet paid enough attention to the formal explanation and systematical theories. In most cases, 'highlighting' is still taken for grant as the use of color and light. As a result, 'highlighting' has been limited to basic viewing aid in most applications.

Therefore, this chapter has attempted to define and classify the existing and potential highlighting techniques. Highlighting covers many disciplines and areas of experiences, like science of cognition, user physiology, aesthetics, human vision study, visualization and visual analytics. The strong theory base is the ground for the evolution of highlighting. To ensure highlighting as lynchpin in visualization and interaction, we should continue the theory development, extend practices of highlighting and advance the user-center evaluation for highlighting. More specifically, it will be beneficial to utilize highlighting visualization to make greater contributions and long term impacts in several aspects. First, with formal evaluation and strong evidence, we can confidently recommend satisfactory highlighting techniques for clients and partners, based on their domain requirements and nature of their data. Second, this research provides some theoretic evidence for professionals to develop more effective visualization tools, in terms of user's needs. Third, it will additionally benefit education and training curriculum development.

REFERENCES

Ahmed, A., Fu, X., Hong, S., Nguyen, Q., & Xu, K. (2009). Visual analysis of history of world cup: A dynamic network with dynamic hierarchy and geographic clustering. *Visual Information Communication*, 25-39. Berlin: Springer. doi:10.1007/978-1-4419-0312-9_2.

Andrew, K., & Heidegger, H. (1998). Information slices: Visualizing and exploring large hierarchies using cascading, semi-circular discs. In *Proceedings of IEEE Symposium on Information Visualization*, 9-12. New Brunswick, NJ: IEEE Press.

Bartram, L., & Ware, C. (2002). Filtering and brushing with motion. *Information Visualization*, *1*(1), 66–79.

Becker, R., & Cleveland, W. (1987). Brushing scatterplots. *Technimetrics*, *29*(2), 127–142. doi: 10.1080/00401706.1987.10488204.

Bederson, B. (2000). *Fisheye menus*. New York: ACM.

Bouthors, V., & Dedieu, O. (1999). Pharos, A collaborative infrastructure for web knowledge sharing. In Abiteboul, , & Vercoustre, (Eds.), *Research and Advanced Technology for Digital Libraries. Lecture Notes in Computer Science* (215-233). Berlin: Springer-Verlag, Inc. doi:10.1007/3-540-48155-9_15.

Huang, M. L., Liang, F. L., Chen, Y. W., Liang, J., & Nguyen, Q. V. (2012). Clutter reduction in multi-dimensional visualization of incomplete data using sugiyama algorithm. In *Proceedings of IEEE Information Visualization Conference*, 93-99. New Brunswick, NJ: IEEE Press.

Huang, M. L., & Liang, J. (2010). Highlighting in information visualization: A survey. In *Proceedings of IEEE Information Visualization Conference*, 79-85. New Brunswick, NJ: IEEE Press.

Huang, M. L., Liang, J., & Nguyen, Q. (2009). A visualization approach for frauds detection in financial market. *IEEE Information Visualization Conference*, 197-202. New Brunswick, NJ: IEEE Press.

Huang, W. (2013). Establishing aesthetics based on human graph reading behavior: Two eye tracking studies. *Personal and Ubiquitous Computing*, *17*(1), 93–105. doi:10.1007/s00779-011-0473-2.

Huang, W., Eades, P., & Hong, S.-H. (2009). A graph reading behavior: Geodesic-path tendency. In *Proceedings of the IEEE Pacific Visualization Symposium*, 137-144. Beijing: IEEE Press.

Huang, W., & Huang, M. L. (2010). Exploring the relative importance of crossing number and crossing angle. In *Proceedings of the 3rd International Symposium on Visual Information Communication*.New York: ACM Press.

Keim, D. A., Mansmann, F., Schneidewind, J., & Ziegler, H. (2006). Challenges in visual data analysis. *Information Visualization*, 9-16.

Kerr, B. (2003). Thread arcs: An email thread visualization. *Citeseer*. Retrieved from http://citeseer.uark.edu:8080/citeseerx/showciting;jsessionid=0BA75E333AE2127F3F70223E43A73075?cid=818372.

Kosara, R. & Miksch. (2001). Semantic depth of field, *Citeseer*. Retrieved from http://citeseer.uark.edu:8080/citeseerx/viewdoc/summary;jsessionid=298F7F0386E377889ECF1B4887C50C5B?doi=10.1.1.24.174.

Liang, J., Nguyen, Q. V., Simoff, S., & Huang, M. L. (2012). Angular treemaps–A new technique for visualizing and emphasizing hierarchical structures. In *Proceedings of IEEE Information Visualization Conference*, 74-80. New Brunswick, NJ: IEEE Press.

Liang, J., Nguyen, Q. V., Simoff, S., & Huang, M. L. (2013). Angular Treemaps. In Banissi, E. (Ed.), *Information Visualization-Techniques, Usability, & Evaluation*. Cambride, UK: Cambridge Scholar Publishing.

MacEachren, A., & Hardisty, . (2003). Supporting visual analysis of federal geospatial statistics. *Communications of the ACM*, *46*(1), 60. doi:10.1145/602421.602452.

Martin, A., & Ward, M. (1995). High dimensional brushing for interactive exploration of multivariate data. In *Proceedings of the 6th Annual Conference on Visualization*. New Brunswick, NJ: IEEE Computer Society.

Nguyen, Q. V., & Huang, M. L. (2004). A focus+context visualization technique using semi-transparency. In *Proceedings of the Fourth International Conference on Computer and information Technology*, 101-108. New Brunswick, NJ: IEEE Press.

Nichols, D., Pemberton, D., Dalhoumi, S., Larouk, O., Belisle, C., & Twidale, M. (2000). DEBORA: Developing an interface to support collaboration in a digital library. In *Proceedings of European Conference on Digital Libraries*, 239-248. Lisbon, Portugal: ECDL Press.

Plumlee, M., & Ware, C. (2006). Zooming versus multiple window interfaces: Cognitive costs of visual comparisons. *ACM Transactions on Computer-Human Interaction*, *13*(2), 209. doi:10.1145/1165734.1165736.

RINA Systems, Inc. (n.d.). Retrieved from http://www.rinafinancial.com/.

Robinson, A. (2009). Visual highlighting methods for geovisualization. *Citeseer*. Retrieved from http://citeseerx.ist.psu.edu/index

Robinson, A., & Center, G. (2006). Highlighting techniques to support geovisualization. *Citeseer*. Retrieved from http://citeseer.uark.edu:8080/citeseerx/viewdoc/summary;jsessionid=C7399B91D98763433F13B57449C2AC90?doi=10.1.1.79.757.

Seo, J., & Shneiderman, B. (2005). A rank-by-feature framework for interactive exploration of multidimensional data. *Information Visualization*, *4*(2), 96–113. doi:10.1057/palgrave.ivs.9500091.

Shi, K., Irani, P., & Li, B. (2005). An evaluation of content browsing techniques for hierarchical space-filling visualizations. In *Proceedings of IEEE Symposium on Information Visualization*, 81-88. New Brunswick, NJ: IEEE Press.

Siirtola, H. & K. J. R. (2006). Interacting with parallel coordinates. *Interacting with Computers, 18*(6), 1278–1309. doi:10.1016/j.intcom.2006.03.006.

Stasko, J., & Zhang, E. (2000). Focus + contest display and navigation techniques for enhancing radial, space-filling hierarchy visualizations. In *Proceedings of IEEE Symposium on Information Visualization*, 57. New Brunswick, NJ: IEEE.

Steinberger, M., Waldner, M., Streit, M., Lex, A., & Schmalstieg, D. (2011). Context–Preserving visual links. *IEEE Transactions on Visualization and Computer Graphics, 17*(12), 2249–2258. doi:10.1109/TVCG.2011.183 PMID:22034344.

ThinkMap Visual Thesaurus. (n.d.). Retrieved from http://www.visualthesaurus.com/.

Villarroel, M. (2006). Visualizing shared highlighting annotations. *HCI Related Papers of Interaction,* (195).

Ware, C., & Bobrow, R. (2004). Motion to support rapid interactive queries on node-link diagrams. *ACM Transactions on Applied Perception, 1*(1), 3–18. doi:10.1145/1008722.1008724.

Ware, C., & Bobrow, R. (2005). Supporting visual queries on medium-sized node-link diagrams. *Information Visualization, 4*(1), 49–58. doi:10.1057/palgrave.ivs.9500090.

Ware, C., & Gilman, A. (2008). *Visual thinking with an interactive diagram*. Berlin: Springer.

Washington D.C. Interactive Map. (n.d.). Retrieved from http://www.cs.umd.edu/class/fall2002/cmsc838s/tichi/fisheye.html.

Chapter 10
The Quest for Clarity:
How Visualization Improves the Usability and User Experience of Contracts

Stefania Passera
Aalto University School of Science, Finland

Helena Haapio
University of Vaasa, Finland & Lexpert Ltd., Finland

ABSTRACT

In today's networked economy, contracts are everywhere. Many of them are watertight and legally perfect documents attempting to refer to every conceivable contingency. For people expected to use or comply with them, such contracts are often difficult to read, comprehend, and/or implement. As an alternative to the current predominantly legal and textual approach, the authors propose a user-centered, visualized approach aimed at better usability and easier implementation. Both consumer and commercial contracts should be communicated in simpler and more user-friendly ways, and we believe that visualization can play a fundamental role in achieving this. This chapter introduces the concept of contract visualization and some early examples produced in this novel field. Results obtained in the first year of a five-year research project, carried out in collaboration with a partner company, indicate preliminary confirmation of positive effects in improving contract usability and related user experience through visualization.

INTRODUCTION

When we hear the words *visual analytics*, what immediately comes to mind is sophisticated computational tools, large datasets, algorithms and digital visual interfaces, all of them playing their part in generating images to represent complex data structures that humans will otherwise have difficulty interpreting. This paper directs attention to the utilization of visualizations in analyzing and communicating complex information using a more 'handcrafted' approach.

DOI: 10.4018/978-1-4666-4309-3.ch010

Depending on whether you ask a computer scientist or a graphic designer, information design means a quite different set of practices and outcomes. One of the Authors of this chapter is a trained graphic designer who is fascinated by the idea of graphic design as a service, a way of displaying information and knowledge in a human-centered, simple and engaging manner.

Many areas of human social life are regrettably suffused with complexity, bureaucracy, dogmatic traditions and a lack of clear communication. One of these areas is contracts and contracting. The other Author of this chapter, a legal practitioner and long-time pioneer in crossing the boundaries of traditional law, has many years of experience in this field, and has always advocated the use of contracts to achieve business success and prevent problems, aims which require simplification and clarity.

The topic of this chapter comes from a genuine desire to conduct research in a multidisciplinary way in order to tackle a specific problem–contract complexity–that has negative effects on both consumers and private and public organizations. In addition to the traditional *reactive* legal perspective on contracts being minimized, other values from a range of disciplines enter the picture: efficiency, effectiveness and value (from business research), promoting successful outcomes, preventing problems, and balancing risk with reward (from *proactive* law and proactive contracting) (Siedel & Haapio, 2011), and user-centeredness and communicativeness (from design research). The novelty in our research is the focus on simplifying knowledge transfer and enhancing shared understanding in contracting by introducing visualizations and elements of information design into the contracting process and documents. We define this research area as *contract visualization*. In terms of sorting information in the belief that complexity can be made

understandable and clarity can be reached through essential, rigorous abstraction (Irwin, 2002), it shares the goals of information design. Contract visualization can also be seen as a subset of the wider research area of knowledge visualization, which can be defined as the creation and transfer of knowledge by visualizations with or without the help of a computer (Burkhard, 2005a), with the aim of supporting cognitive processes in generating, representing, structuring, retrieving, sharing and using knowledge (Tergan, Keller, & Burkhard, 2006).

The benefits of visualization in supporting evidence analysis, explanation, and reasoning have been extensively described in the literature, especially by Tufte (1983, 1990, 1997, 2006), while other authors have begun investigating the possibilities of applying visualization and collaborative, co-located visualizing activities to managerial and organizational practices (e.g. Bresciani, Eppler & Tan, 2011; Roos, Bart & Statler, 2004; Eppler & Platts, 2009; Platts & Tan, 2004). These previous theoretical contributions, together with abundant evidential knowledge from the field of graphic design, constitute the basis for our hypothesis that beneficial results can be expected to flow from the application of visualization in contracts.

Even though visualizations started appearing in legal and contractual documents in recent years, very little research has been conducted so far and the work that has been done has not been systematic. This book chapter has three goals: to define the theoretical motivations behind contract visualization and the practical problems it seeks to tackle, to introduce an overview of the examples of early legal and contract visualizations that inspired our research, and to present the results of an experimental evaluation that appears to confirm the positive effects of visualization on the usability and user experience of contracts.

BACKGROUND

The ability to understand and use contracts in collaborative relationships is increasingly important. Most companies nowadays work in collaboration with other companies, and the added value delivered to end customers depends on a complex network of actors. As the purpose of contracts is to describe and guide the roles, responsibilities and performance of such actors, they are complex in nature even when they try to be as clear as possible (Passera & Haapio, 2011a). This complexity often overloads the cognitive abilities of readers (Hagedorn & Hesen, 2009; Posner, 2010) and reveals that most contracts do not match their users' needs and show bad cognitive ergonomics. (Passera & Haapio, 2011b) For the people involved, this can lead to job dissatisfaction. For the companies they work for, it can lead to missed opportunities, sour and uncooperative business relationships, and even to long-drawn out disputes and litigation.

But who are these users? They can be divided into two major groups: the legal community and the business community. To date, the focus of contract drafters and scholars has been predominantly on the needs of the former: legal practitioners and researchers, judges, arbitrators and teachers of law. Most of the discussion about using contracts has been about applying them in court, after a dispute has arisen.

For a young lawyer just out of law school, the goal of contract design is almost certainly a contract that is as close to perfect as possible: legally-binding, enforceable, unambiguous, and providing solutions for all imaginable contingencies (Pohjonen & Visuri, 2008). The goal for them is the contract itself. In contrast, the business community requires a different approach because the goal is successful implementation. Signing a contract is just the beginning of the process of creating value together with suppliers, partners and customers (Ertel, 2004). Contracts do not make things happen–people do. In both commercial contracts and public procurement, to agree on desired outcomes and the activities needed to achieve them, key people on both sides have to be able to capture, elaborate, structure, communicate, access and use information and knowledge. Then 'reality' arrives and contracts have to be implemented through concrete actions: people in project delivery teams need to know how work should be carried out and people with financial responsibility need to know how much is due to whom and when. In the field, contracts are seldom easy for users to understand and implement, and contract interpretation remains the largest single source of contract litigation between business firms (Schwartz & Scott, 2010). If the parties involved do not truly understand their roles and the implications of the actions they take, the contract–a piece of paper with a signature–cannot achieve miracles and make the transaction and relationships it defines successful.

In organizational settings, contracts pose at least two challenges, one at the level of individuals and the other at social level. The first challenge follows from the fact that contracts are seldom easy for their users in the field, most of whom have no legal training, to access, understand and to implement. If contract complexity overloads their readers' cognitive abilities and contract implementation consequently fails, it would be wrong to maintain that such contracts are perfect. Quite the opposite, they are not fit for purpose. According to the cognitive load theory (Sweller, van Merrienboer, & Paas, 1998), three types of cognitive load exist (intrinsic, extraneous, germane). Dense, text-only contracts do not help in reducing this load: the task of reading long, difficult documents is time-taking and requires concentration (intrinsic load), the language and terminology used to represent the information may not be self-evident to the reader (extraneous load), and efforts to understand and learn the information provided are often far from being intuitive and unconscious (germane load).

One solution would be to move from legalese to plain language. A number of studies confirm the benefits of this approach and its preferred status among many groups of readers – clients (Adler, 1991), judges (Kimble, 2006), and the public (Plain Language Institute of British Columbia, 1993). On the other hand, conventional (especially Anglo-American) drafters of contracts still consider legalese superior. They talk about the benefits of using language that has been tested. For them, legalese has a clearly established and settled meaning. The reference here is to language that has been the subject of litigation. But why rely on language that resulted in litigation? While such language may help to win a battle in court, it does not help those who want to avoid such conflict to reach successful business outcomes. There is also little scientific evidence to support the use of legalese. Common arguments employed focus on the difficulties of adopting plain language (Tiersma, 2006), rather than explaining why legalese is superior from a cognitive, communicational or even practical (i.e. efficiency/effectiveness) perspective. In this light, rather than a substantiated choice, legalese appears to be more a professional convention grounded in tradition and sustained by the difficulty of achieving change. While we welcome and support the use of plain language, we do not believe that plain language alone would suffice to make contracts unambiguous and simple to use in everyday practice.

Contracts often attempt to communicate intangible and complex information. To add an extra layer of difficulty, the fact that clauses refer regularly to other clauses means they resemble hypertext, making it impossible to retrieve all the relevant knowledge from a single location. Text, even in its plainer forms, is not a good tool for communicating the abstract relationships hidden in a document such as the structure of the document itself or the implementation processes it seeks to describe. Also, it does not provide or illustrate a logical structure for making sense of correlated, but scattered, information. According to Keller and Grimm (2005), visualizing such sense-making structures can help reduce external cognitive load because users do not then have to autonomously develop mental structures for managing this information. Visualizations can serve as a basis for externalized cognition (Scaife & Rogers, 1996) and enhance readers' processing ability.

The second challenge is that even though the individuals whose actions are defined in a contract must understand what is required of them, this is not enough when the context of use is a heterogeneous group of people. Different individuals have to communicate, collaborate and synchronize their activities in order to produce and deliver what has been agreed. All these interactions are carried out in a social context. In which different actors collect, negotiate and share meanings. Such processes can be viewed through the lens of knowledge management, an approach that stresses the importance of knowledge creation, capture and transfer in keeping an organization effective, innovative and competitive (Burkhard, 2005b). Knowledge is embedded in culture, systems, artefacts, and individuals and can be managed through four processes (Alavi & Leidner, 2001), its creation, its storage and retrieval, its transfer, and its application. These stages can also be used to describe the contracting process. In which knowledge concerning the goals, scope and terms of a specific form of collaboration is first collected and created through negotiations, then recorded or stored in a contract. Contract implementation, the most important phase of all, is about retrieving and applying such knowledge. As all members of the teams involved must become aware of what is required of them, the process used to transfer this knowledge must be an effective one.

According to Burkhard (2005b), for knowledge to be transferred and then applied, it must be conveyed to individuals in the correct context. Such contexts are extremely heterogeneous. In different organizations, and even in different departments within the same organization, there is a clear risk that the parties involved in a discussion are not actually talking about the same issue, even though all of them believe they are: different practices, cultures and business needs influence the ways that people think. Maintaining an awareness of this invisible, tacit and complex factor at all times is very hard. Also, this is clearly not the type of information best expressed using text or clauses in a contract. Inter-company understanding appears to be a typical case in which the knowledge transfer process is difficult and sticky (Von Hippel, 1994), because the knowledge being exchanged is complex and causally ambiguous (Szulanski, 2000). Eppler (2004) identified chasms of knowledge between experts and managers that can be bridged with the help of *knowledge communication* the deliberate activity of interactively conveying and co-constructing insights, assessments, experiences or skills through verbal or non-verbal means.

This is where visualization enters the picture: even though most of the contracts written today are text-only, they could benefit from the years of research and practice in the field of information design and knowledge visualization which demonstrate convincingly how visual elements can work in parallel with text to enrich and clarify its meaning. Burkhard (2005b) also suggested that knowledge transfer can rely on the powerful and innate human ability to effectively process visual representations. Visualizations can make the invisible visible, help to illustrate relationships and patterns, focus the attention of readers and support recall, coordinate individual thoughts and activities, and illustrate different courses of action. These benefits mean that visualization can be part of a practical solution for tackling issues connected with both cognitive overload and knowledge transfer.

To summarize, even though communication between the parties involved is a vital aspect of successful business relationships, the focus of today's contract designers and drafters continues to be on legal risk allocation, rather than on how best to communicate the deal that has been made and the resulting relationship, together

with its terms, to those who need to understand and implement it. A mental exercise for reconsidering this attitude would be to view contracts and contract visualizations as boundary objects, artefacts–not necessarily physical ones–serving as negotiating interfaces between communities, practices and people communicating and working together through them (Star & Griesemer, 1989). If the focus is shifted towards collaboration and successful working practices, a comprehensive rethink of the types of instruments and tools being used and consideration of whether they have been consciously designed to be fit for purpose is imperative. The requirement for contracts to express essential information in a user-centered and user-friendly way becomes even clearer, because if there is any misunderstanding, the parties involved cannot simply do their best and attempt to keep their promises.

The remainder of this book chapter develops two main topics. Firstly, we provide an overview of early examples of contract-related visualizations which. In addition to having inspired our research, show how such techniques can be successfully applied, as well as having a user-friendly 'look and feel'. Secondly, we introduce our case study. In which a prototype visualized contract was developed and tested with users. Our experimental evaluation focused on assessing whether visualized contracts provide improved usability and a better user experience than contracts in the traditional, text-only form.

THE QUEST FOR CLARITY AND USER-FRIENDLINESS IN CONTRACTS

Beyond Text in Legal Design: Early Examples

Some pioneers have already gone beyond text in the design of legal documents. In Central Europe, the visualization of legal information has developed into a research field in its own right. In German-speaking countries, the terms legal visualization (Rechtsvisualisierung), visual legal communication, visual law and multisensory law have all been used to describe this growing field of research and practice. (Brunschwig, 2011, 2001)

In the United States, the use of visualizations has been studied, for example. In the context of improving comprehension of jury instructions (Semmler & Brewer, 2002; Dattu 1998) and in facilitating the making of complex decisions connected with dispute resolution (Siedel, 1992). Visualization has also been observed in the role of a persuasion tool in a variety of settings from the courtroom (Feigenson & Spiesel, 2009; Solomon, 2006) to the boardroom.

Recently, visual elements such as timelines and photos have even made their way into court decisions in both Europe and the United States. In Sweden, a judgment of the Court of Appeal for Western Sweden (2009) includes two timeline images showing the chain of events which is crucial to understanding the facts of the case. This particular judgment won the Plain Swedish Crystal 2010, a plain language award, not only for being written in a pedagogical and innovative manner, having a clear structure, good paragraphing, clarifying summaries and subheadings, but also for the fact that reading it was facilitated by bullet points and images (Språkrådet, 2010). In the United States, an Opinion by Judge Richard Posner of the Chicago-based 7th U.S. Circuit Court of Appeals uses the ostrich metaphor to criticize lawyers who ignore court precedent. Two photos are included in this opinion: one of an ostrich with its head buried in the sand, another of a man in a suit with his head buried in the sand. (Posner, 2011)

In Canada in 2000, recognizing the need for new ways to generate public interest in the law, the Government commissioned a White Paper proposing a new format for legislation. This document by David Berman (2000), a visual communication designer, also introduced the concept of using diagrams to help describe laws. While creating a flowchart diagram, Berman's team also revealed inconsistencies not accounted for in the legislation, suggesting that if rendering laws in diagrammatic form was part of the drafting process, the resulting legislation could in some instances be substantively improved. (Berman, 2000)

Another convincing example of visualizing legal rules is the Street Vendor Project, work carried out by designer Candy Chang in collaboration with the Center for Urban Pedagogy in New York. After noting that the rulebook [of legal code] is intimidating and hard to understand by anyone, let alone someone whose first language is not English, the project prepared *Vendor Power!*, a visual Street Vendor Guide that makes city regulations accessible and understandable (Figure 1). Together with a modest amount of text, the guide features diagrams illustrating vendors' rights and the rules which are most commonly violated. (Chang, n.d.)

Figure 1. Excerpt from Vendor Power!–A visual guide to the rights and duties for street vendors in New York City Project description available at http://welcometocup.org/Projects/MakingPolicy-Public/VendorPower

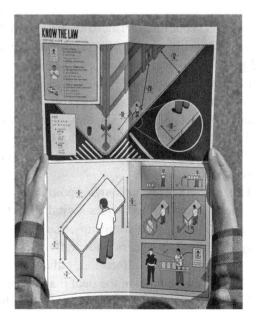

Visualization is also applied with educational intent in the Wolfram Demonstrations Project, an open-code resource that uses dynamic computation to illuminate concepts in science, technology, mathematics, art, finance, and a remarkable range of other fields (Wolfram Demonstrations Project, n.d.). The project includes a rich library of visual and interactive demonstrations taken from the field of law, including a clarification of the so-called 'Battle of Forms'. Such a battle arises in the not uncommon situation where one company makes an offer using a pre-printed form containing its standard terms, and the other party responds with its own form and set of standard terms. The Wolfram Demonstrations platform allows users to choose various details of the case, with the output showing the most likely judicial finding as to whether a contract exists and the terms of that contract, together with a graph explaining the argument that will be advanced in support of that judicial finding. (The Wolfram platform can be tested at: http://demonstrations. wolfram.com/VisualizingLegalRulesBattleOfTheForms/).

With such obvious benefits, why is more visual material not seen used in contracts, contract negotiations, and in communications about contracts? One of the reasons for the dominance of text could well be the fact that with few exceptions, lawyers are accustomed to conveying their thoughts and ideas using nothing but words (Siedel & Haapio, 2011).

Research related to legal risks in the context of contracts conducted at the Faculty of Law in the University of Oslo provides an exception: using icons and diagrams illustrating legal risk, both a graphical modeling language and a method for proactive legal analysis were developed. (Mahler, 2010) In a case study, a group of lawyers, managers, and engineers were asked to use the method to analyze the risks connected with a contract proposal. The results of the case study showed that the diagrams were perceived as being very helpful in communicating risk-related aspects

amongst the study participants. On the other hand, the need for simplicity and usability also resulted in some limitations and the need for a system in which graphical and natural-language elements are combined to allow improved decision-making (Mahler, 2010).

Flowcharts appear to be a useful tool for clarifying information which is complex and possibly ambiguous, not only because they offer a simple and easily recognizable method for displaying questions and answers, but also because the method is familiar to business audiences. Jones and Oswald (2001; Jones, 2009) provide examples of how flowcharts can be successfully used to clarify contractual information, showing concrete examples of how elements such as the logic of contract structure, the actors involved, and clauses such as contract duration and indemnification can be visualized, as well as explaining why this should be done. Another example, from the UK, is the NEC family of contracts for procuring works, services and supply, together with associated guidance notes and flowcharts which make understanding them easier. Originally known as the *New Engineering Contract*, NEC has been widely praised for its collaborative, integrated and practical approach to procurement (NEC, n.d.).

That the flowchart approach is both flexible and replicable in other sets of terms and conditions is shown by an ongoing experiment developed by one of the Authors in collaboration with Kuntaliitto, the Association of Finnish Local and Regional Authorities (Pohjonen & Koskelainen, 2012). With the help of icons and flowcharts, this project is creating a freely available visual guide to the General Terms of Public Procurement in Service Contracts (Ministry of Finance, 2009). Figure 2 is one example—a flowchart that describes in visual form the situation in which a defective service has been supplied. In the flowchart, the implications of different actions are explored and the logic adopted in the contract for resolving the problem is shown. Readers can easily identify the situation at hand, and then use the flowchart to quickly check the preferred course of action and possible risks. Each block displayed in the chart is marked with the number of the clause in which the original information (in text form) can be found. After obtaining an overview and an initial orientation regarding the subject using the flowchart, users can proceed to reading the text for necessary details. In addition, as no contract is perfect, the flowchart also illustrates some limitations by pointing out cases in which the text of the JYSE 2009 Services General Terms do not provide a solution. Highlighting limitations of this type helps the parties involved to make informed decisions and agree separately on such points if they consider this to be important.

A different context in which examples of legal visualization can be found is the digital world: usage licenses, copyright and data privacy are now everyday issues which have an impact on everyone connected to the web. For example, Creative Commons licenses use simple, recognizable icons which can be clicked on to reveal a plain-language version of the relevant legal code (Creative Commons, n.d.). Users are informed about the possibilities and limitations of sharing, remixing and including the licensed content in free or commercial work (Figure 3). If additional information is required, the full text in legalese is also available and just one click away. This 'layered' approach is user-centric because it envisions use by different readers with different skills and knowledge needs.

Another experiment involving icons was carried out by Aza Raskin, a guru in interface design, for Mozilla. The set of Privacy Icons developed by Raskin can be used by websites to clarify the ways in which users of the website are agreeing to allow their personal data to be used (Figure 3). The inspiration for this work was twofold: the desire for simplicity in the Creative Commons approach to icons, and attempts to raise awareness about the attributes in privacy policy and terms of service that people should care about (Raskin,

n.d.). As well as providing users with a more transparent service, utilization of the Privacy Icons can also enhance the brand image of websites that wish to differentiate themselves in terms of their privacy-related good practice.

In the light of a growing number of examples, visualizations appear to be finding their way into the communication of law-related messages and documents – a development which has been promoted by Colette R. Brunschwig (2001, 2011) and other pioneers for quite some time. On the other hand, contract visualization research and practice are still in a seminal phase, with most authors concentrating on theoretical suggestions or the presentation of examples.

To date, the number of tests conducted on contract visualization techniques to clearly assess their benefits in terms of cognition and attention levels, and memory retention, is small. Kay and Terry (2010) have experimented with textured agreements, which they describe as visually redesigned agreements that employ factoids, vignettes, and iconic symbols, with the aim of increasing the time that users spend reading the End-User License Agreements (EULAs) shown during software installation. The measures they are proposing indicate that visualization techniques increase the levels of interest displayed by readers and related attention spans.

An experiment was conducted to assess the usability of the Canadian Employment Insurance Act (GLPi & Schmolka, 2000), after it had been redesigned following the plain language and plain information design principles proposed in the already-mentioned White Paper by Berman (2000). In this case, which is not about a contract but a piece of legislation, the visualized version of the document also performed better than the traditional text-based one. Unfortunately, because the variables involved were not measured separately, this experiment failed to clearly distinguish between the benefits resulting from the use of plain language and those associated with visualization.

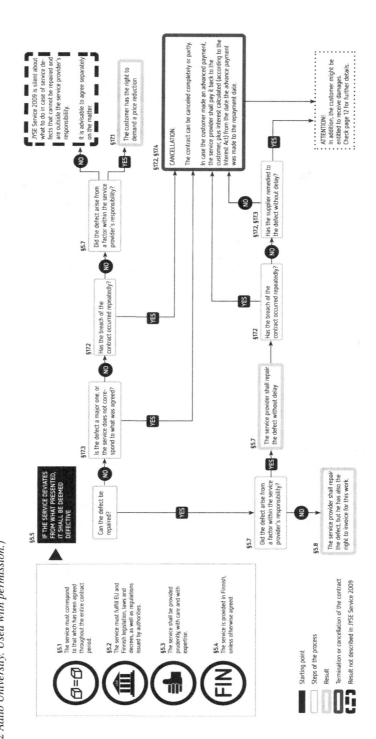

Figure 2. Flowchart visualizing contract clauses dealing with defects in service provision: extract from a visual guide (draft version) to the General Terms of Public Procurement in Service Contracts (Ministry of Finance, 2009) Work in progress (© 2012 Aalto University. Used with permission.)

Figure 3. Examples of icons used for the rapid communication of complex content on the Web. Top: The Creative Commons Licence icons and the Creative Commons licence rationale. Bottom: Mozilla Privacy Icons by Aza Raskin
(© 2010. Aza Raskin. Used with permission.)

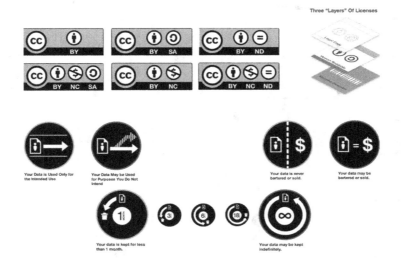

The field of contract visualization still lacks adequate empirical data on the methods, tools and best practices to be employed in implementing visualization techniques when drafting contracts, as well as data that supports the efficiency and effectiveness of this type of approach. Our goal is to move forward from what might be called the preliminary examples stage and extend the discourse by prototyping visual contracts in suitable contexts, collecting feedback from users, and analyzing the impact of contract visualization.

The aim of the case study and experimental evaluation presented in the next section of this chapter is to provide initial empirical data on the benefits of contract visualization. The experiment was the first in a series which, by using the same methodology but different contracts relevant to different groups of users, is seeking to assess whether contracts which employ visualization techniques really do make use by their target groups easier. The generic concept of easiness has been translated into two main testable measures drawn from the design tradition and commonly used to evaluate whether a specific artefact matches the needs of its user group. The first measure,

usability, is used to assess the functionality and fitness for purpose of the contract document. The second measure, User experience (UX), is used in assessing the overall quality of interaction between user and artefact, and can therefore be used to investigate more widely the expectations of contract users, their perceptions and their subsequent experiential evaluations. It is our belief that by optimizing usability and the user experience, user-friendly contracts can be created which both support understanding and promote engagement with the content.

Case Study: Designing and Testing a Visual Contract Prototype with Users

The focus of this case is the experimental evaluation of a prototype B2B contract that contains visualizations. To minimize any threat to the general validity of the results, it was important to work with actual users in a real setting, testing documents as similar as possible to those already in use. The case study was carried out in cooperation with a Finnish company operating in the metals and engineering sector. On the company side, the case owners came from the sourcing department. Both the company and its case owners were conscious of the need to identify and employ novel methods of involving suppliers in delivering better levels of quality to end customers.

Preliminary interviews and workshops provided a rich qualitative background and a better understanding of the contract-related problems being experienced. For example, suppliers perceived the company's current terms and contract templates to be complicated and inflexible, which translated into sourcing personnel experiencing difficulty in negotiating forms of collaboration that were truly based on mutual trust and engagement. Other problems identified included common bottlenecks in the delivery process and specific contract clauses that were often subject to misinterpretation.

A second element in the preliminary analysis was a survey of the contract templates used in such negotiations. All the examples assessed typically consisted of text with almost no formatting apart from a simple table of contents and capitalized headings. As in many other contract templates, no attention had been given to typographical elements such as font size, font type and margins, all of which are factors known by graphic designers to have a significant effect on both legibility (the degree of recognizability of individual letters, a function of typeface design) and readability (the ease with which text can be read and understood, which depends on factors such as line length, kerning, indentations, point size, justification and so on).

Listening to contract users and their stories about real-life contracting events was an important step in deciding on the direction for the design intervention. Aims included improving the typography and document layout, highlighting key sections of the document by using visual techniques such as colors and bold text, and introducing charts and diagrams to explain the text in a way that was more user-friendly. The text of the contract was redrafted by the case company's in-house legal counsel in order to make it shorter and simpler. As each round of visual and textual suggestions went through iterative cycles involving feedback from users, they were able to both comment on the direction of the intervention and steer it according to their real-life needs. The result of this process was a credible prototype of a visual contract template. While text in the document was based on the original contract template, it did not reflect any particular business case. This was important at a later stage in the test procedure, as rather than relying on their familiarity with previous cases, participants were able to provide responses that were more genuine and immediate.

The main visual features of the contract prototype (Figures 4 and 5) can be summarized as follows:

- Better readability through the use of shorter text lines and wider margins
- Better legibility through use of the Utopia typeface rather than Arial. Utopia is both more legible and more condensed, which means that more text can be placed on a page even when shorter lines are used to improve readability
- Color and positioning used to highlight the headings in each clause
- Key terms and concepts in the text highlighted by using bold type
- Bulleted lists used to state the long lists of elements previously contained in text paragraphs
- The use of color coding in the table of contents to highlight recurring topics and the overall document structure
- The inclusion of charts, diagrams, timelines and flowcharts to clarify selected sections of the contract text (including a timeline to clarify the validity and termination clause, a flowchart providing an overview of the process, and photographs to indicate how the purchased materials should be packaged)

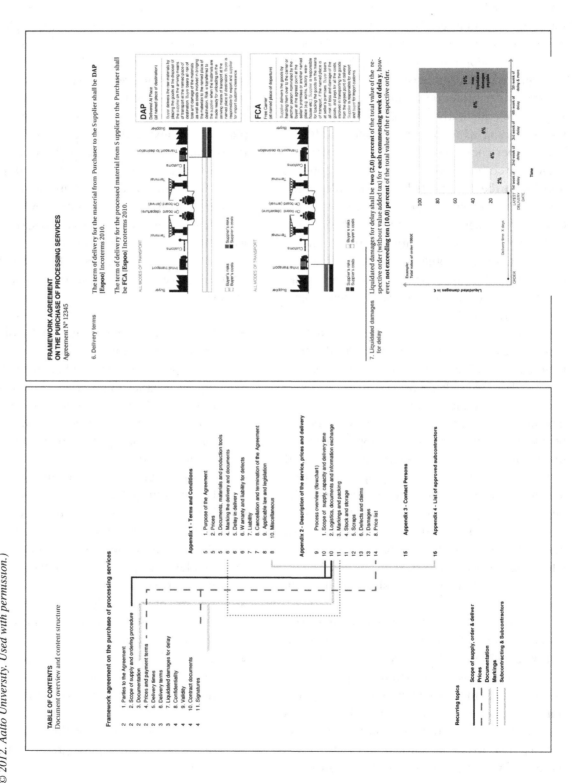

Figure 4. Example pages from a Framework Agreement: color-coded table of contents (bottom) and document layout including a delivery terms diagram and a liquidated damages bar chart (top) (© 2012. Aalto University. Used with permission.)

Figure 5. Examples of visualized clauses in a Framework Agreement: validity (top) and storage conditions (bottom)
(© 2012. Aalto University. Used with permission.)

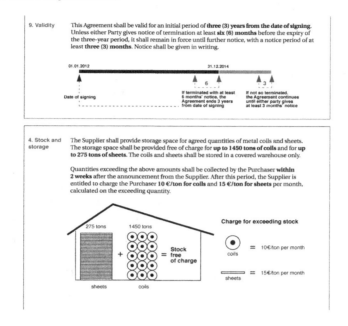

Hypotheses

When the prototype contract with visualized elements was ready, it was tested. The goal was to assess whether the new visual version was easier to use and more user-friendly than the previous text-only version. Values associated with the terms easier and more user-friendly emerged from the preliminary interviews with contract users and can be categorised as follows:

1. Faster to read
2. Easier to understand
3. Less complicated to skim through
4. Information less complicated to identify
5. Helping to avoid misunderstandings and mistakes
6. Reduced levels of frustration

These values are easy to associate with two important measures used in assessing successful designs: usability and User experience (UX). Usability has been defined as the extent to which a product can be used by specified users to achieve specified goals with effectiveness, efficiency, and satisfaction in a specified context of use (ISO 9241-11, 1998). Often associated with functionality, the domain of usability focuses on the degree to which a task is performed effectively and efficiently. Preliminary interviews with the case study participants revealed that the existing text-only contracts they used were long and difficult to read, and that due to their complexity, misunderstandings among different contract readers were a frequent occurrence. For contract users to efficiently and effectively perform their work, quicker reading, easier understanding and making fewer mistakes are all important elements. Both reading speed and correct understanding are metrics that can reveal how usable a contract is, and also allow for quantitative comparisons between different contract versions. The goal of improved contract usability through the inclusion of visual elements–contract visualization–was therefore conceptualized into the following experimental hypotheses:

- **H1:** Visualized contracts support faster reading and information finding
- **H2:** Visualized contracts support more accurate understanding of the information provided

The second concept, User experience (UX), has its origins in research into user-centered design (Usability Professionals' Association [UPA], n.d.). In general terms, UX can be defined as [e]very aspect of the user's interaction with a product, service or company that make up the user's perceptions of the whole (Nuutinen, Seppänen, Mäkinen & Keinonen, 2011). In addition to the pragmatic needs that are mostly addressed by usability, UX attempts to satisfy users' emotional, hedonic and contextual needs. Even though an experience as such cannot be designed, it is possible to design for an improved user experience by providing suitable tools, evidences (Shostack, 1977) or scaffolds that users can employ when building their own experience (Sanders, 2002). In our case, the experience of working with contracts was often described by participants as complicated and frustrating. Their enthusiasm for contracts was limited and they were not willing to spend a lot of time on them, and negative past experiences affected their future expectations. Contracts were viewed as a necessary evil, and most of the participants indicated that they would avoid having to handle them if this were possible.

UX is a dynamic concept, and it can be expressed as experience before usage (anticipated UX), experience during usage (momentary UX), experience after usage (episodic UX) and experience over time (cumulative UX) (Roto, Law, Vermeeren, & Hoonhout, 2011). In our experiment, a single contract usage event was adopted as the unit of analysis, and participants were not asked to verbalize their experience while reading the contract document because this would have affected their concentration and disrupted the verisimilitude of the task. It was therefore only possible to measure and compare the anticipated

UX and the episodic UX. Hypotheses on the impact of visualization on these two dimensions were expressed as:

- **H3:** Visualized contracts provide a more positive user experience than text-only contracts
- **H4:** Visualized contracts affect users' expectations in a positive manner

Test Procedure

The test procedure was a partial repetition in structure and approach, of the test used to assess the usability of the redesigned Canadian Employment Insurance Act (GLPi & Schmolka, 2000). This piece of legislation was redrafted in plain language, with flowcharts, enhanced typography and layout all helping to enhance the clarity and readability of the information it contained. We considered this approach to be a suitable precedent for our case study. With a few modifications and additions, the testing procedure used for assessing the usability of the redesigned Canadian Employment Insurance Act proved suitable for testing our four hypotheses.

The test utilizes two methods of data collection: a self-administered questionnaire in three parts (before, during, and after using a contract), and a follow-up focus group discussion. Our study took place in December 2011 and January 2012 with three different sessions being organized. As in the original study, different user groups were involved to allow data to be gathered from all relevant stakeholders. Study respondents were drawn in roughly equal numbers from four company departments: five from legal, six from sourcing, six from sales, and five from supply chain management, and these 22 respondents were then divided into an experimental group and a control group, the first using a visualized contract and the second using a text-only contract. None were involved in giving feedback during the contract redesign phase, and respondents were only able to view the contract for the first time during the test to ensure that the feedback they gave was uncompromised. On the other hand, the respondents can still be considered to be informed users, because of their familiarity with the original contract templates and the types of agreement used in their company, all of which made up the raw material for our redesign. Working with informed users was a necessary condition for maintaining a reasonable degree of realism in the experimental setting and being able to trust the resulting data. The goal of assessing usability and UX was to optimize the contract design for real-world users. The respondents were small in number, yet selecting large statistical samples would not have been meaningful in this context. In our case study, the characteristics and skills of the people who were the respondents was more important than their number.

The structure of the test reflects the different aspects dealt with in our four hypotheses. In the first part. In addition to general questions such as age, gender and field of expertise, we asked the respondents to indicate on a 7-point scale how difficult they expected it to be (1 = not difficult at all, 7 = extremely difficult) to answer comprehension questions about what is agreed in a contract. This figure was taken as an indication of their general expectations. Respondents were then handed one of the two contract versions and asked to skim through it quickly. After this, they were asked to indicate how difficult they expected it to be to answer comprehension questions about what was agreed in that contract: this figure was taken as indicating the anticipated UX.

During the second part of the test, members of the experimental group were asked to answer eight comprehension questions with the help of the visualized contract, while members of the control group were asked to answer the same questions using a text-only version of the same contract. Even though the two contract versions were different in appearance, their text content was identical to avoid interference by other variables, and to more surely allow any difference

in the results to be attributed to the presence or absence of visual treatment. During this part of the test, both respondents' speed in providing each answer and the number of correct answers they gave were recorded.

In the third part of the test, respondents were asked to indicate how difficult it was to actually answer the comprehension questions about what was agreed in the contract they had been given. This figure was taken as indicating the episodic UX. They were then given the other version of the contract and allowed to look at both versions at the same time. Finally, they were asked to express a preference regarding how different aspects of the contract were handled in the two versions.

Respondents then participated in focus group sessions. One of the Authors facilitated these discussions, following a semi-structured interview format and prompting participants to feel free about expressing their impressions, their thoughts and their feedback. As qualitative data was required in order to understand the motivations behind contract users' preferences, and to discover what experiences and thoughts the visualized contract provoked, the focus group sessions were recorded and transcribed. Even though the participants were not native English speakers and their comments included linguistic errors, we decided to report them in their original form without making corrections.

Results of the Experimental Evaluation

In terms of both speed and accuracy, members of the experimental group using the visualized contract performed, on average, better than members of the control group using the text-only contract. The percentage of correct answers given in the experimental group was 71.9% compared to 60% in the control group (Figure 6). The average time per answer given was lower (i.e. they answered more quickly) for users of the visualized contract (mean = 164.26 seconds, SD = 105.8) than for

Figure 6. From left to right: 1) Correct answers (% of the total number of answers given per group), 2) Average time taken in answering a question (seconds with standard deviation), 3) Questions skipped because the respondent could not locate the necessary information (% of the total number of answers given per group)

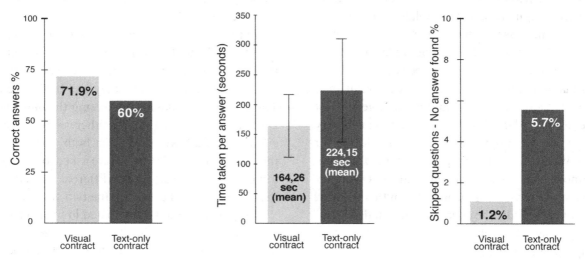

the text-only contract users (mean = 224.15, SD = 172.95). During the test, if they felt that they really could not find the required information, respondents had the possibility of pressing an 'emergency' button and abandoning an attempt to answer a question: this situation occurred four times in the control group (5.7% of the total number of answers given in the group), but only once in the experimental group (1.2% of the total number of answers given in the group).

During the focus group discussions, participants identified which visual elements helped improve the usability of the contracts they had been working with. Some of the related observations were made many times: for instance, the red lateral headings were considered clearer, the key terms highlighted in bold helped in finding relevant information, a less-dense layout made the contract more readable, topic-sensitive color-coding in the table of contents helped in identifying recurrent topics and where they could be found, and the visualizations employed gave hints about the content of the surrounding text, which made locating needed information faster as its location

was easier to recall, "From the first glance I already remembered … so when the question came I remembered straightaway where I saw it." A visual approach was also seen as a useful way of supporting understanding: some respondents said, "It's understandable from text also, but [visualization] helps you to understand it faster or even clearer," or, "If it's only text, I think I need to read it a couple more times before I really understand what is says."

In terms of individual expectations and perceived difficulty, the visualized version of the contract appeared to be regarded as more user-friendly while also inspiring greater confidence among users. Before seeing the contract to be used, the initial expected difficulty in answering comprehension questions in the experimental group averaged 3.42 (SD = 0.62) on a 7-point scale (1 = not difficult at all, 7 = extremely difficult) and 3.80 (SD = 1.03) in the control group (Figure 7). After skimming through their assigned contract versions, members of the experimental group anticipated an average difficulty of 3.50 (SD = 1.26), while the average for the control group

Figure 7. Perceived difficulty in contract utilization (self-assessed). Comparison between the experimental (visualized contract) and control (text-only contract) groups before the contract was viewed, after it was viewed, and after it had been used

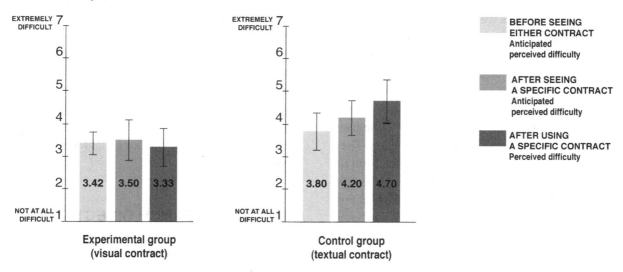

was 4.20 (SD = 1.07). Actual working with the visualized contract suggested an experience comparable to expectations, while working with the text-only version suggested an experience that was somewhat more difficult than expected. A clearer trend emerged after considering the perceived level of difficulty declared after the comprehension questions: the average for the experimental group (visualized contract) was slightly lower at 3.33 (SD = 1.17), while the average for the control group (text-only contract) rose to 4.70 (SD = 1.34). These results are also relevant in experiential terms, since despite the fact that the text in both contract versions was identical, and therefore in theory equally easy (or difficult) to understand, the presence of visualizations appeared to inspire responses that were less negative.

Data collected during the focus group sessions revealed some of the participants' reasons for preferring the visual version of the contract, "One picture tells more than thousand words, It is not always clear 'what is what' in the text, so I liked these pictures because they help, [the contract] became more interesting to see, It is more inviting, It is more readable, It is easier to find [answers],"

and, "When the text confuses me I always need to read it few times. But if there is also an image that explains it, then reading one time is enough." Several of the factors highlighted were related to improved contract usability, but comments from the focus session participants revealed how this had also a positive effect on the usage experience. Their descriptions of the visualized contract as more interesting and more inviting indicates that contracts were probably not considered (or expected) to be interesting or inviting in any way. Visualizations seemed to provide a more positive experience, which was able to catch the attention of previously disillusioned users and engage them in new ways.

Another point worth noting is that contract visualizations could help companies in communicating specific values and improving the levels of trust and collaboration with suppliers. Test respondents were asked to compare the two contract versions by imagining that each had been drafted by a different company. They were then asked which values they associated with the hypothetical companies that had drafted the different contracts. Most respondents appeared to associate visualized contracts with more-trustworthy, innovative, and quality-oriented organizations. Other brand values inferred for the companies creating visualized contracts were openness to collaboration, transparency, and honesty (Table 1). In the focus group sessions, additional thoughts relating to company values and image emerged, and the participants tried to imagine what it would feel like to be working with actual visual contracts. One participant said, "It could increase the trust felt by the business people of the other party. They would know that we are trying to make the contract in a way that everybody really understands what is in it." Other participants added, "[visualization offers] some support to ensure that we are being clear about all the important points, or gather all the opinions about certain [matters]," and also, "It's much easier to start a discussion with new persons." Some respondents also saw visualization as a tool for collaboration during the contracting process, since, "Visualizations need to be done together with the other contract party."

Another value considered important was transparency. Respondents viewed visualization as beneficial, because, "Making both sides understand what was agreed is always good." During the focus group sessions, a common opinion expressed by respondents was that visual contracts could act as good marketing tools, especially in a sales setting, because they would allow greater differentiation from competitors and deliver better customer service. Some respondents said they would be proud to adopt visualized contracts in their organization, "It would be quite nice to be the first ones who are using visualizations, and showing that we are a top company also in this." Another comment made was that their company could be seen as, "The only one that has different contracts."

FUTURE RESEARCH DIRECTIONS

From a theory-construction viewpoint, the results of our case study are a preliminary but encouraging addition to the field of knowledge visualization. They support the view that visualization has positive effects in knowledge-intensive organizational tasks (Bresciani, 2011; Platts & Tan, 2004). From a practical perspective, feedback provided by the test respondents will help in further developing prototypes for visualized contracts and promoting visual approaches within our partner company, as well as having provided valuable experience

Table 1. Perceived brand image. A comparison of the values suggested by a visualized contract and a text-only contract.

What Idea do You get About the Company that Drafted this Contract? What Values Do You Think It Holds?	The Company that Drafted the Text-Only Contract	The Company that Drafted the Visual Contract	Both Companies	None of the Companies
It is an innovative, quality-oriented organization	0%	100%	0%	0%
It is a trustworthy, reliable partner	14%	63%	23%	0%
They are truly open to collaboration	0%	77%	23%	0%
They truly make an effort to communicate with the other party	0%	95%	5%	0%
They value clarity in business	5%	68%	17%	0%
They respect their contractors	5%	59%	31%	5%
They aim at efficiency	14%	68%	18%	0%
They aim at effectiveness	9%	72%	19%	0%

in launching upcoming case studies with other organizations.

Establishing new research cases is a necessary step in increasing the validity and reliability of the results obtained. Firstly, in order to make generalizations, the number of test respondents must be larger. Secondly, any sample drawn from a single organization is only representative of that organization. Employing the same research methods in public and private organizations from different industrial sectors could provide better insight into the general applicability of our results, and also be useful in identifying industry-specific user needs. Thirdly, many different types of contracts exist and can only roughly be categorized as B2B, B2C or public procurement contracts, long-term or short-term contracts, sales of goods or services contracts, and so on. Depending on the nature of each contractual relationship and exactly what has been agreed, many individual typologies exist in each of these contract families. Experimenting with different types of contract in such contexts can be expected to reveal both similarities and specificities, and also help us in determining which consistent findings can be generalized.

One important aspect of our work is cooperation with real users in real-life cases, not only as a way of engaging them in our research activity and providing, in return, interesting results that can improve their working practices, but also as a way of increasing the reliability of our research results. This follows Yin's recommendations for case study research (2009), in which significant analytical sampling is preferred over statistical population sampling. Our fundamental assumption is that if different users who use different contracts to accomplish different tasks all perceive the same benefits from integrating visualization techniques into their contracts, then visualization can be isolated and identified as the reason for improvement. From a design perspective, involving anyone who is not a real user of the contract being tested would not make much sense because good design is contextual to who uses it.

Although university students (a wide and easily-accessible population for researchers) would be suitable subjects when working with, for instance, a student housing tenancy agreement or a phone service agreement, they would probably not be the right people to listen to if the subject being investigated is purchase contracts for industrial equipment or industrial services.

Returning to theoretical viewpoints, actively interacting with real users has proved helpful in expanding both the focus of our studies and our research questions. Investigating contract usability and user experience is only a first step. To gauge the proper potential that lies in contract visualization, we should focus on the actual social interactions which constitute the context in which contracts are planned, created and used. One research question that is certainly worth asking concerns collaboration: do visual contracts work as better boundary objects, enabling more effective information and knowledge transfer? The experimental work we have done so far has taken account of individual understanding, but the next step is to check whether such understanding actually has an impact on social interactions. A second interesting question is whether visualized contracts can have a positive influence on organizational performance by providing better tools for collaboration. Measuring such an effect will be particularly tricky, because organizational performance is affected by a multitude of elements: even if contract visualization brings benefits, these could be hard to identify or negated by other forces at play. A last question, and not a trivial one, is which skills and tools are needed for the concrete adoption of contract visualization as a routine organizational practice. Our goal would not be for companies to have to rely on visual designers every time they strike a deal: we would like managers and lawyers to be able to produce the necessary visualizations autonomously and without being fearful of what they would probably call their inability to draw. The aim is not beautiful images but visuals which are simple and functional. Lawyers and business users should have access to better digital drawing tools than the selection now available to them, and more importantly, should learn to think and communicate in visual terms. Our future research work will involve investigating what is required to provide non-designers with basic visual literacy skills and how their acquisition of visual thinking skills can be promoted.

CONCLUSION

This chapter has provided an overview of some of the common problems that contract users encounter in utilizing complex contracts. We have shown how issues connected with cognitive overload and unclear communication not only make it harder to carry out the tasks which make up one's job, but can even jeopardize organizational performance. Misinterpretations and unintentional errors can easily lead to non-performance, to late or inadequate performance, and in the worse case to claims and litigation. Contracts can in fact be user-*un*centered, not only because of their overly-legalistic logic and language that is a poor match for the abilities of most of their non-legal-background users, but also because of a significant lack of balance which places the emphasis on their drafting rather than on communicating their content and goals. We believe that much can be achieved in terms of clearer communication: both simpler language and clearer logic are necessary steps, but if content communication is taken seriously, why not draw on the advantages offered by different modes of communication? As it can support both interpretation and reasoning, we feel that visualization is an effective way of communicating information which is both abstract and complex.

According to the initial results of the tests we have conducted, our hypotheses on the beneficial role played by visualization in contracts appear to be verified. In terms of usability, test respondents using a visual contract were able to reply to questions faster and provided more correct answers than the control group (H1 and H2). Many respondents expressed the view that visualizations made contract reading more fluent because they supported content visibility, text comprehension and information recall. In addition, as they restated and communicated concepts in alternative ways, visualizations were viewed as a means which clarified and highlighted sections of the text. In terms of user experience, visualized contracts appear to provide a better first impression than traditional text-only ones, and such positive impression was confirmed also after test respondents had used the contract (H3 and H4). Trends in the experimental group indicate that initial expectations and subsequent experience are essentially comparable when using a visualized contract, but in the control group, the initial feeling that a traditional text-only contract will be difficult to use appears to get worse once it actually has been used. Avoiding this type of negative surprise could be a first step towards re-engaging existing users and changing their attitude towards contracts in the long term. Our results, however, suggest that there is more to be gained, as the respondents in our tests appeared to associate positive brand values with a visualized contract. Using visualized contracts in a sales setting could help differentiate a company from its competitors and win over new customers.

Further research and a wider range of examples are required to allow the envisioning of both accurate frameworks for contract visualization and concrete practices and methods. Our ongoing research work aims to provide both, while at the same time raising general awareness about the importance of user-centeredness and effective communication in the field of contracting. Visualization offers ways of empowering users whose job it is to make sense of complex contracts. The visual breakdown of intricate arguments and logical structures, together with visual descriptions of often intricate processes can promote a more analytical approach to the text components in contracts. Rather than struggling with initial sense-making, the clearer understanding supported by visualization enables more sophisticated insights and decision-making. For organizations, this translates into better business opportunities and fewer problems down the road. In the case of individuals, it means that personal choices will be better informed and working with contracts will become less demanding.

ACKNOWLEDGMENT

Support for this research was provided by the FIMECC research programme User Experience & Usability in Complex Systems (UXUS), financed by Tekes, the Finnish Funding Agency for Technology and Innovation, and by participating companies.

REFERENCES

Adler, M. (1991). Bamboozling the public. *New Law Journal*. Retrieved from http://www.clarity-international.net/downloads/Bam.pdf.

Alavi, M., & Leidner, D. (2001). Review: Knowledge management and knowledge management systems: Conceptual foundations and research issues. *Management Information Systems Quarterly*, *25*(1), 107–136. doi:10.2307/3250961.

Berman, D. (2000). Toward a new format for Canadian legislation–Using graphic design principles and methods to improve public access to the law. *Human Resources Development Canada and Justice Canada*. Retrieved from http://www.davidberman.com/NewFormatForCanadianLegislation.pdf.

Bresciani, S. (2011). *Visualizing Knowledge for Organizational Communication within and Across Cultures*. (PhD thesis). Lugano, Switzerland, Università della Svizzera italiana.

Bresciani, S., Eppler, M., & Tan, M. (2011). Communicating strategy across cultures with visualization: An experimental evaluation. In *Proceedings of Academy of Management 2011 Annual Meeting*. San Antonio, TX: AOM Press.

Brunschwig, C. R. (2001). *Visualisierung von rechtsnormen–Legal design*. (Doctoral thesis). Zurich, Switzerland, Universität Zürich.

Brunschwig, C. R. (2011). Multisensory law and legal informatics–A comparison of how these legal disciplines relate to visual law. *Jusletter IT*. Retrieved from http://jusletter-eu.weblaw.ch/issues/2011/104/article_324.html.

Burkhard, R. A. (2005a). *Knowledge Visualization: The Use of Complementary Visual Representations for the Transfer of Knowledge. A model, a Framework, and Four New Approaches*. (PhD thesis). Zurich, Switzerland, Eidgenossische Technische Hochschule ETH.

Burkhard, R. A. (2005b). Towards a framework and a model for knowledge visualization: Synergies between information and knowledge visualization. In S.-O. Tergan, & T. Keller (Eds.), Lecture Notes in Computer Science, Vol. 3426: Knowledge and Information Visualization: Searching for Synergies. (238–255). Heidelberg, Germany: Springer. doi: doi:10.1007/11510154_13.

Chang, C. (n.d.). Street vendor guide. *Accessible City Regulations*. Retrieved from http://candychang.com/street-vendor-guide

Court of Appeal for Western Sweden. (2009). *Judgement in case number B 1534-08*. Hovrätten för Västra Sverige, Göteborg. Retrieved from http://www.domstol.se/Domstolar/vastrahovratten/Kristalldom.pdf.

Creative Commons. (n.d.). *About the licenses–Creative commons*. Retrieved from http://creativecommons.org/licenses.

Dattu, F. (1998). Illustrated jury instructions: A proposal. *Law and Psychology Review, 22,* 67–102.

Eppler, M. J. (2004). *Knowledge communication problems between experts and managers. An analysis of knowledge transfer in decision processes.* Retrieved from http://doc.rero.ch/lm .php?url=1000,42,6,20051020101029-UL/1_ wpca0401.pdf.

Eppler, M. J., & Platts, K. (2009). Visual strategizing: The systematic use of visualization in the strategic-planning process. *Long Range Planning, 42*(1), 42–74. doi:10.1016/j.lrp.2008.11.005.

Ertel, D. (2004). Getting past yes: Negotiating as if implementation mattered. *Harvard Business Review, 82*(11), 60–68. PMID:15559446.

Feigenson, N., & Spiesel, C. (2009). *Law on display. The digital transformation of legal persuasion and judgment.* New York: New York University Press.

GLPi & Schmolka. V. (2000). *Results of usability testing research on plain language draft sections of the employment insurance act. Justice Canada and Human Resources Development Canada.* Retrieved from http://www.davidberman.com/ wp-content/uploads/glpi-english.pdf.

Hagedorn, J., & Hesen, G. G. (2009). Contractual complexity and the cognitive load of R&D alliance contracts. *Journal of Empirical Legal Studies, 6*(4), 818–847. doi:10.1111/j.1740-1461.2009.01161.x.

Irwin, T. (2002). *Information design: What is it and who does it?* Retrieved from http://www. aiga.org/resources/content/1/8/9/3/documents/ AIGA_Clear_InformationDesign.pdf.

ISO 9241-11. (1998). Ergonomic requirements for office work with visual display terminals (VDTs). *Part 11: Guidance on Usability.* Retrieved from http://www.iso.org/iso/catalogue_detail. htm?csnumber=16883.

Jones, H. W. (2009). Envisioning visual contracting: Why non-textual tools will improve your contracting. *Contracting Excellence, 2*(6), 27–31. Retrieved from http://www.iaccm.com/userfiles/ file/CE_2_6_press_new.pdf.

Jones, H. W., & Oswald, M. (2001). Doing deals with flowcharts. *ACCA Docket, 19*(9), 94–108.

Kay, M., & Terry, M. (2010). Textured agreements: Re-envisioning electronic consent. In L. F. Cranor (Ed.), *Proceedings of the Sixth Symposium on Usable Privacy and Security.* Redmond, WA: ACM. doi:10.1145/1837110.1837127

Keller, T., & Grimm, M. (2005). The impact of dimensionality and color coding of information visualizations. In S.-O. Tergan & T. Keller (Eds.), Lecture Notes in Computer Science, Vol. 3426: Knowledge and information visualization: searching for synergies. (167–182). Heidelberg, Germany: Springer. doi: doi:10.1007/11510154_9.

Kimble, J. (2006). *Lifting the fog of legalese.* Durham, NC: Carolina Academic Press.

Mahler, T. (2010). *Legal Risk Management–Developing and Evaluating Elements of a Method for Proactive Legal Analyses, with a Particular Focus on Contracts.* (Doctoral thesis). Oslo, Norway: University of Oslo.

Ministry of Finance. (2009). *General Terms of Public Procurement in service contracts JYSE 2009 Service.* Helsinki, Finland. Retrieved from http://www.vm.fi/vm/en/04_publica- tions_and_documents/01_publications/08_other_ publications/20100217Genera/JYSE_2009_ser- vices.pdf.

NEC. (n.d.). *What is the NEC? Promoting best practice procurement. Achieving excellence in the procurement of works, services and supply.* Retrieved from http://www.neccontract.com/ documents/WhatistheNEC.pdf.

Nuutinen, M., Seppänen, M., Mäkinen, S. J., & Keinonen, T. (2011). User experience in complex systems: Crafting a conceptual framework. In *Proceedings of the 1st Cambridge Academic Design Management Conference.* Cambridge, UK: Cambridge University Press.

Passera, S., & Haapio, H. (2011a). User-centered contract design: New directions in the quest for simpler contracting. In R. F. Henschel (Ed.), *Proceedings of the 2011 IACCM Academic Symposium for Contract and Commercial Management* (80–97). Ridgefield, CT: The International Association for Contract and Commercial Management. Retrieved from http://www.iaccm.com/admin/docs/docs/HH_Paper.pdf.

Passera, S., & Haapio, H. (2011b). Facilitating collaboration through contract visualization and modularization. In A. Dittmar & P. Forbrig (Eds.), *Designing Collaborative Activities. ECCE 2011, European Conference on Cognitive Ergonomics*, 57-60. Rostock, Germany: Universitätsdruckerei. doi: 10.1145/2074712.2074724.

Plain Language Institute of British Columbia. (1993). *Critical opinions: The public's view of lawyers' documents*. Vancouver: Plain Language Institute.

Platts, K., & Tan, K. H. (2004). Strategy visualisation: Knowing, understanding, and formulating. *Management Decision*, 42(5/6), 667–676. doi:10.1108/00251740410538505.

Pohjonen, S., & Koskelainen, K. (2012). Visualization in trialogic public procurement contracting. In E. Banissi, S. Bertschi, C. Forsell, J. Johansson, S. Kenderdine, F. T. Marchese, ... & G. Venturini (Eds.), *Proceedings of 16th International Conference on Information Visualisation* (383–388). Montpellier, France: IEEE Press. doi: 10.1109/IV.2012.70.

Pohjonen, S., & Visuri, K. (2008). Proactive approach in project management and contracting. InHaapio, H (Ed.), *A Proactive Approach to Contracting and Law* (75–95). Turku, Finland: International Association for Contract and Commercial Management & Turku University of Applied Sciences.

Posner, E. A. (2010). ProCD vs. Zeidenberg and Cognitive Overload in Contractual Bargaining. *The University of Chicago Law Review. University of Chicago. Law School*, 77(4), 1181–1194. Retrieved from http://ssrn.com/abstract=1499414.

Posner, R. (2011). Opinion in the united states court of appeals for the seventh circuit no. 11-1665. *Gonzalez-Servin v. Ford Motor Co.* Retrieved from http://www.abajournal.com/files/DG0R2WE8.pdf.

Raskin, A. (n.d.). *Privacy icons: Alpha release.* Retrieved from http://www.azarask.in/blog/post/privacy-icons.

Roos, J., Bart, V., & Statler, M. (2004). Playing seriously with strategy. *Long Range Planning*, 37(6), 549–568. doi:10.1016/j.lrp.2004.09.005.

Roto, V., Law, E., Vermeeren, A., & Hoonhout, J. (Eds.). (2011). User experience white paper: Bringing clarity to the concept of user experience. *Result from Dagsthul Seminar on Demarcating User Experience.* Retrieved from http://www.allaboutux.org/files/UX-WhitePaper.pdf.

Sanders, E. B.-N. (2002). *Scaffolds for experiencing in the new design space.* In Institute for Information Design Japan IIDj (Eds.), *Information Design.* Retrieved from http://www.maketools.com/articles-papers/ScaffoldsforExperiencing_Sanders_03.pdf.

Scaife, M., & Rogers, Y. (1996). External cognition: how do graphical representations work? *International Journal of Human-Computer Studies*, 45(2), 185–213. doi:10.1006/ijhc.1996.0048.

Schwartz, A., & Scott, R. E. (2010). Contract interpretation redux. *The Yale Law Journal*, *119*(5), 926–965. Retrieved from http://ssrn.com/abstract=1504223.

Semmler, C., & Brewer, N. (2002). Using a flow-chart to improve comprehension of jury instructions. *Psychiatry, Psychology and Law*, *9*(2), 262–270. doi:10.1375/pplt.2002.9.2.262.

Shostack, G. L. (1977). Breaking free from product marketing. *Journal of Marketing*, *41*(2), 73–80. doi:10.2307/1250637.

Siedel, G., & Haapio, H. (2011). *Proactive law for managers: A hidden source of competitive advantage*. Farnham, UK: Gower.

Siedel, G. J. (1992). Interdisciplinary approaches to alternative dispute resolution. *Journal of Legal Studies Education*, *10*(2), 141–169. doi:10.1111/j.1744-1722.1992.tb00226.x.

Solomon, S. H. (2006). *Visuals and visualisation: Penetrating the heart and soul of persuasion*. DOAR Litigation Consulting. Retrieved from http://tillers.net/solomon.pdf.

Språkrådet. (2010). Press release: Plain crystal 2010. *CSN and the Court Of Appeal For Western Sweden*. http://www.sprakradet.se/7121.

Star, S. L., & Griesemer, J. R. (1989). Institutional ecology, 'translations,' and boundary objects: Amateurs and professionals in Berkeley's Museum of Vertebrate Zoology. *Social Studies of Science*, *19*(3), 387–420. doi:10.1177/030631289019003001.

Sweller, J., van Merrienboer, J. J. G., & Paas, F. G. W. C. (1998). Cognitive architecture and instructional design. *Educational Psychology Review*, *10*(3), 251–296. doi:10.1023/A:1022193728205.

Szulanski, G. (2000). The process of knowledge transfer: A diachronic analysis of stickiness. *Organizational Behavior and Human Decision Processes*, *82*(1), 9–27. doi:10.1006/obhd.2000.2884.

Tergan, S.-O., Keller, T., & Burkhard, R. A. (2006). Integrating knowledge and information: Digital concept maps as a bridging technology. *Information Visualization*, *5*(3), 167–174. doi:10.1057/palgrave.ivs.9500132.

Tiersma, P. M. (2006). Some myths about legal language. *Law, Culture, and the Humanities, 2*(1), 29–50. doi:10.1191/1743872106lw035oa.

Tufte, E. (1983). *The visual display of quantitative information*. Cheshire, CT: Graphics Press.

Tufte, E. (1990). *Envisioning information*. Cheshire, CT: Graphics Press.

Tufte, E. (1997). *Visual explanations: Images and quantities, evidence and narrative*. Cheshire, CT: Graphics Press.

Tufte, E. (2006). *Beautiful evidence*. Cheshire, CT: Graphics Press.

Usability Professionals' Association UPA. (n.d.). Glossary. *Usability Body of Knowledge*. Retrieved from http://www.usabilitybok.org/glossary.

Von Hippel, E. (1994). Sticky information and the locus of problem solving: Implications for innovation. *Management Science, 40*(4), 429–439. doi:10.1287/mnsc.40.4.429.

Wolfram Demonstrations Project. (n.d.). Retrieved from http://demonstrations.wolfram.com.

Yin, R. K. (2009). Applied social research methods series: *Vol. 5. Case study research: Design and methods* (4th ed.). Thousand Oaks, CA: SAGE.

ADDITIONAL READING

Barton, T. D., Berger-Walliser, G., & Haapio, H. (2011). Visualization: Seeing contracts for what they are, and what they could become. In R. F. Henschel (Ed.), *Proceedings of the 2011 IACCM Academic Symposium for Contract and Commercial Management* (3–15). Ridgefield, CT: The International Association for Contract and Commercial Management. Retrieved from http://ssrn.com/abstract=2005434.

Becker, J., Heddier, M., & Knackstedt, R. (2011). Towards business process modeling in business contracting–Analyzing collaboration contracts as a field of application for process models. In *Proceedings of the 2012 45th Hawaii International Conference on System Sciences HICSS '12*. 4376–4385. Washington, DC: IEEE Press. doi:10.1109/HICSS.2012.601.

Berger-Walliser, G., Bird, R. C., & Haapio, H. (2011). Promoting business success through contract visualization. *The Journal of Law. Business Ethics (Oxford, England)*, *17*, 55–75. Retrieved from http://ssrn.com/abstract=1744096.

Chisnell, D. (Ed.). (2012). *Field guides to ensuring voters intent, Vol. 1: Designing usable ballots.* Available from http://civicdesigning.org/wp-content/uploads/2012/06/Field-Guide-Vol-011.pdf.

Chisnell, D. (Ed.). (2012). *Field guides to ensuring voters intent, Vol. 2: Writing instructions voters understand.* Available from http://civicdesigning.org/wp-content/uploads/2012/06/Field-Guide-Vol-021.pdf.

Chisnell, D. (Ed.). (2012). *Field guides to ensuring voters intent, Vol. 3: Testing ballots for usability.* Available from http://civicdesigning.org/wp-content/uploads/2012/06/Field-Guide-Vol-031.pdf.

Chisnell, D. (Ed.). (2012). *Field guides to ensuring voters intent, Vol. 4: Effective poll workers material.* Available from http://civicdesigning.org/wp-content/uploads/2012/06/Field-Guide-Vol-041.pdf.

Finnegan, M., & Haapio, H. (2012). Communicating contracts in split seconds: Using visual tools to make leadership pay attention. *Contract Management*, *52*(7), 26–43.

Haapio, H. (2010). Visualising contracts and legal rules for greater clarity. *The Law Teacher*, *44*(3), 391–394. doi:10.1080/03069400.2010.527126.

Haapio, H. (2011). Communicating contracts: When text alone is not enough. *Clarity–Journal of the International Association Promoting Plain Legal Language*, *65*, 33–36.

Haapio, H. (2011). Contract clarity through visualization – Preliminary observations and experiments. In E. Banissi, S. Bertschi, R. A. Burkhard, U. Cvek, M. J. Eppler, C. Forsell, ... & T. G. Wyeld (Eds.), *15th International Conference on Information Visualisation* (337–342). Los Alamitos, CA: IEEE Computer Society. doi:10.1109/IV.2011.70.

Haapio, H. (2012). Making contracts work for clients: towards greater clarity and usability. In E. Schweighofer, F. Kummer, & W. Hötzendorfer (Eds.), *Transformation Juristischer Sprachen Transformation of Legal Languages. Tagungsband des 15. Internationalen Rechtsinformatik Symposions IRIS 2012 Proceedings of the 15th International Legal Informatics Symposium* (389–396). Vienna, Austria: Österreichische Computer Gesellschaft OCG.

Haapio, H. (in press). Contract clarity and usability through visualization. In Marchese, F. T., & Banissi, E. (Eds.), *Knowledge visualization currents: From text to art to culture.* London, UK: Springer. doi:10.1007/978-1-4471-4303-1_4.

Haapio, H., Berger-Walliser, G., Walliser, B., & Rekola, K. (2012). Time for a visual turn in contracting? *Journal of Contract Management, 10*, 49–57.

Haapio, H., & Passera, S. (2012). Reducing contract complexity through visualization: A multi-level challenge. In E. Banissi, S. Bertschi, C. Forsell, J. Johansson, S. Kenderdine, F. T. Marchese, ... & G. Venturini (Eds.), *16th International Conference on Information Visualisation, IV2012, 11–13 July 2012, Montpellier, France* (370–375). Los Alamitos, CA: IEEE Computer Society. doi: 10.1109/IV.2012.68.

Halliday, M. A. K. (1994). *An introduction to functional grammar*. London: Arnold.

Kaltenbacher, M. (2004). Perspectives on multimodality: From the early beginnings to the state of art. *Information Design Journal, 12*(3), 190–207. doi:10.1075/idjdd.12.3.05kal.

Kay, M. (2010). *Techniques and Heuristics for Improving the Visual Design of Software Agreements*. (Master Thesis) Waterloo, ON, Canada, University of Waterloo.

Kelley, P. G., Bresee, J., Cranor, L. F., & Reeder, R. W. (2009). A nutrition label for privacy. In L. F. Cranor (Ed.), *Proceedings of the 5th Symposium on Usable Privacy and Security*. Mountain View, CA: ACM Press. doi:10.1145/1572532.1572538.

Kong, K. C. C. (2006). A taxonomy of the discourse relations between words and visuals. *Information Design Journal, 14*(3), 207–230. doi:10.1075/idj.14.3.04kon.

Kress, G. R., & Van Leeuwen, T. (2006). *Reading images: The grammar of visual design* (2nd ed.). Abingdon, UK: Routledge.

Passera, S. (2012). Enhancing contract usability and user experience through visualization–An experimental evaluation. In E. Banissi, S. Bertschi, C. Forsell, J. Johansson, S. Kenderdine, F. T. Marchese, ... & G. Venturini (Eds.), *16th International Conference on Information Visualisation* (376-382). Montpellier, France: IEEE Press. doi: 10.1109/IV.2012.69.

Rekola, K., & Boucht, K. (2011). Visualizing service contracts–The case of an equipment manufacturer. In E. Banissi, S. Bertschi, R. A. Burkhard, U. Cvek, M. J. Eppler, C. Forsell, ... & T. G. Wyeld (Eds.), *15th International Conference on Information Visualisation* (359–364). London: IEEE Press. doi: 10.1109/IV.2011.35.

Rekola, K., & Haapio, H. (2009). Better business through proactive productization and visualization of contracts. *Contracting Excellence, 2*(5), 17–19. Available from http://www.iaccm.com/userfiles/file/CE_2_5_press_C2(1).pdf.

Siedel, G. J., & Haapio, H. (2010). Using proactive law for competitive advantage. *American Business Law Journal, 47*(4), 641–686. doi:10.1111/j.1744-1714.2010.01106.x.

(2005). In Tergan, S.-O., & Keller, T. (Eds.). Lecture Notes in Computer Science: *Vol. 3426. Knowledge and Information Visualization: Searching for Synergies*. Heidelberg, Germany: Springer. doi:10.1007/b138081.

Waller, R. (1987). *The Typographic Contribution to Language. Towards a Model of Typographic Genres and Their Underlying Structures*. (PhD thesis). Reading, UK: University of Reading. Retrieved from http://www.robwaller.org/RobWaller_thesis87.pdf.

Waller, R. (2011a). *Information Design: How the Disciplines Work Together*. (Technical paper). Reading, UK: University of Reading. Retrieved from http://www.simplificationcentre.org.uk/downloads/papers/SC14DisciplinesTogether.pdf.

Waller, R. (2011b). *What makes a good document? The criteria we use*. (Technical paper). Reading, UK: University of Reading. Retrieved from http://www.simplificationcentre.org.uk/downloads/papers/SC2CriteriaGoodDoc_v2.pdf

Wogalter, M. S., & Laughery, K. R. (1996). WARNING! Sign and label effectiveness. *Current Directions in Psychological Science, 5*(2), 33–37. doi:10.1111/1467-8721.ep10772712.

KEY TERMS AND DEFINITIONS

Contract Usability: The extent to which a contract can be utilized by specified users to perform their tasks and to achieve their goals with effectiveness, efficiency and satisfaction, given a specified context of use. The concept focuses on user performance: in this research, the performance by user groups with non-legal backgrounds using contracts as part of their everyday work.

Contract User Experience: The way a user feels about using a contract. The concept focuses on the overall experiences, values, meanings, thoughts and feelings perceived by the user when working with a contract. User experience, when positive, contributes to engaging users in a certain activity: in this case. In reading a contract and acting upon it.

Contract Visualization: A subset of knowledge visualization which utilizes infographics and other information design methods to make contracts clearer and more user-friendly

Knowledge Visualization: A field of study and practice that investigates the power of visual formats to support the cognitive processes of generating, structuring, sharing and retrieving knowledge

Proactive Contracting: A field of research and practice that uses contracting processes and documents to merge Proactive Law with contract, quality and risk management in order to promote successful outcomes, prevent problems and balance risk with reward

Proactive Law: A future-oriented approach that uses the law to promote successful outcomes and prevent problems, unlike traditional law, which is oriented to the past and mainly uses legal rules to react to past failures

User-centered Contract: A contract that is designed and drafted focusing on the knowledge needs of different user groups (with both legal and non-legal backgrounds), their cognitive capabilities and the contexts where the contract will be used

Chapter 11

Articulate:
Creating Meaningful Visualizations from Natural Language

Yiwen Sun
University of Illinois at Chicago, USA

Andrew Johnson
University of Illinois at Chicago, USA

Jason Leigh
University of Illinois at Chicago, USA

Barbara Di Eugenio
University of Illinois at Chicago, USA

ABSTRACT

This chapter presents an approach to enable non-visualization experts to craft advanced visualizations through the use of natural language as the primary interface. The main challenge in this research is in determining how to translate imprecise verbal queries into effective visualizations. To demonstrate the viability of the concept, the authors developed and evaluated a prototype, Articulate, which allows users to simply ask the computer for questions about their data and have it automatically generate visualizations that answer these questions. The authors discovered that by relieving the user of the burden of learning how to use a complex interface, they enable them to focus on articulating better scientific questions and wasting less time in producing unintended visualizations.

INTRODUCTION

Nearly one third of the human brain is devoted to processing visual information. Vision is the dominant sense for the acquisition of information from our everyday world. It is therefore no surprise that visualization, even in its simplest form, remains the most effective means for converting large volumes of raw data into insight. Over the past three decades, much has been investigated in the design of sophisticated visualization tools in a variety of disciplines. However, the effort end-users have to make to craft a meaningful visualization using these tools has been mostly

DOI: 10.4018/978-1-4666-4309-3.ch011

overlooked. The users of such tools are usually lay people or domain experts with marginal knowledge of visualization techniques. When exploring data, they typically know what questions they want to ask, but often do not know, or do not have the time to learn, how to express these questions into a series of interactions that produce an effective visualization.

A 2008 National Science Foundation report "Enabling Science Discoveries through Visual Exploration" (Ebert, 2008) also noted that one of the main barriers hindering the adoption of advanced visualization tools is the steep learning curve associated with them. 2010 findings by Grammel (2010) showed that novices to Information Visualization still tended to use traditional bar, line and pie charts over other chart types by more than 70% because of their familiarity with them. Modern visualization tools offer such an expansive array of capabilities that they can only be wielded by an expert trained in visualization. In some ways it is like expecting someone to know how to build a house by simply sending them to Home Depot.

Meanwhile, the 2008 NSF report noted "there is a strong desire for conversational interfaces that facilitate a more natural means of interacting with science." In other words, scientists "simply" want to tell the computer what they want to see and have it just create it. They do not want to have to become visualization experts. Even a decade ago this would have seemed far-fetched, but today we are seeing renewed interest in the use of natural language as an interface to computing. For example, survey results according to search engines like Ask.com show that a third of search queries are entered as natural language questions rather than keywords. Siri, the intelligent personal assistant on iPhone 4S, allows users to send messages, schedule meetings, and place phone calls by directly speaking into their smartphones. The field of natural language processing has made great strides in the last decades, with a variety of models that are able to understand the meaning of sentences in recommender systems, educational technology and health applications.

This inspired us to consider the use of a conversational interface for the automatic generation of visualizations. A system such as this would allow an end-user to pose natural language inquiries, and then let the system assume the burden of creating the most appropriate visual representation of the inquiry. It is hoped that such a capability can potentially reduce the learning curve necessary for effective use of visualization tools, and thereby expand the population of users who can successfully conduct visual analysis. Note however that in this work we are not simply translating explicit visualization commands such as *"make a plot of temperature vs pressure"*- though it is certainly possible within the context of this research. Instead the expectation is that our approach will enable a user to ask deeper questions about data, such as *"what is the correlation between temperature and depth with temperature below zero"*, without having to follow or memorize a strict grammar or command structure, as has been in the past. Furthermore users will be able to ask follow-up questions where the computer has some knowledge of what has already been asked and visualized. Therefore the fundamental value of this approach is that it enables the end-users to focus on the scientific question they are trying to ask rather than the specific visualization task they are trying to perform.

The remainder of this chapter is organized as follows. We first describe prior work in related fields. Then we explain in detail our methodology for translating conversation into a precise visualization. Next, we present details of our user studies. While the initial prototype produces information visualizations, we will also explain and show through a case study how the approach is conceptually extensible to scientific visualizations as well. Lastly we outline directions for future work.

BACKGROUND

The problem of deriving a meaningful visualization from natural language highlights many interesting areas for computer science research. It involves researching the steps needed to translate and classify spoken queries that can then be meaningfully visualized. It also involves discovering how to create, modify and explain visualizations automatically, and understanding the benefits and issues related to such an approach.

As creating visualizations remains a skilled and time-consuming task, researchers began to investigate computational approaches to simplify the crafting process. One of the early pieces of work was Mackinlay's APT system (Mackinlay, 1986). It introduced a composition algebra to describe various graphical encoding and developed expressiveness and effectiveness criteria to ensure meaningful design. The SAGE system (Roth, 1994) extended the concepts of APT, providing a richer set of data characterizations and generating a wider range of composite views through interaction. The previous work on automatic presentation focused primarily on single views of data; however, Show Me (Mackinlay, 2007) provided support for small multiple views. It included an integrated set of user interface commands and default settings that automatically generate small multiple views based on VizQL–an algebraic specification language. Users place data fields into columns and rows in the interface panel to specify VizQL commands. In order to generate insightful visualizations, an understanding of the relationships between columns and rows is needed. While the above work focused on identifying and encoding data in discrete graphics, there is another trend in addressing the issues of communicating with users in visual discourse. Feiner's Apex system (Feiner, 1985) set the foundational work in this area. It attempted to automatically create visual discourses-a series of animated visual illustrations for explaining complex information to users. His work was extended in IMPROVISE (Zhou, 1998), which used an AI planning-based approach to automatically design and create such discourses.

In recent years, related approaches have targeted specific application domains, rather than proposed a more general methodology. Kerpedjiev and Roth introduced AutoBrief (Kerpedjiev, 2001), a system that automatically summarizes transportation schedules as text and graphs. In this system, they proposed a set of rules to map communicative goals to low-level operational tasks, such as lookup or compare. However, the system only focused on generating explanations of problems and relations existing in the data but not in response to user's ad-hoc requests. Gilson et al. (2008) proposed an approach for automatic generation of visualizations via ontology mapping and applied the approach to web data for music. The web data was first mapped to domain ontology, and then projected to visual representation ontology, which was finally depicted as a specific visualization using external visualization toolkits. The mapping between domain and visual representation ontologies was represented by semantic bridging ontologies, which were defined from expert knowledge. By comparison, our approach uses a more flexible meta-learning algorithm to automatically translate language into visualization intentions. Another interesting approach is VisMashup (Santos, 2009), which simplified the creation of customized visualization applications with a pipeline. Once the pipeline is constructed, the application can be generated automatically. While this infrastructure enables an application designer to assemble custom applications quickly, the designer still needs some visualization background to build up the pipeline from components or templates. Although *Articulate* shares some of these same goals, it goes a step further by allowing the users to verbally articulate what they want to see with minimal a priori knowledge of how to use the user interface.

A decade ago the possibility of widespread use of speech interaction seemed far-fetched, for both cognitive and technical reasons. Shneiderman (2000) argued that speech input has limited value in human-computer interaction except in niche applications-such as for the disabled or answering service systems. The key criticism cited was that problem-solving and recall competed with speech articulation and interpretation in their use of working memory. However, Dennett (1991) argues that problem solving is in fact enhanced when more areas of the brain are engaged such as when you are speaking and hearing your own words (i.e. thinking a problem out loud). Hanks (2010) argued that "Humans are social animals, and language is the instrument of their sociability, as well as the vehicle of their thought processes." Language interfaces in a variety of settings, from educational technology to health care, have been shown to improve the user's experience and performance (Grasso, 1998; Hallet, 2008; Kersey, 2009; Schulman, 2009).

Technically, the considerable renewed interest in the use of speech and natural language as an interface to computing is due in large part to significant computing power and new powerful statistical models that are brought to improve speech recognition and natural language interpretation. Google's director of research Peter Norvig, believes that being able to converse with computers is "the future". NLP, the processing of language beyond the recognition of words in speech, also made great strides in the last decade, with a variety of models that are used to understand the meaning of sentences, as shown by successes such as that of IBM Watson which defeated the two best human champions in Jeopardy! and Wolfram Alpha - a knowledge engine developed by Wolfram Research that is capable of responding to natural language based questions with computed answers and relevant visualizations instead of a list of web pages as a traditional search engine provides. Additionally, a number of speech-based computational models have been developed that help users to access information using a conver-

sational paradigm. JUPITER (Zue, 2000b) for example allows users to obtain worldwide weather forecast information over the phone using spoken dialogue. It is a mixed initiative system (Zue, 2000a) that requires zero user training, and accepts a large range of user inputs. This approach has been extended to similar domains where the vocabulary is sufficiently limited to support practical conversational paradigm, such as travel planning (Seneff, 2000) or health information access (Sherwani, 2007).

Recent work in the information visualization community has applied various design principles to the automatic generation of visualizations though none had used natural language nor approached scientific visualizations. *Articulate* attempts to combine these advanced techniques together in exploring how to automatically translate natural, and potentially ill-defined, conversational language into meaningful visualizations of data in a generalizable way that enables users who are not visualization experts to make use of modern advances in visualization.

THE APPROACH

In brief, the approach involves: extracting syntactic and semantic information from a verbal query; applying a supervised learning algorithm to automatically translate the user's intention into explicit commands; and finally, determining an appropriate type of visualization based on the translated commands and properties of the metadata (see Figure 1.)

To demonstrate the concept is viable, we developed a small prototype - *Articulate*. There are three essential parts to its framework: the Data Parser, the Input Translator, and the Visualization Executer. The Data Parser collects information on the attribute names of the data and their data types. The Input Translator takes natural language queries spoken by the user and translates them into a set of commands that follows a precise grammar, which we call SimVL (Simplified Vi-

Figure 1. A conceptual pipeline for translating imprecise verbal queries into visualizations

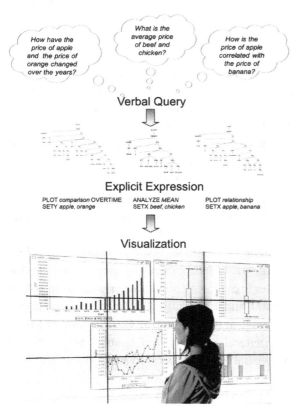

Figure 2. Basic workflow in the input translator

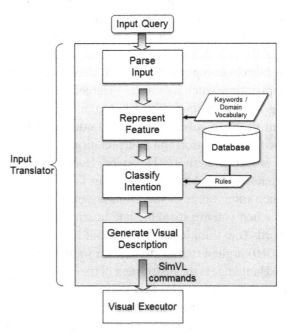

sualization Language)–analogous to small subset of Wilkinson's Grammar of Graphics (2000). The precise SimVL commands and information on the properties of various types of visualization, are given to a Visualization Executer which determines the most appropriate visualization to produce. Figure 2 outlines the major components of the Input Translator. In what follows, we present the ideas underlying these major components.

Parsing the Input Stream

The user's initial input to the system is a natural language query. The query sentence is parsed into a syntax tree where leaf nodes store the words and internal nodes show the part-of-speech or phrasal labels. This tree provides an intuitive perception of the structure of the sentence (Figure 3). Ad-

ditionally, a dependency diagram is obtained via the Stanford Parser (Klein, 2003) to describe the grammatical relationships between pairs of words. Using these structures, the function of each word can be identified which helps to recognize the feature of the query.

Ideally when articulating a query, the user will mention an attribute name as it appears in the raw data. But in reality this is not always the case, as discovered in our earlier study (Sun, 2010). For example, in a dataset regarding average food prices, data values may include apple, orange and banana. However users may pose queries such as: "*compare the price of fruit*". Clearly, searching for the exact data value in the query will not lead to a desired result. Hence, meta-data properties are gathered such as data units and semantic relations, which provide a brief context for interpreting the data. To obtain the semantic relations, we use WordNet (Miller, 1995), a lexical database that groups English words into sets of cognitive synonyms (synsets) and expresses various semantic relations between these synsets. Using this,

Figure 3. An example of syntax tree and dependency diagram parsed from a sample sentence

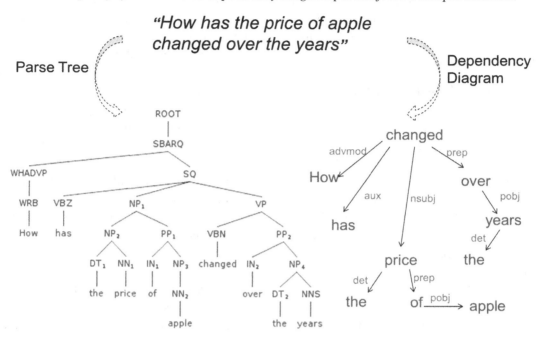

we can expand each attribute into an insightful meta-word and send that to the Visualization Executer to help determine the most appropriate graph to produce.

Representing Syntactic and Semantic Features

The results from the language parsing step provide complex information about the features of the query. Some of the information is not essential in the procedure of identifying the user's general intention. Hence, we defined six categories of keywords: *comparison, relationship, composition, distribution, statistics* and *manipulation*, to represent the semantics of user's general intentions. The keywords in each dictionary are selected according to empirical knowledge and domain vocabulary. For example, *associate, correlate, link, relate, relevant* are often used in the queries intended for tasks regarding relationship or connection between two or more variables, so they are entered into the relationship dictionary.

Besides that, the findings from the preliminary user study show that some queries were not correctly answered due to the ambiguity of query's feature. It is possible to improve feature identification by capturing the syntactic characteristics of those queries. Through close examination, several shallow linguistic features were found that might help the classification of the query, for example clause type, query contains a comparative or superlative adjective or adverb, query contains a cardinal number, and query contains a quantifier.

Based on the above syntactic and semantic feature analysis, a smaller feature space is derived to represent the most important aspects of the query. This feature space is defined as a fourteen-dimensional space. Each dimension describes one feature found in the query. Specifically, the features are: comparison, relationship, composition, distribution, statistics, manipulation, time-series, visual_primitive, superlative, cardinal, quantifier, filter, clause_type, and number_of_attributes. The first twelve are Boolean values. For instance, if a query involves the comparison between two data attributes, the comparison feature is tagged as true, and the number_of_attributes is declared as 2. In this way, a query sentence can be simply represented as a feature vector.

Classifying the Intended Tasks

The feature vector essentially identifies the words that describe the intended visualization. It does not however guarantee that the user is sufficiently precise in their use of their wording. Therefore the feature vector is given to a task classifier that attempts to derive the user's true intent. Three widely used supervised learning algorithms were considered for this classification job: Decision Tree, Bayesian Network and Support Vector Machine. Each model generated by one machine-learning algorithm can be regarded as an expert. It is more reliable to take into account the opinions of several experts rather than relying on only one judgment. Therefore, we combined a decision tree inducer, a Bayesian network learner, and a support vector machine to form a meta-learner, which takes the majority votes from the three basic classifiers. This meta-learner was formed by applying the meta-learning method over a corpus of sample queries tagged into seven classes of visualizations, based on Shneiderman's task taxonomy (Shneiderman, 1996) and Abela's chart classification model (Abela, 1981).

The visualization task recognized using the meta-learner gives the user a solution based on the limited training corpus. However it may not always be the "best" choice. To help users find the truly intended visualization, a means to allow *Articulate* to suggest alternative visualizations was explored. The algorithm employed to select candidates for suggestion is based on a context-aware meta-classifier. This classifier is similar to the idea used in task classification process discussed above, in which a decision tree inducer, a Bayesian network learner, and a support vector machine are combined together. But different from the task classifier, the immediately preced-

ing tasks were taken into account as context for suggestion, which maintains the coherence of attention in successive tasks.

Given a successful classification, and having identified the attributes to be visualized, a set of precise commands in the form of SimVL is generated. Recall that SimVL is our formal grammar for describing visualization tasks in a precise manner. SimVL's commands comprise four categories: sketch commands, analysis commands, manipulation commands and filter commands. Sketch commands consist of commands that describe the semantics of general visualization tasks, which often perform the actual task of drawing a graph. Analysis commands consist of tasks that involve the use of statistical methods such as taking the average or standard deviation. Manipulation commands describe ways to alter an existing visualization- such as remapping colors to data attributes. Lastly, filter commands are mainly used to select the desired pieces of data.

Obtaining Meaningful Visual Results

The Visualization Executer reads the SimVL command, as well as the properties of various types of visualizations, and uses a heuristic algorithm to choose the most appropriate visualization to execute (Sun, 2012). Just as a visualization expert might weigh the pros and cons of different graphs in the determination of a desired plot type, the Executer works as an agent carrying out a similar reasoning process. For sketch commands, the choice of a specific visualization is contingent upon factors including the property of the data (such as the number of variables, data types, and whether the variables change over time), and the effectiveness of different visual primitives (such as position, length, direction, area, volume, shading and color saturation). Figure 4 gives an example. For analysis commands, which usually focus on the statistical features of data (such as minimum, maximum, average, percentile), a box-and-whisker chart is a convenient way of graphically depicting

Figure 4. Result for sketch and filter commands translated from "how has MPG changed since 1970" with regard to a 1983 ASA Data Expo dataset on automobiles

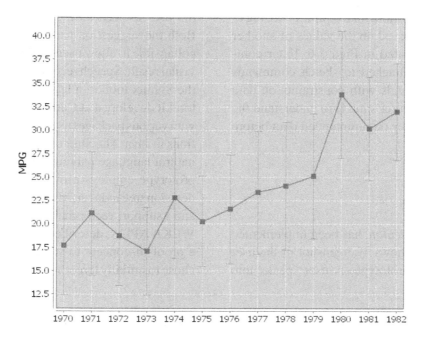

Figure 5. Result for analysis commands translated from "what is the average MPG by country of origin" with regard to the same dataset as Figure 4

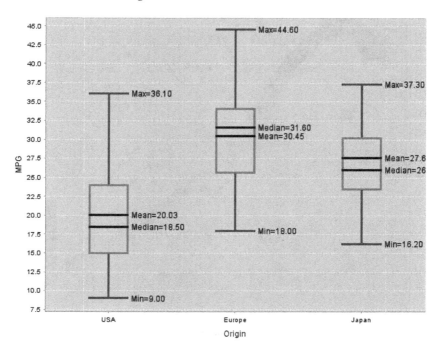

these features, as illustrated in Figure 5. Manipulation commands are typically adjustments made to an existing visualization, for example choosing to color data points based on the values of another attribute, as illustrated in Figure 6. Filter commands are often attached to sketch commands or analysis commands with constraints on data values, so the Executer's job is to understand the constraints and filter out unintended data before plotting it.

EVALUATION

A prototype of *Articulate* has been implemented in Java. Figure 7 shows a screenshot of the user interface for the prototype. A user speaks into the system without any a priori knowledge of a grammar and the translated text is displayed to the user as well as the resulting visualization. Both the suggestion panel and data window are collapsible to allow users to focus on the intended visual result. Speech recognition is achieved using the Sphinx toolkit, a leading speech recognition toolkit developed at Carnegie Mellon University with various packages used to build speech applications in Java. The Stanford Parser is leveraged for natural language parsing. The task classification prototype employs a meta-learner combining a decision tree inducer, a Bayesian network learner, and a support vector machine implemented using WEKA API. As described earlier, since this is only a proof-of-concept to validate the approach, we chose to initially target simple visualizations such

Figure 6. Result for manipulation commands translated from "can you color the points by pH" following a query "what is the correlation between depth and temperature" with regard to a 10-attribute hydrological dataset

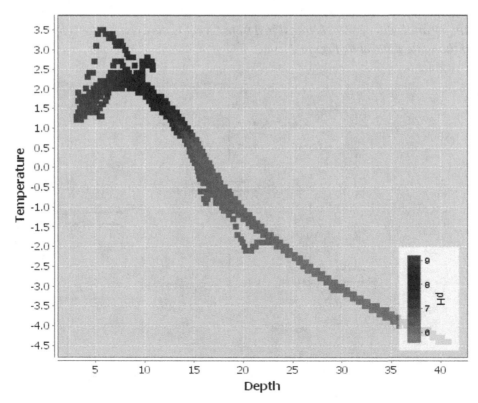

Figure 7. The user interface for the articulate system

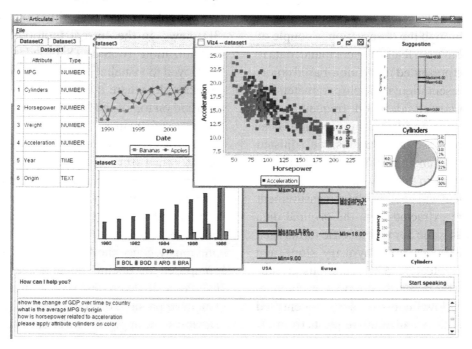

as bar charts, scatter plots, and so forth. Therefore we employed the JFreeChart and Prefuse graph engines to perform the graph generation.

We conducted a preliminary study to evaluate the viability of our approach. The study consisted of a comparison between users of *Articulate* versus a popular graphing tool such as Microsoft Excel. Subjects in the experiment were provided with a number of datasets ranging from hydrologic data to census data and were given 20 minutes to perform 3 tasks: find meaningful correlations among the data attributes; find as many trends as possible about the data; find other interesting features about the data. We tracked the number of graphs produced, their types, and the duration needed to create a graph that resulted in a discovery. The findings were highly encouraging. We found that at least half of the Excel users had to create more than one chart and call additional Excel functions (such as sort, min, max) to describe a query that could have been expressed with a single sentence in *Articulate*. Furthermore, on average users took twelve times longer to realize a graph for a query in Excel than in Articulate.

Case Study

While the initial prototype focuses on producing information visualizations, this methodology can be applied to scientific visualizations by adjusting certain steps in the framework. The experience of a case study for the Endurance application illustrates this idea.

ENDURANCE (Environmentally Non-Disturbing Under-ice Robotic ANtarctiC Explorer) is a NASA funded project involving the development of an Autonomous Underwater Vehicle (AUV) capable of generating 3-D bio-geochemical datasets in the extreme environment of a perennially ice-covered Antarctic dry valley lake, which offers a blend of statistical as well as scientific visualization problems. In addition, they have been using the visualization tools developed in our lab to support the analysis of the data coming from the ENDURANCE mission.

The first step in the expansion of *Articulate* towards the ENDURANCE application is to understand their usage scenario. Preliminary observations of interactions between a visualization expert and several of the participating domain scientists using the existing visualization tool were conducted. Through the observation, a couple of distinctive behavioral features were found: data is preferred to be presented in location-based color-coded 3D representation; multiple parameters are plotted and compared side by side frequently; data are often selected or filtered by time and location. Based on these observations, we adjusted the *Articulate* system in certain aspects. The first adjustment occurs in the meta-data deriving step: all the biological and geo-chemical measurement parameters are extracted from the original data files, as well as some domain specific terms used by the scientists, such as bathymetry, slope, and scale. Secondly, feature representations are tailored to reflect the domain scenario. For example, a couple of shallow linguistic cues are identified to distinguish 3D visualization requests from 2D counterparts, such as the appearance of keywords like 3D, volumetric, bathymetry in a query. Finally,

in the Visualization Executer, adaptions are made in the graph reasoning algorithm to accommodate 3D views. In the current prototype, VTK (the Visualization Toolkit) (Schroeder, 2006) was employed to visualize scalar data. Figure 8 gives an example, where a 2D lake map with grids is overlaid on top of the 3D glyphs to highlight the location information.

Before given access to *Articulate*, the domain scientists had to interact with a visualization expert to create various visualizations needed in their data analysis. With the help of *Articulate*, scientists were able to use language to create visualizations and modify those that have been created previously. Since the framework of *Articulate* is composed of distinct modules, each of them handles a single process such as data processing, language parsing, or graph generation; it is very flexible to be applied to different domain science by adjusting certain modules in the framework.

Figure 8. 3D visualization for the query "Show me the relationship between depth and CDOM in a 3D view"

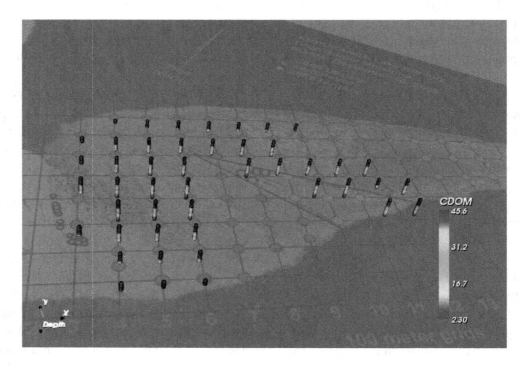

User Study

The framework of *Articulate* has a number of theoretical advantages. However, the success of an approach will ultimately depend on whether the users perceive improvements in their experience. For that reason we designed a between-subject experiment to discover whether the users using *Articulate* can: produce more appropriate visualizations and fewer irrelevant visualizations, and make discoveries that would not have occurred otherwise. Seventeen post-graduate subjects participated in the study. Each of them was presented with multi-country wealth and health development data extracted from Gapminder World's data repository. The participants were expected to perform three tasks at two different levels of complexity (two simple direct tasks and one complex open-ended task):

- **Task 1:** What are the top 2 countries that emit most CO2 recently?
- **Task 2:** Is there any big difference between the trends of Japan and Philippines?
- **Task 3:** Based on this data set which attribute(s) do you think are important factors to life expectancy?

Subjects were asked to make verbal queries to *Articulate* to explore the data and summarize their findings based on the visual results showing on the display.

All participants completed the tasks, but their total completion time varied (mean = 26.8 minutes, SD = 9.3) and the number of queries initiated were different (mean = 8, SD = 3.4). To investigate the different behavior and the effectiveness of the system, we performed statistical analysis on the factor of query per task, which measured the number of queries user initiated to complete each task. We wanted to find out if the number of queries was related with the type of task. A one-way analysis of variance (ANOVA) with $\alpha = 0.05$ was used for this analysis. For task 1 and 2, on average about 1.5 queries were needed to solve the problem, which clearly showed the efficiency of the system. Task 3 required more queries (mean=4.8) to solve due to its complexity. The ANOVA result also indicated that the level of complexity of the task had a significant impact on the number of queries user initiated ($F_{2,48} = 12.45$, $p < 0.0001$).

Furthermore, we analyzed the subjective ratings in the post-study survey pertaining to the effectiveness of the suggestion function. The rating is based on a 5 point Likert scale (1 = Never helpful; 5 = Always helpful). The result was positive (mean=3.7, SD=0.8). The main reason subjects liked the suggestion function was that it provided alternative visualizations that gave insights on different perspectives of the data, which could potentially help users find their solution quickly.

Learning any new system can increase cognitive burden, and in this case, that means the transition from mind-hand coordination to mind-mouth coordination. In this study, we were encouraged to find that all of the subjects were able to alter their working styles to adapt to the new environment. Their feedback on using *Articulate* compared with other traditional visual analytic tools showed that the subjects were more favorable towards the natural language guided interface:

I think being able to just speak my question instead of having to type it is very helpful.

In other tools like Excel I have to put in the data, find the right chart, make everything organized. But for this, I asked a question, it pulls the data for me. It gives me easier access to different types of graphs without me having to go back and fill in the place again.

I like the suggestions because they were not necessarily things I was looking for myself. … Most of time it understood what I was looking for, but it also brought in things that I wasn't looking for that ended up being helpful. It did a good job translating my requests but also giving me alternatives.

FUTURE RESEARCH DIRECTIONS

The work presented in this chapter offers a new approach for automatically creating visualizations from verbal descriptions; however, there are still limitations that need to be addressed. For example, in the current graph engine, only standard 2D graphs and plots, and basic 3D scalar visualizations are supported, which we fully intend to extend in the future, to accommodate more advanced visualization techniques such as those commonly used in scientific visualization (for instance volumetric or streamline visualizations).

Another direction in this research is to provide a textual or verbal explanation to the user on how and why the resulting visualization was derived by the system. When answering the user's questions, which may include requests for information about how to visualize the data and requests for clarification on what the visualization represents, *Articulate* needs access to its own knowledge about the implementation of the current visualization, such as the mapping from data attribute to visual primitives. Providing explanations of the visualization can help users learn visualization techniques they did not know before, and make better understanding about the data.

In terms of interaction modality, enabling gesture input as a complementary interface to voice input is a promising area to investigate. During a conversational interaction, verbal communication is often enhanced or further clarified through a variety of different gestures. As observed in the user study, subjects tend to point and gesture to the screen when saying "this", "these", "here" in deictic expressions. Recognizing pointing gestures can help the interpretation of references used in the verbal description. With devices such as a multi-touch screen and optical trackers (such as the Kinect or Leap), it will be relatively easy to extend *Articulate's* framework with the gesture interaction.

Lastly, one of the emerging trends in large scale data visualization is the use of display-rich environments (Figure 9) to facilitate the integration and interpretation of multiple visualizations simultaneously (Leigh, 2012). A natural language and gesture based interface is ideally suited to such an environment where the traditional mouse and keyboard are typically cumbersome.

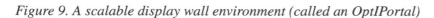

Figure 9. A scalable display wall environment (called an OptIPortal)

CONCLUSION

This chapter has demonstrated *Articulate*-a generalized approach for the creation and modification of meaningful visualizations from user's imprecise verbal descriptions. Unlike traditional visualization tool, this approach brings together natural language processing, machine learning and visualization techniques, to enable the interaction with speech, hence relieve the users of the burden of having to learn how to use a complex interface for their data exploration.

The major components of *Articulate* include: Data Parser, Input Translator, and Visualization Executer. A Data Parser collects information from the data file and prepares them in metadata formats to provide a brief context for interpreting user's interests. The Input Translator recognizes the intended data and translates user's natural language descriptions into specific visualization tasks expressed in a formal grammar. These explicit expressions together with the impact of various graphical primitives guide the Visualization Executer in determining the most appropriate graph. A key benefit of this approach is that it enables the end-users to focus on the scientific question they are trying to ask rather than the specific operations that must be performed to produce a representative visualization.

The contributions of this research are three-fold: First, the incorporation of a speech interface and natural language parser enables the user to "tell" the computer what they want to see, and have the system intelligently create the graph rather than having to struggle with yet another esoteric user-interaction device.

Second, the introduction of a meta-learning algorithm to automatically interpret a user's intent based on linguistic features. We devised a multi-dimensional feature space to represent both syntactic and semantic characteristics of a verbal query. The query is then converted to a feature vector, which is mapped to a visualization task by applying a supervised learning algorithm, and finally translated into explicit graphical commands.

Third, the capability of suggesting related queries and visualizations. Besides the primary recommended visualization, a list of "next-best" candidates are provided to the users, which take into account their previous preferences. Such context-aware suggestions can potentially help them consider alternative perspectives on the data that they may not have originally envisioned.

Formal studies via between-subject experiments were conducted to evaluate the approach. *Articulate* users took less time and created fewer charts to produce a desired result as compared to using a popular graphing program. The studies also showed this approach was able to provide meaningful visualizations to the user, help them make discoveries that would not have occurred to them otherwise, and eventually speed up their data exploration process.

The presented research results, although far from constituting a complete set, offer direction for the future investigation of the automatic generation of data visualization in a natural interaction environment. As the technology needed for building such environments becomes more affordable, we will likely see natural language interfaces permeate a broad range of everyday use cases. Since the Internet has made it possible for everyday citizens to access vast amounts of data instantaneously and at very low cost. There is tremendous interest amongst researchers in the visualization community finding better ways to harness data to make it useful to individuals, businesses, and companies. The work described here will contribute greatly to that effort by making it possible for non-visualization experts to be able to leverage modern advances in visualization and help them interpret data that is growing exponentially in scale and complexity.

REFERENCES

Abela, A. (1981). *Advanced presentations by design: Creating communication that drives action.* San Francisco, CA: Pfeiffer.

Dennett, D. (1991). *Consciousness explained.* New York: Little, Brown, and Company.

Ebert, D., Gaither, K., & Gilpin, C. (2008). Enabling science discoveries through visual exploration. *NSF Workshop Report.* Washington, D.C.: National Science Foundation.

Feiner, S. (1985). APEX: An experiment in the automated creation of pictorial explanations. *IEEE Computer Graphics and Applications,* 5(11), 29–37. doi:10.1109/MCG.1985.276329.

Gilson, O., Silva, N., Grant, P. W., & Chen, M. (2008). From web data to visualization via ontology mapping. *Computer Graphics Forum,* 27(3), 959–966. doi:10.1111/j.1467-8659.2008.01230.x.

Grammel, L., Tory, M., & Storey, M.-A. (2010). How information visualization novices construct visualizations. *IEEE Transactions on Visualization and Computer Graphics,* 16(6), 943–952. doi:10.1109/TVCG.2010.164 PMID:20975131.

Grasso, M. A., Ebert, D. S., & Finin, T. W. (1998). The Integrality of speech in multimodal interfaces. *ACM Transactions on Computer-Human Interaction,* 5(4), 303–325. doi:10.1145/300520.300521.

Hallett, C. (2008). Multi-modal presentation of medical histories. In *Proceedings of the 13th International Conference on Intelligent User Interfaces,* 80–89. New York: ACM Press.

Hanks, P. (2010). How people use words to make meanings. In *Proceedings of the 7th International Workshop on Natural Language Processing and Cognitive Science, 3(13).*

Kaufmann, E., & Bernstein, A. (2007). How useful are natural language interface to the semantic web for casual end-users? In *Proceedings of the 6th International Semantic Web Conference,* 281–294. Berlin: Springer.

Kerpedjiev, S., & Roth, S. F. (2001). Mapping communicative goals into conceptual tasks to generate graphics in discourse. *Knowledge-Based Systems,* 14(1), 93–102. doi:10.1016/S0950-7051(00)00100-3.

Kersey, C., Di Eugenio, B., Jordan, P. W., & Katz, S. (2009). Knowledge co-construction and initiative in peer learning interactions. *In Proceedings of the 14th International Conference on Artificial Intelligence in Education.* Brighton, UK: IOS Press.

Klein, D., & Manning, C. D. (2003). Accurate unlexicalized parsing. In *Proceedings of the 41st Meeting of the Association for Computational Linguistics,* 423-430. Cambridge, MA: MIT Press.

Leigh, J., Johnson, A., Renambot, L., Peterka, T., Jeong, B., et al., & Sun, Y. (2012). Scalable resolution display walls. *Proceedings of the IEEE,* (99).

Mackinlay, J. D. (1986). Automating the Design of graphical presentations of relational information. *ACM Transactions on Graphics,* 5(2). doi:10.1145/22949.22950.

Mackinlay, J. D., Hanrahan, P., & Stolte, C. (2007). Show me: Automatic presentation for visual analysis. *IEEE Transactions on Visualization and Computer Graphics,* 13(6). doi:10.1109/TVCG.2007.70594 PMID:17968057.

Miller, G. A. (1995). WordNet: A Lexical Database for English. *Communications of the ACM,* 38(11), 39–41. doi:10.1145/219717.219748.

Roth, S. F., Kolojejchick, J., Mattis, J., & Goldstein, J. (1994). Interactive graphic design using automatic presentation knowledge. In *Proceedings of the SIGCHI Conference on Human Factors in Computing Systems*, 112-117. New York: ACM Press.

Santos, E., Lins, L., Ahrens, J., Freire, J., & Silva, C. (2009). VisMashup: Streamlining the creation of custom visualization applications. *IEEE Transactions on Visualization and Computer Graphics*, *15*(6), 1539–1546. doi:10.1109/TVCG.2009.195 PMID:19834231.

Schroeder, W., Martin, K., & Lorensen, B. (2006). *The visualization toolkit: An object-oriented approach to 3D graphics* (4th ed.). Clifton Park, NY: Kitware, Inc. Publishers.

Schulman, D., & Bickmore, T. (2009). Persuading users through counseling dialogue with a conversational agent. In *Proceedings of the 4th International Conference on Persuasive Technology*, 1-8. New York: ACM Press.

Seneff, S., & Polifroni, J. (2000). Dialogue management in the mercury flight reservation system. *In Proceedings of ANLP/NAACL 2000 Workshop on Conversational Systems*, 11-16. Seattle, WA: Academic Press.

Sherwani, J., Ali, N., Tongia, R., Rosenfeld, R., Memon, Y., Karim, M., & Pappas, G. (2007). HealthLine: Towards speech-based access to health information by semi-literate users. In *Proceedings of Speech in Mobile and Pervasive Environments*. New York: ACM Press.

Shneiderman, B. (1996). The eyes have it: A task by data type taxonomy for information visualizations. In *Proceedings of the IEEE Symposium on Visual Languages*, 336-343. New Brunswick, NJ: IEEE Press.

Shneiderman, B. (2000). The limits of speech recognition. *Communications of the ACM*, *43*(9), 63–65. doi:10.1145/348941.348990.

Sun, Y. (2012). *Articulate: Creating Meaningful Visualizations from Natural Language*. (Doctoral dissertation). Chicago, University of Illinois.

Sun, Y., Leigh, J., Johnson, A., & Lee, S. (2010). Articulate: A semi-automated model for translating natural language queries into meaningful visualizations. In *Proceedings of 10th International Symposium on Smart Graphic*, 184-195. New York: ACM Press.

Wilkinson, L. (2005). *The grammar of graphics* (2nd ed.). Berlin: Springer.

Zhou, M., & Feiner, S. (1998). IMPROVISE: Automated generation of animated graphics for coordinated multimedia presentations. In *Proceedings of Second International Conference on Cooperative Multimodal Communication*, 43-63. New York: ACM Press.

Zue, V., & Glass, J. R. (2000a). Conversational interfaces: Advances and challenges. In *Proceedings of the IEEE*, 1166-1180. New Brunswick, NJ: IEEE Press.

Zue, V., Seneff, S., Glass, J. R., Polifroni, J., Pao, C., Hazen, T. J., & Hetherington, L. (2000b). JUPITER: A telephone-based conversational interface for weather information. *IEEE Transactions on Speech and Audio Processing*, *8*(1), 85–96. doi:10.1109/89.817460.

ADDITIONAL READING

Amar, R., Eagan, J., & Stasko, J. (2005). Low-level components of analytic activity in information visualization. In *Proceedings of the IEEE Symposium on Information Visualization*, 111-117. New Brunswick, NJ: IEEE Press.

Bavoil, L., Callahan, S., Crossno, P., Freire, J., Scheidegger, C., Silva, C., & Vo, H. (2005). Vistrails: Enabling interactive multiple-view visualizations. In *Proceedings of IEEE Conference on Visualization*, 135–142. New Brunswick, NJ: IEEE Press.

Bostock, M., & Heer, J. (2009). Protovis: A graphical toolkit for visualization. *IEEE Transactions on Visualization and Computer Graphics*, *15*(6), 1121–1128. doi:10.1109/TVCG.2009.174 PMID:19834180.

Chih, C., & Parker, D. (2008). The persuasive phase of visualization. In *Proceedings of the 14th ACM SIGKDD International Conference on Knowledge Discovery and Data Mining.*, New York: ACM Press.

Cleveland, W. S., & McGill, R. (1984). Graphical perception: Theory, experimentation, and application to the development of graphical methods. *Journal of the American Statistical Association*, *79*(387), 531–554. doi:10.1080/01621459.1984.10478080.

Di Eugenio, B., Zefran, M., Ben-Arie, J., Foreman, M., Chen, L., et al., & Ma, K. (2010). Towards effective communication with robotic assistants for the elderly: Integrating speech, vision, and haptics. In *Proceedings of Dialog with Robots, AAAI 2010 Fall Symposium*. Arlington, VA: AAAI Press.

Duke, D. J., Borgo, R., Wallace, M., & Runciman, C. (2009). Huge data but small programs: visualization design via multiple embedded DSLs. In *Proceedings of the 11th International Symposium on Practical Aspects of Declarative Languages*, 31-45. Savannah, GA: Springer.

Duke, D. J., Brodlie, K. W., Duce, D. A., & Herman, I. (2005). Do you see what i mean? *IEEE Computer Graphics and Applications*, *25*(3), 6–9. doi:10.1109/MCG.2005.55 PMID:15943083.

Gotz, D., & Wen, Z. (2009). Behavior-driven visualization recommendation. In *Proceedings of the 14th International Conference on Intelligent User Interfaces*. New York: ACM.

Gotz, D., & Zhou, M. (2008). *Characterizing users' visual analytic activity for insight provenance. IEEE Visual Analytics, Science, and Technology*. Columbus, OH: IEEE Press.

Hall, M., Frank, E., Holmes, G., Pfahringer, B., Reutemann, P., & Witten, I. H. (2009). The WEKA data mining software: An update. *SIGKDD Explorations*, *11*(1). doi:10.1145/1656274.1656278.

Hansen, C. D., & Johnson, C. D. (2005). *The visualization handbook*. Amsterdam: Elsevier.

Harris, R. L. (2000). *Information graphics. A comprehensive illustrated reference*. Oxford, UK: Oxford University Press.

Heer, J., & Bostock, M. (2010). Declarative language design for interactive visualization. *IEEE Transactions on Visualization and Computer Graphics*, *16*(6), 1149–1156. doi:10.1109/TVCG.2010.144 PMID:20975153.

Heer, J., Card, S. K., & Landay, J. A. (2005). Prefuse: A Toolkit for interactive information visualization. In *Proceedings of the SIGCHI conference on Human factors in computing systems*, 421-430, Portland, OR: ACM Press.

Keim, D. (2012). Information visualization and visual data mining. *IEEE Transactions on Visualization and Computer Graphics*, *8*(1), 1–8. doi:10.1109/2945.981847.

Munzner, T., Johnson, C., Moorhead, R. H., Rheingans, P., & Yoo, T. S. (2006). NIH-NSF visualization research challenges report summary. *IEEE Computer Graphics and Applications*, *26*(2), 20–24. doi:10.1109/MCG.2006.44 PMID:16548457.

Stolte, C., Tang, D., & Hanrahan, P. (2002). Polaris: A system for query, analysis, and visualization of multidimensional relational databases. *IEEE Transactions on Visualization and Computer Graphics*, 8(1), 52–65. doi:10.1109/2945.981851.

Tufte, E. R. (1983). *The visual display of quantitative information*. Cheshire, CT: Graphics Press.

Tufte, E. R. (2006). *Beautiful evidence*. Cheshire, CT: Graphics Press.

Viegas, F. B., Wattenberg, M., van Ham, F., Kriss, J., & McKeon, M. (2007). ManyEyes: A site for visualization at internet scale. *IEEE Transactions on Visualization and Computer Graphics*, *13*(6), 1121–1128. doi:10.1109/TVCG.2007.70577 PMID:17968055.

Ward, M., Grinstein, G., & Keim, D. (2010). *Interactive data visualization: Foundations, techniques, and applications*. Natick, MA: A K Peters.

Ware, C. (2004). *Information visualization: Perception for design*. New York: Morgan Kaufmann.

Wehrend, S., & Lewis, C. (1990). A problem-oriented classification of visualization techniques. In *Proceedings of the 1st Conference on Visualization*, 139-143. New Brunswick, NJ: IEEE Press.

Witten, I. H., Frank, E., & Hall, M. A. (2011). *Data mining: Practical machine learning tools and techniques* (3rd ed.). New York: Morgan Kaufmann.

Chapter 12
Visualization of Human Behavior Data:
The Quantified Self

Alessandro Marcengo
Telecom Italia, Italy

Amon Rapp
University of Torino, Italy

ABSTRACT

Although in recent years the Quantified Self (QS) application domain is growing, there are still some palpable fundamental problems that relegate the QS movement in a phase of low maturity. The first is a technological problem, and specifically, a lack of maturity in technologies for the collection, processing, and data visualization. This is accompanied by a perhaps more fundamental problem of deficit, bias, and lack of integration of aspects concerning the human side of the QS idea. The step that the authors tried to make in this chapter is to highlight aspects that could lead to a more robust approach in QS area. This was done, primarily, through a new approach in data visualization and, secondly, through a necessary management of complexity, both in technological terms and, for what concerns the human side of the whole issue, in theoretical terms. The authors have gone a little further stressing how the future directions of research could lead to significant impacts on both individual and social level.

1. INTRODUCTION

Knowledge of the self is the mother of all knowledge. So it is incumbent on me to know my self, to know it completely, to know its minutiae, its characteristics, its subtleties, and its very atoms.
Khalil Gibran

In this chapter our proposal is to outline some aspects of human behavior generated data in the light of a specific research branch, the so called Quantified Self (QS) area. We think that time has come to sketch current status and new directions in a field that even being explored for years, only recently, also thanks to some technological

DOI: 10.4018/978-1-4666-4309-3.ch012

advances, is finding its practical application. We will analyze the first attempts to trace and represent human activity through the description of some experiments in this direction (e.g. LifeLog DARPA Project, MyLifeBits Microsoft Project, etc.). The chapter will then describe the most important application fields of QS, in order to draw a clear picture of the current situation and to give an overview of the most promising sectors in which this approach will be developed in the coming years.

In particular, we will describe the distinctive means to monitor and render human behavior and the applications aimed to persuade people to change their practices of everyday life, in areas related to health, mood and fitness but also with few references to sports, training, social networking, transportation, consumptions, emotions and communications.

The chapter will cover then two fundamental problems of the QS today, the technological problems and the theoretical problems both in terms of data visualization of large dataset and in terms of behaviour change theories that still make difficult to adopt a non-purely empirical QS approach. Will be then drawn the directions to handle these problems toward a more robust and credible QS scenario through new ways of representing data and new directions in the management of complexity, both on the technological side and on the human side of the topic. Then we will go further considering future directions of research with both individual and social impacts.

2. WHAT IS THE QUANTIFIED SELF?

The QS is a school of thought which aims to use the increasingly invisible technology means in order to acquire and collect data on different aspects of the daily lives of people. These data can be "input" from the outside (such as the calories or the CO_2 consumed), or they can be "states" (as the mood or the oxygen level in the blood) or parametric indicators of performance or activity (such as the kilometers run, the mail sent, or the mp3 heard). The purpose of collecting this data is the self-monitoring and the self-reflection oriented to some kind of change or improvement (behavioral, psychological, medical, etc.).

It is immediately evident how this approach, which we will analyze in more details in the following pages, raises a series of theoretical problems (for example, what are the foundations of human behaviour change?) but even before a series of technological issues. How can this data be collected (input)? With what kind of sensors? And above all, how this knowledge can be returned to the user (output)? With what kind of data visualization techniques? In this short arc, from doing an action (recorded by a sensor and stored by a database) to have the "image" of that action (displayed on a screen), there are about 200 years of research studies in different fields.

Just to do a little bit of history of this topic, the whole spectrum of toolset, application and technical approaches related to this type of thinking has taken different names over time. It can be found in literature as "Personal Informatics," "Personal analytics," "Self Tracking," and "Living by Numbers" according to the focus on what has been emphasized by each definition.

Considering only the QS sunrise, the movement was founded in 2007 by the editors of "Wired" Gary Wolf and Kevin Kelly, with the purpose of creating collaboration between users and manufacturers involved in the development of self-knowledge through self-tracking technology. In 2008, the same Wolf and Kelly opened the site "quantifiedself.com". In 2010, Wolf spoke at TED Conference, and in May 2011 in Mountain View the movement held the first conference specifically on QS.

There are some basic points that define the QS movement: the data collection, the displaying of these data, and the cross linking of these data in order to discovery some possible correlations. The interest that is developing in these years around this current is also evidenced by the proliferation of gadgets that are appearing in trade shows such as CES (Consumer Electronic Association) or conference sponsors among which it is possible to find names such as Vodafone, Philips and Intel.

The whole issue seems to revolve around the question *"Who am I?"* The supporters of the QS think that the answer lies in our daily activities and hence the need to quantify any behavior, taking photos of everything is eaten or drank, recording the distances covered, monitoring the pattern of REM/NREM sleep, noting the "mood of the day", storing the blood pressure and heart rate, and so on.

According to this fundamental question, is maybe necessary to underline what we mean by "Self" that perhaps is something too often left aside. The notion of "Self" has been a central aspect of many personality theories, including those of Sigmund Freud, Alfred Adler, Carl Jung, Carl Rogers, and Abraham H. Maslow. In Carl Jung's concept the self is a totality consisting of conscious and unconscious contents that dwarfs the ego in scope and intensity. The maturation of the self is the individuation process, which is the goal of any healthy personality. Many years later Rogers theorized that a person's self-concept determines his behaviour and his relation to the world, and that therapeutic improvement occurs only when the individual changes his own self-concept. Maslow's theory of self-actualization was based on a hierarchy of needs and emphasized the highest capacities or gratifications of a person. Nowadays a simple "common sense" definition of "Self" is *"one's identity, character, abilities, and attitudes, especially in relation to persons or things outside oneself or itself"* (Definition of Self, 2012a), while amongst the more "academic" definitions we can find this kind of descriptions: *"The individual as the object of his own reflective consciousness; the man viewed by his own cognition as the subject of all his mental phenomena, the agent in his own activities, the subject of his own feelings, and the possessor of capacities and*

character; a person as a distinct individual; a being regarded as having personality" (Definition of Self, 2012b).

The concept of "self" is central in all human history since the emergence of consciousness. The ability to reflect on oneself is central to each of us as human beings. The fundamental human question *"Who am I?"* is exactly the research of our "Self".

3. ROOTS OF QUANTIFIED SELF MOVEMENT

The idea to record the personal physical activity and psychological and emotional "states", through technology (spread sheet, digital pictures, etc.) has roots that can be traced to the mid-90s: the practice of lifelogging, *"a form of pervasive computing consisting of a unified digital record of the totality of an individual's experiences, captured multimodally through digital sensors and stored permanently as a personal multimedia archive"* (Dodge & Kitchin, 2007), is the one that comes closest to the idea of QS and finds in people like Steve Mann, professor at the University of Toronto, its precursors. Mann, a pioneer in the field of wearable devices, since 1994 decided to stream his daily life 24 hours a day. EyeTap (2012), the name of his project, consists of a wearable device allowing storage of all that the user sees, making possible to record a complete photographic memory of everything happens to himself. Furthermore, EyeTap displays information to the user itself, altering the visual perception of the wearer and creating in this way a kind of augmented reality (Mann, 2004). In essence, users can "build" reality by altering the visual perception of the environment and the visual appearance of the sight by adding or modifying what they are seeing: this mediation of reality can be done in real time or in a following phase, going to retrieve what was recorded and applying to it the desired changes (Nack, 2005). Around the experience of Mann has developed, over the years, a community of lifeloggers (or globbers, as they call themselves) that aim to visually record everything that happens around them during their daily life: this community has reached the amount of 200 thousand units.

If EyeTap was one of the first individual projects designed to record all individual's perceptions on a digital media, "MyLifeBits" (Gemmell et al., 2006) was the first attempt, supported by the industry (Microsoft Company), to aspire to the complete recording of all the experiences of a human being. Conceived in 1998 as a tool to record daily life events, MyLifeBits aims to preserve the whole life of its creator: Gordon Bell. Bell decided to store in digital format everything with which he came into contact during his day: articles, CDs, letters, events, notes, sounds, conversations and photos. Bell, then began his experience of digitalization, still needed a human assistant to catalog and digitalize all the items flowing in his life. However, even all materials digitalized, Bell still not had the chance to use them due to the limitations of the software available at that time (Bell & Gemmell, 2007). MyLifeBits was designed to bring order and create links between the various data collected and stored by Bell, taking advantage of a metadata system in order to make possible the navigation in these huge amounts of heterogeneous data. For instance the system is able to generate automatic links, by correlating the GPS location of Bell, continuously recorded throughout the day, with the time and date of a photo taken by the same Bell. Nevertheless, MyLifeBits records his telephone calls and the programs playing on his radio and television, automatically stores a copy of every Web page he visits and a transcript of every instant message he sends or receives. With the aid of a "SenseCam", a wearable device developed by Microsoft Research (Hodges et al., 2006) that automatically takes pictures when its sensors indicated that the user want to photograph, Bell preserves the image relating to the surrounding environments in which he moves, the people he meets, the significant moments of his life. In fact, Gordon Bell realized the pioneer idea of Vannevar Bush that since 1945, in his article "As We May Think" (Bush, 1945), envisioned a tool (the Memex–abbreviation for Memory Extender) able to store and catalog, using the microfilm technology, all the documents that an individual faces in the course of his life. The Memex should have been able to generate automatic annotation and create links between documents similarly to the process of human associative memory. Today MyLifeBits is evolving towards a continuous connection with any kind of sensors, able to automatically generate data regarding the displacements of Bell, his health and his physiological parameters. However, the limit of the Bell's project is in his strong individual connotation because it was designed by and for its creator: a system tailored to the constant recording of Bell's daily life that had more the virtue of pointing the way, rather than to seek a large scale diffusion on consumer market.

"Total Recall", instead, is a Lifelog research project of the Internet Media Lab of the University of Southern California, that starts from a different perspective (Internet Multimedia Lab, 2004). The basic idea of this system is to increase the memory of people through the storing of experiences, events and knowledge relating to an individual or a multitude of individuals. Using a large amount of sensors, a microphone and a camera mounted on a pair of glasses or in a necklace, Total Recall aims to record the world from a personal point of view, allowing on demand to recover the data collected through customizable searching, analysis, and querying of this data. Total Recall was designed from the beginning to have a wide range of applications, all aimed at gathering information about an individual with the purpose of making evident data and elements that usually do not rise to his knowledge. For example, in the health care area, the system can monitor the daily diet of a diabetic person, reporting any risk situations or correlating these data with the visited environments by the same individual in order to identify specific allergies: the data, flowing continuously from the patient, can also help clinicians to fine tune the diagnosis and the treatments (Cheng et al. 2004).

All these attempts show how from the first half of the 90s the idea of recording the life of an individual and to return it back in some visual form was spreading in the world of industrial and academic research. Worth a note, however, "LifeLog" as the first government project aimed at monitoring and recording the lives of individuals with also potential military applications. LifeLog was a project developed by the Defense Advanced Research Projects Agency (DARPA) recognized as a system capable of collecting information on an individual, on its activities, its states and its relationship. The goal of LifeLog was to trace the entire life of an individual: his monetary transactions and his purchases, the contents of his phone calls, sent and received emails and messages, his movements (traced by a GPS signal), and even biomedical data related to his physical health (obtainable through specific wearable sensors). In the original concept the system could have been used in stand-alone mode as a sort of journal or recorder of individual memories, allowing the user to search and retrieve information and experiences related to his past in the form of images, sounds, videos. LifeLog Project was closed in 2004, due to privacy problems raised by the public opinion. However, during his short life it made the people imagine a future in which military commands would have been equipped with systems for continuous recording of their experiences, able to access their own data and to re-trace what happened to them (Allen, 2008).

All these early research efforts, trying to build applications for continuously tracking parameters about the whole human behavior, have found some obstacles in the availability, the complexity and the cost of the technology (O'hara et al., 2006) as well as in issues concerning ethics and privacy (Mayer-Schönberger, 2009). Only recently, technological advances in networks, sensors, search and storage seem to have changed this situation. How we will see, the birth of a number of academic projects and a considerable amount of commercial tools capable of tracking individual parameters of people's lives (then recomposing them in significant views) seems to make at least closer a credible QS scenario.

4. QUANTIFIED SELF PROMISES

Wolf in his famous speech at the TED (Wolf, 2010) opened his talk reciting a series of numbers. The time he woke up (6:10 am), his average beats per minute (61), his blood pressure (127/74), how many minutes of exercise he had (0), how many milligrams of caffeine he had been drinking (600), how many milliliters of alcohol (0), and such other numbers.

The statement Wolf pronounced was: *"If we want to act more effectively in the world, we have to get to know ourselves better."* This phrase, that actually at first glance seems to make sense, looks naïve to a more detailed analysis. Is not enough to know "things" (data) because this is able to produce some sort of change. This is a naïve thought that as we will see has its origin in partial or outdated psychological paradigms. What we now know for sure is that the human brain is not a "rational computer", that given some data produces the "best" answer for that data. In a word, this rationalist model would work perhaps for Mr. Spock of Startrek (the rational, non-affective, vulcanian) but not for humans that are most dependent for their decisions by emotions, complex social cognition and even pre-cognitive processing that in data visualization drive the attentive focus.

Looking at the current QS scenario the impression is that this knowledge is shortly considered in favor of a "wow effect" or an aesthetic presentation. Hence the suspicion is that nowadays QS is not something oriented to build knowledge toward a purpose, but instead a way to collect data, like collecting butterflies, beer caps, etc. something that end in itself. The flavor is that QS supporters are more interested in collecting numbers, and putting them in some sort of neat filing cabinets (usually called infographics) than anything else. The risk is that the data do not help people to reach a personal goal, but their collection becomes a goal in itself, losing the big picture and the original motivations that should guide QS applications.

In fact, the interesting point of the whole QS movement is the ability to change something (for the better) in people's lives. But often this discussion is simplified in this kind of statements: *"by seeing my data I have more information and this allows me to make better choices. Furthermore if the graph is nice I will like more to collect my data"*. In fact there are a number of mechanisms that govern the behavior change and them are numerous and complex. In the following sections we will see some key moments related to the study of human psychology seeing how some of these are used from time to time in QS application often without even realizing it.

Although Gary Wolf sometimes called the QS as *"the next step in human development"* stressing that having greater awareness of one's data is a form of action against choice standardization imposed by TV, advertising, various media, etc., and a sort of re-appropriation of the individual self-determination, QS still looks like something very embryonic. In fact there are some fundamental problems yet to be solved. On the one hand some technological problems, but these are not of great concern, because the technological evolution is a fairly linear and predictable process. Those who appear the problems to be addressed in a deeper manner appear instead of a higher order of theoretical order. The huge amount of data that can generate a QS scenario poses major challenge in the manipulation of this information and in the displaying of these data. It will be discussed in the next sections how far we are from having a knowledge applied to data visualization for large amounts of data and how we have to develop

innovative solutions that take into account the ability of our brain to perceive data in a more natural way, as is done with the complexity of the natural world.

A second and even more profound problem is the lack of a true theory of behaviour change, or rather the existence of knowledge modules used in a more or less conscious way by QS applications but without an actual theoretical corpus that can be used by designers. There is therefore a theoretical problem that does not allow, besides some personal experiments in some application domain, to say which is the mechanism of operation that given some data should produce a change and consequently what should be considered in a QS application to produce a different personal behaviour.

In order to make more clearness, there will be in the next section a brief review of the elements that somehow seem to have a role in the QS as behaviour change engine and how these contribute to give a general impression of utility, though each has a different role in different application fields and for different people.

5. CURRENT APPLICATION FIELD OF QUANTIFIED SELF

Today there are more and more widespread applications and research projects related to the self tracking of people's behavior. Regardless the particular application domain (e.g. health, fitness, mood, goals and time management) most of these tools can be outlined to tracking: a physiological state (e.g. body temperature, and breathing), a state of mind (e.g. thinking patterns, mood), a location (e.g. environment, travel), time (e.g. time intervals, performance time), people (people you are with, interactions). To collect these data, applications that spin around the QS movement may resort today to direct measurement (using wearable and/or environmental sensors), inference (using semantic reasoning and algorithms: some data can deduce or infer others) or self-reporting (requiring manual data entry). In this section we will review three of the domains in which the QS idea seemed to realize most successfully in recent years: health, mood and fitness.

5.1. Healthcare

There is a growing trend in consumer market to develop sensors and services that support self-tracking of data concerning health. At moment users can access a variety of services and applications that collect, analyze and display statistics about a diverse range of parameters and behaviors related to their health. Although there are studies that seek to correlate these parameters with each other or with the context in which these behaviors are produced (Bentley et al., 2012), typically these tools now detect a single parameter or health-related behavior of the individual, often relying on a device able to measure it, storing it on a website where the user can view changes over time and compare them with those of other users. These services are intended to improve the health condition of the patient and help him to live a more salubrious life by changing its behavior in a positive direction. Although it is more and more common trying to find new ways to influence current and future health behaviors (e.g. using "past-self" avatar able to "give birth" to the past behavior of a person, or improving self-efficacy of the patient's presenting "reminders of success" when a failure occurs [Ramirez & Hekler, 2012], or even more by using game mechanics related to the world of social media [HealthMonth, 2012]), the more common used methods today can be traced back to the display of data about current behaviors and the presentation of information about the progress towards a particular short or long term goal.

Most part of the services are not targeted to specific diseases but rather aim to facilitate the health reporting of individuals suffering from dif-

ferent disorders, trying, with the support of a social network, to facilitate the exchange of information between patients, providing disease progression, drug prescriptions and symptom tracking. The most famous is PatientsLikeMe (2012), founded in 2004, that today gathers more than 160 thousand registered patients: it allows to record the symptoms of their disease in order to find patients in similar conditions and to exchange information about the effectiveness of the treatments and the evolution of their medical symptoms. As well CureTogether (2012) allows to compare the effectiveness of thousands of treatments to find the best solution for one's own health needs and Health Tracking Network (2012) aims to get people to work together to monitor common illnesses and discover factors related to them, using a system of self-reporting and collecting information from third party tracking tools. HealthEngage (2012) instead appears as an aggregator of health data about individuals, able to trace the general condition of the patient, the medicine he has to take, his daily diet and any chronic disease he has, importing information from different free tools; HealthVault (2012), a Microsoft service, can arrange in one place all medical information relating to an individual, providing forms of data visualizations that should help patients to take more conscious decisions about their health; ReliefInsite (2012), finally, allows to track pain conditions and store them in a journal that can also serve the medical staff to reconstruct the patient's condition.

Related to this kind of services there are more specific applications that can monitor physiological trends and behaviors related to a specific chronic disease: DiaMedics (2012), DIALOG (2012), and SugarStats (2012) are all services that can monitor the health of a patient with diabetes, providing statistics, community support and collaborative sharing to motivate and improve health; while Asthmapolis (2012) uses a specific sensor to track spatially and temporally asthma attacks of a patient and the quantity of medicines he takes.

The use of specific sensors and dedicated devices is also implemented by applications that are able to track physiological parameters continuously throughout the day. Glasswing allows to measure non-invasively hemoglobin (2012). SenseWear (2012), as well as Fitbit (2012) and Zeo (2012), collect and analyze information related to physical activity performed by the patient and sleep behaviors: the tracker monitors how many times and for how long the patient wake up during the night providing information on the quantity and quality of sleep patterns. Other research projects, on the academic side, such as Lullaby (Kay et al. 2011) set more ambitious targets and, using a variety of different sensors (e.g. sensors for air quality, noise, RGB light, infrared camera) seek to integrate the monitoring of physiological parameters with the environmental factors that can affect the sleep of the patient. In the end, BAM Labs (2012) uses a non-intrusive system, called Touch-free Life Care (TLC), which, through an under-the-mattress biometric sensor, collects motion, heart and breathing rate without attaching anything to the body.

Taking advantage of a small but growing number of consumers who prefer to skip costs and delays of specialist medical consultations to order their laboratory tests, some companies have begun to offer services of medical lab tests, making it possible not only to order directly from their websites the desired analyzes, but also to keep track over time of the variations in the parameters analyzed, as the level of cholesterol or glucose in the blood. MyMedLab (2012) and Private MD Lab Services (2012) are two examples of services that are part of a more general trend that is bringing individuals to care for themselves health status, tracking, storing and managing their physiological parameters, in collaboration with health peers and in co-care with physicians. QS applications make it possible, and at the same time are a symptom of a change that is arising in the health care, toward a patient-driven health care characterized by *"having an increased level of information flow,*

transparency, customization, collaboration and patient choice and responsibility-taking, as well as quantitative, predictive and preventive aspects" (Swan, 2009).

Finally, companies like 23andMe (2012) Pathway (2012), Knome (2012), Navigenics (2012) deCODEme (2012) have begun to offer tracking of DNA profiles to their clients: tracing the sequence of one million "snips" (snips are the current unit in personal genomics and are the part of the gene researchers have noticed that varies between individuals), these companies provide a series of numbers and letters that can be related to some aspects of their health and their genetic past. These genetic data can then be shared on network sites like Personal Genome Project (2012) or compared with the information contained in wikis as SNPedia (2012). As Gary Wolf noticed in his article Genomic Openness (Wolf, 2008) the field of Personal Genomics, or the ability to track data about their genes, is located at the edge of the field action of the QS. If the aim of the movement of the QS is the tracking of the physical and psychological "self" to make changes in behavior or take action to improve conditions (e.g. health) is not yet clear how knowledge of genome parts can lead to this result even if people like it. Melanie Swan from DIY Genomics (2012) advocates this strategy to develop a form of personalized preventive medicine (Swan, 2011)). The complexity in correlating these data with elements relating to personal health or personal phenotype makes to foresee that only an open sharing of raw genetic data and mass public collaboration could lead to some kind of knowledge advancement in the future.

5.2. Mood

Today, the mood tracking area is having increasing consideration. Applications and services related to this field are intended to help users to increase their awareness and understanding of all the factors that influence their "mood states" and their mental health. These applications, through different kind of visualizations, are able to track changes in mood over time and identify patterns and correlations with environmental and social factors, in order to facilitate the identification of variables that can affect the mental states of the person.

It is possible to find applications such as Track Your Happiness (2012) a research project of Mart Killingsworth at Harvard University: it allows you to draw the happiness of people asking them on a regular basis, via email or sms, what they are doing and how happy they feel at that time (through questions like: *"How happy are you right now?"*, *"Do you want to do what you're doing?"*, *"Do you have to do what you're doing?"*, *"Where are you?"*, *"Are you alone?"*). Reports inform the user about the changes in his happiness over time and what possible factors have had an influence on it. Happy Factor (2012) asks the user about their happiness by sending text messages: these data are recorded on a scale from 1 to 10 also associating them with some notes about activities carried out at that particular time. The application is then able to return in visual form history, average happiness for days, months and a frequency chart of words used in the notes from happiest to unhappiest. On the same mechanism is based MoodPanda (2012): happiness rating on a 0-10 scale, and optionally adding a brief twitter-like comment on what's influencing the mood.

Other services instead, such Moodscope (2012) and MoodTracker (2012), aim to measure, track and share the mood not only onto the happiness dimension. The first, for instance, uses a simple card game for tracking daily mood, brings out what can have a positive or negative influence about it and allows to share data with a list of trusted friends who can support the person in order to improve his overall mood. Both applications are designed not only for the common people, but especially for those suffering from depression and bipolar disorder. Even FindingOptimism (2012) is a service that has the purpose of increasing the understanding of the factors that can affect the mental health of the individual, helping to identify the "triggers" that affect the patient, and the early warning signs of new episodes of mental disorder, favoring the filling of a wellness plan with detailed strategies for dealing with events related to his disorder. Less oriented to the therapeutic scope is Gotta Feeling (2012) that aims to track the emotions of the user with the purpose to share them on his social networks; it, however, uses a different model, asking the user to indicate what are the emotions he feels choosing from 10 different categories and connecting them to a more precise list of words that express the feeling: the reports keep track of all the registered feelings, places and people to whom they were linked.

Finally, some services use dedicated devices to track and return the overall mood of the user. This is the case of Rationalizer (2012) a kind of "emotional mirror" in which the user sees the intensity of his feelings, with the purpose of improving his financial decisions which should be less emotionally charged and more rationally founded. Rationalizer consists of two dedicated devices. The EmoBracelet measure the intensity of the user's emotion, in the form of arousal level, through a galvanic skin response sensor. The level of arousal is shown as a light pattern that is both on EmoBracelet both on the second device, the EmoBowl (a kind of light dish that displays different light patterns). The higher the level of arousal more intense will be the dynamic light pattern, larger the number of graphical elements of the pattern, greater their speed, the more intense their color. BodyMonitor (2012) instead is a research project of the Leibniz-Institut for Sozialwissenschaft, which, using a wearable armband, measures heart rate and skin conductance, to determine the emotional state of the user. In the end StressEraser (2012) is a portable biofeedback device designed with the aim of reducing the stress of the user synchronizing his heartbeat with his respiratory rate: the device displays heart rate variability on a graphical display, suggesting how to control breath using visual cues.

5.3. Fitness

Self-tracking wearable devices are increasingly used in the consumer market (especially in the fitness arena) to track calorie consumption and daily physical activity and to support self-awareness and healthy behaviors. These devices automatically recognize positive behaviors (such as walking) tracking changes over time: the underlay idea is that having always-available displays could be useful to increase the individual's awareness about individual physical activity level and this could be valuable particularly when people try to change their habits (Consolvo et al., 2008). In this sense, the fitness area is the one that most uses dedicated devices (or smartphones) able to track physical activity and physiological parameters to improve physical well-being. All these systems can monitor the entire daily physical activity or can be addressed to the tracking of some specific sports.

Nike + iPod Sport Kit (2012) is perhaps the today most widely used tracking system of physical activities in the consumer market, and consists of a suite of interconnected devices like Nike + running shoes, Nike + Sensor, iPod Nano, iPod touch, or iPhone. The Nike + sensors can be integrated into the Nike + shoes transmitting the frequency of your steps into the user Apple device, who can see time, distance, pace, and calories burned. The system also allows to load physical performances into the nikeplus.com site where stats regarding physical activity can be shared and compared with those of other users. On the same principles is based the Adidas service Micoach (2012) that through the SPEED_CELL™ is able to track running speed, distance run and heart rate providing real time digital coaching, interactive training and post-workout analysis of pace, distance and stride rate. Runkeeper (2012) instead uses the GPS built into the iPhone of the user to track run, the distance, duration, speed and calories, preserving the history of run and showing progress and objectives.

Other service solutions are able to track more parameters and behaviors simultaneously correlating them. Jawbone UP System (2012) uses a wrist wearable motion detector interfaced with an iPhone application permitting to track daily physical activity and sleep behaviors, reminding to the user when it should make some exercise and waking him up at the right time. Even Fitbit (2012) is a device that can be worn throughout the day, allowing to track physical activity and sleep patterns. Once the data is collected, the user can view them on a website or mobile application. Fitbit has also been used by university research projects to identify unhealthy behaviors and intervene at the appropriate time to correct them. Fitbit+ uses Fitbit technology to identify sedentary moments in the day and prompt users to take walking breaks (Pina et al., 2012). BodyBugg (2012) uses a series of sensors such as an accelerometer, a skin-temperature sensor, a galvanic skin response sensor and a heat sensor to measure physical exercise in order to track how many calories the body has used during a physical activity. And it is right on eating behavior that many applications have been developed in the field of QS. They are capable of tracking daily weight changes and monitor the diet of the user. MyFitnessPal (2012) allows to keep track of daily diet by simply adding to the personal food journal the foods eaten during the day and available in the database of the system. The display of eating habits and calorie consumption, combined with the support of a social network of users, should provide motivation to adopt strategies to reduce body weight. Loseit (2012) and My Calorie Counter (2012) are based on the same principle of tracking the eating habits through self-reporting and viewing statistics that could make people more aware of how they behave every day. The Withings scales (2012) instead track daily weight, body mass index and fat mass index: the user smartphone can then display statistics showing significant changes during the time period selected.

6. QUANTIFIED SELF FUNDAMENTAL PROBLEMS

6.1. Technological Limits for Collection, Processing and Visualization of Large Dataset

At present the increasing miniaturization of electronic modules and processing power of microprocessors, the developments in sensor technologies, the new potentials offered by displays and micro-displays, the advances of mobile networks and the new models of dynamic data visualization focus to make large amounts of data accessible in a lesser amount of pixels and with littler attentional effort from the user.

On the data collection side nowadays the wearable computing, the body sensor networks, the RFID tags allow to gather information, in an automatic way, making possible to envision the opportunity of a constant monitoring of the individual behavior. The data collected by these technologies can today also be stored and structured (through semantic reasoning techniques) in almost tangible "knowledge", manipulable and usable for different purposes. The appearance on the market of very large screen and highly innovative technologies, such as 3D printing, enable the exploration of new ways of viewing data and in some case the physical materialization of them.

Sensors available on the market today allow to monitor a variety of physical, biochemical and physiological parameters of the individuals as well as the environments in which they are moving at a very affordable price and with a very low power consumption. For example, from the perspective of physiological and biochemical parameters are increasingly spreading sensors for measuring heart rate, blood pressure, respiratory rate, temperature, muscle and brain activity (e.g. Shaltis et al., 2006) and Corbishley & Rodriguez-Villegas (2008)), while the development of flexible circuits insertable within tissues is allowing the integration of these sensors also in wearable device scenarios

(Barbaro et al., 2010). In addition, accelerometers, gyroscopes and magnetometers integrated in wearable devices are now used to track the movements of people, and the data available from these sensors can be combined with information from other ambient sensors, such as motion sensors placed in a domestic environment, in order to determine, for instance, the type of activity performed by an individual (Bonato et al., 2012). All these sensors are often integrated in a sensor network that relies on modern wireless communication networks. In recent years numerous standards are born for wireless communication networks that fulfill the requirements of miniaturization and low cost / low power consumption of transmitters and receivers. Not only the development of IEEE 802.15.4/ZigBee (ZigBee Alliance, 2012) and Bluetooth, but also of IEEE 802.15.4a standard based on Ultra-Wide-Band (UWB) impulse radio made possible to foresee a set of sensor network applications with a high data rate (Zhang et al., 2009) easily deployable in many kind of environments. In addition, the need to transmit the data gathered from the sensors to a terminal that can process them, such as a mobile phone or a personal computer, can now be easily met by GSM or 3G communication mobile networks and soon by new LTE networks. The actual and future smartphones look like the ideal platform for applications that have to continuously monitor individual data. They have built-in large computing capacity and excellent graphic displays, are equipped with motion sensors, GPS systems capable of tracking the movements of individuals, and networking technologies, able to connect with the surrounding environment in order to become hubs for body area networks (BAN). Moreover, smartphones are always brought on by their users, eliminating the disadvantage of having to bring dedicated devices for recording specific daily activities and behaviors (Rawassizadeh et al., 2012).

On the data storage and processing side, the linear increasing in capacity, make now possible to store and process an amount of data just unthinkable few years ago. Today, one terabyte hard drive is available on the market at less than $ 100 and may contain all the written information we come in contact in the course of a lifetime (by mail, books, web pages). Twenty years from now, we will be able to buy at the same price 250 terabytes of storage sufficient to store ten thousand hours of video and tens of millions of photographs: a capacity able to meet the needs of recording of one hundred years of life (Bell & Gemmell, 2007). If the increasing miniaturization of digital media will continues to proceed according to Moore's Law, in 70 years will double around 47 times and in 2072 the physical space of storage needed to contain all the experiences of a lifetime will be the size of a grain of sand (Dix, 2002). In addition, all collected and stored data can now be structured semantically, using reasoning rules (possible to the increasing computational power of todays processors) to extract relevant information in response to complex queries. Ontologies and systems that can automatically annotate data with metadata can provide a structure to the information collected (e.g. Gruber, 1995; Guarino. 1998) and also extract knowledge from large stores of unstructured data allowing the surfacing of relationships, patterns and connections. The extreme evolution of this approach permits to envision the possibility of retrieving links to specific items similarly to the retrieval mechanisms of human associative memory (O'Hara et al., 2006)

On the data visualization side technological advances are taking two opposite directions. On the one hand are increasingly available at a lesser cost very large screens capable of ensuring access to large amounts of data and allowing interaction with them quickly in order to gain understanding and take decisions faster; on the other hand there is a growing effort to find new ways to maximize the amount of information visible in a limited space, due to the growing popularity of smartphones and tablets as first choice devices for human behavior tracking applications (Few, 2009). Today are available many possible configurations

of large displays. The Cave Automatic Virtual Environment (CAVEs™) is a projection-based display system (e.g. Mechdyne CAVETM Virtual Reality, 2012) with a resolution of 100 megapixels or higher. La Cueva Grande, is a five-sided slot with 33 projectors for a resolution of 43 mega-pixels (Canada et al., 2006) which surround the viewer with an immersive environment: they are commonly composed of four large wall displays arranged as a cube (Cruz-Neira et al., 1993). There are also monitor-based wall displays that combining the resolution of LCD monitors can get to reach a comprehensive resolution of hundreds megapixels (e.g. LambdaVision, a wall of 5 x 11 LCD panels with about 100 megapixels spread over a width of 5 meters [Renambot et al., 2012] and hyperwall composed by 49 LCD panels tiled in a 7x7 array [Sandstrom, 2003]): however, these configurations have the problem of not providing a continuous display, being interrupted by screen bezels (Thelen, 2010). There are then projector based systems that combines multiple computer projectors arranged in a grid in order to project on very large screens (e.g. the ten Sony SXRD 4K SRX-S110 projectors combined to create an image of approximately 88 Megapixels in ITC's Michigan Control Room (2012) and Visblock™ (2012)). The projectors resolution is increasing, as they are steady progress to optimize the calibration for example on color gamut matching, luminance matching and image blending. (Ni et al., 2006) Finally, are increasingly widespread in the consumer market stereoscopic displays that can display 3D images using special glasses or even autostereoscopic displays that eliminate the need to wear glasses to get the 3D visualization effect (e.g. AU Optronics prototype of autostereoscopic technology [Information Displays, 2012]). Although the costs of these devices are progressively going down, so that it is possible to imagine in the near future their massive spread, outside a research context, even in the consumer market (both for very large LCD monitor, and for autostereoscopic 3D display), commercial tools that aim to track the behavior of people and return back significant views are watching today mainly to the market of mobile devices to convey their services. The advent of high resolution micro-displays, such the 4" Retina Displays of Iphone5 (1136x640 resolution), or the 9.7" of the new iPad (with a resolution of 2048x1536), pushes the research towards new visualization solutions, such as interactive dashboards able to deal to the relative narrowness of the display surface of these devices.

The spread of human behaviors tracking applications on mobile devices poses today serious technical issues that are currently not fully resolved. The mobile devices, even if their ability to collect, process and display data is constantly increasing, suffer from both the small size of displays and the limited processing power, which limits the amount of data that can be managed locally and prevents the use of computationally expensive algorithms; the extreme segmentation of the smartphones and tablet market also rise the problem of the severe variability between different models in terms of performance and input peripherals (Burigat & Chittaro, 2007). Moreover, the mobile context introduces a number of problems in relation to fixed devices: on the one hand, the physical environment can affect the data visualization on the display (e.g. mobile devices can be used in different light condition that may vary from the bright light of the sun to the total darkness affecting so the perception of colors), on the other hand the mobility context makes it difficult to focus user attention on the device, because of the activities that are often performed at the same time that transform the use of the device in a secondary task (Chittaro, 2007).

However, other technological problems are shared by applications that rely both on fixed and mobile environment. One of the central issues is that often users and systems have to deal with digital data coming from various sources in heterogeneous forms and formats (Whittaker et al., 2012). In particular, this problem is related to the capacity of storing large amounts of information

not only limited to textual data but also multimedial. Search and retrieval of textual information is now relatively simple, but other media present major problems about framing queries and organization of memory stores, and adding text annotations requires a great effort, often not covering the entire range of possible meanings that can convey an image or a sound: furthermore the future possibility to integrate new types of information (such as olfactory and haptic) poses new problems of integration between different "media" and how these heterogeneous information can be indexed, searched and retrieved (O'Hara et al., 2006). Last but not least, there is the central problem of how to handle this immense amount of information, because the possibility of capturing vast arrays of data is not yet balanced by the possibility of an efficient and really meaningful search, and this can overwhelm users in their effort to retrieving valuable information from large clusters of data (Abigail & Whittaker, 2010).

The technological problem as we have seen is quite relevant, even if the trend line makes it probable that this will have less and less importance in the future. What appear instead the most worrying aspects of the QS field are at a higher level. What is missing is some convincing positions about how to return people with sufficient clarity and sense the data they collect and how to structure a model of human behavior change that in front of these data makes possible to use them in the desired direction.

6.2. Theoretical Limits in Perception and Cognition

6.2.1. Data Visualization

The data visualization is the way in which all the data collected are rendered and made available to the user. How the data "appears" is the first step that data make in the user brain, so it is important to consider all the studies on perception, reading charts, organization of complex data, because this first step is crucial in the pathway that data make into cognition. How data visualization is realized is able to modify and affect subsequent processing of the same data. The manner in which data are presented has a huge importance and is strongly influenced by the model of knowledge that is embraced: this is the reason why we will treat this aspect first and the cognition aspect later.

The first theoretical foundations that are available to help designers to organize information on a perceptive point of view are the Gestalt principles. The associationist psychology considered perception as the sum of more simple stimuli linked directly to the physiological substrate of the sensory systems. With the development and consolidation of Gestalt psychology, the center of the investigation on the perceptual processes passes from the previous elementaristic conception to a more complex notion of perception as result of interaction and global organization of various components. Gestalt, using a phenomenological approach to perception, canonizes a series of perceptual laws independent from external experience (hence not connected with learning processes) and present since birth.

These laws analyze the figural organization taking into account the separation of figure from background (by color, density, texture, contour). Wolfgang Köhler, the father of Gestalt psychology, suggested the following laws:

1. **Law of Superposition**: The forms above are figures. In order to distinguish an overlap is necessary that there is evidence of depth.
2. **Law of the Occupied Area:** The separate zone which occupies minor extension tends to be seen as a figure, while the wider as background. This mechanism for the identification of objects in the background works even if the closure is incomplete.
3. **Law of Perceptual Organization on the Basis of Common Destiny:** This mechanism of closeness is salient not only at the level of modification of the space, but also of time.

Further studies related to Gestalt psychology aimed to postulate general laws oriented to synthesize multiple items in a single global perception:

1. Simplicity or "good form" law which summarizes the whole logic of perception. Data are organized in the simplest and more consistent way possible, according to previous experiences.
2. Similarity law states that for elements arranged in a disorderly way, those who are similar tend to be perceived as a form, separated from the background. The perception of the figure is as strong as stronger the items similarity.
3. Continuity Law states that a perceptual unit emerge between the elements that offers the least number of irregularities or interruptions, being equal other features.

Other studies have instead explored the figural elements used for the perception of the third dimension. It is in fact linked to the motion perception. The main indicators are identified:

- The relative magnitude (the largest object is the closest)
- Brightness
- The linear and aerial perspective

The laws of perception are considered innate because are not the result of learning, although it is demonstrated that there is a developmental progression in the development of perceptions. From the first months the baby is able to recognize colors and shapes (especially the human figure), but only later he acquires the "perceptual constancy", the ability to link a shape or figure already known, with a different one in which he recognizes characteristics of similarity (e.g. a statue associated with a person).

These laws are easily testable in everyday life and it is easy to have a direct evidence with optical effects. But they are only the basis of knowledge useful for improving the data visualization for human perception. Instead the purpose of data visualization as a discipline is to display parametric information essentially with a twofold perspective: on the one hand to better understand the data, on the other to extract evidence non-extractable otherwise. There are a lot of hidden meanings behind each set of data. To discover these meanings is necessary that the visualization choices of this data set are functional to the emergence of these meanings. When we say that "a picture is worth a thousand words" means just that that image is effective to convey with a single glance all the meaning hidden in a thousand words or a thousand numbers. But how to choose for the best visualization? Again we are dealing with a problem that has its basis in the theoretical research on perception and cognition, that is about how humans can see, filter, store, learn, retrieve complex content. But for the moment let's stop at the first step, we will see the basic theories of cognition in the following paragraphs. Speaking instead about perception we have already mentioned the fundamental Gestalt laws but what other theoretical elements we have to provide a good visualization to the users? Much of what is now the data visualization we owe to Descartes that in the 17th century invented the coordinate axes that in some extent are the first and most basic form of visualization of a set of two-dimensional data. In the modern sense the first significant contributions are due to William Playfair that as early as the 18th century began to develop almost all types of graphics that are still in use (bar charts, pie charts, etc.). There are no other significant contributions until the work "Semiologie Graphique" of Jacques Bertin in 1967 in which for the first time we found a complete reflection about the best ways to represent different kind of information. Then there is the fundamentals work of Tukey (1977), of Tufte (1983), and of Card et al. (1999), the most advanced in defining the best way of representation. Last but not least for a complete and comprehensive work on data visualization and its bases, see the work of Colin

Ware-Visual Thinking for Design (2008). All the attention to the way we represent the data has only one purpose: that our eyes can distinguish good information and our brain can understand it. All this can be done simply running back on the results of 100 years of experimental psychology studies. Despite this knowledge has always been available, it has not been used very much. In the last 10-15 years it has been developed a number of products designed right to give meaning to data, but in fact simply based on covering data with shining graphic work with purely aesthetic value, not considering even some basic requirements that a good visualization must have to be considered a good one. We can resume them in few statement (Few, 2010). A good visualization:

- Must clearly indicate relationships
- Must represent quantities accurately
- Must make it possible to easily compare the quantities
- Must clearly show the ordering of values
- Must encourage people to use the information

These simple requirements inform us about the quality of visualization, and for example, show us how pie charts are not suitable for many types of data, or like sometimes the old bar charts are much more efficient. If a visualization does not meet these criteria is not suitable for that particular type of data.

The motivation to make better visualization is to make possible a primary processing already at the perceptual level, without having even turn on the cognitive processing level. It is a form of cognitive economy that allows us to already have all the information we need with fewer resources. The Gestalt laws mentioned at the beginning of paragraph are based right on this economical concept. But today there are interesting studies that come from the fields of neuroscience that provide material even more interesting (Guidano, 1983). The first research area is the pre-attentive visual processing. It is a sort of pre attentional processing that occurs before the data arrives at a consciousness level. It is made by particular neuronal structures able to perceive length orientation, but also by more complex properties such as shading, groupings and three-dimensional orientation.

The second broader research area is about the mechanisms that govern attention and memory. In particular for the attention, latest studies have shown that the attentional processes focus only on some parts of the scene. Also data visualization techniques should be able to govern their points of attentional salience organizing the data meant to be conveyed almost like a "real world" (Rensink, 2002). These aspects, together with the dynamic views required to manipulate large data sets (nowadays we are limited to organize levels starting from an overview, providing filtering and zooming features), introduce how the entire discipline of data visualization, specially if linked with QS large dataset, should become a discipline of data interaction rather than simple data visualization. In the next paragraphs we will see how storytelling in some extent represents a solution that includes both the aspect of interaction with the real world (fostering pre attentive elaboration), and the complexity of managing large amounts of data. Roambi (2012) a company specialized in data visualization is going in this direction with its latest product Roambi Flow that allows "to tell" data to the intended audience.

After this theoretical analysis on data visualization let's move on to what are the theoretical foundations of behaviour change theory that implicitly (sometimes without awareness) are used by many applications of QS.

6.2.2. Behavior Change Theories

As mentioned previously, one of the fundamental problems of QS is that it does not have a well-structured and well-established theoretical basis. QS is nowadays mostly a series of experiences more or less significant where, an application,

in a certain domain, worked at a certain time for someone in particular. Basically it is not a generalizable or falsifiable approach according to scientific criteria (Popper & Eccles, 1977). It is a pragmatic and empirical approach which carries with it the limitation of not progressing beyond few single anecdotal cases and takes the risk of disappearing or becoming irrelevant. On the other hand, today's technology makes QS look very modern, but in a variety of fields the habit of data recording in order to find relationships between variables and to drive changes it's quite an old idea, at least dating back to the birth of the industrial age. In the medical, financial, industrial fields since decades it is custom to fill graphs and spreadsheets, and also on a personal level in many biographies is possible to find peculiar a way to organize self-knowledge through manual annotation of notes an tables and filling of summary sheets.

The most innovative aspect is perhaps, more than anything else, that QS, taking advantage of new technological devices, frees the individual from the burden to personally record every data. But there is another aspect of substantive novelty. As long as you remain in the domain of financial or political science the change process driven by new knowledge emerged by data seems easier to implement according to a rationalistic model. When we move in the domain of personal and individual change, things get complicated. What are the rules that govern the individual change? Are they so clear? Can we put them in a structured system that can predictably drive the change? In part yes and in part not yet. The various paradigms that have developed over 20th century and are still evolving thanks to the neurosciences have precisely tried to answer these questions. Some pieces of knowledge are now part of these simplified change theories that are implicitly implemented (often misused and distorted) within many QS applications. In the following lines there is a brief summary of the paradigms borrowed by this "naïve change theory".

6.2.2.1. Behaviorism and the Positive/Negative Reinforcement

Who has tried to do fitness with the Nintendo Wii Fit will have noticed that by according to his performance the system will critique you if the performance is poor or on the contrary praise you if it is positive. The system simply seeks to introduce a positive or negative reinforcement providing paradigm derived from behaviorism. Behaviorism was originally developed by psychologist John Watson at the beginning of the twentieth century, based on the assumption that explicit behavior is the only unit of analysis to be studied scientifically by psychology, because it is directly observable by the researcher. The mind is thus seen as a black box, a black box whose inner workings are unknowable and, in some respects, irrelevant: what really matters for behaviorists is to have a thorough understanding of empirical and experimental relationships between certain types of stimuli (environment) and certain types of responses (behavior). Within this broad approach, emphasis is placed on particular aspects. One of the major assumptions is the mechanism of the conditioning, according to which the repeated association of a stimulus, said neutral stimulus, with a response that is not directly related to it, will ensure that, after a period of time, such stimulus will follow the conditioned response. The famous experiment of Pavlov's dog that everyone knows makes reference to this type of mechanism.

Skinner with his writings "The Behavior of Organisms" (1938) and "Science and Human Behavior" (1953) laid the foundation for the discovery of the laws and of the most important paradigms of matter, giving rise to a new way of conceiving the causes and enabling thus to enlarge significantly the possibilities to influence the observable behavior. His great merit is in fact to have found that human behavior is predictable and controllable through an appropriate management of two classes of stimuli from the physical environment: "antecedent" stimuli that the body receives before implementing a behavior and "result" stimuli that the body receives immediately after the behavior has been put in place. After the discoveries of Skinner, a growing number of researchers have progressively developed many techniques for behavioral change in almost all areas of application and, from the mid-seventies, even within organizations and in the specific field of work safety.

In North America, the birthplace of the QS, this behaviorist perspective strongly permeates the environment especially in the common sense psychology. In terms of QS, this paradigm was translated using positive or negative reinforcement depending on the behavior to drive. An example is the badge gaining, the collection of awards, such as elements of positive reinforcement (e.g. Foursquare, Nike +) or, conversely, the blame, the criticism, etc. if the behavior is not consistent with the purposes of the application. This mechanism is well documented but, as the same latest generation behaviorists have stressed, is not rigidly determined. There are in fact a number of intervening variables that change or at least modulate the Stimulus-Response (S-R) arc. For example, it is necessary for the user to perceive correctly the reinforcement, to understand it, to weight it, to check if is relevant for him and so on. In the case of Nike +, the praise that arrives from the system or by the community can have a totally different weight for two different people, or even for the same person at different times of his life or even of his day.

Recognizing excessive simplicity and rigidity of the behaviorist paradigm, some behavioral psychologists, called "neo behaviorists", proposed some corrective premises (the so-called "intervening variables of the SR process") opening the way for further development of cognitive psychology. The evident role of internal and external variables in determining the behavior demonstrated by many experiments paved the way for at least two other types of theoretical contributions to the behaviour change topic: cognitivism introducing the internals variables and social psychology introducing the externals variables influencing behavior.

6.2.2.2. Cognitivism the Role of Mind

At a QS meetup a speaker explain: *"I use the Nike + app on my iPhone. I find it motivates me to run more, try and run faster than previous PB's and Generally lets me check up on myself for further improvements. Couple this with Their website of the same name and I now have a 24week plan for running a marathon. Good times"* (Guardian, 2010). Some athletes or coaches (in various sports) have been doing things like this for decades: keeping daily written notes on workouts, feelings before and after, bodyweight, body temperature, sleep, nutrition, techniques used etc. using then that data for statistical analysis. This is a classic example of self-monitoring model deriving from early cognitivist model of feedback engine (TOTE) as we will see below.

Cognitivism is sometimes considered an evolution of behaviorism because it introduces more complexity in the S-R arc recovering the concept of mind (the black-box originally excluded by behaviorism). Cognitivist focus is on the mind as an intermediate element between the behavior and purely neurophysiological brain activity. The mind operations are metaphorically compared to that of a software that processes information (input) coming from the outside, giving in return information (output) in the form of knowledge representation and semantic and cognitive networks. Perception, learning, reasoning, problem solving, memory, attention, language, and emotions are mental processes studied by cognitive psychology (Neisser, 1967). In the early cognitivist models, processing was conceived as a process that occurs in subsequent stages, finished one step the "system" move to the next, and so on. In the '70s were presented new models that put in evidence both the possibility of feedback of a processing

stage to the previous ones, and the possibility to activate operations of the next stage without previous ones had already processed their information.

Another important aspect was the emphasis on specific objectives targeted by mental processes. The behavior was now conceived as a series of acts guided by cognitive processes for the solution of a problem, with constant adjustments to ensure the best solution. The notion of "feedback", developed by cybernetics became central in this conception of behavior directed toward a goal. The experimental psychologist of language G. Miller with his works brought to a real turning point in the representation of behavior: the behavior was seen now as the product of a data-processing system, driven by the development of a plan helpful to solve a problem, in certain sense like a computer (Miller et al., 1960). In this new model the behavior was therefore not an epiphenomenon of a reflex arc (sensory input, processing, motor output), but the result of a process of continuous retroactive monitoring of the behavior plan according to the TOTE unit (test, operate, test, exit). The final act (exit) does not follow directly to a sensory input or a motor command, but it is the result of previous environmental conditions verification (test), intermediate operations (operate) and new tests (test). In the feedback model is expected that to complete a specific goal there are some verification stages and then an exit from the plan (if the goal is reached) or new operations (if the goal is not reached). This model is also implicitly widely used in QS application. The concept is that if there is a goal that the application advocates, it is possible through constant quantification (test) show to the user how far away he is from and so drive him to focus and continue the action (operate) toward the goal or stop it when the same goal is reached (exit).

The concept of the mind as a computer based on feedback engine underlies many QS applications and in a certain extent is also one of their main limitations. Knowing how far from a goal we are is certainly informative in itself; however it is not enough to motivate a behavior in a generalizable way (for instance the fact that I know what my sleep patterns are, hardly makes me change the time that I go to bed). There are other variables that can intervene: for instance external social variables.

6.2.2.3. Social Psychology: The Role of External Variables

Many applications of QS refer to a social and interpersonal dimension both in agonistic terms, the cases in which there is a gaming dimension and for example the most virtuous climb a rank (many applications of energy savings are based on this example) and in cooperative terms, where many people work together to obtain an objective valuable for all (for instance in many healthcare QS applications).

Social psychologists typically explain human behavior in terms of interaction between mental states and social situations. In the famous heuristic formula of Kurt Lewin (1951) behavior (C) is seen as a function (F) of the interaction between the person (P) and the environment (A). "Social" is an interdisciplinary domain that bridges the gap between psychology and sociology. During the years immediately following the Second World War, there was frequent collaboration between psychologists and sociologists. In recent years, the two disciplines are increasingly specialized and isolated from each other, with sociologists focusing on "macro variables" (social structure). Nevertheless, sociological approaches to social psychology remain an important counterpart to psychological research in this area. Cognitive strategies are influenced by our relationships with others, our expectations on their reactions, from belonging to a group or another, membership of which brings us to the definition of who we are and our social identity. In particular, the group is a unit with its overall social identity, which determines what each member expects from others in terms of behaviors. This social identity is then linked to the social identity of the group members. Our identity is, in fact, largely a function of our belonging to different social groups.

7. TOWARD A MORE ROBUST APPROACH IN QUANTIFIED SELF

7.1. New Model of Data Visualization: Telling Stories

In recent years, much research has focused on the role that storytelling can play in data visualization. Often are also been highlighted the great similarities that a good data visualization has with the ability to tell engaging stories through images. Since 2001, Gershon & Page (2001) predicted that the technology could have used different genres and media to convey information in a story-like manner. However, since what makes data visualization different from other types of visual storytelling is the complexity of the content that needs to be communicated (Wojtkowski & Wojtkowski, 2002), to effectively use storytelling are necessary skills like those familiar to movie directors, beyond a technical expert's knowledge of computer engineering and computer science (Gershon & Page, 2001). At present applications that attempted to implement narrative elements within data visualization scope are very few (e.g Heer et al., 2008; Eccles et al., 2007). Moreover, since none of these seems to go beyond the incorporation of some superficial narrative mechanisms in the flow of data visualization, also the researches carried out appear to be limited to the enumeration of stylistic and narrative mechanics, but decontextualized from their original media. Edward Segel and Jeffrey Heer (2008), for example, analyzing several case studies of narrative visualizations, identify three divisions of features (genres, visual narrative tactics, and narrative structures) that can be considered patterns for narrative visualization. Genres identify established visual structures that can be used to communicate data, such as comic strips, slide shows, and film / video / animation; visual narrative tactics are instead visual devices that assist and facilitate the narrative; while narrative structures are mechanisms that assist the narrative. Nevertheless, the analogy with stories seems to be hard. As Zach Gemignani (2012) underlines many of the key elements of the stories are not present in data visualization: characters, a plot, a beginning and an end. On the other hand data visualizations have characteristics that are missing from the traditional storytelling. As interactive means data visualizations allow users to explore in an active and dynamic way the data to find insights by themselves. For these reasons Gemignani notes that the data visualization today has nothing to do with telling a story more than with accompanying the audience in a guided conversation.

However, the QS field seems to offer new opportunities for the use of storytelling in data visualization. Visualizing human behavior is in a certain extent to put in the center of the visualization the subject as individual. Finding new ways to make alive these data, to make them meaningful in the eyes of the person they belong to, seems to be the real challenge that QS must face. In this sense a huge importance can gain one of the key elements of storytelling, the character, through which the story takes a perspective and a point of view. Aggregating data about personal behavior in the form of a fictional character can be seen as a way to give sense, in two ways, as meaning and as direction. The direction is firstly temporal from the past to the future, and through the overcoming of continuous testing and objectives, key elements in narratological theory (e.g. Greimas, 1987; Propp, 1927), sets in motion a narrative development that can really bring, no more superficially, but essentially, data visualization to a new level closer to the storytelling. From this point of view today video games seem the more suitable media narrative forms from which to take inspiration for the creation of new ways to display behavioral

data. Video games in fact have managed to create a form of interactive narrative where hypertext narrative had failed, managing to involve deeply the audience while leaving the user the power to influence the story told. Although not leaving a completely open narrative, which, as noted by Jesse Schell in his book (2008), is difficult to achieve both in technical and design terms, as well as difficult to use, video games, especially in the form of MMORPGs (Massively Multiplayer Online Role-Playing Games), leave broad room for their users to build the mirror of themselves in dynamic ways. Growing his own virtual avatar on different form and sizes depending on the choices made, users can, within these worlds, see themselves from different perspectives in a logic that encourage reflection about the actions taken, the objectives achieved, and the changes that they have produced on own subjectivity and identity. From these media products, therefore, the QS can draw on design strategies, tactics, forms of representation, and temporal evolution that in the near future could revolutionize the display of human behavior data.

7.2. Managing Complexity in Technology and People

We can understand the management of complexity in both directions, one more technological and one more human. Let's see them separately.

7.2.1. Technological Side

What today is missing is a platform that integrates all the data a person collect during his daily activities, a complete, adequate, integrated, picture of the individual. Nowadays there are only a small amount of recorder that manage certain parameters to render them in different and separate applications. In this sense, the technological complexity that QS will have to face in the future years is the tracking of many different kind of data and the integration of them in meaningful visualizations.

In a certain sense is the rediscovery of the original ambitions of Lifelogging depicted in the first paragraphs but on a massive and more pervasive seamless plan. We could call it the "ultimate lifelogging scenario".

Some examples in this sense already exist: for instance Capzels (2012) uses social storytelling to allow users to create chronological slideshows containing photos, videos and slide decks located on a timeline. LifeLapse (2012) is an iPhone app that lets you take a photo every 30 seconds tying your iPhone to the neck. The preserved images can then be seen one by one or mounted in a video that evokes the recorded life experience. If in these two applications build from scratch the lifelogging experience require an active intervention by the user to continuously record his life experience, other applications such as your. flowingdata (2012) and Daytum (2012) exploit the popular micro-blogging site Twitter as input mechanism to trace the daily life of users. Daytum allows you to collect, categorize and communicate your everyday data through the storage and display of personal statistics related to the daily events, providing various forms of statistical display, as pie charts, bar charts, timelines, and so forth. Your. flowingdata captures the lives of users using data from Twitter. Following @YFD on Twitter the user can begin to record his experiences simply sending a tweet to @YFD. Data about what the user eats, sees and more generally experiences are recorded by the system in order to be displayed on the application site. Display modes range from timelines to charts, also integrating experimental visualizations that allow the user to find cross-correlations between data, to explore durations between a start and stop actions and to use calendar visualizations, which displays the frequency of an action on a given day through the intensity of color (Yau & Hansen, 2010).

However, lifelogging systems are still suffering some difficulties to spread on the consumer market and it seems quite far away the possibility to see in the next future an application that can be used by all users to really record all aspects of a person's life, as it was hoped by the first pioneering research projects of the lifeloggers. Although the miniaturization of sensors and chips, such as audio recorders and cameras, makes possible now to integrate them into common smartphones, these applications seem destined to remain for some time prerogative of academic research projects. This is partly due the excessive involvement of the user that is necessary today (through self-reporting or manual annotation of recorded media) in order to record all the experiences of his life. Research projects try also to address another technological problem: how to cope with the difficulties of recovering significant data in the enormous amount of information that can be recorded in an extensive lifelogging scenario. For instance Poyozo is an automatic journal able to generate summaries and statistics displays from heterogeneous activity data, integrating this information into a calendar trying to create a meaningful narrative life for the user (Moore et al., 2010). Or like in an interesting research project of the Aizu University, trying to overcome the problem of information overload storing only the significant highlights of a lifetime, without requiring active intervention by the user. This system automatically saves significant events for a group of people if their emotional arousal (detected by a heart rate monitor and compared through a peer-to-peer network) exceeds a certain threshold (Gyorbiro et al., 2010).

7.2.2. Human Side

Another level of complexity that we must address is that about the complexity that drives behaviors (Guidano, 1987). We have to accept that human action is not simply driven by rationality but also from infinite variables that affect the final behavior. We all know that is not enough just to look at the weight on the balance (awareness) to make us want to do more sport or eating less. We have to take into account the human complexity. An attempt in this direction is carried out by the second cognitivism which introduces greater complexity compared to the first theoretical assumptions. This development suggests how the reading of the "reality", the "world", is in fact very personal and can lead to different meaning depending on who is "reading". There is a shift from a realistic/objective paradigm to a subjective one. Human behavior becomes so the result of an articulated and variously structured cognitive process of information processing.

The most recent results on the analysis of cognitive processes focus these dynamics in the social and interpersonal contexts in which the thought develops. This approach based on cognitivism, defined as social cognitive theory, studies the interaction between cognition and social context. Great importance in this theoretical core is attributed to the reflections of Albert Bandura (1986) about cognitive-emotional processes, who sees that these processes express themselves through behaviors. There is essentially a complete re-evaluation of interpersonal and emotional components as human action drivers.

Let's consider just one the many examples of QS interpreted as "augmented awareness". Asthmapolis (2012) links sensors attached to the inhalers used by patients with asthma to smartphones. These sensors gather data on where and when they are used. Recording this information helps patients identify the triggers that make their conditions worse. The concept seems simple: more data lead to greater awareness and make possible the anticipation. In fact, looking at this example the impression is that the driver of who decides to rely on Asthmapolis is more emotional, driven by the concern, the fear and the attempt to gain control on this. One of the main fear mastery strategies is to seek information to improve or prevent damage to ourselves, or even to prevent the stress of uncertainty. It is what is called in psychology coping strategy: looking frantically for information, for new data. Collecting personal information is an effective coping strategy that manage the emotional stress of the disease. The

real driver of those who use this form of QS is not the rational data collection in order to develop more knowledge, at least not only that, there is also (and maybe is even more crucial) in the application adoption, the coping strategy to decrease in a certain extent the fear given by their disease condition. Fear is not instead what guides those who collect their own fitness data: in this case the motivational mechanism underlying the emotional matrix will be linked rather to the positive emotions related to competitive motivational systems. In this sense we speak about taking into account the human complexity, to really address the full spectrum of human behaviour drivers.

8. FUTURE RESEARCH DIRECTIONS

Future research directions should start from what is stated in the preceding paragraph, a different management of technological and human complexity and new ways to address this complexity keeping in mind that the real and final purpose of the QS is the personal and social improvements.

8.1. Individual Impact

Let's consider this example. A QS supporter claims to have lost 20 kg of his 100 by either writing the word "lethargic" or "energised" on a flash card at 3pm every day for 18 months, depending on how he felt: *I gradually noticed that my perception of some foods shifted from thinking they were delicious to starting to feel their heaviness and the effects they were going to have on me. The act of paying greater attention has an effect on your behaviour* (Guardian, 2011). What we see in this example again is not an example of augmented awareness; it is rather a gradual reorganization of the "Self", through the focusing on the connection between behavior and the mood, the emotional component ("lethargic" or "energised") linked to the behavior (food consumption) (Damasio, 1999). The effect of this focusing is well known as instrument of change in psychology and therapy under different names and has its theoretical bases in Cognitive Behavioral Therapy (CBT) and even more in the post rationalist paradigm. The studies that have helped to define the post-rationalist paradigm have pointed out that it is not possible to have a unique idea of an objective reality. Echoing comments made by Ricoeur (1992) and Morin (2003) the reality is quite captured through a reading that is in large part subjective and in which are critical, even more than the rational, the emotional and affective components. The reality is then reconstructed on the basis of emotional and cognitive tools available to the person at some point of his life cycle. The focus is so shifted from what is valid or common for all individuals to subjective experience.

As Guidano (1991) evidenced the varied and changeable flow of experience inbound is compared with the pre-existing mental configurations that act as frames of reference. Any knowledge of external reality, as well as data from the QS, trigger subjective mode of experience, from which are then extracted the personal knowledge and the vision of the world. There is thus a dialogic dimension of continuous mutual influence between the "Self" and the narration of incoming data that continuously restructure the same "Self". This means that the data that I collect and how they are presented to me, on the one hand will be seen in a different way depending on the current emotional and cognitive configuration but on other hand will also contribute to define it. So we are in a scenario where the data really have a role in building the "Self" and the personal identity (Guidano & Liotti, 1987). This is especially true if we speak about data that reflect our mental activity in terms of thought, action and emotional aspects. There are already some examples in this regard. Dream-Board (2012) is a platform that collects dreams and renders a graphic story of dream activities, quantifying characters, mood, recurring figures, etc. Because the dream, as many studies proved, is a mental activity among the others (Fosshage,

1997) this kind of restitution contributes to develops new meanings to some cognitive restructuring and actual construction "self". This is a greater self-knowledge but not in the trivial terms of knowing more "things" in a quantitative way, but instead to know more in the terms expressed by Gibran in the sentence quoted at the beginning of the chapter, in a qualitative way.

8.2. Social Impacts

On a social level again an example is the social dimension of the management of our data and the return of favorable options. It is possible in this case to extend the QS concept, toward Quantified family, Quantified cities, Quantified country. We can take for example the case of our travel habits, consumption trends, all the personal health or needs that we express individually and that nowadays are totally disconnected from others individuality. The aggregate use of this data for statistical analysis in order to provide solutions based on these analyzes would be essential in order to optimize, in a social sense, many of the resources that are now wasted. Of course, this opens a hot topic for QS: privacy and ethical issues. In fact, the described scenario is already happening partly for our consumption behaviors: all our "Consumption Self" is already recorded by third parties, not for social purposes but for profiling and customization to encourage further consumption.It should therefore paid much attention to this type of use of information even when it is done for social purposes. An example of this was a research project of UCLA (2011) who built a stress app for young mothers oriented at personalized health care based on a phone's GPS system,. The purpose of the research was noble, to develop a pilot program based on Android smartphones technology to monitor assess, and treat participants. The device was able (thanks to the accelerometer on board) to track the location and the movement in detail. All these data clearly started to become an issue so as to include the use of a "personal data vaults" a digital lock box run by a third-party intermediary. Beside the privacy issue some QS companies are already going in this "social" direction. For instance Zeo databases now contains more than 400,000 nights of sleep. Cure Toghether is the site where thousands of patients can post and compare their own symptoms and treatments for more than 500 diseases. For example thanks to the posting on CureTogheter the aggregation of the data showed that people who have had vertigo in association with migraine had four times more likely to have side effects using the Imitrex (a medicine for migraine) than those who did not had vertigo. It is obvious that the critics of this approach point out that all the intervening variables does not make this data reliable, making this exchange of the same value of a chat bar and not a form of medical research. However, it remains the great value of the enormous amount of data collected.

9. CONCLUSION

In this chapter we set ourselves the aim of defining the growing movement of QS in the light of the two words that compose the name itself. In fact, we have seen how under other names a similar technological ambition was seen at least since the mid 90's. Many are the experimental projects that have sought to rely on technology to quantify the "Self", or at least the human behavior in the world. This original ambition was declined in the last years according to various purposes some of which still unclear, unrealistic or naïve. Although many are the application domains of QS (we outlined in paragraph 5 those related to healthcare, mood management, and fitness), are still palpable some fundamental problems that relegate the QS movement in a phase of low maturity. The first is a technological problem and specifically a lack of maturity in technologies for the collection, processing and data rendering. This is accompanied by a perhaps more fundamental

problem of deficit, bias and lack of integration of aspects concerning the human side of the QS idea. There are in fact some theoretical aspects that still to be understood about how to render meaningfully the representation of the large amounts of data that an integrated QS scenario produces (despite some theoretical elements are already available but often not applied in favor of the banality of a simple "wow effect"). But there are also and above some theoretical limits on the most fundamentals goals of QS: change, improvement, transformation. Just the difficulty in having an effective theory of human behaviour change, that is now fragmented between modules from behaviorism, from cognitivism, from social psychology theories, makes the deployments of QS application so unexpectedly ineffective, unsatisfactory or irrelevant. The step that we tried to make in this chapter is to highlight aspects that could lead to a more robust approach in QS area. Primarily through modes of data representation, taking into account the limitations and potential of human pre-attentional processing, identifying in studies on storytelling approach a possible way to reach a new form of QS data visualization. Secondly, through a necessary management of complexity, both in terms of technology (toward "ultimate lifelogging" scenarios that integrate and create value between different data of areas today addressed vertically) both in theoretical terms for what concerns the human side of the whole issue (thereby integrating social and emotional components in an all-embracing theory of human behavior change). We have gone a little further stressing how the future directions of research could lead to significant impacts on both individual and social level. On the one hand by configuring the QS as a tool to support the personal constant construction of the individual "Self" (a kind of mirror in constant communication with our identity) and on the other driving the aggregation of QS data at a sufficient level to be able to extract knowledge and new social services propositions based on statistical analyzes (for instance in

Healthcare, Mobility, Energy sector). In conclusion are necessary some considerations about the possible risks that QS scenarios can generate especially considering its possible massive use. The privacy risks combined with ethical issues related to social control scenarios lead up to a glimpse of dystopia in which in the name of a "superior" aggregate knowledge the individual is excluded from any kind of the decisions, even minimal, concerning him.

REFERENCES

23andMe. (2012) Retrieved from https://www.23andme.com/.

Abigail, S., & Whittaker, S. (2010). Beyond total capture: A constructive critique of lifelogging. *Communications of the ACM, 53*(5), 70–77. doi:10.1145/1735223.1735243.

Adidas service Micoach. (2012). Retrieved from http://www.adidas.com/us/micoach/.

Allen, A. L. (2008). Dredging-up the past: Lifelogging, memory, and surveillance. *The University of Chicago Law Review. University of Chicago. Law School, 75*(1), 47–74.

Asthmapolis. (2012). Retrieved from http://asthmapolis.com/.

BAM Labs. (2012). Retrieved from http://bamlabs.com/product/.

Bandura, A. (1986). *Social foundations of thought and action*. Englewood Cliffs, NJ: Prentice-Hall.

Barbaro, M. (2010). Active devices based on organic semiconductors for wearable applications. *IEEE Transactions on Information Technology in Biomedicine, 14*(3), 758–766. doi:10.1109/TITB.2010.2044798 PMID:20371414.

Bell, G., & Gemmell, J. (18 February 2007). A digital life. *Scientific American Magazine*. Retrieved from http://www.scientificamerican.com/article.cfm?id=a-digital-life.

Bentley, F. (2012). Personal health mashups: Mining significant observation from wellbeing data and context. In *Proceedings of CHI2012 Workshop on Personal Informatics in Practice: Improving Quality of Life Through Data*. New York: ACM Press.

BodyBugg. (2012). Retrieved from http://www.bodybugg.com/.

BodyMonitor. (2012). Retrieved from http://bodymonitor.de.

Bonato, P. (2012). A review of wearable sensors and systems with application in rehabilitation. *Journal of Neuroengineering and Rehabilitation, 9*(21).

Burigat, S., & Chittaro, L. (2007). Geographic data visualization on mobile devices for user's navigation and decision support activities. In Belussi, (ed.), *Spatial Data on the Web-Modeling and Management*. Berlin: Springer. doi:10.1007/978-3-540-69878-4_12.

Bush, V. (1945). As we may think. *Atlantic Monthly, 176*(1), 101–108.

Canada, C. (2006). La cueva grande: A 43-megapixel immersive system. In *Proceedings of Virtual Reality Conference 2006*. New Brunswick, NJ: IEEE Press.

Capzels. (2012). Retrieved from http://www.capzles.com/.

Card, S. K. (Ed.). (1999). *Readings in information visualization: Using vision to think*. San Francisco: Morgan Kaufmann.

Cheng, W. C. (2004). Total recall: Are privacy changes inevitable? In *Proceedings of CARPE 2004 First ACM Workshop on Continuous Archival and Retrieval of Personal Experiences*. New York: ACM

Chittaro, L. (2006). Visualizing information on mobile devices. *IEEE Computer*, *39*(3), 34–39. doi:10.1109/MC.2006.109.

Colin, W. (2008). *Visual thinking: For design*. San Francisco: Morgan Kaufmann.

Consolvo, S. (2008). Flowers or a robot army? Encouraging awareness & activity with personal, mobile displays. In *Proceedings of the 10th International Conference on Ubiquitous Computing: UbiComp 08*, 54-63. New York: ACM Press.

Corbishley, P., & Rodriguez-Villegas, E. (2008). Breathing detection: Towards a miniaturized, wearable, battery-operated monitoring system. *IEEE Transactions on Bio-Medical Engineering*, *55*(1), 196–204. doi:10.1109/TBME.2007.910679 PMID:18232362.

Cruz-Neira, C. (1993). Surround-screen projection-based virtual reality: The design and implementation of the cave. In *Proceedings of ACM SIGGRAPH*. New York: ACM Press.

CureTogether. (2012). Retrieved from http://curetogether.com/.

Damasio, A. R. (1999). *The feeling of what happens: Body and emotion in the making of consciousness*. London: Harcourt Inc..

Daytum. (2012). Retrieved from http://www.daytum.com/.

deCODEme. (2012). Retrieved from http://www.decodeme.com/.

Definition of Self. (2012a). Retrieved from http://www.yourdictionary.com/self-definition.

Definition of Self. (2012b). Retrieved from http://en.academic.ru/dic.nsf/cide/156773/Self.

DIALOG. (2012). Retrieved from http://4thmainhealth.com/.

DiaMedics. (2012). Retrieved from http://www.martoon.com/Diamedic/Diamedic/Overview.html.

Dix, A. (2002). The ultimate interface and the sums of life*? Interfaces*, *50*(16).

DIY Genomics. (2012). Retrieved from http://diygenomics.org/.

Dodge, M., & Kitchin, R. (2007). Outlines of a world coming into existence: pervasive computing and the ethics of forgetting. *Environment and Planning. B, Planning & Design*, *24*, 431–445. doi:10.1068/b32041t.

DreamBoard. (2012). Retrieved from http://www.dreamborad.com.

Eccles, R. (2007). Stories in geotime. In *Proceedings of IEEE Symposium on Visual Analytics Science and Technology*, 2007. New Brunswick, NJ: IEEE Press.

EyeTap. (2012). Retrieved from http://eyetap.org/.

Few, S. (2009). *Data visualization past, present and future. Innovation in Action Series*. Armonk, NY: IBM.

Few, S. (2010). Data visualization for human perception. In: Mads& Friis (Eds.), *Encyclopedia of Human-Computer Interaction*. Aarhus, Denmark: The Interaction Design Foundation. Retrieved from http://www.interaction-design.org/encyclopedia/data_visualization_for_human_perception.html.

FindingOptimism. (2012). Retrieved from http://www.findingoptimism.com/.

Fitbit. (2012). Retrieved from http://www.fitbit.com/.

Fosshage, J. L. (1997). The organizing functions of dream mentation. *Contemporary Psychoanalysis*, *33*(3), 429–458.

Gemignani, Z. (2012). *Juice analytics*. Retrieved from http://www.juiceanalytics.com/writing/data-visualization-as-storytelling-a-stretched-analogy/.

Gemmell, J. (2006). MyLifeBits: A personal database for everything. *Communications of the ACM*, *49*(1), 88–95. doi:10.1145/1107458.1107460.

Gershon, N. D., & Page, W. (2001). What storytelling can do for information visualization. *Communications of the ACM*, *44*(8), 31–37. doi:10.1145/381641.381653.

Glasswing. (2012). Retrieved from http://www.orsense.com/product.php?ID=38.

Gotta Feeling. (2012). Retrieved from http://gottafeeling.com/.

Greimas, A.-J. (1987). *On meaning: Selected writings in semiotic theory*. Minneapolic, MN: University of Minnesota Press.

Gruber, T. R. (1995). Toward principles for the design of ontologies used for knowledge sharing? *International Journal of Human-Computer Studies*, *43*(5-6), 907–928. doi:10.1006/ijhc.1995.1081.

Guardian. (2010). Retrieved from http://www.guardian.co.uk/science/2011/dec/02/psychology-human-biology?newsfeed=true.

Guarino, N. (1998), Formal ontology in information systems. In *Proceedings of FOIS '98*. Amsterdam, IOS Press.

Guidano, V. F. (1987). *Complexity of the self*. New York: Guilford.

Guidano, V. F. (1991). *The self in process*. New York: Guilford.

Guidano, V. F., & Liotti, G. (1986). *Cognitive processes and emotional disorders*. New York: Guilford.

Gyorbiro, N. (2010). Collaborative capturing of significant life memories? In *Proceedings of CHI 2010 Worksho-Know Thyself: Monitoring and Reflecting on Facets of One's Life*. New York: ACM Press.

Happy Factor. (2012). Retrieved from http://howhappy.dreamhosters.com/.

Health Tracking. (2012). Retrieved from Network http://www.healthtracking.net/.

HealthEngage. (2012). Retrieved from http://www.healthengage.com/.

HealthMonth. (2012). Retrieved from http://healthmonth.com.

Health Vault. (2012). Retrieved from http://www.microsoft.com/en-gb/healthvault/default.aspx.

Heer, J. (2008). Graphical histories for visualization: Supporting analysis, communication, and evaluation. *IEEE Transactions on Visualization and Computer Graphics*, *14*(6), 1189–1196. doi:10.1109/TVCG.2008.137 PMID:18988963.

Hodges, S. (2006). L. SenseCam: A Retrospective Memory Aid. [Berlin: Springer.]. *Proceedings of UBICOMP*, *2006*, 81–90.

Information Display: Display Week. (2012). *Review Issue*, 28.

Internet Multimedia Lab at the University of Southern California. (2004). *Total recall: A personal information management system*. Retrieved from http://bourbon.usc.edu/iml/recall/.

ITC's Michigan Control Room. (2012). Retrieved from http:/ / pro.sony.com / bbsccms / assets / files / micro / sxrd / articles / ITC_IGI_SXRD_CASE_STUDY.pdf.

Jawbone UP System. (2012). Retrieved from http://jawbone.com/up.

Kay, M. (2011). Lulaby: Environmental sensing for sleep self-improvement. In Proceedings of *CHI2011 Workshop on Personal Informatics*. New York: ACM Press.

Knome. (2012). Retrieved from http://www. knome.com/.

Lewin, K. (1951). *Field theory in social science; Selected theoretical papers*. New York: Harper & Row.

LifeLapse. (2012). Retrieved from http://www. lifelapse.com/.

Loseit. (2012) Retrieved from http://www.loseit. com/.

Mann, S. (2004) Continuous lifelong capture of personal experiences with eyetap. In *Proceedings of 1st ACM Workshop on Continuous Archival and Retrieval of Personal Experiences*. New York: ACM Press.

Mayer-Schönberger, V. (2009). *Delete: The virtue of forgetting in the digital age*. Princeton, NJ: Princeton University Press.

Mechdyne. (n.d.). Retrieved from http://www. mechdyne.com/cave.aspx.

Miller, G. A. (1960). *Plans and the structure of behavior*. New York: Holt, Rhinehart, & Winston. doi:10.1037/10039-000.

MoodPanda. (2012). Retrieved from http://Mood-Panda.com/.

Moodscope. (2012). Retrieved from http://www. moodscope.com/login.

MoodTracker. (2012). Retrieved from https:// www.moodtracker.com/.

Moore, B. (2010). Assisted self reflection: Combining lifetracking, sensemaking, & personal information management. In *Proceedings of CHI 2010 Workshop-Know Thyself: Monitoring and Reflecting on Facets of One's Life*. New York: ACM Press.

Morin, E. (2003). *La méthode: L'humanité de l'humanité-L'identité humaine*. Paris: Le Seuil, Nouvelle Èdition, coll. Points.

My Calorie Counter. (2012). Retrieved from http:// my-calorie-counter.com/calorie_counter.asp.

MyFitnessPal. (2012). Retrieved from http://www. myfitnesspal.com/.

MyMedLab. (2012). Retrieved from https://www. mymedlab.com/.

Nack, F. (2005). You must remember this. *IEEE MultiMedia*, *12*(1), 4–7. doi:10.1109/ MMUL.2005.17.

Navigenics. (2012). Retrieved from http://www. navigenics.com/.

Neisser, U. (1967). *Cognitive psychology*. New York: Appleton-Century-Crofts.

Ni, T. (2006). A survey of large high-resolution display technologies, techniques, and applications. In *Proceedings of the IEEE Conference on Virtual Reality*. New Brunswick, NJ: IEEE Press.

Nike + iPod Sport Kit. (2012) Retrieved from http://www.apple.com/ipod/nike/.

O'Hara, K. (2006). Memories for life: A review of the science and technology. *Journal of the Royal Society, Interface*, *3*, 351–365. doi:10.1098/ rsif.2006.0125 PMID:16849265.

Pathway. (2012). Retrieved from https://www. pathway.com/.

PatientsLikeMe. (2012). Retrieved from http:// www.patientslikeme.com/.

Personal Genome Project. (2012). Retrieved from http://www.personalgenomes.org.

Pina, L. R. (2012). Fitbit+: A behavior-based intervention system to reduce sedentary behavior. In Popper & Eccles (Eds.), The Self and the Brain. London: Springer International.

Private MD Lab Services. (2012). Retrieved from https://www.mymedlab.com/.

Propp, V. (1927). *Morphology of the folktale. Transactions of Laurence Scott* (2nd ed.). Austin, TX: University of Texas Press.

Ramirez, E. R., & Hekler, E. (2012). Digital histories for future health. In *Proceedings of CHI2012 Workshop on Personal Informatics in Practice: Improving Quality of Life Through Data.* New York: ACM Press.

Rationalizer. (2012). Retrieved from http://www.mirrorofemotions.com/.

Rawassizadeh, R. (2012). *UbiqLog: A generic mobile phone based life-log framework. Personal and Ubiquitous Computing, 2012.* London, UK: Springer.

ReliefInsite. (2012). Retrieved from http://www.reliefinsite.com/.

Renambot, L. (2012). *Lambdavision: Building a 100 megapixel display.* Retrieved from www.evl.uic.edu/cavern/sage/pubs/LambdaVision-light.pdf.

Rensink, R. A. (2002). Internal vs. external information in visual perception. In *Proceedings of the Second International Symposium on Smart Graphics. Smart Graphics, 2,* 63-70

Ricoeur, P. (1992). *Oneself as another.* Chicago: University of Chicago Press.

Roambi. (2012). Retrieved from http://www.roambi.com.

Runkeeper. (2012). Retrieved from http://runkeeper.com/.

Sandstrom, T. (2003). The hyperwall. In *Proceedings of the Conference on Coordinated and Multiple Views in Exploratory Visualizations.* New Brunswick, NJ: IEEE Press.

Schell, J. (2008). *The art of game design: A book of lenses.* Burlington, MA: Elsevier.

Segel, E., & Heer, J. (2010). Narrative visualization: Telling stories with data. *IEEE Transactions on Visualization and Computer Graphics, 16*(6), 1139–1148. doi:10.1109/TVCG.2010.179 PMID:20975152.

SenseWear. (2012). Retrieved from http://sensewear.bodymedia.com/.

Shaltis, P. A. (2006). Wearable, cuff-less PPG-based blood pressure monitor with novel height sensor. In *Proceedings of IEEE Engineering in Medicine and Biology Society.* New Brunswick, NJ: IEEE Press. doi:10.1109/IEMBS.2006.260027.

Skinner, B. F. (1938). *The behavior of organisms: An experimental analysis.* New York: Appleton-Century.

Skinner, B. F. (1953). *Science and human behavior.* New York: Macmillan.

SNPedia. (2012). Retrieved from http://www.snpedia.com/index.php / SNPedia.

StressEraser. (2012). Retrieved from http://www.stresseraser.com.

SugarStats. (2012). Retrieved Sfrom https://sugarstats.com/.

Swan, M. (2009). Emerging patient-driven health care models: An examination of health social networks, consumer personalized medicine, and quantified self-tracking. *International Journal of Environmental Research and Public Health, 6*(2), 492–525. doi:10.3390/ijerph6020492 PMID:19440396.

Swan, M. (2011). *Genomic self-hacking.* Retrieved from http://quantifiedself.com/2011/11/melanie-swan-on-genomic-self-hacking/.

Thelen, S. (2010). Advanced visualization and interaction techniques for large high-resolution displays. In Middel, Ariane (eds.), *Visualization of Large and Unstructured Data Sets-Applications in Geospatial Planning, Modeling, and Engineering*, 19 (73-81). Berlin: DFG.

Track Your Happiness. (2012). Retrieved from http://www.trackyourhappiness.org/.

Tufte, E. R. (1983). *The visual display of quantitative information*. Cheshire, CT: Graphics Press.

Tukey, J. W. (1977). *Exploratory data analysis*. Boston: Addison-Wesley.

UCLA. (2011). Retrieved from http://www.cens.ucla.edu/pub/ParticipatoryOpenMhealth-Apple-DE080711.pdf.

Visblock™. (2012). Retrieved from http://www.visbox.com/visblock.html.

Whittaker, S. (2012). Socio-technical lifelogging: Deriving design principles for a future proof digital past. *Human-Computer Interaction*, *27*, 37–62.

Withings scales. (2012). Retrieved from http://www.withings.com/.

Wojtkowski, W., & Wojtkowski, W. G. (2002). Storytelling: Its role in information visualization. In *Proceedings of European Systems Science Congress*. New Brunswick, NJ: IEEE Press.

Wolf, G. (2008). *Genomic openness*. Retrieved from http://quantifiedself.com/2008/01/genomic-openness/.

Wolf, G. (2010). *Ted talk*. Retrieved from http://www.ted.com/talks/gary_wolf_the_quantified_self.html.

Yau, N., & Hansen, M. (2010). your.flowingdata: Personal data collection via twitter. In *Proceedings of CHI 2010 Workshop-Know Thyself: Monitoring and Reflecting on Facets of One's Life*. New York: ACM Press.

Your.flowingdata. (2012). Retrieved from http://your.flowingdata.com/.

Zeo. (2012). Retrieved from http://www.myzeo.com/sleep/.

Zhang, J. (2009). UWB systems for wireless sensor networks. *Proceedings of the IEEE*, *97*(2), 313–331. doi:10.1109/JPROC.2008.2008786.

ZigBee Alliance. (2012). Retrieved from http://www.zigbee.org.

KEY TERMS AND DEFINITIONS

Gestalt: It means "form", and in gestalt psychology it means that perception is a result of interaction and global organization of various components, emphasizing that the whole is greater than the sum of its part.

Lifelog: The practice of digital recording of the totality of an individual's experiences.

Massively Multiplayer Online Role-Playing Games: It is a class of role-playing video games in which a huge number of users play together in a shared virtual world.

Personal Informatics: It is another way to call the Quantified Self, a class of tools that support people to collect personal information for the aim of self-monitoring.

Reinforcement: It is a term in the behaviorist paradigm for a process of strengthening the probability of a specific response.

Chapter 13
From Data–Centered to Activity–Centered Geospatial Visualizations

Olga Buchel
Western University, Canada

Kamran Sedig
Western University, Canada

ABSTRACT

As geospatial visualizations grow in popularity, their role in human activities is also evolving. While maps have been used to support higher-level cognitive activities such as decision-making, sense making, and knowledge discovery, traditionally their use in such activities has been partial. Nowadays they are being used at various stages of such activities. This trend is simultaneously being accompanied with another shift: a movement from the design and use of data-centered geospatial visualizations to activity-centered visualizations. Data-centered visualizations are primarily focused on representation of data from data layers; activity-centered visualizations, not only represent the data layers, but also focus on users' needs and real-world activities—such as storytelling and comparing data layers with other information. Examples of this shift are being seen in some mashup techniques that deviate from standard data-driven visualization designs. Beyond the discussion of the needed shift, this chapter presents ideas for designing human-activity-centered geospatial visualizations.

INTRODUCTION

Geospatial visualizations are digital geographic and/or spatial maps to which users or designers can link their data. Due to the widespread availability of map application programming interfaces (e.g., Google Maps, Google Earth, Bing Maps, OpenStreetMap, and others), geospatial visualizations have become common tools in many human activities. Climatologists, biologists, linguists, literary researchers, business analysts, real-estate agents, journalists, historians, librarians,

DOI: 10.4018/978-1-4666-4309-3.ch013

archivists, geologists, social scientists, educators, archaeologists, health and medical professionals, and others have adopted various types of maps for data visualization (Shandler, 2012; Bailey et al., 2012; Boggs et al., 2012; Nunn & Bentley, 2012; Xie & Pearson, 2010; Skiba, 2007). Broadly, designers create geospatial visualizations using three approaches. First approach is taken by those who design simple Web 2.0 tools such as Fusion Tables, Flickr, Historypin, or SIMILE Widgets. Second approach is taken by those who, having more advanced programming skills, use data-centered models, developed by geovisualization and information visualization researchers, to design time maps, coordinated displays, and dynamic query interfaces. Third approach is taken by those who design activity-centered geospatial visualizations—examples of which include Historypin, an online, user-created archive of historical photos and personal recollections (Historypin, n.d.) and Marine Map decision support tool (South Coast Regional Stakeholder Group, n.d.). These visualizations are geared towards supporting user tasks and activities. The first two approaches result in more-or-less data-centered visualizations, and the third approach is intended to produce human-activity-centered visualizations. The distinction between data-centered and activity-centered visualizations lies in the focus of their designs. Whereas data-centered visualizations are primarily focused on and concerned with representing empirically or mathematically derived data values, activity-centered visualizations focus on representations and interactions that support user's goals, needs, and real-world tasks and activities. As there is scarcity of research with regard to how to design activity-centered geospatial visualizations, in this chapter, we discuss how geospatial visualizations can be made more activity-centered and suggest some ideas and techniques.

In this chapter, human activities refer to "clusters of actions and decisions that are done for a purpose" (Saffer, 2010,). Tracing one's genealogy,

deciding about a real-estate purchase, making sense of medical records, or finding the cause of a disease outbreak are examples of human activities. Activities may range from simple ones, such as finding a specific location or retrieving driving directions, to complex ones, such as determining the cause and effect in natural phenomena or drawing conclusions about the data coming from multiple sensors or map layers. A single activity may involve many tasks and subtasks (Sedig & Parsons, 2013). For example, determining the causes of some social activities (e.g., riots or strikes) may involve a number of visual comparisons of several map layers with the locations of riots and strikes, reading newspaper articles and social media messages about them, and determining proximity to some important landmarks. As such, it can be seen that there are differences between the complexity of higher-level activities that people perform and the less complex lower-level computational and preparatory tasks that help them complete these activities.

Understanding user tasks and activities is essential for the effective design of activity-centered visualizations. Geospatial visualizations should be designed such that they support users to tell spatio-temporal stories, to make comparisons between different data, to draw extrapolations from data, to generate hypotheses, to observe trends in data, and to perform other tasks that collectively give rise to more complex activities at hand. Ideally, these visualizations should create conditions whereby users would not assume that maps can only provide limited "snapshots of reality" (Cartwright, 2009), nor that they are not able to support high-level sense-making activities (Elias et al., 2008). Sedig and Parsons (2013) suggest that one of the main roles that computational tools, such as these interactive visualizations, can play is epistemic—that is, they should support, extend, partner, and supplement the cognitive functionings and activities of their users, activities, such as decision-making, learning, problem solving, and analytical reasoning. With this in mind, geospatial visualizations can be thought of as tools that can and should support epistemic activities of users.

Identifying tasks in human activities is, however, challenging. Firstly, higher-level cognitive activities are neither clearly defined, nor easily understood. Compared to mundane tasks (such as operating an airline booking system, using an ATM, or checking out a library book), higher-level cognitive activities are complex, difficult to observe, interwoven with various other tasks and subtasks, and situated within intricate social contexts and networks (Casner, 1991; Rogers & Ellis, 1994; Sedig & Parsons, 2013). Secondly, few real-world human activities start with the use of maps. For example, genealogical researchers start looking for information in books, gazetteers, articles, pamphlets, and other sources; they consult maps only at the end of their search (USGS, 2002). Geospatial visualizations, however, can change the flow of users' activities. For example, while 20 years ago no one could even think about searching for business-related information on digital maps, today geospatial search engines are so ubiquitous that many find it difficult to locate business information without them.

The remainder of this chapter focuses on the gap between data-centered and activity-centered designs. We will explore how traditional data-centered visualization designs fail to facilitate higher-level human activities, and how they can be rendered more suitable through activity-centered design. The next section provides background information about the roles and characteristics of different components of map application programming interfaces in geospatial visualizations. The overview section presents an overview of popular geospatial visualizations that have had a significant impact on the design of other visualizations. The section about tasks, activities, and interactions introduces theoretical underpinnings of tasks and activities. An example of real-world human activity—specifically real-estate decision-making—is

given in the next section. This section highlights why data-centered visualizations fail to support them. Using the real-estate example, the section that follows discusses some design considerations that can make data-centered visualizations more suited to human tasks and activities. Finally, the concluding section provides a summary of the ideas discussed in the chapter.

COMPONENTS OF MAP APPLICATION PROGRAMMING INTERFACES

Before discussing design principles, we discuss the different layers of geospatial visualizations, where layers refer to different strata of representations and geospatial visualizations are created by combining these layers.

Data Layer

The data layer (in GIS parlance also known as a vector layer) consists of points, lines, and polygons, typically used to characterize distinct entities such as houses, roads, or districts (United Nations, 2000). This layer can have a composite structure, as it can include gazetteers (i.e., spatial data) as well as metadata (i.e., properties or attributes of data). The former is a dictionary of geographic locations containing information about location names, types, and coordinates. The latter contains information about the source, temporal coverage, and other properties of the metadata, though not necessarily the information entities themselves. Gazetteers and metadata can have cross-references to each other. For example, metadata can be linked to locations described in a gazetteer.

Base Map Layer

The base map layer contains geographical reference information upon which the data layer may be plotted for purposes of comparison or geographical correlation (Robinson et al., 1995). Preferences for base maps differ depending on the user's background and purpose. For example, epidemiologists use demographic maps for the presentation of aerial data, relating disease rates to spatial areas in the hope of finding "clues of aetiological significance" (Forster, 1966). Demographic maps provide epidemiologists with information about the size of the population at risk, indicate rates and locations of diseases in local populations, and allow weighting of local differences (Forster, ibid.).

Map application programming interfaces most commonly provide road, satellite, or aerial maps as a base layer; however, these are not necessarily the most suitable representations for supporting users' tasks. As Hill (2006) and Elias et al. (2005) have suggested, base map layers should display boundaries or landmarks that are familiar to users and be tailored to their tasks and activities—that is, they should be activity-centered and fit the user and the task, and not provide pre-packaged data-centered maps.

Google Maps Layers

Google Maps has additional thematic data layers, including Wikipedia, Demographics, YouTube, Panoramio, Weather, and Bicycling layers, which enhance base maps and enrich users' understanding of location. These are developed by third-party programmers and are available as open-source data. The Panoramio and YouTube layers augment users' understanding of places through imagery and video. The Wikipedia layer helps users to explore unknown locations with crowd-sourced descriptions by integrating location information from the web. The Demographics layer "contain[s] United States census information … from recent years as well as 5-year projections of many data fields" (Google Developers, 2012a). It can be used for showing population size, age, race, household income, marital status, household size, and other

demographics. The Weather and the Bicycling layers facilitate understanding of local weather and bicycle trails.

Other Layers

Besides base map layers, many mashups merge multiple KML[1] or GeoRSS[2] files and present them as a single map layer (Elias et al., 2005), where a mashup is the combination of several data sources in one interface. While individual files may have small regional coverage, synthesized files can create layers that cover the whole world. For example, GeoRSS news files, amassed from various websites and RSS feeds, can be combined into one large news map.

Layers differ in the structure and characteristics of their interactions. Data layers, for example, are the most malleable. They can be decomposed into individual metadata properties which can be grouped, regrouped, filtered, or transformed in many different ways. Data properties can be used for developing symbols and other representations, or they can be grouped and used for creating more generalized derived representations (e.g., heat maps). Base layers and additional layers are not as flexible as data layers. In base map layers, designers can change certain aesthetic properties, such as hue, lightness, saturation, gamma, visibility, and color; modify content by adding or removing feature types, such as administrative, landscape, road, transit, and water features; and add or remove labels for all these features. However, base layers do not contain any metadata about individual properties of feature types, as these properties can be available via a different API; that is, markers in Wikipedia, Weather, GeoRSS, Panoramio, and other layers can be made clickable, but will not have information about individual articles or images. For this reason, markers cannot be grouped or filtered by subject, language, or any other properties.

OVERVIEW OF POPULAR GEOSPATIAL VISUALIZATIONS

In this section, we review the most popular types of geospatial visualizations described in the literature. These types are not mutually exclusive; designers combine them. Although these geospatial visualizations vary in complexity, their designs share a common shortcoming: they are data-centered, not activity-centered.

Geographic Information Retrieval Visualizations

Visualizations for geographic information retrieval usually have a simple conceptual design. Users interact with such visualizations by searching for spatial objects in certain locations and browse the retrieved results on a map. Such visualizations are often used to display news, library collections, real-estate listings, and retrieval results in geospatial search engines. They excel at making geospatial relationships visible: showing spatial diffusion, proximity, and relationships (such as overlaps, is-part-of, touches, and others). However, when the results are retrieved, these visualizations do not support the tasks that often are essential constituent parts of analytical reasoning and sense making activities. Upon retrieval, users usually need to perform further actions and tasks, such as gather, group/regroup, transform, filter, compare, and annotate. Retrieval visualizations seldom support these user-needed actions and tasks.

Time Maps

Cartographers and geovisualization researchers have developed several conceptualizations of time and space (e.g., Peuquet, 2002; Hägerstrand, 1982; Andrienko, 2003; Kraak, 2003). Whereas in simpler time maps, visualizations are based on linear time models, in more sophisticated spatio-temporal models, visualizations are based on a space-time cube (Kraak, 2003). Simple time maps show changes in objects both on a map and a timeline, and are favoured by digital humanists, linguists, and health and earth science researchers (for an example, see CSTA, 2013). In the cube model, the x- and y-axes form a map, the z-axis represents time, and events and processes are projected onto x-, y-, and z-axes accordingly. Since this model is rather complicated, it only has a few implementations (see, e.g., Huisman et al., 2009).

Geographic time (i.e., time that can be observed on a map) has many different conceptualizations including world time, valid time, user-defined time (Peuquet, 2002), absolute time (universe time), cyclical time, ordinal time, and time analogous to distance (Vasiliev, 1997). In some real-world activities, a frame of reference for time is not geographic time, and users have alternative models of time and space. For example, in narratives, people discretize space and events in time by the objects and the events in time. They connect representations of space and time by segments, temporally in the case of space, causally in the case of events (Tversky, 2004).

Simple time maps can represent time in the form of text, a bar, a clock, or a combination of these, where users can interactively switch between them (Edsall, 2001). Edsall also describes a "time coil" representation that resembles a telephone cord with linearity along its length and cyclical behaviour in the coil (Edsall, 2001). Peuquet (2002) suggests that time can also have branching lines for overlapping periods.

Time maps can help users answer questions about the existence of objects and their locations in space, as well as the existence of events and their duration, frequency, sequence, or location in time (Edsall, 2001; Kraak, Edsall, & MacEachren, 1997). Users can select objects, times, or locations, and observe how objects change over time and compare phenomena (Andrienko, Andrienko, & Gatalsky, 2005; Plaisant, 2005). None of these provide mechanisms for performing for elaborate interactions to support higher-level activities.

Maps with Dynamic Queries

Dynamic query interfaces allow provide users with the ability to formulate queries by directly manipulating and adjusting of sliders which results in immediate, dynamic display of found information items (Williamson & Schneiderman, 1992). These interfaces show continuous visual representation of information objects. Sliders represent values of the properties of the entities in a database, and visual entities in the displayed visualization area are a subset of the entities from the database. Such geospatial visualizations help users dynamically locate information items, filter unwanted information, detect trends, and notice exceptions (outliers). However, these are only basic tasks.

Coordinated Displays

Coordinated displays focus on the visualization of multiple properties including geographic space and time. Representations in coordinated geospatial visualizations include synchronized geospatial maps, semantic views, and timelines. They can facilitate spatial data mining and discovery of patterns and trends (Guo & Mennis, 2009), help maintain situational awareness (MacEachren et al., 2010), and assist knowledge construction (MacEachren et al., 1999). An example of coordinated displays is the Health GeoJunction web portal (GEOVISTA Studio, 2007), which has a digital map synchronized with a Tag Cloud and a timeline. All individual views (the map, Tag Cloud, and timeline) are generated from the entire collection of documents, and represent the collection from different perspectives (i.e., it is easy to establish relationships between representations of entities in one view with different representations of the same entities in another view). These displays highlight relations among properties, including geographic space, time, and topics, and can provide comprehensive overviews of the data from different perspectives (Andrienko &

Andrienko, 2007). As such, change to any of the properties in one display affects the representations in other displays and causes them to get updated. For example, a change in a range on a time slider causes simultaneous changes in the Tag Cloud and on the map. These visualizations are suitable for making sense of the spatial distribution of objects and their properties, but are less useful for non-spatial information. Problems include lack of screen space and complex, cognitively overwhelming and counterintuitive interfaces (Baldonado et al., 2000).

The geospatial visualizations described in this section can display rich data layers, in which objects can be grouped, selected, transformed, sliced, and divided. These design models support visual, retrieval, and exploratory tasks; however, they generally fail at assisting users to carry out more complex real-life activities.

TASKS, ACTIVITIES, AND INTERACTIONS

Activities and tasks are best understood in the context of Activity Theory (Kaptelinin & Nardi, 2009). Activity Theory offers a conceptual framework that accommodates diversity along a number of dimensions. This theory not only accounts for higher-level activities, real-world interactions, and work contexts, but also integrates technical, cognitive and social perspectives. It proposes that activities are mediated by tools as well as users' interaction with tools. Activities, tasks, and interactions are defined next.

Activities

As we mentioned earlier in this chapter, human activities refer to "clusters of actions and decisions that are done for a purpose" (Saffer, 2010, p. 35). Examples include real-estate decision-making, exploratory data analysis, disease monitoring, and knowledge discovery[3]. Each of these higher-level activities relies on a number of smaller actions and decisions carried out in tasks (Sedig & Parsons, 2013).

Tasks

Tasks are conscious processes undertaken in the fulfillment of a goal. They can be recursively broken down into subtasks. For example, finding neighbours in a space, measuring distances or estimating travel time.

Interactions

Interactions refer to low-level actions that users perform on objects and the responses of those objects, which enable users to adjust information to suit their epistemic, cognitive, and contextual needs and preferences (Sedig & Parsons, 2013). Interactions enable different properties, elements, relations, and layers to be probed, made explicit, and available on demand, thereby making the visualizations better suited to the needs and preferences of users (ibid.).

Activities consist of tasks and interactions in a given context; however, they are more than their sum. Rather, they are purposeful and planned by subjects through interaction with the environment (Kaptelinin & Nardi, 2009). For example, when planning a trip to a new destination, users study maps; learn the history of the location and its landmarks; find a place to stay and eat; estimate and measure distances to places of interest; create itineraries; make changes to their itineraries when they start the trip and get a better understanding of distances and the environment, and so on.

AN EXAMPLE OF A HUMAN ACTIVITY

In this section, we illustrate the limitations of data-centered designs (described in Section 3) through an example of a human activity in the context of real-estate decision-making.

Data-driven visualizations for real-estate decision-making are typically designed as maps augmented with dynamic queries or as geographic information retrieval tools. Examples of mashups can be found at http://www.realtor.ca/, http://www.housingmaps.com, http://www.realtor.ca/, and other web sites. These visualizations typically answer questions about distances and housing properties, such as how far this is house from work or grocery stores, how long it takes to get to school, how big the house is, and how many bedrooms the house has. But real-estate decisions are not only about distances and time. Decisions are made by a variety of stakeholders performing a wide range of activities. Stakeholders include home buyers, renters, builders, brokers, bankers, business analysts, and public agencies. Oftentimes these people are interested in much more than properties and distances for their decisions. These decisions require information which is unavailable in real-estate listings.

In general, real-estate decisions can be divided into corporate and residential. In corporate real-estate decision-making, location, interior design, space layout, lease obligations, nearby amenities and complementary facilities all play a decisive role (Gibler, Black, & Moon, 2002). Schmenner (1982) further identifies labour costs, potential for labour unionization, proximity to markets, supplies, and resources, and concerns for quality of life. Plaut and Pluta (1983) and Bartik (1985) add business climate, employment, and services to the list, and further, Rabianski, DeLisle, & Carn (2001) identify labour force, income and other taxes on corporations, fees, changes and special assessments, development regulations and controls, utilities and infrastructure, public and transportation services, cost of living, and community as factors influencing decision-making about corporate real-estate.

Corporations also take aggregation of related businesses and industries into account, as it leads to greater cross-firm synergies and improved supply-chain management (Rabianski, DeLisle, & Carn, ibid.). The importance of agglomeration is demonstrated by Shilton and Stanley's study (1999), which found high geographic clustering among Fortune 500 firm headquarters. Some firms relocate to cities with high labor supply and low cost of living (Alli, Ramirez, & Yung, 1991), while others seek to reduce costs without compromising growth or sales (Manning, Rodriguez, & Ghosh, 1999).

Concerns in residential real-estate can be grouped along the following activities: (1) planning, (2) construction and development, (3) finance, including construction lending, property taxation, and assessment, (4) property management, (5) risk management, (6) marketing, and (7) regulatory compliance (Peterson, 1998). Residential real-estate buyers and sellers often use information not available in visualizations. For example, Northcraft and Neal (1987) observed that real-estate buyers make 'comparison computations' by assessing the number, age and condition of comparable properties, those already sold in the area, and other potential buyers. Similar characteristics of real-estate sellers within a neighborhood also tend to have like effects on real-estate transactions within that geographic area (see Can 1992; Dubin 1992; Can & Megbolugbe 1997). A summary of factors affecting real-estate decision-making can be found in Zeng and Zhou (2001), who distinguish among environmental, social and personal factors. Environmental factors include slope, elevation, vegetation, parks and natural reserves, rivers and beaches, floodplains, dump/hazardous sites or other pollution. Social factors include demographics, housing prices and proximity to shopping centers, railway stations, schools, hospitals, theatres, roads, bus stops, railway, power-lines and airports. Lastly, personal factors refer to income, place of work, location of relatives, household size, value of mortgage, and preferred population group.

Other stakeholders, such as business analysts or real-estate agents, may also be involved in real-estate tasks and activities. For example, real-estate analysts look at changes in the spatial diffusion of prices to identify the origin and spread of bubbles (Roehner, 1997), while real-estate agents utilize storytelling, a task for marketing properties and communities.

Prior to map application programming interfaces becoming widely available, a few geographic information systems designed in the 1980s and 1990s attempted to support some of the aforementioned tasks and activities (see Belsky, Can, & Megbolugbe, 1996; Thrall & Amos, 1996; Barnett & Okoruwa, 1993; Beaumont, 1991; Hall, 1993; Thrall, Fandrich, & Thrall, 1995). These systems facilitated tasks and interactions that helped users make well-informed decisions about real-estate properties. For example, Francica (1993) and Kochera (1994) describe applications that allow users to determine whether a property is located in an area prone to natural disasters (e.g., floods or earthquakes) and calculate rates based on neighborhood crime rates, and distances to fire hydrants, fire stations, and police stations. Other applications allow users to access detailed site measurements and sales data, project population trends, identify market areas, estimate their potential, and measure their penetration (Robbins 1996; Rodriguez, Sirmans, & Marks 1995).

Nowadays, however, these tasks and activities are not supported by data-centered geospatial visualization designs. Data-centered visualizations support visual, exploratory, and analytical tasks about houses, estates, and rental properties, but largely exclude information about natural disasters, crime rates, distances, historical sales data, demographics, population trends, and natural or man-made features. This failure can be ascribed to at least two things. First and most important is the lack of designs that take into account human activities. Second is that, even though there is a tsunami of data, the data is scattered and difficult to collect in one place. In the next section, we present some considerations about task and activity-centered design and propose it as a means of improving time maps, coordinate displays, dynamic query interfaces, and other geospatial visualizations.

ACTIVITY-CENTERED DESIGN CONSIDERATIONS

In this section, we discuss the advantages of activity-centered designs found in some mashups. Specifically, we examine the role of enhanced base maps, historical data, and storytelling techniques. These design considerations are not only useful for real-estate mashups, but also for various other activity contexts involving the use of geospatial visualizations.

Enhanced Base Maps

The use of road maps as base maps in real-estate mashups provides limited support for making decisions about housing, since they contain no information about communities (e.g., crime rates, school quality, population trends, and demographics), environment (e.g., vegetation, parks and natural reserves, rivers and beaches, floodplain, dump/hazardous sites), or proximity to places of interest (e.g., shops, railway stations, schools, hospitals, theatres, roads, bus stops, and power-lines). The paucity of information contained in mashups persists, despite recommendations by some researchers (Francica, 1993; Kochera, 1994; Anselin, 1998)—this despite the fact that real-estate decision-making is an ideal area for designers to take advantage of Google Maps layers, Google Maps Styled Maps (Google Developers, 2012b), and other open source layers. For example, the Google Maps Demographics layer can provide information about population size, household income, marital status, age and race, while GeoRSS news layers from local newspapers can provide links to local news and police reports. Designers can assist users in understanding the environmental, cultural, and social affordances of locations by enriching base maps with various features (e.g., administrative, geographical, roads, and transit) and points of interest (e.g., attractions, businesses, government buildings, medical facilities, parks, places of worship, schools, and sports

complexes). The OpenHazardMap layer, currently being developed as an addition to OpenStreetMap, can provide information about natural disasters (e.g., floods, avalanches, seismic activities, storms, forest fires, landslides, and volcanoes) and industrial disasters (e.g., dangerous material transport). Visualizations can also include KML layers showing boundaries of real-estate zones, giving buyers a better understanding of the extent of local communities, thereby making such visualizations more activity-centered.

Since geographical correlations between data layers and base maps can be made, designers may replace base maps with some other layers to help users carry out computational comparisons. For example, Matt Stiles, a journalist for The Guardian, has used an additional layer featuring "indices of deprivation" to demonstrate a correlation between riots and poverty in London, England. His map, shown in Figure 1, indicates the locations of riots with red markers mapped over the "indices of deprivation" base map. In this map, deep red areas represent higher degrees of poverty while blues indicate more income. This base map helps reveal the link between poverty and riot incidence.

The 'indices of deprivation' base map can be used to highlight similar relationships in real-estate listings, helping buyers make extrapolations about houses for sale, depending on the level of income of neighborhoods.

Historical Data

To further assist decision-making, geovisualization researchers suggest adding historical data, including proprietary records of project vacancy rates, rental rates, property appreciation rates over time, historical census data, and national housing survey data (Peterson, 1998). Despite challenges in finding and linking historical data to maps, there are thousands of GeoRSS layers, listings, and feeds that can be archived daily and used later for retrospective analyses. The archived data can form "sedimentation layers", a recent technique

Figure 1. Map of London riots over 'indices of deprivation' base map.© 2011 Matt Stiles Used with permission

that progressively aggregates streaming data from feeds and generates and updates visualizations (Huron et al., 2012). These data can be used for the design of graphs and charts for individual locations, allowing the development of sales dashboards for real-estate zones.

Additionally, historical information can be discovered in historical maps in library collections, commonly residing on library servers, and largely neglected in geospatial visualizations. For example, real-estate maps can utilize Fire Insurance maps as their base maps. These are large-scale print maps that encode detailed information about real-estate properties, including outlines and exterior types of buildings, housing numbers, parcel lot boundaries, locations of windows and doors, street names and widths, and various landscape features. Architects, realtors, urban planners and developers, environmental assessors, genealogists, geographers, and historians often use them to understand the historical use of a parcel of land, assess property taxes, or estimate the damages incurred by natural disasters. Pictured below is The Sanborn Fire Insurance map for Reno, Nevada,

dated April 1899. It shows the commercial center of the city, including the railroad tracks and train station, several hotels, a variety of businesses, most of which were constructed in brick (encoded in pink), "China Town" on the Truckee River, and legal houses of prostitution labeled "Female Boarding" (description adapted from Library of Congress, 2010).

A short comparison of Figure 2 to the aerial photograph of the same area in Figure 3 reveals that the railroad tracks, train station, and the Truckee River are still present, but the "China Town" and the "Female Boarding" houses are replaced with a plaza (across from Reno City Hall), Men Wielding Fire Restaurant, and Choque's Construction company. Hence, the fire insurance map helps users understand how Reno has changed over time and highlights the usefulness of insurance maps in understanding the history of real-estate properties.

Studies report that real-estate buyers often have questions about the history of a parcel of land prior to purchase, in particular, property lines, Indian reservations, historical property occupancy and use, and watersheds (Elias et al., 2008).

Figure 2. Sanborn Fire Insurance Map for Reno, Nevada, April 1899

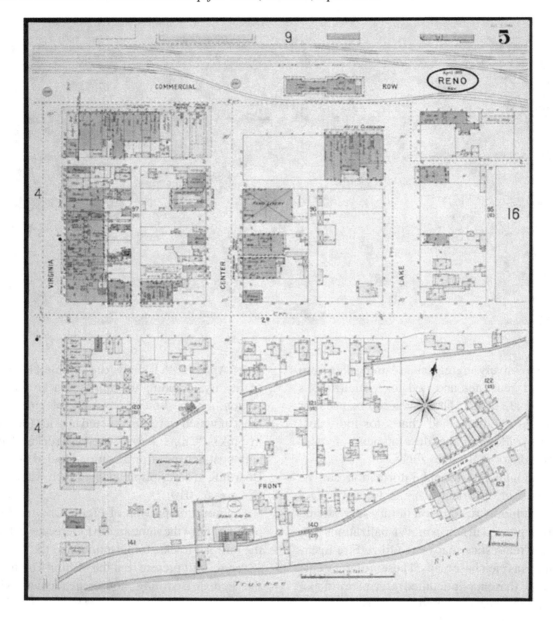

Adding insurance maps to such visualizations can help real-estate buyers answer these questions, hence making them more activity-centered.

An example of how historical maps can be used with map application programming interfaces can be found in the mashups created by the Cartifacts company (e.g., http://maps.cartifact.com/lany/). The Cartifacts mashups for New York and Los Angeles merge historical maps with the modern maps by allowing users to interact with the map through a magic lens tool (see Figure 4). As users move the lens over the map, the historical layers appear on top of the modern maps. This technique offers many benefits to users. It allows for different representations to be correctly aligned relative to each other, hence preserving the geospatial rela-

Figure 3. Aerial view of Reno, Nevada, in Google Maps, December, 2012

tionship between the two maps. It enables users to relate features between the two maps by their spatial positions. It also enables users to control the focus by reducing the number of objects that fit into the lens. Ultimately, it allows users to learn local history of estates from historical maps, saving them a trip to a library or an archive.

Putting print maps in the context of geospatial visualizations can be challenging, however. The problem is that print maps are characterized by varying orientations and projections suitable to the scale, locale, and terrain of the map. For this reason, it is difficult to align locations on historical maps with locations on digital maps. To

Figure 4. Cartifacts mashup with the magic lens © 2009, Cartifact, Inc. Used with permission

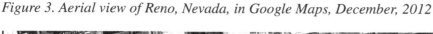

overcome alignment problems, designers can use tools such as Georeferencer (http://www.georeferencer.org/) that can help adjust projections and orientations of scanned maps.

Stories

Stories are essential for content marketing, organizational decision-making (O'Connor, 2002; Fleming, 2001), knowledge sharing (Sole & Wilson, 2002), and other higher-level cognitive activities. Stories can guide users through "unknown territories" and help them understand the relationships among entities in a geographical context (Cartwright, 2009).

Although maps can facilitate storytelling (Turner, 2006), data-centered geospatial visualizations often fail to communicate their affordances, including where users should start and the kinds of discoveries that are available to them (Andrienko & Andrienko, 2007). Despite being interactive, they are insufficient for understanding stories about changes in data because they do little to highlight related facts, events, or other layers of information to users. Without these relationships cognitive activities such as drawing conclusions, generation of hypotheses, decision-making, sense making, knowledge discovery, and understanding physical landscapes, are weakened (Isbister & Doyle, 1999).

Visualizations that facilitate storytelling use techniques that are often overlooked in data-centered design. These include Graphic Scripts (Monmonier, 1989), movies (Cartwright, 2009), interactive tours, narratives, and metaphors (Cartwright & Hunter, 1999). Graphic Scripts are series of representations and text statements that guide users from one information source to another, ensuring no essential information is missed. Such metaphors as The Storyteller, The Navigator, The Guide, The Sage, The Data Store, and The Fact Book allow for designing different scripts (Cartwright & Hunter, 1999). For example, the Guide takes the user and leads him or her to important

and relevant information. The Navigator describes the map's role as a tool to assist users in finding where information is located. The Sage connects the user to experts in the field. The Data Store and the fact Book link to additional information about locations. The Storyteller tells users a multimedia story about local history.

Unlike timelines or other sliders used in data-centered visualizations, interactive tours do not force visitors to pass by all locations in a visualization, but guide them only through a series of selected destinations. Depending on the nature of users' tasks and activities, tours can be designed as geographical, trails, direct, attribute, or similarity walks. In attribute and similarity walks, users search for objects with similar attributes to those already selected (Card et al., 1999). Geographic walks can be based on alphabetic or geographic proximity of locations (Cunliffe et al., 1997), while tours can take different forms: users can walk, fly (Sedig & Sumner, 2006), navigate by a 'magic' subway, via warp drives, worm holes (Dieberger, 1994; Kay, 1990), or ocean currents (Benyon & Höök, 1997). The choice of mode of navigation in tours depends on the tasks and activities of users. For example, those planning a trip might choose a flying mode while geologists exploring the Earth's core would investigate holes drilled at the ocean floor.

Figure 5 shows a snapshot from 'The March on Washington' Tour in Historypin (Historypin, n.d.). Historypin differs from traditional data-centered collections of images of space and time in that its purpose is to "lead users step-by-step through a series of pieces of content, telling a story, exploring a place or walking through time" (Historypin Team, n.d.). The timeline visualization is activity-relevant and helps users establish historically relevant spatial relationships and match locations between the Street View in which they are immersed and the photographs superimposed upon it. To understand how a location has changed over time, users can change the opacity of the photograph overlay. This interaction helps users identify differences and similarities between old photographs and a recent Street View, locate historical landmarks on modern maps, and pinpoint modern landmarks on the historical backdrop. For example, while the photograph in Figure 5 below shows a crowd in front of the Washington Monument, in the Street View it appears to be gone, as the name Odeon does not appear on it.

All elements in the tour are linked to a navigation ribbon that guides users to the next step. Users can click on the thumbnails on the ribbon or use 'Previous' and 'Next' buttons to walk through the tour. Each element in the tour has its own description and explanation of how it is related to the rest of the tour.

The difficulty of integrating stories into geospatial visualizations depends on the granularity of the stories, which, in turn, is contingent upon user tasks and activities. Story details can be created at the macro and micro levels. Macro stories focus on entire cities, nations, or even the world, while micro stories narrate a particular part of a city, including communities, ethnicities, genders, or individual residents (Ball-Rokeach, Kim, & Matei, 2001). Stories can be user-generated or can come from layers. For example, the Wikipedia layer has numerous macro and micro stories about locations. The challenge is to understand how to relate and overview these stories. Despite the challenges, stories are useful for many tasks and activities and when added to data-centered visualizations can make them more activity-centered, and hence more human-centered.

CONCLUSION

In this chapter, we have discussed data-centered geospatial visualization designs and how they often fail to provide enough support for real-world human activities of their users. The main problem with such designs is that their primary focus is the data layer component of the visualizations. This layer usually allows users to perform visual and exploratory tasks facilitated by access to gazetteers and metadata. By doing so, such data-

Figure 5. A snapshot from 'The March on Washington' Tour by US National Archives featuring 'The Washington Monument during March on Washington' (NARA identifier 595342) shared on Historypin. com by the US National Archives © 2013 Historypin Used with permission

centered designs often overlook other real-world high-level activities that users need to perform, such as geographical correlations, complex decisions involving historical data, and storytelling. Examples in this chapter demonstrate that these activities and their constituent tasks and subtasks often require interaction with additional representations (e.g., base maps, historical data, and other information), without which users cannot process or understand trends and patterns in geospatial visualizations. Therefore, when conceptualizing activity-centered visualizations, it is crucial to take the following into consideration: 1. Account for information representations and interactions; 2. Pay proper attention to additional information sources that help people draw conclusions, make decisions, and solve problems, and 3. Understand how people link and process information. Equally important, we need to open up possibilities for research to investigate what additional information and interactions should be combined in activity-centered designs. Such research can help visualization researchers better understand the conceptual principles for design of geospatial visualizations.

REFERENCES

Alli, K., Ramirez, G. G., & Yung, K. K. (2001). Withdrawn spin-offs: An empirical analysis. *Journal of Financial Research*, *24*(4), 603–616.

Andrienko, G., & Andrienko, N. (2007). Coordinated multiple views: A critical view. *In Proceedings of the Fifth International Conference on Coordinated and Multiple Views in Exploratory Visualization*, (72-74). Zurich, Switzerland: Institute of Electrical and Electronics Engineers (IEEE).

Andrienko, N., Andrienko, G., & Gatalsky, P. (2005). Impact of data and task characteristics on design of spatio-temporal data visualization tools. In A. MacEachren, M.-J. Kraak, & J. Dykes (Eds.), Exploring Geovisualization (201-222). New York: Elsevier, Ltd. doi:doi:10.1016/B978-008044531-1/50428-0 doi:10.1016/B978-008044531-1/50428-0.

Bailey, J. E., Whitmeyer, S. J., & De Paor, D. G. (2012). Geological Society of America Special Papers: *Vol. 492. Introduction: The application of google geo tools to geoscience education and research* (pp. vii–xix). doi:10.1130/2012.2492(00).

Baldonado, M. Q., Woodruff, A., & Kuchinsky, A. (2000). Guidelines for using multiple views in information visualization. *Proceedings of the Working Conference on Advanced Visual Interfaces,* (110-119). New York: ACM.

Ball-Rokeach, S. J., Kim, Y. C., & Matei, S. (2001). Storytelling neighborhood: Paths to belonging in diverse urban environments. *Communication Research*, *28*(4), 392–428. doi:10.1177/009365001028004003.

Barnett, A. P., & Okoruwa, A. A. (1993). Application of geographic information systems in site selection and location analysis. *The Appraisal Journal*, *61*, 245–245.

Beaumont, J. R. (1991). GIS and market analysis. In Maguire, D. J., Goodchild, M. F., & Rhind, D. W. (Eds.), *Geographical Information Systems: Principles and Applications (139–51)*. New York: Wiley.

Belsky, E., Can, A., & Megbolugbe, I. (1998). A primer on geographic information systems in mortgage finance. *Journal of Housing Research*, *9*(1), 5–31.

Benyon, D., & Höök, K. (1997). Navigation in information spaces: supporting the individual. Nordby (ed.) *Proceedings of the IFIP TC13 International Conference on Human-Computer Interaction*, (39-46). London: Chapman and Hall.

Boggs. (2012). Grotto creek, front ranges, canadian cordillera: An example of google earth models. *Geoscience Canada, 39*(2).

Can, A. (1992). Specification and estimation of hedonic housing price models. *Regional Science and Urban Economics, 22*(3), 453–474. doi:10.1016/0166-0462(92)90039-4.

Can, A., & Megbolugbe, I. (1997). Spatial dependence and house price index construction. *The Journal of Real Estate Finance and Economics, 14*, 203–222. doi:10.1023/A:1007744706720.

Card, S. K., Mackinlay, J. D., & Shneiderman, B. (Eds.). (1999). *Readings in information visualization: Using vision to think*. San Francisco: Morgan Kaufman Publishers.

Cartwright, W. (2009). Applying the theatre metaphor to integrated media for depicting geography. *The Cartographic Journal, 46*(1), 24–35. doi:10.1179/000870409X415561.

Cartwright, W. E., & Hunter, G. J. (1999). Enhancing the map metaphor with multimedia cartography. InCartwright, , Peterson, , & Gartner, (Eds.), *Multimedia Cartography* (257-270). Heidelberg, Germany: Springer-Verlag. doi:10.1007/978-3-662-03784-3_24.

Casner, S. (1991). A task-analytic approach to the automated design of graphic presentations. *ACM Transactions on Graphics, 10*, 111–151. doi:10.1145/108360.108361.

CSTA. (2013). The spatial history project. *Stanford University*. Retrieved from http://www.stanford.edu/group/spatialhistory/cgi-bin/site/index.php.

Cunliffe, D., Taylor, C., & Tudhope, D. (1997). Query-based navigation in semantically indexed hypermedia. *Proceedings of the Eighth ACM Conference on Hypertext*, 87-95. Southampton, UK: ACM Press.

Dieberger, A. (1994). *On Navigation in Textual Virtual Environments and Hypertext*. (Unpublished doctoral dissertation). Vienna, Austria, Vienna University of Technology.

Dubin, R. A. (1992). Spatial autocorrelation and neighborhood quality. *Regional Science and Urban Economics, 22*(3), 433–452. doi:10.1016/0166-0462(92)90038-3.

Edsall, R. M. (2001). *Interacting with Space and Time: Designing Dynamic Geovisualization Environments*. (Unpublished doctoral dissertation). Philadelphia, The Pennsylvania State University.

Elias, M., Elson, J., Fisher, D., & Howe, J. (2008). Do I live in a flood basin? Synthesizing ten thousand maps. In *Proceedings of the 2008 Conference on Human Factors in Computing Systems*, 255-264. New York: ACM Press.

Fleming, D. (2001). Narrative leadership: Using the power of stories. *Strategy and Leadership, 29*(4), 34.

Forster, F. (1966). Use of a demographic base map for the presentation of areal data in epidemiology. *British Journal of Preventive & Social Medicine, 20*, 165–171. PMID:5969679.

Francica, J. R. (1993). *Profiting from a geographic information system. GIS World*. Hoboken, NJ: Wiley.

Gibler, K. M., Black, R. T., & Moon, K. P. (2002). Time, place, space, technology, and corporate real-estate strategy. *Journal of Real Estate Research, 24*(3), 235–262.

Google Developers. (2012a). Demographics layer. *Google Maps API for Business*. Retrieved from https://developers.google.com/maps/documentation/business/demographics.

Google Developers. (2012b). Styled maps. *Google Maps JavaScript API v3*. Retrieved from https://developers.google.com/maps/documentation/javascript/styling.

Guo, D., & Mennis, J. (2009). Spatial data mining and geographic knowledge discovery: An introduction. *Computers, Environment and Urban Systems, 33*(6), 403–408. doi:10.1016/j.compenvurbsys.2009.11.001.

Hägerstrand, T. (1982). Diorama, path, and project. *Tijdschrift voor Economische en Sociale Geografie, 73*(6), 323–339. doi:10.1111/j.1467-9663.1982.tb01647.x.

Hall, P. R. (1993). The role of GIS in targeted and database marketing for packaged goods. *GIS in Business Conference Proceedings,* 65–76. Boston: GIS World.

Hill, L. (2006). *Georeferencing: The geographic associations of information*. Cambridge, MA: MIT Press.

Historypin. (n.d.). A global community collaborating around history. *Historypin*. Retrieved from http://www.historypin.com/.

Historypin Team. (n.d.). What are tours? *Historypin*. Retrieved from http://www.historypin.com/tours/.

Huisman, O., Feliciano Santiago, I. T., Kraak, M. J., & Retsios, V. (2009). Developing a geovisual analytics environment for investigating archaeological events: Extending the space time cube. *Cartography and Geographic Information Science, 36*(3), 225–236. doi:10.1559/152304009788988297.

Isbister, K., & Doyle, P. (1999). Touring machines: Guide agents for sharing stories about digital places. In *Proceedings of Workshop on Narrative Intelligence.* Cape Cod, MA: AAAI Press.

Kaptelinin, V., & Nardi, B. A. (2009). *Acting with technology: Activity theory and interaction design*. Cambridge, MA: MIT Press.

Kay, A. (1990). User interface: A personal view. In Laurel, (ed.), *The Art of Human-Computer Interface Design*. Cambridge, MA: Addison-Wesley.

Kochera, A. (1994). Home characteristics and property insurance. *Housing Economics, 42*(12), 9–12.

Kraak, M. J. (2003). The space-time cube revisited from a geovisualization perspective. In *Proceedings of the 21st International Cartographic Conference: Cartographic Renaissance*. Durban, South Africa. International Cartographic Association (ICA).

Kraak, M.-J., Edsall, R., & MacEachren, A. (1997). Cartographic animation and legends for temporal maps: Exploration and or interaction. In *Proceedings of the 18th International Cartographic Conference,* 253-261. Stockholm: International Cartopgraphic Association.

Library of Congress. (2010). Fire insurance map, sheet 5. *American Treasures of the Library of Congress: Reason*. Retrieved from http://www.loc.gov/exhibits/treasures/trr016.html.

MacEachren, A., Wachowicz, M., Edsall, R., & Haug, D. (1999). Constructing knowledge from multivariate spatiotemporal data: Integrating geographic visualization (GVis) with knowledge discovery in database (KDD) methods. *International Journal of Geographical Information Science, 13*(4), 311–334. doi:10.1080/136588199241229.

MacEachren, A. M., Jaiswal, A. R., Robinson, A. C., Pezanowski, S., Savelyev, A., et al., & Blanford, J. (2011). Senseplace2: Geotwitter analytics support for situational awareness. In *Proceedings of IEEE Conference on Visual Analytics Science and Technology,* 181–190. New Brunswick, NJ: IEEE Press.

Manning, C., Rodriguez, M., & Ghosh, C. (1999). Devising a Corporate facility location strategy to maximize shareholder wealth. *Journal of Real-Estate Research. American Real-Estate Society, 17*(3), 321–340.

Monmonier, M. (1989). Graphic scripts for the sequenced visualization of geographic data. In *Proceedings of GIS/LIS 189*, 381-389. Orlando, FL: CUPR Press.

NComVA. (n.d.). National and regional statistical visualization. *NCOMVA.* Retrieved from http://www.ncomva.com/solutions/national-and-regional-statistical-visualization/.

Nivala, A.-M., Brewster, S., & Sarjakoski, L. T. (2008). Usability evaluation of web mapping sites. *The Cartographic Journal, 45*(2), 129–138. doi:10.1179/174327708X305120.

Northcraft, G. B., & Neale, M. A. (1987). Experts, amateurs, and real-estate: An anchoring-and-adjustment perspective on property pricing decisions. *Organizational Behavior and Human Decision Processes, 39*(1), 84–97. doi:10.1016/0749-5978(87)90046-X.

Nunn, J. A., & Bentley, L. (2012). Visualization of spatial and temporal trends in Louisiana water usage using google fusion tables. *Geological Society of America,* 492.

O'Connor, E. S. (2002). Storied business: Typology, intertextuality, and traffic in entrepreneurial narrative. *Journal of Business Communication, 39*(1), 36–54. doi:10.1177/002194360203900103.

Peterson, K. (1998). Development of spatial decision support systems for residential real-estate. *Journal of Housing Research, 9*(1), 135–156.

Peuquet, D. J. (2002). *Representations of space and time.* New York: The Guildford Press.

Plaisant, C. (2005). Information visualization and the challenge of universal usability. In A. MMacEachren, , M.-J. Kraak, & JDykes, (Eds.), *Exploring geovisualization* (53-82). New York: Elsevier Ltd. doi:10.1016/B978-008044531-1/50421-8.

Rabianski, J., DeLisle, J., & Carn, N. (2001). Corporate real-estate site selection: A community specific information framework. *Journal of Real Estate Research, 22*(1), 165–197.

Reno, Nevada. (1899). *Sheet #5.* New York: Sanborn Map and Publishing Company. Retrieved from: http://www.loc.gov/exhibits/treasures/trr016.html.

Robbins, M. L. (1996). *Spatial decision support systems for automated residential property valuation: A discussion of an actual installed system. Research and Business Uses of Geographic Information Systems in Housing and Mortgage Finance.* Washington, DC: Fannie MaeResearch Roundtable Series.

Robinson, A. H., Morrison, J. L., Muehrcke, P. C., Kimerling, A. J., & Guptill, S. C. (1995). *Elements of cartography.* New York: John Wiley and Sons.

Rodriguez, M., Sirmans, C. F., & Marks, A. (1995). Using geographic information systems to improve real-estate analysis. *Journal of Real Estate Research, 10*(2), 163–172.

Rogers, Y., & Ellis, J. (1994). Distributed cognition: An alternative framework for analyzing and explaining collaborative working. *Journal of Information Technology, 9*(2), 119–128. doi:10.1057/jit.1994.12.

Saffer, D. (2010). *Designing for interaction* (2nd ed.). Berkeley, CA: New Riders Press.

Schmenner, R. (1982). *Making business location decisions*. Englewood Cliffs, NJ: Prentice Hall.

Sedig, K., & Parsons, P. (2013). (in press). Interaction design for complex cognitive activities with visual representations: A pattern-based approach. *AIS Transactions on Human-Computer Interaction*.

Sedig, K., & Sumner, M. (2006). Characterizing interaction with visual mathematical representations. *International Journal of Computers for Mathematical Learning, 11*(1), 1–55. doi:10.1007/s10758-006-0001-z.

Shandler, J. (2012). United states holocaust memorial museum. *The Journal of American History*, 1228–1230. doi:10.1093/jahist/jar642.

Skiba, D. (2007). Nursing Education 2.0: are mashups useful for nursing education? *Nursing Education Perspectives, 5*, 286–288. PMID:17944264.

Sole, D., & Wilson, D. G. (2002). Storytelling in organizations: The power and traps of using stories to share knowledge in organizations. *LILA, Harvard, Graduate School of Education*. Retrieved from http://www.providersedge.com/docs/km_articles/Storytelling_in_Organizations.pdf.

South Coast Regional Stakeholder Group. (n.d.). *MarineMAP decision support tool*. Retrieved from http://southcoast.marinemap.org/marinemap/.

Studio, G. E. O. V. I. S. T. A. (2007). Health geojunction. *GEOVISTA*. Retrieved from http://www.apps.geovista.psu.edu/hgj/#.

Thrall, G. I., & Amos, P. (1996). *GIS within real-estate and related industries. Research and Business Uses of Geographic Information Systems in Housing and Mortgage Finance*. Washington, DC: Fannie Mae Research Roundtable Series.

Thrall, G. I., Fandrich, J., & Thrall, S. (1995). The location quotient: Descriptive geography for the community reinvestment act. *Geographical Information Systems, 5*(6), 18–22.

Turner, A. (2006). *Introduction to neogeography. Short Cuts*. Sebasapol, CA: O'Reilly Media.

Tversky, B. (2004). Narratives of space, time, and life. *Mind & Language, 19*(4), 380–392. doi:10.1111/j.0268-1064.2004.00264.x.

United Nations. (2000). *Handbook on geographic information systems and digital mapping*. New York, Series F No. 79. Retrieved http://unstats.un.org/unsd/publication/SeriesF/SeriesF_79E.pdf.

USGS. (2002). Using maps in genealogy: Fact sheet 099-02. *USGS Science for a Changing World*. Retrieved from http://egsc.usgs.gov/isb/pubs/factsheets/fs09902.html.

Vasiliev, I. R. (1997). Mapping time: Discussion of historical attempts to define time, and integration of time information into diagrams of geographic data. *Cartographica, 34*(2), 1–44. doi:10.3138/D357-234G-2M62-4373.

Williamson, C., & Shneiderman, B. (1992). The dynamic homefinder: Evaluating dynamic queries in a real-estate information exploration system. In *Proceedings* of *ACM SIGIR'92 Conference*, 338-346. Copenhagen, Denmark: ACM Press.

Xie, B., & Pearson, G. (2010). Usability testing by older americans of a prototype google map web site to select nursing homes. In *Proceedings of the 43rd Hawaii International Conference on System Sciences*. Hawaii: IEEE Press.

Zeng, T. Q., & Zhou, Q. (2001). Optimal spatial decision-making using GIS: A prototype of a real-estate geographical information system (REGIS). *International Journal of Geographical Information Science, 15*(4), 307–321. doi:10.1080/136588101300304034.

ADDITIONAL READING

Aanensen, D. M., Huntley, D. M., Feil, E. J., & Spratt, B. G. (2009). EpiCollect: Linking smartphones to web applications for epidemiology, ecology, and community data collection. *PLoS ONE*, *4*(9). doi:10.1371/journal.pone.0006968 PMID:19756138.

Alexander, B. (2006). Web 2.0: A new wave of innovation for teaching and learning? *EDUCAUSE Review*, *41*(2), 32.

Birkin, M., Chen, H., Clarke, M., Keen, J., Rees, P., & Xu, J. (2005). Moses: Modelling and simulation for e-social science. In *Proceedings of First International Conference on E-Social Science*. Manchester, UK: IEEE Press. Retrieved from: http://www.allhands.org.uk/2005/proceedings/papers/341.pdf.

Blower, J. D., Bretherton, D., Haines, K., Liu, C., & Santokhee, A. (2006). Exploring large marine datasets using an interactive website and google earth. *AGU Fall Meeting Abstracts, 1*, 8.

Cheung, K. H., Yip, K. Y., Townsend, J. P., & Scotch, M. (2008). HCLS 2.0/3.0: Health care and life sciences data mashup using Web 2.0/3.0. *Journal of Biomedical Informatics*, *41*(5), 694. doi:10.1016/j.jbi.2008.04.001 PMID:18487092.

Engard, N. C. (Ed.). (2009). *Library mashups: Exploring new ways to deliver library data*. Medford, NJ: Information Today, Inc..

Franklin, E. C. (2011). Rapid development of a hybrid web application for synthesis science of symbiodinium with Google Apps. In *Proceedings of the Environmental Information Management Conference*, 44-48. Santa Barbara, California: UCSB Press. doi:10.5060/D2NC5Z4X.

Gallo, T., & Waitt, D. (2011). Creating a successful citizen science model to detect and report invasive species. *Bioscience*, *61*(6), 459–465. doi:10.1525/bio.2011.61.6.8.

Gibbins, H., & Buyya, R. (2006). Gridscape II: A customizable and pluggable grid monitoring portal and its integration with google maps. In *Fifth International Conference on Grid and Cooperative Computing*, 257-265. New Brunswick, NJ: IEEE Press.

Goolsby, R. (2010). Social media as crisis platform: The future of community maps/crisis maps. *ACM Transactions on Intelligent Systems and Technology*, *1*(1), 7. doi:10.1145/1858948.1858955.

Hsu, W. K., Huang, P. C., Chang, C. C., Chen, C. W., Hung, D. M., & Chiang, W. L. (2011). An integrated flood risk assessment model for property insurance industry in taiwan. *Natural Hazards*, *58*(3), 1295–1309. doi:10.1007/s11069-011-9732-9.

Jiang, B. & Yao, X. (2010). Geospatial analysis and modeling of urban structure and dynamics: An overview. *Geospatial Analysis and Modelling of Urban Structure and Dynamics*, 3-11.

Kono, N., Arakawa, K., Ogawa, R., Kido, N., Oshita, K., & Ikegami, K. et al. (2009). Pathway projector: Web-based zoomable pathway browser using KEGG atlas and google maps API. *PLoS ONE*, *4*(11). doi:10.1371/journal.pone.0007710 PMID:19907644.

Kristensson, P. O., Dahlback, N., Anundi, D., Bjornstad, M., Gillberg, H., & Stahl, J. et al. (2009). An evaluation of space time cube representation of spatiotemporal patterns. *IEEE Transactions on Visualization and Computer Graphics*, *15*(4), 696–702. doi:10.1109/TVCG.2008.194 PMID:19423892.

Leydesdorff, L., & Bornmann, L. (2012). Mapping (USPTO) patent data using overlays to google maps. *Journal of the American Society for Information Science and Technology*, *63*(7), 1442–1458. doi:10.1002/asi.22666.

Liechti, R., Gleizes, A., Kuznetsov, D., Bougueleret, L., Le Mercier, P., Bairoch, A., & Xenarios, I. (2010). *OpenFluDB, a database for human and animal influenza virus. Oxford Database.* Oxford, UK: Oxford University.

López-de-Ipiña, D., García-Zubia, J., & Orduña, P. (2006). Remote control of Web 2.0-enabled laboratories from mobile devices. In *Proceedings of Second IEEE International Conference on e-Science and Grid Computing,* 123-123. New Brunswick, NJ: IEEE Press.

Ma, X., Carranza, E. J. M., Wu, C., & van der Meer, F. D. (2012). Ontology-aided annotation, visualization, and generalization of geological time scale information from online geological map services. *Computers & Geosciences, 40*(3), 107–119. doi:10.1016/j.cageo.2011.07.018.

Nagarajan, M., Gomadam, K., Sheth, A., Ranabahu, A., Mutharaju, R., & Jadhav, A. (2009). Spatio-temporal-thematic analysis of citizen sensor data: Challenges and experiences. [New Brunswick, NJ: IEEE Press.]. *Proceedings of Web Information Systems Engineering-WISE, 2009,* 539–553.

Pejic, A., Pletl, S., & Pejic, B. (2009). An expert system for tourists using google maps API. In *Proceedings of 7th International Symposium on Intelligent Systems and Informatics,* 317-322. New Brunswick, NJ: IEEE Press.

Pettit, C., Bishop, I. D., Borda, A., Uotila, P., Sposito, V., et al., & Russel, A. B. M. (2009) An E-science approach to climate change adaptation. In Ostendorf, Baldock, Bruce, Burdett, & Corcoran. (Eds.), *Proceedings of the Surveying & Spatial Sciences Institute Biennial International Conference* (1123-1134). Adelaide, Australia: Surveying & Spatial Sciences Institute.

Roth, R. E. & Ross, K. S. (2012). Extending the google maps API for event animation mashups. *Cartographic Perspectives,* (64), 21-40.

Tsai, Y. H. E. (2011). PhyloGeoViz: A web-based program that visualizes genetic data on maps. *Molecular Ecology Resources, 11*(3), 557–561. doi:10.1111/j.1755-0998.2010.02964.x PMID:21481214.

Wang, A., Jun, Z., & Jiang, W. (2009). Useful resources integration based on google maps. In *Proceedings of 4th International Conference on Computer Science & Education,* 1044-1047. New Brunswick, NJ: IEEE.

Worthington, J. P., Silvertown, J., Cook, L., Cameron, R., Dodd, M., & Skelton, P. et al. (2012). Evolution MegaLab: A case study in citizen science methods. *Methods in Ecology and Evolution, 3,* 303–309. doi:10.1111/j.2041-210X.2011.00164.x.

Yi, Q., Hoskins, R. E., Hillringhouse, E. A., Sorensen, S. S., Oberle, M. W., Fuller, S. S., & Wallace, J. C. (2008). Integrating open-source technologies to build low-cost information systems for improved access to public health data. *International Journal of Health Geographics, 7*(1), 29. doi:10.1186/1476-072X-7-29 PMID:18541035.

KEY TERMS AND DEFINITIONS

Activities: Human activities refer to clusters of actions and decisions that are done for a purpose.

Activity-Centered Visualizations: Activity-centered visualizations, not only represent the data layers, but also focus on users' needs, and real-world tasks and activities—such as storytelling and comparing data layers with other information.

Base Map Layers: Base map layers contain geographical reference information upon which the data layers may be plotted for purposes of comparison or geographical correlation.

Coordinated Displays: Coordinated displays visualize multiple properties of the data layer. Representations in coordinated geospatial visualizations include synchronized geospatial maps, semantic views, and timelines.

Data-Centered Visualizations: Data-centered visualizations are primarily focused on representation of data from data layers.

Data Layer: A data layer consists of points, lines, and polygons, typically used to characterize distinct entities such as houses, roads, or districts.

Geographic Information Retrieval Visualizations: Visualizations for geographic information retrieval. Users interact with such visualizations by searching for spatial objects in certain locations and browse the retrieved results on a map.

Geospatial Visualizations: Geospatial visualizations are digital geographic and/or spatial maps to which users or designers can link their data.

Google Maps Layers: Examples of Google Maps layers include Wikipedia, Demographics, YouTube, Panoramio, Weather, and Bicycling layers, which enhance base maps and enrich users' understanding of location.

Tasks: Tasks are conscious processes undertaken in the fulfillment of a goal.

Time Maps: Maps with timelines.

ENDNOTES

[1]   KML is the OpenGIS encoding standard (OGC KML) for managing the display of data in Google Maps.

[2]   GeoRSS is a standard for encoding location in feeds of content, such as news articles, audio blogs, video blogs and text blog entries. See Chinese Canadian Immigrant Pipeline, 1912-1923 and Arrests of Italian Jews, 1943-1945 projects at the Center for Spatial and Textual Analysis (2013) or National and Regional Statistical Visualization at NComVA (n.d.). ed interchangeably.

Chapter 14
An Information Visualization-Based Approach for Exploring Databases:
A Case Study for Learning Management Systems

Celmar Guimarães da Silva
School of Technology, University of Campinas, Brazil

ABSTRACT

Learning Management Systems (LMS) may use Information Visualization techniques and concepts for presenting their large amounts of data, in order to ease the monitoring and analysis of students learning process problems. Nonetheless, the generally adopted approaches are based on presenting data obtained by predefined database queries only, which does not consider unforeseen situations derived from final user's knowledge about e-learning domain. Therefore, the purpose of this work is to provide a resource for LMS users to define and execute queries related to these unforeseen situations. This resource is a prototype by which users may access a remote LMS database, create their own queries by selecting database attributes they want to analyze, and represent query results by means of automatically selected interactive graphical representations. User evaluations indicate that the approach is appropriate and points out possible enhancements.

1. INTRODUCTION

Providing user-level access to data stored in a database is not an easy task. It is not just a matter of providing connectivity from a system to a local or remote database. In fact, it is related also to how a user may query the database, and how he/she may interpret the returned results.

Querying a database requires that the user has gained much knowledge of database theory. This requirement includes, at least, concepts of table fields and tuples, primary and foreign keys,

DOI: 10.4018/978-1-4666-4309-3.ch014

entities and relationships. It also requires that the user masters a database query language such as SQL. Even more, querying requires that the user knows what kind of data is stored in the database, in order to define what to query. Given these restrictions, the user's task of querying a database requires a cognitive overload which may not be dismissed, in part because typical users have not such theoretical knowledge and do not even know about the internal organization of the database to be queried. In fact, typical users are not interested in this kind of technicality, but instead they just want to obtain an answer for a question related to a system stored data.

When analyzing answers provided by a Data-Base Management System (DBMS) for a query, one may think that the mostly common alphanumeric, table-based answer format is enough for answering users' questions. Even though this format is sufficient for obtaining some specific data, it may be difficult to get a data overview and to detect patterns, trends and outliers present in the data. Graphical and interactive representations of data, as proposed by the Information Visualization area (InfoVis, for short) (Card et al., 1999), are suitable for this kind of analysis. They may provide distinct levels of data overview, details on demand, and interactive capabilities of data reorganization and filtering, among other useful resources. For example, interactive filtering techniques (such as dynamic queries [Shneiderman, 1994]) afford user controls for selecting relevant data and for querying details, providing fast answers, and without the need to learn command-line querying syntax. When applied together, filtering and other techniques may enhance users' formulation of an internal model about the data under analysis.

Both difficulties—how users may query a database and how to represent query results in a useful way for them—may be analyzed from distinct scenarios, which may have distinct kinds of users with distinct computer-related and data-analysis-related skills. In this chapter, those difficulties were analyzed within a Learning Management System (LMS) scenario, in which there are students and teachers involved in learning activities. LMS are virtual environments that enable and mediate communications among participants of courses. These systems group distinct computer-based resources, like electronic mails, chat rooms, resources for publishing readings and for delivering activities' results, among others. Each resource manages and saves different kinds of data, like messages, published contents, and participant data.

In this scenario, analyzing LMS data is an important task for monitoring students' learning process, making possible to detect its potential problems. For example, participants with few accesses to the LMS, or those who do not interact with other course participants represent situations that can reveal problems related to an adopted course methodology.

Different researches try to overcome the analysis difficulty by applying InfoVis concepts and techniques, in order to graphically and interactively present LMS data. Some examples of these researches are: InterMap visual representations of course participants interaction (Romani, 2000), France et al.'s interactive activity diagram for learning scenarios (2005), and GISMO (Mazza & Milani, 2005) and CourseVis (Mazza & Dimitrova, 2005) representation of students' social, behavioral and cognitive aspects. Nonetheless, these researches show data that are obtained by predefined database queries, and so these data fit specific analysis situations. Unforeseen situations derived from final user's knowledge about e-learning domain are not considered by these researches, which do not provide ways for this user to inform the system about the data he/she wants to analyze.

Overcoming those difficulties related to querying databases and understanding query results may provide an important way for analyzing LMS data. In the LMS scenario, the presented difficulties may be summarized by two questions:

1. How to enable a user to inform the LMS what datasets he/she needs to analyze?

2. How to enable this user to get these data from the LMS, in order to analyze and understand them?

This chapter presents a proposed solution for these questions. This solution enables LMS users, each with distinct data analysis needs, to define different data combinations that they want to analyze, instead of using only system predefined queries. The solution uses database concepts of universal relation model (Ullman, 1982) for enabling users to choose database fields to be queried, without the need to know the queried LMS database internal organization. Besides, these concepts are also used for executing a query derived from this field choice in LMS database. Query results are automatically converted into interactive graphical representations by InfoVis techniques, avoiding user's concerns about developing a graphic representation that is appropriate for these data analysis. This chapter summarizes some results of Silva's doctoral thesis (Silva, 2006) and extends a previously published paper (Silva & Rocha, 2007).

The next sections are organized as follows. Section 2 presents a theoretical background on InfoVis and database universal relation model, which is necessary for understanding the proposed solution. It also summarizes how recent works apply InfoVis to LMS. The adopted solution is presented in Section 3, which describes the two systems composing the prototype–the JInfoVis and the LMS Database Explorer. This section also presents prototype's general architecture, implementation, and initial evaluation. Section 4 presents future research directions. Section 5 concludes the chapter and presents future works.

2. BACKGROUND

This section presents some theoretical background which this chapter refers to. It is organized in three parts: Section 2.1 presents InfoVis concepts used

by this work; Section 2.2 presents how InfoVis is used in the context of LMS; and Section 2.3 presents the database concept of Universal Relation Model.

2.1. InfoVis

Visual mapping (Card et al., 1999) (i.e. how to transform a data table into a visual structure that users can analyze and understand) is an important process for InfoVis. Given a data table, this process represents all its data by marks into a visual structure, which can be a heatmap, a node-link diagram or a bar chart, among many others. Marks can be dots, lines, circles or other visual elements. A visual mapping associates each data table attribute (or variable) to a graphical property (color, shapes, textures, orientation etc.) or to a spatial property (e.g., its position with relation to a defined axis, or its proximity to other marks). For example, if circles are used as marks for representing users of a system, circle size may represent a variable "quantity of accesses" (how many times each user accessed this system).

Data table variables can be classified according to its semantics and its functional dependencies of other variables. Based on Card et al. (1999), Spence (2001), and Ware (2004), variables can be semantically classified into three main categories: nominal (set of elements without specific order), ordinal (set of elements with a specific order relation among them), and quantitative (set of elements with a numerical scope, and that support arithmetical operations). Considering functional dependencies aspects, each data table variable can also be defined as input or output variable, according to Spence (2001). Input variables are the variables that functionally determine the rest of data table's variables, which are called output variables.

Mackinlay (1986) points out two criteria which help defining a visual mapping for a data table: expressiveness and effectiveness. In order to achieve expressiveness, a visual structure must express exactly all data table information (i.e. all data table information, and only this information without representing additional incorrect data). Effectiveness is a criterion related to how fast a user can interpret data and easily distinguish them, with the lowest possible interpretation errors. One may compare graphical properties' effectiveness according to the data categories they represent (e.g. size is more effective than colors for showing quantitative information). Card et al. (1999, Table 1.23) present a table of relative effectiveness of retinal properties.

After representing data into a visual structure, users can interact with it in order to extract more information from it, which could not be done statically. Details-on-demand, distortions, viewpoint controls and marks rearrangement are examples of interaction techniques. Users can use radio buttons, sliders and range-sliders, among other controls, for selecting relevant data and discard irrelevant ones. In this sense, dynamic queries (Shneiderman, 1994) are an important interaction technique for users to control visual query parameters, and quickly generate a visual representation of query results. Some of their advantages are: avoiding the need of knowing command-line syntax; minimizing syntax errors when the user defines his/her query; and making it easier to construct an internal model or cognitive map about data under analysis, because query formulation and results exhibition are fast (Spence, 2001; Shneiderman, 1994).

All these and other techniques and concepts may be applied to some domain in order to represent its data and enable decision making. In this sense, next subsection presents some works that applies InfoVis to the LMS domain.

2.2. InfoVis Applied to LMS

This subsection presents a set of works that shows synergies between InfoVis and e-learning. Silva's thesis (Silva, 2006) presents additional details about some of them.

TelEduc (Rocha et al., 2002) is a LMS that uses some InfoVis related techniques in order to enable a distinction among "silent and present" students and really "absent" ones, a needed differentiation for tracking a full-distance course. In this sense, the InterMap (Interaction Map) tool (Romani, 2000) uses node-link diagrams, heatmaps and bar charts, among other visual structures, for graphically representing course participants interaction into TelEduc communication tools (Mail, Chat, and Discussion Forums). A similar objective lead TelEduc development team to create a tool called Access (Silva & Rocha, 2004), which stores and presents course participants accesses to the course starting page and to the TelEduc tools available for that course. TelEduc is an open source LMS that has been developed since 1997 by the Nucleus of Informatics Applied to Education and the Institute of Computing, both at University of Campinas.

Access and InterMap tools highlight questions that are also addressed by Hardless and Nulden (1999). According to them, e-learning-based course instructors report difficulties in perceiving what is happening in their courses. Hardless and Nulden propose a software called Activity Visualization, which aims to reduce this kind of "blindness". It uses heatmaps for showing course participants' access and messages along the time. However, it is not possible to conclude from their paper whether their software provides an interactive heatmap, neither what LMS it was connected to.

GISMO (Mazza & Milani, 2005) and Course-Vis (Mazza & Dimitrova, 2005) represent Moodle and WebCT course data, respectively. Both use heatmaps and histograms for representing students' social, behavioral and cognitive aspects, such as: data about participants' accesses to LMS courses or resources (contents), data about tasks and quizzes, and data about participants' discussions. GISMO also provides interactive controls for manipulating the visual structure (for time interval selection and for selecting students, groups, resources, etc.).

Mazza (2006) presents an interactive system that enable Moodle administrators to compare the intensity of access to Moodle tools in many offered courses. It provides a representation based on pixel-oriented techniques, and enables administrators to select courses, time intervals and aggregation unit (daily, monthly, etc.) for access count.

Tzoumakas and Theodoulidis (2005) focus not just on visual representations of course participants' interaction, but also on representations of interactions between students and resources, and between students and software. Force-directed and radial graphs represent these interaction types, whose data is provided by WebCT e-learning environment logs.

Saltz et al. (2004) propose visual structures for helping instructors to perceive students participation in online discussions and to detect students with difficulties for creating an active dialog. The proposed solution, called "social student graph", is a node-link diagram whose nodes are students and whose directed edges represent messages sent to a specific student under analysis. Node size and form represents, respectively, the amount of sent messages and the participant role in the course (instructor or student). The proposed visual structure, however, does not have interactive features neither is connected to a LMS.

Otsuka and Rocha (Otsuka, 2006; Otsuka & Rocha, 2007) use non-interactive graphics for helping instructors to assess LMS students participation in a formative assessment process. Their multi-agent system represents different LMS data, such as: relevance of messages sent by course participants; students participation regularity in an activity; amount of messages and comments sent by participants; time of activity delivery by students (in relation to activity deadline); and students' performance. All these data is represented visually as bar charts, line charts and pie charts.

Foroughi and Taponecco (2005) propose bar charts and spiral-based visual structures for representing and contrasting attributes such as time spent by students to resolving problems and students' performance. These graphics present interactive features such as zoom, rotation, brushing and navigation through the available visual

structures. Gómez-Aguilar et al. (2009) also use an interactive spiral timeline; their spiral present a histogram of activities (among other elements) along the time. It is improved by background bars that present the intensity of activities in higher units of time than the used by the histogram. Filtering and alternative views of data are also available.

France et al. (2005) use simultaneous representation of an activity diagram for a learning scenario and a set of LMS-related logs, in order to enable student behavior analysis. Their system employs focus+context techniques for representing these logs.

The aim of Nguyen, Huang and Hintz works (Nguyen & Huang, 2005; Huang et al., 2005) is helping to understand data stored in LiveNet collaborative learning environment. They focus on representing relationships among different collaborative objects, such as activities, contents, and participant groups. These relationships are presented by means of hierarchical representations based on encapsulation and connection techniques used simultaneously.

Klerkx et al. (2004) study how to use InfoVis techniques for easing object search into a learning content management system. Different search strategies are enabled by InfoVis techniques for representing hierarchical data, such as the above mentioned encapsulation and connection ones.

Hijón-Neira & Velázquez-Iturbide (2008) use a subset of Prefuse visualizations for representing diverse LMS data, including: a scatterplot showing the evolution of the amount of work done by students; a fisheye-based textual description of student accesses; a node-link diagram that groups students according to their grades; a Prefuse's "data mountain" representation with the temporal evolution of accesses; and a "data mountain" with characteristics of students' computing equipment and geographical location.

Hijón-Neira et al. (2008) use Spotfire for analyzing students interactions with a LMS (Merlin), trying to correlate access patterns, course period (morning or evening) and exam performance.

They neither present how data was transferred from LMS to Spotfire, nor the characteristics of the users who used Spotfire for analysis.

Martín et al. (2011) presented a module of a LMS whose pie charts present percentages of time spent by users for concluding exercises and their correctness. These exercises may be selected by an outline. They point out that other visual representations are available but their paper does not present them.

Teutsch and Bourdet (2010) state the importance of visualizing three dimensions of LMS data: participants, calendar (time) and scenario (the course structure itself, composed by tasks, content and methods of participation [activities]). They propose to analyze pairs of these dimensions, represented as axes of a kind of scatterplot. Another dimension may be represented by mark colors.

France et al. (2006) propose a visualization system which represents three views: classroom, student and activity view. They use Chernoff faces for representing students: face characteristics are mapped to the number of student logs and the time spent by the students doing some exercise. In "classroom view", Venn diagrams group students that are doing the same activity, and colors indicate group delay for accomplishing the activity. The "student view" present a scatterplot of number of logs accumulated per minute by a student in order to complete course activities; this view also compares this number with an histogram of average number of logs from other students in the same activities. The "activity view" presents a scatterplot correlating time spent per each course participant for accomplishing an activity, and average time of a student relative to the classroom average time of doing exercises. It aims to help teachers to analyze if students are spending more time than usual to conclude an activity.

Gómez-Aguilar et al. (2008) uses Prefuse for presenting some visual representations for LMS elements (participants, logs and data stored by Moodle tools), such as a node-link diagram connecting these elements and a word cloud about forum messages. A more recent work of Gómez-Aguilar et al. (2011) presents a tag cloud integrated to a wave-graph and a bar-graph for representing the frequency of words in LMS tools along the time.

Gómez-Aguilar et al. (2010) surveyed some InfoVis works related to the use of visualization for representing the learning content and learning objects, for organizing and managing learning objects, and for representing the learning process in order to better understand it.

A comparison of the characteristics of these works reveals a common aspect: each one deals with visualization solutions implemented for helping users with specific analysis needs. This way, users whose needs were not contemplated by the previous works still have arduous effort for collecting LMS data from the available user interfaces and for organizing them into a chart, so as to better understand the data. Section 3 presents a possible solution for this problem. Before it, the next subsection introduces the Universal Relation Model for a better understanding of the remainder of the chapter.

2.3. Universal Relation Model

As the introduction section states, this work aims to enable users to query a LMS database without the need to know its internal organization. This objective is shared with some Database researches, which aim to isolate users from the need to know the data's logical structure (such as tables, registers, entities and relationships). These researches use the concept of universal relation model for doing this kind of logic isolation. A database universal relation is a hypothetical relation whose schema is composed by all attributes from all relation schemas of a database (Ullman, 1982). For the user who defines the query, it seems that the database has just one big relation (the universal relation) to which he/she may send queries. For the DBMS that supports this model, it is necessary to convert each universal relation-based query into a query that can be executed in the relational model. This conversion mechanism, called query interpretation, frequently needs to define lossless joins that were not defined in the original query. This join definition is the heart of query interpretation algorithms, and defines the sense of the query and, consequently, the sense of its result.

3. PROPOSED SOLUTION

The presented background on InfoVis and Database enables constructing a solution for the LMS querying problem, stated at the beginning of this chapter. It is possible to help LMS users to obtain answers to questions related to its analysis, in two ways:

1. Enabling users to define their queries as a set of LMS database attributes, selected by the user among all table attributes, and without need to know the database internal organization. Query interpretation algorithms may transform the selected attribute set (considered as a universal relation query) into a relational query, which enables it to be executed in LMS database.

2. Enabling them to visualize graphically and interactively the query results, helping them to analyze and understand these results, and to get the desired answer. This solution also determines that the system itself, instead of the user, can define suitable graphical representations for the results.

This solution was divided into the following six steps:

1. The system shows LMS database attributes, so users may select some of them. Database tables are not shown for users, because they must see the database as a single universal relation. Attributes derived by applying aggregate functions (quantity, maximum,

minimum, sum and average) to other database attributes may also be selected. All attributes are shown with descriptive names instead of their original names.

2. After the user selects a non-empty set of attributes, the system analyzes the selected attributes and verifies how functional dependencies relate them in the database. The observation of primary, alternative and foreign keys in the database schema infers these functional dependencies.

3. Based on the selected attributes, on their categories, and on their functional dependence-based relationships, the system chooses a visual structure (among the available ones) that it understands as a best-fit choice for showing query results, taking into consideration expressiveness and effectiveness concepts. In this step, user can go back to step 1 and modify the selected attribute set, or else he/she can continue to the next step.

4. Based on the selected attributes, the system prepares and executes an SQL query for getting the asked data. This step uses universal relation theories for join inference if necessary.

5. After query execution, the system uses the system-selected visual structure for showing the obtained data.

6. The system enables the user to explore the visual structure by means of dynamic query-based controls and functionalities. The user may reorganize data, filter them and ask for details about them.

In order to provide this solution, a prototype was planned and implemented. This prototype has two main parts: LMS Database Explorer, which provides attribute selection and query interpretation capabilities; and JInfoVis, which provides graphical and interactive representation of results, and which is used by LMS Database Explorer. Both prototype modules are described in the following subsections.

3.1. LMS Database Explorer

The Learning Management System Database Explorer (or LMS Database Explorer, for short) is a system which aims at giving users the capability of querying a LMS database even if they know neither database concepts nor the database itself. It is related to all six steps of the presented solution, but specially to the former three, which will be detailed in this section. Section 3.2 will detail the latter three, which are more related to JInfoVis.

3.1.1. Showing Database Attributes

In order to enable users to choose a subset of the database attributes – the first step of the solution – the system must show all those attributes. However, the attributes names may have often no meaning for user, even if concatenated with their table names (e.g., Mail.message_id). Attribute names must then be converted into meaningful and unambiguous descriptions for enabling users to select attributes which are appropriated for their queries.

Grouping attributes by some subject is also necessary for helping users find what attributes they may select. This work considers that users have experience in using a LMS, and then the LMS concept of *tools* (Mail, Discussion Forums, Whiteboard, Support Material etc.) should be well-known. Based on this fact, it is proposed that the system groups LMS attributes by tools.

The attribute selection step also must take care of ethical and security-related questions. If all database attributes are available for users' queries, they would be able to acquire login and password data from other users. Another equally undesired situation is that users would find it possible to obtain other users' private data, such as personal messages and contents stored in the LMS. Blocking users to select specific attributes such as login, password and mail messages helps to solve this problem.

Sometimes it is also necessary to summarize the values of some attributes. For example, the analyst may not be interested in each forum message, but in the quantity of forum messages. Another example is the observation of when the users' most recent accesses to the LMS happened, and not each one of their accesses. Taking this into consideration, it is necessary to provide users the possibility of selecting values calculated by aggregation functions, such as sum, average, maximum value and minimum value. This chapter calls this kind of pseudo-attributes *derived attributes*, which are actually result columns of aggregation-function-related queries. For differentiation purposes, attributes that are originally available in the database will be called non-derived attributes.

3.1.2. Analyzing Selected Attributes

Given that a user has selected a set of attributes, the system must understand some characteristics of these attributes in order to propose a graphical and interactive representation, which will represent the dataset related to them.

The first characteristic to consider is the semantic category of the attributes, a concept already presented in Section 2. Database schemas define attributes in terms of data types (integer, float, string etc.), which are not sufficient for defining the data semantic category. Hence, it is necessary to provide this kind of metadata for each database attribute.

Beyond classifying database attributes, it is also necessary to categorize derived attributes, given that users may select them. In order to address this problem, one should first consider which aggregation functions may be applied to which attributes, given that their semantic categories may block the use of some functions. As an example, it does not make sense to apply an average function on nominal values, but one may apply it on quantitative values without problem. The latter situation will produce a derived attribute which is

Table 1. Categories of aggregation functions' output attributes, according to input attribute categories. Adapted from Spence (2001, p. 68, Tables 5.1 and 5.2)

Aggregation Functions	Input Attribute's Categories		
	Nominal	Ordinal	Quantitative
count	quantitative	quantitative	quantitative
min, max	(unavailable)	ordinal	quantitative
sum, avg	(unavailable)	(unavailable)	quantitative

also quantitative. Therefore, given the categories of each aggregate function input attributes, it is possible to state what the output attribute category is, as presented in Table 1.

Another analysis one must do before choosing a visual structure is how the selected attributes are interrelated. This relationship may be defined in terms of *functional dependencies*, a well known concept of database area. Consider a database relation R and two attribute sets of R, called X and Y. If one verifies that $t_1(Y)=t_2(Y)$ for any couple of tuples t_1 and t_2 for which $t_1(X)=t_2(X)$, then this situation characterizes that X functionally determines Y (which is denoted by X→Y). This concept of functional dependency may be transitive: if A→B and B→C, then A→C, according to Armstrong's transitivity rule (Elmasri & Navathe, 2000). Therefore, a well defined database may be understood as a directed graph, whose nodes are non-derived attributes and whose edges are functional dependencies.

In order to consider derived attributes and universal relation model, one may apply also the following functional dependency rules:

1. An attribute set functionally determines each of its attributes (which is derived from Armstrong's reflexivity rule [Elmasri & Navathe, 2000]).

2. A derived attribute functionally determines only itself.

3. A primary or alternative key from a table functionally determines other table attributes (which is derived from the concept of key).

4. Consider a foreign key F which points to a primary or alternative key K. Following a universal relation model, each attribute of F merges with an equivalent attribute of K through a natural join. Therefore, F→K and K→F.

5. Consider a derived attribute D, which results from an aggregation function applied to an attribute set A. Therefore, A→D. Observe that D does not exist in the real database, and consequently this functional dependency only may be defined after query definition.

6. Let A and B be two distinct attributes, such that A→B and ¬(B→A), either transitively or not. Therefore, there is a value of B for each value of A, and many values of A may exist for each value of B. Let D be a derived attribute, such that A→D (as presented by the rule #5). Therefore, there is a value of D for each value of A. From both situations, many values of D may be indirectly related to each value of B through A. Consequently, grouping values of B by values of D make sense, and then B→D.

Rule #6 deserves an example. Suppose that class, teacher and student are some universal relation attributes, such that *class→teacher* and ¬*(teacher→class)*. Suppose that *class→number_of_students* (a derived attribute generated by a count function applied to student). Given that each teacher possibly teaches more than a class and each class has a number of students, then each teacher teaches a number of students. Therefore, there is a functional dependency *teacher→number_of_students*.

The presented rules, together with functional dependency original ones, enable the system to calculate functional dependencies from non-derived and derived attributes. As the following subsection presents, system uses these dependencies for defining which visual structures to use.

3.1.3. Choosing Visual Structures

The previous step analyzed some important characteristics of selected attributes, nominally functional dependencies and semantic categories. Based on these characteristics, the system must propose a visual structure for representing data. Among all available visual structures, the chosen structure must be one that better fits data, that is, one with the highest effectiveness and expressiveness related to attributes semantic categories and functional dependencies.

The available visual structures considered in this work are bar charts and heatmaps (which may be considered as starfield displays or even double-entry tables), and they are available for use in JInfoVis. Given these visual structures, it is necessary to define which structure to use, and how to do the visual mapping among its graphical properties and selected attributes.

First, it is necessary to understand that *each available visual structure has its own expressiveness*, that is, a capability of expressing exactly a specific type of input data. Consequently, expressiveness criteria restrict which datasets may be represented by which visual structure. For example, a bar chart, as implemented by JInfoVis, has a horizontal axis H which express nominal or ordinal values, and a vertical axis V which express only quantitative values. Besides, for each value of V there is only one corresponding value of H. It is equivalent to affirm that H→V.

An equivalent analysis may be applied to heatmaps. The heatmap implemented by JInfoVis has a horizontal axis H and a vertical axis V. Both may express nominal, ordinal or quantitative values, and a functional dependency between H and V is not necessary. Optionally, a legend L may exist, and it may represent quantitative or ordinal values (other heatmap implementations may also support nominal values). JInfoVis heatmap represents a single output value for a pair of input values, one from H and other from V. Therefore, it has a functional dependency HV→S. Figure 1 represents thumbnails of the three presented possibilities of visual structures.

The presented analysis is related with visual mapping, which maps data table variables into graphical properties. However, one must think about *how database selected attributes are related to these variables*. A first and intuitive approach is to associate directly each attribute to a variable. Consequently, this solution works as if each attribute was mapped to an axis or to a legend.

A second and a little bit less intuitive approach is to map more than an attribute to a single variable. Suppose that attributes $A_1,..., A_n$ are mapped to data table variables $V_1,...,V_n$, respectively. Besides, suppose that a data transformation originates a new data table, in which $V_1,..., V_n$ are demoted to values of a new variable W. All cases of the previous data table are then redefined, in such a way that values of each variable V_i are merged

Figure 1. Visual structures: (a) bar chart, (b) simple heatmap, (c) heatmap with legend

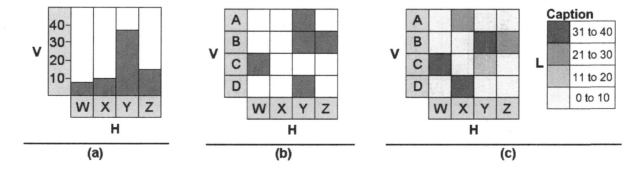

into a single value. W is represented as an axis in the visual structure, which consequently shows all attributes A_1,..., A_n. Figure 2 exemplifies this second approach. It is important to highlight that all attributes A_1,..., A_n must be similar enough to enable demotion; for example, all attributes may be quantitative ones.

Given the functional dependencies among user-selected attributes, semantic categories of attributes, expressiveness of available visual structures and relationship between attributes and data table variables, it is possible to verify if there are available visual structures able to represent the results from the user-defined query. If there is more than one structure available, it is also possible to choose the one that better fits the data.

When considering expressiveness criteria, a visual structure is able to represent the results of a query if two conditions are obeyed. The first one is that a subset (S) of the attribute set functional dependencies (A) must match the set of visual structure functional dependencies (F), in order to provide a minimally necessary expressiveness. The more S and F matching functional dependencies, the higher the expressiveness. For example, suppose that $\{X{\to}Y\}$ is the set of functional dependencies of the attribute set $\{X,Y\}$. Bar charts' functional dependencies set is $\{H{\to}V\}$, which matches exactly $\{X{\to}Y\}$ if X is mapped to

H and Y is mapped to V. The heatmap functional dependencies set for a two-variable case is an empty set, but this does not block a heatmap from representing X and Y relationship. In this case, both bar chart and heatmap may represent the attribute set $\{X,Y\}$. However, the bar chart is more expressive than the heatmap in this case, because the bar chart expresses the $X{\to}Y$ dependency, but the heatmap does not.

The second expressiveness condition is that a data table variable (which may represent a single database attribute or a set of attributes) only may be mapped to a graphical attribute (axis or legend) that matches its semantic category. In the previous example related to bar charts, X must be nominal or ordinal (because H has this restriction), and Y must be quantitative (because V has this restriction). If these characteristics do not happen, it is necessary to use the next available visual structure, even if it is less expressive than the former.

Effectiveness must also be considered for defining a visual mapping. Concerning this, this chapter presents an approach that prioritizes the use of spatial position of marks in the visual structure. This approach defines that input variables have priority to be mapped to spatial axes. This characteristic privileges the visual comparison of data related to distinct values of a same input variable.

Figure 2. Multiple variables (V1,..., Vn) are mapped to a new variable W. In (a), each variable Vi determines a quantitative value (the variable "Quantity") In (b), {Vi,A} determines a variable represented by color

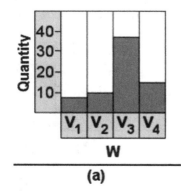

(a)

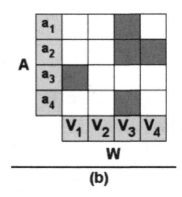

(b)

Another feature of the proposed effectiveness approach is related to heatmap legend colors. Legend represents an output ordinal variable. Consequently, values of a quantitative attribute must be classified in order to be represented by legends, and therefore this classified attribute becomes ordinal. Distinct color sets are used for distinct variable categories. Quantitative or ordinal variables are mapped to color brightness, and hue and saturation are kept constant. Ordinal temporal variables, however, uses new-leaves color for representing recent values, and old-leaves color for old ones. The former decision is based on the effectiveness of bright for representing quantitative and ordinal values (Card et al., 1999). The latter is based on Tufte's work (Tufte, 1990), which suggests using colors found in nature, given our familiarity with them, their coherence and harmony.

Taking in consideration these expressiveness and effectiveness criteria and all the definitions presented in this chapter, the following algorithm chooses a visual structure and a related visual mapping for a given set of user-selected attributes.

1. Define X as the user-selected attributes.
2. Identify all sink attributes. A sink attribute is an attribute functionally determined by all other user-selected attributes, transitively or not.
3. If X has just a single sink attribute, this attribute will be mapped to an output variable, because it is defined by all other selected attributes. In this case:
    a. Lasting attributes will be mapped as input variables.
    b. If there is only one input variable (and therefore only two attributes were selected), two situations may happen:
        i. If the output variable is quantitative and the input variable is ordinal or nominal, create a bar chart. Its horizontal and vertical axes must represent the input and

output variables, respectively, which respects the bar chart restriction $H \rightarrow V$. (End.)

ii. Otherwise, create a heatmap without legends. Its vertical and horizontal axes must represent the input and output variables, respectively. (End.)

c. If there are 2 input variables, and the output variable is not nominal:
    i. Create a heatmap with legend. Its horizontal and vertical axes must represent both input variables, and the legend must represent the output variable. This configuration obeys the heatmap restriction $HV \rightarrow L$. (End.)

d. Otherwise, there are not visual structures available, suitable for representing query results. (End.)

4. If X does not have a sink attribute, only one of the following situations must happen:
    a. If all X attributes are quantitative, create a bar chart. Merge all X attributes into a single input variable. Map this variable to the bar chart horizontal axis. The vertical axis represents quantities related to each X attribute, which constitutes an output variable generated by merging. (End).
    b. If all X attributes are ordinal temporal, create a heatmap without legend. Similarly to the previous situation, merge all X attributes into a single variable. However, map this variable to the vertical axis instead of the horizontal one. The horizontal axis must be mapped to time, which constitutes an output variable generated by merging. (End.)
    c. Consider an attribute A such that A $\notin$ X. If all X attributes determine A, create a heatmap without legend. Map

A to an output variable, which must be mapped to the horizontal axis. As in previous steps, merge X attributes into a single variable, and map this variable to the vertical axis. (End.)

d. Consider that X has only 2 selected attributes, A and B, and that there is an attribute C, which functionally determines both. In this case, take A and B as input variables. A new binary output variable O is defined by a function f, defined as follows: given $a \in A$ and $b \in B$, define f(C,a,b)=true if there exists $c \in C$ such that a, b and c share at least one of the universal relation tuples; otherwise, f(C,a,b)= false. Create a heatmap without legend, whose axes map A and B. The output variable O determines the existence or absence of marks in each possible coordinate of the heatmap.

e. Otherwise, there are no available visual structures suitable for representing query results. (End.)

5. Otherwise, if there are more than one sink attribute, there are no available visual structures suitable for representing query results. (End.)

Figure 3 summarizes this algorithm. It is important to highlight that the presented algorithm considers only heatmaps and bar charts as available visual structures. Future extensions of this algorithm must consider other possible visual structures.

3.1.4. Alternative Visual Structures for Selected Data

Shneiderman (1996) states in his Visual Information Seeking Mantra–"overview first, zoom and filter, then details on demand"-a data navigational approach by which users should first see a overview of the data and then navigate through the details.

JInfoVis approach agrees with this mantra, but with a slight different way of providing details.

Among the visual structures provided by JInfoVis, heatmap is the one that represents more variables at the same time (three, when using legends), and then it is the most general one. If a user asks for details of a heatmap line or column, the result for this kind of query also must be effectively represented. Suppose that A, B and C are three variables visually mapped to the vertical axis, horizontal axis and legends of a heatmap, respectively. If the user asks details about a value $a_1 \in A$, he/she is not interested in other values of A, and therefore A does not need to be represented at the heatmap. Removing A from it, there is a free vertical axis at the heatmap. In order to provide a more effective visual mapping of data, C should move from legends to this vertical axis. Variable A may be mapped to a single-value selection filter, closer to the heatmap, and with a_1 as a preselected value. If C is an ordinal or nominal variable, the previous solution fits well. However, if C is a quantitative variable, it is more expressive to represent B and C through a bar chart instead of a heatmap. Figure 4 shows this situation.

Indeed, this kind of operation does not reveal more data (and, therefore, should not be called a "detail-on-demand" operation), but it aims to enable a correct visual comparison of the selected data.

As presented, LMS Database Explorer defines a visual structure (and its related visual mapping) for representing user's query results. JInfoVis, presented in the following section, is responsible for executing queries, drawing visual structures and enabling user interactions.

3.2. JInfoVis

JInfoVis is an Information Visualization toolkit prototype. It provides infrastructure for querying a database and for showing visual structures and associated widgets for users. JInfoVis was created in the context of LMS data analysis, aiming to ease

Figure 3. Summarized decision tree for choosing a visual structure

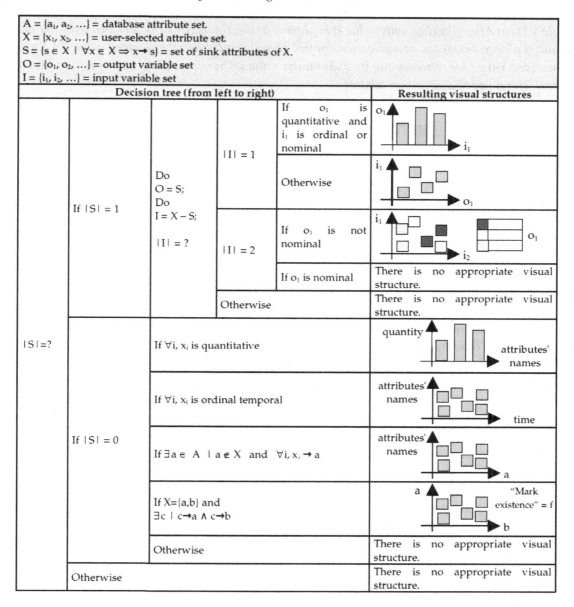

observation of data relevant for analyzing user behaviors and for course-related decision making. Despite this, JInfoVis may be used in other data analysis contexts which are not related to LMS.

JInfoVis was conceived according to a set of principles defined by the authors' previous experience on using InfoVis concepts at TelEduc, and by analysis about more intense use of InfoVis techniques for visually representing LMS data. These principles, considered as requirements for defining JInfoVis, are presented in the following subsections. Some considerations about how to show attributes for users are also presented.

Figure 4. Example of accessing more detailed views of data (a) A heatmap representing two variables by axis (V1,V2) and a third one by legend (V3) A user asks details about the selected line (value B of variable V1) (b) After filtering, only value B is present at the Y-axis (c) V1 is removed from the graphic itself and is placed besides it, at a selection control This control shows the selected value B V3 may use the dismissed Y-axis for representing its quantitative values Therefore, the visual structure becomes a bar chart with a coupled selection control

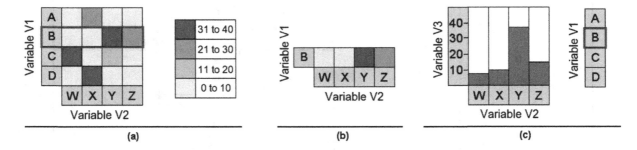

3.2.1. InfoVis-Related Characteristics

The following InfoVis-related requirements determined JInfoVis development:

- Avoid excessive use of numeric representation of data, in order to reduce users' cognitive effort for data comprehension.

- Enable users to access different levels of data generalization, as presented in Section 3.1.4. JInfoVis does not define what visual structure may represent details about data selected in another visual structure. However, it enables programmers to define what happens when the user asks details about a subset of the presented data, and here programmers may invoke a second visual structure or any kind of detail information.

- Also according to Shneiderman's mantra, provide for users filtering capabilities, such as dynamic query filters (Ahlberg & Shneiderman, 1994) and direct selection mechanisms, in order to hide irrelevant data.

- Provide data reordering capabilities for users, obeying visual structure organization.

Spence (2001) points out that this kind of rearrangement may provide new insights about data.

- Use simple visual structures, with few variables, in order to ease data understanding. Given that heatmaps may represent two or three variables, and bar charts two variables, these are the visual structures implemented by JInfoVis, as already mentioned in this chapter. Node-link diagrams are also implemented by JInfoVis, but they were not used in the context of this work.

- Ease dataset comparison by users, avoiding motor and cognitive overhead. In order to accomplish this, the following sub-requirements (related to direct manipulation concept) must be attended:
  - Enable users to define query parameters about data to be analyzed, and provide in the same query window the data resulted from query execution.
  - Provide responsive interaction (Spence, 2001), reflecting instantaneously into the presented dataset each query parameter change.
  - Provide query parameter change by user interaction through keyboard

(e. g. entering a data interval) or by pointing devices (e. g. dragging a range slider).

○ Provide undo and redo capabilities.

3.2.2. Query Execution Requirements

One of the JInfoVis responsibilities is executing queries in the LMS database. The main requirements related to this task are:

- Allow for querying LMS database every time it is necessary–and not just at application startup – because JInfoVis interactions may demand more data after presenting a visual structure.

- Avoid querying LMS database frequently.

- Provide secure and remote querying capabilities, because LMS database will not be stored in the users' computers, but in a remote server.

- Allow for the execution of interpretation algorithms for querying LMS databases according to the universal relation model. An interpretation algorithm related to an attribute set X must determine a set of lossless joins among the database relations which contain X. This requirement is an LMS Database Explorer demand.

3.2.3. Preparing Data for User Comprehension

In order to enable users to understand a dataset, it is relevant to prepare data before presenting them. This is necessary because a database may have attributes and values that make sense only for database and system designers, and not for system users. Concerning this, this section presents situations which must be taken into consideration for enhancing user understanding about data.

The already presented concerning about showing attribute names (Section 3.2) also applies to the time when attributes will be presented by JInfoVis. This may happen when many attributes are mapped to a single variable, and hence attribute names are presented at the visual structure axes.

This only-understandable-by-programmers problem related to attributes names also applies to attribute values. These values may be system-defined codes related to system states (e.g., single-character attributes such as "N," "R," and "A" are not directly meaningful for users but, for a mail system, they may represent new, read and answered messages, respectively). Meaningful descriptions of these values must be presented for users instead of the original values, in order to enhance their understanding about data. Similarly, the attributes null values also may have an implicit meaning that must be clarified for the user.

Substitute keys require also some attention. A substitute key (defined by Date (1986) as "substitute") is a system-defined immutable single-attribute primary key, e.g. an auto-increment attribute. Once its values only matters for the system itself and not for users, a simple approach (A) is avoiding users to select this kind of attribute. A second approach (B) is presenting each of these attributes for users (because they represent a single database table tuple), but showing values of another attribute which is more relevant for users than the primary key artificial codes. For example, suppose a database table *User(user-id, name, address, phone-number)*; if a user asks for user-id values, the system may show name values instead, which are more descriptive than user-id codes.

Foreign key attributes that point to substitute keys also have system-defined values, and hence they may be transformed into descriptive values by the same A and B approaches, previously presented. (E.g. if a user asks for user-id values of the table *Participation(user-id, class-id)*, and Participation.user-id is a foreign key that points to User.user-id, the system may present User.name values instead of Participation.user-id ones, according to B approach). Indeed, B was the approach implemented by JInfoVis.

In order to meet all of the stated problems, JInfoVis must have access to LMS database metadata which must hold descriptions of attributes values and names. JInfoVis must also access LMS database schema in order to analyze tables' foreign and substitute keys.

3.3. Prototype architecture

Both JInfoVis and LMS Database Explorer were implemented according to the architecture presented in Figure 5. In this architecture, the LMS database and its metadata are stored in the LMS server. A JInfoVis module called Request, which mediates the acquisition of data from the database, is a servlet that also resides in the LMS server. The remaining system runs in the users' web browser as a Java applet.

According to the presented architecture, LMS Database Explorer initially gets LMS database metadata. After a user asks a query, LMS Database Explorer interacts with JInfoVis (through Request module); the former informs the latter about the query to be executed in the LMS database. The request module executes the query, obtains its results and feed them back with the information. When LMS Database Explorer receives these results, it stores these data in the Internal Structure module, which stores the data into a specific data structure. Finally, LMS Database Explorer uses Visual Structure module for defining what visual structure will be connected to the stored data, that is, which data must be shown by the defined visual structure. User interactions may ask more details about a data subset. LMS Database Ex-

plorer answers this event with another visual structure, which demands a new dataset. Hence, the request-and-show cycle restarts.

The system uses TelEduc (Rocha et al., 2002) as its subjacent LMS, and accesses its database and its related metadata. Given that neither JInfoVis nor LMS Database Explorer depends on TelEduc implementation, the overall system works also with another LMS whose data persistence layer is managed by a relational DBMS. Future developments may connect the implemented system to another LMS, such as Moodle and TIDIA-Ae.

3.4. Implemented Prototype

The prototype system was implemented according to the previously presented characteristics, and the following figures depict it. In Figure 6, a user executes LMS Database Explorer. This figure shows a list of LMS database attributes related to the subject Discussion Forums ("Fóruns de Discussão", in Portuguese). He chooses the following attributes: "discussion forums messages date", "discussion forums", and "discussion forums messages – quantity". At the bottom of the figure, the system informs that a heatmap is available for interconnecting the selected attributes values.

When user press the "Show graph" ("Exibir gráfico", in Portuguese) button, the system runs a query on the LMS database and then shows Figure 7, which illustrates JInfoVis in action. It shows the selected database attributes as elements of a heatmap, which presents the quantity of forum messages (represented as color) by forums (at y-axis) and by message date (at x-axis).

Figure 5. System architecture

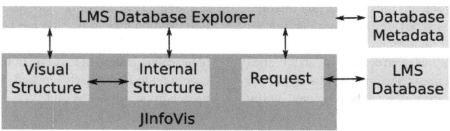

304

Figure 6. User selecting LMS database attributes

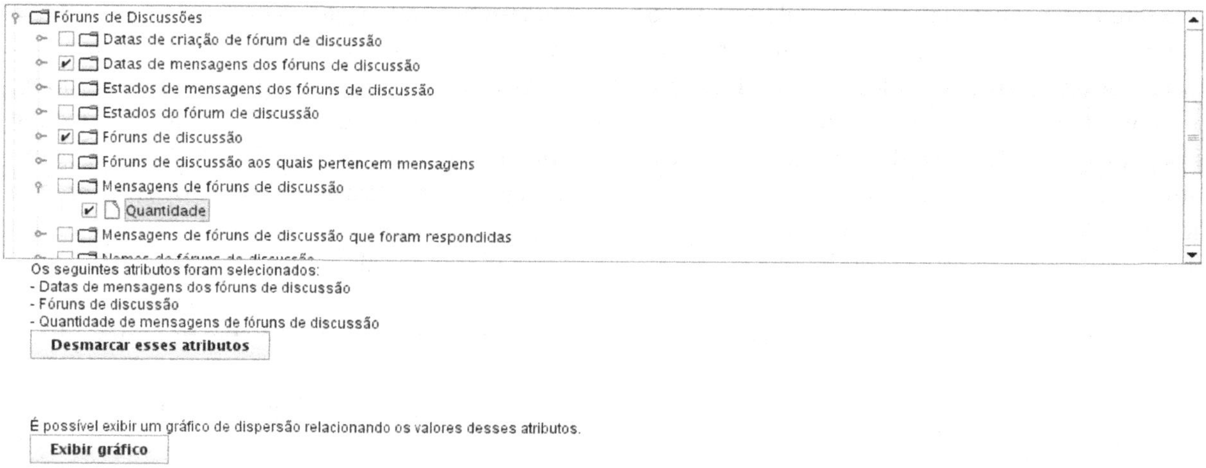

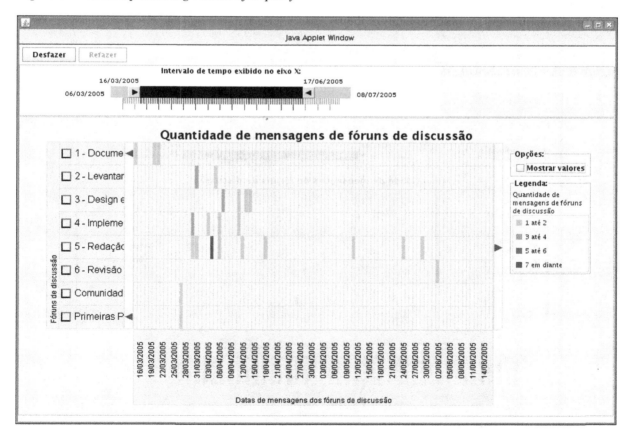

Figure 7. A heatmap showing results of a query

If user asks an alternative view for a dataset presented at a heatmap line or column, LMS Database Explorer defines a new visual structure for better presenting the selected data. Figure 8 presents this situation, in which a user selects another view for a heatmap line (a selected discussion forum). The visual structure used for presenting this view is a bar chart with the remaining attributes ("discussion forums messages date" and "discussion forums messages – quantity"). An available listbox enable user to change what discussion forum the presented data refers to.

3.5. Prototype Evaluation

The implemented prototype was evaluated through a preliminary evaluation with three phases. In the first one, a set of LMS-related questions to be answered in the following phases was defined. In phase II, the author used the prototype for trying to answer the proposed questions. Phase III was a study case with users, in order to analyze their difficulty for using the prototype when answering the proposed questions. A detailed version of this evaluation is documented elsewhere (Silva, 2006).

Four users were involved in this evaluation; two of them are graduated in Computing and the other two in Education. All users have strong experience with e-learning courses offered through TelEduc, and provided valuable commentaries and suggestions about the software.

In phase I, these users and the author proposed questions to be answered by the prototype. Their experience with e-learning courses inspired them to come up with relevant questions in this context. A heterogeneous list of questions was proposed, with 5 questions proposed by the author, and 34 by the users. The following list presents some of these questions:

1. What participants are recently accessing the e-learning environment?

Figure 8. Bar chart showing data presented by the fifth line of previous heatmap

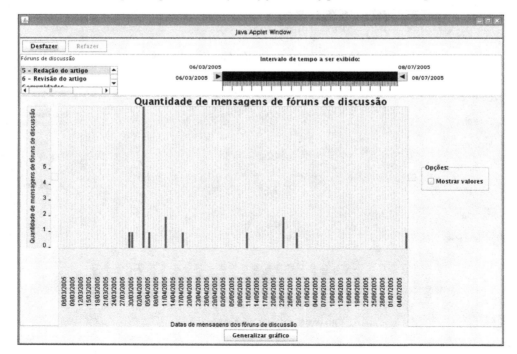

2. How intense has message sending at the Forum Discussion been by participant in the course?

3. How course participants have been talking to each other at the Chat tool?

4. How many (and which) students stopped to access the environment?

5. How many (and which) students have been using communication tools?

6. Which participant commented the production of which other participants?

7. What tools were more used by each user in a defined period?

8. What type of communication takes place more often: student-student or teacher-student? Is there equilibrium? (Analyze these types of communication in distinct periods of the course).

The heterogeneity of the proposed questions reinforces the necessity of a flexible tool like the proposed one, which tries to fit not only predefined questions about LMS, but also new questions created on demand.

In phase II, the author tried to answer the proposed questions. From the 34 proposed questions, 7 were not considered for the study because their answers would need either some data that are not stored in the LMS database, or data from functionalities that were incorporated to LMS after the prototype development. From the remaining 27 questions, 11 (40.7%) were completely answered, 9 (33.3%) were partially answered, and 7 (26.0%) were not answered.

Figure 9 presents an example of the completely answered question "How many (and which) students have been using communication tools?". In order to answer it, three database attributes were selected: "users' most recently date accesses", "tools accessed by users", and "users that accessed TelEduc, or one of its tools". For these selected attributes, the prototype generated a heatmap in which tools are presented at the Y axis, users at the X axis, and data accesses by color. Light green represents most recent accesses. Given this figure, the author could see the communication-related tools, its related light green cells and their respective students.

Questions that were partially answered or not answered at all are related to absent functionalities, such as calculating percentages or mathematical expressions combining distinct attributes values. They were also related to the selection of attribute sets to which the prototype did not know how to generate a graphical representation. Some questions also revealed little system inconsistencies to be corrected.

The objectives of the third evaluation phase were 1) to analyze how difficult it was expressing queries through database attribute selection; 2) to analyze how difficult it was answering these queries, using the prototype-selected graphical representations; and 3) to obtain opinions about the prototype, which includes suggestions for its improvement. For this phase, user interactions with the prototype were recorded. These recordings enabled further analysis about which attributes were selected in order to answer each question, and about what output graph users expected to be presented by the prototype. It was also collected users' comments made along and after the prototype use.

All four users tried to answer the 5 questions elaborated by the author, except one user, which tried to answer only 4. From these 19 attempts, 16 (84%) generated a graph that helped users to answer these questions, either completely or partially.

Each user also tried to answer the questions he/she had created in phase one of this evaluation process. From these 26 questions, 14 (53.8%) were completely or partially answered (34.6% were completely answered and 19.2% were partially answered), and 12 (46.2%) were not answered.

As an example, Figure 10 shows a user answering the question "What was the intensity of Discussion Forums messages sent by participant in the course?". The user first selected two attributes – "Discussion Forums messages–quantity"

Figure 9. Most recent date of LMS tools accesses

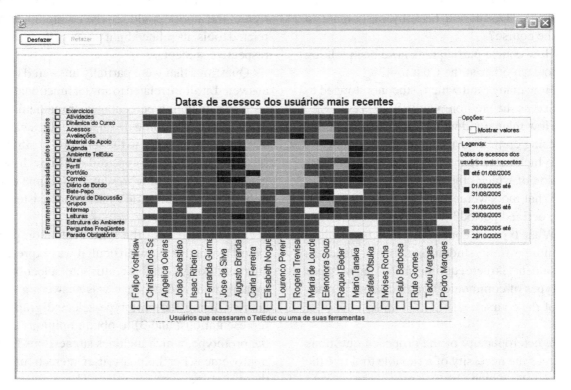

and "Users who wrote forums messages". The prototype then shows a bar chart with the quantity of forum messages by message author.

Users also filled in a post-use evaluation form. Their answers show that they had a good impression of the prototype. Those users agree that the prototype helps to analyze TelEduc data. According to the evaluation, users did not consider answering a query by the prototype a hard task. Their answer revealed that the presented visual representations were relevant and that the controls for data filtering and selection were very useful. Users' main suggestions in this evaluation were for taking care with attributes description (specially avoiding ambiguous attribute names), quantity of available attributes and prototype usability.

4. FUTURE RESEARCH DIRECTIONS

As presented in the Section 2, there is a multitude of LMS, including some open source systems such as TelEduc and Moodle. *Ad hoc* solutions have been developed for some of them in order to attend specific user needs of monitoring and/or assessing course participants. This chapter presents an approach which is, as far as I know, the only one that deals the problem of visually revealing data in a more general way.

In the other hand, the amount of software and APIs for data visualization is increasing. Nowadays programmers have good visualization APIs such as Prefuse, JIT, Data-Driven Documents and Google Chart Tools, which implement lots of interactive visual representations, mainly in Java and JavaScript. These tools are important accelerators for the prototyping and development of InfoVis solutions for e-learning and other domains.

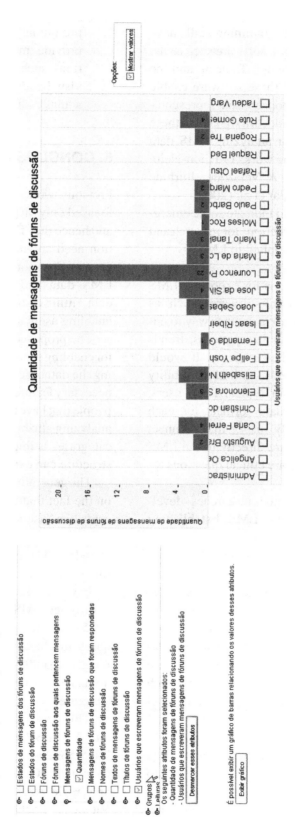

Figure 10. A user answers the question "What was the intensity of Discussion Forums message sent by course participant?" At the left, attribute selection screen At the right, graphical representation generated by the users attribute-based query This representation shows the number of messages sent by course participant into Discussion Forums tool

Besides, users without programming skills have available good visualization software such as the commercial tools Spotfire and Tableau, and the IBM Many Eyes site; all these software enable users to insert data and choose visual representations for representing it. Indeed, a signal that these software may be used for analyzing LMS data was just pointed out by the works of Hijón-Neira et al. (2008), Hijón-Neira & Velázquez-Iturbide (2008), and Gómez-Aguilar et al. (2008).

Therefore, it is worth to indicate some emerging and possible future directions for research and development in InfoVis applied to LMS:

- Providing mechanisms for exporting LMS data to visualization software (such as Tableau and Spotfire) is another way to enable teachers to visualize patterns, trends and outliers into their courses. It would be necessary to study both the usability of these software for typical LMS users, and the adequate data formats for each software. Optionally, users may connect visualization software directly to the LMS database, but there are ethical questions related to this option.

- Each of the presented researches developed tools for a single LMS. Establishing a common interface (such as an API or a web service) for obtaining data from LMS would improve software reuse and enable InfoVis tool exchange among distinct LMS. In this sense, SCORM (ADL, 2009) and AICC guidelines (AICC, 2004) are starting points for defining how to exchange learning resources; however, these works do not seem to deal with data such as accesses to LMS and interaction between course participants.

- E-learning and computer science researchers should direct efforts for evaluating the real impacts of adopting InfoVis tools into LMS scenario. There are lots of proposed visualizations but some works did only preliminary evaluation steps. One should provide more reliable answers for questions such as what are the most relevant visualizations for e-learning and how they actually affect this scenario.

5. CONCLUSION

Previous works from InfoVis related to LMS focused only on predefined subsets of LMS data, and hence they fit only a subset of users' information need about LMS stored data. This chapter presented a more general solution for querying LMS data and for representing the obtained data, fitting distinct LMS data analysis needs and enabling users to graphically analyze these data.

The proposed solution uses universal relation for enabling users to specify queries without knowing the database internal organization, which is a necessary feature for enabling the prototype use by people that have no database knowledge. Besides, analyzing attributes functional dependencies and categories is important for mapping what visual structure can express an attribute set.

The generality of the proposed solution resides on the fact that it is not connected to LMS concepts like "users", "discussion forum messages," or "tools", but to LMS databases and related metadata. Therefore, one may create extensions for connecting other LMS to the prototype.

Future works may focus on: using the prototype with other LMS (like TIDIA-Ae (Beder et al., 2005)) and with new TelEduc tools; enhancing query mechanisms and usability; internationalizing; expanding the tool for other knowledge domains; and implementing and using more visual structures.

This research was supported by CAPES and FAPESP (processes 2004/08233-5 and 2005/56629-8). Author thanks University of Campinas' General Coordination for its valuable reviews. He also thanks Prof. Dr. Heloisa Vieira da Rocha for all guidance provided for the author through his entire undergraduate and doctoral studies; Nucleus of Informatics Applied to Education (NIED) and Institute of Computing (IC) of University of Campinas, where this work was developed; and School of Technology, where this chapter was written.

REFERENCES

Advanced Distributed Learning–ADL. (2009). SCORM® 2004 4th edition-content aggregation model (CAM), version 1.1. *Department of Defense, United States of America.* Retrieved from http://www.adlnet.gov/capabilities/scorm/scorm-2004-4th.

Ahlberg, C., & Shneiderman, B. (1994). Visual information seeking: Tight coupling of dynamic query filters with starfield displays. In *Proceedings of ACM Conference on Human Factors in Computing Systems*, 313-317. New York: ACM Press.

AICC. (2004). CMI guidelines for interoperability, revision 4.0. *AICC CMI Subcommittee.* Retrieved from http://www.aicc.org/joomla/dev/index.php?option=com_content&view=article&id=64&Itemid=28.

Beder, D. M., Otsuka, J. L., Silva, C. G., Silva, A. C., Talarico, N., et al., & Silva, J. C. A. (2005) The TIDIA-Ae portfolio tool: A case study of its development following a component-based layered architecture. In *Proceedings of 2nd Workshop TIDIA FAPESP*. São Paulo, Brazil: FAPESP Press.

Card, S. K., Mackinlay, J. D., & Shneiderman, B. (1999). *Readings in information visualization: Using vision to think*. San Francisco: Morgan Kaufman Publishers.

Date, C. J. (1986). *An introduction to database systems, 1* (4th ed.). Boston: Addison-Wesley.

Elmasri, R., & Navathe, S. (2000). *Fundamentals of database systems* (3rd ed.). Boston: Addison Wesley.

Foroughi, R., & Taponecco, F. (2005). A visualization tool for student assessment and evaluation in online learning. In *Proceedings of IADIS International Conference on Applied Computing*, 68-73. IADIS Press.

France, L., Heraud, J.-M., Marty, J.-C., & Carron, T. (2005). Help through visualization to compare learners' activities to recommended learning scenarios. In *Proceedings of the Fifth IEEE International Conference on Advanced Learning Technologies*, 476-480. Washington, DC: IEEE Press.

France, L., Heraud, J.-M., Marty, J.-C., Carron, T., & Heili, J. (2006). Monitoring virtual classroom: visualization techniques to observe student activities in an e-learning system. In *Proceedings of the Sixth International Conference on Advanced Learning Technologies*, 716-720. Washington, DC: IEEE Press.

Gómez-Aguilar, D. A., Conde-González, M. Á., Therón, R., & García-Peñalvo, F. J. (2011). Revealing the evolution of semantic content through visual analysis. In *Proceedings of the 11th IEEE International Conference on Advanced Learning Technologies*, 450-454. Washington, DC: IEEE Press.

Gómez-Aguilar, D. A., Guerrero, C. S., Sanchez, R. T., Therón, R., & García-Peñalvo, F. J. (2010). Visual analytics to support e-learning. In Rosson (Ed.), Advances in Learning Processes (207-228). Rijeka, Croatia: InTech. doi:doi:10.5772/7932 doi:10.5772/7932.

Gómez-Aguilar, D. A., Therón, R., & García-Peñalvo, F. (2008). Understanding educational relationships in Moodle with ViMoodle. In *Proceedings of the Eighth IEEE International Conference on Advanced Learning Technologies*, 954-956. Washington, DC: IEEE Press.

Gómez-Aguilar, D. A., Therón, R., & García-Peñalvo, F. (2009). Semantic spiral timelines used as support for e-learning. *Journal of Universal Computer Science*, 15(7), 1526–1545.

Hardless, C., & Nulden, U. (1999). Visualizing learning activities to support tutors. In *Proceedings of Conference on Human Factors in Computing Systems (CHI)*. Pittsburgh, Pennsylvania: ACM Press.

Hijón-Neira, R. Velázquez-Iturbide, J. Á., Barn, B., & Oussena, S. (2008). A comparative study on the analysis of students interactions in e-learning. In *Proceedings of Eighth IEEE International Conference on Advanced Learning Technologies*, 20-22. Washington, DC: IEEE Press.

Hijón-Neira, R., & Velázquez-Iturbide, J. Á. (2008). How to improve assessment of learning and performance through interactive visualization. In *Proceedings of Eighth IEEE International Conference on Advanced Learning Technologies*, 472-476. Washington, DC: IEEE Press.

Huang, M. L., Nguyen, Q. V., & Hintz, T. (2005). Attributed graph visualization of collaborative workspaces. In *Proceedings of the Computer Graphics, Imaging and Vision: New Trends (CGIV)*, 155-161. Washington, DC: IEEE Press.

Klerkx, J., Duval, E., & Meire, M. (2004). Using information visualization for accessing learning object repositories. In *Proceedings of the Eighth IEEE International Conference on Information Visualisation (IV)*, 465-470. Washington, DC: IEEE Press.

Mackinlay, J. D. (1986). Automating the design of graphical presentations of relational information. *ACM Transactions on Graphics*, 5(2), 110–141. doi:10.1145/22949.22950.

Martín, M., Álvarez, A., Fernández-Castro, I., Reina, D., & Urretavizcaya, M. (2011) Experiences in visualizing the analysis of blended-learning interactions to support teachers. In *Proceedings of 11th IEEE International Conference on Advanced Learning Technologies*, 265-266. Washington, DC: IEEE Press.

Mazza, R. (2006). A graphical tool for monitoring the usage of modules in course management systems. In *Proceedings of Visual Information Expert Workshop*. Paris, VIEW Press.

Mazza, R., & Dimitrova, V. (2005). Generation of graphical representations of student tracking data in course management systems. In *Proceedings of the 9th IEEE International Conference on Information Visualisation*. London: IEEE Press.

Mazza, R., & Milani, C. (2005). Exploring usage analysis in learning systems: gaining insights from visualisations. In *Proceedings of the 12th International Conference on Artificial Intelligence in Education (AIED)*, 65-72. Amsterdam: IOS Press.

Nguyen, Q. V., & Huang, M. L. (2005). EncCon: An approach to constructing interactive visualization of large hierarchical data. *Information Visualization*, 4(1), 1–21. doi:10.1057/palgrave. ivs.9500087.

Otsuka, J. L. (2006). *Multi-Agent Model to Formative Assessment Support at Learning*. (Doctoral thesis). Campinas, Brazil, University of Campinas.

Otsuka, J. L., & Rocha, H. V. (2007). A multi-agent formative assessment support model for learning management systems. In *Proceedings of the 7th IEEE International Conference on Advanced Learning Technologies*. Niigata, Japan: IEEE Press.

Rocha, H. V., Kropiwiec, D. D., Fukaya, S. M., Neto, J. C., Gayard, L. A., et al., & Ferreira, T. B. (2002). TelEduc project: Technology research and development for distance learning. In *Proceedings of IX Brazilian Association of Distance Education International Congress of Distance Learning*. Available at http://www.teleduc.org.br/artigos/premio_abed2002.pdf.

Romani, L. A. S. (2000). *InterMap: Tool for Visualizing Interaction in Distance Learning Environments on Web*. (Master thesis). Campinas, Brazil, University of Campinas.

Saltz, J. S., Hiltz, S. R., & Turoff, M. (2004). Student social graphs: Visualizing a student's online social network. In *Proceedings of ACM Conference on Computer Supported Collaborative Work (CSCW)*. Chicago: ACM Press.

Shneiderman, B. (1994). Dynamic queries for visual information seeking. *IEEE Software*, *11*(6), 70–77. doi:10.1109/52.329404.

Shneiderman, B. (1996). The eyes have it: A task by data type taxonomy for information visualizations. In *Proceedings of IEEE Symposium on Visual Languages*, 336-343. Washington, DC: IEEE Press.

Silva, C. G. (2006). *Learning Management Systems' Database Exploration by Means of Information Visualization-Based Query Tools*. (Doctoral thesis). Campinas, Brazil, University of Campinas.

Silva, C. G., & Rocha, H. V. (2004). Contributions of information visualization for distance learning area. In *Proceedings of VI Brazilian Symposium on Human Factors in Computing Systems (IHC)*. Curitiba, Brazil: IHC Press.

Silva, C. G., & Rocha, H. V. (2007). Learning management systems' database exploration by means of information visualization-based query tools. In *Proceedings of Seventh International Conference on Advanced Learning Technologies (ICALT)*, 543-545. Washington, DC: IEEE Press.

Spence, R. (2001). *Information Visualization* (1st ed.). Boston: Addison-Wesley.

Teutsch, P., & Bourdet, J.-F. (2010). How to see training paths in learning management systems? In *Proceedings of 10th IEEE International Conference on Advanced Learning Technologies*, 349-351. Washington, DC: IEEE Press.

Tufte, E. R. (1990). *Envisioning information*. Chechire, CT: Graphics Press.

Tzoumakas, V., & Theodoulidis, B. (2005). Force based visualizations for instructor support. In *Proceedings of the Fifth IEEE International Conference on Advanced Learning Technologies (ICALT)*, 452-456. Washington, DC: IEEE Press.

Ullman, J. D. (1982). *Principles of database systems* (2nd ed.). Washington, DC: Computer Science Press.

Ware, C. (2004). *Information visualization: Perception for design*. San Francisco: Morgan-Kaufmann Publishers.

ADDITIONAL READING

Advanced Distributed Learning–ADL. (2009). *ADL web site*. Retrieved from http://www.adlnet.org/.

Affero. (2011). *AulaNet–Pioneer, innovator, and complete LMS*. Retrieved from http://www.eduweb.com.br/aulanet/.

AICC. (2004). *Aviation industry CBT committee (AICC) web site*. Retrieved from http://www.aicc.org.

Bakharia, A., & Dawson, S. (2011). Snapp: A bird's-eye view of temporal participant interaction. In *Proceedings of the 1st International Conference on Learning Analytics and Knowledge (LAK)*, 168-173. New York: ACM.

Berkeley Institute of Design. (2012). *Prefuse–Interactive information visualization toolkit.* Retrieved from http://prefuse.org.

Blackboard. (2012). *Blackboard site.* Retrieved from www.blackboard.com.

Bostock, M. (2012). D3.js–Data-driven documents. Web site. Retrieved from http://d3js.org.

Costagliola, G., Fuccella, V., Giordano, M., & Polese, G. (2009). Monitoring online tests through data visualization. *IEEE Transactions on Knowledge and Data Engineering, 21*(6), 773–784. doi:10.1109/TKDE.2008.133.

Dario, D. (2010). *Application of Techniques of Information Visualization to Support Formative Assessment in E-Learning Systems.* (Master dissertation). Campinas, Brazil, University of Campinas.

Dokeos Company. (2012). *Dokeos–Open source e-learning.* Retrieved from http://www.dokeos.com.

Donath, J., Karahalios, K., & Viégas, F. (1999). Visualizing conversation. *Journal of Computer-Mediated Communication 4*(4). Retrieved from http://dx.doi.org/10.1111/j.1083-6101.1999.tb00107.x.

Eskildsen, S., Rodil, K., & Rehm, M. (2012). Visualizing learner activities with a virtual learning environment: Experiences from an in situ test with primary school children. In *Proceedings of the IEEE International Conference on Advanced Learning Technologies (ICALT)*, 660-661. Washington, DC: IEEE Press.

García-Solórzano, D., Morán, J. A., Cobo, G., Monzo, C., Santamaría, E., & Melenchón, J. (2012). Educational monitoring tool based on faceted browsing and data portraits. In *Proceedings of the 2nd International Conference on Learning Analytics and Knowledge*, 170-178. New York: ACM.

Gomez-Aguilar, D., Conde-Gonzalez, M., Theron, R., & Garcia-Peñalvo, F. (2011). Supporting moodle-based lesson through visual analysis. *Human-computer interaction–INTERACT 2011. Lecture Notes in Computer Science, 6949*, 604–607. doi:10.1007/978-3-642-23768-3_93.

Google. (2012). *Google chart tools.* Retrieved from https://developers.google.com/chart.

Hemphill, L., & Teasley, S. D. (2010). Overherd: Designing information visualizations to make sense of students' online discussions. In *Proceedings of the 9th International Conference of the Learning Sciences-Volume 2*, 302-303. New York: ACM Press.

Hijón-Neira, R., & Velázquez-Iturbide, J. Á. (2011). Merlin-Mo, An interactions analysis system for Moodle. In *Proceedings of the 16th Annual Joint Conference on Innovation and Technology in Computer Science Education*, 340-340. New York: ACM Press.

IBM. (2012). *Many eyes.* Retrieved from http://www-958.ibm.com/software/data/cognos/many-eyes.

LRN. (2012). *LRN–Learn, research, network.* Retrieved from http://dotlrn.org.

LTSC. (2012). *IEEE learning technology standards committee (LTSC) web site.* Retrieved from http://www.ieeeltsc.org.

Mazza, R. (2004). *Using Information Visualisation to Facilitate Instructors in Web-based Distance Learning.* (Ph.D. Thesis). Lugano, Switzerland, University of Lugano.

Mazza, R. (2010). Visualization in educational environments. In Romero, Ventura, Pechenizkiy, & Backer (eds.). Handbook of Educational Data Mining (9-26). New York: CRC Press. doi:doi:10.1201/b10274-4 doi:10.1201/b10274-4.

Mazza, R., & Nidola, M. (2012). *GISMO–Graphical interactive student monitoring tool for moodle*. Retrieved from http://gismo.sourceforge.net.

Moodle. (2012). *Moodle–Project site*. Retrieved from www.moodle.org.

NIED/UNICAMP. (2012). *TelEduc–Project site*. Retrieved from www.teleduc.org.br.

Rabbany, R., Takaffoli, M., & Zaïane, O. R. (2011). Social network analysis and mining to support the assessment of online student participation. *ACM SIGKDD Explorations Newsletter, 13*(2), 20–29. doi:10.1145/2207243.2207247.

Rocha, H. V., Oeiras, J. Y., & Romani, L. A. S. (2001). Communication, visualization and social aspects involved on a virtual collaborative learning environment. *Journal of Three Dimensional Images, 15*(3), 122–126.

Romani, L. A. S., & Rocha, H. V. (2000). Interaction map: Information visualization techniques in web-based distance education environments. *Technical Report (IC-00-17)*. Campinas, Brazil: Institute of Computing, University of Campinas. Retrieved from http://www.ic.unicamp.br/~reltech/2000/00-17.pdf.

Sakai Foundation. (2012). *Sakai Project–Collaboration and learning–For educators by educators*. Retrieved from http://www.sakaiproject.org.

SenchaLabs. (2011). *JavaScript InfoVis toolkit*. Retrieved from http://thejit.org.

Tableau Software. (2012). *Tableau Software web site*. Retrieved from http://www.tableausoftware.com.

TIBCO Software. (2012). *TIBCO spotfire–Business intelligence analytics software & data visualization*. Retrieved from http://spotfire.tibco.com.

Xiong, R., & Donath, J. (1999). PeopleGarden: Creating data portraits for users. In *Proceedings of the 12th Annual ACM Symposium on User Interface Software and Technology (UIST)*, 37-44. New York: ACM Press.

Zhang, H., Almeroth, K., Knight, A., Bulger, M., & Mayer, R. (2007). Moodog: Tracking students' online learning activities. In *Proceedings of World Conference on Educational Multimedia, Hypermedia and Telecommunications*, 4415-4422. Chesapeake, VA: AACE Press.

KEY TERMS AND DEFINITIONS

CMI: Computer Managed Instruction. Another name for LMS.

CMS: Content Management System. Sometimes this name is used as a synonym of an entire LMS or of a subset of its tools.

DBMS: Database Management System.

Heatmap: A matrix whose cells are colored according to their values.

InfoVis: Information Visualization.

LMS: Learning Management System.

SCORM: Shareable Content Object Reference Model.

VLE: Virtual Learning Environment. Another name for LMS.

WebCT: An old LMS which was merged with Blackboard LMS.

Chapter 15

Visualizing Information–Triage:
A Speculative and Metaphoric Interface for Making Sense of Online Searching

Liese Zahabi
Weber State University, USA

ABSTRACT

In many ways, the promise of the Internet has been overshadowed by a sense of information overload and anxiety for many users. The production and publication of online material has become increasingly accessible and affordable, creating a confusing glut of information users must sift through to locate exactly what they want or need. Even a fundamental Google search can often prove paralyzing. In this chapter, the author examines the points at which design plays a role in the online search process, reconciles those points with the nature of sensemaking and the limitations of working memory, and suggests ways to support users with an information-triage system. The author then describes a speculative online searching prototype that explores these issues and the possibilities for information-triage.

INTRODUCTION

The Complications of Complexity

Search engines like Google allow users access to unimaginable amounts and types of complex information, but the ways in which search results are visualized often makes comparing and contrasting these results difficult. In many ways, the promise of the Internet—easily sharing information via a network of globally connected hyperlinks—has been overshadowed for many users by a sense of

information overload and anxiety. The production and publication of online material has become increasingly accessible and affordable, creating a confusing glut of information users must sift through to locate exactly what they want or need. Moreover, the visual display of this information has remained woefully un-designed, under-designed, and/or unconsidered.

Generations of people who have been trained to passively accept information from sources of vetted authority are now interacting with a dynamic system of globally linked information, raising slip-

DOI: 10.4018/978-1-4666-4309-3.ch015

pery questions that are no longer easy to answer. Is an article in the Encyclopedia Britannica on augmented reality equal to an entry in Wikipedia? Can a blog posting about diabetes be more informative than an appointment with your doctor? In the shifting context of the Internet, credibility and authority should never be assumed, but often are.

Information overload is not a new problem. People have been inundated with increasing levels of information since the Industrial Revolution and the explosion of printed material and resulting mass-media that came along with it (Wright, 2007). What *has* changed in the last twenty years is the ease of access to an unchecked flood of information. According to Clay Shirky (2008), Internet technology writer and academic, what we are experiencing today is not really information overload—it is filter failure. Filters that developed over the last few hundred years to deal with large amounts of information have started to break down as the Internet has moved society from a process of top-down edited publication to one of bottom-up open-source dissemination. Design can (and should) engage with this issue to develop better tools and systems, helping users understand and filter the information they encounter online. One method, which has yet to be fully explored, is information-triage.

The concept of information-triage is derived from the medical process of sorting through and prioritizing patients for care. The word originates from the old French verb *trier*, and means to sift, separate, or select; traditionally, three discrete categories for sorting were used (Merriam-Webster, 2012). A medical triage practitioner must quickly recognize, sort, categorize, and prioritize the status of a given patient—usually in a hierarchically driven and methodical way. Each new case is moved through a system following scripted sets of criteria, allowing less critical cases to be dealt with as time allows, and the most critical cases to be dealt with immediately (O'Meara, 2007).

The concept of triage migrated to the computing and business world as tasks and jobs became increasingly complex, and the amounts of available and accessible data grew exponentially. Other HCI (Human Computer Interaction) and Information Science researchers have begun investigating a related concept known as *document triage*, the manual process of briefly reading through multiple source documents, and quickly making decisions regarding relevance and saliency. These quick decisions allow a user to sort through large quantities of initial documents, which are then explored in more detail depending on user goals and needs (Geng, Laramee, Loizides, & Buchanan, 2011).

However, researchers have found that the document triage process is imperfect, and many users miss relevant sources and connections when using current document search and display technology (Buchanan & Owen, 2008). Information-triage is the selecting, sorting and categorizing of different kinds of information, while document triage is the process of selecting, sorting and categorizing sets of whole documents. These concepts are certainly related, and many aspects of the search process in general are affected by a user's ability to successfully conduct triage.

Part of the anxiety Internet users feel has to do with the shifting nature of the human attention span and the limits of working memory. As users engage with data and information online, they are bombarded with multiple levels of layered material and alternate avenues of discovery. The user encounters countless screens, ads, and links, which are all competing for attention. These short bursts of disjointed data are distracting for even the most focused user, and over time users often forget what they were searching for in the first place. When attempting to gather information to aid an important decision—especially when a search yields conflicting opinions—this chaotic atmosphere can prove paralyzing.

However, users are not without some inherent tools—one human ability being investigated and incorporated into interfaces is *sensemaking*. Studies related to this concept are currently being conducted in many different disciplines including medicine, geography, organizational communications, management and HCI (Pirolli & Russell, 2011). By integrating the findings from sensemaking research into the design of search engine interfaces, users can be given explicit tools to utilize in intuitive and flexible ways.

In this chapter, I will: examine current methods for search result visualization; explore and address the points at which design plays a role in the online search process; investigate those points in relation to the nature of sensemaking and the limitations of working memory; and suggest one way to visualize search results within a metaphorical and speculative interface design that would allow users to benefit from both the use of information-triage, and specifically designed data visualization.

BACKGROUND AND MOTIVATIONS

Content and Visual Analyses of Existing Search Engines

I have conducted an analysis of ten of the most commonly used search engines: Google, Bing, Yahoo, Ask.com, AOL, MyWebSearch, Blekko, Lycos, Dogpile and WebCrawler (eBiz/MBA, 2012). This analysis included an examination of the same six elements of interface design and functionality:

1. Initial search page
2. Search term assistance
3. Search results interface
4. System settings/preferences
5. Advanced search options
6. Basic image search

The analysis found that all ten of the search engines are quite similar in setup, function and overall experience. Most of the interfaces begin with a simple search box page, show results in pages of lists, and have some personal setting

options. A few of the search engines include large photographs, article listings, and popular news stories on the initial search page. Of the ten search engines analyzed, most report on their results pages that they are in some way pulling results from, or powered by, Google. This fact helps to explain why so many of the search engine interfaces are strikingly similar.

All ten of the search engines display results in nearly identical ways. Generally, the interfaces default to showing ten results per display page, with navigation at the bottom that allow users to move on to subsequent pages. Each result listing consists of a title, a URL and some synopsis text pulled from the website listed. The typefaces and styling for this text are identical for all search engines analyzed. In part, this sameness is due to conventions traced back to the first iterations of HTML, and to cultural expectations that have built up over the last few decades.

Most of the search engines, especially the most popular two, Bing and Google, emphasize sponsored results, which are not clearly differentiated from the non-sponsored results. For the most part, these results are labeled as "Ads" in small type, and generally appear in three locations: at the top of the search result listings, in a column on the right-hand side of the interface, and often at the bottom of the page. Some of the interfaces place a lightly shaded box behind these ads, but in all cases the typefaces, style and kinds of language used are identical to the search results themselves. This raises questions and concerns about the credibility and motivations of all the sources listed, as well as the search engines themselves. Users cannot easily distinguish between these two types of inherently different information.

The analysis also found that overall, advanced searches are shallow and limited. None of the ten search engines allows a user to search-within-a-search to narrow her results. Some of the search engines do offer help pages to assist the user with search basics, but in general these pages are difficult to find and poorly organized. Bing and Google offer reasonably robust search help once the pages are found and accessed. The assumption seems to be that users will just type in search terms based on conversational phrases or questions, rather than Boolean phrases or other types of advanced search methods that Information Science professionals utilize.

Of the ten interfaces analyzed, only Google and Blekko truly allow for a faceted search. A faceted search is the assignment of multiple categories and tags to an object, enabling the categories and tags to be ordered in multiple ways. Google allows users to sort result listings by location and time ranges, as well as a somewhat confusing list of specific filter criteria: Sites with Images, Related Searches, Visited Pages, Not Yet Visited, Dictionary, Reading Level, Personal, Nearby, Translated Foreign Pages, and Verbatim. These options are not all self-explanatory, and feel like a list generated by multiple requests or ideas over time and cobbled together, rather than a cohesive and understandable system. Blekko allows users to sort result listings by location and a system of user assigned "slash tags"—labels that users choose and apply to specific results according to whatever criteria they choose. The other search engines allow users to sort by large context categories, but not more specific criteria. Since none of these systems allow for a true search-within-a-search, the facets and distinctions aren't robust enough to help a user narrow her search effectively and efficiently.

Overall, these search engines, especially Google, excel at cataloging the web and returning increasingly accurate results. But the functionality and visualization of both the interface and results is poorly developed, and in many cases, a hindrance to a user's cognitive abilities and needs. When faced with a solid and utterly homogeneous screen of text, most users have trouble discerning among the returned results, because visual, spatial, cognitive and sensemaking cues are not utilized in any meaningful way.

Working Memory: For Better and For Worse

Our brains are overflowing with information—tasks, memories, ideas, conversations—which comes at us in a steady stream from technology, media, other people and our environment. We have an undeniably impressive ability to manage immense amounts of this information on a daily basis. But even as we cope, when the steady stream becomes heavier and faster, we are left feeling uneasy, anxious and overloaded.

Our ability to process complex information is related to how well we can focus our attention, which is directly linked to the capacity and limitations of our working memory. As our brains overflow and our tasks become more complex and taxing, we discover that working memory can be very limited indeed. Alan Baddeley, a professor of psychology at the University of York, defined the term working memory. Working memory is "a limited capacity temporary storage system that underpins complex human thought" (Baddeley, 2007). It allows the brain to actively hold, and temporarily capture information, and is part of what makes attentional control, focusing on one object or concept while ignoring others, possible.

Working memory is what allows us to temporarily remember a phone number or verbal directions to a friend's house. It allows us to solve a math problem or to think through the steps needed to complete a process. This is the workhorse of our cognition, allowing us to move through information and situations without having to commit everything we encounter to long-term memory.

Working memory operates in conjunction with short-term memory. Short-term memory is a storage system for information on a short-term basis, while working memory is the active manipulation and use of that information. Long-term memories are created through the short-term memory system. These memories generally occur when a sensory stimulus proves particularly powerful or engaging, or through active and conscious rehearsal or memorization techniques. Long-term memories are considered lasting and enduring. They are part of a complex retrieval system, allowing users to call them forward as desired—although this process is imperfect, as anyone who has claimed an answer was "on the tip of my tongue" can attest.

Baddeley has constructed a model to explain working memory, which is based on clinical findings centered on dual-task experiments. When a user was asked to complete tasks involving two of the three 'perceptual domains' in the model—verbal information and language, visual information, and narrative and time based information— she was able to complete both tasks simultaneously nearly as well as when the tasks were attempted separately. However, when a user was asked to carry out more than one task within the *same* perceptual domain she found it significantly harder. Therefore, Baddeley posited, there must be some kind of interference when a user attempts to process too much information in one perceptual domain at a time. This explains why most people are able to draw while listening to music or someone speaking, but unable to comprehend someone speaking to them while simultaneously watching the news on TV.

Working memory also has an overall limited capacity. At some point, it becomes full and cannot hold any more information. New pieces of information can be taken in but only through the loss of another piece of information. An example of this concept at work is the everyday shopping list. Your mother asks you to go to the store to pick up just a few things. She verbally lists off the items for you: a loaf of bread, a carton of eggs, a quart of milk, and a stick of butter. This list is fairly short. You repeat back the items and might rehearse the list once or twice on the way to the store but have no problems remembering without a written list.

Now imagine she asks you to remember thirteen items instead of four. Even if you try to rehearse this list several times, chances are you will forget

something. This is because you have filled your working memory. Typically, people can easily store four to seven items in their working memory. But at some point, the storage is full, and you need to employ another strategy to help you retain and recall the information.

The limitations of working memory have many implications for the task of searching online. Attempting to make sense of multiple search results at the same time can fill the capacity of working memory, creating a sense of unease or confusion for a user. This is specifically difficult because of the way most of the search engine interfaces are designed. The structure of the pages, the use of barely styled lists of text, and the repetitive sameness of page after page of blue and black type on a white background don't allow users to effectively discriminate relevant results. Within the distracting and overwhelming world of the connected laptop or mobile phone, these limitations are pushed even further. Most of the search interfaces found online have not been designed to help users with this cognitive limitation.

Sensemaking: Processing and Understanding Information

Sensemaking is a cognitive process that has been studied in several different knowledge domains including medicine, policy making, understanding geographical influences on patterns of data, and the intelligence community. Simply stated, sensemaking allows humans to make sense of complex information and data encountered in the world around them. Pirolli and Russell discuss the implications for sensemaking in terms of HCI in their introduction to an issue of the *Human-Computer Interaction Journal* dedicated to the topic:

Sensemaking involves not only finding information but also requires learning about new domains, solving ill-structured problems, acquiring situation awareness, and participating in social exchanges of knowledge. In particular, the term encompasses the entire gamut of behavior surrounding collecting and organizing information for deeper understanding (Pirolli & Russell, 2011).

Pirolli and Russell go on to discuss three perspectives currently being posited in the literature regarding sensemaking:

- **Representation Construction Model of Sensemaking:** This model organizes the sensemaking process along an axis of structure and effort, and focuses on smaller sub-tasks within the larger search goal; specifically these sub-tasks are organized into those related to "foraging" and "sensemaking"; the model follows a recursive process of a user's interactions with information which include searching, making connections, supporting those connections with evidence, and reevaluation.

- **Data/Frame Perspective of Sensemaking:** This model uses the idea of "frame" construction, and explores how users encounter data, try to place that data within a frame, and then reconstruct those frames as needed to make sense of the information; this perspective comes from outside the world of HCI, but closely relates to the idea of "context" used within HCI and design research.

- **Collaborative Sensemaking:** This perspective investigates how teams of researchers and other types of workers make sense of information as they work together; this research also explores the difficulties faced by teams and how the members find focus as both individuals and team-members.

All three perspectives have ramifications for the research in this chapter. The first describes a methodical process users employ or could employ; the second explores the importance of framing and reframing information into different contexts

and understandings; and the third examines the social and collaborative aspects of sensemaking, which have been present on the Internet since its beginning, but are just starting to be exploited in truly intentional ways. Ntuen, Park, and Gwang-Myung (2010) further characterize sensemaking in the following ways: as an aspect of foraging, or seeking and collecting information that seems pertinent to the task at hand; as a way humans attempt to fuse information together, making connections and finding ways to explain strange juxtapositions or information that is surprising in some way; and as the comprehension of context.

Several examples of interface prototypes that incorporate concepts from sensemaking research have been recently designed. Examples include interfaces: to help military experts make decisions (Ntuen, Park, & Gwang-Myung, 2010); to support geographic analysts (Tomaszewski, Blanford, Ross, Pezanowski, and MacEachren, 2011); and to engage self-directed student learners in the process of completing tasks related to education (Butcher & Sumner, 2011). In all three cases, the interfaces designed focus on giving a user the power of spatially organizing information she has already located and decided was important. The interfaces utilize many spatial cues, cordoning sections off into different boxes for different task-purposes. The designs also integrate drag-and-drop techniques to help users intuitively understand the movement and sorting of information. Two of the interfaces integrate maps and charts, enabling users to plot information points using these types of schematics.

Overall, these three interface examples do not address the need for triage to occur at the site of the search engine itself, where raw data is being initially chosen and collected. While the systems do acknowledge the creation of spatial understandings of visual data, the designs do not go much further beyond organizing the space into multiple divisions and boxes. Other types of visualization and organization could be employed to further address the cognitive needs of users.

Information-Triage: Defining the Term

As the role of multi-tasking is being applied to more professions and activities, methods for 'cutting through the clutter' become integral to even basic tasks. Finding ways to sift through all the text, images and multi-layered links of the Internet in order to drill down to exactly what you need, exactly when you need it, has become a necessity. While the ways in which we're interacting with information are quickly changing, our need and desire to sort through it all remains the same. This is where the idea of triage is useful.

Triage is generally, and almost exclusively, associated with the medical practice of sorting and prioritizing patients based on the urgency of their need for care. Several triage systems are available for medical practitioners. These typically consist of colorful and meticulously codified tags and a course to teach triagers how to use the system efficiently and quickly. This extremely structured process is built around routine. Each time a triager encounters a patient, she moves through the same series of steps. She carefully records pertinent data and has been trained to be both methodical and unemotional as she moves through a disaster area, emergency room, or doctor's office. Patients are typically ranked along a four- or five-point scale to determine severity of injury and the urgency of immediate care (FitzGerald, Jelinek, Scott, & Gerdtz, 2010).

A visual analysis of several of these triage systems revealed that they use similar techniques and visual conventions, which include the use of color-coding (using primary colors); icons; simple geometric shapes; roman numerals; fill-ins and check-boxes; strong visual hierarchy; charts; arrows; and perforated sections containing bar-codes. Furthermore, all of the tags analyzed read from top to bottom, used little text, and were double-sided. These tags are designed to move the triager through her routine step-by-step, alternately asking her to examine the patient and catalog specific injuries, check and document vital signs, and to then use this information to prioritize care.

Triaging Information: Data as Patient

Information-triage is the process of sorting, grouping, categorizing, prioritizing, storing, and retrieving information in order to make sense and use of it. Peter Lunenfeld, media theorist and professor of media design, discusses this notion of information-triage: "Info-triage is more art than science, a practice that involves the weighing of options and the measuring of time. We tend to think of time in relation to efficiency, but info-triage is about more than job performance, it is a practice devoted to mindfulness...[it] is not so much about efficiency as the culling of the distraction in the search for meaning" (Lunenfeld, 2011). In this context, information-triage is not merely a sorting technique, but also, a type of curation.

Several methods of information curation currently exist online. Search engines offer a fundamental form: they seek out sites based on key words and phrases, and display the results back to the user in a hierarchical fashion. Sites like Google allow users to look through an abbreviated version of the Internet, making it possible to find particular pieces of information relatively quickly and easily. In fact, since their inception over ten years ago, today's users of search engines would likely define them as indispensable. It is difficult to remember what the Internet was like before their implementation.

Google created another useful interface for curation with iGoogle, a customizable 'personalized' homepage. Users can place widgets on their page containing information as diverse as the weather report, today's news headlines, games, and interesting images from other sites like Flickr. iGoogle offers a holding place for information and content that a user would normally have to visit multiple separate websites to view. It acts as a catchall, a single drawer the user can access to keep the content she deems most important to her close at hand. And, when this content exists within one portal, there are fewer chances for the user to become distracted by non-relevant material. iGoogle is both a display of choice and a buffer from distraction. Lunenfeld posits, "Info-triage accepts the psychological insight that those confronted with a vast array of options are often less satisfied than those who select between a smaller set of alternatives" (Lunenfeld, 2011). Ultimately, what this notion of info-triage offers is a sense of abbreviation—a threshing out of the chaff—allowing a user to focus on what is actually wanted or needed at any given time.

The concept and underlying process of information-triage are directly borrowed from the medical context, but the metaphor can only carry so far. If medical triage is about maximizing the number of survivors, treating those most likely to recover or eventually be healthy, then what is info-triage ultimately attempting to do? 'Save' only the most useful or pertinent information? What happens to the information deemed unworthy or beyond help? Information given up for 'dead' could later prove crucial to a user's purpose. Should an information-triage system give the option to 'resurrect' information? If a user's search task is less urgent, can info-triage still be useful?

A significant distinction between medical triage and information-triage is the motivation behind the act. Medical triagers are motivated by a sense of emergency, duty and the greater good. They are confronted with an overwhelming and grave situation and have been trained to move through survivors or patients quickly, assessing which category each patient falls into. They must act with a sense of urgency because lives are on the line. The motivations behind information-triage are quite different, as this concept functions on a much less visceral level. Generally, no one's life is at stake, and even when information is messy, it is much less so than human bodies. Info-triage allows for mistakes and uncertainty, and is greatly enhanced through the power and efficiency of computers and databases.

Information-triage can also be described in these two ways: triage as *noun* (a result, or a display of information that has been triaged) and as *verb* (the system or process of triaging information). This is an important distinction because the concept of triage can be helpful in both aspects. Providing triage as a result allows a user to understand information more easily. It offers a focus, a filtering, a distillation. Providing triage as a process allows a user to think through a search. It supports her with tools and criteria with which to evaluate the information she encounters. These two aspects are useful for different kinds of situations, users, tasks, and timeframes.

What Does Information-Triage Look Like?

Info-triage can take many different forms, some subtle, some overt. The emotional qualities of these triage experiences can also be quite different. Below are three examples of current digital information-triage. Each offers up a slightly different flavor of this term.

Ommwriter

Attempting to write a text on a personal computer can be deceptively difficult. Because writing software like Word exists as a window, functioning among many other windows and the Internet, the temptation to procrastinate is great. The functional yet chaotic nature of the desktop makes it difficult for a user to focus. Herraitz Soto & Co. has created a soothing environment for writing, which addresses these difficulties, called Ommwriter. The website for this product defines the software as, "a simple text processor that firmly believes in making writing a pleasure once again, vindicating the close relationship between writer and paper. The more intimate the relation, the smoother the flow of inspiration" (Ommwriter, 2010).

The software operates as a bare bones, full-screen text editor with a decidedly Zen look and feel. The designers of the interface have stripped away any superfluous frills or functions, leaving a writing environment that is relaxing and quiet. A text box is automatically generated in the center of the screen, a handful of options float off to one side, and an optional background image keeps the environment from feeling too stark. The overall effect soothes and provides focus, especially because the user has to save her text and close the program before she can use another piece of software or her web browser. This basic limitation forces the user to think twice before trying to multi-task or procrastinate.

Of course, the usefulness of Ommwriter is limited and much of the appeal is in its novel aesthetic presentation. The tools to manipulate the text are basic, and the software does not include a spellchecker. Most writers require and desire far more robust support and tools. However, just the mere act of simplifying the interface and displaying it full-screen creates a sense of focus.

Viewzi

Co-founded in 2006 by Brandon Cotter and Chris Mancini in Dallas, Texas, Viewzi (please note, this site is now defunct) offered Internet searchers a legitimate alternative to Google. The co-founders described this search engine as, "a new and highly visual way to search that brings all your favorite stuff together in one place." Viewzi operated as a mass search engine aggregator, culling results from Ask, Google, MSN, and Yahoo. However, the real charm (and usefulness) of Viewzi lay in its multiple ways to view results. The website offered nineteen different view modes, some open-ended and some specific.

Many of the view modes were so specific that the usefulness was limited, for instance Celebrity Photos, Songs, or Recipes. These modes allowed the user to sort through these particular types of media in novel and visual ways, but did not facilitate overall research or making meaningful connections. However, these modes provided info-triage at a highly specific level. If a user clicked on the Recipes view mode, her search results were culled from four popular cooking sites, not just the Internet at large. The effect of this specificity meant that the user may have missed out on several hundreds of thousands of recipes from the overall Internet, but the search results she did receive were likely to be more useful.

Three of the more general types of searches on Viewzi were particularly interesting examples of info-triage: the Power Grid, the Web Screenshot, and the 4 Sources. These three view modes reconfigured results, normally seen in a static list, in a dynamic and visual way. The overall effect was a display that had been filtered and prioritized.

The *Power Grid* pulled search results from Yahoo and Google and placed them on a six-by-three grid. This view mode also allowed users to move, hide, open (launch) and star (highlight) pages through mouse clicks and key-strokes. Users were also given the option to view results as either text or home-page screen shots. This mode created a visual snapshot of the total search results, allowing the user to view them just eighteen at a time, and also provided a mechanism with which to sort and eliminate results in an intuitive way.

The *Web Screenshot* was one of the simplest, most focused ways to view search engine results. This mode displayed each result one at a time as a home-page screen shot, annotated with synopsis text, the site URL, as well as where the result came from (Yahoo, Google, MSN, etc.), and how many other results came from that same source. The user was able to move through the results fairly quickly using the arrow keys on her keyboard, and the overall effect of viewing results in isolation allowed a user to focus on one thing at a time. However, if a search returned a large number of results, or if the search query wasn't specific, the interface quickly became cumbersome. The Web Screenshot offered triage through isolation and annotation.

The *4 Sources* mode allowed a user to compare her search results by search engine source. Results were color coded, and the user was able to select which sources she wanted to include in her search. This simple interface allowed for quick comparison between search engines and enabled the user to see where results overlapped among sources. Furthermore, this kind of comparison and visual overlap allowed a user to begin evaluating the credibility of sources.

Viewzi engaged users with a dynamic, visual set of displays and interfaces. The end result offered information-triage through prioritizing, visualizing, isolating, annotating and comparing search results. However, these interfaces are only hinting at the usefulness and power of information-triage, and the site itself has unfortunately disbanded and hasn't yet been resurrected.

Flipboard

Created in 2010 for the iPad, and recently expanded to several other mobile tablet-style devices, Flipboard is an app that allows users to digitally thumb through multiple streams of content found on the Internet in a cohesive and striking interface. Data, news stories, blog posts, entries on social media sites, is gathered from the Internet and flows into a simple, magazine-style display.

When a user initially downloads Flipbook onto a device, they are asked to choose content topics to personalize their experience. These topics include: News, Business, Tech & Science, Audio, Video, Cool Curators, Photos & Design, Living, Entertainment, Sports, Style, Travel and Local. Within each of these content topics, a user can further curate the kinds of content she would like to see. For example, under Tech & Science, users can choose to view: Space, Apps, Apple News, and Tech; or users can choose to view content from specific blogs and sources like the *New York Times*. This process of selecting from large

categories of information and curating a personal experience allows a user to triage the content found on the Internet, creating an abbreviated and specialized space.

However, the real charm of Flipboard lies in the gestural interface. The content is labeled according to the topics initially chosen by the user, and then poured into a templated design created to look like the pages of a magazine. The focus here is on presenting multiple stories per page, and including images and headlines to allow a user to quickly move through a large amount of content at once. The user peruses the interface by flipping through the pages with a flick of her finger. New content is continually added to the front pages, and a small navigation bar at the bottom shows the user where she is spatially within the stream of material.

Flipboard allows users to triage information in two ways: by choosing the kinds of content to be included in viewing sessions, and by showing the content in a specific and familiar way. However, the interface is set up to feel like a magazine-reading experience, encouraging browsing and casual reading behaviors, rather than enabling a user to power through a great deal of precise information to reach a specific search goal. Flipboard allows for curation, but encourages a more random and unintentional grazing-based environment.

Our User, Ourselves

We know that working memory is directly related to how well we can focus our attention. We know that it is limited and when full, a user feels overwhelmed and anxious. We know that this anxiety, and the complexity of the online atmosphere make it difficult for some users to make careful, rational decisions. We know that a user's understanding of information in a search relates to a concept called sensemaking, but that the tools available online do not take this into account.

- Our user is bombarded with information.
- She is often pressed for time.
- Her life is full of distraction and multi-tasking.
- She finds it hard to focus on the task at hand, and her thoughts wander.
- Finding conflicting information about an important topic can leave her feeling confused and paralyzed.
- The current options for online searching do not adequately address our user's limitations of time, focus, or working memory.

MISE EN PLACE: AN ONLINE SEARCH INTERFACE PROTOTYPE

This speculative interface prototype is based on the idea of *mise en place* (French for "everything in its place") that chefs and cooks use to organize—and triage—their process, kitchen, ingredients, time, and space while cooking. Essentially, *mise en place* is a methodical, focused way to arrange all the elements in place before the main event begins, enhancing competency and providing efficiency through established expectations.

Mise en Place is proposed as an online interface, housed within a web browser that aggregates search results from other search engines (Viewzi, 2010). The system allows the user to organize and state the purpose of her search, and then displays visually coded results of her search query. These results are labeled according to large categories generated by the system, and a gradient of credibility generated by other users of the system. The interface is meant to be friendly and comforting, creating an environment that will allow users to make sense of search results and find focus.

Methods

The development of the *Mise en Place* interface began with a content and visual analysis of current manifestations of Internet search engines and in-terfaces, and connected those interfaces to the idea of information-triage. The analysis was created as a visual document that allowed for comparisons among current search systems. This process also created conditions for the discernment of patterns regarding what is and is not functioning within the domain of online search. The main problems found were in these areas:

1. Helping users organize their overall search
2. Helping users formulate concise and reliable search terms
3. Helping users quickly and visually understand search results
4. Helping users find patterns and make connections within large search result pools

At the same time, a review of current related research was conducted. This review focused on issues within the fields of interface and interaction design, cognitive issues including working memory and search behavior, the use of mental and cognitive models through sensemaking, theory regarding the organization of information in an online context, and visualization techniques for this type of information and data.

Next, the content domain of nutrition was chosen, based on the complexity of available information online, and the emotional nature of making decisions regarding nutrition. Finding results that seem trustworthy and reliable are more difficult during a search of this nature, and that complexity was needed to help develop a more robust and realistic prototype. Once the context was specified, user analysis was conducted—Who might be searching for information about nutrition? What are the different needs and goals related to an online search in this context? What kinds of behavior might be exhibited? A matrix was then created, which listed out possible behaviors and needs of potential users, including: things people are looking for, attributes of users, kinds of decisions, consequences, motivations, problems of attention, and problems of working memory.

Content from the persona matrix helped to create a series of specific personas for the prototype that typified sets of behaviors and needs encapsulated in personalities and characters that felt like real people. The personas were written and refined, and given names, backstories and head-shots. Narrative scenarios of use were then developed to start to explore how the personas would use the prototype during a typical day. Finally, visual studies and various prototypes were developed, edited, compared and culled, and then refined using a typical iterative design process.

An animated walk-though of the *Mise en Place* interface prototype may be viewed here: http://vimeo.com/11885160.

Preliminary user testing is currently being conducted, using paper and digital Flash prototypes and both obtrusive and unobtrusive user observation. Findings from this testing have yet to be compiled and analyzed. The *Mise en Place* prototype continues to be shaped and refined, and other speculative prototype interfaces are under development.

Design Details of the Mise en Place Prototype

A Metaphorical Interface

This interface utilizes the metaphor of a chef's *mise en place,* enabling the design to take on certain characteristics to help users manage space and give them a greater sense of control. A chef using *mise en place* gathers all the ingredients needed for a recipe into one space, measures these items out into small containers, and then organizes them according to the steps of a given recipe. The items generally included in this organization are actual ingredients, spices, utensils, and other cooking apparatus like pots, pans and appliances. *Mise en place* helps the chef establish a sense of control and creates a specific abbreviated space for all involved elements as well as the activity of cooking.

Mise en place enables the chef to manage space, content and activity in a powerful and meaningful way. She can make sure all the needed ingredients are present and measured out correctly; she can execute sub-activities in the process ahead of time; and she can be methodical and organized. This example of triage permits the chef to confidently execute her recipe, while allowing for some freedom to experiment and play with a dish. She can rely on her system, on the structure of *mise en place*, and try out variations to the recipe or cooking methods as desired. Without the system, cooking is far more chaotic.

Overall Visualization and Organization

The visualization and organization of this prototype attempt to embody the idea of *mise en place* in several ways. The structure of the interface is uncluttered and employs a strong and obvious grid. Important elements are placed at the top of the screen so the user has no trouble locating them. Search results appear in a large panel, can be previewed in small rollover windows, and can be viewed within a large lightbox-style window that appears on top of the main interface screen and has its own navigation. All elements appear within the current space of the screen so the user never has to scroll, and the interface itself is completely flat in structure—users never leave the space of the main screen or get lost in a series of links and tabs.

The typefaces and color palette were chosen to feel friendly but reliable. The icons and other visual elements were designed to reinforce this sense of ease and trust. The images and symbols are simple, recognizable, and familiar—yet are not often seen in the context of other search engines.

All these design choices help make the *Mise en Place* prototype distinct from other existing search engine options.

Taken together, all the elements are designed to provide the user with a sense of control and comfort, and to help her stay visually and spatially oriented in one space that she can easily understand and navigate.

Orienting and Preparing the User for Search

When the user first comes to the *Mise en Place* interface, she encounters a simple screen with a mottled blue background, the name of the interface at the top left, and three simple options at the top of the screen: *save, new search* and *saved search.* When the user chooses new search, she is then prompted by the system to determine what kind of search she is conducting. A small box near the top animates open, and the system asks: *What is your _____?* When the user hovers her mouse pointer over the blank, a list appears offering the

following options: *question, problem, idea, goal* and *issue.* (Figure 1) By offering up this targeted list, the system prompts the user to reflect on the current needs for this particular search—this kind of reflection helps give her focus.

Once the user chooses a word for the blank, the system restates this initial question using the response; for example: *What is your question?* A cursor begins to blink under the question, signaling to the user that she needs to provide a beginning question, for example: *How can I safely introduce a gluten-free diet to my daughter?* This question or statement now animates to a larger size, and becomes a part of the upper portion of the interface itself—enabling the user to view and review the question as she continues her search, helping her maintain focus. Finally, a search box appears in the upper left corner of the interface, with another blinking cursor. The user is able to view her focused question and then choose a specific term to search, for example: *gluten-free.* The search box is similar to those found across the Internet, making it familiar and understand-

Figure 1. The interface asks the user to define her search as an information goal

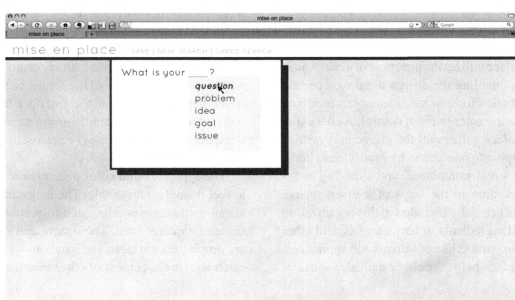

able, yet the insertion of a focused search-goal as a prominent part of the interface introduces an unusual and useful element.

The Search Activity and Results

Now several new areas animate onto the screen: a *sort* tab, a color-coded *categories* list, a set of trustworthiness *symbols,* and an area for *search breadcrumbs* (a list of the searches undertaken during this search session, in the order the terms were entered). The sort tab is a personal area for the user to save and organize search results she deems important or wants to bookmark. A more detailed description of this area will be discussed further below.

The categories list helps to triage results into the following large system categories: *advocacy and opinion*; *explanatory and reference*; *practical and how-to*; *commerce and shopping*; and *latest and breaking*. These system categories are assigned using several criteria including meta-data, keyword relationships, and feedback from other system users.

The trustworthiness symbols are based on a gradient of reliability assigned by other system users. As users encounter sites within the search space, they are asked to assign ratings according to this gradient. The most trustworthy sites would be graded with a *smiley face*, while somewhat trustworthy sites would be graded with a *check mark*. Sites deemed somewhat untrustworthy would be graded with an *X*, and highly untrustworthy would be graded with a *skull and crossbones*. The final trustworthiness symbol is a *question mark*, which describes a site that has yet to be graded, or that users are unsure of.

Both the system categories and the trustworthiness gradient are initial attempts at creating a system of triage for the user, and are likely imperfect. A system with a social/participatory component such as this would demand a certain amount of flexibility, allowing users to give input regarding both types of filtering, helping to refine

the system over time. This is an area of the interface that will be further addressed in subsequent iterations and prototypes.

Next, the *results* themselves would animate onto the screen, falling from the top into a large white box that dominates the interface. (Figure 2) The search results are rendered as small squares, each colored according to category and displaying a symbol according to the trustworthiness gradient. All the search results are organized into a tightly spaced grid, ten results high and twenty results wide. These numbers were chosen deliberately—by creating columns of ten, users are equipped to quickly estimate the number of sites shown. The initial state for the results is to show the highest ranked page (according to the page-rankings of the source search engine) in the top left corner, and the lower ranked pages in the bottom right corner.

The user may view a small thumbnail of the homepage for each search result by hovering over it. (Figure 3) The thumbnails are contained in boxes, colored according to the appropriate system category, which also display the title and URL for the search result. If the user clicks on one of these thumbnails, a large lightbox-style frame appears on top of the main interface. This frame contains: the website itself, which is completely navigable; the appropriate color- and symbol-coded search result from the main interface in the upper right-hand corner; and a simple navigation system. This allows the user to open up any of the individual search results to view a particular website, and then quickly flip through the others according to how the results are organized in the main interface itself. (Figure 4)

The Info-Triage Sorting Functions

The sorting functions of the *Mise en Place* interface allow users to triage search results in a powerful way. If a user clicks on the bounding box for the system categories list, the current search results will rearrange themselves according to those cat-

Figure 2. Search results are displayed as visually labeled squares organized in a grid, permitting the user to find patterns within the data

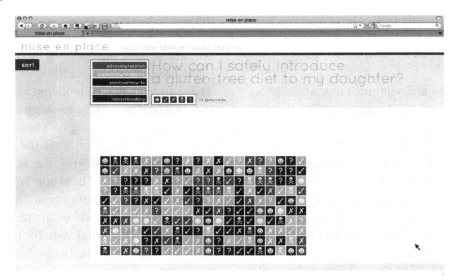

egories, displayed in separate columns in the same order as the list. If a user clicks on the bounding box for the trustworthiness symbols, the search results will rearrange themselves accordingly. If a user clicks on both boxes, the results will be sorted both by category and symbol: the categories sorted vertically into columns, and the symbols sorted horizontally into rows (Figure 5).

The user can also choose to discard whole categories and trustworthiness symbols by clicking on those individual elements within the bounding boxes. If, for example, the user decides she does not want to include results from the *commerce and shopping* category, she can click on that element within its bounding box and all the search results labeled as *commerce and shop-*

Figure 3. The user may view a thumbnail of each website with a hover behavior

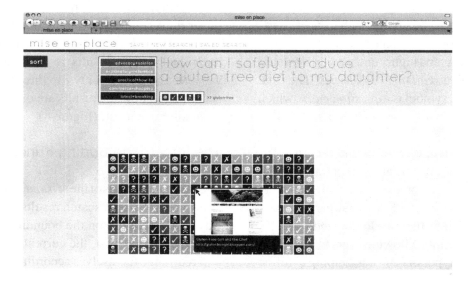

Figure 4. The user may view and navigate through the websites themselves in a lightbox-style frame

ping will float down off the bottom edge of the interface—now they have been discarded. In the same way, the user can choose to discard all search results labeled with an *X* and a *skull and crossbones*. Once results have been discarded, the elements within the bounding boxes are grayed out, and the remaining search results re-organize into neat columns and rows (Figure 6).

Figure 5. The search results are sorted into columns and rows according to both the large system categories and the trustworthiness symbols

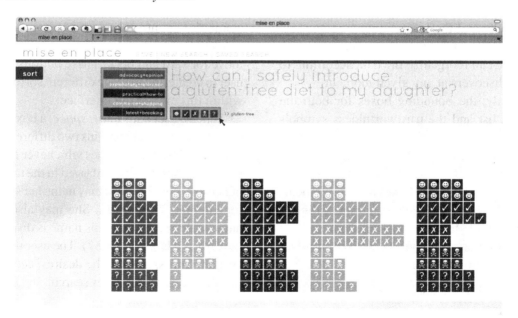

Figure 6. The user can discard categories as desired, and the results rearrange themselves accordingly

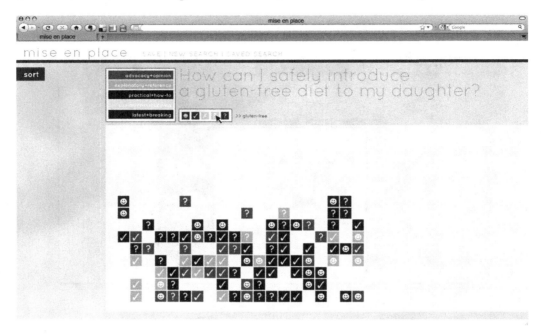

These simple sorting and filtering techniques allow the user to quickly see patterns within the search results, make large organizational decisions about which results to keep and discard, and continue to reconfigure the results during the search as needed or desired. The sorting functions also reveal connections among the categorization of the results and the information contained on the websites themselves—as the user explores the results, she can reorganize the data according to what she discovers at any given moment.

Currently, the bounding boxes for both the categories list and the trustworthiness symbols don't have compelling affordance. When a user hovers over these boxes, they will appear active, but otherwise, the interface doesn't intuitively signal to the user what those boxes and the elements within them will do. As always, a user willing to investigate will discover the functionality, but this is another area that will be revised in future interface iterations and prototypes.

The Personal Sort Area

The final element of the interface is the *personal sort area*. This area is accessed through a tab at the top left corner of the interface labeled *sort*. When the user clicks on the sort tab, it animates to the right, revealing a sort bar. This bar contains elements to control the sort area: an *add button*, a *delete button*, and two *navigational buttons* to move forward and back. These buttons allow the user to create and manage different sorting spaces within this area of the interface.

When a user adds a *sort space*, a box animates onto the screen that contains two different images of dishes. The user chooses whichever image she prefers, and that dish is enlarged in the top portion of her sort area. The user may name her sort space, for example: *Definitions*. She may also edit the name later or delete it. This name is displayed on the dish as a label (Figure 7). The user may create as many sort spaces as she desires, according to the changing needs of her search.

Figure 7. The personal sort area allows the user to set up specific sort spaces to help meaningfully organize saved results

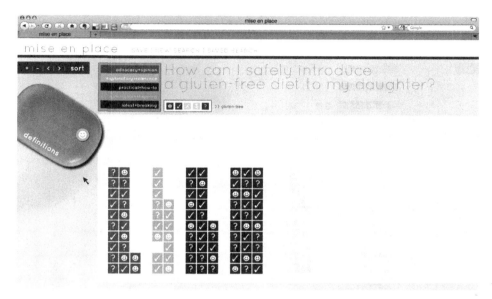

Now the user may collect search results from the main interface and place them on the dish in her sort area. This is executed through a simple and intuitive click and drag. When the user drags a search result into her sort space, it changes from a square into a circle. This state change signals to the user that this particular result has been saved in her personal sort space. As she drags results into her space, the interface leaves holes where those results were. This ensures that the user doesn't attempt to drag the same result into her sort space more than once.

When finished, the user clicks on the sort tab again, which closes the personal sort area. Any search results that have been saved into the sort area now appear as circles within the main interface. The user can easily see which results she has decided to save, can compare these to the rest of the results, and can continue reorganizing everything with the sorting functions of the system (Figure 8).

Saving Entire Searches and Sessions

The *Mise en Place* interface also allows users to *save* their searches and search sessions. As the user interacts with the interface during a search session, the system will keep track of the main focus statement (*How can I safely introduce a gluten-free diet to my daughter?*) as well as all the search terms investigated. Moreover, the system will also keep track of the search results sorted into the personal sort area for a given search. When the user is ready to take on a different search, or set a new search-goal, she can simply start a new search. In this way, the interface system can scale and maintain flexibility for the different search needs of a given user, and for multiple types of users.

Addressing Needs Through Info-Triage

The *Mise en Place* interface encourages the user to sort through her search results. She can easily conduct mass sorts using the basic category

Figure 8. Results that have been saved to the user's personal sort area change into circles in the main interface

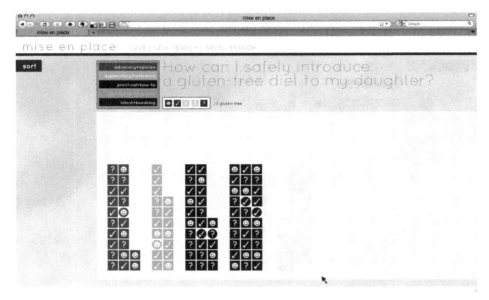

and symbol menus, and she can discard types of results that aren't relevant to her search. The user can also choose to utilize her personal *sort* area, creating categories and affinities that fit particular and unique criteria.

Typically, search engines return results that look identical, are purely language-based, and attempt to be objectively neutral. The *Mise en Place* interface endeavors to color these same search results using sets of meaningful criteria, allowing a user to understand specific aspects of her results before she chooses to explore them. This also permits users to see and understand many more results at once, eliminating the tendency of only viewing the first few pages of results found on search engines like Google.

The *Mise en Place* interface addresses information-triage in these ways:

- The system gives the user the agency to make decisions and choices throughout the search process and offers visual and strategy support along the way.

- The system keeps the user focused on one step at a time and provides reassurance that ideas and information are not being lost in the shuffle; everything is saved and stored for the user to find again.

- The system addresses working memory by visually displaying information in digestible bits and allowing the user to sort through and make sense of her results as needed.

CONCLUSION

One challenge encountered in the creation of this interface was exploring how intuitive it should be. Where is the balance between robust and practical functionality, and minimal and intuitive interaction? By providing a simple set of tools and sorting functions, the *Mise en Place* interface attempts to create the possibility for many different kinds of interactions and experiences for users.

The concept of triage cannot simply be lifted whole from the medical discipline and pasted directly onto the discipline of information science or interaction design. The metaphor simply won't hold. Instead, my conception of information-triage echoes that of Peter Lunenfeld, "[it] is not so much about efficiency as the culling of the distraction in the search for meaning" (2011). Information-triage should enable users to intuitively comprehend and curate the material they encounter online.

As I have argued, the concept of information-triage has two facets. It can be thought of as a verb (process), and as a noun (display of results). By articulating this difference, I was able to design variations of both facets and explore what might happen to user experience when the balance of power between system and user shifts. However, these two facets should be explored further—I plan to continue investigating these issues in future interfaces and user testing.

Further research should also be done to answer questions within the following unresolved issues:

Balance

- How can we balance the needs of each individual user within the process of searching on a vast and chaotic Internet?
- What kinds of interfaces should we construct to balance a user's needs for efficiency, speed, relevance and ease of comprehension?
- How can we account for the great differences among users— even among one user's different types of searches?

Credibility

- How can we triage source credibility to allow a user to understand commonalities and differences, yet help eliminate or minimize what is superfluous?
- Who decides which sources are superfluous and what criteria should be used?

- What is the mechanism and structure for tagging these sources?
- How can we quickly signal to a user the differences between types of sources?

Relevance

- How much information-triage does the average user require? How much is too much?
- Do we need uncompromising diligence and vigilance, or can information-triage happen ambiently through interfaces and computerized tools?
- How can we continue to build interfaces that enable users to find information that is contextually relevant to them, without leaving out information that is surprising or creates innovative juxtapositions?

FUTURE RESEARCH DIRECTIONS

The Complexity Continues

As citizens, organizations and companies continue adding to the large masses of content online, users will continue to feel overwhelmed unless interfaces are created to specifically address user needs and limitations. The visualization of information in an online-search context can take many different shapes and forms, and is just starting to be investigated in ways that strive to help support users within the limits of cognition and understanding. Currently, these forms are exploring spatial and gestural ways to aid users, but more work should be done to create interfaces that are metaphorical and uniquely visual in nature as well.

HCI, human cognition, information science and computer science professionals need to work with designers and other experts to start merging the disparate bodies of research being produced that currently swirl around the main idea of helping users triage and understand information. Future research directions should employ collaborative groups of the above-mentioned professionals in the act of creating multiple speculative interfaces around this and other pertinent concepts. The visualization of search results online has remained stultified and static for nearly a decade, hopefully this is just the beginning of new user-centered forms and cognitively aesthetic designs taking shape.

REFERENCES

AOL. (2012). *AOL, Inc.* Retrieved from http://www.aol.com/.

Ask.com. (2012). Retrieved from http://www.ask.com/.

Baddeley, A. (2007). *Working memory, thought, and action.* New York: Oxford University Press. doi:10.1093/acprof:oso/9780198528012.001.0001.

Blekko. (2012). *Blekko, Inc.* Retrieved from http://blekko.com/.

Buchanan, G., & Owen, T. (2008). Improving skim reading for document triage. In *Proceedings of the Second International Symposium on Information Interaction in Context*, 83-88. New York: ACM.

Butcher, K. R., & Sumner, T. (2011). Self-directed learning and the sensemaking paradox. *Human-Computer Interaction*, *26*, 123–159. doi:10.1080/07370024.2011.556552.

eBiz/MBA. (2012). *Top 15 most popular search engines.* Retrieved from http://www.ebizmba.com/articles/search-engines.

FitzGerald, G., Jelinek, G. A., Scott, D., & Gerdtz, M. F. (2010). Emergency department triage revisited. *Emergency Medicine Journal*, *27*, 86–92. doi:10.1136/emj.2009.077081 PMID:20156855.

Flipboard. (2012). *Flipboard, Inc.* Retrieved from http://flipboard.com/.

Geng, Z., Laramee, R. S., Loizides, F., & Buchanan, G. (2011). Visual analysis of document triage data. In *Proceedings of International Conference on Information Visualization Theory and Applications*. Vilamoura, Algarve, Portugal: INSTICC Press.

Google. (2012). Retrieved on from https://www.google.com/.

Herraiz Soto & Co. (2010). *Ommwriter.* Retrieved from http://ommwriter.com.

Infospace, Inc. (2012). *Dogpile.* Retrieved from http://www.dogpile.com/info.dogpl/search/home.

Lunenfeld, P. (2011). *The secret war between downloading and uploading: Tales of the computer as culture machine.* Cambridge, MA: MIT Press.

Lycos. (2012). *Lycos, Inc.* Retrieved from http://www.lycos.com/.

Merriam-Webster. (2012). Triage. *Online Dictionary.* Retrieved from http://www.merriam-webster.com/dictionary/triage.

Microsoft. (2012). *Bing.* Retrieved from http://www.bing.com/.

MyWebSearch. (2012*). Mindspark interactive network, inc.* Retrieved from http://home.mywebsearch.com/.

Ntuen, C. A., Park, E. H., & Gwang-Myung, K. (2010). Designing an information visualization tool for sensemaking. *International Journal of Human-Computer Interaction*, *26*(2-3), 189–205. doi:10.1080/10447310903498825.

O'Meara, M., Porter, K., & Greaves, I. (2007). Triage. *Trauma*, *9*, 111. doi:10.1177/1460408607084180.

Pirolli, P., & Russell, D. M. (2011). Introduction to this special issue on sensemaking. *Human-Computer Interaction*, *26*, 1–8. doi:10.1080/07370024.2011.556557.

Shirky, C. (2008). It's not information overload. It's filter failure. *Web 2.0 Expo New York*. Retrieved from http://web2expo.blip.tv/file/1277460.

Tomaszewski, B., Blandford, J., Ross, K., Pezanowski, S., & MacEachren, A. M. (2011). Supporting geographically-aware web document foraging and sensemaking. *Computers, Environment and Urban Systems*, *35*, 192–207. doi:10.1016/j.compenvurbsys.2011.01.003.

Viewzi. (2010). *Viewzi, inc.* Retrieved from http://www.viewzi.com/.

WebCrawler. (2012). *Infospace, inc.* Retrieved from http://www.webcrawler.com/.

Wright, A. (2007). *Glut: Mastering information through the ages*. Washington, DC: Joseph Henry P..

Yahoo. (2012). *Yahoo! inc.* Retrieved from http://www.yahoo.com/.

ADDITIONAL READING

Ariely, D. (2009). *Predictably irrational*. New York: Harper Collins.

Aumer-Ryan, P. (2009). Information triage: Factors affecting credibility judgments of web-based resources. *Bulletin of IEEE Technical Committee on Digital Libraries*, *5*(3), 1–9.

Bates, M. (1989). The design of browsing and berrypicking techniques for the online search interface. *Online Review*, *13*, 407–424. doi:10.1108/eb024320.

Bates, M. (1990). Where should the person stop and the information search interface start? *Information Processing & Management*, *26*(5), 575–591. doi:10.1016/0306-4573(90)90103-9.

Batetelle, J. (2005). *The search: How google and its rivals rewrote the rules of business and transformed our culture*. New York: The Penguin Group.

Kahneman, D. (2011). *Thinking, fast and slow*. New York: Farrar, Straus, and Giroux.

Klanten, R., Bourquin, N., Ehmann, S., & van Heerden, F. (2008). *Data flow: Visualising information in graphic design*. Berlin: Gestalten.

Klingberg, T. (2009). *Overflowing brain: Information overload and the limits of working memory*. New York: Oxford University Press.

Kolko, J. (2007). *Thoughts on interaction design*. Boston: Brown Bear LLC.

Lakoff, G. (1990). *Women, fire, and dangerous things: What categories reveal about the mind*. Chicago: University of Chicago.

McCandless, D. (2009). *The visual miscellaneum: A colorful guide to the world's most consequential trivia*. New York: Collins Design.

Moggridge, B. (2007). *Designing interactions*. Cambridge, MA: The MIT Press.

Morville, P. (2005). *Ambient findability*. Sebastopol, CA: O'Reilly.

Norman, D. A. (1994). *Things that make us smart: Defending human attributes in the age of the machine*. Boston: Addison Wesley Company.

Promorock Design. (2011) *Information triage table design*. Retrieved from http://promorock.com/ux-projects/information-triage-table-design/.

Weinberger, D. (2007). *Everything is miscellaneous: The power of the new digital disorder*. New York: Times Books.

Zhang, Y. (2008). The influence of mental models on undergraduate students' searching behavior on the Web. *Information Processing & Management*, *44*, 1330–1345. doi:10.1016/j.ipm.2007.09.002.

KEY TERMS AND DEFINITIONS

Data: Any piece of information in its raw form; information that has not been made sense of.

Information: Any data or piece of information that has been made sense of; data that has been given context.

Information-Triage: The process of retrieving, sorting, evaluating and prioritizing information in order to make sense and use of it.

Mise en Place: The act of organizing materials and activities prior to preparing a meal, done by a chef or cook in a systematic way.

Search Engine: An interface housed within an Internet browser that retrieves websites and other kinds of data from the Internet based on specific terms or phrases.

Sensemaking: The cognitive process of taking in information from various sources and trying to make sense of it.

Working Memory: The limited cognitive ability of humans to retain small amounts of information over a short period of time without committing that information to long-term memory.

Chapter 16
A Framework for Developing Diagram Applications

Wei Lai
Swinburne University of Technology, Australia

Weidong Huang
CSIRO ICT Centre, Sydney, Australia

ABSTRACT

This chapter presents a framework for developing diagram applications. The diagrams refer to those graphs where nodes vary in shape and size used in real world applications, such as flowcharts, UML diagrams, and E-R diagrams. The framework is based on a model the authors developed for diagrams. The model is robust for diagrams and it can represent a wide variety of applications and support the development of powerful application-specific functions. The framework based on this model supports the development of automatic layout techniques for diagrams and the development of the linkage between the graph structure and applications. Automatic layout for diagrams is demonstrated and two case studies for diagram applications are presented.

1. INTRODUCTION

A graph typically consists of a set of nodes and a set of edges where a node is drawn as a point and an edge is drawn as a line. We are more interested in diagrams which refer to practical graphs. In a practical graph, nodes (e.g. boxes and circles) representing objects take some spaces. They are not abstract points in a classical graph. Diagrams are commonly used to model relations in information systems and software engineering. Examples are data flow diagrams, state transition diagrams, flow charts, PERT charts, organization charts, Petri nets, entity-relationship diagrams, and UML diagrams.

A number of graph drawing algorithms have been developed, these algorithms are listed in (Battista et al 1999). These algorithms produce aesthetically pleasing abstract graph drawings, where nodes are just points in the plane. In prac-

DOI: 10.4018/978-1-4666-4309-3.ch016

tice, nodes have many attributes; for example, in a UML diagram, a node has several textual labels in several fields. These attributes need to be represented graphically, for instance, as shapes, sizes, and colors. We call this kind of graph where nodes vary in shape and size a practical graph.

Most diagrams in applications are practical graphs (e.g. UML diagrams). Diagrams are widely used in information visualization. The motivation for information visualization is that relational information, once handled textually, is now commonly displayed and manipulated with diagrams. We call this kind of information visualization using diagram displays and manipulations *diagram applications*. Diagram applications can be divided into two categories:

1. Those which focus on translation of textual information into a diagram, such as translation of a program to a flow chart, and translation of URL relations to a web graph.
2. Those which focus on semantic interpretation of diagrams, such as interpretation of a flow chart to execute a program, code generation from a UML diagram, and using diagrams for data mining.

Both categories of applications need diagram layout interfaces. It is critical to have an efficient tool for creating diagram layout interfaces. Although there are some software tools (such as Visual Basic, Xlib, and Motif) for windows and GUI programming, they are very low-level and not efficient for interactive diagram applications. These tools support building those interface components, such as menus, scrolling bars, dialog boxes, and so on. However, they are not efficient to support building diagram layout interfaces.

Most existing CASE (Computer Aided Software Engineering) tools, such as Rational Rose (7), provide graphical editors for drawing UML diagrams. However, these tools were designed for UML diagram applications only and they cannot be used for various diagram applications. Also, these CASE tools do not efficiently support automatic

diagram layout. Automatic layout can release the user from the time-consuming and detail-intensive chore of generating a readable diagram.

This chapter presents a framework for developing diagram applications. It includes the investigation of a robust model for diagrams to solve the problems mentioned above. This model can support automatic layout techniques for diagrams and the development the linkage between the diagram structure and applications.

The critical issue is that what kind of model is suitable to represent diagrams where nodes vary in size and shape and can support the development of diagram layout functions? Is current classical graph model sufficient in playing this role? Can current graph drawing algorithms be applied to diagram layout? In next section, the background is introduced for classical graph model and graph drawing algorithms, and the questions above will be answered.

2. BACKGROUND

Many graph drawing algorithms (Battista et al., 1999) have been developed for abstract graph automatic layout. They are based on the classical graph model, that is, G=(V, E), where V is a set of abstract nodes (points) and E is a set of edges (lines). However, there is little work have been done on automatic layout for practical graphs (i.e. diagrams) used in real world applications, especially for nodes varying in size and shape in practice.

The most difficult problem for diagram interfaces is *layout*-assigning a position for each node and a curve for each edge. The assignment must be chosen to make the resulting picture easy to understand and easy to remember. A good layout can be like a picture-worth a thousand words; a poor layout can confuse or mislead the user. This problem is called the *graph drawing problem*. A number of graph drawing algorithms have been developed. They produce aesthetically pleasing graph layouts (see Figure 1a). These algorithms

Figure 1. An example of overlapping nodes

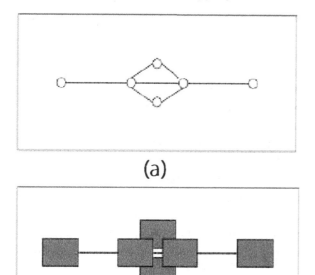

(a)

(b)

can be applied to draw those graphs where the sizes of nodes are very small. This is because such algorithms were often originally designed for *abstract graphs* where nodes take up little or no space. However, in applications, the images of nodes are circles, boxes, diamonds and similar shapes, and may contain a considerable amount of text and graphics. Sometimes nodes may represent subgraphs, and may be quite unpredictable in size and shape. Applying such algorithms to *practical graphs* (i.e. diagrams) where nodes vary in shape and size may result in overlapping nodes and/or edge-node intersections (see Figure 1b).

Another example is illustrated in Figure 2; replacing the abstract nodes in Figure 2 (a) with rectangles gives the overlapping nodes in Figure 2 (b). But the layout we need should be Figure 2 (c). For practical graphs, the size of nodes should be taken into account in the development of automatic layout techniques. What kind of functions should be developed to suitable for diagram layout?

If we cannot make use of existing drawing algorithms for displaying diagrams in practice, we have to develop specific drawing approach for a specific type of diagrams. For example, to display a UML diagram, a specific approach is developed (Storrle, 2012).

Figure 2. Layout of a class diagram

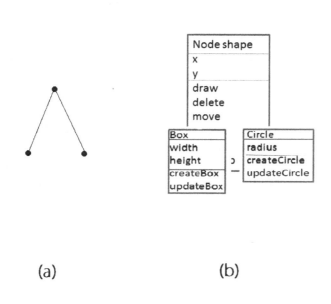

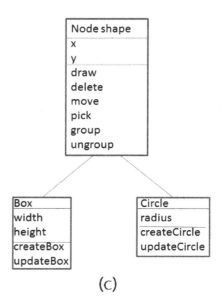

(a)   (b)   (c)

Based on the analysis above, it is obviously the classical graph model is not suitable for representing diagrams used in practice. A robust model for diagrams (layout and applications) should be investigated. In next section, the model for diagrams is presented.

3. A MODEL FOR DIAGRAMS

In this section, we present the model for diagrams and a generic approach for automatic diagram layout.

3.1. The Model

A robust structure for diagrams has been investigated. This structure can represent a wide variety of applications and support the development of powerful application-specific functions (including layout functions and the functions for the linkage between the graph structure and applications).

This kind of structure should include geometrical information for diagrams and support the development of automatic layout functions. We call this structure the *practical graph model*.

The model is combined with the approaches on generic graph grammars (Ong & Kurth, 2012; Rekers & Schurr, 1995) and cluster graphs (Huang & Lai, 2006). In order to represent a variety of diagrams in application, basic components of diagrams should be defined. These basic components can be used to construct compound components. A diagram component is defined as

$$C = (r, L_r, P_r, I_r, E_r)$$

which consists of a single *root* node r, a set of *inside* nodes I_r, and a set of relationships E_r between elements of I_r. The root node r *includes* the graph $G_r = (I_r, E_r)$.

If I_r is empty, the component is a basic component. Otherwise it is a compound component. For example, the root node r of the component *statement* is a rectangle with label "*if_statement*". Its inside node set I_r consists of an entry point node, an exit point node, a condition node, and two component nodes (corresponding to '*yes*' and '*no*' of the condition node); the set E_r is a set of relationships between the inside nodes.

L_r and P_r define a component's *logical part* and *physical part*. The logical part can be used to communicate with applications. The semantic connection between the application and the logical part can be set up. One connection is visualization in the application; for instance, the application data represented by syntactic rules in text can be translated into the logical part of the diagram component. Another is semantic interpretation of the diagram on the screen, which is achieved by semantically interpreting the logical part of the diagram component. For example, the mapping between a program in a specific language and the logical part can be achieved by invoking an application-specific function.

The purpose of the physical part is purely for illustration-it is only an image of reality. The semantic connection between the application and the physical part is rather loose. The application may or may not influence the physical part: the semantics of the application can be illustrated in the physical part, but the basic purpose of the physical part is to *clarify* meaning, not to *define* meaning. For example, a node image mapping function can easily be defined from geometric information for the node: position (x, y), size (w, h) and node image mode (like a box). In direct manipulation, when a node image is selected by the mouse, the corresponding node can be found by the position matched. The physical part defines a diagram's graphical appearance. For a diagram component, its physical part is related to a diagram layout function.

That is, diagram layout functions would operate on the diagram component's physical part; the application linkage mechanism would be related to diagram component's logical part.

The framework is based on this practical graph model. We have developed a prototype platform of the framework. This platform can allow the developers to interactively construct a diagram component by testing diagram layout/editing functions they developed.

3.2. Development of Automatic Layout for Diagrams

The development of layout functions should consider the node's shape and size. If a node's shape is a box, its size is decided by its width and height. If a node's shape is not a box, such as an oval, a circle, or a diamond, it can be bounded in a box (see Figure 3). That is, its bounding box decides

Figure 3. A node's size is based on its bounding box

its size. To draw a node's shape, a specific shape drawing function can be used. In the processing of solving overlapping nodes and edge-node intersections, a node's size is based on its bounding box.

Our approach to automatic layout for practical graphs has two steps, as follows.

1. Apply an abstract graph layout function to the graph.
2. Use post-processes to avoid overlaps of node images and edge-node intersections by rearranging the graph layout generated by step 1.

Figure 4. An abstract graph layout

Step 1 is to make use of existing abstract graph drawing algorithms which are available in (Battista et al., 1999).

Step 2 refers to rearrange and adjust the graph generated by step 1. The rearrangement should also preserve the original "structure" of the graph. In the other words, the user's mental map of the graph (Eades et al., 1991, 1995) should be preserved. Step 2 needs to address the problems of overlapping nodes and edge-node intersections.

The critical part of our approach is to remove overlapping nodes and edge-node intersections. We use the techniques (Lai & Eades, 1992, 2002) for removing overlaps of node images and edge-node intersections. We have experimented with these techniques using many sets of overlapping nodes and found that it is quite effective. An example of using these techniques is shown below.

Figure 4 shows a graph layout generated by an abstract graph layout algorithm - the "spring" algorithm (Eades, 1984). Figure 5 shows the result of replacing the nodes with rectangles, which gives not only the overlapping nodes but edge-node intersections. Figure 6 is the result of applying the force-scan algorithm (Lai & Eades, 2002) for removing overlaps of node images and edge-node intersections.

Layout adjustment and *Dynamic methods* for diagram editing have been studied (Eades et al., 1991, 1995; Lai & Eades, 1992, 2002). A change in the combinatorial graph (made either by the user or the application) should induce a change in the layout on the screen. However, the layout should not change so much as to disturb the user's "mental map" of the diagram. Some mathematical models of "mental map" have been defined

Figure 5. A practical graph

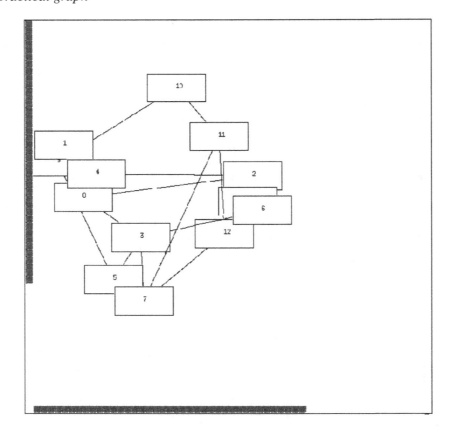

Figure 6. Layout adjustment

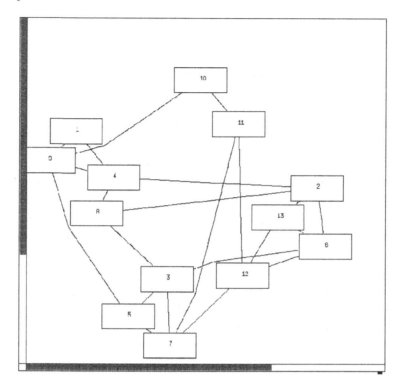

and some algorithms (Lai & Eades, 1992, 2002) developed for rearranging a diagram while preserving its "mental map". We have developed some dynamic methods for practical graph layout without changing the "mental map". Some efficient algorithms have been developed for removing overlapping nodes and edge-node intersections.

The user interface includes abstract graph drawing algorithms and layout adjustment algorithms for removing overlapping nodes and edge-node intersections. We mainly focus on the development of automatic layout techniques for practical graphs based on this platform.

4. TWO CASE STUDIES

As mentioned above, a platform has been developed based on the framework. We use this platform to do some case studies for applications,

as this platform can also allow the developers to develop functions for the linkage between the graph structure's logical part and applications. For example, different applications can be translated into abstract objects and relations in the graph structure by using different language parsers. To test and evaluate this framework for diagrams, two case studies have been developed.

4.1. Web Graph Visualization and Navigation

Each URL in the webspace is treated as a node and a link between two URLs is an edge. The graph using these nodes and edges is called web graph.

A specific function (web site parser) is developed to support the construction of Web sub-graphs by communicating with Web sites over the Internet. It can quickly search the entire neighbourhood of the focused node to form a Web sub-graph.

The Web site parser analyses the HTML file of the Web site corresponding to the focused node and extracts the hyperlinks embedded in the Web site to form nodes and edges for the Web sub-graph. To reduce the complexity of the Web graph, an information filter is developed to remove unnecessary information (edges and nodes) generated by the parser and only retains the essential part which the user requires. The web graph is mapped to the logical part of the practical graph model. The physical part of the model supports the web graph display. Actually, only the sub-graph is displayed based on the user's focus. The Web sub-graph user interface maintains the user's orientation for Web exploration and it also reduces the cognitive effort required to recognise the change of views. This is done by connecting successive displays of the subset of the Web graph and by smoothly swapping the displays via animation according to the user's navigation of the web graph. Figure 7 shows an example of a web site and its web sub-graph.

4.2. Visualization of Program Flowcharts

A source code parser is developed for converting a Pascal program source code to the flowchart drawing structure. The parser scans the source code from top to bottom and convert each statement to corresponding flowchart component (i.e. the graph's logic part). The graph's physical part is responsible for its layout.

For example, suppose that the user wants to expand the contents of node, the right statement_block within the if_statement, to see more details. After a mouse action, the function DynamicLayout is invoked to operate on this node (statement_block). First the graph included by this node is displayed and it replaces the node statement_block in the diagram (see Figure 8a); then the whole diagram (the graph included by statement_block) is rearranged (see Figure 8b) - this is achieved by the function DynamicLayout.

Figure 7. A web site and its web sub graph

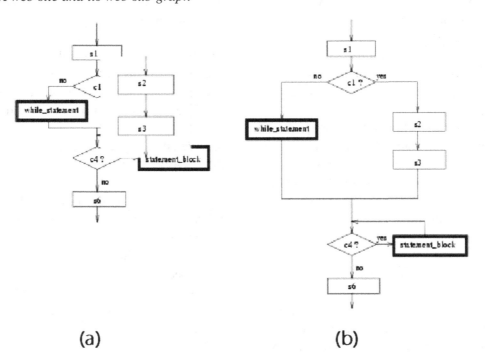

(a)   (b)

Figure 8. An example of supporting dynamic layout

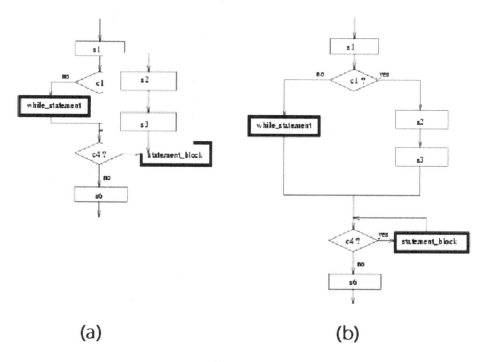

(a)   (b)

Figure 9 shows the flowchart visualization for Pascal is in action.

5. FUTURE WORK

More efficient methods will be further investigated for the layout of diagrams used in real world applications and more case studies will be developed. In practically, an application will be developed for UML diagrams visualization and code generation. Through this case study, we can test the semantic interpretation of the practical graph model. That is, the logical part can be used as a linkage between UML diagrams and code generation.

Figure 9. An example of flowchart visualization

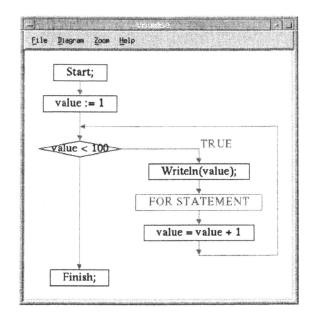

REFERENCES

Battista, G. D., Eades, P. R., Tamassia, R., & Tollis, I. (1999). *Graph drawing: Algorithms for the visualization of graphs*. Upper Saddle River, NJ: Prentice Hall.

Eades, P. (1984). A heuristic for graph drawing. *Congressus Numerantium*, *42*, 149–160.

Eades, P., Lai, W., Misue, K., & Sugiyama, K. (1991). Preserving the mental map of a diagram. [Sesimbra, Portugal: Academic Press.]. *Proceedings of COMPUGRAPHICS*, *91*, 34–43.

Eades, P., Lai, W., Misue, K., & Sugiyama, K. (1995). Layout adjustment and the mental map. *Journal of Visual Languages and Computing*, (6): 183–210.

Huang, X., & Lai, W. (2006). Clustering graphs for visualization through node similarities. *Journal of Visual Languages and Computing*, (17): 225–253. doi:10.1016/j.jvlc.2005.10.003.

Lai, W., & Eades, P. (1992). Algorithms for disjoint node images. *Australian Computer Science Communications*, *14*(1), 253–265.

Lai, W., & Eades, P. (2002). Removing edge-node intersections in drawings of graphs. *Information Processing Letters*, *81*, 105–110. doi:10.1016/S0020-0190(01)00194-6.

Ong, Y., & Kurth, W. (2012). A graph model and grammar for multi-scale modelling using XL. In *Proceedings of 2012 IEEE International Conference on Bioinformatics and Biomedicine Workshops* 1-8. Washington, DC: IEEE Press.

Rekers, J., & Schurr, A. (1995). A graph grammar approach to graphical parsing. In *Proceedings of IEEE Symposium on Visual Languages (VL'95)*. Darmstadt, Germany: IEEE Press.

Storrle, H. (2012). On the impact of layout quality to understanding UML diagrams: Diagram type and expertise. In *Proceedings of IEEE Symposium on Visual Languages and Human-Centric Computing*, 49-56. Innsbruck, Austria: IEEE Press.

Chapter 17
Community Management Matters:
Advanced Visual Analytics for Online Community Managers

John McAuley
Centre for Next Generation Localization, Trinity College, Ireland

Alex O'Connor
Centre for Next Generation Localization, Trinity College, Ireland

Dave Lewis
Centre for Next Generation Localization, Trinity College, Ireland

ABSTRACT

Online communities provide technical support for organisations on a range of products and services. These communities are managed by dedicated online community managers who nurture and help the community grow. While visual analytics are increasingly used to support a range of data-intensive management processes, similar techniques have not been adopted into the community management field. Although relevant tools exist, the majority is developed in the lab, without conducting a domain analysis or eliciting user requirements, or is designed to support more general analytic tasks. In this chapter, the authors describe a case study in which we design, develop, and evaluate a visual analytics application with the help of Symantec's online community management team. The authors suggest that the approach and the resulting application, called Petri, is an important step to promoting online community management as a strategic and data-driven process.

DOI: 10.4018/978-1-4666-4309-3.ch017

1. INTRODUCTION

Over the last number of years, large organisations have recognised the benefit in hosting online communities that promote products and services and assist in the provision of technical support. These communities help to reduce the organisation's overhead, as it is the community members, and not the organisation's technical support department, that handle questions from other product and service users. The role of the online community manager has emerged as integral to this strategy. It is their job to ensure that the community develops in a productive fashion, that anti-social behaviour is kept to a minimum and that pro-active users are encouraged and in the promoted to positions of influence in the community. At the same time, the community manager must encourage "peering", whereby members of the community, and not the organisation's staff, answer questions from other community members. Active or prolific users are often then rewarded with affiliation programmes, access to new products or services, or in some cases, jobs, contracts and new positions.

The growing trend in strategic and operational management is to make use of advanced analytic technologies that provide insight into large volumes of data and thus support a more informed or data-centric approach to decision-making (Lohr, 2012). The online community manager is in an ideal position to take advantage of this trend. Community interactions are stored in online databases, which are accessible, generally, by public or private APIs. Moreover, the online community and social analytics literature is replete with new applications and technologies that could help the community manager to identify users of potential (H. Welser, Cosley, Kossinets, & Lin, 2011), spot points of conflict (Kittur & Kraut, 2010) and deepen their understanding of community dynamics (Suh, Chi, Kittur, & Pendleton, 2008). As yet, however, these tools have not been widely adopted by online community managers and either remain as part of a growing academic literature or are employed by researchers or data analysts. Furthermore, very few, if any, of these applications are designed from the perspective of the online community manager. Instead, researchers tend to develop a novel community metric and asses its utility across multiple datasets (Chan & Hayes, 2010; Wagner, Rowe, Strohmaier, & Alani, 2012) or design a new visualisation and use it to discover and thus explain certain community phenomenon (Wattenberg, Viégas, & Hollenbach, 2007).

Our position is that a human-centred design approach is required to shift visual analytics from the research community into the practice of online community management. In supporting this position, we conducted a case study with Symantec's online community management team in Dublin, Ireland. We drew on Munzner's nested model for design and validation to guide and to an extent formalise the design process (Munzner, 2009). The model consists of four nested layers, domain analysis, data/operation abstraction design, encoding/interaction technique design and finally algorithm design, and provides a rigorous way to construct and validate human-centred visualisations. While Munzner suggests validation over evaluation, we tend to adopt both methods, applying validation at certain points during the design process but then completing a final evaluation of the application with members of the community team (five in total). We tried to apply this model in as faithful a way as possible but were restricted by the amount of access we had to the team. We held five sessions in total with the community management team. The first two workshops were used to gather requirements and to sketch out some initial designs (Domain Analysis and Operation Design). The third workshop helped to validate the initial mock-ups and reject some alternative designs (Encoding/Interaction Design). In the fourth workshop, we identified the features that were used for clustering the community into meaningful cultures, which is discussed in more detail later in this chapter (Algorithm design). These cultures were then validated in discussions with the community manger that is responsible for that particular community. The fifth and final session took the form of an explorative evaluation, following the qualitative methodology proposed by Dix (Ellis & Dix, 2006). At each point, we aimed to validate the application with the intended user community, a more grounded approach that avoids drawing subjects from the lab (Isenberg, Zuk, & Collins, 2008). In total, the research was conducted over a ten month period, from January 2012 to October 2012. Next, we briefly describe the community, on which the visual analytics application was based, and then provide an outline of the chapter.

1.1. The Community

The community is a non-English speaking technical support forum that is hosted by Symantec. The forum was started in December 2009. At the time of writing, the community had approximately 7000 users. The aim of the forum is to provide technical support on a range of products and services. Thus, the majority of activity is goal driven–users seek answers to specific technical questions. The forum is hosted by an external software provider. Their service is typical of online Q&A communities. To ask a question, a user initiates a thread on a relevant board. To answer, users submit replies. If the reply answers the question to a sufficient degree, the first user, who originally asked the question, will (or at least should) accept the reply as an answer. Other users who experience similar technical problems can draw on the answer, while also having access to the chain of reasoning (replies by other users) that contributed to the answer along the way. Users can give "kudos" to other users in the community. Kudos is a way of rewarding a user for a particular action, whether this involves asking an interesting question or submitting a well crafted answer, and helps to raise the profile of effective contributors. The community is managed by a dedicated online

community manger. Her role is to facilitate the community, and to answer questions that are not addressed by other members of the community.

1.2. Chapter Outline

The chapter is outlined as follows: First, we discuss background in which we focus on how online community visualisation has been addressed to date, outlining the advantages and disadvantages of each. We pay particular attention to the target audience of each approach; who, for example, was the visualisation designed to support and in what context was the visualisation to be applied. The context of the application advances the discussion from describing information with graphics to the application of the visualisation in specific organisational contexts. Next, we present a case study, which is divided into three parts: domain analysis, design and evaluation. In the domain analysis, we report on three workshops that were held with the community management team. The aim of the first workshop was to develop a better understanding of the process of community management, as a set of operational and strategic directives, and to understand the requirements that the team had in terms of a visual analytics application. The second and third workshops were used to gather feedback on initial designs. Next, we present Petri. We justify our design decisions with reference to the requirements, and conclude with an evaluation of the tool.

2. BACKGROUND

While there are a substantial number of applications and research prototypes available that can be used to visualise social media and online community data, none of these are developed to specifically address the process of online community management. Existing approaches fall generally within one of two categories: Activity-based visualisation, which is based on attribute or statistical data, and network-based visualisation, which is based on communication or connection data. Under network-based visualisation, there are further sub-categories, including tools that have Graphical User Interfaces (GUI) or tools that are based on programming environments or Application Programming Interfaces (API)(Henry & Fekete, 2006). The second sub-category is highly configurable yet complex and requires a substantial level of in-depth expert knowledge or expertise. In this section, we briefly analyse each category. We consider the end-user and how appropriately the application supports end-user tasks.

2.1. Activity-Based Visualisation

Activity-based visualisation presents the community as either definable groups or repeated patterns of user activity. The advantage of this approach is that it draws upon the user's perceptual capabilities to isolate and associate significant patterns and related features. This is in contrast to network-based visualisations, which generally rely on mathematical algorithms such as spring or force-directed layouts, to position the nodes and arcs in 2D space and thus improve graph readability.

Newsgroup crowds and Authorlines are two early examples of activity-based visualisation that enabled the identification of social roles in the Usenet online community (such as "Answer person," "Pollinator," or "Debater") (Viégas & Smith, 2004). While this work made a significant contribution to online community research, there are some limitations to approach to visualisation. Newsgroup crowds is a multivariate scatter plot that, while effective, is restricted to conveying four variables at a time, size, colour and coordinates. A fifth variable, shape, could be added but can serve to clutter the resulting visualisation. While this may be sufficient, there is much more information collected about a user that could improve the granularity of the resulting representation. Also, despite the use of transparency, occlusion remains an issue, as users with a similar profile can overlap and make identification and selection difficult. Finally, from the perspective of this work, the visualisations were developed to support exploration and discovery by casual users and were not designed from the perspective of the online community manager.

Other work by Viégas et al. found that visualising personal email archives prompted reflection and storytelling in casual users (Viégas, Boyd, Nguyen, Potter, & Donath, 2004). While the domain is different, salient aspects of the approach remain relevant for online community datasets. Users can, for instance, explore their email exchange or social interactions from a temporal perspective. However, the visualisations were not developed to support external analysis but instead were designed to promote personal reflection. As a result, the visual composition is more expressive and has less fidelity than expected from an analytic application. For instance, occlusion remains problematic and the use of animation is not based on increasing the level of insight but instead aims to emphasise the ebb and flow of personal communication.

HistoryFlow (Viégas, Wattenberg, & Dave, 2004; Viégas, Wattenberg, Kriss, & Ham, 2007) and Chromograms (Wattenberg et al., 2007) are two novel visualisations that were designed to explore Wikipedia. While the first exposes the edit activity of users on Wikipedia pages, the second exposes the edit activity of Wikipedia editors (described as Wikipedians by [Panciera & Halfaker, 2009]). These visualisations were used by the authors to support inductive analysis (Kimmerle, Moskaliuk, Harrer, & Cress, 2010), so that the authors could explore and then explain, posit hypotheses about or draw conclusions from Wikipedia as a large scale socio-technical phenomenon. Each visualisation design is specific to this purpose and is, thus, removed from the needs of a community manger or other community stakeholders. Having said this, their contribution is significant and the Chromogram, as a novel visual construct, has been adopted by other community researchers (Masli, Priedhorsky, & Terveen, 2011).

In contrast, Comtella (Vassileva & Sun; 2007) and Codesaw (Gilbert & Karahalios; 2007, 2009) are two social visualisations that were designed to support specific user groups. The aim of Comtella is to motivate users and increase participation rates in a peer-based sharing community, while Codesaw was designed to improve team coordination in Open Source Software (OSS) teams. While the work on Comtella has provided evidence to suggest that participation rates can be increased through the introduction of social visualisations, from an analytic perspective, the approach is quite limited. The visualisation, which draws heavily on Erickson's design principles (Erickson, 2003), is based on an evocative metaphor, described by the author "as a summer night's sky", and only one or possibly two visual variables are used when communicating activity to the user (size and colour). Also, as with any visualisation that lies beyond the experience of the user, the authors found that the interface needed some explanation. In this respect, a scatter plot, as proposed by Viégas previously, could be more useful, particularly when approached from an analytic perspective. The design of Codesaw, on the other hand, is of more interest, as the authors decided upon a user-centred design approach and consulted the intended user group from the outset. The resulting artefact is quite effective at illustrating the contrasting work practice of an OSS development team – the communications patterns versus the code-based contributions. However, Codesaw is designed for a small community (8 in total) and there is no way to select and, thus, analyse user behaviour from a larger online community. Naturally, this presents a problem when wishing to address communities of scale.

Finally, some researchers have created "legible" and "intuitive" visualisations or "data portraits" that convey, in a qualitative sense, the rich social features of users and communities. This work includes People Garden (Xiong & Donath, 1999), Loom (Donath, Karahalios, & Viégas, 1999), Loom2 (Boyd, Ramage, & Donath, 2002) and anthropomorphic visualisations (Perry & Donath, 2004). While certainly interesting, the integrity of the visualisation is always questionable given that the designer attributes additional meaning with often evocative metaphors. The result is more impressionistic than realistic, and may, as a consequence, not serve the purposes of the community manager (which is to comprehend in as faithful a way as possible the behaviour of their community). Also, each approach was designed to support exploration and discovery by casual users and there was little consultation with user groups or communities during the design process.

2.2. Network-Based Visualisation

There are a number of work-bench-type applications, such as R, NetworkX with Gephi and GraphViz, currently available that can be used to analyse and visualise network data. Even the most user-friendly of these applications, however, are methodologically-driven (requiring the use of "recipes" to get started) and are designed to support the explorative analysis of network data, often from the perspective of a data scientist or professional analyst. In addition, users require some programming knowledge to parse and assemble the graphs, which can lie beyond the skill-set of the regular online community manager. While applications, such as Orion (Heer & Perer, 2011) and NodeXL (Bonsignore et al., 2009; Smith et al., 2009), help to mitigate these concerns, there still remains the need for the user to understand how to apply the appropriate analytic methodology. Certainly, NodeXL, based on Microsoft's Excel software, is a step in the right direction, in terms of broadening a user community; however it remains a comprehensive analytic tool. While programming is not required, an understanding of social network analysis is; as is an understanding of how to methodically approach the analytic process. For a novice, getting to grips with the application involves a period of trial and error. And while it has been shown that students can quickly understand and thus apply NodeXL to analyse social media data, the demonstration was undertaken within a tutorial setting with the aid of an experienced tutor. How an online community manager would adjust to the introduction of NodeXL, thus, remains an open question.

Less complex network applications, such as Vizster (Heer & Boyd, 2005) and ICTA (Gruzd & Haythornthwaite, 2008), provide users with access to online community data as visualised social networks. While certainly more intuitive, Vizster was designed to support "playful discovery" of community networks, from the perspective of the casual end-user, and was not designed from the perspective of the online community manager. Having said this, Vizster's approach to the interactive exploration of community networks remains quite innovative. ICTA (Internet Community Text Analyzer), on the other hand, is a content-based approach to the analysis and visualisation of online community data. Unlike other network visualisations, ICTA extracts usernames from community posts and then creates a social network based on those names and the connections between the posts. The authors argue that the use of a name carries increased significance and thus provides another way to evaluate the community's network. Both Vizster and ICTA only support exploration, however, and while explorative analysis is important for discovery, from our analysis we learned that community managers require the ability to shift from explorative to confirmative analysis, when validating the choice of super-user for example. Shifting modes of analysis requires precise information delivered to the user in different formats at different times.

Researchers have also investigated the use of matrix-based representations to visualise social connections in groups and communities. While less popular than node-link diagrams, matrices have some advantages, namely that they not only show the connections between users but also show incidents where there are no connections between users, thus, the user is privy to how groups are communicating and also not communicating. Matrices can also be used to illustrate temporal shifts more effectively than node-link diagrams due to the nodes having a fixed position in space. Van Ham et al. Developed Honeycomb, a scalable matrix-based visualisation, to address the communications of large organisations (such as IBM). They found meaningful communications across the entire organisation, using varying degrees of resolution, such as country and business division. One advantage of this approach is that it provides the user with a single reference model, unlike a composite of metrics and visualisation interfaces like NodeXL. However, the authors focused on emphasising the benefits of matrices over node-link diagrams, as opposed to addressing how matrices could be adopted by non-expert users, such as online community managers, in other analytic scenarios. In contrast, Henry's work with social science researchers sought to establish how matrices could be used to support their work practice (Henry & Fekete, 2006). Taking a user-centred design approach, Henry characterised the domain of the social science researchers, drafted up a set of requirements and then designed and developed a matrix-based visualisation environment to address their needs. While not specific to the domain of online community management, the approach to design, coupled with the goal of applying visualisation to support an existing user-community, illustrates how to create meaningful visualisation environments for non-expert users (i.e. non-professional analysts).

Finally, the use of network or matrix-based visualisation places an overriding emphasis on the connection, a view that was first established by the sociologist Georg Simmel (Marin & Wellman, 2010), over the other characteristics of the social group. This view has gained considerable currency in online community research, which is, to some degree, driven by the ease of access to electronic records and early publications, such as (Danyel Fisher, Smith, & Welser, 2006; Turner, Smith, Fisher, & Welser, 2005), which helped to illustrate the benefits of the approach. While network data is important, it provides just one perspective, which can be supported with the addition of other visualisations. As suggested by Fernanda Viégas, "we usually understand things better we have more than one way of looking at them" (F.B. Viégas & Donath, 2004).

3. DOMAIN ANALYSIS

Initially, we presented some of our previous work to the team in Symantec. We described the aim of this work, which was to provide reflective support to online communities (McAuley, O'Connor, & Lewis, 2012), and discussed, in broader terms, how we thought visualisation could support the role of the community manager. In a way, much of this discussion was driven from the literature, as we had little working knowledge of how the community manager went about their daily routine. We had conducted some informal interviews with community managers from other organisations, but their approach to community management varied greatly. In some instances, their role was quite casual, and the process of community management had not been formalised into strategic or operational directives. Also, in some cases, the notion of visualising a community to support the management process had been met with little interest. They found it difficult to conceive of a use for such as tool. As a result, the aim of the domain analysis was for us to find out as much about the team's internal work process as it was to elicit a set of design requirements.

During the domain analysis, we conducted three workshops in total. The first two workshops involved three members of the team, including the manager of the community, and the principle researcher, and were aimed at understanding the team's management processes and their need for a visual analytics tool. The third and final workshop included an additional member of the team and

a second researcher, and was used to present and get feedback on initial designs, and to identify a feature set for clustering users in the community into a set of cultures. While we aimed to video each workshop, some of the team felt more comfortable with audio, thus the audio was recorded for each workshop. In this section, we present and discuss the findings from each of the three workshops.

3.1. First Workshop

The aim of the first workshop was to develop a general understanding of how the team underwent the process of community management and to establish how they thought visual analytics could support this process. We divided the workshop into two stages. In the first stage, we addressed the following questions:

- What is the process of community management?
- How do you currently analyse or evaluate community activity?
- How do you envision visual analytics supporting the community manager?

Each question was considered open-ended and used to guide discussion. The principal researcher facilitated and took notes. In the second stage, the team sketched out some initial design ideas on a white board, which were then brainstormed as a group. Here we describe both stages of the workshop.

3.1.1. What is the Process of Community Management?

From the outset, it was highlighted that the process of community management was not to suppress or control the community, which as the literature highlights can reduce contribution rates (Preece, 2000), but to support and encourage pro-social behaviour. The aim, it was emphasised, is to reinforce, and not undermine, the sense of community. For example, the community manager mentioned that over the two years since the community started, she has only banned one user. Rarely, have the community experienced anti-social behaviour to the point that it needed to be addressed on a broader scale or at a policy level. The team were more interested in increasing "conversion" rates. Conversion is the term used to describe the process of converting a user from "detractor" to "supporter". A detractor is someone who discredits a product or service or, possibly, contributes to the community in a negative way. A "promoter", on the other hand, is someone who either promotes the company's products and services or helps out in the forum.

Aside from converting detractors to promoters, members of the team were interested in improving "peer support" in the community. Peer support is the term used to describe when a user, who is not a member of Symantec's staff, answers a question belonging to another user in the community. Thus peers, regular or casual community members, provide the required technical support, which in turn, reduces the burden on the organisation's technical support department. Coupled with increasing conversion, improving peer support is considered as instrumental to the organisation's community strategy.

Regularly, community managers will present cases to the management team about specific conversions (amongst other noteworthy incidents and events) in their respective communities. These presentations help to reinforce successful management practice by allowing the team discuss how best address difficult or troublesome situations (Brown & Duguid, 1991). Also, the idea of "conversion" is an identifiable practice that can be readily communicated to management, which helps to validate, and justify, the online community strategy.

3.1.2. How Do You Currently Analyse or Evaluate Community Activity?

The community software provider, that host Symantec's online communities, provides a measure of community health called the "community health index". This is a weekly report that outlines the community's current standing. The participants do not find this measure particularly useful however. Rather they described the measure as too "coarse" or having "no value-add" and thus unrepresentative of how they understand the progression of their communities. It was also identified that community health is very difficult to measure, and that striving for a single measure, as opposed to a composite of different yet related measures, is often meaningless. Nevertheless, currently, there is no generally accepted way for the community manger to assess status or evaluate activity. They did indicate that ratios, such as posts to number of threads, can be used to make "snap judgements" on different users but that those judgements would need further validation. Users can have high thread-to-post ratio yet, qualitatively, contribute very little to the community. Conversely, low thread-to-post ratios may indicate "ranters"-users who are active one thread posting negatively about a specific topic.

3.1.3. How Do You Envision Visual Analytics Supporting the Community Manager?

In answering this question, the team identified four main objectives for the visual analytics application:

Detractors

The team were interested in detractors. Detractors are users who post negative comments about Symantec products or services. Automatically identifying negative comments in social media communities is difficult however, due to the nuance of language and the context of use. While structural or social-network features, such as reply-to-networks, can help to identify cliques of dissatisfied users (through the analysis of detractor comments and voting patterns for example), realising the sentiment of the content in the first place, requires some form of textual analysis. The difficulties of sentiment were discussed at some length. A member of the team, who had experience of sentiment analysis in other projects, suggested avoiding this approach entirely due to the "inaccuracies" and difficulties that it presented previously. They suggested that the information provided in the visualisation must be "reliable" and "actionable" and that, because sentiment is too nuanced a concept to address at this point, identifying detractors (if addressed at all) should be deferred to future iterations of the tool. Nevertheless, the ability to reveal colluders, users who support vocal detractors, was identified as important by a member of the team. Also the ability to reveal sock puppets, users who create alternate accounts with the aim of gaming the system or trolling other users (Gazan, 2009; Suh, Chi, Pendleton, & Kittur, 2007), was suggested by the team.

Peer Support

Part of the online community strategy is to increase peer support. Peer support involves members of the community answering questions about Symantec products and services. As discussed, this reduces the burden of effort on the community manager, or other officially appointed community members, which in turn reduces the cost of providing technical support. The team were interested in questions and metrics around peer-support, such as, how much support in the community can be considered peer support? And is change in peer support evident over time? They were also interested in identifying users that could contribute more in terms of answers, to the community. One of the team mentioned that while she knows her community very well, she felt that there could still be

users, who have untapped potential, and thus slip through the net because she was unable to identify that potential early enough. Being able to identify users that could provide a greater contribution to the community is important.

Cultures

The team were interested in partitioning the community into several different "cultures" with each culture representing a degree or level of contribution to the community. To take a simple example from the first workshop, as illustrated in Figure 1, the culture "newbie" could represent those that have just joined the community. The visitor culture could represent someone who visits the community regularly, asking questions but not contributing answers. The culture "regular contributor" could represent an active user who both asks and answers questions and the culture "guru" could represent the most knowledgeable users who are few in number but answer many questions. These sorts of demographics are common in Q&A forums, amongst other types of online communities, and have been addressed in the literature on the identification of social roles (Chan & Hayes, 2010; Crowston & Howison, 2005; Golder & Donath, 2004; Kelly, Fisher, & Smith, 2006; Malouf & Mullen, 2008; Welser et al., 2011; Welser, Gleave, Fisher, & Smith, 2008). The difference with this approach is that the team was interested in identifying users that have the capacity to contribute to the community in a more meaningful way and then converting those users from one culture to the next over a sustained period of time. In this capacity, a user who starts out as a newbie could end up as a contributor or indeed a guru (to return to our previous example) through the encouragement and support of the community manager. While similar frameworks have been proposed, most notably Preece and Shneiderman's reader-to-leader framework (Preece & Shneiderman, 2009), we have yet to find an actual implementation of this approach in the online community literature.

Figure 1. An illustration of community cultures, as presented by one of the team in the first workshop In this image, a user starts out as a newbie Over time, that user becomes a visitor, develops into a regular contributor and then emerges as a guru This is an "ideal" trajectory, from the perspective of an online community manager, for a user in a technical support forum

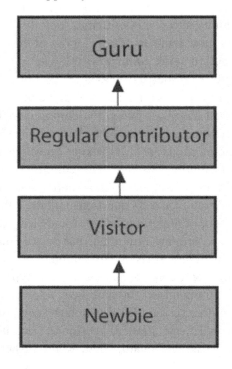

User Paths

The team were also interested in the notion of a user's path. A member of the team described a user's path as "a logical path, which is based on increased levels of activity". The team hypothesised the "Gurus" could have "ideal" paths and that these paths could be used to compare and contrast different user trajectories over time. If, for example, the community manager is interested in promoting a user to the position of Guru, she could use the path visualisation to confirm and thus validate her decision. Similarly, the path visualisation could be used to communicate this decision to the rest of the team or to upper man-

agement and thus illustrate the effectiveness of the online community strategy.

In the second stage of the workshop, the team sketched some ideas on a whiteboard that were then discussed as a group (see Figure 2). We concentrated on visualising community cultures, which would provide a high-level overview of the community, and then user paths, which would describe a user's trajectory through the community. It was decided that the community culture visualisation would be the community manager's first contact with the visualisation tool. From there the community manager could select users that are of interest and then "carry her analysis forward" by comparing user paths using other visualisations methods. Coordinating these visualisations (North, 2000) was suggested but discarded, due to screen dimensions and the quantity of information being presented.

3.1.4. Implications

Certainly, the outcome of this session has several implications for the role of the community manager and the practice of online community management: Firstly, they will be able to extend the practice of "conversion" to other community cultures beyond that of detractor. Secondly, they will be able to assess, in an approximate fashion, the outcome of any intervention with the community. For example, if a certain activity is targeted at a specific set of users, and that activity is promoted and rewarded, what is the rate of conversion of users to the next culture? This will allow them to answer questions such as, who should be promoted? How successful was that intervention with the community? Are there gold standard approaches to encouraging certain users or dealing with specific cultures? Thirdly: Visual analytics will be considered a key component of the community management process, enabling the community manager to not only analyse the activity of the community but also assess their own interventions, and the result of those interventions, with the community.

Figure 2. The results from the second stage of the first workshop held with the community management team General ideas and initial designs as proposed during brainstorming 1. Cultures as articulated by the participants in the first workshop Cultures are defined by their levels of contribution, from newbie to visitor to contributor 2. Analysing different user actions 3. A team member's initial diagram of community cultures 4. Initial sketch of user paths

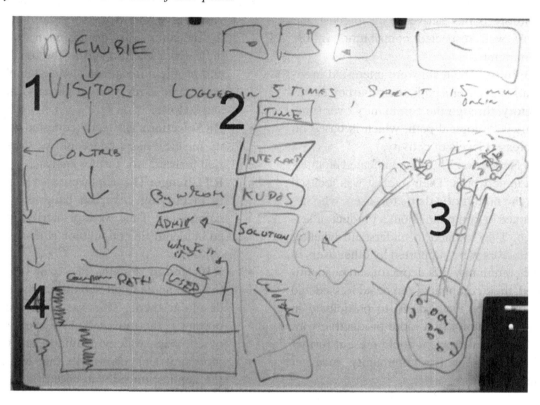

4. DESIGN REQUIREMENTS

Having completed the first workshop, we drafted a set of design requirements.

- **R1 Multiple Visualisations**: The team suggested that Petri consist of both global and local visualisations. The global visualisation provides access to the entire community, while the local visualisation allows the user to drill down into data and compare different user paths. In this mode of analysis, the user shifts between explorative and confirmative tasks. First she explores the global visualisation to select users of interest and then confirms her se-

lection using the local visualisation. Over time, the global visualisation can support both kinds of tasks, the global view confirming that a user has migrated into a new culture while also allowing the community manager explore the community. In this way, the manager can build a more comprehensive mental-model of the how the community is organised and how specific users contribute to the community.

- **R2 Cultures**: The global view should automatically cluster the community into meaningful representations called "cultures". Each culture should represent a collective position in the community. While there is a lot of work being conducted on identifying social roles in online communities, the aim of this approach is to partition users by their level contribution coupled with the level of peer recognition. This is a linear trajectory that extends from users who are barley active to the highest and most well respected contributors in the community.

- **R3 Paths**: The team were interested in visualising a user's path, their journey or trajectory, through the community over time. This is "a logical path, which is based on increased levels of activity."

- **R4 Networks:** The team indicated an interest in networks. Their interest was focused on the notion of a detractor–users who denounce or complain about a product or service. They wanted to understand whether detractors were supported by other users in the community. If a detractor can be identified, their complaints can be addressed and they can be encouraged to participate in the community in a more productive way. Cliques of detractors could present further difficulties for the community manager also.

- **R5 Outliers**: As with the use of most visual analytic applications, community managers are interested in identifying, and if necessary filtering for, outliers. In this case, an outlier is someone on the periphery of a particular culture, or someone who has just moved from one culture to another.

- **R6 Interaction**: The ability to interact with the application, to adjust the scope of time and filter for specific users, was also highlighted. Animation was discussed at some length but considered superfluous to the analytic process. Parameter fine-tuning, whereby a user adjusts the feature set or the parameters of the clustering algorithm, was discussed but considered as excessively complex, considering the domain analysis, and would require further inves-

tigation beyond the scope of the current study. However, the ability to pan, zoom, search and filter was requested to enable traversal of the dataset.

- **R7 Profile Information**: Aside from providing access to the user's pattern of activity, the community management team also indicated a need to access the user's general profile information such as number of posts, time of registration, time of last visit, and so forth.

- **R8 Selection:** The team requested the ability to select users that could be then "carried forward" for further analysis.

- **R9 Change:** The team were also interested in identifying changing patterns in their community. They were primarily interested in identifying population shifts between cultures.

- **R10 Design**: Finally, the team suggested that the application should have a certain design aesthetic. This was considered important if the tool was to be used as part of a broader strategy. Similarly, and from a more practical perspective, they asked that the application be web-based or have the ability to run on a tablet. This is because managers use tablets to quickly share observations and insights with other members of their team. Thus, a web-based approach would help improve the possibility of adoption and the dissemination of findings. While these are practical considerations, and usually reserved as implementation details, their inclusion illustrates the requirements needed for the adoption of visual analytics into regular work practice.

5. DESIGN WORKSHOPS

In the next two workshops, we focused on producing an initial set of designs, validating those designs as mock-ups presented to the team, selecting a set of features for the clustering process and then validating the cultures from the perspective of the community manager.

5.1. Second Workshop

In the second workshop, the researcher gave a brief presentation on relevant approaches to information visualisation. All of the examples that were used in the presentation were based on the requirements gathered during the first workshop. Only a couple of the examples were related specifically to online communities. Having completed the presentation, the researcher handed out an information sheet that detailed different ways to visualise a community's culture or a user's path. The sheet presented an illustration of the visualisation on the left and a textual description of the visualisation on the right as illustrated in Figure 3.

The team addressed each visualisation in turn, with each member providing their opinion of the approach, and then we discussed the advantages and disadvantages of each visualisation as a group. The aim was to see if there was a preference for a certain type of visualisation outside of what had been discussed previously. Also, it provided some alternative representations that the team had not previously encountered but could help understand the problem from a different perspective. The rest of the workshop was used to address some initial sketches, to clarify the different interactive techniques and to discuss possible alternative visualisations.

5.2. Third Workshop

The third workshop had two specific goals: To validate our initial designs (as illustrated in Figure 4) and to identify a set of features that could be used to cluster the community into meaningful cultures. We presented the mock-ups to the team, which involved providing the rationale for our design decisions, and held a discussion on the approach to clustering. Some initial work on the clustering had been completed at this point, so the general idea was presented and discussed at some length. Communicating the idea behind the clustering was also discussed. Very obscure measure renders the visualisation less comprehensible, thus it was important to create a model that community managers can understand. Following the workshop, we drafted up all the metrics, numbering over 60 in total, which could be used as features in clustering. This was then reduced to a smaller set as discussed in more detail in section 6.1.1.

Figure 3. A sheet of visualisation examples used to guide discussion and present alternative approaches during the second workshop

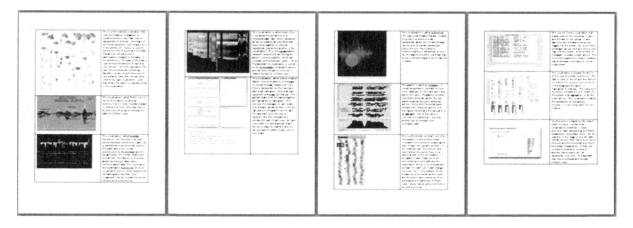

As regards the visualisations, the team felt comfortable with how the cultures were represented (see Figure 4). At the time, there was no discernible order to how each culture was positioned on the screen. The team suggested that the position of each culture should convey some meaning. One member of the team suggested that the ordering of the cultures should be represented in the visualisation–from newbie to guru for example. They had mixed views on representing lurkers (which are the largest of the cultures in Figure 4). One member of the team thought lurkers were the most interesting culture but that they occupied a lot of screen real estate and commanded a lot perceptual attention if they are not to be used in the actual application. The paths visualisation was less well received. It was described as non-intuitive and overly complex. It was suggested that a more familiar approach be considered. As result, we discussed timelines, sparklines and small multiples as an alternative and more familiar representation.

6. DESIGN OF PETRI

Petri is an initial attempt to develop a visual analytic application that can support, and thus be integrated into, the work practice of an online community manager. In this section, we present the application's main features. We describe each visualisation, justifying our design decisions with reference to the user requirements (see section 4). We also present our approach to partitioning and then ordering the community into number of discrete cultures.

6.1. Visualsiation1: Cultures

Initially, we choose a scatter plot, varying the hue of visual variable according to their culture (Bertin, 1983). However, the resulting visualisation was sparse, and required the use of "jitter" to reduce occlusion. Further, the visualisation posed some interesting questions as to how the tool would be used in practice. It was felt that a scatter plot

Figure 4. Some initial mock-ups The cultures visualisation (on the left) is close to how the cultures are represented in later versions of Petri The paths visualisation (on the right) was rejected as noisy and non-intuitive In this visualisation, the users are represented by profile images on the left and their activity is presented like a heat map stretching left to right

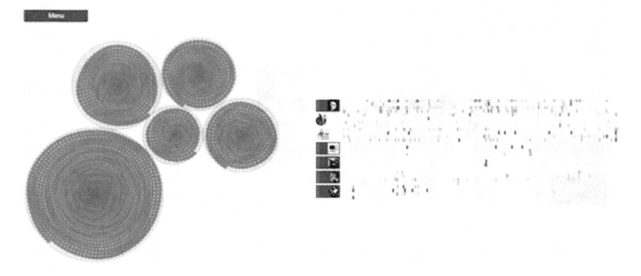

would be more suited to the sorts of explorative analysis performed by a data analyst, at the point of "inventory and classification" (Bertin, 1983b) for example, as opposed to a tool that is used at regular intervals by a community manager. In the latter case, the dataset remains the same and the task may shift from explorative to confirmative as time progresses (in addressing simple questions, such as, have we more gurus this week than last? Are there more pragmatists this week than last week? [These are two community cultures]). Even having enclosed each culture using convex hull (and quadratic spline for smoothing), the occluded and dispersed data points remained problematic. The community manager would have to seek out each culture when addressing the tool and comparing cultures, as regards their size and population, would also be difficult. The approach, we observed, would not help the user build a sufficient mental model of the community, particularly as the tool is to be used at regular intervals over time.

Comparing change (R9) in cultures over time is not addressed in this chapter, but, as discussed, this requirement contributed to the choice of technique. The culture visualisation, given the static position of each culture and the reliance on size to illustrate population, can be used in a small multiple display to illustrate change in the community's structure over time. This is not reported in this chapter however; as we did not address it in the evaluation, and is thus considered in future work.

We re-organised the layout and composition of the visualisation. We drew together each culture, as illustrated in Figure 5 and ordered each culture in a spiral (clockwise) orientation according to their level of contribution (From Pragmatist to Guru). Thus, each culture has a fixed spatial position. We varied the saturation of each culture (using a degree of blue) and provided a legend. We used a circle packing algorithm, as discussed in (Wang, Wang, Dai, & Wang, 2006) to avoid occlusion,

thus ensuring that each user is perceptible. This approach also accounted for interaction and guaranteed that the community manager could click on, and, thus, retrieve the details of a user at any point (R8). Also, the community manager could filter different users based on last visit or registration date or search for a particular user with a given username. We sized and ordered each user according to their distance from the medoid (centre of their cluster), thus outliers appear larger and to the outskirts of the culture (R5), than closely related users, who are packed together at the centre of the culture. Although the size of a visual variable has less efficacy than its spatial position, which is generally considered the "fundamental substrate" of visualisation (Munzner, 2000), we felt this approach was appropriate, given the requirements of the management team. One drawback, however, is that the community manager is provided with no information on how closely a user may be related to a second culture or how a user is related to a user from a second culture. How useful this information is to a community manager, who is not an experienced data analyst, is speculative, and could serve to confuse rather than clarify their analysis.

6.1.1. Algorithm

The aim of the cultures visualisation is to partition the community into different cultures and visualise those cultures for the online community manager. Although the term "culture" was proposed by participants in the first workshop, the term social role is more commonly used in the online community literature. Generally, social roles are informal social positions taken up by users in an online community and are based upon "repeated interactions and mutually agreed upon practices" (Golder & Donath, 2004). Familiar social roles include lurker (someone who does not actively engage with the community) and troll (someone who baits other users into argu-

Figure 5. Petri Cultures Visualisation 1. Interactive dispaly with different cultures organised in a clock-work configuration: pragmatist, peer, apprentice and guru, 2. Individual users, organised according to the distance from the medoid of their cluster The larger the glyph, the further the user is from the centre. Exceptionally large glyphs are outliers, 3. Selected users. These users are "carried forward" by the communtiy manager for analysis, 4. Search functionality, 5. Date selector, 6. Filters (only available when the communty manager zooms into a culture), 7. User Profile Data (R7)

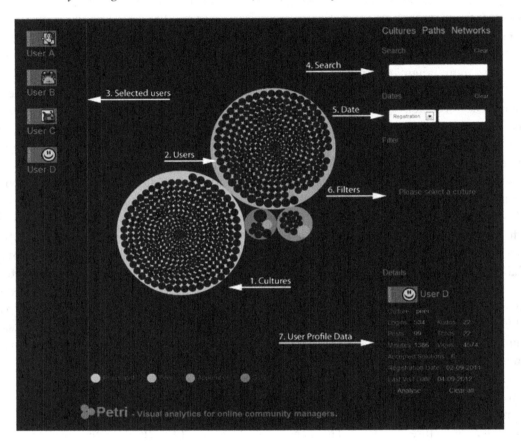

ments). However, over the last number of years, researchers have used a combination activity and social network visualisations to reveal a number of additional social roles, such as answer person, debater (Usenet) and technical editor (Wikipedia) (Fisher et al., 2006; Kelly et al., 2006; Viégas & Smith, 2004; Welser et al., 2011; Welser et al., 2008). Our conception of a culture may be a little different from the social role proposed by Golder and Donath in that we are interested in identifying points along a linear trajectory (see Figure 1) that can be used to gauge a user's increasing level of contribution.

Initially, we followed the approach proposed by Chan and Hayes (Chan & Hayes, 2010) in which they use a number of social network measures, coupled with activity ratios, to cluster and partition a large online community into a number of different user roles. However, we found it difficult to communicate the nature of these user roles to the community management team because they are based on a combination of complex (social network) measures. Also, there is no indication of a clear trajectory, which users can follow from lurker to guru using this approach as the categorisation is skewed by the structural position of the user in the community. Consequently, we removed the social network measures, and concentrated, instead, on identifying a number of activity based ratios that could be used to illustrate an increasing level contribution. We focused on ratios that indicate productive contribution, such as number of replies submitted to a thread that the user did not start, and peer recognition, such as amount of kudos attributed to a user over-time.

The company's software provider collects over 60 metrics on each member of the community. These metrics range from the conventional, such as number of logins and number of minutes spent online, to the more obscure such as arbitrary points and view productivity. As with most forum software, certain metrics are immediately useful, such as number of posts or number of replies versus number of initiated threads, however, we validated our feature selection with participants from the community management team (fourth session). With the help of one of the participants, we reduced the 60 metrics to 15, and identified 7 of those 15 as supplementary, and to be used

only if we had difficulty in producing meaningful clusters with the initial set. Adding more features to clustering will not, however, guarantee more meaningful results, but the supplementary features can be used to replace some of the initial set.

The resulting 15 features are shown in Table 1.

As with the majority of online community populations, the distribution of activity is heavily skewed. Generally, this resembles a power law (called Pareto's law) in which roughly 80% of all posts in a community are contributed by 20% of the population (Anderson, 2006; Morzy, 2009). Some communities are more heavily skewed than others, and distributions can range from 90%/10% to 99%/1%. Essentially, our aim was to remove marginal users form the population, thus "cutting the tail", and then partitioning the remaining distribution into a number of discrete yet ordered "bands", with each band representing an increasing level of user contribution. This reduces the noise for clustering, but also helps the community manager to focus on the users who are active in the community. First, we choose users who

Table 1. The final set of primary and supplementary features drawn up with a member of Symantec team

	Primary Features	Explanation
1.	Initiated Threads	Total number of threads initiated
2.	Posts	Number of posts
3.	Message views	Total number of message views
4.	Replies	Number of replies
5.	Accepted solutions	Number of accepted solutions
6.	Minutes spent online	Total number of minutes spent online
7.	Registration time	Time of registration
8.	Kudos received	Kudos received by other users in the community
	Supplementary Features	Explanation
9.	Logins	Total number of logins
10.	Solved threads to threads ratio	Threads to solved threads ratio
11.	Total posts per thread	Number of posts per thread
12.	Solutions marked	Number of posts that are marked as a solution
13.	Number of private messages sent	Number of private messages sent
14.	Last visit time	Last time the user visited the site
14.	Kudos given	Kudos attributed to other users in the community

submitted more than three posts to the community, which reduced the population to 879. Next, we converted all the above features into percentages of the overall population and then normalised the dataset. So, for example, the percentage replies of a specific user was calculated by comparing the number of replies that user submitted to the community against all replies submitted by all users to the community, while percentage of kudos received is calculated against all the kudos that is distributed in the system. This allows us to situate each user in relation to other users in the community. We created one additional feature–the percentage of threads that a user contributes a reply to, which they did not initiate. This is an important addition as it indicates peer-based activity–users contributing to threads that they did not

initiate with a question. We choose principal component analysis, to reduce the dimensionality of the dataset, and then used agglomerative hierarchical clustering, as it does not require pre-defining the number of clusters (see Table 2). A similar approach was first applied by Chan and Hayes to decompose communities into user roles, as discussed above, and is detailed in a practical way in (Husson, Le, & Pages, 2010).

Clustering partitioned the community into 19 different clusters as described in Table 1. Next, we evaluated and then aggregated the clusters by the commonality of their features resulting in a set of easily describable cultures. These clusters had to be communicated to the user of Petri so the aim was not produce too fine-grained a representation.

Table 2. Cluster statistics. The middle columns provide the means of the nine features for the 19 clusters The first column is the cluster number and the last column is the population of the cluster N.B. Cl in the first column stands for the "Cluster", the cluster number.

Cl	Replies	Accepted Solutions	Initiated Threads	Kudos Received	Posts	Views	Minutes	Threads	Non-initiate	Size
1	0.75	0	0.25	0	0.016878	0.0006482	0.0086079	0.02281022	0	2
2	0.75	0	0.25	0	0.0168776	0.00055733	0.0084206	0.03910323	0.0162930	7
3	0.7365501	0.01617632	0.2755102	0.00070837	0.0168776	0.0006183	0.0126181	0.033982571	0.00844779	49
4	0.7398325	0.01544103	0.2601674	0.0010518	0.02132720	0.00109018	0.01671008	0.0468646	0.0182481	55
5	0.7423309	0.01993561	0.2576691	0.00260733	0.0281690	0.0013686	0.02034079	0.05718662	0.02377403	71
6	0.77012406	0.00941295	0.2298759	0.0013963	0.02068134	0.00091810	0.0143510	0.0374177	0.0126973	203
7	0.78590876	0.010722941	0.21409125	0.00214747	0.03091037	0.00192022	0.0395176	0.08266423	0.03576642	132
8	0.7936631	0.0249115	0.20633694	0.00337846	0.04587342	0.00241718	0.0395176	0.08266423	0.0357664	125
9	0.7985033	0.03023245	0.2014966	0.00370691	0.0555487	0.0035999	0.0385052	0.1067430	0.04384877	103
10	0.8492664	0.0557137	0.1507336	0.0099084	0.0794506	0.0006438	0.0767692	0.1494797	0.088086	94
11	0.873083	0.2251818	0.1269164	0.0491727	0.349252	0.0205566	0.2371149	0.9103351	0.6822329	22
12	0.9675596	1.6749233	0.0324404	0.293108	0.7264416	0.0454212	0.9015536	14.94069	2.4026764	6
13	0.986842	0.070771	0.013158	0.02314	0.962025	0.051323	2.087226	1.117701	1.04927	1
14	0.959016	1.98159	0.040984	0.485942	1.544304	0.059372	1.577933	4.425182	4.083029	1
15	0.833368	2.642132	0.166323	0.539935	2.41490	0.084248	0.964431	7.010341	4.77794	3
16	0.991286	5.095541	0.008143	0.766516	3.911392	0.221030	6.677768	13.20712	13.01323	2
17	0.816449	5.732484	0.183551	2.296656	4.206751	0.583894	8.340355	14.59854	10.42427	1
18	0.987507	15.28662	0.012493	1.700798	8.105485	0.315316	3.804482	24.74909	24.20164	1
19	0.989204	18.25902	0.010796	2.302441	9.379747	0.52056	8.977342	22.71898	22.17153	1

This resulted in 4 cultures:

1. **Pragmatist (Clusters 1–7):** Users that ask a question and then receive an answer. Generally, they do not contribute to other threads that they have not initiated. They receive very little kudos and are mainly in the community to seek an answer to a question. These users make up the majority of active users in the community.
2. **Peer (Clusters 8–10):** Users that contribute to threads that they have not initiated. However, they receive little recognition from their peers, by way of kudos, and have lower contribution rates than the apprentice culture. This group shows some potential.
3. **Apprentice (Clusters 11–12):** Users that make a recognisable contribution to the community, participating in more threads than they initiate, thereby contributing more answers than questions. They have also begun to receive recognition in the form of kudos, views and accepted solutions from the rest of the community.
4. **Guru (Clusters 13–19):** Finally, gurus contribute the most to the community. They are highly knowledgeable and skilled users that receive the most peer recognition in the form of the kudos, views and accepted solutions.

6.1.2. Interaction

We sought to provide straightforward and intuitive ways for the user to improve the readability and representation of the visualisation (R6). Thus, the user can pan and zoom, search (using auto-suggest) and filer out users on a range of different attributes (number of logins, posts, kudos, threads, views and date or registration or date of last visit). Filters can only be applied once the community manager has zoomed into a specific culture (see Figure 6). This is because there is a significant gulf between the contribution rates of users in the different cultures. For example, one of the top contributors, who is a guru, logged in over 3050 times at the time of writing. This is in contrast to the majority of pragmatists who have logged in less than 30 times. Filters can be combined to isolate users within a specific set of parameters, for example, users that have received a certain level of kudos combined with a certain number of posts. The overall approach reflects Shneiderman's highly cited visual information-seeking mantra, overview first, pan, zoom and filter, details on demand (Shneiderman, 1996) and allows the manager to traverse the community in a intuitive manner. We felt that this was important. While we discussed the possibilities of parameter adjustment, reordering and automatic clustering

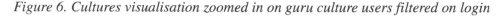

Figure 6. Cultures visualisation zoomed in on guru culture users filtered on login

in the workshops, we decided against it in this iteration. The results of these techniques can be difficult to interpret and can require much trial-and-error on behalf of the user, which is something we aimed to avoid. Further refinement is required before implementation and evaluation of this sort of interaction.

6.1.3. Selection

In Petri, we implemented a relatively simple selection function to fulfil the requirement (R8) and provide the community manager with a way to select users for further analysis (see Figure 7). Selected users are presented to the community manager in the top left of the visualisation interface and are persisted across the cultures, paths and network visualisations. At both the cultures and networks interface, the community manager is able to add additional users for analysis.

6.2. Visualisation 2: Paths

In Petri, the community manager is able to analyse and compare how users develop over time (R3). A user's path is an aggregation of any recorded productive action that is committed during their

time in the community. Other actions, such as giving and receiving kudos, are also included in the user's path as these actions signify social exchange and peer recognition by the community as a whole. So, for example, initiating a thread or replying to a thread, are both social actions that contribute to a user's path, as are having a solution accepted, giving kudos, receiving kudos and posting to threads that the user did not initiate (as this is considered peer-based behaviour). Initially, we considered the user path as an invariant represented by two components – aggregated actions over time (Bertin, 1983c). We used a time-series to represent this information, reducing the number of categories in the time component to intervals of four months (since the forum began). We avoided cumulative frequencies so that the graph would present the general tendency of a user's contribution since joining the community (see Figure 8).

6.2.1. Interaction

While this approach facilitates comparison, and supports confirmatory analysis, it is quite limited in scope. The community manger is unable to assess how exactly an individual user contributes to the community. They are unable to answer

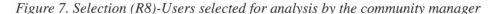

Figure 7. Selection (R8)-Users selected for analysis by the community manager

Figure 8. Path visualization. In this image, the communtiy manager is comparing the combined contribution rates of four users The user's path (considered as an aggregation of all productive activtiy in the community) is presented on a time-series At a glance the most active contributors are perceptable, however, the approach also allows the community manager compare their contribution rates with other users

questions such as: Does this user post replies or initiate threads? Or, do their replies receive kudos from other users? Further, a user's path may be heavily skewed by a single action and that single action is not presented to the community manager in the context of the user's other actions. However, to provide this context, we had to re-address the construction of the visualisation. Our objective was to provide a second visualisation that would draw from the first, and thus have a similar design aesthetic, yet provide the ability to compare and contrast a user's actions over time.

For example, a community manager could asses a user's replies versus their kudos received or their number of posts versus their number of replies. To do this, we had to add a third component to the visualisation in a way that would not (excessively) increase the complexity of the visualisation and thus reduce retention. We drew some inspiration from CodeSaw, as discussed in section 2.1, and introduced a third component (see Figure 9) as an inverted time-series positioned under the x-axis. Now the visualisation resembles a stacked graph (Heer, Bostock, & Ogievetsky, 2010). Using the

Figure 9. Filtered path visualisation In this image, the community manager is comparing the paths of four different users Non-initialised threads are in orange and received kudos is in blue The representation enables the community manager to quickly evaluate how useful a user's contribution is considered by the community over time

interactive filters (R6), the community manager is able to "drill into" a user's path, reducing the path to their individual actions and then comparing those actions over time. We used animation to transition between the time-series (Complete Paths) and the stacked graph (Individual Actions).

6.3. Visualsiation 3: Ego-Centric Networks

Community managers are also interested in networks (R4). The use of networks as a way to visualise the community was proposed by a member of the team in the first workshop. However, the issue of addressing large graphs was also raised (graphs of over 150 nodes can be problematic). As opposed to visualising the entire graph, Petri provides access to the ego-centric (directed and 1 degree) network of selected users (Fisher, 2005). This approach enables the community manager to explore the immediate social network of any selected user, from the dual perspective of the kudos and the reply-to graphs. This helps the community manager to answer questions such as "Who kudoed this user?" or "Is there significant communication between a subset of users?" or

"Have two users unusually high levels of kudos exchange?" Applying relatively simple network analysis in this way, furnishes the community manager with another perspective from which to consider the interactions of their community.

6.3.1. Interaction

Petri allows the community manager to filter out users based on the number of connections (R6). So, for example, the community manager can focus on a user who has been "kudoed" by another user over a particular threshold (see Figure 10). This enables the community manager to isolate users based on specific communication patterns. While this approach does not attempt to automatically identify detractors or sock puppets, as was discussed in the first workshop, it does allow the community manager to confirm their suspicions about particular patterns of user activity. This can be a powerful tool in combating against negative or potentially disruptive behaviour in the community. In this network visualisation, the community manager can also select other users from the network and examine then their paths and networks (R8).

Figure 10. Network Visualisation In this image the user is analysing the ego-centric networks of four users She is looking at their kudos network and has filtered out any connections that are fewer than 74 kudos

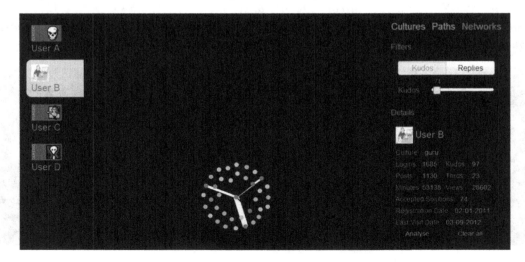

7. EVALUATION

We evaluated Petri with five members of Symantec's community management team (2 women and 3 men). The evaluation took place over a single day at the Symantec offices in Dublin. Three of the team, who participated in the evaluation, were involved in the initial design sessions. The other two were aware of the project but had not participated previously. All five participants were familiar with the community; however, one of the participants was more involved with Symantec's enterprise communities than the company's technical support forums. The aim of the evaluation was to critically asses the usability and usefulness of the Petri visual analytics tool.

7.1. Methodology

We drew on three sources to help define our methodology. The first was Ellis and Dix's approach to exploratory analysis in which they argue for less performance-based, in favour of more exploratory-based, evaluation strategies for information visualisation systems. In this paper, domain experts are considered to as "worth their weight in gold" (Ellis & Dix, 2006) and exploring the visualisation without predetermined tasks is favoured. The second was Isenberg et al.'s paper on grounded evaluation strategies, in which the authors argue for conducting the evaluation in the context of its intended use (Isenberg et al., 2008). Both papers suggest a qualitative, and chiefly observational, approach to evaluation, which is germane giving the size and required expertise of the user group. The third and final source is Andrew's short paper on evaluating information visualisation (Andrews, 2006) in which he suggests selecting the "correct users" and applying the "correct tasks" on a stable visualisation environment.

7.2. Procedure

The five sessions were conducted back-to-back and each session was videoed for analysis later. First, we asked three preliminary questions to establish the participant's familiarity with the community and, more generally, their understanding of visualisation tools and visual analytics systems. Next we asked them to complete some simple explorative tasks. In previous studies we observed that, even with highly motivated participants, loosely described yet open-ended tasks help guide the participant through the evaluation. Asking the participant to simply "explore the visualisation and tell me what you observe" can, at times, leave participants uncertain about what to do next which in turn requires intervention from a facilitator. However, very narrow tasks can have the opposite effect, as the participant does not explore or learn from the visualisation, and, as a consequence, the results are limited to the prescribed tasks (North, 2006). We defined five loosely-focused and open-ended tasks to help guide each participant through the evaluation. They were informed that each task was considered explorative, there was no correct answer, and that we were not observing completion time. Also, if they wished to pursue their own interests or objectives, irrespective of the tasks, we suggested they do so. Each participant was encouraged to think aloud and describe any insights or observations (Saraiya, North, & Duca, 2005; Yi, Kang, Stasko, & Jacko, 2008) they come across whilst using the tool. Having completed the tasks, or having felt they have thoroughly explored the community, each participant was asked to circle five characteristics of the system (drawing from the product desirability table in (Benedek & Miner, 2002). Each characteristic was then used as a discussion point in a post evaluation interview, which was coupled with a set of open-ended questions. Each session lasted between one and one and a half hour. We analysed the video of each session and used content analysis, in an approach similar to (Heer, Viégas, & Wattenberg, 2009), to first code and then evaluate the usefulness of the tool. We used inductive content analysis to draft an initial code book, which consisted of eleven categories. Next, using two coders, we categorised the transcribed video. This process involved two individual sessions to reach a satisfactory kappa coefficient of 0.81. We do not use North's insight based methodology, although this is an approach that is gaining in popularity (Boyandin, Bertini, & Lalanne, 2012), as a larger sample is required and a longer evaluation strategy to obtain statistically significant results.

7.3. Results

In this section, we present the results of the video analysis, and then we discuss the post evaluation interview. We were interested in understanding how useful and usable participants found Petri but also aimed to assess whether any observational cycles were evident in how they went about their analysis. Finally, we identified, and categorised, any usability issues that participants encountered during their session.

7.3.1. Video Analysis

Each user set about the tasks differently. One participant, for example, started the first task but then abruptly abandoned it and just explored the visualisation, in an attempt, primarily, to find users that she found interesting. Having participated in earlier design sessions, some participants had one goal in mind, to identify potential gurus. In two cases, the entire evaluation was driven by that goal. The other two participants followed the prescribed tasks more judiciously. However, they were much less familiar with the community.

Usefulness

To assess usefulness, we wished to answer questions such as: Did users learn something about the community when using Petri? What cycles of analysis did Petri facilitate? Can Petri help a community manager make decisions about their community? What actions would a user suggest having used Petri? We triangulated answers from the video analysis and exit interview.

The large majority of comments that participants made during the evaluation were observational (Figure 11), these are self-evident, are of interest, yet do not signify a deep level of insight. Some of the most interesting uses of the tool came when a participant sought out a user of interest. For instance, one participant, who manages the community, searched for a user because she "wanted to see how he was doing". She had contact with him before and thought he might be "Guru material". She found the user and then analysed his path. She said "but he seems to be getting a good bit of kudos. Maybe it is not extensive but..." Later on she chose a second user that is also of interest to her. She examined both their paths simultaneously. She commented, "I was wondering is he guru material, but now I can see he is not very active. I remember seeing him around a lot but obviously not much anymore." This helps to validate her decision as regards the potential of this user. She then commented on the second user's path: "This girl here is quite active. I don't know is she guru material but she seems quite motivated so maybe in the future." Clicking on accepted solutions for these two users, she commented "Ok she (the second user) has gave [sic] a lot of replies but has no accepted solutions otherwise it is quite regular." The ability to quickly asses how a user contributes, and how their contribution is received, enables the community manager to validate their decisions on promotion in the community. The participant indicated that this is quite important because "it always happens that you make wrong decisions (about the promotion of users) and you

Figure 11. Content analysis of transcribed video Categories are not mutually exclusive

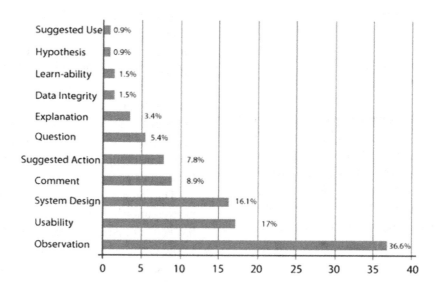

cannot revert back because you do not want them on your back but that is just the way it is." Being able to validate the selection process qualitatively, through interaction with users, and quantitatively, through analysis with Petri, helps to act against these sorts of problems.

Similarly another participant filtered for users who just joined the community this year. Finding a user that is particularly active, she says "whether she would recommend him as a guru. He looks very active across a couple of threads. Only one solution. It is doubtful that he is a guru. It depends what he is doing? If those five threads were people continuing asking questions and him answering it or if it is about him moaning about the last release and people kudoing him for it, I don't know". Again, this approach to analysis reflects the experience of the previous participant. While the tool can assist in the validation, qualitative analysis remains important.

Usability

Overall, users found Petri usable. They found that each visualisation was legible and comprehensible. Several times, however, participants expressed some confusion with a specific aspect of a visualisation (25% of usability issues). For example, one participant had not encountered a stacked graph before and, thus, found the interactive path visualisation difficult to interpret. She said she preferred the time-series as this was an approach she had used regularly on a personal running application. The approach to the cultures visualisation required further explanation, particularly in relation to how outliers were represented. The majority of usability issues (36% of usability issues) arose around the user selection process. Simple actions, such as adding or removing single users at each stage of analysis, were expected. Participants also expected a context menu when they right clicked a user's glyph. Similarly, several participants tried to hold the shift or ctrl key and then click on several glyphs in a row to select multiple users. More details, better labelling, or the ability to interrogate the actual numbers, was also identified as an issue by some participants (11%). There were some issues as regards terminology (17%) as participants found certain words and descriptions confusing (especially the word "analyse" used to select a user for analysis).

Finally, some participants felt that the navigation did not accurately reflect the analytic methodology (6%) and in two cases filtering by date caused confusion (5%).

7.3.2. Interviews

Although the analysis helped us evaluate the utility of Petri, we also wanted to better understand the context in which the tool would be applied. We conducted a short exit interview with each participant, in which we drew upon the themes of utility, design, improvement and the process of community management. Here we briefly discuss the interviews:

Usefulness

All users indicated that they found Petri to be useful. Several focused on explicit aspects of Petri. One of the participants said that even in a short time that the evaluation took place, she can "say immediately now, how many gurus there are, how sparse they are. Proportionally, how much they contribute. The other thing you can tell right away is that they are not alike. Gurus are their own people; they are not cookie-cutters. The tool could be very insightful for encouraging users, and provide key indicators." Others commented on how quickly they came to terms with the interface, as it was "easy to find", "inviting" and "straightforward", suggesting that the tool was easy to learn and had a low barrier to use.

Interestingly, users had differing opinions on the approach to categorising cultures. While one participant queried the "use-case" behind having a pragmatist culture, a second suggested that the pragmatist culture may be of most interest, as this is the body of users that they wish to engage in peer-based activity. One of the participants, who is not engaged with any one community but oversees strategy, said that Petri would give her much more "visibility" into the community and would provide grounds for validating the decision-making of her community mangers.

Design and Presentation

Not many participants used the network visualisation. One participant said that she found ego-centric network too restrictive, she said "it might be too focused on the individual, it does not tell me anything about whole network look like", and that she would prefer the ability to explore the whole of the network, even if that was a very large and dense graph. Another suggested that the network should be composed of the users that are selected for further analysis.

The category of lurker was discussed also. Two participants identified that it was important to have an understanding of the proportion of lurkers in the community even if that category is overly represented in the culture visualisation. Having the ability to show/hide lurkers was mentioned.

Improving Petri

Some participants discussed the methodology around the application of Petri. One participant suggested that there is a clear methodology associated with the use of Petri, which involves observing shifts in cultures and then drilling into user's paths and networks. This, however, is not clear from the design and could benefit from a better description. She suggested that, at present, it looks as if these three functions are in "parity". Some participants also expressed dissatisfaction with the network functionality. As mentioned previously, they found it less useful than the other two visualisations and indicated that they would have preferred access to the entire network as opposed to the ego-centric visualisations provided in Petri.

Other aspects of the tool were also discussed. The concept of "linking" was proposed by several participants, whereby the user could easily traverse between Petri and the forum whilst maintaining the context of analysis. This is important for a community manger to assess the "quality" of a user's contribution, and while similar approaches have been implemented in previous work (Zhu & Chen, 2008), this feature was not discussed in previous sessions. Interaction was also raised in relation to the path visualisation. Two participants specifically asked for better "drill down" and required the ability to reduce and increase the span of analysis. Flagging employees, who are active across the entire forum, was also suggested.

Finally, the scrutability of the visualisation was also highlighted. While in general the participants responded positively to the interface, two participants asked to see the "actual numbers", to support their understanding of what is presented in the visualisation and to assist in their analysis.

The Process of Community Management

We were interested to see whether participants thought Petri could help facilitate current community management practices at Symantec. We asked about adoption, and specifically sought to establish how Petri could fit into their current workflow. While participants noted the value of the tool, they were a little unsure of how it could be adopted in practice. Reflecting on this, one of the participants commented:

Possibly, it is very cool, forward looking and it has potential. The community manager on her day to day job, when she has ten things on her plate, typically, she will look for something to improve productivity. This is a "more big" [sic] picture tool. Would it be used on a day to day basis? I think there would be a novelty to it first but then I think it has to offer something that drives productivity or would require a very strong individual use case.

Another suggested that community managers require a more reflective approach to the process of community management more generally, and thought Petri could add value in this context. She described it in this way:

Community managers have very particular things to think about, i.e. their everyday list of issues to be addressed. But they have to have a more abstract view. It's like, say you were raising a child, and you have to look after it day-to-day, and you fed it and you clothed it and all those things. But, if you have a more abstract view of child development, then you have other things to think about that aren't apparent on a day to day meter. Have reflexives set in, has cognitive learning set in, has speech happened? You know, it is a different process and I don't think we have that learning for community managers to step back and say, well really, given the development curve of a community we should be here and we are not.

This same participant suggested that while the analysis of one community is interesting, comparing communities may provide much more fruitful results.

Decisions about guru selection were considered by other participants. Some participants suggested that Petri could reduce the time required to assess new candidates because you would not be "required to read all the posts and assess the user's contribution" and that the tasks could be completed in "no-time at all". One participant went on to describe how she would use the tool in practice:

If I wanted to determine a new guru, and I didn't really know who, if there were three people who were potential gurus, I could use this to see how active are they and then go back to the forums to see how much quality they are providing.

She would not use the tool daily but probably "weekly" or "bi-weekly" and "it could provide you with the metrics if you want to make a case for a specific user". Another participant queried the adoption of such tools given, generally speaking, the technical knowledge of online community managers. She suggested that adoption of such advanced visual analytic tools could meet with some resistance from those less technical.

8. LIMITATIONS

In pursuing a human-centred approach to visualisation, we sought to include users into the design process as much as we possibly could. We drew on Munzner's nested model for design to identify points at which feedback, and thus iteration, could be realised, namely, abstraction, interaction and algorithmic design. While our aim was to pursue this model in as methodical a way as possible, collaborating with a busy team, that travel widely and attend to a company's entire community strategy, presented some practical difficulties. We would have liked, for instance, to carry out additional workshops to further refine initial sketches (visual encodings) and to identify alternative, and possibly more adept, interactive strategies (addressing interaction). Following the domain analysis, mapping the user requirements to different visual presentations, as discussed in (Card & Mackinlay, 1997), or using a taxonomy, as discussed in (Tory & Moller, 2004), may have helped formalise our design process further. For the reader, a taxonomic approach could help clarify certain design decisions, while for the reviewer; such an approach could provide the grounds for better critical analysis. In future work, this is something that the authors will address. Our approach to algorithmic design was initially presented in the third workshop, as discussed, and then later refined through discussions (both face-to-face and over email) with the community management team. We do not claim that each iteration, as described in this chapter, validated the approach we took, but that each iteration provided further justification for our entire design. The evaluation conducted at the end of the process helped to assess the degree of usefulness of the overall system.

There are also some limitations as regards to the generalisability of Petri. While the community in question is small, given the scope of the organisations other online communities, participants had asked in early workshops could this tool be easily ported to other communities? Certainly, the clustering is generalisable and can be reapplied to other datasets, once, that is, a degree of noise is accounted for and thus filtered out. In the case of Petri, we only included users who had posted over three times to the community. Of course, there are other issues when visualising datasets of scale. From a technical standpoint, handling a huge dataset can be problematic, particularly if the visualisation requires interaction such as pan, zoom and filter and thus cannot be pre-rendered. Approaches such as "multiscale data aggregation", as applied in Google maps and used by Elmqvist et al. for their work on Zame (Elmqvist, Do, Goodell, Henry, & Fekete, 2008), can allow the user zoom into various sections of a large dataset. But how this tool would be used in practice is an open question. Could a community manager use this tool in regular intervals to assess how a given policy is proceeding, especially given the size of some popular online communities? Better interactive strategies would be required, and ways to quickly and intelligently reduce the dimensionality of the dataset needed. We developed Petri to dovetail into the community management process, so that the community manager could regularly asses the results of their intervention with the community. Such an approach may be much less possible with large online communities; however, this could be addressed with future work.

9. FUTURE RESEARCH DIRECTIONS

Immediate directions for future work include the implementation of small multiples (Tufte, 2001), that will support the analysis of change in the community's cultures over time. It was our intention to pursue this aspect of the application having completed an initial evaluation, as it can be evaluated independently of the rest of the application. Also, integration of Petri with the actual forum software, to allow the community manager to qualitatively substantiate any quantitative assessment is also required. This has been raised in early studies (Viégas & Smith, 2004) but was not addressed in this implementation. Furthermore, given the negative reception to the ego-centric visualisation there is scope to re-address how to convey network information in Petri. Certainly, approaches such as Vizster, discussed in section 2.2, could be useful in this context.

While we have partitioned the community in quite a coarse grained manner, there is scope to develop a categorisation scheme that operates at a much finer level of resolution. This could be a significant contribution to the analysis of online communities; as such an approach can be reapplied to any forum that has a similar socio-technical infrastructure–users, boards, threads, replies and kudos. In fact, this data structure makes up for the vast majority of question and answer communities on the web. Furthermore, we did not provide the ability for the community manager to alter the parameters of the clustering algorithm used to partition the community. Advancing analytics in this direction, so that non-professional analysts can progressively carry-out increasingly complex computational tasks, within, of course, a clearly defined scope, is not well understood at present. However, as visual analytics shifts into the main stream, this presents an opportunity for future work.

The ultimate indication of success for Petri is adoption and it is clear from the evaluation that more work is required before Petri could be adopted into the workflow of the community manager. It is also clear, however, that given the busy schedule of a professional community manager, it is difficult to assess how visual analytics could be successfully adopted in practice. While participants recognised the benefits of Petri, and some even suggested re-addressing the process of

online community management given the application of such tools, the need to provide solutions that improve productivity is always pressing. Moreover, to understand if visual analytic tools, such as Petri, can support the role of community manager on a long term basis, and provide a more analytic approach to online community management, further, principally longitudinal, evaluation is required.

Finally, as regards the methodology, while Muzner's model supports an informed design process-one that is both aware of the design space and the incremental procedures required to construct a useful visual analytics application - the model does not account for deployment or address how the tool is adapted when used in practice. In most cases there is a need to amend the application, or at least alter varying aspects of the application, once deployed. While a focus on design is precedent, it is also important to factor in the social and organisational issues that can impact the success of any deployment. Other models, such as (Dou, Butkiewicz, Bier, & Ribarsky, 2011), may prove a useful addition in this context.

10. CONCLUSION

In this chapter we described a case study in which we designed, developed and evaluated a visual analytics tool to support the management of online communities. The tool was designed to encourage a more analytic approach to online community management, which is based on cycles of observation and intervention. In designing the tool we adopted Muzner's nested methodology for visualisation design and validation and conducted several interviews and design workshops with Symantec's online community team. From these sessions we drafted a set of requirements that were then used to inform the design of the resulting visual analytics application, called Petri. Petri enables the community manager to analyse their community from multiple perspectives, shifting between phases of explorative and confirmative analysis, and to identify users that could prove valuable to the community as it evolves over time. We presented the results of an explorative evaluation, conducted with five members from the community management team, and found the visualisation tool was both useful and usable. Nevertheless, questions were raised in exit interviews as to how the tool would perform in practice.

We made the following contributions:

- First, we proposed a novel approach to online community management, which is based on cycles of observation and intervention, and is supported by the application of advanced visual analytic tools.
- Second, we presented a set of design requirements that can be readdressed by other researchers interested in online community visualisation.
- Third, we presented Petri, a novel visual analytics tool that was designed, developed and evaluated with Symantec's online community management team.

Finally, we outlined several directions for future work. While the evaluation presented in the paper helps to establish the utility or the tool, there is scope to evaluate how this application would perform in practice. Adoption is not based solely on utility and usability, however, but is also based on the social and organisational context in which the tool is deployed. To shift visual analytics from the research community into the hands of community practitioners there is a need to address not only how the tool is designed but also how the tool is deployed in practice. This, of course, requires a greater degree of commitment from an online community manager and would include a longitudinal research methodology such as Multi-dimensional In-depth Long-term Case Study (MILC), as outlined in Shneiderman and Plaisant (Ben Shneiderman & Plaisant, 2006).

ACKNOWLEDGMENT

This research is supported by the Science Foundation Ireland (Grant 07/CE/I1142) as part of the Centre for Next Generation Localisation (www.cngl.ie) at Trinity College Dublin. Thanks to members of the Symantec community management team for their participation in this research.

REFERENCES

Anderson, C. (2006). *The long tail: Why the future of business is selling less of more*. New York: Hyperion.

Andrews, K. (2006). Evaluating information visualisations. In *Proceedings of the 2006 AVI Workshop On Beyond Time And Errors: Novel Evaluation Methods For Information Visualization*, 1–5. New York: ACM Press.

Archambault, D., Purchase, H., & Pinaud, B. (2010). Animation, small multiples, and the effect of mental map preservation in dynamic graphs. *IEEE Transactions on Visualization and Computer Graphics*, 17(4), 539–552. doi:10.1109/TVCG.2010.78 PMID:20498503.

Bacon, J. (2009). *The art of community: Building the new age of participation (Theory in practice)*. Sebastopol, CA: O'Reilly Media.

Bederson, B. (1999). Does animation help users build mental maps of spatial information? In *Proceedings of the 1999 IEEE Symposium on Information Visualization, 11*, 28. Washington, DC: IEEE Press.

Benedek, J., & Miner, T. (2002). Measuring desirability: New methods for evaluating desirability in a usability lab setting. In *Proceedings of Usability Professionals*. New York: ACM Press.

Bertin, J. (1983a). *The retinal variables. Semiology of Graphics: Diagrams, Networks, Maps (65)*. Madison, WI: The University of Wisconsin Press.

Bertin, J. (1983b). *Colour Variation. Semiology of Graphics: Diagrams, Networks, Maps (91)*. Madison, WI: The University of Wisconsin Press.

Bertin, J. (1983c). *Diagrams involving two components. Semiology of Graphics: Diagrams, Networks, Maps (195)*. Madison, WI: The University of Wisconsin Press.

Bonsignore, E. M., Dunne, C., Rotman, D., Smith, M., Capone, T., Hansen, D. L., & Shneiderman, B. (2009). First steps to netviz nirvana: Evaluating social network analysis with NodeXL. In *Proceedings of International Conference on Computational Science and Engineering*, 332–339. New York: ACM Press.

Boyandin, I., Bertini, E., & Lalanne, D. (2012). A qualitative study on the exploration of temporal changes in flow maps with animation and small multiples. *Computer Graphics Forum*, *31*(3.2), 1005–1014.

Boyd, D., Ramage, D., & Donath, J. (2002). Developing legible visualizations for online social spaces. In *Proceedings of the 35th Annual Hawaii International Conference on System Sciences*, 1060–1069. Washington, DC: IEEE Press.

Brown, J. S., & Duguid, P. (1991). Organizational learning and communities-of-practice: Toward a unified view of working, learning, and innovation. *Organizational Learning*, *2*(1), 40–57.

Butler, B., Sproull, L., Kiesler, S., & Kraut, R. (2007). Community effort in online groups: Who does the work and why. In S. PWeisband, (Ed.), *Leadership at a Distance* (171–195). Florence, KY: Psychology Press.

Card, S. K., & Mackinlay, J. (1997). The structure of the information visualization design space. In *Proceedings of VIZ '97: Visualization Conference, Information Visualization Symposium and Parallel Rendering Symposium*, 92–99. Washington, DC: IEEE Press.

Chan, J., & Hayes, C. (2010). Decomposing discussion forums using user roles. In *Proceedings of the Second Web Science Conference*. Raleigh, NC: ACM Press.

Crowston, K., & Howison, J. (2005). The social structure of free and open source software development. *First Monday*, *10*(2). doi:10.5210/fm.v10i2.1207.

Donath, J. (2007). Signals in social supernets. *Journal of Computer Mediated Communication*, *13*(1).

Donath, J., Karahalios, K., & Viégas, F. (1999). Visualizing conversation. In *Proceedings of the 32nd Annual Hawaii International Conference on Systems Sciences, 32*, 9. Hawaii: IEEE Press.

Dou, X. W. W., Butkiewicz, T., Bier, E. A., & Ribarsky, W. (2011). A two-stage framework for designing visual analytics system in organizational environments. In *Proceedings of 2011 IEEE Conference on Visual Analytics, Science, and Technology*, 251–260. Providence, RI: IEEE Press.

Ellis, G., & Dix, A. (2006). An explorative analysis of user evaluation studies in information visualisation. In *Proceedings of the 2006 AVI Workshop on Beyond Time and Errors: Novel Evaluation Methods for Information Visualization*, 109–116. Venice, Italy: AVI Press.

Elmqvist, N., Do, T.-N., Goodell, H., Henry, N., & Fekete, J.-D. (2008). ZAME: Interactive Large-Scale Graph Visualization. In *Proceedings of IEEE Pacific Visualization Symposium*, 215–222. Kyoto: IEEE Press.

Erickson, T. (2003). Designing visualizations of social activity: Six claims. In *Proceedings of CHI EA '03 CHI '03 Extended Abstracts on Human Factors in Computing Systems*, 846–847. Ft. Lauderdale, FL: ACM Press.

Fisher, D. (2005). Using egocentric networks to understand communication. *IEEE Internet Computing*, *9*(5), 20–28. doi:10.1109/MIC.2005.114.

Fisher, D., Smith, M., & Welser, H. T. (2006). You are who you talk to: Detecting roles in usenet newsgroups. In *Proceedings of the 39th Annual Hawaii International Conference on System Sciences*. Washington, DC: IEEE Press.

Gazan, R. (2009). When online communities become self-aware. In *Proceedings of Conference on Hawaii International System Sciences*. Washington, DC: IEEE Press.

Gilbert, E., & Karahalios, K. (2007). CodeSaw: A social visualization of distributed software development. In *Proceedings of the 11th IFIP TC 13 International Conference on Human-Computer Interaction-Volume Part II*, 303–316. New York: HCIR Press.

Gilbert, E. & Karahalios, K. (2009). Using social visualization to motivate social production. *IEEE Transactions on Multimedia-Special section on communities and media*, *11*(3), 413–421.

Golder, S. A., & Donath, J. (2004). Social roles in electronic communities. *Internet Research*, *5*, 19–22.

Gruzd, A., & Haythornthwaite, C. (2008). The analysis of online communities using interactive content-based social networks. *In Proceedings of the American Society for Information Science and Technology Conference*, 523–527. Paris: ICSU Press.

Heer, J., Bostock, M., & Ogievetsky, V. (2010). Visualisation: A Tour through the visualization zoo: A survey of powerful visualization techniques, from the obvious to the obscure. *ACM Queue; Tomorrow's Computing Today*, *8*(5), 20.

Heer, J., & Boyd, D. (2005). Vizster: Visualizing online social networks. In *Proceedings of IEEE Symposium on Information Visualization*, 32–39. Minneapolis, MN: IEEE Press.

Heer, J., & Hellerstein, J. (2009). Data Visualization and social data analysis. In *Proceedings of the VLDB Endowment*, 1656–1657.

Heer, J., & Perer, A. (2011). Orion: A system for modeling, transformation and visualization of multidimensional heterogeneous networks. In *Proceedings of 2011 IEEE Conference on Visual Analytics Science and Technology*, 51–60. Providence, RI: IEEE Press.

Heer, J., Viégas, F., & Wattenberg, M. (2009). Voyagers and voyeurs: Supporting asynchronous collaborative visualization. *Communications of the ACM-Rural Engineering Development*, *52*(1), 87–97. doi:10.1145/1435417.1435439.

Henry, N., & Fekete, J.-D. (2006). MatrixExplorer: A dual-representation system to explore social networks. *IEEE Transactions on Visualization and Computer Graphics*, *12*(5), 677–684. doi:10.1109/TVCG.2006.160 PMID:17080787.

Holten, D. (2006). Hierarchical edge bundles: Visualization of adjacency relations in hierarchical data. *IEEE Transactions on Visualization and Computer Graphics*, *12*(5), 741–748. doi:10.1109/TVCG.2006.147 PMID:17080795.

Husson, F., Le, S., & Pages, J. (2010). *Exploratory multivariate analysis by example using r*. New York: CRC Press. doi:10.1201/b10345.

Isenberg, P., Zuk, T., & Collins, C. (2008). Grounded evaluation of information visualizations. In *Proceedings of the 2008 Workshop on Beyond time and errors: Novel Evaluation Methods for Information Visualization*, 1–8. Florence, Italy: ACM Press.

Kelly, J. W., Fisher, D., & Smith, M. (2006). Friends, foes, and fringe: Norms and structure in political discussion networks. In *Proceedings of the 2006 International Conference on Digital Government Research*, 412–417. San Diego, CA: ACM Press.

Kimmerle, J., Moskaliuk, J., Harrer, A., & Cress, U. (2010). Visualizing co-evolution of individual and collective knowledge. *Information Communication and Society*, *13*(8). doi:10.1080/13691180903521547.

Kittur, A., & Kraut, R. E. (2010). Beyond wikipedia: Coordination and conflict in online production groups. In *Proceedings of the 2010 ACM Conference on Computer Supported Cooperative Work*, 215–224. Savannah, GA: ACM Press.

Lohr, S. (2012). The age of big data. *The New York Times*. New York.

Malouf, R., & Mullen, T. (2008). Taking sides: User classification for informal online political discourse. *Internet Research*, *18*(2), 177–190. doi:10.1108/10662240810862239.

Marin, A., & Wellman, B. (2010). Social network analysis: An introduction. In Carrington, P., & Scott, J. (Eds.), *Handbook of Social Network Analysis*. London: Sage.

Masli, M., Priedhorsky, R., & Terveen, L. (2011). Task specialization in social production communities: The case of geographic volunteer work. In *Proceedings of ICWSM*, 217–224. Palo Alto, CA: AAAI Press.

McAuley, J., O'Connor, A., & Lewis, D. (2012). Exploring reflection in online communities. In *Proceedings of the 2nd International Conference on Learning Analytics and Knowledge*, 102–110. Vancouver, BC: ACM Press.

Morzy, M. (2009). On mining and social role discovery in internet forums. In *Proceedings of 2009 International Workshop on Social Informatics*, 74–79. Warsaw, Poland: IEEE Press.

Munzner, T. (2000). *Interactive Visualization of Large Graphs and Networks*. (Unpublished doctoral thesis). Stanford, CA, Stanford University.

Munzner, T. (2009). A nested model for visualization design and validation. *IEEE Transactions on Visualization and Computer Graphics*, *15*(6), 921–928. doi:10.1109/TVCG.2009.111 PMID:19834155.

North, C. (2000). Snap-together visualization: Can users construct and operate coordinated visualizations? *International Journal of Human-Computer Studies*, *53*(5), 715–739. doi:10.1006/ijhc.2000.0418.

North, C. (2006). Toward measuring visualization insight. *IEEE Computer Graphics and Applications*, *26*(3), 6–9. doi:10.1109/MCG.2006.70 PMID:16711210.

O'Keffe, P. (2008). *Managing online forums: Everything You need to know to create and run successful community discussion boards, 320.* Saranac, NY: AMACOM.

Panciera, K., & Halfaker, A. (2009). Wikipedians are born, not made: A study of power editors on Wikipedia. In *Proceedings of the ACM 2009 International Conference on Supporting Group Work*, 51–60. Sanibel Island, FL: ACM Press.

Perry, E., & Donath, J. (2004). Anthropomorphic visualization: A new approach for depicting participants in online spaces. In *Proceedings of CHI EA '04 CHI '04 Extended Abstracts on Human Factors in Computing*, 1115–1118. Vienna, Austria: ACM Press.

Preece, D. J. (2000). *Online communities: Designing usability and supporting sociability.* Hoboken, NJ: Wiley.

Preece, J., & Shneiderman, B. (2009). The reader-to-leader framework: Motivating technology-mediated social participation. *AIS Transactions on Human-Computer Interaction*, *1*(1), 13–32.

Robertson, G., Fernandez, R., Fisher, D., Lee, B., & Stasko, J. (2008). Effectiveness of animation in trend visualization. *IEEE Transactions on Visualization and Computer Graphics*, *14*(6), 1325–1332. doi:10.1109/TVCG.2008.125 PMID:18988980.

Saraiya, P., North, C., & Duca, K. (2005). An insight-based methodology for evaluating bioinformatics visualizations. *IEEE Transactions on Visualization and Computer Graphics*, *11*(4), 443–456. doi:10.1109/TVCG.2005.53 PMID:16138554.

Shneiderman, B. (1996). The eyes have it: A task by data type taxonomy for information visualizations. In *Proceedings of 1996 IEEE Symposium on Visual Languages*, 336–343. Washington, DC: IEEE Press.

Shneiderman, B., & Aris, A. (2006). Network visualization by semantic substrates. *IEEE Transactions on Visualization and Computer Graphics*, *12*(5), 733–740. doi:10.1109/TVCG.2006.166 PMID:17080794.

Shneiderman, B., & Plaisant, C. (2006). Strategies for evaluating information visualization tools: Multi-dimensional in-depth long-term case studies. In *Proceedings of the 2006 AVI Workshop on Beyond Time and Errors: Novel Evaluation Methods for Information Visualization*, 1–7. Philadelphia: ACM.

Smith, M. A., Shneiderman, B., Milic-Frayling, N., Mendes Rodrigues, E., Barash, V., Dunne, C., & Capone, T. (2009). Analyzing (social media) networks with NodeXL. In *Proceedings of the Fourth International Conference on Communities and Technologies-C&T '09*, 255. New York: ACM Press.

Suh, B., Chi, E. H., Kittur, A., & Pendleton, B. A. (2008). Lifting the veil: Improving accountability and social transparency in wikipedia with wikidashboard. In *Proceeding of the Twenty-Sixth Annual SIGCHI Conference on Human Factors in Computing Systems*, 1037–1040. Florence, Italy: ACM Press.

Suh, B., Chi, E. H., Pendleton, B. A., & Kittur, A. (2007). Us vs. them: Understanding social dynamics in wikipedia with revert graph visualizations. In *Proceedings of 2007 IEEE Symposium on Visual Analytics Science and Technology*, 163–170. Washington, DC: IEEE Press.

Tory, M., & Moller, T. (2004). Rethinking visualization: A high-level taxonomy. In *Proceedings of IEEE Symposium on Information Visualization*, 151–158. Washington, DC: IEEE Press.

Tufte, E. R. (2001). *Data denstiy and small multiples. The Visual Display of Quantitative Information (42)*. Cheshire, CT: Graphics Pr.

Turner, T. C., Smith, M. A., Fisher, D., & Welser, H. T. (2005). Picturing usenet: Mapping computer-mediated collective action. *Journal of Computer Mediated Communication*, *10*(4).

Tversky, B., Bauer, J., Betrancourt, M., De Europe, A., & St-Martin, M. (2002). Animation: Can it facilitate? *International Journal of Human-Computer Studies*, *57*(4), 247–262. doi:10.1006/ijhc.2002.1017.

Van Ham, F., Schulz, H., & Dimicco, J. M. (2009). Honeycomb: Visual analysis of large scale social networks. In *Proceedings of the 12th IFIP TC 13 International Conference on Human-Computer Interaction: Part II*, 429–442. Uppsala, Sweden: Springer.

Vassileva, J., & Sun, L. (2007). Using community visualization to stimulate participation in online communities. *E-Service Journal*, *6*(1), 3–39. doi:10.2979/ESJ.2007.6.1.3.

Viégas, F. B., Boyd, D., Nguyen, D. H., Potter, J., & Donath, J. (2004). Digital artifacts for remembering and storytelling: Posthistory and social network fragments. In *Proceedings of the 37th Annual Hawaii International Conference on System Sciences*, 109–118. Washington, DC: IEEE Press.

Viégas, F. B., & Donath, J. (2004). Social network visualization: Can we go beyond the graph. In *Proceedings of Workshop on Social Networks, 4*, 6–10. Chicago: ACM Press.

Viégas, F. B., & Smith, M. (2004). Newsgroup crowds and authorlines: Visualizing the activity of individuals in conversational cyberspaces. In *Proceedings of the 37th Hawaii International Conference on System Sciences*. Washington, DC: IEEE Press.

Viégas, F. B., Wattenberg, M., & Dave, K. (2004). Studying cooperation and conflict between authors with history flow visualizations. In *Proceedings of the SIGCHI Conference on Human Factors in Computing Systems*, 575–582. Vienna, Austria: ACM Press.

Viégas, F. B., Wattenberg, M., Kriss, J., & Ham, F. V. (2007). Talk before you type: Coordination in wikipedia. In *Proceedings of the 40th Annual Hawaii International Conference on System Sciences* (78). Hawaii: IEEE Press.

Wagner, C., Rowe, M., Strohmaier, M., & Alani, H. (2012). Ignorance isn't bliss: An empirical analysis of attention patterns in online communities. In *Proceedings of IEEE International Conference on Social Computing*. Amsterdam: IEEE Press.

Wang, W., Wang, H., Dai, G., & Wang, H. (2006). Visualization of large hierarchical data by circle packing. In *Proceedings of the SIGCHI Conference on Human Factors in computing Systems-CHI '06*, 517–520. New York: ACM Press.

Wattenberg, M., & Kriss, J. (2006). Designing for social data analysis. *IEEE Transactions on Visualization and Computer Graphics*, *12*(4), 549–557. doi:10.1109/TVCG.2006.65 PMID:16805263.

Wattenberg, M., Viégas, F., & Hollenbach, K. (2007). Visualizing activity on wikipedia with chromograms. In *Proceedings of the 11th IFIP TC 13 International Conference on Human-Computer Interaction-Volume Part II*, 272–287. Rio de Janeiro: Springer.

Welser, H., Cosley, D., Kossinets, G., & Lin, A. (2011). Finding social roles in wikipedia. In *Proceedings of the 2011 iConference*, 122–129. Seattle, WA: JALT.

Welser, H. T., Gleave, E., Fisher, D., & Smith, M. (2008). Visualizing the signatures of social roles in online discussion groups. Journal of Social Structure, 8.

Xiong, R., & Donath, J. (1999). PeopleGarden: Creating data portraits for users. In *Proceedings of the 12th Annual ACM Symposium on User Interface Software and Technology*, 37–44. Asheville, NC: ACM Press.

Yi, J. S., Kang, Y., Stasko, J. T., & Jacko, J. A. (2008). Understanding and characterizing insights: how do people gain insights using information visualization? In *Proceedings of the 2008 Workshop on Beyond Time and Errors: Novel Evaluation Methods for Information Visualization*, 1–6. Florence, Italy: ACM Press.

Zhu, B., & Chen, H. (2008). Communication-garden system: Visualizing a computer-mediated communication process. *Decision Support Systems*, 45(4), 778–794. doi:10.1016/j.dss.2008.02.004.

Chapter 18
A Programmer–Centric and Task–Optimized Object Graph Visualizer for Debuggers

Anthony Savidis
Institute of Computer Science-FORTH, Greece & University of Crete, Greece

Nikos Koutsopoulos
Institute of Computer Science-FORTH, Greece

ABSTRACT

Today, existing graph visualizers are not popular for debugging purposes because they are mostly visualization-oriented, rather than task-oriented, implementing general-purpose graph drawing algorithms. The latter explains why prominent integrated development environments still adopt traditional tree views. The authors introduce a debugging assistant with a visualization technique designed to better fit the actual task of defect detection in runtime object networks, while supporting advanced inspection and configuration features. Its design has been centered on the study of the actual programmer needs in the context of the debugging task, emphasizing: 1.) visualization style inspired by a social networking metaphor enabling easily identify who deploys objects (clients) and whom objects deploy (servers); 2.) inspection features to easily review object contents and associations and to search content patterns (currently regular expressions only); and 3.) interactively configurable levels of information detail, supporting off-line inspection and multiple concurrent views.

INTRODUCTION

Debugging is the systematic process of detecting and fixing bugs within computer programs and can be summarized (Zeller, 2005) by two main steps, bug detection and bug fixing, as outlined under Figurer 1. The examination of the runtime state requires inspection of object contents, associations and dependencies.

DOI: 10.4018/978-1-4666-4309-3.ch018

Figure 1. The overall workflow of the debugging process

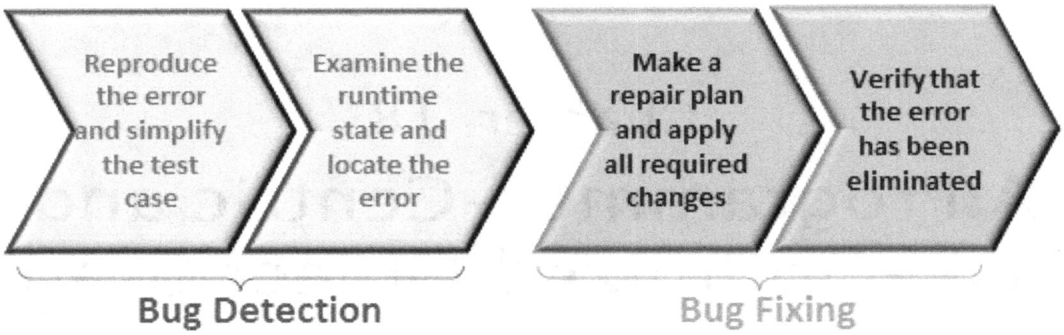

The latter is a difficult task, even for small-scale applications, where traditional graph visualizations proved to be rather ineffective. The remark is justified by the fact that most popular commercial IDEs like Visual Studio (Microsoft) and IntelliJ IDEA (Jet Brains) do not provide them, while open source IDEs like Eclipse and NetBeans have a couple of relevant third-party plug-ins which are rarely used. But still, during debugging, objects remain the primary information unit for gaining insights (Yi et al., 2008) on how errors infect the runtime state. Interestingly, while the notion of visualization generally receives positive attention, relevant implementations failed to essentially improve the state examination process.

We argue that this is due to the primary focus of present tools on visualization, adopting general-purpose rendering algorithms being the outcome of graph drawing research, however, lacking other sophisticated interactive features.

More specifically, general graph drawing algorithms aim to better support supervision and pattern matching tasks through the display of alternative clustering layouts. This can be valuable when visualizing static features like class hierarchies, function dependencies and recursive data structures. However, during the debugging process the emphasis is shifted towards runtime state analysis involving primarily state exploration and comparison tasks, requiring detailed and advanced inspection facilities. We argue that the inability to systematically address this key issue explains the failure of object graph visualizers in the context of general-purpose debugging. As we discuss later, most existing tools are no more than mere implementations of graph drawing algorithms. Our primary goal is to provide interactive facilities which improve the runtime state examination process for defect detection. This goal is further elaborated into three primary design requirements:

- Visualization style inspired by a social networking metaphor enabling easily identify who deploys objects (clients) and whom objects deploy (servers)
- Inspection features to easily review object contents and associations and to search content patterns (currently regular expressions only)
- Interactively configurable levels of information detail, supporting off-line inspection and multiple concurrent views

The reported work (i-views) has been implemented as a debugger plug-in on top of the Sparrow IDE for the Delta programming language being publicly available (Savidis, 2010). This language has been chosen for ease of implementation, since it offers an XML-based protocol for extracting object contents during runtime (Savidis & Lilis, 2009). Overall, our results may be applied to any other debugging tool.

BACKGROUND

Graphs have been widely deployed in the context of object-oriented visualizations (Lange & Nakamura, 1997) for various purposes, besides debugging, such as: tracing of dynamic object-allocation characteristics, revealing static ownership-based object relationships (Hill et al., 2002), tracking event generation in event-based systems (Kranzlmuller et al., 1996), and investigating object constraints (Muller, 2000). General purpose visualization toolkits exists too, such as Prefuse (Heer et al., 2005) for visualization of large-scale data offering predefined layout algorithms, and the work of (Hendrix et al., 2004) for visualizing data structures in a lightweight IDE. Another state visualization tool is HDPV (Sundararaman & Back, 2008) whose purpose is to provide a global image of the stack, heap and the static data segment in a way reflecting the precise set of object instances during runtime. It offers an option to animate the changes in the memory state in response to instruction execution, assuming users will perceive potential state anomalies by observing state snapshots and eventually lead to defect detection. The emphasis of such previous tools is primarily put in enabling visualization while letting users navigate and explore in a free manner, rather than providing interactive layouts optimized for the particular task at hand being debugging.

Tools offering interactive object graphs exclusively for the debugging process exist for various languages. Memory visualization tools such as those by Aftandilian et al. (2010), De Pauw and Sevitsky (1999), and Reiss (2009) are essentially memory graph visualizers targeted in displaying memory usage by programs, enabling programmers to detect memory leaks or identify memory corruption patterns. They are low-level since their focus is on memory maps and memory analysis, while fundamental program notions like objects and associations (clients and servers) are not handled. A tool working on objects is DDD (GNU,

2009), however, it allows incremental expansion only for referent (outgoing / server) structures.

Comparing with previous work, it is clear that all existing tools focus merely on the graph drawing quality rather than on optimizing the primary task being object state inspection for defect detection. As a result, while they tend overall offer attractive visualizations, those are not perfectly aligned with the typical activity patterns programmers actually perform during debugging. As an example, none of the existing tools allows to identify directly the clients and servers of an object, information being very critical when examining error propagation patterns.

In our approach, the previous has been treated as a primary requirement and played a key role in designing a layer-based graph visualization style. Additionally, we treated inspection as a genuine data mining process by providing users with facilities not met in existing tools, including: bookmarking, text search, lens tools, concurrent views, off-line inspection, dropping interactively examined objects, and configurable visualization parameters in real-time.

DEBUGGING TASK DETAILS

Our graph visualization approach does not adopt a generic graph drawing algorithm (Battista et al., 1999), like those provided by GraphViz (Gansner & North, 1999), but is explicitly designed for defect detection in object networks. We elaborate on the design details of our method showing that it is primarily task-oriented, rather than supervision-oriented or comprehension-oriented as with most graph visualizers.

More specifically, the bug detection process is initiated from a starting object on which the undesirable symptoms are initially observed. Then, an iterative process is applied with essentially two categories of analysis activities to detect state corruption and identify malicious code (see Figure 2, to part). In this context, programmers will

Figure 2. (Top) flowchart of the bug detection task and (bottom) typical debugger tree views

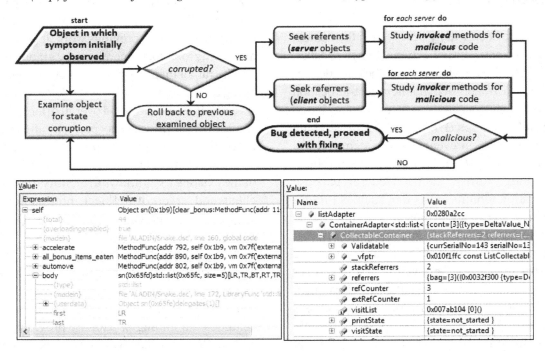

usually have to further inspect objects by seeking referent objects (outgoings links) from a starting object. Such referent inspection is well supported by existing visualizers like DDD (GNU, 2010) or HeapViz (Aftandilian et al., 2010). However, it is also supported by common tree views (like those of Figure 2, bottom part), which, due to their ease of use, remain at present the most preferable inspection tool.

Once the type and level of state corruption is verified on an object, the analysis proceeds so as to identify the offensive code. For the latter, all use sites of infected objects must be investigated since they constitute potentially malicious code. For this step referrer objects (incoming links) should be manually traced. Since many infected objects may coexist, it is crucial to *allow programmers quickly switch back and forth to referent/referrer inspection for different objects*.

This step is the most critical and most demanding part of debugging known as the bug

finding process. Only when the offensive statement is eventually found the defect detection step completes and the bug fixing process is initiated. Based on the previous remarks, we follow with the design details of our object graph visualizer.

PROGRAMMER CENTRIC DESIGN

To better support defect detection in object networks, visualizers should support referrer and referent inspection since they directly affect the generation and propagation of defects. In particular (see Figure 3, top part), objects are infected if a method with an offensive statement is invoked by clients (step 1).

Such an infection is propagated when servers (referents) are used by (step 2), or clients (referrers) are using an infected object (step 3). Based on the characteristics of the debugging process we focused on a visualization method allowing

Figure 3. (Top) defect generation and propagation in object networks and (bottom) a typical digraph and a layered graph for node (1)

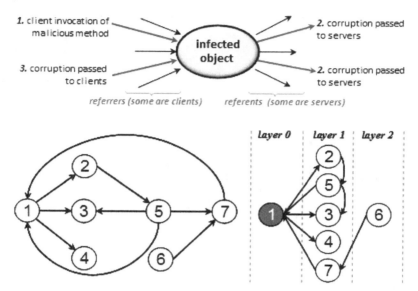

improved inspection practices for detecting object anomalies. We observed that given an object, all its direct referrers and referents are essentially its close runtime peers, semantically playing as either clients or servers. If such an inner social circle for objects is directly traceable it becomes easier to examine the actual level of infection.

Following this concept, given a starting object A and a maximum social distance N we introduce layers of social peers by the rules: (i) all direct referrers and referents of A are put in *layer 1*; (ii) *layer i+1* contains the direct referrers and referents of objects from *layer i* not included in *layer i* or *layer i-1*; and (iii) when *layer i+1* becomes empty the process terminates.

An example is provided under Figure 3 (bottom part) showing how from a typical directed graph we get a layered graph, for a given starting node. In a layered graph the runtime peers of an object fall either in its own layer or a neighbor one. Every layer encompasses the client and server objects of its previous and next layers. By tracing layers, clients of clients or servers of servers are easily tracked down. Typically, from a starting node, the number of subsequent layers to visit during

inspection is usually small, while the number of objects within layers may get very large. It should be noted that the layered view is not designed to offer a generally more attractive, or easier to assimilate, image of the graph. It is a task-specific visualization technique which for a mission other than debugging may be proved to be suboptimal.

INTERACTIVE OBJECT GRAPH VISUALIZER

The detailed software architecture of the interactive object graph visualizer is provided under Figure 4 and a general snapshot of the system used in real practice is shown within Figure 5 (objects are shown with full contents as tables with slot–value pairs). Although the default view is crowded with crossing / overlapping edges, we will briefly discuss how this is handled via the large repertoire of interactive configuration and inspection features allowing programmers to inspect object contents and identify potential state faults. We discuss the key features below.

Figure 4. Software architecture of the visualizer

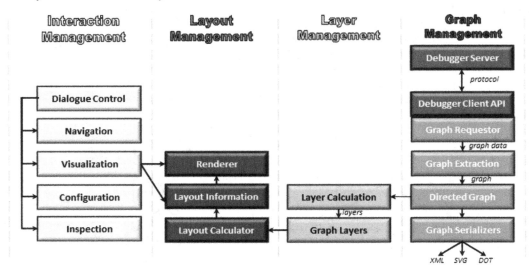

Adjustable Lens View

The main view offers zooming and resizing to enable inspect the object graph from different view scales and with varying view sizes. Similarly, the lens view scale and size (see Figure 6) can be separately adjusted. The latter, combined with the main view, offers two independent levels of detail for the inspection process. One of the most typical uses of the lens view during the inspection phase relates to the snapshot of Figure 6: 1.) the main view is chosen with a high zoom-out factor enabling to supervise the largest part of the graph although with a low-level of information detail;

Figure 5. Two parallel inspection sessions with different configurations

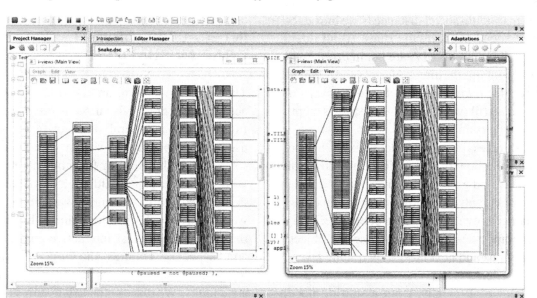

Figure 6. The lens view in various (adjustable) view scales

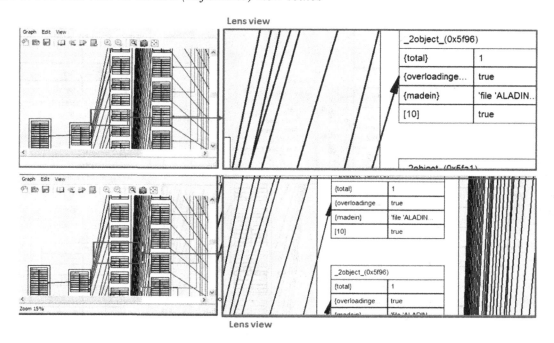

2.) the lens view is configured to combine a large view size (window) with a high zoom-in factor to offer an increased level of detail; and 3.) the lens is dragged across the main view to inspect object contents and their respective associations.

Content Tooltips, Text Search, and Goto Source

As we discuss later, the visualization can be configured in various ways, such as displaying full object contents (all slots shown) or only the object reference identifier. The latter, while it makes the resulting graphs visually less crowded, it also reduces the conveyed information content. For this purpose, content tooltips allow to quickly view object contents (see Figure 7). Also, under a zoom-out factor (value is configurable, default is 30%), the tooltips will remain active even if full contents are shown. Another feature is text search which, amongst others, enables to immediately spot objects with content-corruption patterns (supporting regular expressions too). As shown

in Figure 7 (right part), with every match, the tool focuses on the target object and highlights the matching slots; the search can be combined with lens views. Finally, the debugger cores of some languages, like the Delta language, are capable to record in every object instance the source point in which it has been originally constructed during execution. If such information is available, the graph viewer offers a *goto source line* option opening in the editor the respective source file and also positioning at precise source line (see Figure 7, up right).

Bookmarking and Path Highlighting

During the inspection process, content analysis and comparison between different objects is frequently performed. The goal is to identify cases where object contents disobey the patterns expected in a correct program execution. For this task, in existing debugging tools, programmers have to apply tedious heuristics.

Figure 7. Content tooltips, text search combined with lens view and go to source

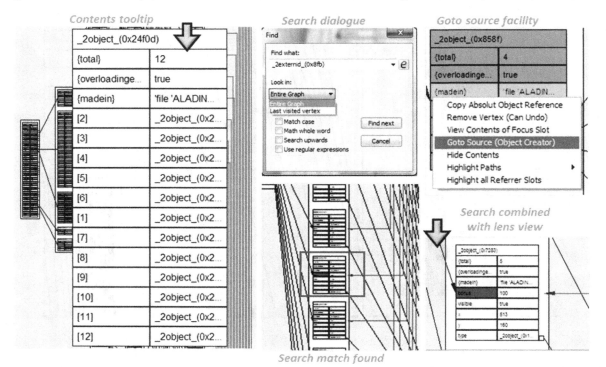

For example, they manually copy contents in an editor, trace another target object in the debugger with which they need to compare, and then switch back and forth between the editor and the debugger inspection tool to identify differences or commonalities. To facilitate such activities, we introduced bookmarks in the graph viewer which record the focus object, view origin, and zooming factor. As a result, when switching context to a bookmark, the view state is restored exactly as it was at the time the bookmark was set. Bookmarked objects are indicated with an extra marker. Another useful facility for debugging is highlighting all client and server reference paths recursively (i.e. clients of clients and servers of servers) for a given object (see Figure 8, upper part). This provides a clear picture of the runtime interactions of an object at a given time. Additionally, the object slots involved in creating a reference path are highlighted as well.

The interactive configuration features of the graph viewer have been designed to enable switching between different levels of information detail. A few examples are provided under Figure 8 (middle and bottom parts) showing the outcome by applying configuration features. They mostly concern the way either objects (vertices) or their associations (edges) are drawn. When combined with other inspection features typical process patterns during debugging are supported. For example, consider path highlighting combined with the ability to hide contents of all objects and the option for selective content expansion on individual objects. This combination allows programmers focus on a specific client-server dependency path, commonly studied when likely corruption patterns are detected. This way, programmers avoid the information overload caused when objects irrelevant to the current investigation context are fully expanded.

Figure 8. Various interaction configuration features in the object graph

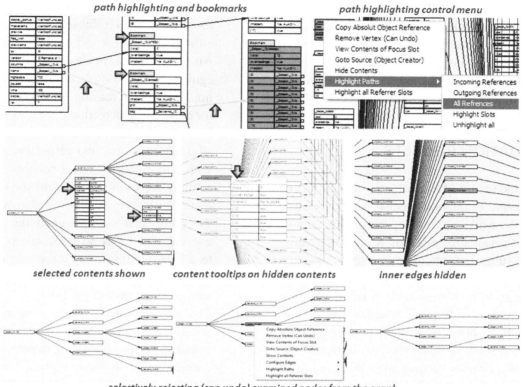

Additionally, it is allowed to drop (with undo support) from the graph any object that is considered of no interest during inspection. This allows programmers incrementally simplify the examined graph, thus eventually keeping only the objects assumed as candidates for state infection.

Concurrent Inspection Sessions

In existing graph / tree view tools, inspection is initiated from a starting object whose content is taken using a language library for communicating with the debugger core. Further requests to the debugger core are made when the user requests graph / tree expansion. Most languages support a single communication session with the core, thus the user-interface is made modal. The lat-

ter disables concurrent inspection sessions from different starting objects, severely restricting the overall inspection process.

Because of the specific structure of layered graphs, semantically related objects of a starting object fall within a usually small number of proximate layers. This property allowed us to overcome the incremental communication bottleneck and support concurrent non-modal inspection sessions. More specifically, the user is initially requested to provide a maximum depth (semantic distance) from a starting node. Then, an intensive communication round with the debugger core takes place for extracting all required objects and their contents. Once completed, the session is terminated and the tool enables the inspection facilities. To gain such information via existing tree or graph views, a large number of incremental expansion steps are needed, involving synchronous communication with the debugger backend. Additionally, because no debugger core is actually deployed during inspection, we allow the graphs to be saved (in XML format) enabling to reopen at any point in time for off-line inspection.

EVALUATION RESULTS

Due to the nature of the domain, the conduct of a systematic evaluation process with users was inevitable, while we dropped the deployment of subjective evaluation methods. More specifically, because subjective evaluation prescribes expert-based analysis we decided that concrete results with programmers involved in actual debugging tasks would provide more valuable and reliable data. In this context, we initially performed early evaluation trials with prototypes; however, the results were rather inconclusive and partial. In particular, we observed that even small discounts on functionality, something mandatory in order to be able carry out such early sessions, tended to seriously affect the way programmers organize debugging activities. As a result, we have decided to firstly fully implement features, and then *test them in combination* with all the features becoming available to programmers. Thus, following user suggestions as well, we treated all *debugging features as a unit*, shifting emphasis to the conduct of an iterative application of *integration, testing and evaluation* processes with real users. The latter was carried out following a scenario-based conduct:

- We introduced various defects within two applications, all causing malfunctions due to propagated object infections, and then we required users to locate them. To enable the extraction of comparative results we had to produce similar errors, however

involving different packages, classes and methods, and then challenged programmers to located offensive statements by either using or not our visualization tool. Also, the bugs were classified in three categories, namely *simple*, *average* and *tough*, implying an increasing level of difficulty for overall bug detection.

- The process was organized with two parallel sessions and two respective groups, with only one group at a running session actually deploying the visualization instrument. With every session we also switched the group that was assigned the task to use the tool to avoid conclusions biased to a group. After every three sessions the groups were reorganized, with about fifteen sessions overall executed.

- The users involved in the sessions were programmers (graduate students) with considerable programming experience and knowledgeable in using typical debugging visualization facilities in popular IDEs like Eclipse, Net Beans and Visual Studio. In total, six students were involved, with two groups of three students per session.

Our conclusions were very interesting regarding the utility of the tool. In particular, they were heavily related to the difficulty level of the bugs, and in some cases indicated a bias due to the required learning curve of the tool. More specifically, for simple bugs most programmers expressed that they found the adoption of such a comprehensive visual instrument to be rather tedious and unnecessary, as they manage to detect infected objects quickly with traditional watches and tree views. One of the ten programmers involved in the study mentioned that the inherent learning effort to use the tool, for detecting simple anomalies, is overall "annoying" in terms of the required investment. Now, when it came to analyzing the results for the bugs of an average complexity scale the conclusions were surprising. Although we did expect some changes, we thought that we could likely get positive feedback only with the tough bugs.

What we observed, and what apparently most of the programmers did in the study, was a very quick shift from the tree views to the layered graphs, even after five to eight repeated inspection trials once failing to capture the originally infected objects. While they expressed that the exploded views with global referent and referrer associations seemed a little crowded in the opening visualization screen, they begun using lenses and configuration features directly and quickly managed to reach infected objects. We asked if they were to abandon the tree views so quickly anyway, irrespective of the presence of the object graphs. All of them responded negatively in an emphatic way. They mentioned that the reason they switched this time so quickly is because they were very eager to find the bug, and they considered that the graph tool with its visual associations would help them to do so. The comparative results for the tough bugs were not very different from the average ones, although it took more time for programmers to locate them (two of them actually failed to identify the bug at all). Finally, in a post analysis session involving the programmers, they mentioned that from their experience, the vast majority of the bugs they are faced in a software project are simple and pretty straightforward to detect. In this case, they would never switch to graph views. However, once bugs get more difficult, it is the psychology of the task that makes them more open to the adoption of tools enabling inspect objects in a more elaborate manner, with the hope that anomalies will be more quickly spotted.

SUMMARY AND CONCLUSION

We have discussed a debugging assistant offering interactive object graphs, putting emphasis on improved visualization, inspection (navigation)

and configuration facilities. The design of the tool was focused on the optimal support of the primary task, rather than on the general-purpose graph drawing applicability as such. This has led to a considerable number of interactive features, each with a distinctive role in object state inspection, not met in existing tools.

As explained earlier, our visualization approach has been also a spin-off of the task analysis process, which emphasized effective and efficient inspection, rather than overall comprehension. The latter is a novel view regarding the utility of graphical debugging aids. In particular, we observed that programmers study object paths based almost exclusively on infection criteria. Practically, views like dynamic object topology and linkage patterns were of less interest during debugging. They seemed to be appropriate for the design stages of a subsystem, to assimilate its runtime behavior, but not during the bug finding process.

Our evaluation trials have shown that programmers tend to spend more time in detailed inspection of object contents, in identifying corruption patterns and in tracking down referrers and referrers. They reported that they prefer alternative drawing tools mostly for static aspects such as class hierarchies and module dependencies. In conclusion, we believe our work offers a novel insight on the design of interactive graph visualizations for debuggers. Further systematic analysis and support of debugging activities in the future may result in more advanced facilities, effectively leading to more usable and useful interactive debugging environments.

REFERENCES

Aftandilian, E., Kelley, S., Gramazio, C., Ricci, N., Su, S., & Guyer, S. (2010). Heapviz: Interactive heap visualization for program understanding and debugging. In *Proceedings of ACM SoftVis 2010*. Salt Lake City, UT: ACM Press.

Battista, D. G., Eades, P., Tamassia, R., & Tollis, I. G. (1999). *Graph Drawing: Algorithms for the Visualization of Graphs*. Upper Saddle River, NJ: Prentice-Hall.

De Pauw, W., & Sevitsky, G. (1999). Visualizing reference patterns for solving memory leaks in java. In *Proceedings of the ECOOP 1999 Conference*. Berlin: Springer.

Gansner, E., & North, S. C. (1999). An open graph visualization system and its applications to software engineering. *Software, Practice & Experience, 30*(11), 1203–1233. doi:10.1002/1097-024X(200009)30:11<1203::AID-SPE338>3.0.CO;2-N.

GNU DDD. (2009). *Data display debugger*. Retrieved from http://www.gnu.org/software/ddd/.

Heer, J., Card, S., & Landay, J. (2005). Prefuse: A toolkit for interactive information visualization. In *Proceedings of the CHI 2005 Conference on Human Factors in Computing Systems*. Portland, OR: ACM Press.

Hendrix, D., Cross, J., & Barowski, L. (2004). An extensible framework for providing dynamic data structure visualizations in a lightweight IDE. In *Proceedings of SIGCSE'04 35th Technical Symposium on Computer Science Education*. New York: ACM Press.

Hill, T., Noble, J., & Potter, J. (2002). Scalable visualizations of object-oriented systems with ownership trees. *Journal of Visual Languages and Computing, 13*, 319–339. doi:10.1006/jvlc.2002.0238.

Kranzlmuller, D., Grabner, S., & Volkert, J. (1996). Event graph visualization for debugging large applications. In *Proceedings of ACM SPDT'96*. Philadelphia: ACM Press.

Lange, D. B., & Nakamura, Y. (1997). Object-oriented program tracing and visualization. *IEEE Computer, 30*(5), 63–70. doi:10.1109/2.589912.

Muller, T. (2000). Practical investigation of constraints with graph views. In *Proceedings of the International Workshop on the Implementation of Declarative Languages*. Paris: Springer.

Reiss, S. (2009). Visualizing the java heap to detect memory problems. In *Proceedings of VISSOFT '09 5th IEEE International Workshop on Visualizing Software for Understanding and Analysis*, 73–80. Washington, DC: IEEE Press.

Savidis, A. (2010). *Delta programming language*. Retrieved from http://www.ics.forth.gr/hci/files/plang/Delta/Delta.html.

Savidis, A., & Lilis, Y. (2009). Support for language independent browsing of aggregate values by debugger backends. *Journal of Object Technology, 8*(6), 159–180. Retrieved from http://www.jot.fm/issues/issue_2009_09/article4.pdf doi:10.5381/jot.2009.8.6.a4.

Sundararaman, J., & Back, G. (2008). HDPV: Interactive, faithful, in-vivo runtime state visualization for C/C++ and Java. In *Proceedings of SoftVis'08 4th Symposium on Software Visualization*, 47–56. New York: ACM Press.

Yi, J. S., Kang, Y., Stasko, J., & Jacko, J. (2008). Understanding and characterizing insights: How do people gain insights using information visualization? In *Proceedings of ACM BELIV '08*. Florence, Italy: ACM Press.

Zeller, A. (2005). *Why programs fail: A guide to systematic debugging*. Boston: Morgan Kaufmann.

Zimmermann, T., & Zeller, A. (2002) Visualizing memory graphs. In Diehl, S (Ed), *Software Visualization* (191-204). New York: Springer. doi:10.1007/3-540-45875-1_15.

Compilation of References

23andMe. (2012) Retrieved from https://www.23andme.com/.

Abela, A. (1981). *Advanced presentations by design: Creating communication that drives action*. San Francisco, CA: Pfeiffer.

Abigail, S., & Whittaker, S. (2010). Beyond total capture: A constructive critique of lifelogging. *Communications of the ACM, 53*(5), 70–77. doi:10.1145/1735223.1735243.

Adachi, Y., Kumano, T., & Ogino, K. (1995). Intermediate representation for stiff virtual objects. In *Proceedings of IEEE Virtual Reality Conference*, 203-210). New Brunswick, NJ: IEEE Press.

Adidas service Micoach . (2012). Retrieved from http://www.adidas.com/us/micoach/.

Adler, M. (1991). Bamboozling the public. *New Law Journal*. Retrieved from http://www.clarity-international.net/downloads/Bam.pdf.

Adobe. (n.d.). ActionScript technology center. *Adobe Developer Connection*. Retrieved from http://www.adobe.com/devnet/actionscript.html.

Advanced Distributed Learning–ADL. (2009). SCORM® 2004 4th edition-content aggregation model (CAM), version 1.1. *Department of Defense, United States of America*. Retrieved from http://www.adlnet.gov/capabilities/scorm/scorm-2004-4th.

Aftandilian, E., Kelley, S., Gramazio, C., Ricci, N., Su, S., & Guyer, S. (2010). Heapviz: Interactive heap visualization for program understanding and debugging. In *Proceedings of ACM SoftVis 2010*. Salt Lake City, UT: ACM Press.

Ahlberg, C., & Shneiderman, B. (1994). Visual information seeking: Tight coupling of dynamic query filters with starfield displays. In *Proceedings of ACM Conference on Human Factors in Computing Systems*, 313-317. New York: ACM Press.

Ahlberg, C., Williamson, C., & Shneiderman, B. (1992). Dynamic queries for information exploration. In *Proceedings of the SIGCHI Conference on Human Factors in Computing Systems*, 619–626. New York: ACM Press. doi:10.1145/142750.143054.

Ahmed, A., Fu, X., Hong, S., Nguyen, Q., & Xu, K. (2009). Visual analysis of history of world cup: A dynamic network with dynamic hierarchy and geographic clustering. *Visual Information Communication*, 25-39. Berlin: Springer. doi:10.1007/978-1-4419-0312-9_2.

AICC. (2004). CMI guidelines for interoperability, revision 4.0. *AICC CMI Subcommittee*. Retrieved from http://www.aicc.org/joomla/dev/index.php?option=com_content&view=article&id=64&Itemid=28.

Alavi, M., & Leidner, D. (2001). Review: Knowledge management and knowledge management systems: Conceptual foundations and research issues. *Management Information Systems Quarterly, 25*(1), 107–136. doi:10.2307/3250961.

Allen, A. L. (2008). Dredging-up the past: Lifelogging, memory, and surveillance. *The University of Chicago Law Review. University of Chicago. Law School, 75*(1), 47–74.

Alli, K., Ramirez, G. G., & Yung, K. K. (2001). Withdrawn spin-offs: An empirical analysis. *Journal of Financial Research, 24*(4), 603–616.

Amar, R., Eagan, J., & Stasko, J. (2005). Low-level components of analytic activity in information visualization. In *Proceedings of IEEE Symposium on Information Visualization*, 111-117. New Brunswick, NJ: IEEE Press.

Amavizca, M., Sánchez, J., & Abascal, R. (1999). 3DTree: Visualization of large and complex information spaces in the floristic digital library. In *Proceedings of the Workshop on Computer Mediated Interaction, 2nd Mexican International Conference on Computer Science*. Pachuca, México: ACM Press.

Anderson, C. (2006). *The long tail: Why the future of business is selling less of more*. New York: Hyperion.

Andersson, P., Rosenqvist, C., & Sahrawi, O. (2007). Mobile innovations in healthcare: customer involvement and the co-creation of value. *International Journal of Mobile Communications*, 5(4), 371–388. doi:10.1504/IJMC.2007.012786.

Andrade, J., & Meudell, P. (1993). Is spatial information encoded automatically in memory? *The Quarterly Journal of Experimental Psychology Section A: Human Experimental Psychology*, 46(2), 365–375. doi:10.1080/14640749308401051 PMID:8316640.

Andrew, K., & Heidegger, H. (1998). Information slices: Visualizing and exploring large hierarchies using cascading, semi-circular discs. In *Proceedings of IEEE Symposium on Information Visualization*, 9-12. New Brunswick, NJ: IEEE Press.

Andrews, A. E., Ratwani, R. M., & Trafton, J. G. (2009). The effect of alert type to an interruption on primary task resumptions. In *Proceedings of HFES*. Boulder, CO: Westview Press.

Andrews, K. (2006). Evaluating information visualisations. In *Proceedings of the 2006 AVI Workshop On Beyond Time And Errors: Novel Evaluation Methods For Information Visualization*, 1–5. New York: ACM Press.

Andrienko, G., & Andrienko, N. (2007). Coordinated multiple views: A critical view. *In Proceedings of the Fifth International Conference on Coordinated and Multiple Views in Exploratory Visualization*, (72-74). Zurich, Switzerland: Institute of Electrical and Electronics Engineers (IEEE).

Andrienko, N., Andrienko, G., & Gatalsky, P. (2005). Impact of data and task characteristics on design of spatio-temporal data visualization tools. In A. MacEachren, M.-J. Kraak, & J. Dykes (Eds.), Exploring Geovisualization (201-222). New York: Elsevier, Ltd. doi:doi:10.1016/B978-008044531-1/50428-0 doi:10.1016/B978-008044531-1/50428-0.

AOL. (2012). *AOL, Inc*. Retrieved from http://www.aol.com/.

Archambault, D., Purchase, H., & Pinaud, B. (2010). Animation, small multiples, and the effect of mental map preservation in dynamic graphs. *IEEE Transactions on Visualization and Computer Graphics*, 17(4), 539–552. doi:10.1109/TVCG.2010.78 PMID:20498503.

Arend, A., Muthig, K., & Wandmacher, J. (1987). Evidence for global feature superiority in menu selection by icons. *Behaviour & Information Technology*, 6(4), 411–426. doi:10.1080/01449298708901853.

Artero, A. O., de Oliverira, M. C. F., & Levkowitz, H. (2004). Uncovering clusters in crowded parallel coordinates visualization. In *IEEE Symposium on Information Visualization*, 81-88. New Brunswick, NJ: IEEE Press.

Ask.com . (2012). Retrieved from http://www.ask.com/.

Asthmapolis . (2012). Retrieved from http://asthmapolis.com/.

Avila, R., & Sobierajski, L. (1996). A haptic interaction method for volume visualization. In *Proceedings of IEEE Symposium on Information Visualization '96*, 197-204. New Brunswick, NJ: IEEE Press.

Aviles, W., & Ranta, J. (1999). Haptic interaction with geoscientific data. In *Proceedings of the Fourth PHANTOM Users Group Workshop*, 78-81. Cambridge, MA: MIT Press.

Axelsson, S. (2005). *Understanding Intrusion Detection Through Visualization*. (Ph.D. thesis). Goteborg, Sweden: Chalmers University of Technology.

Bacon, J. (2009). *The art of community: Building the new age of participation (Theory in practice)*. Sebastopol, CA: O'Reilly Media.

Baddeley, A. (2007). *Working memory, thought, and action*. New York: Oxford University Press. doi:10.1093/ac prof:oso/9780198528012.001.0001.

Baer, M., & Ellis, J. B. (1998). Designing audio aura. In *Proceedings of CHI*. New York: ACM Press.

Bailey, J. E., Whitmeyer, S. J., & De Paor, D. G. (2012). Geological Society of America Special Papers: *Vol. 492. Introduction: The application of google geo tools to geoscience education and research* (pp. vii–xix). doi:10.1130/2012.2492(00).

Bajaj, C. L., Pascucci, V., & Schikore, D. R. (1997). The contour spectrum. In *Proceedings of Visualization '97*. New Brunswick, NJ: IEEE Press.

Baldonado, M. Q., Woodruff, A., & Kuchinsky, A. (2000). Guidelines for using multiple views in information visualization. *Proceedings of the Working Conference on Advanced Visual Interfaces,* (110-119). New York: ACM.

Ball-Rokeach, S. J., Kim, Y. C., & Matei, S. (2001). Storytelling neighborhood: Paths to belonging in diverse urban environments. *Communication Research, 28*(4), 392–428. doi:10.1177/009365001028004003.

Balsamiq Studios. (2013). *Rapid wireframing tool*. Retrieved from http://www.balsamiq.com/.

BAM Labs. (2012). Retrieved from http://bamlabs.com/product/.

Bandura, A. (1986). *Social foundations of thought and action*. Englewood Cliffs, NJ: Prentice-Hall.

Barabasi, A.-L. (2010). *Bursts: The hidden pattern behind everything we do*. Retrieved from http://dl.acm.org/citation.cfm?id=1941887.

Baranovsky, D. (n.d.). *GRaphael-Jevascript library*. Retrieved from http://g.raphaeljs.com/.

Barbaro, M. (2010). Active devices based on organic semiconductors for wearable applications. *IEEE Transactions on Information Technology in Biomedicine, 14*(3), 758–766. doi:10.1109/TITB.2010.2044798 PMID:20371414.

Barnett, A. P., & Okoruwa, A. A. (1993). Application of geographic information systems in site selection and location analysis. *The Appraisal Journal, 61*, 245–245.

Bartram, L., & Ware, C. (2002). Filtering and brushing with motion. *Information Visualization, 1*(1), 66–79.

Bartram, L., Ware, C., & Calvert, T. (2003). Moticons: Detection, distraction, and task. *International Journal of Human-Computer Studies, 58*(5), 515–545. doi:10.1016/S1071-5819(03)00021-1.

Basdogan, C., Ho, C., Slater, M., & Srinivasa, M. (1998). The role of haptic communication in shared virtual environments. In *Proceedings of the Fourth PHANTOM Users Group Workshop*. Cambridge, MA: MIT Press.

Battista, D. G., Eades, P., Tamassia, R., & Tollis, I. G. (1999). *Graph Drawing: Algorithms for the Visualization of Graphs*. Upper Saddle River, NJ: Prentice-Hall.

Beaudouin-Lafon, M. (2004). Designing interaction, not interfaces. In: *Proceedings of AVI '04 The Working Conference on Advanced Visual Interfaces,* 15-22. New York: ACM Press.

Beaumont, J. R. (1991). GIS and market analysis. In Maguire, D. J., Goodchild, M. F., & Rhind, D. W. (Eds.), *Geographical Information Systems: Principles and Applications (139–51)*. New York: Wiley.

Becker, R., & Cleveland, W. (1987). Brushing scatterplots. *Technimetrics, 29*(2), 127–142. doi:10.1080/00401706.1987.10488204.

Beder, D. M., Otsuka, J. L., Silva, C. G., Silva, A. C., Talarico, N., et al., & Silva, J. C. A. (2005) The TIDIA-Ae portfolio tool: A case study of its development following a component-based layered architecture. In *Proceedings of 2nd Workshop TIDIA FAPESP*. São Paulo, Brazil: FAPESP Press.

Bederson, B. (1999). Does animation help users build mental maps of spatial information? In *Proceedings of the 1999 IEEE Symposium on Information Visualization, 11*, 28. Washington, DC: IEEE Press.

Bederson, B. (2000). *Fisheye menus*. New York: ACM.

Bell, G., & Gemmell, J. (18 February 2007). A digital life. *Scientific American Magazine*. Retrieved from http://www.scientificamerican.com/article.cfm?id=a-digital-life.

Belsky, E., Can, A., & Megbolugbe, I. (1998). A primer on geographic information systems in mortgage finance. *Journal of Housing Research, 9*(1), 5–31.

Benedek, J., & Miner, T. (2002). Measuring desirability: New methods for evaluating desirability in a usability lab setting. In *Proceedings of Usability Professionals*. New York: ACM Press.

Bentley, F. (2012). Personal health mashups: Mining significant observation from wellbeing data and context. In *Proceedings of CHI2012 Workshop on Personal Informatics in Practice: Improving Quality of Life Through Data*. New York: ACM Press.

Benyon, D., & Höök, K. (1997). Navigation in information spaces: supporting the individual. Nordby (ed.) *Proceedings of the IFIP TC13 International Conference on Human-Computer Interaction*, (39-46). London: Chapman and Hall.

Berman, D. (2000). Toward a new format for Canadian legislation–Using graphic design principles and methods to improve public access to the law. *Human Resources Development Canada and Justice Canada*. Retrieved from http://www.davidberman.com/NewFormatForCanadianLegislation.pdf.

Bernsen, N. O. (1993). Modality theory: Supporting multimodal interface design. In *Proceedings of ERCIM Workshop on Multimodal Human-Computer Interaction*. Cambridge, MA: MIT Press.

Bertin, J. (1983). *Semiology of graphics: Diagrams, networks, maps*. Milwaukee, WI: ESRI Press.

Bertin, J. (1983a). *The retinal variables. Semiology of Graphics: Diagrams, Networks, Maps (65)*. Madison, WI: The University of Wisconsin Press.

Bertin, J. (1983b). *Colour Variation. Semiology of Graphics: Diagrams, Networks, Maps (91)*. Madison, WI: The University of Wisconsin Press.

Bertin, J. (1983c). *Diagrams involving two components. Semiology of Graphics: Diagrams, Networks, Maps (195)*. Madison, WI: The University of Wisconsin Press.

Bideau, B., Multon, F., Kulpa, R., Fradet, L., Arnaldi, B., & Delamarche, P. (2004). Virtual reality, a new tool to investigate anticipation skills: Application to goalkeeper and handball thrower duel. *Neuroscience Letters*, *372*(1-2). PMID:15531100.

Blajenkova, O., Kozhevnikov, M., & Motes, M. A. (2006). Object-spatial imagery: A new self-report imagery questionnaire. *Applied Cognitive Psychology*, *20*(2), 239–263. doi:10.1002/acp.1182.

Blazhenkova, O., Becker, M., & Kozhevnikov, M. (2011). Object–spatial imagery and verbal cognitive styles in children and adolescents: Developmental trajectories in relation to ability. *Learning and Individual Differences*, *21*(3), 281–287. doi:10.1016/j.lindif.2010.11.012.

Blazhenkova, O., & Kozhevnikov, M. (2009). The new object-spatial-verbal cognitive style model: Theory and measurement. *Applied Cognitive Psychology*, *23*(5), 638–663. doi:10.1002/acp.1473.

Blazhenkova, O., & Kozhevnikov, M. (2010). Visual-object ability: A new dimension of non-verbal intelligence. *Cognition*, *117*(3), 276–301. doi:10.1016/j.cognition.2010.08.021 PMID:20887982.

Blekko. (2012). *Blekko, Inc.* Retrieved from http://blekko.com/.

Bodnar, A., Corbett, R., & Nekrasovski, D. (2004). AROMA: Ambient awareness through olfaction in messaging application. In *Proceedings of ICMI*. New York: ACM Press.

BodyBugg . (2012). Retrieved from http://www.bodybugg.com/.

BodyMonitor . (2012). Retrieved from http://bodymonitor.de/.

Boggs. (2012). Grotto creek, front ranges, canadian cordillera: An example of google earth models. *Geoscience Canada, 39*(2).

Bomberger, N., Rhodes, B., Seibert, M., & Waxman, A. (2006). Associative learning of vessel motion patterns for maritime situation awareness. In *Proceedings of 9th International Conference on Information Fusion*. New Brunswick, NJ: IEEE Press.

Bonato, P. (2012). A review of wearable sensors and systems with application in rehabilitation. *Journal of Neuroengineering and Rehabilitation*, *9*(21).

Bonsignore, E. M., Dunne, C., Rotman, D., Smith, M., Capone, T., Hansen, D. L., & Shneiderman, B. (2009). First steps to netviz nirvana: Evaluating social network analysis with NodeXL.In *Proceedings of International Conference on Computational Science and Engineering*, 332–339. New York: ACM Press.

Borst, W. (1997). *Construction of Engineering Ontologies for Knowledge Sharing and Reuse*. (Dissertation). Enschede, The Netherlands, University of Twente.

Bostock, M. (2012). *Data-driven documents*. Retrieved from http://d3js.org/.

Bostock, M., Ogievetsky, V., & Heer, J. (2011). D³ data-driven documents. *IEEE Transactions on Visualization and Computer Graphics*, *17*(12), 2301–2309. doi:10.1109/TVCG.2011.185 PMID:22034350.

Bouthors, V., & Dedieu, O. (1999). Pharos, A collaborative infrastructure for web knowledge sharing. InAbiteboul, , & Vercoustre, (Eds.), *Research and Advanced Technology for Digital Libraries. Lecture Notes in Computer Science* (215-233). Berlin: Springer-Verlag, Inc. doi:10.1007/3-540-48155-9_15.

Bowman, D., Kruijff, E., LaViola, J., & Poupyrev, I. (2004). *3D user interfaces: Theory and practice*. Upper Saddle River, NJ: Addison-Wesley.

Boyandin, I., Bertini, E., & Lalanne, D. (2012). A qualitative study on the exploration of temporal changes in flow maps with animation and small multiples. *Computer Graphics Forum*, *31*(3.2), 1005–1014.

Boyd, D., Ramage, D., & Donath, J. (2002). Developing legible visualizations for online social spaces. In *Proceedings of the 35th Annual Hawaii International Conference on System Sciences*, 1060–1069. Washington, DC: IEEE Press.

Bresciani, S. (2011). *Visualizing Knowledge for Organizational Communication within and Across Cultures*. (PhD thesis). Lugano, Switzerland, Università della Svizzera italiana.

Bresciani, S., Eppler, M., & Tan, M. (2011). Communicating strategy across cultures with visualization: An experimental evaluation. In *Proceedings of Academy of Management 2011 Annual Meeting*. San Antonio, TX: AOM Press.

Brewster, S. A. (1995). The development of a sonically-enhanced widget set. In *Proceedings of EWHCI'95 International Centre for Scientific and Technical Information*, 126-129. Moscow: MIT Press.

Brodlie, K., Osorio, R. A., & Lopes, A. (2012). A review of uncertainty in data visualization. InDill, J, Earnshaw, R, Kasik, D, Vince, J, & Wong, P. C. (Eds.), *Expanding the Frontiers of Visual Analytics and Visualization* (81-109). Berlin: Springer. doi:10.1007/978-1-4471-2804-5_6.

Brown, J. S., & Duguid, P. (1991). Organizational learning and communities-of-practice: Toward a unified view of working, learning, and innovation. *Organizational Learning*, *2*(1), 40–57.

Bruls, M., Huizing, K., & Wijk, J. (1999) Squarified treemaps, In *Proceedings of the Joint Eurographics and IEEE TCVG Symposium on Visualization*. New Brunswick, NJ: IEEE Press.

Brunschwig, C. R. (2001). *Visualisierung von rechtsnormen–Legal design*. (Doctoral thesis). Zurich, Switzerland, Universität Zürich.

Brunschwig, C. R. (2011). Multisensory law and legal informatics–A comparison of how these legal disciplines relate to visual law. *Jusletter IT*. Retrieved from http://jusletter-eu.weblaw.ch/issues/2011/104/article_324.html.

Bruzzese, D., & Davino, C. (2008). Visual mining of association rules. In *Visual Data Mining* (103–122). Berlin: Springer-Verlag. doi:10.1007/978-3-540-71080-6_8.

Bryson, S. (1996). Virtual reality in scientific visualization. *Communications of the ACM*, *39*(5), 62–71. doi:10.1145/229459.229467.

Buchanan, G., & Owen, T. (2008). Improving skim reading for document triage. In *Proceedings of the Second International Symposium on Information Interaction in Context*, 83-88. New York: ACM.

Buchel, O. (2011). Designing map-based visualizations for collection understanding. In *Proceeding of the 11th Annual International ACM/IEEE Joint Conference on Digital Libraries*. New York: ACM Press. doi:10.1145/1998076.1998169.

Burdea, G., & Coiffet, P. (1994). *Virtual reality technology*. New York: John Wiley & Sons, Inc..

Burigat, S., & Chittaro, L. (2007). Geographic data visualization on mobile devices for user's navigation and decision support activities. InBelussi, (ed.), *Spatial Data on the Web-Modeling and Management*. Berlin: Springer. doi:10.1007/978-3-540-69878-4_12.

Burkhard, R. A. (2005a). *Knowledge Visualization: The Use of Complementary Visual Representations for the Transfer of Knowledge. A model, a Framework, and Four New Approaches*. (PhD thesis). Zurich, Switzerland, Eidgenossische Technische Hochschule ETH.

Burkhard, R. A. (2005b). Towards a framework and a model for knowledge visualization: Synergies between information and knowledge visualization. In S.-O. Tergan, & T. Keller (Eds.), Lecture Notes in Computer Science, Vol. 3426: Knowledge and Information Visualization: Searching for Synergies. (238–255). Heidelberg, Germany: Springer. doi: doi:10.1007/11510154_13.

Burnett, S. A., & Lane, D. M. (1980). Effects of academic instruction on spatial visualization. *Intelligence*, *4*(3), 233–242. doi:10.1016/0160-2896(80)90021-5.

Bush, V. (1945). As we may think. *Atlantic Monthly*, *176*(1), 101–108.

Butcher, K. R., & Sumner, T. (2011). Self-directed learning and the sensemaking paradox. *Human-Computer Interaction*, *26*, 123–159. doi:10.1080/07370024.2011.556552.

Butler, B., Sproull, L., Kiesler, S., & Kraut, R. (2007). Community effort in online groups: Who does the work and why. In S. PWeisband, (Ed.), *Leadership at a Distance* (171–195). Florence, KY: Psychology Press.

Cai, Y. & de M. Franco, R. (2009). Interactive visualization of network anomalous events. In: *Computational Science, 5544*, 450–459. Berlin: Springer.

Can, A. (1992). Specification and estimation of hedonic housing price models. *Regional Science and Urban Economics*, *22*(3), 453–474. doi:10.1016/0166-0462(92)90039-4.

Can, A., & Megbolugbe, I. (1997). Spatial dependence and house price index construction. *The Journal of Real Estate Finance and Economics*, *14*, 203–222. doi:10.1023/A:1007744706720.

Canada, C. (2006). La cueva grande: A 43-megapixel immersive system. In *Proceedings of Virtual Reality Conference 2006*. New Brunswick, NJ: IEEE Press.

Capzels. (2012). Retrieved from http://www.capzles.com/.

Card, S. K., & Mackinlay, J. (1997). The structure of the information visualization design space. In *Proceedings of VIZ '97: Visualization Conference, Information Visualization Symposium and Parallel Rendering Symposium*, 92–99. Washington, DC: IEEE Press.

Card, S. K. (Ed.). (1999). *Readings in information visualization: Using vision to think*. San Francisco: Morgan Kaufmann.

Card, S. K., Mackinlay, J. D., & Shneiderman, B. (1999). *Readings in information visualization: Using vision to think*. San Francisco: Morgan Kaufman Publishers.

Card, S. K., Moran, T. P., & Newell, A. (1983). *The psychology of human-computer interaction*. Hillsdale, NJ: Lawrence Erlbaum.

Card, S., Mackinlay, J. D., & Shneiderman, B. (1999). *Readings in information visualization: Using vision to think*. San Francisco: Morgan Kaufmann Publishers.

Carpenter, S., Fortune, J. L., Delugach, H. S., Etzkorn, L. H., Utley, D. R., Farrington, P. A., & Virani, S. (2008). Studying team shared mental models. In P. J. Ågerfalk, H. Delugach, & M. Lind (Eds.), *Proceedings of the 3rd International Conference on the Pragmatic Web: Innovating the Interactive Society, Uppsala, Sweden* (41-48). New York: ACM.

Carr, H. (2004). *Topological Manipulation of Isosurfaces*. (PhD Thesis). Vancouver, BC, Canada, University of British Columbia.

Carr, H., & Snoeyink, J. (2003). *Path seeds and flexible isosurfaces using topology for exploratory visualization*. In *Proceedings of the Symposium on Data Visualisation*. New Brunswick, NJ: IEEE Press.

Carr, H., Snoeyink, J., & Axen, U. (2003). Computing contour trees in all dimensions. *Computational. Geometry. Theory & Applications*, *24*(2), 75–94.

Carr, H., Snoeyink, J., & Panne, M. V. D. (2004). Simplifying flexible isosurfaces using local geometric measures. In *Proceedings of Visualization '04*. New Brunswick, NJ: IEEE Press. doi:10.1109/VISUAL.2004.96.

Cartwright, W. (2009). Applying the theatre metaphor to integrated media for depicting geography. *The Cartographic Journal*, *46*(1), 24–35. doi:10.1179/000870409X415561.

Cartwright, W. E., & Hunter, G. J. (1999). Enhancing the map metaphor with multimedia cartography. InCartwright, , Peterson, , & Gartner, (Eds.), *Multimedia Cartography* (257-270). Heidelberg, Germany: Springer-Verlag. doi:10.1007/978-3-662-03784-3_24.

Casey, M. B., Winner, E., Brabeck, M., & Sullivan, K. (1990). Visual-spatial abilities in art, maths, and science majors: Effects of sex, family handedness, and spatial experience. In Gilhooly, K. J., Keane, M. T. G., Logie, R. H., & Erdos, G. (Eds.), *Lines of Thinking: On the Psychology of Thought* (*Vol. 2*, pp. 275–294). West Sussex, UK: John Wiley & Sons Ltd..

Casner, S. (1991). A task-analytic approach to the automated design of graphic presentations. *ACM Transactions on Graphics*, *10*, 111–151. doi:10.1145/108360.108361.

Cedilnik, A., & Rheingans, P. (2000). Procedural annotation of uncertain information. In *Proceedings of Visualization '04*. New Brunswick, NJ: IEEE.

Chan, J., & Hayes, C. (2010). Decomposing discussion forums using user roles. In *Proceedings of the Second Web Science Conference*. Raleigh, NC: ACM Press.

Chan, A., MacLean, K., & McGrenere, J. (2008). Designing haptic icons to support collaborative turn-taking. *International Journal of Human-Computer Studies*, *66*, 333–355. doi:10.1016/j.ijhcs.2007.11.002.

Chang, C. (n.d.). Street vendor guide. *Accessible City Regulations*. Retrieved from http://candychang.com/street-vendor-guide

Chang, M., Leggett, J. J., Furuta, R., Kerne, A., Williams, J. P., Burns, S. A., & Bias, R. G. (2004). Collection understanding. In *Proceedings of the 4th ACM/IEEE-CS Joint Conference on Digital Libraries*, 334–342. New York: ACM. doi:10.1145/996350.996426.

Chen, K. W., Heng, P. A., & H., S. (2000). Direct haptic rendering of isosurface by intermediate representation. In *Proceedings of ACM Symposium on Virtual Reality Software and Technology VRST*, 188-194. New York: ACM Press.

Cheng, W. C. (2004). Total recall: Are privacy changes inevitable? In *Proceedings of CARPE 2004 First ACM Workshop on Continuous Archival and Retrieval of Personal Experiences*. New York: ACM

Chittaro, L. (2006). Visualizing information on mobile devices. *IEEE Computer*, *39*(3), 34–39. doi:10.1109/MC.2006.109.

Clegg, T., Gardner, C., Williams, O., & Kolodner, J. (2006). Promoting learning in informal learning environments. In *Proceedings of the 7th International Conference on Learning Sciences*, 92-98. Bloomington, IN: International Society of the Learning Sciences.

Cockburn, A., & Brewster, S. A. (2005). Multimodal feedback for the acquisition of small targets. *Ergonomics*, *48*(9), 1129–1150. doi:10.1080/00140130500197260 PMID:16251152.

Colin, W. (2008). *Visual thinking: For design*. San Francisco: Morgan Kaufmann.

Consolvo, S. (2008). Flowers or a robot army? Encouraging awareness & activity with personal, mobile displays. In *Proceedings of the 10th International Conference on Ubiquitous Computing: UbiComp 08*, 54-63. New York: ACM Press.

Corbishley, P., & Rodriguez-Villegas, E. (2008). Breathing detection: Towards a miniaturized, wearable, battery-operated monitoring system. *IEEE Transactions on Bio-Medical Engineering*, *55*(1), 196–204. doi:10.1109/TBME.2007.910679 PMID:18232362.

Coulson, T., Shayo, C., Olfman, L., & Rohm, C. E. T. (2003). ERP training strategies: Conceptual training and the formation of accurate mental models. In *Proceedings of the 2003 SIGMIS Conference on Computer Personnel Research*, 87-97. Philadelphia, PA: ACM.

Court of Appeal for Western Sweden. (2009). *Judgement in case number B 1534-08*. Hovrätten för Västra Sverige, Göteborg. Retrieved from http://www.domstol.se/Domstolar/vastrahovratten/Kristalldom.pdf.

Creative Commons. (n.d.). *About the licenses–Creative commons.* Retrieved from http://creativecommons.org/licenses.

Cross, N. (2011). *Design thinking: Understanding how designers think and work.* Oxford, UK: Berg Publishers.

Crowston, K., & Howison, J. (2005). The social structure of free and open source software development. *First Monday, 10*(2). doi:10.5210/fm.v10i2.1207.

Cruz-Neira, C. (1993). Surround-screen projection-based virtual reality: The design and implementation of the cave. In *Proceedings of ACM SIGGRAPH.* New York: ACM Press.

CSTA. (2013). The spatial history project. *Stanford University.* Retrieved from http://www.stanford.edu/group/spatialhistory/cgi-bin/site/index.php.

Cunliffe, D., Taylor, C., & Tudhope, D. (1997). Query-based navigation in semantically indexed hypermedia. *Proceedings of the Eighth ACM Conference on Hypertext,* 87-95. Southampton, UK: ACM Press.

Cunningham, S. J., & Bennett, E. (2008). Understanding collection understanding with collage. In *Proceedings of the 11th International Conference on Asian Digital Libraries: Universal and Ubiquitous Access to Information,* 367–370. Berlin: Springer-Verlag. doi:10.1007/978-3-540-89533-6_46.

CureTogether. (2012). Retrieved from http://curetogether.com/.

Czerwinski, M., Cutrell, E., & Horvitz, E. (2000). *Instant messaging and interruption: Influence of task type on performance.* In *Proceedings of OZCHI.* New York: ACM Press.

Dahlbom, A., & Niklasson, L. (2007). Trajectory clustering for coastal surveillance. In *Proceedings of the 10th International Conference on Information Fusion.* QC, Canada: IEEE Press.

Damasio, A. R. (1999). *The feeling of what happens: Body and emotion in the making of consciousness.* London: Harcourt Inc..

Dantzich, M. V., Robbins, D., Horvitz, E., & Czerwinski, M. (2002). *Scope: Providing awareness of multiple notifications at a glance.* In *Proceedings of AVI.* New York: ACM Press.

D'Argembeau, A., & Van der Linden, M. (2004). *Influence of affective meaning on memory for contextual information.* Washington, DC: American Psychological Association. doi:10.1037/1528-3542.4.2.173.

Date, C. J. (1986). *An introduction to database systems, 1* (4th ed.). Boston: Addison-Wesley.

Dattu, F. (1998). Illustrated jury instructions: A proposal. *Law and Psychology Review, 22,* 67–102.

Davis, S., & Bostrom, R. (1992). An experimental investigation of the roles of the computer interface and individual characteristics in the learning of computer systems. *International Journal of Human-Computer Interaction, 4*(2), 143–172. doi:10.1080/10447319209526033.

Davis, T. J., & Keller, C. P. (1997). Modeling and visualizing multiple spatial uncertainties. *Computers & Geosciences, 23*(4), 397–408. doi:10.1016/S0098-3004(97)00012-5.

Daytum. (2012). Retrieved from http://www.daytum.com/.

De Pauw, W., & Sevitsky, G. (1999). Visualizing reference patterns for solving memory leaks in java. In *Proceedings of the ECOOP 1999 Conference.* Berlin: Springer.

deCODEme . (2012). Retrieved from http://www.decodeme.com/.

Definition of Self . (2012a). Retrieved from http://www.yourdictionary.com/self-definition.

Definition of Self . (2012b). Retrieved from http://en.academic.ru/dic.nsf/cide/156773/Self.

Dehnadi, S., Bornat, R., & Adams, R. (2009). *Meta-analysis of the effect of consistency on success in early learning of programming.* Paper presented at Psychology Programming Interested Group (PPIG) Annual Workshop. Retrieved from http://www.ppig.org/papers/21st-dehnadi.pdf.

Demšar, U. 2006. *Data Mining of Geospatial Data: Combining Visual and Automatic Methods.* (Ph.D. thesis). Stockholm, Royal Institute of Technology (KTH).

Denham, P. (1993). Nine- to fourteen-year-old children's conception of computers using drawings. *Behaviour & Information Technology, 12*(6), 346–358. doi:10.1080/01449299308924399.

Dennerlein, J., & Yang, M. C. (1999). Perceived musculoskeletal loading during use of a force-feedback computer mouse. In *Proceedings of Human Factors and Ergonomics Conference.* Thousand Oaks, CA: Sage Publishers.

Dennerlein, J., & Yang, M. C. (2001). Haptic force feedback devices for the office computer: Performance and musculoskeletal loading issues. *Human Factors, 43*(2), 278–286. doi:10.1518/001872001775900850 PMID:11592668.

Dennett, D. (1991). *Consciousness explained.* New York: Little, Brown, and Company.

DIALOG . (2012). Retrieved from http://4thmainhealth.com/.

DiaMedics. (2012). Retrieved from http://www.martoon.com/Diamedic/Diamedic/Overview.html.

Dieberger, A. (1994). *On Navigation in Textual Virtual Environments and Hypertext.* (Unpublished doctoral dissertation). Vienna, Austria, Vienna University of Technology.

Diggle, P., Heagerty, P., Liang, K.-Y., & Zeger, S. (2002). *Analysis of longitudinal data.* New York: Oxford University Press.

Dix, A. (2002). The ultimate interface and the sums of life*? Interfaces, 50*(16).

DIY Genomics . (2012). Retrieved from http://diygenomics.org/.

Djurcilova, S., Kima, K., Lermusiauxb, P., & Pang, A. (2002). Visualizing scalar volumetric data with uncertainty. *Computers & Graphics, 26*(2), 239–248. doi:10.1016/S0097-8493(02)00055-9.

Dodge, M., & Kitchin, R. (2007). Outlines of a world coming into existence: pervasive computing and the ethics of forgetting. *Environment and Planning. B, Planning & Design, 24*, 431–445. doi:10.1068/b32041t.

Doherty, A. R., & Smeaton, A. F. (2008). Automatically segmenting lifelog data into events. In *Proceedings of WIAMIS.* New Brunswick, NJ: IEEE Press.

Donath, J., Karahalios, K., & Viégas, F. (1999). Visualizing conversation. In *Proceedings of the 32nd Annual Hawaii International Conference on Systems Sciences, 32*, 9. Hawaii: IEEE Press.

Donath, J. (2007). Signals in social supernets. *Journal of Computer Mediated Communication,13*(1).

Dou, X. W. W., Butkiewicz, T., Bier, E. A., & Ribarsky, W. (2011). A two-stage framework for designing visual analytics system in organizational environments. In *Proceedings of 2011 IEEE Conference on Visual Analytics, Science, and Technology, 251*–260. Providence, RI: IEEE Press.

Downs, R., & DeSouza, A. (Eds.). (2006). *Learning to think spatially: GIS as a support system in the K-12 curriculum.* Washington, D.C.: National Academies Press.

DreamBoard . (2012). Retrieved from http://www.dreamborad.com.

Dubin, R. A. (1992). Spatial autocorrelation and neighborhood quality. *Regional Science and Urban Economics, 22*(3), 433–452. doi:10.1016/0166-0462(92)90038-3.

Durbeck, L. J., Macias, N. J., Weinstein, D. M., Johnson, C. R., & Hollerbach, J. M. (1998). Scirun haptic display for scientific visualization. In *Proceedings of Third Phantom Users Group Workshop.* Cambridge, MA: MIT Press.

Eades, P. (1984). A heuristic for graph drawing. *Congressus Numerantium, 42*, 149–160.

Eades, P., Lai, W., Misue, K., & Sugiyama, K. (1991). Preserving the mental map of a diagram.[Sesimbra, Portugal: Academic Press.]. *Proceedings of COMPU-GRAPHICS, 91*, 34–43.

Eades, P., Lai, W., Misue, K., & Sugiyama, K. (1995). Layout adjustment and the mental map. *Journal of Visual Languages and Computing*, (6): 183–210.

Ebert, D., Gaither, K., & Gilpin, C. (2008). Enabling science discoveries through visual exploration. *NSF Workshop Report.* Washington, D.C.: National Science Foundation.

eBiz/MBA. (2012). *Top 15 most popular search engines.* Retrieved from http://www.ebizmba.com/articles/search-engines.

Ecamm. (2013). Supercharge your mail dock icon. *DockStar.* Retrieved from www.ecamm.com/mac/dockstar.

Eccles, R. (2007). Stories in geotime. In *Proceedings of IEEE Symposium on Visual Analytics Science and Technology, 2007.* New Brunswick, NJ: IEEE Press.

Edlund, J., Gronkvist, M., Lingvall, A., & Sviestins, E. (2006). Rule-based situation assessment for sea surveillance. In *Proceedings of SPIE Conference on Multisensor, Multisource Information Fusion: Architectures, Algorithms and Applications, 624,* 1–11. Bellingham, WA: SPIE Press.

Edsall, R. M. (2001). *Interacting with Space and Time: Designing Dynamic Geovisualization Environments.* (Unpublished doctoral dissertation). Philadelphia, The Pennsylvania State University.

Eickhoff, S. B., Laird, A. R., Grefkes, C., Wang, L. E., Zilles, K., & Fox, P. T. (2009). Coordinate-based activation likelihood estimation meta-analysis of neuroimaging data: A random-effects approach based on empirical estimates of spatial uncertainty. *Human Brain Mapping, 30*(9), 2907–2926. doi:10.1002/hbm.20718 PMID:19172646.

Ekbia, H. R. (2008). *Artificial dreams: The quest for non-biological intelligence.* New York: Cambridge University Press. doi:10.1017/CBO9780511802126.

Elias, M., Elson, J., Fisher, D., & Howe, J. (2008). Do I live in a flood basin? Synthesizing ten thousand maps. In *Proceedings of the 2008 Conference on Human Factors in Computing Systems,* 255-264. New York: ACM Press.

Ellis, G., & Dix, A. (2006). An explorative analysis of user evaluation studies in information visualisation. In *Proceedings of the 2006 AVI Workshop on Beyond Time and Errors: Novel Evaluation Methods for Information Visualization,* 109–116. Venice, Italy: AVI Press.

Elmasri, R., & Navathe, S. (2000). *Fundamentals of database systems* (3rd ed.). Boston: Addison Wesley.

Elmqvist, N., Do, T.-N., Goodell, H., Henry, N., & Fekete, J.-D. (2008). ZAME: Interactive Large-Scale Graph Visualization. In *Proceedings of IEEE Pacific Visualization Symposium,* 215–222. Kyoto: IEEE Press.

Eppler, M. J. (2004). *Knowledge communication problems between experts and managers. An analysis of knowledge transfer in decision processes.* Retrieved from http://doc.rero.ch/lm.php?url=1000,42,6,20051020101029-UL/1_wpca0401.pdf.

Eppler, M. J., & Platts, K. (2009). Visual strategizing: The systematic use of visualization in the strategic-planning process. *Long Range Planning, 42*(1), 42–74. doi:10.1016/j.lrp.2008.11.005.

Erickson, T. (2003). Designing visualizations of social activity: Six claims. In *Proceedings of CHI EA '03 CHI '03 Extended Abstracts on Human Factors in Computing Systems,* 846–847. Ft. Lauderdale, FL: ACM Press.

Ertel, D. (2004). Getting past yes: Negotiating as if implementation mattered. *Harvard Business Review, 82*(11), 60–68. PMID:15559446.

Evans, C., & Cools, E. (2011). Applying styles research to educational practice. *Learning and Individual Differences, 21*(3), 249–254. doi:10.1016/j.lindif.2010.11.009.

EyeTap . (2012). Retrieved from http://eyetap.org/.

Fabrikant, S. I., Montello, D. R., Ruocco, M., & Middleton, R. S. (2004). The distance-similarity metaphor in network-display spatializations. *Cartography and Geographic Information Science, 31*(4), 237–252. doi:10.1559/1523040042742402.

Fauvet, N., Ammi, M., & Bourdot, P. (2007). Experiments of haptic perception techniques for computational fluid dynamics. In *Proceedings of International Conference on Cyberworlds CW '07,* 322-329. New Brunswick, NJ: IEEE Press.

Fayyad, U., Grinstein, G., & Wierse, A. (Eds.). (2002). *Information visualization in data mining and knowledge discovery.* San Francisco: Morgan Kaufmann Publishers Inc..

Feigenson, N., & Spiesel, C. (2009). *Law on display. The digital transformation of legal persuasion and judgment.* New York: New York University Press.

Feiner, S. (1985). APEX: An experiment in the automated creation of pictorial explanations. *IEEE Computer Graphics and Applications, 5*(11), 29–37. doi:10.1109/MCG.1985.276329.

Fein, R. M., Olson, G. M., & Olson, J. S. (1993). A mental model can help with learning to operate a complex device. InAshlund, S, Mullet, K, Henderson, A, Hollnagel, E, & White, T (Eds.), *INTERACT '93 and CHI '93 Conference Companion on Human Factors in Computing Systems* (157-158). Amsterdam: ACM Press. doi:10.1145/259964.260170.

Ferey, N., Bouyer, G., Martin, C., Bourdot, P., Nelson, J., & Burkhardt, J. M. (2008). User needs analysis to design a 3d multimodal protein-docking interface. In *Proceedings of IEEE Symposium on 3D User Interfaces 3DUI*, 125-132. New Brunswick, NJ: IEEE Press.

Few, S. (2010). Data visualization for human perception. In: Mads& Friis (Eds.), *Encyclopedia of Human-Computer Interaction*. Aarhus, Denmark: The Interaction Design Foundation. Retrieved from http://www.interaction-design.org/encyclopedia/data_visualization_for_human_perception.html.

Few, S. (2009). *Data visualization past, present and future. Innovation in Action Series*. Armonk, NY: IBM.

Fikkert, W., D'Ambros, M., Bierz, T., & Jankun-Kelly, T. (2007). Interacting with visualizations. Human-Centered Visualization Environments (77-162). Berlin: Springer. doi:doi:10.1007/978-3-540-71949-6_3 doi:10.1007/978-3-540-71949-6_3.

Finding Optimism . (2012). Retrieved from http://www.findingoptimism.com/.

Fisher, D., Smith, M., & Welser, H. T. (2006). You are who you talk to: Detecting roles in usenet newsgroups. In *Proceedings of the 39th Annual Hawaii International Conference on System Sciences*. Washington, DC: IEEE Press.

Fisher, D. (2005). Using egocentric networks to understand communication. *IEEE Internet Computing*, *9*(5), 20–28. doi:10.1109/MIC.2005.114.

Fitbit. (2012). Retrieved from http://www.fitbit.com/.

FitzGerald, G., Jelinek, G. A., Scott, D., & Gerdtz, M. F. (2010). Emergency department triage revisited. *Emergency Medicine Journal*, *27*, 86–92. doi:10.1136/emj.2009.077081 PMID:20156855.

Fitzpatrick, P. J. (1997). Understanding and forecasting tropical cyclone intensity change with the Typhoon Intensity Prediction Scheme (TIPS). *Weather and Forecasting*, *12*(4), 826–846. doi:10.1175/1520-0434(1997)012<0826:UAFTCI>2.0.CO;2.

Fitzpatrick, P. J. (1999). *Natural disasters, hurricanes: A reference handbook*. Santa Barbara, CA: ABC-CLIO.

Fleming, D. (2001). Narrative leadership: Using the power of stories. *Strategy and Leadership*, *29*(4), 34.

Flipboard. (2012). *Flipboard, Inc.* Retrieved from http://flipboard.com/.

Foroughi, R., & Taponecco, F. (2005). A visualization tool for student assessment and evaluation in online learning. In *Proceedings of IADIS International Conference on Applied Computing*, 68-73. IADIS Press.

Forster, F. (1966). Use of a demographic base map for the presentation of areal data in epidemiology. *British Journal of Preventive & Social Medicine*, *20*, 165–171. PMID:5969679.

Fosshage, J. L. (1997). The organizing functions of dream mentation. *Contemporary Psychoanalysis*, *33*(3), 429–458.

France, L., Heraud, J.-M., Marty, J.-C., & Carron, T. (2005). Help through visualization to compare learners' activities to recommended learning scenarios. In *Proceedings of the Fifth IEEE International Conference on Advanced Learning Technologies*, 476-480. Washington, DC: IEEE Press.

France, L., Heraud, J.-M., Marty, J.-C., Carron, T., & Heili, J. (2006). Monitoring virtual classroom: visualization techniques to observe student activities in an e-learning system. In *Proceedings of the Sixth International Conference on Advanced Learning Technologies*, 716-720. Washington, DC: IEEE Press.

Francica, J. R. (1993). *Profiting from a geographic information system. GIS World*. Hoboken, NJ: Wiley.

Friedes, D. (1974). Human information processing and sensory modality: Cross-modal functions, information complexity, memory, and deficit. *Psychological Bulletin*, *81*(5), 284–310. doi:10.1037/h0036331 PMID:4608609.

Fua, Y.-H., Ward, M. O., & Rundensteiner, E. A. (1999). Hierarchical parallel coordinates for exploration of large datasets. In *Proceedings of IEEE Visualization*, 43-50. New Brunswick, NJ: IEEE Press.

Fung, B. C. M., Wang, K., & Ester, M. (2003). *Hierarchical document clustering. Encyclopedia of Data Warehousing and Mining*. Hershey, PA: IGI Global.

Galyean, T. A., & Hughes, J. F. (1991). Sculpting: An interactive volumetric modeling technique. In *Proceedings of the 18th Annual Conference on Computer Graphics and Interactive Techniques*, 267-274. New York: ACM Press.

Gansner, E., & North, S. C. (1999). An open graph visualization system and its applications to software engineering. *Software, Practice & Experience, 30*(11), 1203–1233. doi:10.1002/1097-024X(200009)30:11<1203::AID-SPE338>3.0.CO;2-N.

Garth, C., & Tricoche, X. (2005). Topology-and feature-based flow visualization: Methods and applications. In *Proceedings of the SIAM Conference on Geometric Design and Computing*. New York: ACM Press.

Gasper, K., & Clore, G. L. (2002). Attending to the big picture: Mood and global versus local processing of visual information. *Psychological Science, 13*(1), 34–40. doi:10.1111/1467-9280.00406 PMID:11892776.

Gazan, R. (2009). When online communities become self-aware. In *Proceedings of Conference on Hawaii International System Sciences*. Washington, DC: IEEE Press.

Gemignani, Z. (2012). *Juice analytics*. Retrieved from http://www.juiceanalytics.com/writing/data-visualization-as-storytelling-a-stretched-analogy/.

Gemmell, J. (2006). MyLifeBits: A personal database for everything. *Communications of the ACM, 49*(1), 88–95. doi:10.1145/1107458.1107460.

Geng, Z., Laramee, R. S., Loizides, F., & Buchanan, G. (2011). Visual analysis of document triage data. In *Proceedings of International Conference on Information Visualization Theory and Applications*. Vilamoura, Algarve, Portugal: INSTICC Press.

Gershon, N. D., & Page, W. (2001). What storytelling can do for information visualization. *Communications of the ACM, 44*(8), 31–37. doi:10.1145/381641.381653.

Gershon, N., Eick, S. G., & Card, S. (1998). Design: Information visualization. *Interactions (New York, N.Y.), 5*, 9–15. doi:10.1145/274430.274432.

Gibler, K. M., Black, R. T., & Moon, K. P. (2002). Time, place, space, technology, and corporate real-estate strategy. *Journal of Real Estate Research, 24*(3), 235–262.

Gilbert, E. & Karahalios, K. (2009). Using social visualization to motivate social production. *IEEE Transactions on Multimedia-Special section on communities and media, 11*(3), 413–421.

Gilbert, E., & Karahalios, K. (2007). CodeSaw: A social visualization of distributed software development. In *Proceedings of the 11th IFIP TC 13 International Conference on Human-Computer Interaction-Volume Part II*, 303–316. New York: HCIR Press.

Gilson, O., Silva, N., Grant, P. W., & Chen, M. (2008). From web data to visualization via ontology mapping. *Computer Graphics Forum, 27*(3), 959–966. doi:10.1111/j.1467-8659.2008.01230.x.

Girgensohn, A., Shipman, F., Turner, T., & Wilcox, L. (2010). Flexible access to photo libraries via time, place, tags, and visual features. In *Proceedings of the 10th Annual Joint Conference on Digital Libraries*, 187–196. New York: ACM. doi:10.1145/1816123.1816151.

Giunchiglia, F., Marchese, M., & Zaihrayeu, I. (2007). Encoding classifications into lightweight ontologies. *Journal on Data Semantics VIII, 4380*(4380), 57–81. Retrieved from http://dx.doi.org/10.1007/978-3-540-70664-9_3.

Glasswing . (2012). Retrieved from http://www.orsense.com/product.php?ID=38.

GLPi & Schmolka. V. (2000). *Results of usability testing research on plain language draft sections of the employment insurance act. Justice Canada and Human Resources Development Canada*. Retrieved from http://www.davidberman.com/wp-content/uploads/glpi-english.pdf.

GNU DDD. (2009). *Data display debugger*. Retrieved from http://www.gnu.org/software/ddd/.

Golder, S. A., & Donath, J. (2004). Social roles in electronic communities. *Internet Research*, *5*, 19–22.

Gómez-Aguilar, D. A., Conde-González, M. Á., Therón, R., & García-Peñalvo, F. J. (2011). Revealing the evolution of semantic content through visual analysis. In *Proceedings of the 11th IEEE International Conference on Advanced Learning Technologies*, 450-454. Washington, DC: IEEE Press.

Gómez-Aguilar, D. A., Guerrero, C. S., Sanchez, R. T., Therón, R., & García-Peñalvo, F. J. (2010). Visual analytics to support e-learning. In Rosson (Ed.), Advances in Learning Processes (207-228). Rijeka, Croatia: InTech. doi:doi:10.5772/7932 doi:10.5772/7932.

Gómez-Aguilar, D. A., Therón, R., & García-Peñalvo, F. (2008). Understanding educational relationships in Moodle with ViMoodle. In *Proceedings of the Eighth IEEE International Conference on Advanced Learning Technologies*, 954-956. Washington, DC: IEEE Press.

Gómez-Aguilar, D. A., Therón, R., & García-Peñalvo, F. (2009). Semantic spiral timelines used as support for e-learning. *Journal of Universal Computer Science*, *15*(7), 1526–1545.

Goodman, E., Stolterman, E., & Wakkary, R. (2011). Understanding interaction design practice. In *Proceedings of Conference on Human Factors in Computing Systems,* 1061-1070. New York: ACM Press.

Google Developers. (2012a). Demographics layer. *Google Maps API for Business*. Retrieved from https://developers.google.com/maps/documentation/business/demographics.

Google Developers. (2012b). Styled maps. *Google Maps JavaScript API v3*. Retrieved from https://developers.google.com/maps/documentation/javascript/styling.

Google . (2012). Retrieved on from https://www.google.com/.

Götschi, T., Sanders, I., & Galpin, V. (2003). Mental models of recursion. In *Proceedings of the 34th SIGCSE Technical Symposium on Computer Science Education* (346-350). Reno, NV: ACM Press.

Gotta Feeling . (2012). Retrieved from http://gottafeeling.com/.

Grammel, L., Tory, M., & Storey, M.-A. (2010). How information visualization novices construct visualizations. *IEEE Transactions on Visualization and Computer Graphics*, *16*(6), 943–952. doi:10.1109/TVCG.2010.164 PMID:20975131.

Grasso, M. A., Ebert, D. S., & Finin, T. W. (1998). The Integrality of speech in multimodal interfaces. *ACM Transactions on Computer-Human Interaction*, *5*(4), 303–325. doi:10.1145/300520.300521.

Greene, J. A., & Azevedo, R. (2007). Adolescents' use of self-regulatory processes and their relation to qualitative mental model shifts while using hypermedia. *Journal of Educational Computing Research*, *36*(2), 125–148. doi:10.2190/G7M1-2734-3JRR-8033.

Greimas, A.-J. (1987). *On meaning: Selected writings in semiotic theory*. Minneapolic, MN: University of Minnesota Press.

Griffith, E. J., Post, F. H., Koutek, M., Heus, T., & Jonker, H. J. J. (2005). Feature tracking in VR for cumulus cloud life-cycle studies. In Kjems & Blach (Eds.), Virtual Environments 2005 (121–128). Natick, MA: A K Peters.

Grigoryan, G., & Rheingans, P. (2004). Point-based probabilistic surfaces to show surface uncertainty. *IEEE Transactions on Visualization and Computer Graphics*, *10*(5), 564–573. doi:10.1109/TVCG.2004.30 PMID:15794138.

Gruber, T. R. (1993). A translation approach to portable ontology specifications. In H. Burkhardt & B. Smith (Eds.) Knowledge Creation Diffusion Utilization, 5, 199–220. doi:doi:10.1006/knac.1993.1008. doi:10.1006/knac.1993.1008.

Gruber, T. R. (1995). Toward principles for the design of ontologies used for knowledge sharing? *International Journal of Human-Computer Studies*, *43*(5-6), 907–928. doi:10.1006/ijhc.1995.1081.

Gruzd, A., & Haythornthwaite, C. (2008). The analysis of online communities using interactive content-based social networks. *In Proceedings of the American Society for Information Science and Technology Conference*, 523–527. Paris: ICSU Press.

Guardian. (2010). Retrieved from http://www.guardian.co.uk/science/2011/dec/02/psychology-human-biology?newsfeed=true.

Guarino, N. (1998), Formal ontology in information systems. In *Proceedings of FOIS '98*. Amsterdam, IOS Press.

Guidano, V. F. (1987). *Complexity of the self*. New York: Guilford.

Guidano, V. F. (1991). *The self in process*. New York: Guilford.

Guidano, V. F., & Liotti, G. (1986). *Cognitive processes and emotional disorders*. New York: Guilford.

Guo, D., & Mennis, J. (2009). Spatial data mining and geographic knowledge discovery: An introduction. *Computers, Environment and Urban Systems, 33*(6), 403–408. doi:10.1016/j.compenvurbsys.2009.11.001.

Gyorbiro, N. (2010). Collaborative capturing of significant life memories? In *Proceedings of CHI 2010 Workshop-Know Thyself: Monitoring and Reflecting on Facets of One's Life*. New York: ACM Press.

Hagedorn, J., & Hesen, G. G. (2009). Contractual complexity and the cognitive load of R&D alliance contracts. *Journal of Empirical Legal Studies, 6*(4), 818–847. doi:10.1111/j.1740-1461.2009.01161.x.

Hägerstrand, T. (1982). Diorama, path, and project. *Tijdschrift voor Economische en Sociale Geografie, 73*(6), 323–339. doi:10.1111/j.1467-9663.1982.tb01647.x.

Hall, P. R. (1993). The role of GIS in targeted and database marketing for packaged goods. *GIS in Business Conference Proceedings,* 65–76. Boston: GIS World.

Hallett, C. (2008). Multi-modal presentation of medical histories. In *Proceedings of the 13th International Conference on Intelligent User Interfaces,* 80–89. New York: ACM Press.

Hand, D. J., Mannila, H., & Smyth, P. (2001). *Principles of data mining. Adaptive computation and machine learning*. Cambridge, MA: The MIT Press.

Hanks, P. (2010). How people use words to make meanings. In *Proceedings of the 7th International Workshop on Natural Language Processing and Cognitive Science, 3*(13).

Happy Factor. (2012). Retrieved from http://howhappy.dreamhosters.com/.

Hardless, C., & Nulden, U. (1999). Visualizing learning activities to support tutors. In *Proceedings of Conference on Human Factors in Computing Systems (CHI)*. Pittsburgh, Pennsylvania: ACM Press.

Harrison-John, G. (1997). *Enhancements to the Data Mining Process*. (Ph.D. thesis). Stanford, CA, Stanford University.

Hasser, C., & Goldenberg, A. (1998). User performance in a GUI pointing task with a low-cost force-feedback computer mouse. In *Proceedings of Seventh Annual Symposium on Haptic Interfaces, International Mechanical Engineering Congress, and Exposition*. Anaheim, CA: IEEE Press.

Hauser, H., Ledermann, F., & Doleisch, H. (2002). Angular brushing of extended parallel coordinates. In *Proceedings of IEEE Symposium on Information Visualization,* 127-130. New Brunswick, NJ: IEEE Press.

Healey, C. G., Tateosian, L., Enns, J. T., & Remple, M. (2004). Perceptually-based brush strokes for non-photorealistic visualization. *ACM Transactions on Graphics, 23*(1), 64–96. doi:10.1145/966131.966135.

Health Tracking. (2012). Retrieved from Network http://www.healthtracking.net/.

HealthEngage. (2012). Retrieved from http://www.healthengage.com/.

HealthMonth. (2012). Retrieved from http://healthmonth.com.

HealthVault. (2012). Retrieved from http://www.microsoft.com/en-gb/healthvault/default.aspx.

Heer, J., & Boyd, D. (2005). Vizster: Visualizing online social networks. In *Proceedings of IEEE Symposium on Information Visualization,* 32–39. Minneapolis, MN: IEEE Press.

Heer, J., & Hellerstein, J. (2009). Data Visualization and social data analysis. In *Proceedings of the VLDB Endowment,* 1656–1657.

Heer, J., & Perer, A. (2011). Orion: A system for modeling, transformation and visualization of multidimensional heterogeneous networks. In *Proceedings of 2011 IEEE Conference on Visual Analytics Science and Technology*, 51–60. Providence, RI: IEEE Press.

Heer, J., Card, S., & Landay, J. (2005). Prefuse: A toolkit for interactive information visualization. In *Proceedings of the CHI 2005 Conference on Human Factors in Computing Systems*. Portland, OR: ACM Press.

Heer, J. (2008). Graphical histories for visualization: Supporting analysis, communication, and evaluation. *IEEE Transactions on Visualization and Computer Graphics*, *14*(6), 1189–1196. doi:10.1109/TVCG.2008.137 PMID:18988963.

Heer, J., Bostock, M., & Ogievetsky, V. (2010). Visualisation: A Tour through the visualization zoo: A survey of powerful visualization techniques, from the obvious to the obscure. *ACM Queue; Tomorrow's Computing Today*, *8*(5), 20.

Heer, J., Viégas, F., & Wattenberg, M. (2009). Voyagers and voyeurs: Supporting asynchronous collaborative visualization. *Communications of the ACM-Rural Engineering Development*, *52*(1), 87–97. doi:10.1145/1435417.1435439.

Heine, C., Schneider, D., Carr, H., & Scheuermann, G. (2011). Drawing Contour trees in the plane. *IEEE Transactions on Visualization and Computer Graphics*, *17*(11), 1599–1611. doi:10.1109/TVCG.2010.270 PMID:21173451.

Helldin, T., & Riveiro, M. (2009). Explanation methods for bayesian networks: review and application to a maritime scenario. In: *3rd Annual Skövde Workshop on Information Fusion Topic*, 11–16. New Brunswick, NJ: IEEE Press.

Helman, J., & Hesselink, L. (1989). Representation and display of vector field topology in fluid flow data sets. *IEEE Computer Graphics and Applications*, *22*(8), 27–36.

Hendrix, D., Cross, J., & Barowski, L. (2004). An extensible framework for providing dynamic data structure visualizations in a lightweight IDE. In *Proceedings of SIGCSE'04 35th Technical Symposium on Computer Science Education*. New York: ACM Press.

Hengl, T., & Toomanian, N. (2006). Maps are not what they seem: Representing uncertainty in soil-property maps. In *Proceedings of 7th International Symposium on Spatial Accuracy Assessment in Natural Resources and Environmental Sciences*. Edgbaston, UK: World Academic Press.

Henry, N., & Fekete, J.-D. (2006). MatrixExplorer: A dual-representation system to explore social networks. *IEEE Transactions on Visualization and Computer Graphics*, *12*(5), 677–684. doi:10.1109/TVCG.2006.160 PMID:17080787.

Herman, I., Melancon, G., & Marshall, M. S. (2000). Graph visualization and navigation in information visualization: A survey. *IEEE Transactions on Visualization and Computer Graphics*, *6*(1), 24–43. doi:10.1109/2945.841119.

Hernández-Bolaños, F. (2010). *UltraVCN: Uso de filtros y características gráficas para la visualización de redes de colaboración*. (Unpublished B.Sc. Thesis). Puebla, Mexico, Universidad de las Américas.

Herraiz Soto & Co. (2010). *Ommwriter*. Retrieved from http://ommwriter.com.

Hess, S. M., Detweiler, M. C., & Ellis, R. D. (1999). The utility of display space in keeping track of rapidly changing information. *Human Factors*, *41*(2), 257–281. doi:10.1518/001872099779591187.

Hijón-Neira, R. Velázquez-Iturbide, J. Á., Barn, B., & Oussena,S. (2008). A comparative study on the analysis of students interactions in e-learning. In *Proceedings of Eighth IEEE International Conference on Advanced Learning Technologies*, 20-22. Washington, DC: IEEE Press.

Hijón-Neira, R., & Velázquez-Iturbide, J. Á. (2008). How to improve assessment of learning and performance through interactive visualization. In *Proceedings of Eighth IEEE International Conference on Advanced Learning Technologies*, 472-476. Washington, DC: IEEE Press.

Hill, L. (2006). *Georeferencing: The geographic associations of information*. Cambridge, MA: MIT Press.

Hill, T., Noble, J., & Potter, J. (2002). Scalable visualizations of object-oriented systems with ownership trees. *Journal of Visual Languages and Computing, 13*, 319–339. doi:10.1006/jvlc.2002.0238.

Historypin Team. (n.d.). What are tours? *Historypin*. Retrieved from http://www.historypin.com/tours/.

Historypin. (n.d.). A global community collaborating around history. *Historypin*. Retrieved from http://www.historypin.com/.

Hodges, S. (2006). L. SenseCam: A Retrospective Memory Aid.[Berlin: Springer.]. *Proceedings of UBICOMP, 2006*, 81–90.

Hoffman, R., Baudisch, P., & Weld, D. S. (2008). Evaluating visual cues for window switching on large screens. In *Proceedings of CHI*. New York: ACM Press.

Holten, D. (2006). Hierarchical edge bundles: Visualization of adjacency relations in hierarchical data. *IEEE Transactions on Visualization and Computer Graphics, 12*(5), 741–748. doi:10.1109/TVCG.2006.147 PMID:17080795.

Hou, X., & Sourina, O. (2011). Six degree-of-freedom haptic rendering for biomolecular docking. In Gavrilova, M., Tan, C., Sourin, A., & Sourina, O. (Eds.), *Transactions on Computational Science XII* (*Vol. 6670*, pp. 98–117). Lecture Notes in Computer ScienceBerlin: Springer. doi:10.1007/978-3-642-22336-5_6.

Howard, R. W. (1995). *Learning and memory: Major ideas, principles, issues, and applications*. Westport, CT: Praeger.

Huang, M. L., & Liang, J. (2010). Highlighting in information visualization: A survey. In *Proceedings of IEEE Information Visualization Conference, 79-85*. New Brunswick, NJ: IEEE Press.

Huang, M. L., Liang, F. L., Chen, Y. W., Liang, J., & Nguyen, Q. V. (2012). Clutter reduction in multi-dimensional visualization of incomplete data using sugiyama algorithm. In *Proceedings of IEEE Information Visualization Conference, 93-99*. New Brunswick, NJ: IEEE Press.

Huang, M. L., Liang, J., & Nguyen, Q. (2009). A visualization approach for frauds detection in financial market. *IEEE Information Visualization Conference, 197-202*. New Brunswick, NJ: IEEE Press.

Huang, M. L., Nguyen, Q. V., & Hintz, T. (2005). Attributed graph visualization of collaborative workspaces. In *Proceedings of the Computer Graphics, Imaging and Vision: New Trends (CGIV), 155-161*. Washington, DC: IEEE Press.

Huang, W., & Huang, M. L. (2010). Exploring the relative importance of crossing number and crossing angle. In *Proceedings of the 3rd International Symposium on Visual Information Communication*.New York: ACM Press.

Huang, W., Eades, P., & Hong, S.-H. (2009). A graph reading behavior: Geodesic-path tendency. In *Proceedings of the IEEE Pacific Visualization Symposium, 137-144*. Beijing: IEEE Press.

Huang, D., Rau, P. P., Su, H., Tu, N., & Zhao, C. (2007). Effects of time orientation on design of notification systems. *Human-Computer Interaction, 4550*, 835–843.

Huang, W. (2013). Establishing aesthetics based on human graph reading behavior: Two eye tracking studies. *Personal and Ubiquitous Computing, 17*(1), 93–105. doi:10.1007/s00779-011-0473-2.

Huang, W., Eades, P., & Hong, S.-H. (2009). Measuring effectiveness of graph visualizations: A cognitive load perspective. *Information Visualization, 8*(3), 139–152. doi:10.1057/ivs.2009.10.

Huang, X., & Lai, W. (2006). Clustering graphs for visualization through node similarities. *Journal of Visual Languages and Computing*, (17): 225–253. doi:10.1016/j.jvlc.2005.10.003.

Huisman, O., Feliciano Santiago, I. T., Kraak, M. J., & Retsios, V. (2009). Developing a geovisual analytics environment for investigating archaeological events: Extending the space time cube. *Cartography and Geographic Information Science, 36*(3), 225–236. doi:10.1559/152304009788988297.

Husson, F., Le, S., & Pages, J. (2010). *Exploratory multivariate analysis by example using r*. New York: CRC Press. doi:10.1201/b10345.

Hutchins, E. (2002). *Cognition in the wild*. Cambridge, MA: MIT Press.

Hwang, F., Keates, S., Langdon, P., & Clarkson, P. J. (2003). Multiple haptic targets for motion-impaired computer users. In *Proceedings of the SIGCHI Conference on Human Factors in Computing Systems,* 41-48. New York: ACM Press.

IBM. (n.d.). Many eyes. *Software Analytics.* Retrieved from http://www-958.ibm.com/.

Ikits, M., Brederson, J., Hansen, C., & Johnson, C. (2003). A constraint-based technique for haptic volume exploration.[New Brunswick, NJ: IEEE Press.]. *Proceedings of IEEE Visualization VIS, 2003,* 263–269.

Information Display: Display Week. (2012). *Review Issue,* 28.

Infospace, Inc. (2012). *Dogpile.* Retrieved from http://www.dogpile.com/info.dogpl/search/home.

Inselberg, A. (1985). The plane with parallel coordinates. *The Visual Computer, 1*(4), 69–91. doi:10.1007/BF01898350.

Inselberg, A. (2009). Parallel coordinates: Interactive visualization for high dimensions. InZudilova- Seinstra, E., Adriaansen, T., & Liere, R. (Ed.), *Trends in Interactive Visualization* (49-78). London: Springer-Verlag. doi:10.1007/978-1-84800-269-2_3.

Internet Multimedia Lab at the University of Southern California. (2004). *Total recall: A personal information management system.* Retrieved from http://bourbon.usc.edu/iml/recall/.

Irwin, T. (2002). *Information design: What is it and who does it?* Retrieved from http://www.aiga.org/resources/content/1/8/9/3/documents/AIGA_Clear_Information-Design.pdf.

Isaac, A. R., & Marks, D. F. (1994). Individual differences in mental imagery experience: Developmental changes and specialization. *The British Journal of Psychology, 85*(4), 479–500. doi:10.1111/j.2044-8295.1994.tb02536.x PMID:7812670.

Isbister, K., & Doyle, P. (1999). Touring machines: Guide agents for sharing stories about digital places. In *Proceedings of Workshop on Narrative Intelligence.* Cape Cod, MA: AAAI Press.

Isenberg, P., Zuk, T., & Collins, C. (2008). Grounded evaluation of information visualizations. In *Proceedings of the 2008 Workshop on Beyond time and errors: Novel Evaluation Methods for Information Visualization,* 1–8. Florence, Italy: ACM Press.

ISO 9241-11. (1998). Ergonomic requirements for office work with visual display terminals (VDTs). *Part 11: Guidance on Usability.* Retrieved from http://www.iso.org/iso/catalogue_detail.htm?csnumber=16883.

ITC's Michigan Control Room . (2012). Retrieved from http:/ / pro.sony.com / bbsccms / assets / files / micro / sxrd / articles / ITC_IGI_SXRD_CASE_STUDY.pdf.

Itten, J. (1970). *The elements of color.* Ravensburg, Germany: Van Nostrand Reinhold Publishing.

Iwata, H., & Noma, H. (1993). Volume haptization. In *Proceedings of IEEE Symposium on Research Frontiers in Virtual Reality,* 16-23. New Brunswick, NJ: IEEE Press.

Iwata, T., & Saito, K. (2004). Visualization of anomaly using mixture model. In *Knowledge-Based Intelligent Information and Engineering System,*624–631. Berlin: Springer. doi:10.1007/978-3-540-30133-2_82.

Jawbone UP System . (2012). Retrieved from http://jawbone.com/up.

Jenkinson, M., & Smith, S. (2001). A global optimisation method for robust affine registration of brain images. *Medical Image Analysis, 5*(2), 143–156. doi:10.1016/S1361-8415(01)00036-6 PMID:11516708.

Jensen, F., Aldenryd, S., & Jensen, K. (1995). Sensitivity analysis in bayesian networks. In *Symbolic and Quantitative Approaches to Reasoning and Uncertainty,*243–250. Berlin: Springer. doi:10.1007/3-540-60112-0_28.

Johansson, F., & Falkman, G. (2007). Detection of vessel anomalies–A bayesian network approach. In *Proceedings of the 3rd International Conference on Intelligent Sensors, Sensor Networks, and Information Processing.* New Brunswick, NJ: IEEE Press.

Johansson, J., Ljung, P., Jern, M., & Cooper, M. (2005). Revealing structure within clustered parallel coordinates displays. In *IEEE Symposium on Information Visualization,* 125-132. New Brunswick, NJ: IEEE Press.

Johnson-Laird, P. N. (1983). *Mental models: Towards a cognitive science of language, inference, and consciousness.* Cambridge, MA: Harvard University Press.

Jones, H. W. (2009). Envisioning visual contracting: Why non-textual tools will improve your contracting. *Contracting Excellence, 2*(6), 27–31. Retrieved from http://www.iaccm.com/userfiles/file/CE_2_6_press_new.pdf.

Jones, H. W., & Oswald, M. (2001). Doing deals with flowcharts. *ACCA Docket, 19*(9), 94–108.

Kahney, H. (1983). What do novice programmers know about recursion. In A. Janda (Ed.), *CHI '83: Proceedings of the SIGCHI Conference on Human Factors in Computing Systems* (235-239). Boston: ACM.

Kahol, K., Tripathi, P., Mcdaniel, T., Bratton, L., & Panchanathan, S. (2006). Modeling context in haptic perception, rendering, and visualization. *ACM Transactions on Multimedia Computing, Communications, and Applications, 2*(3), 219–240. doi:10.1145/1152149.1152153.

Kalnikaite, V., & Whittaker, S. (2012). Recollection: How to design lifelogging tools that help locate the right information. *Human-Computer Interaction: The Agency Perspective Studies in Computational Intelligence,* 329-348. Berlin: Springer. doi:10.1007/978-3-642-25691-2_14.

Kanai, H., Tsuruma, G., Nakada, T., & Kunifuji, S. (2008). Notification of dangerous situation for elderly people using visual cues. In *Proceedings of IUI.* New York: ACM Press.

Kaptelinin, V., & Nardi, B. A. (2009). *Acting with technology: Activity theory and interaction design.* Cambridge, MA: MIT Press.

Katifori, A., Halatsis, C., Lepouras, G., Vassilakis, C., & Giannopoulou, E. (2007). Ontology visualization methods-A survey. *ACM Computing Surveys, 39*(4), 10. doi:10.1145/1287620.1287621.

Kaufmann, E., & Bernstein, A. (2007). How useful are natural language interface to the semantic web for casual end-users? In *Proceedings of the 6th International Semantic Web Conference,* 281–294. Berlin: Springer.

Kay, M. (2011). Lulaby: Environmental sensing for sleep self-improvement. In Proceedings of *CHI 2011 Workshop on Personal Informatics.* New York: ACM Press.

Kay, M., & Terry, M. (2010). Textured agreements: Re-envisioning electronic consent. In L. F. Cranor (Ed.), *Proceedings of the Sixth Symposium on Usable Privacy and Security.* Redmond, WA: ACM. doi:10.1145/1837110.1837127

Kay, A. (1990). User interface: A personal view. In Laurel, (ed.), *The Art of Human-Computer Interface Design.* Cambridge, MA: Addison-Wesley.

Keim, D. A., Mansmann, F., Schneidewind, J., & Ziegler, H. (2006). Challenges in visual data analysis. *Information Visualization,* 9-16.

Keim, D. (2002). Information visualization and visual data mining. *IEEE Transactions on Visualization and Computer Graphics, 7*(1), 1–8. doi:10.1109/2945.981847.

Keim, D. A., Mansmann, F., & Thomas, J. (2009). Visual analytics: How much visualization and how much analytics. *SIGKDD Explorations, 11*(2).

Keller, T., & Grimm, M. (2005). The impact of dimensionality and color coding of information visualizations. In S.-O. Tergan & T. Keller (Eds.), Lecture Notes in Computer Science, Vol. 3426: Knowledge and information visualization: searching for synergies. (167–182). Heidelberg, Germany: Springer. doi: doi:10.1007/11510154_9.

Kelly, J. W., Fisher, D., & Smith, M. (2006). Friends, foes, and fringe: Norms and structure in political discussion networks. In *Proceedings of the 2006 International Conference on Digital Government Research,* 412–417. San Diego, CA: ACM Press.

Keqin, W., Zhanping, L., Song, Z., & Moorhead, R. J. (2010). Topology-aware evenly spaced streamline placement. *IEEE Transactions on Visualization and Computer Graphics, 16*(5), 791–801. doi:10.1109/TVCG.2009.206 PMID:20616394.

Kerpedjiev, S., & Roth, S. F. (2001). Mapping communicative goals into conceptual tasks to generate graphics in discourse. *Knowledge-Based Systems, 14*(1), 93–102. doi:10.1016/S0950-7051(00)00100-3.

Kerr, B. (2003). Thread arcs: An email thread visualization. *Citeseer.* Retrieved from http://citeseer.uark.edu:8080/citeseerx/showciting;jsessionid=0BA75E333AE2127F3F70223E43A73075?cid=818372.

Kerren, A., Stasko, J., Fekete, J.-D., & North, C. (2007). Workshop report: Information visualization–human-centered issues in visual representation, interaction, and evaluation. *Information Visualization, 6,* 189–196.

Kerr, S. T. (1990). Wayfinding in an electronic database: The relative importance of navigational cues vs. mental models. *Information Processing & Management, 26*(4), 511–523. doi:10.1016/0306-4573(90)90071-9.

Kersey, C., Di Eugenio, B., Jordan, P. W., & Katz, S. (2009). Knowledge co-construction and initiative in peer learning interactions. *In Proceedings of the 14th International Conference on Artificial Intelligence in Education.* Brighton, UK: IOS Press.

Keuning, H. (2003). *Augmented Force Feedback to Facilitate Target Acquisition in Human-Computer Interaction.* (Ph.D. thesis). Eindhoven, The Netherlands, University of Eindhoven.

Khan, A., Matejka, J., Fitzmaurice, G., & Kurtenbach, G. (2005). *Spotlight: Directing users' attention on large displays.* In *Proceedings of CHI.* New York: ACM Press.

Kharchenko, V., & Vasylyev, V. (2002). Application of the intellectual decision making system for vessel traffic control. In *Proceedings of 14th International Conference on Microwaves, Radar, and Wireless Communications, 2,* 639–642. New Brunswick, NJ: IEEE Press.

Kim, S. C., & Kwon, D. S. (2007). Haptic and sound grid for enhanced positioning in a 3D virtual environment. In *Proceedings of Second International Workshop of Haptic and Audio Interaction Design,* 98-109. Seoul, South Korea: HAID Press.

Kimble, J. (2006). *Lifting the fog of legalese.* Durham, NC: Carolina Academic Press.

Kimmerle, J., Moskaliuk, J., Harrer, A., & Cress, U. (2010). Visualizing co-evolution of individual and collective knowledge. *Information Communication and Society, 13*(8). doi:10.1080/13691180903521547.

Kirsch, I. S., & Jungeblut, A. (1986). *Literacy: Profiles of america's young adults.* Princeton, NJ: Educational Testing Service.

Kirsh, D. (2010). Thinking with external representations. *AI & Society, 25*(4), 441–454. doi:10.1007/s00146-010-0272-8.

Kittur, A., & Kraut, R. E. (2010). Beyond wikipedia: Coordination and conflict in online production groups. In *Proceedings of the 2010 ACM Conference on Computer Supported Cooperative Work,* 215–224. Savannah, GA: ACM Press.

Klatzky, R., & Lederman, S. (1995). Identifying objects from a haptic glance. *Perception & Psychophysics, 57,* 1111–1123. doi:10.3758/BF03208368 PMID:8539087.

Klein, D., & Manning, C. D. (2003). Accurate unlexicalized parsing. In *Proceedings of the 41st Meeting of the Association for Computational Linguistics,* 423-430. Cambridge, MA: MIT Press.

Klerkx, J., Duval, E., & Meire, M. (2004). Using information visualization for accessing learning object repositories. In *Proceedings of the Eighth IEEE International Conference on Information Visualisation (IV),* 465-470. Washington, DC: IEEE Press.

Knome. (2012). Retrieved from http://www.knome.com/.

Kochera, A. (1994). Home characteristics and property insurance. *Housing Economics, 42*(12), 9–12.

Kohonen, T. (1990). The self-organizing map. *Proceedings of the IEEE, 78*(9), 1464–1480. doi:10.1109/5.58325.

Korner, O., Schill, M., Wagner, C., Bender, H. J., & Mnner, R. (1999). Haptic volume rendering with an intermediate local representation. In *Proceedings of the 1st International Workshop on the Haptic Devices in Medical Applications,* 79-84. Cambridge, MA: MIT Press.

Kosara, R. & Miksch. (2001). Semantic depth of field, *Citeseer.* Retrieved from http://citeseer.uark.edu:8080/citeseerx/viewdoc/summary;jsessionid=298F7F0386E377889ECF1B4887C50C5B?doi=10.1.1.24.174.

Kosara, R., Miksch, S., Hauser, H., Schrammel, J., Giller, V., & Tscheligi, M. (2002). *Useful Properties of Semantic Depth of Field for Better F+C Visualization.* In *Proceedings of the Symposium on Data Visualisation.* New Brunswick, NJ: IEEE Press.

Kozhevnikov, M., Blazhenkova, O., & Becker, M. (2010). Trade-off in object versus spatial visualization abilities: Restriction in the development of visual-processing resources. *Psychonomic Bulletin & Review, 17*(1), 29–35. doi:10.3758/PBR.17.1.29 PMID:20081157.

Kozhevnikov, M., Hegarty, M., & Mayer, R. E. (2002). Revising the visualizer-verbalizer dimension: Evidence for two types of visualizers. *Cognition and Instruction, 20*(1), 47–77. doi:10.1207/S1532690XCI2001_3.

Kozhevnikov, M., Kosslyn, S., & Shephard, J. (2005). Spatial versus object visualizers: A new characterization of visual cognitive style. *Memory & Cognition, 33*(4), 710–726. doi:10.3758/BF03195337 PMID:16248335.

Kraak, M. J. (2003). The space-time cube revisited from a geovisualization perspective. In*Proceedings of the 21st International Cartographic Conference: Cartographic Renaissance.* Durban, South Africa. International Cartographic Association (ICA).

Kraak, M.-J., Edsall, R., & MacEachren, A. (1997). Cartographic animation and legends for temporal maps: Exploration and or interaction. In *Proceedings of the 18th International Cartographic Conference,* 253-261. Stockholm: International Cartopgraphic Association.

Kraiman, J. B., Arouh, S. L., & Webb, M. L. (2002). Automated anomaly detection processor. In Sisti & Trevisani (Eds.), *Proceedings of SPIE: Enabling Technologies for Simulation Science VI* (128–137). Bellingham, WA: SPIE Press.

Kranzlmuller, D., Grabner, S., & Volkert, J. (1996). Event graph visualization for debugging large applications. In *Proceedings of ACM SPDT'96.* Philadelphia: ACM Press.

Lai, W., & Eades, P. (1992). Algorithms for disjoint node images. *Australian Computer Science Communications, 14*(1), 253–265.

Lai, W., & Eades, P. (2002). Removing edge-node intersections in drawings of graphs. *Information Processing Letters, 81,* 105–110. doi:10.1016/S0020-0190(01)00194-6.

Lai-Yuen, S. K., & Lee, Y. S. (2005). Computer-aided molecular design (CAMD) with force-torque feedback. In *Proceedings of the Ninth International Conference on Computer Aided Design and Computer Graphics,* 199-204. New Brunswick, NJ: IEEE Press.

Lam, H., Bertini, E., Isenberg, P., Plaisant, C., & Carpendale, S. (2012). Empirical studies in information visualization: Seven scenarios. *IEEE Transactions on Visualization and Computer Graphics, 18*(9), 1520–1536. doi:10.1109/TVCG.2011.279 PMID:22144529.

Lange, D. B., & Nakamura, Y. (1997). Object-oriented program tracing and visualization. *IEEE Computer, 30*(5), 63–70. doi:10.1109/2.589912.

Laramee, R. S., & Kosara, R. (2007). Human-centered visualization environments: Future challenges and unsolved problems. In A. Kerren, A. Ebert, & J. Meyer (Eds.), Human-Centered Visualization, Lecture Notes in Computer Science, Tutorial Volume 4417 (231–254). Berlin: Springer Verlag.

Lassila, O., & McGuinness, D. (2001). The role of frame-based representation on the semantic web. *Linköping Electronic Articles in Computer and Information Science, 6*(5), 2001. Retrieved from http://www.ksl.stanford.edu/KSL_Abstracts/KSL-01-02.html.

LaViola, J. J. Prabhat, Forsberg, A. S., Laidlaw, D. H., & van Dam, A. (2009). Trends in interactive visualization. In E. Zudilova-Seinstra (Ed.), Virtual Reality-Based Interactive Scientific Visualization Environments (317-328). London: Springer-Verlag.

Lawrence, D., Lee, C., Pao, L., & Novoselov, R. (2000). Shock and vortex visualization using a combined visual/haptic interface.[New Brunswick, NJ: IEEE Press.]. *Proceedings of Visualization, 2000,* 131–137.

Laxhammar, R. (2008). Anomaly detection for sea surveillance. In *Proceedings of the 11th International Conference on Information Fusion,* 47–54. Cologne, Germany: IEEE Press.

Laxhammar, R., Falkman, G., & Sviestins, E. (2009). Anomaly detection in sea traffic-A comparison of the gaussian mixture model and the kernel density estimator. In *Proceedings of the 12th International Conference on Information Fusion,* 756–763. New Brunswick, NJ: IEEE Press.

Lecuyer, A., Coquillart, S., Kheddar, A., Richard, P., & Coiffet, P. (2000). Pseudo-haptic feedback: Can isometric input devices simulate force feedback? In *Proceedings of the IEEE Virtual Reality 2000 Conference,* 83-90. New Brunswick, NJ: IEEE Press.

Lederman, S. J., & Klatzky, R. L. (1987). Hand movements: A window into haptic object recognition. *Cognitive Psychology*, *19*(3), 342–368. doi:10.1016/0010-0285(87)90008-9 PMID:3608405.

Leigh, J., Johnson, A., Renambot, L., Peterka, T., Jeong, B., et al., & Sun, Y. (2012). Scalable resolution display walls. *Proceedings of the IEEE*, (99).

Lewin, K. (1951). *Field theory in social science; Selected theoretical papers*. New York: Harper & Row.

Liang, J., Nguyen, Q. V., Simoff, S., & Huang, M. L. (2012). Angular treemaps–A new technique for visualizing and emphasizing hierarchical structures. In *Proceedings of IEEE Information Visualization Conference*, 74-80. New Brunswick, NJ: IEEE Press.

Liang, J., Nguyen, Q. V., Simoff, S., & Huang, M. L. (2013). Angular Treemaps. In Banissi, E. (Ed.), *Information Visualization-Techniques, Usability, & Evaluation*. Cambride, UK: Cambridge Scholar Publishing.

Library of Congress. (2010). Fire insurance map, sheet 5. *American Treasures of the Library of Congress: Reason*. Retrieved from http://www.loc.gov/exhibits/treasures/trr016.html.

LifeLapse . (2012). Retrieved from http://www.lifelapse.com/.

Light, L. L., & Berger, D. E. (1974). Memory for modality: Within-modality discrimination is not automatic. *Journal of Experimental Psychology*, *103*(5), 854–860. doi:10.1037/h0037404.

Linn, M. C., & Petersen, A. C. (1985). Emergence and characterization of sex differences in spatial ability: A meta-analysis. *Child Development*, *56*(6), 1479–1498. doi:10.2307/1130467 PMID:4075870.

Liu, Z., & Stasko, J. T. (2010). Mental models, visual reasoning and interaction in Information Visualization: A top-down perspective. *IEEE Transactions on Visualization and Computer Graphics*, *16*(6), 999–1008. doi:10.1109/TVCG.2010.177 PMID:20975137.

Livnat, Y., Agutter, J., Moon, S., Erbacher, R. F., & Foresti, S. (2005). A visual paradigm for network intrusion detection. In *Proceedings of the 2005 IEEE Workshop on Information Assurance and Security*, 92–99. New Brunswick, NJ: IEEE Press.

Loftin, R. B., Chen, J., & Rosenblum, L. (2004). Visualization using virtual reality.InHansen, C, & Johnson, C (Eds.),*Visualization Handbook* (479-489). Amsterdam: Elsevier.

Lohman, D. F., & Nichols, P. D. (1990). Training spatial abilities: Effects of practice on rotation and synthesis tasks. *Learning and Individual Differences*, *2*(1), 67–93. doi:10.1016/1041-6080(90)90017-B.

Lohr, S. (2012). The age of big data. *The New York Times*. New York.

Lorensen, W. E., & Cline, H. E. (1987). Marching cubes: A high resolution 3d surface construction algorithm. In *Proceedings of the 14th Annual Conference on Computer Graphics and Interactive Techniques*,163-169. New York: ACM Press.

Loseit . (2012) Retrieved from http://www.loseit.com/.

Löwgren, J., & Stolterman, E. (2004). *Thoughtful Interaction Design: A Design Perspective on Information Technology*. Cambridge, MA: MIT Press.

Lundin, K., Ynnerman, A., & Gudmundsson, B. (2002). Proxybased haptic feedback from volumetric density data. In *Proceedings of the Eurohaptic Conference,* 104-109. Edinburgh, UK: University of Edinburgh Press.

Lunenfeld, P. (2011). *The secret war between downloading and uploading: Tales of the computer as culture machine*. Cambridge, MA: MIT Press.

Lycos. (2012). *Lycos, Inc.* Retrieved from http://www.lycos.com/.

Ma, L., Ferguson, J., Roper, M., & Wood, M. (2007). Investigating the viability of mental models held by novice programmers. In *Proceedings of the 38th SIGCSE Technical Symposium on Computer Science Education* (499-503).Covington, KY: ACM.

MacEachren, A. M., Jaiswal, A. R., Robinson, A. C., Pezanowski, S., Savelyev, A., et al., & Blanford, J. (2011). Senseplace2: Geotwitter analytics support for situational awareness. In *Proceedings of IEEE Conference on Visual Analytics Science and Technology,* 181–190. New Brunswick, NJ: IEEE Press.

MacEachren, A. M. (1992). Visualizing uncertain information. *Cartographic Perspective*, *13*(3), 10–19.

MacEachren, A., & Hardisty, . (2003). Supporting visual analysis of federal geospatial statistics. *Communications of the ACM, 46*(1), 60. doi:10.1145/602421.602452.

MacEachren, A., Wachowicz, M., Edsall, R., & Haug, D. (1999). Constructing knowledge from multivariate spatio-temporal data: Integrating geographic visualization (GVis) with knowledge discovery in database (KDD) methods. *International Journal of Geographical Information Science, 13*(4), 311–334. doi:10.1080/136588199241229.

Mackinlay, J. D. (1986). Automating the design of graphical presentations of relational information. *ACM Transactions on Graphics, 5*(2), 110–141. doi:10.1145/22949.22950.

Mackinlay, J. D., Hanrahan, P., & Stolte, C. (2007). Show me: Automatic presentation for visual analysis. *IEEE Transactions on Visualization and Computer Graphics, 13*(6). doi:10.1109/TVCG.2007.70594 PMID:17968057.

MacLean, K. E. (2000). Designing with haptic feedback. In *Proceedings of IEEE International Conference on Robotics and Automation,* 783-788. New Brunswick, NJ: IEEE Press.

Maglio, P. P., & Campbell, C. S. (2000). Tradeoffs in displaying peripheral information. In *Proceedings of CHI.* New York: ACM Press.

Mahler, T. (2010). *Legal Risk Management–Developing and Evaluating Elements of a Method for Proactive Legal Analyses, with a Particular Focus on Contracts.* (Doctoral thesis). Oslo, Norway: University of Oslo.

Malouf, R., & Mullen, T. (2008). Taking sides: User classification for informal online political discourse. *Internet Research, 18*(2), 177–190. doi:10.1108/10662240810862239.

Mann, S. (2004) Continuous lifelong capture of personal experiences with eyetap. In *Proceedings of 1st ACM Workshop on Continuous Archival and Retrieval of Personal Experiences.* New York: ACM Press.

Manning, C., Rodriguez, M., & Ghosh, C. (1999). Devising a Corporate facility location strategy to maximize shareholder wealth. *Journal of Real-Estate Research. American Real-Estate Society, 17*(3), 321–340.

Manovich, L. (2008). *Introduction to info-aesthetics.* Retrieved from http://goo.gl/NFLvy.

Manovich, L. (2010). *What is visualization?* Retrieved from http://www.datavisualisation.org/2010/11/levmanovichwhat-is-visualization/.

Mansmann, F. (2008). *Visual Analysis of Network Traffic: Interactive Monitoring, Detection, and Interpretation of Security Threats.* (Ph.D. thesis). Konstanz, Germany, Universität Konstanz.

Mantovani, G. (1996). Social context in HCI: A new framework for mental models, cooperation, and communication. *Cognitive Science, 20*(2), 237–269. doi:10.1207/s15516709cog2002_3.

Marin, A., & Wellman, B. (2010). Social network analysis: An introduction. In Carrington, P., & Scott, J. (Eds.), *Handbook of Social Network Analysis.* London: Sage.

Mark, W., Randolph, S., Finch, M., Verth, J. V., & Taylor, R. M. (1996). Adding force feedback to graphics systems: Issues and solutions. In *Proceedings of Computer Graphics,* 447-452. Amsterdam: IOS Press. doi:10.1145/237170.237284.

Martin, A., & Ward, M. (1995). High dimensional brushing for interactive exploration of multivariate data. In *Proceedings of the 6th Annual Conference on Visualization.* New Brunswick, NJ: IEEE Computer Society.

Martín, M., Álvarez, A., Fernández-Castro, I., Reina, D., & Urretavizcaya, M. (2011) Experiences in visualizing the analysis of blended-learning interactions to support teachers. In *Proceedings of 11th IEEE International Conference on Advanced Learning Technologies,* 265-266. Washington, DC: IEEE Press.

Masli, M., Priedhorsky, R., & Terveen, L. (2011). Task specialization in social production communities: The case of geographic volunteer work. In *Proceedings of ICWSM,* 217–224. Palo Alto, CA: AAAI Press.

Mayer, R. E., & Moreno, R. (1998). *A cognitive theory of multimedia learning: Implications for design principles.* Paper presented at the CHI-98 Workshop on Hyped-Media to Hyper-Media, Los Angeles, CA.

Mayer, R. E. (2002). Multimedia learning. *Psychology of Learning and Motivation, 41*, 85–139. doi:10.1016/S0079-7421(02)80005-6.

Mayer, R. E. (2011a). Does styles research have useful implications for educational practice? *Learning and Individual Differences*, *21*(3), 319–320. doi:10.1016/j.lindif.2010.11.016.

Mayer, R. E. (2011b). Applying the science of learning to multimedia instruction. In Mestre, J. P., & Ross, B. H. (Eds.), *The Psychology of Learning and Motivation* (*Vol. 55*, pp. 77–108). Amsterdam: Elsevier. doi:10.1016/B978-0-12-387691-1.00003-X.

Mayer, R. E., Heiser, J., & Lonn, S. (2001). Cognitive constraints on multimedia learning: When presenting more material results in less understanding. *Journal of Educational Psychology*, *93*(1), 187–198. doi:10.1037/0022-0663.93.1.187.

Mayer, R. E., & Moreno, R. (2003). Nine ways to reduce cognitive load in multimedia learning. *Educational Psychologist*, *38*(1), 43–52. doi:10.1207/S15326985EP3801_6.

Mayer-Schönberger, V. (2009). *Delete: The virtue of forgetting in the digital age*. Princeton, NJ: Princeton University Press.

Mazza, R. (2006). A graphical tool for monitoring the usage of modules in course management systems. In *Proceedings of Visual Information Expert Workshop*. Paris, VIEW Press.

Mazza, R., & Dimitrova, V. (2005). Generation of graphical representations of student tracking data in course management systems. In *Proceedings of the 9th IEEE International Conference on Information Visualisation*. London: IEEE Press.

Mazza, R., & Milani, C. (2005). Exploring usage analysis in learning systems: gaining insights from visualisations. In *Proceedings of the 12th International Conference on Artificial Intelligence in Education (AIED)*, 65-72. Amsterdam: IOS Press.

McAuley, J., O'Connor, A., & Lewis, D. (2012). Exploring reflection in online communities. In *Proceedings of the 2nd International Conference on Learning Analytics and Knowledge*, 102–110. Vancouver, BC: ACM Press.

McCormick, E. J., & Sanders, M. S. (1982). *Human factors in engineering and design*. New York: Mcgraw-Hill.

McCrickard, D. S., Catrambone, R., Chewar, C. M., & Stasko, J. T. (2003). Establishing tradeoffs that leverage attention for utility:empirically evaluating information display in notification systems. *International Journal of Human-Computer Studies*, *58*, 547–582. doi:10.1016/S1071-5819(03)00022-3.

McCrickard, D. S., & Chewar, C. M. (2003). Attuning notification design to user goals and attention costs. *Communications of the ACM*, *46*(3), 67–72. doi:10.1145/636772.636800.

McCrickard, D. S., Czerwinski, M., & Bartram, L. (2003). Introduction: Design and evaluation of notification user interfaces. *International Journal of Human-Computer Studies*, *58*, 509–514. doi:10.1016/S1071-5819(03)00025-9.

McFarlane, D. C. (2002). Comparison of four primary methods for coordinating the interruption of people in human-computer interaction. *Human-Computer Interaction*, *17*, 63–139. doi:10.1207/S15327051HCI1701_2.

Mechdyne. (n.d.). Retrieved from http://www.mechdyne.com/cave.aspx.

Menelas, B., Ammi, M., & Bourdot, P. (2008). A flexible method for haptic rendering of isosurface from volumetric data. In *Proceedings of the 6th International EuroHaptics Conference on Haptics*. Berlin Springer-Verlag.

Menelas, B., Ammi, M., Pastur, L., & Bourdot, P. (2009). Haptical exploration of an unsteady flow. In *Symposium on Haptic Interfaces for Virtual Environment and Teleoperator Systems EuroHaptics Conference World Haptics*, 232-237. Berlin: Springer.

Menelas, B., Fauvet, N., Ammi, M., & Bourdot, P. (2008). Direct haptic rendering for large datasets with high gradients. In *Proceedings of the 2008 Ambi-Sys Workshop on Haptic User Interfaces in Ambient Media Systems, 1-9.* New Brunswick, NJ: IEEE Press.

Menelas, B., Picinali, L., Katz, B. F. G., & Bourdot, P. (2010). Audio haptic feedbacks for an acquisition task in a multitarget context. In *Proceedings of IEEE Symposium on 3D User Interface,* 51-54. New Brunswick, NJ: IEEE Press.

Menelas, B., Picinali, L., Katz, B. F. G., Bourdot, P., & Ammi, M. (2009). Haptic audio guidance for target selection in a virtual environment. In *Proceedings of 4th International Haptic and Auditory Interaction Design Workshop,* 1-2. HAID.

Menelas, B.-A. J. & Otis, J.-D., M. (2012) Design of a serious game for learning vibrotactile messages. In Proceedings of *International Workshop on Haptic Audio Visual Environments and Games, 124-129.* New Brunswick, NJ: IEEE Press.

Menelas, B.-A. J. (2012). Interactive analysis of cavity-flows in a virtual environment. In *ACM 28th Spring Conference on Computer Graphics,* 1-6). New York, ACM Press.

Meneses, C. J., & Grinstein, G. G. (2001). Visualization for enhancing the data mining process.[Bellingham, WA: SPIE Press.]. *Proceedings of the Society for Photo-Instrumentation Engineers, 4384,* 126–137. doi:10.1117/12.421066.

Merriam-Webster. (2012). Triage. *Online Dictionary.* Retrieved from http://www.merriam-webster.com/dictionary/triage.

Microsoft. (2012). *Bing.* Retrieved from http://www.bing.com/.

Miller, G. A. (1960). *Plans and the structure of behavior.* New York: Holt, Rhinehart, & Winston. doi:10.1037/10039-000.

Miller, G. A. (1995). WordNet: A Lexical Database for English. *Communications of the ACM, 38*(11), 39–41. doi:10.1145/219717.219748.

Miller, N. E. (1948). Theory and experiment relating psychoanalytic displacement to simulus-response generalization. *Journal of Abnormal and Social Psychology, 43,* 155–178. doi:10.1037/h0056728.

Ministry of Finance. (2009). *General Terms of Public Procurement in service contracts JYSE 2009 Service.* Helsinki, Finland. Retrieved from http://www.vm.fi/vm/en/04_publications_and_documents/01_publications/08_other_publications/20100217Genera/JYSE_2009_services.pdf.

Molitor, S., Ballstaedt, S.-P., & Mandl, H. (1989). Problems in knowledge acquisition from text and pictures. InMandl, H, J. R, , & Levin, (Eds.), *Advances in Psychology, volume 58: Knowledge Acquisition from Text and Pictures* (3-35). Amsterdam: North-Holland. doi:10.1016/S0166-4115(08)62145-7.

Monk, C. A. (2004). The effect of frequent and infrequent interruptions on primary task resumption. *Human Factors, 48*(3), 295–299. doi:10.1177/154193120404800304.

Monmonier, M. (1989). Graphic scripts for the sequenced visualization of geographic data. In *Proceedings of GIS/LIS 189,* 381-389. Orlando, FL: CUPR Press.

MoodPanda . (2012). Retrieved from http://MoodPanda.com/.

Moodscope . (2012). Retrieved from http://www.moodscope.com/login.

MoodTracker . (2012). Retrieved from https://www.moodtracker.com/.

Moore, B. (2010). Assisted self reflection: Combining lifetracking, sensemaking, & personal information management. In *Proceedings of CHI 2010 Workshop-Know Thyself: Monitoring and Reflecting on Facets of One's Life.* New York: ACM Press.

Moreno, R., & Mayer, R. E. (1999). Cognitive principles of multimedia learning: The role of modality and contiguity. *Journal of Educational Psychology, 91*(2), 358–368. doi:10.1037/0022-0663.91.2.358.

Morin, E. (2003). *La méthode: L'humanité de l'humanité- L'identité humaine.* Paris: Le Seuil, Nouvelle Èdition, coll. Points.

Morzy, M. (2009). On mining and social role discovery in internet forums. In *Proceedings of 2009 International Workshop on Social Informatics*, 74–79. Warsaw, Poland: IEEE Press.

Muelder, C., Ma, K.-L., & Bartoletti, T. (2005). Interactive visualization for network and port scan detection. In *Proceedings of 2005 Recent Advances in Intrusion Detection*, 1–20. New Brunswick, NJ: IEEE Press.

Muller, T. (2000). Practical investigation of constraints with graph views. In *Proceedings of the International Workshop on the Implementation of Declarative Languages*. Paris: Springer.

Munzner, T. (2000). *Interactive Visualization of Large Graphs and Networks.* (Unpublished doctoral thesis). Stanford, CA, Stanford University.

Munzner, T. (2009). A nested model for visualization design and validation. *IEEE Transactions on Visualization and Computer Graphics*, *15*(6), 921–928. doi:10.1109/TVCG.2009.111 PMID:19834155.

My Calorie Counter . (2012). Retrieved from http://my-calorie-counter.com/calorie_counter.asp.

MyFitnessPal . (2012). Retrieved from http://www.my-fitnesspal.com/.

MyMedLab . (2012). Retrieved from https://www.mymedlab.com/.

MyWebSearch. (2012*). Mindspark interactive network, inc.* Retrieved from http://home.mywebsearch.com/.

Nack, F. (2005). You must remember this. *IEEE Multi-Media*, *12*(1), 4–7. doi:10.1109/MMUL.2005.17.

Nardi, B. A., & Zarmer, C. L. (1990). *Beyond models and metaphors: Visual formalisms in user interface design.* Palo Alto, CA: Hewlett-Packard Laboratories.

Navigenics . (2012). Retrieved from http://www.navigenics.com/.

NComVA. (n.d.). National and regional statistical visualization. *NCOMVA*. Retrieved from http://www.ncomva.com/solutions/national-and-regional-statistical-visualization/.

NEC. (n.d.). *What is the NEC? Promoting best practice procurement. Achieving excellence in the procurement of works, services and supply.* Retrieved from http://www.neccontract.com/documents/WhatistheNEC.pdf.

Neisser, U. (1967). *Cognitive psychology.* New York: Appleton-Century-Crofts.

Nesbitt, K. (2003). *Designing Multi-Sensory Displays for Abstract Data.* (Ph.D. thesis). Sydney, Australia, University of Sydney.

Newcombe, N. S., & Stieff, M. (2012). Six myths about spatial thinking. *International Journal of Science Education*, *34*(6), 955–971. doi:10.1080/09500693.2011.588728.

Newcombe, N. S., Uttal, D. H., & Sauter, M. (in press). Spatial development. In Zelazo, P. (Ed.), *Oxford Handbook of Developmental Psychology.* New York: Oxford University Press. doi:10.1037/e537272012-075.

Nguyen, Q. V., & Huang, M. L. (2004). A focus+context visualization technique using semi-transparency. In *Proceedings of the Fourth International Conference on Computer and information Technology*, 101-108. New Brunswick, NJ: IEEE Press.

Nguyen, Q. V., & Huang, M. L. (2005). EncCon: An approach to constructing interactive visualization of large hierarchical data. *Information Visualization*, *4*(1), 1–21. doi:10.1057/palgrave.ivs.9500087.

Ni, T. (2006). A survey of large high-resolution display technologies, techniques, and applications. In *Proceedings of the IEEE Conference on Virtual Reality.* New Brunswick, NJ: IEEE Press.

Nichols, D., Pemberton, D., Dalhoumi, S., Larouk, O., Belisle, C., & Twidale, M. (2000). DEBORA: Developing an interface to support collaboration in a digital library. In *Proceedings of European Conference on Digital Libraries*, 239-248. Lisbon, Portugal: ECDL Press.

Nielson, G. M., & Franke, R. (1997). Computing the separating surface for segmented data. In *Proceedings of the 8th Conference on Visualization*, 229-233. Los Alamitos, CA: IEEE Press.

Nike + iPod Sport Kit. (2012) Retrieved from http://www.apple.com/ipod/nike/.

Nivala, A.-M., Brewster, S., & Sarjakoski, L. T. (2008). Usability evaluation of web mapping sites. *The Cartographic Journal*, *45*(2), 129–138. doi:10.1179/174327708X305120.

Nokia Research Center. (2012). *Nokia mobile data challenge*. Retrieved from http://research.nokia.com/page/12000.

Norman, D. A. (1983). Some observations on mental models. InGentner, D, & Stevens, A. L. (Eds.), *Mental Models* (7-14). Hillsdale, NJ: Lawrence Erlbaum Associates.

North, C. (2000). Snap-together visualization: Can users construct and operate coordinated visualizations? *International Journal of Human-Computer Studies*, *53*(5), 715–739. doi:10.1006/ijhc.2000.0418.

North, C. (2006). Toward measuring visualization insight. *IEEE Computer Graphics and Applications*, *26*(3), 6–9. doi:10.1109/MCG.2006.70 PMID:16711210.

Northcraft, G. B., & Neale, M. A. (1987). Experts, amateurs, and real-estate: An anchoring-and-adjustment perspective on property pricing decisions. *Organizational Behavior and Human Decision Processes*, *39*(1), 84–97. doi:10.1016/0749-5978(87)90046-X.

Novotńy, M., & Hauser, H. (2006). Outlier-preserving focus+context visualization in parallel coordinates. *IEEE Transactions on Visualization and Computer Graphics*, *12*(5), 893–900. doi:10.1109/TVCG.2006.170 PMID:17080814.

Ntuen, C. A., Park, E. H., & Gwang-Myung, K. (2010). Designing an information visualization tool for sensemaking. *International Journal of Human-Computer Interaction*, *26*(2-3), 189–205. doi:10.1080/10447310903498825.

Nunn, J. A., & Bentley, L. (2012). Visualization of spatial and temporal trends in Louisiana water usage using google fusion tables. *Geological Society of America*, 492.

Nuutinen, M., Seppänen, M., Mäkinen, S. J., & Keinonen, T. (2011). User experience in complex systems: Crafting a conceptual framework. In *Proceedings of the 1st Cambridge Academic Design Management Conference*. Cambridge, UK: Cambridge University Press.

O'Connor, E. S. (2002). Storied business: Typology, intertextuality, and traffic in entrepreneurial narrative. *Journal of Business Communication*, *39*(1), 36–54. doi:10.1177/002194360203900103.

O'Hara, K. (2006). Memories for life: A review of the science and technology. *Journal of the Royal Society, Interface*, *3*, 351–365. doi:10.1098/rsif.2006.0125 PMID:16849265.

O'Keffe, P. (2008). *Managing online forums: Everything You need to know to create and run successful community discussion boards, 320*. Saranac, NY: AMACOM.

O'Meara, M., Porter, K., & Greaves, I. (2007). Triage. *Trauma*, *9*, 111. doi:10.1177/1460408607084180.

Oakley, I., Adams, A., Brewster, S., & Gray, P. (2002). Guidelines for the design of haptic widgets. In *Proceedings of British Computer Society Conference on Human-Computer Interaction*, 195-212. HCIRN Press.

Oakley, I., McGee, M. R., Brewster, S., & Gray, P. (2000). Putting the feel in 'look and feel'. In *Proceedings of SIGCHI Conference on Human Factors in Computing Systems*, 415-422. New York: ACM Press.

Okamura, A. M., & Cutkosky, M. R. (2001). Feature detection for haptic exploration with robotic fingers. *The International Journal of Robotics Research*, *20*(12), 925–938. doi:10.1177/02783640122068191.

Ong, Y., & Kurth, W. (2012). A graph model and grammar for multi-scale modelling using XL. In *Proceedings of 2012 IEEE International Conference on Bioinformatics and Biomedicine Workshops* 1-8. Washington, DC: IEEE Press.

Onut, I. V., Zhu, B., & Ghorbani, A. A. (2004). A novel visualization technique for network anomaly detection. In *Proceedings of the 2nd Annual Conference on Privacy, Security, and Trust*, 167–174. New York: ACM Press.

Otsuka, J. L. (2006). *Multi-Agent Model to Formative Assessment Support at Learning*. (Doctoral thesis). Campinas, Brazil, University of Campinas.

Otsuka, J. L., & Rocha, H. V. (2007). A multi-agent formative assessment support model for learning management systems. In *Proceedings of the 7th IEEE International Conference on Advanced Learning Technologies*. Niigata, Japan: IEEE Press.

Otto, M., Germer, T., Hege, H.-C., & Theisel, H. (2010). Uncertain 2D vector field topology. *Computer Graphics Forum*, 2(29), 347–356. doi:10.1111/j.1467-8659.2009.01604.x.

Oviatt, S. L., & Cohen, P. R. (2000). Multimodal interfaces that process what comes naturally. *Communications of the ACM*, 43(3), 45–50. doi:10.1145/330534.330538.

Palmerius, K. L. (2007). Direct Volume Haptics for Visualization. (Ph.D. Thesis). Linkoping, Sweden, Linkoping University.

Panciera, K., & Halfaker, A. (2009). Wikipedians are born, not made: A study of power editors on Wikipedia. In *Proceedings of the ACM 2009 International Conference on Supporting Group Work*, 51–60. Sanibel Island, FL: ACM Press.

Paneels, S., & Roberts, J. C. (2009). Review of designs for haptic data visualization. *IEEE Transactions on Haptics*, 3(2), 119–137. doi:10.1109/TOH.2009.44.

Pang, A., Wittenbrink, C., & Lodha, S. (1997). Approaches to uncertainty visualization. *The Visual Computer*, 13(8), 370–390. doi:10.1007/s003710050111.

Pao, L. Y., & Lawrence, D. A. (1998). Synergistic visual/haptic computer interfaces. In *Proceedings of Japan/USA/Vietnam Workshop on Research and Education in Systems, Computation, and Control Engineering*, 155-162. New York: CRC Press.

Pascucci, V., Cole-McLaughlin, K., & Scorzelli, G. (2004). Multi–resolution computation and presentation of contour tree. In *Proceedings of the IASTED Conference on Visualization, Imaging, and Image*. Calgary, AB: ACTA Press.

Passera, S., & Haapio, H. (2011a). User-centered contract design: New directions in the quest for simpler contracting. In R. F. Henschel (Ed.), *Proceedings of the 2011 IACCM Academic Symposium for Contract and Commercial Management* (80–97). Ridgefield, CT: The International Association for Contract and Commercial Management. Retrieved from http://www.iaccm.com/admin/docs/docs/HH_Paper.pdf.

Passera, S., & Haapio, H. (2011b). Facilitating collaboration through contract visualization and modularization. In A. Dittmar & P. Forbrig (Eds.), *Designing Collaborative Activities. ECCE 2011, European Conference on Cognitive Ergonomics*, 57-60. Rostock, Germany: Universitätsdruckerei. doi: 10.1145/2074712.2074724.

Pastore, R. S. (2009). The effects of diagrams and time-compressed instruction on learning and learners' perceptions of cognitive load. *Educational Technology Research and Development*, 58(5), 485–505. doi:10.1007/s11423-009-9145-6.

Patcha, A., & Park, J.-M. (2007). An overview of anomaly detection techniques: Existing solutions and latest technological trends. *Computer Networks*, 51(12), 3448–3470. doi:10.1016/j.comnet.2007.02.001.

Pathway. (2012). Retrieved from https://www.pathway.com/.

PatientsLikeMe. (2012). Retrieved from http://www.patientslikeme.com/.

Pauly, M., Mitra, N. J., & Guibas, L. (2004). Uncertainty and variability in point cloud surface data. In *Proceedings of Eurographics Symposium on Point-Based Graphics*. New Brunswick, NJ: IEEE Press.

Payne, S. J. (2003). Users' mental models: The very ideas. In Carroll, J. M. (Ed.), *HCI models, theories, and frameworks: Toward a multidisciplinary science* (135-156). San Francisco: Morgan Kaufmann Publishers. doi:10.1016/B978-155860808-5/50006-X.

Perer, A., & Shneiderman, B. (2008). Integrating statistics and visualization: Case studies of gaining clarity during exploratory data analysis. In M. Burnett, M. F. Costabile, T. Catarci, B. DeRuyter, D. Tan, M. Czerwinski, & A. Lund (Eds.), Human-Computer Interaction (265–274). Florence, Italy: ACM Press. doi:doi:10.1145/1357054.1357101. doi:10.1145/1357054.1357101.

Perry, E., & Donath, J. (2004). Anthropomorphic visualization: A new approach for depicting participants in online spaces. In *Proceedings of CHI EA '04 CHI '04 Extended Abstracts on Human Factors in Computing*, 1115–1118. Vienna, Austria: ACM Press.

Personal Genome Project. (2012). Retrieved from http://www.personalgenomes.org.

Persson, P., Cooper, M., Tibell, L., Ainsworth, S., Ynnerman, A., & Jonsson, B. H. (2007). Designing and evaluating a haptic system for biomolecular education. In *Proceedings of IEEE Virtual Reality Conference,* 171-178. New Brunswick, NJ: IEEE Press.

Peterson, K. (1998). Development of spatial decision support systems for residential real-estate. *Journal of Housing Research*, *9*(1), 135–156.

Peuquet, D. J. (2002). *Representations of space and time.* New York: The Guildford Press.

Pfaffelmoser, T., Reitinger, M., & Westermann, R. (2011). Visualizing the positional and geometrical variability of isosurfaces in uncertain scalar fields. In *Proceedings of Eurographics/IEEE Symposium on Visualization.* New Brunswick, NJ: IEEE Press.

Picinali, L., Menelas, B., Katz, B. F. G., & Bourdot, P. (2010). Evaluation of a haptic/audio system for 3D targeting tasks. In *Proceedings of 128th Convention of the Audio Engineering Society.* New York: AES Press.

Pina, L. R. (2012). Fitbit+: A behavior-based intervention system to reduce sedentary behavior. In Popper & Eccles (Eds.), The Self and the Brain. London: Springer International.

Piringer, H., Berger, W., & Hauser, H. (2008). Quantifying and comparing features in high-dimensional datasets. In *Proceedings of the International Conference on Information Visualization,* 240-245. New Brunswick, NJ: IEEE Press.

Pirolli, P., & Card, S. K. (1999). Information foraging. *Psychological Review*, *106*(4), 643–675. doi:10.1037/0033-295X.106.4.643.

Pirolli, P., & Russell, D. M. (2011). Introduction to this special issue on sensemaking. *Human-Computer Interaction*, *26*, 1–8. doi:10.1080/07370024.2011.556557.

Plain Language Institute of British Columbia. (1993). *Critical opinions: The public's view of lawyers' documents.* Vancouver: Plain Language Institute.

Plaisant, C. (2005). Information visualization and the challenge of universal usability. In A. MMacEachren, , M.-J. Kraak, & JDykes, (Eds.), *Exploring geovisualization* (53-82). New York: Elsevier Ltd. doi:10.1016/B978-008044531-1/50421-8.

Plaisant, C., Shneiderman, B., Doan, K., & Bruns, T. (1999). Interface and data architecture for query preview in networked information systems. *ACM Transactions on Information Systems*, *17*(3), 320–341. doi:10.1145/314516.314522.

Platts, K., & Tan, K. H. (2004). Strategy visualisation: Knowing, understanding, and formulating. *Management Decision*, *42*(5/6), 667–676. doi:10.1108/00251740410538505.

Plumlee, M., & Ware, C. (2006). Zooming versus multiple window interfaces: Cognitive costs of visual comparisons. *ACM Transactions on Computer-Human Interaction*, *13*(2), 209. doi:10.1145/1165734.1165736.

Pohjonen, S., & Koskelainen, K. (2012). Visualization in trialogic public procurement contracting. In E. Banissi, S. Bertschi, C. Forsell, J. Johansson, S. Kenderdine, F. T. Marchese, ... & G. Venturini (Eds.), *Proceedings of 16th International Conference on Information Visualisation* (383–388). Montpellier, France: IEEE Press. doi: 10.1109/IV.2012.70.

Pohjonen, S., & Visuri, K. (2008). Proactive approach in project management and contracting. InHaapio, H (Ed.), *A Proactive Approach to Contracting and Law* (75–95). Turku, Finland: International Association for Contract and Commercial Management & Turku University of Applied Sciences.

Posner, R. (2011). Opinion in the united states court of appeals for the seventh circuit no. 11-1665. *Gonzalez-Servin v. Ford Motor Co.* Retrieved from http://www.abajournal.com/files/DG0R2WE8.pdf.

Posner, E. A. (2010). ProCD vs. Zeidenberg and Cognitive Overload in Contractual Bargaining. *The University of Chicago Law Review. University of Chicago. Law School*, *77*(4), 1181–1194. Retrieved from http://ssrn.com/abstract=1499414.

Pöthkow, K., & Hege, H.-C. (2011). Positional uncertainty of isocontours: Condition analysis and probabilistic measures. *IEEE Transactions on Visualization and Computer Graphics, 17*(10), 1393–1406. doi:10.1109/TVCG.2010.247 PMID:21041883.

Pousman, Z., & Stasko, J. (2006). A taxonomy of ambient information systems: Four patterns of design. In *Proceedings of AVI*. New York: ACM Press.

Pousman, Z., & Stasko, J. T. (2007). Data in everyday life. *IEEE Transactions on Visualization and Computer Graphics, 13*(6), 1145–1152. doi:10.1109/TVCG.2007.70541 PMID:17968058.

Preece, D. J. (2000). *Online communities: Designing usability and supporting sociability*. Hoboken, NJ: Wiley.

Preece, J., & Shneiderman, B. (2009). The reader-to-leader framework: Motivating technology-mediated social participation. *AIS Transactions on Human-Computer Interaction, 1*(1), 13–32.

Private MD Lab Services. (2012). Retrieved from https://www.mymedlab.com/.

Proal, C., Sánchez, J. A., & Fernández, L. (2000). UVA: 3D representations for visualizing digital collections. In *Proceedings of the Third International Conference on Visual Computing*, 185–192. Mexico City: IEEE Press. Retrieved from http://ict.udlap.mx/pubs/UVA2000.pdf.

Processing 2. (n.d.). *Processing.org*. Retrieved from http://processing.org/.

Propp, V. (1927). *Morphology of the folktale. Transactions of Laurence Scott* (2nd ed.). Austin, TX: University of Texas Press.

Qian, X., Yang, Y., & Gong, Y. (2011). The art of metaphor: A method for interface design based on mental models. In *Proceedings of the 10th International Conference on Virtual Reality Continuum and Its Applications in Industry* (171-178). Hong Kong: ACM.

Qu, H., Chan, W., Xu, A., Chung, K., Lau, K., & Guo, P. (2007). Visual analysis of the air pollution problem in Hong Kong. *IEEE Transactions on Visualization and Computer Graphics, 13*(6), 1408–1415. doi:10.1109/TVCG.2007.70523 PMID:17968091.

Rabianski, J., DeLisle, J., & Carn, N. (2001). Corporate real-estate site selection: A community specific information framework. *Journal of Real Estate Research, 22*(1), 165–197.

Ramirez, E. R., & Hekler, E. (2012). Digital histories for future health. In *Proceedings of CHI2012 Workshop on Personal Informatics in Practice: Improving Quality of Life Through Data*. New York: ACM Press.

Ramos, A., Sánchez, J. A., & Hernández-Bolaños, F. (2010). OntoStarFish: Visualization of collaboration networks using starfields, ontologies, and fisheye views. In *Proceedings of the 3rd Mexican Workshop on Human Computer Interaction*, 44–53. San Luis Potosí, México: Universidad Politécnia de San Luis Potosí. Retrieved from http://dl.acm.org/citation.cfm?id=1978702.1978713.

Raskin, A. (n.d.). *Privacy icons: Alpha release*. Retrieved from http://www.azarask.in/blog/post/privacy-icons.

Rationalizer . (2012). Retrieved from http://www.mirrorofemotions.com/.

Ratwani, R. M., & Trafton, J. G. (2008). Spatial memory guides task resumption. *Visual Cognition, 16*(8), 1001–1010. doi:10.1080/13506280802025791.

Rauterberg, M. (1992). An empirical comparison of menu-selection (CUI) and desktop (GUI) computer progrmas carried out by beginners and experts. *Behaviour & Information Technology, 11*, 227–236. doi:10.1080/01449299208924341.

Rawassizadeh, R. (2012). *UbiqLog: A generic mobile phone based life-log framework. Personal and Ubiquitous Computing, 2012*. London, UK: Springer.

Reiss, S. (2009). Visualizing the java heap to detect memory problems. In *Proceedings of VISSOFT '09 5th IEEE International Workshop on Visualizing Software for Understanding and Analysis*, 73–80. Washington, DC: IEEE Press.

Rekers, J., & Schurr, A. (1995). A graph grammar approach to graphical parsing. In *Proceedings of IEEE Symposium on Visual Languages (VL'95)*. Darmstadt, Germany: IEEE Press.

ReliefInsite . (2012). Retrieved from http://www.reliefinsite.com/.

Renambot, L. (2012). *Lambdavision: Building a 100 megapixel display*. Retrieved from www.evl.uic.edu/cavern/sage/pubs/LambdaVision-light.pdf.

Reno, Nevada. (1899). *Sheet #5*. New York: Sanborn Map and Publishing Company. Retrieved from: http://www.loc.gov/exhibits/treasures/trr016.html.

Rensink, R. A. (2002). Internal vs. external information in visual perception. In *Proceedings of the Second International Symposium on Smart Graphics. Smart Graphics, 2*, 63-70

Rensink, R. A. (2002). Change detection. *Annual Review of Psychology, 53*, 245–577. doi:10.1146/annurev.psych.53.100901.135125 PMID:11752486.

Rheingans, P., & desJardins, M. (2000). Visualizing high-dimensional predictive model quality.[New Brunswick, NJ: IEEE Press.]. *Proceedings of IEEE Visualization, 2000*, 493–496.

Rhodes, B. J., Bomberger, N. A., Zandipour, M., Waxman, A. M., & Seibert, M. (2007b). Cognitively-inspired motion pattern learning & analysis algorithms for higher-level fusion and automated scene understanding. In *Military Communications Conference (MILCOM 2007)*, 1–6. New Brunswick, NJ: IEEE Press.

Rhodes, B., Bomberger, N., & Zandipour, M. (2007a). Probabilistic associative learning of vessel motion patterns at multiple spatial scales for maritime situation awareness. In: *10th International Conference on Information Fusion*, 1–8.

Rhodes, B., Bomberger, N., Seibert, M., & Waxman, A. (2005). Maritime situation monitoring and awareness using learning mechanisms. *Military Communications Conference, 1*, 646–652. New Brunswick, NJ: IEEE Press.

Rhodes, P. J., Laramee, R. S., Bergeron, R. D., & Sparr, T. M. (2003). Uncertainty visualization methods in isosurface rendering. In *Proceedings of Eurographics*. New Brunswick, NJ: IEEE Press.

Ricoeur, P. (1992). *Oneself as another*. Chicago: University of Chicago Press.

Rieh, S. Y., Yang, J. Y., Yakel, E., & Markey, K. (2010). Conceptualizing institutional repositories: Using co-discovery to uncover mental models. In *Proceedings of the Third Symposium on Information Interaction in Context*, 165-174. New York: ACM.

RINA Systems, Inc. (n.d.). Retrieved from http://www.rinafinancial.com/.

Rips, L. J. (1986). Mental muddles. InBrand, M, & Harnish, R. M. (Eds.), *The Representation of Knowledge and Belief* (258-286). Tucson, AZ: The University of Arizona Press.

Risko, E. F., Anderson, N. C., Lanthier, S., & Kingstone, A. (2012). Curious eyes: Individual differences in personality predict eye movement behavior in scene-viewing. *Cognition, 122*(1), 86–90. doi:10.1016/j.cognition.2011.08.014 PMID:21983424.

Ristic, B., Scala, B. L., Morelande, M., & Gordon, N. (2008). Statistical analysis of motion patterns in AIS data: Anomaly detection and motion prediction. In *Proceedings of 11th International Conference of Information Fusion*. New Brunswick, NJ: IEEE Press.

Riveiro, M., Falkman, G., & Ziemke, T. (2008). Improving maritime anomaly detection and situation awareness through interactive visualization. In *Proceedings of 11th International Conference on Information Fusion*, 47–54. New Brunswick, NJ: IEEE Press.

Riveiro, M., Falkman, G., Ziemke, T., & Kronhamn, T. (2009). Reasoning about anomalies: A study of the analytical process of detecting and identifying anomalous behavior in maritime traffic data. InTolone, , & Ribarsky, (Eds.), *SPIE Defense, Security, and Sensing. Visual Analytics for Homeland Defense and Security.Volume 7346*. Orlando, FL: SPIE Press.

Rizzo, A., & Bacigalupo, M. (2004) Scenarios: heuristics for actions. In *Proceedings of XII European Conference on Cognitive Ergonomics*. York, UK: EACE.

Roambi. (2012). Retrieved from http://www.roambi.com.

Robbins, M. L. (1996). *Spatial decision support systems for automated residential property valuation: A discussion of an actual installed system. Research and Business Uses of Geographic Information Systems in Housing and Mortgage Finance*. Washington, DC: Fannie MaeResearch Roundtable Series.

Robertson, G., Fernandez, R., Fisher, D., Lee, B., & Stasko, J. (2008). Effectiveness of animation in trend visualization. *IEEE Transactions on Visualization and Computer Graphics*, *14*(6), 1325–1332. doi:10.1109/TVCG.2008.125 PMID:18988980.

Robinson, A. (2009). Visual highlighting methods for geovisualization. *Citeseer*. Retrieved from http://citeseerx.ist.psu.edu/index

Robinson, A., & Center, G. (2006). Highlighting techniques to support geovisualization. *Citeseer*. Retrieved from http://citeseer.uark.edu:8080/citeseerx/viewdoc/summary;jsessionid=C7399B91D98763433F13B57449C2AC90?doi=10.1.1.79.757.

Robinson, A. H., Morrison, J. L., Muehrcke, P. C., Kimerling, A. J., & Guptill, S. C. (1995). *Elements of cartography*. New York: John Wiley and Sons.

Rocha, H. V., Kropiwiec, D. D., Fukaya, S. M., Neto, J. C., Gayard, L. A., et al., & Ferreira, T. B. (2002). TelEduc project: Technology research and development for distance learning. In *Proceedings of IX Brazilian Association of Distance Education International Congress of Distance Learning*. Available at http://www.teleduc.org.br/artigos/premio_abed2002.pdf.

Rodriguez, M., Sirmans, C. F., & Marks, A. (1995). Using geographic information systems to improve real-estate analysis. *Journal of Real Estate Research*, *10*(2), 163–172.

Rogers, Y., & Ellis, J. (1994). Distributed cognition: An alternative framework for analyzing and explaining collaborative working. *Journal of Information Technology*, *9*(2), 119–128. doi:10.1057/jit.1994.12.

Romani, L. A. S. (2000). *InterMap: Tool for Visualizing Interaction in Distance Learning Environments on Web*. (Master thesis). Campinas, Brazil, University of Campinas.

Roos, J., Bart, V., & Statler, M. (2004). Playing seriously with strategy. *Long Range Planning*, *37*(6), 549–568. doi:10.1016/j.lrp.2004.09.005.

Roth, S. F., Kolojejchick, J., Mattis, J., & Goldstein, J. (1994). Interactive graphic design using automatic presentation knowledge. In *Proceedings of the SIGCHI Conference on Human Factors in Computing Systems*, 112-117. New York: ACM Press.

Roto, V., Law, E., Vermeeren, A., & Hoonhout, J. (Eds.). (2011). User experience white paper: Bringing clarity to the concept of user experience. *Result from Dagsthul Seminar on Demarcating User Experience*. Retrieved from http://www.allaboutux.org/files/UX-WhitePaper.pdf.

Roy, J. (2008). Anomaly detection in the maritime domain. In *Proceedings of SPIE, Volume 6945,* 69450W 1–14. Bellingham, WA: SPIE Press.

Rumelhart, D. E. (1984). Schemata and the Cognitive System. In Wyer, R. S. Jr, & Srull, T. K. (Eds.), *Handbook of Social Cognition* (*Vol. 1*, pp. 161–188). Hillsdale, NJ: Lawrence Erlbaum Associates.

Runkeeper. (2012). Retrieved from http://runkeeper.com/.

Ruspini, D. C., Kolarov, K., & Khatib, O. (1997). The haptic display of complex graphical environments. In *Proceedings of the 24th Annual Conference on Computer Graphics and Interactive Techniques,* 345-352. New York: ACM Press.

Sadarjoen, I. A., & Post, F. H. (2000). Detection, quantification, and tracking of vortices using streamline geometry. *Computers & Graphics*, *24*(3), 333–341. doi:10.1016/S0097-8493(00)00029-7.

Saffer, D. (2010). *Designing for interaction* (2nd ed.). Berkeley, CA: New Riders Press.

Sahner, J., Weinkauf, T., & Hege, H.-C. (2005). Galilean invariant extraction and iconic representation of vortex core lines. In *Proceedings of EuroVis*. New Brunswick, NJ: IEEE Press.

Salimun, C., Purchase, H. C., Simmons, D. R., & Brewster, S. (2010). The effect of aesthetically pleasing composition on visual search performance. In *Proceedings of the 6th Nordic Conference on Human-Computer Interaction: Extending Boundaries,* 422–431. New York: ACM Press.

Saltz, J. S., Hiltz, S. R., & Turoff, M. (2004). Student social graphs: Visualizing a student's online social network. In *Proceedings of ACM Conference on Computer Supported Collaborative Work (CSCW)*. Chicago: ACM Press.

Sánchez, J. A., Medina, M., Starostenko, O., Benitez, A., & Domínguez, E. (2012). Organizing open archives via lightweight ontologies to facilitate the use of heterogeneous collections. In *Proceedings of ASLIB, 64,* 46–66. New York: Emerald Press. doi:10.1108/00012531211196701

Sánchez, J. A., Quintana, M., & Razo, A. (2007). Star-fish: Starfields+ fisheye visualization and its application to federated digital libraries. In *Proceedings of the 3rd Latin American Conference on Human-Computer Interaction*. Rio de Janeiro, Brazil: HCIR Press. Retrieved from http://clihc.org/2007/papers/StarFish_ID38_longpaper.pdf.

Sánchez, J. A., Twidale, M. B., Nichols, D. M., & Silva, N. N. (2005). Experiences with starfield visualizations for analysis of library collections. In *Proceedings of the Conference on Visualization and Data Analysis, 5669*, 215–225. San Jose, CA: SPIE Press.

Sanders, E. B.-N. (2002). *Scaffolds for experiencing in the new design space*. In Institute for Information Design Japan IIDj (Eds.), *Information Design*. Retrieved from http://www.maketools.com/articles-papers/Scaffoldsfor-Experiencing_Sanders_03.pdf.

Sandstrom, T. (2003). The hyperwall. In *Proceedings of the Conference on Coordinated and Multiple Views in Exploratory Visualizations*. New Brunswick, NJ: IEEE Press.

Santos, E., Lins, L., Ahrens, J., Freire, J., & Silva, C. (2009). VisMashup: Streamlining the creation of custom visualization applications. *IEEE Transactions on Visualization and Computer Graphics, 15*(6), 1539–1546. doi:10.1109/TVCG.2009.195 PMID:19834231.

Sanyal, J., Zhang, S., Bhattacharya, G., Amburn, P., & Moorhead, R. (2009). A user study to compare four uncertainty visualization methods for 1D and 2D datasets. *IEEE Transactions on Visualization and Computer Graphics, 15*(6), 1209–1218. doi:10.1109/TVCG.2009.114 PMID:19834191.

Sanyal, J., Zhang, S., Dyer, J., Mercer, A., Amburn, P., & Moorhead, R. J. (2010). Noodles: A tool for visualization of numerical weather model ensemble uncertainty. *IEEE Transactions on Visualization and Computer Graphics, 16*(6), 1421–1430. doi:10.1109/TVCG.2010.181 PMID:20975183.

Saraiya, P., North, C., & Duca, K. (2005). An insight-based methodology for evaluating bioinformatics visualizations. *IEEE Transactions on Visualization and Computer Graphics, 11*(4), 443–456. doi:10.1109/TVCG.2005.53 PMID:16138554.

Savidis, A. (2010). *Delta programming language*. Retrieved from http://www.ics.forth.gr/hci/files/plang/Delta/Delta.html.

Savidis, A., & Lilis, Y. (2009). Support for language independent browsing of aggregate values by debugger backends. *Journal of Object Technology, 8*(6), 159–180. Retrieved from http://www.jot.fm/issues/issue_2009_09/article4.pdf doi:10.5381/jot.2009.8.6.a4.

Scaife, M., & Rogers, Y. (1996). External cognition: how do graphical representations work? *International Journal of Human-Computer Studies, 45*(2), 185–213. doi:10.1006/ijhc.1996.0048.

Schell, J. (2008). *The art of game design: A book of lenses*. Burlington, MA: Elsevier.

Schmenner, R. (1982). *Making business location decisions*. Englewood Cliffs, NJ: Prentice Hall.

Schmidt, G. S., Chen, S.-L., Bryden, A. N., Livingston, M. A., Osborn, B. R., & Rosenblum, L. J. (2004). Multidimensional visual representations for underwater environmental uncertainty. *IEEE Computer Graphics and Applications, 24*(5), 56–65. doi:10.1109/MCG.2004.35 PMID:15628101.

Schneider, D., Wiebel, A., Carr, H., Hlawitschka, M., & Scheuermann, G. (2008). Interactive comparison of scalar fields based on largest contours with applications to flow visualization. *IEEE Transactions on Visualization and Computer Graphics, 14*(6), 1475–1482. doi:10.1109/TVCG.2008.143 PMID:18988999.

Schroeder, W., Martin, K., & Lorensen, B. (2006). *The visualization toolkit: An object-oriented approach to 3D graphics* (4th ed.). Clifton Park, NY: Kitware, Inc. Publishers.

Schulman, D., & Bickmore, T. (2009). Persuading users through counseling dialogue with a conversational agent. In *Proceedings of the 4th International Conference on Persuasive Technology*, 1-8. New York: ACM Press.

Schwartz, A., & Scott, R. E. (2010). Contract interpretation redux. *The Yale Law Journal, 119*(5), 926–965. Retrieved from http://ssrn.com/abstract=1504223.

Sedig, K., & Parsons, P. (2013). (in press). Interaction design for complex cognitive activities with visual representations: A pattern-based approach. *AIS Transactions on Human-Computer Interaction*.

Sedig, K., & Sumner, M. (2006). Characterizing interaction with visual mathematical representations. *International Journal of Computers for Mathematical Learning*, *11*(1), 1–55. doi:10.1007/s10758-006-0001-z.

Segel, E., & Heer, J. (2010). Narrative visualization: telling stories with data. *IEEE Transactions on Visualization and Computer Graphics*, *16*(6), 1139–1148. doi:10.1109/TVCG.2010.179 PMID:20975152.

Seibert, M., Rhodes, B. J., Bomberger, N. A., Beane, P. O., Sroka, J. J., et al., & Tillson, R. (2006). SeeCoast port surveillance. In *Proceedings of SPIE, Volume 6204: Photonics for Port and Harbor Security II*. Orlando, FL: SPIE Press.

Sellen, A. J., & Whittaker, S. (2010). Beyond total capture: A constructive critique of lifelogging. *Communications of the ACM*, *53*(5), 70–77. doi:10.1145/1735223.1735243.

Semmler, C., & Brewer, N. (2002). Using a flow-chart to improve comprehension of jury instructions. *Psychiatry, Psychology and Law*, *9*(2), 262–270. doi:10.1375/pplt.2002.9.2.262.

Seneff, S., & Polifroni, J. (2000). Dialogue management in the mercury flight reservation system. *In Proceedings of ANLP/NAACL 2000 Workshop on Conversational Systems*, 11-16. Seattle, WA: Academic Press.

SenseWear . (2012). Retrieved from http://sensewear.bodymedia.com/.

Seo, J., & Shneiderman, B. (2005). A rank-by-feature framework for interactive exploration of multidimensional data. *Information Visualization*, *4*(2), 96–113. doi:10.1057/palgrave.ivs.9500091.

Shaltis, P. A. (2006). Wearable, cuff-less PPG-based blood pressure monitor with novel height sensor. In *Proceedings of IEEE Engineering in Medicine and Biology Society*. New Brunswick, NJ: IEEE Press. doi:10.1109/IEMBS.2006.260027.

Shandler, J. (2012). United states holocaust memorial museum. *The Journal of American History*, 1228–1230. doi:10.1093/jahist/jar642.

Shearer, C. (2000). The CRISP-DM model: The new blueprint for data mining. *Journal of Data Warehousing*, *5*(4), 13–22.

Sherwani, J., Ali, N., Tongia, R., Rosenfeld, R., Memon, Y., Karim, M., & Pappas, G. (2007). HealthLine: Towards speech-based access to health information by semi-literate users. In *Proceedings of Speech in Mobile and Pervasive Environments*. New York: ACM Press.

Shi, K., Irani, P., & Li, B. (2005). An evaluation of content browsing techniques for hierarchical space-filling visualizations. In *Proceedings of IEEE Symposium on Information Visualization*, 81-88. New Brunswick, NJ: IEEE Press.

Shirky, C. (2008). It's not information overload. It's filter failure. *Web 2.0 Expo New York*. Retrieved from http://web2expo.blip.tv/file/1277460.

Shneiderman, B. (1996). The eyes have it: A task by data type taxonomy for information visualizations. In *Proceedings of 1996 IEEE Symposium on Visual Languages*, 336–343. Washington, DC: IEEE Press.

Shneiderman, B., & Plaisant, C. (2006). Strategies for evaluating information visualization tools: Multi-dimensional in-depth long-term case studies. In *Proceedings of the 2006 AVI Workshop on Beyond Time and Errors: Novel Evaluation Methods for Information Visualization*, 1–7. Philadelphia: ACM.

Shneiderman, B. (1994). Dynamic queries for visual information seeking. *IEEE Software*, *11*(6), 70–77. doi:10.1109/52.329404.

Shneiderman, B. (2000). The limits of speech recognition. *Communications of the ACM*, *43*(9), 63–65. doi:10.1145/348941.348990.

Shneiderman, B. (2002). Inventing discovery tools: Combining information visualization with data mining. *Information Visualization*, *1*(1), 5–12.

Shneiderman, B., & Aris, A. (2006). Network visualization by semantic substrates. *IEEE Transactions on Visualization and Computer Graphics*, *12*(5), 733–740. doi:10.1109/TVCG.2006.166 PMID:17080794.

Shostack, G. L. (1977). Breaking free from product marketing. *Journal of Marketing*, *41*(2), 73–80. doi:10.2307/1250637.

Siedel, G. J. (1992). Interdisciplinary approaches to alternative dispute resolution. *Journal of Legal Studies Education*, *10*(2), 141–169. doi:10.1111/j.1744-1722.1992.tb00226.x.

Siedel, G., & Haapio, H. (2011). *Proactive law for managers: A hidden source of competitive advantage.* Farnham, UK: Gower.

Siirtola, H. (2000). Direct manipulation of parallel coordinates. In *Proceedings of the International Conference on Information Visualisation*, 373-378. New Brunswick, NJ: IEEE.

Siirtola, H. & K. J. R. (2006). Interacting with parallel coordinates. *Interacting with Computers*, *18*(6), 1278–1309. doi:10.1016/j.intcom.2006.03.006.

Silva, C. G. (2006). *Learning Management Systems' Database Exploration by Means of Information Visualization-Based Query Tools.* (Doctoral thesis). Campinas, Brazil, University of Campinas.

Silva, C. G., & Rocha, H. V. (2004). Contributions of information visualization for distance learning area. In *Proceedings of VI Brazilian Symposium on Human Factors in Computing Systems (IHC)*. Curitiba, Brazil: IHC Press.

Silva, C. G., & Rocha, H. V. (2007). Learning management systems' database exploration by means of information visualization-based query tools. In *Proceedings of Seventh International Conference on Advanced Learning Technologies (ICALT)*, 543-545. Washington, DC: IEEE Press.

Silva, N. N., Sanchez, J. A., Proal, C., & Rebollar, C. (2003). Visual exploration of large collections in digital libraries. In *Proceedings of the Latin American Conference on Human-Computer Interaction*, 147–157. New York: ACM Press. Retrieved from http://portal.acm.org/citation.cfm?id=944519.944535.

Skiba, D. (2007). Nursing Education 2.0: are mashups useful for nursing education? *Nursing Education Perspectives*, *5*, 286–288. PMID:17944264.

Skinner, B. F. (1938). *The behavior of organisms: An experimental analysis.* New York: Appleton-Century.

Skinner, B. F. (1953). *Science and human behavior.* New York: Macmillan.

Slocum, T. A., McMaster, R. B., Kessler, F. C., & Howard, H. H. (2009). *Thematic cartography and geovisualization.* Upper Saddle River, NJ: Prentice Hall.

Smale, S. (1961). On gradient dynamical systems. *The Annals of Mathematics*, *71*(1), 199–206. doi:10.2307/1970311.

Smith, M. A., Shneiderman, B., Milic-Frayling, N., Mendes Rodrigues, E., Barash, V., Dunne, C., & Capone, T. (2009). Analyzing (social media) networks with NodeXL. In D. Hansen, B. Shneiderman, M. Smith, & R. Ackland (Eds.), *Proceedings of the Fourth International Conference on Communities and Technologies-CT 09* (255–264). New York: ACM Press. doi:10.1145/1556460.1556497.

SNPedia . (2012). Retrieved from http://www.snpedia.com/index.php / SNPedia.

Sohn, B. S., & Chandrajit, B. (2006). Time-varying contour topology. *IEEE Transactions on Visualization and Computer Graphics*, *12*(1), 14–25. doi:10.1109/TVCG.2006.16 PMID:16382604.

Sole, D., & Wilson, D. G. (2002). Storytelling in organizations: The power and traps of using stories to share knowledge in organizations. *LILA, Harvard, Graduate School of Education*. Retrieved from http://www.providersedge.com/docs/km_articles/Storytelling_in_Organizations.pdf.

Solomon, S. H. (2006). *Visuals and visualisation: Penetrating the heart and soul of persuasion.* DOAR Litigation Consulting. Retrieved from http://tillers.net/solomon.pdf.

South Coast Regional Stakeholder Group. (n.d.). *Marine-MAP decision support tool.* Retrieved from http://southcoast.marinemap.org/marinemap/.

Spence, R. (2001). *Information Visualization* (1st ed.). Boston: Addison-Wesley.

Spot The Difference. (2013). Retrieved from Spotthedifference.com.

Språkrådet. (2010). Press release: Plain crystal 2010. *CSN and the Court Of Appeal For Western Sweden.* http://www.sprakradet.se/7121.

Staggers, N., & Kobus, D. (2000). Comparing response time, errors, and satisfaction between tex-based and graphical user interfaces during nursing order tasks. *Journal of the American Medical Informatics Association, 7,* 164–176. doi:10.1136/jamia.2000.0070164 PMID:10730600.

Stanford Visual Group. (2010). Protovis-A graphical approach to visualization. *Protovis.* Retrieved from http://mbostock.github.com/protovis/.

Star, S. L., & Griesemer, J. R. (1989). Institutional ecology, 'translations,' and boundary objects: Amateurs and professionals in Berkeley's Museum of Vertebrate Zoology. *Social Studies of Science, 19*(3), 387–420. doi:10.1177/030631289019003001.

Stasko, J., & Zhang, E. (2000). Focus + contest display and navigation techniques for enhancing radial, space-filling hierarchy visualizations. In *Proceedings of IEEE Symposium on Information Visualization,* 57. New Brunswick, NJ: IEEE.

Steed, C. A., Swan, J. E., II, Jankun-Kelly, T. J., & Fitzpatrick, P. J. (2009). Guided analysis of hurricane trends using statistical processes integrated with interactive parallel coordinates. In *Proceedings of IEEE Symposium on Visual Analytics Science and Technology,* 19-26. New Brunswick, NJ: IEEE Press.

Steed, C. A., Fitzpatrick, P. J., Jankun-Kelly, T. J., Yancey, A. N., & Swan, J. E. II. (2009). An interactive parallel coordinates technique applied to a tropical cyclone climate analysis. *Computers & Geosciences, 35*(7), 1529–1539. doi:10.1016/j.cageo.2008.11.004.

Steed, C. A., Fitzpatrick, P. J., Swan, J. E. II, & Jankun-Kelly, T. J. (2009). Tropical cyclone trend analysis using enhanced parallel coordinates and statistical analytics. *Cartography and Geographic Information Science, 36*(3), 251–265. doi:10.1559/152304009788988314.

Steinberger, M., Waldner, M., Streit, M., Lex, A., & Schmalstieg, D. (2011). Context–Preserving visual links. *IEEE Transactions on Visualization and Computer Graphics, 17*(12), 2249–2258. doi:10.1109/TVCG.2011.183 PMID:22034344.

Storrle, H. (2012). On the impact of layout quality to understanding UML diagrams: Diagram type and expertise. In *Proceedings of IEEE Symposium on Visual Languages and Human-Centric Computing,* 49-56. Innsbruck, Austria: IEEE Press.

StressEraser . (2012). Retrieved from http://www.stresseraser.com.

Studio, G. E. O. V. I. S. T. A. (2007). Health geojunction. *GEOVISTA.* Retrieved from http://www.apps.geovista.psu.edu/hgj/#.

SugarStats . (2012). Retrieved Sfrom https://sugarstats.com/.

Suh, B., Chi, E. H., Kittur, A., & Pendleton, B. A. (2008). Lifting the veil: Improving accountability and social transparency in wikipedia with wikidashboard. In *Proceeding of the Twenty-Sixth Annual SIGCHI Conference on Human Factors in Computing Systems,* 1037–1040. Florence, Italy: ACM Press.

Suh, B., Chi, E. H., Pendleton, B. A., & Kittur, A. (2007). Us vs. them: Understanding social dynamics in wikipedia with revert graph visualizations. In *Proceedings of 2007 IEEE Symposium on Visual Analytics Science and Technology,* 163–170. Washington, DC: IEEE Press.

Sun, Y. (2012). *Articulate: Creating Meaningful Visualizations from Natural Language.* (Doctoral dissertation). Chicago, University of Illinois.

Sun, Y., Leigh, J., Johnson, A., & Lee, S. (2010). Articulate: A semi-automated model for translating natural language queries into meaningful visualizations. In *Proceedings of 10th International Symposium on Smart Graphic,* 184-195. New York: ACM Press.

Sundararaman, J., & Back, G. (2008). HDPV: Interactive, faithful, in-vivo runtime state visualization for C/C++ and Java. In *Proceedings of SoftVis'08 4th Symposium on Software Visualization,* 47–56. New York: ACM Press.

Swan, M. (2011). *Genomic self-hacking*. Retrieved from http://quantifiedself.com/2011/11/melanie-swan-on-genomic-self-hacking/.

Swan, M. (2009). Emerging patient-driven health care models: An examination of health social networks, consumer personalized medicine, and quantified self-tracking. *International Journal of Environmental Research and Public Health*, 6(2), 492–525. doi:10.3390/ijerph6020492 PMID:19440396.

Sweller, J., van Merrienboer, J. J. G., & Paas, F. G. W. C. (1998). Cognitive architecture and instructional design. *Educational Psychology Review*, 10(3), 251–296. doi:10.1023/A:1022193728205.

Szulanski, G. (2000). The process of knowledge transfer: A diachronic analysis of stickiness. *Organizational Behavior and Human Decision Processes*, 82(1), 9–27. doi:10.1006/obhd.2000.2884.

Tableau. (2013). Free data visualization software. *Tableau Public*. Retrieved from http://www.tableausoftware.com/public.

Takahashi, S., Takeshima, Y., & Fujishiro, I. (2004). Topological volume skeletonization and its application to transfer function design. *Graphical Models*, 66(1), 24–49. doi:10.1016/j.gmod.2003.08.002.

Teoh, S. T., Zhang, K., Tseng, S., Ma, K., & Wu, S. F. (2004). Combining visual and automated data mining for near-realtime anomaly detection and analysis in BGP. In *Proceedings of the 2004 ACM Workshop on Visualization and Data Mining for Computer Security*, 35–44. New York: ACM Press.

Tergan, S.-O., Keller, T., & Burkhard, R. A. (2006). Integrating knowledge and information: Digital concept maps as a bridging technology. *Information Visualization*, 5(3), 167–174. doi:10.1057/palgrave.ivs.9500132.

Teutsch, P., & Bourdet, J.-F. (2010). How to see training paths in learning management systems? In *Proceedings of 10th IEEE International Conference on Advanced Learning Technologies*, 349-351. Washington, DC: IEEE Press.

Theisel, H., Rössl, C., & Seidel, H.-P. (2003a). Combining topological simplification and topology preserving compression for 2D vector fields. In *Proceedings of Pacific Graphics*. New Brunswick, NJ: IEEE Press. doi:10.1109/PCCGA.2003.1238287.

Theisel, H., Rössl, C., & Seidel, H.-P. (2003b). Using feature flow fields for topological comparison of vector fields. In *Proceedings of Vision, Modeling, and Visualization*. New Brunswick, NJ: IEEE Press.

Theisel, H., & Seidel, H.-P. (2003). Feature flow fields. In *Proceedings of Data Visualization*. New Brunswick, NJ: IEEE Press.

Theisel, H., Weinkauf, T., Hege, H.-C., & Seidel, H.-P. (2005). Topological methods for 2D time-dependent vector fields based on stream lines and path lines. *IEEE Transactions on Visualization and Computer Graphics*, 11(4), 383–394. doi:10.1109/TVCG.2005.68 PMID:16138549.

Thelen, S. (2010). Advanced visualization and interaction techniques for large high-resolution displays. InMiddel, Ariane (eds.), *Visualization of Large and Unstructured Data Sets-Applications in Geospatial Planning, Modeling, and Engineering*, 19 (73-81). Berlin: DFG.

ThinkMap Visual Thesaurus. (n.d.). Retrieved from http://www.visualthesaurus.com/.

Thomas, J. J., & Cook, K. A. (Eds.). (2005). *Illuminating the path: The research and development agenda for visual analytics*. Los Alamitos, CA: IEEE Press.

Thomas, J., & Cook, K. (Eds.). (2005). *Illuminating the Path: The Research and Development Agenda for Visual Analytics*. Los Alametos, CA: IEEE Computer Society.

Thrall, G. I., & Amos, P. (1996). *GIS within real-estate and related industries. Research and Business Uses of Geographic Information Systems in Housing and Mortgage Finance*. Washington, DC: Fannie Mae Research Roundtable Series.

Thrall, G. I., Fandrich, J., & Thrall, S. (1995). The location quotient: Descriptive geography for the community reinvestment act. *Geographical Information Systems*, 5(6), 18–22.

Tierny, J., Gyulassy, A., Simon, E., & Pascucci, V. (2009). Loop surgery for volumetric meshes: Reeb graphs reduced to contour trees. *IEEE Transactions on Visualization and Computer Graphics*, 15(6), 1177–1184. doi:10.1109/TVCG.2009.163 PMID:19834187.

Tiersma, P. M. (2006). Some myths about legal language. *Law, Culture, and the Humanities*, 2(1), 29–50. doi:10.1191/1743872106lw035oa.

Tomaszewski, B., Blandford, J., Ross, K., Pezanowski, S., & MacEachren, A. M. (2011). Supporting geographically-aware web document foraging and sensemaking. *Computers, Environment and Urban Systems, 35*, 192–207. doi:10.1016/j.compenvurbsys.2011.01.003.

Tory, M., & Moller, T. (2004). Rethinking visualization: A high-level taxonomy. In *Proceedings of IEEE Symposium on Information Visualization*, 151–158. Washington, DC: IEEE Press.

Track Your Happiness . (2012). Retrieved from http://www.trackyourhappiness.org/.

Trafton, J. G., Altmann, E. M., Brock, D. P., & Mintz, F. E. (2003). Preparing to resume an interrupted task: Effects of prospecting goal encoding and restrospective rehearsal. *International Journal of Human-Computer Studies, 58*, 583–603. doi:10.1016/S1071-5819(03)00023-5.

Tricoche, X. (2002). *Vector and Tensor Field Topology Simplification, Tracking and Visualization*. (Dissertation). Kaiserslautern, Germany, University of Kaiserslautern.

Tufte, E. (1983). *The visual display of quantitative information*. Cheshire, CT: Graphics Press.

Tufte, E. (1990). *Envisioning information*. Cheshire, CT: Graphics Press.

Tufte, E. (1997). *Visual explanations: Images and quantities, evidence and narrative*. Cheshire, CT: Graphics Press.

Tufte, E. (2006). *Beautiful evidence*. Cheshire, CT: Graphics Press.

Tufte, E. R. (1983). *The visual display of quantitative information*. Cheshire, CT: Graphics Press.

Tufte, E. R. (1990). *Envisioning information*. Chechire, CT: Graphics Press.

Tufte, E. R. (2001). *Data denstiy and small multiples. The Visual Display of Quantitative Information (42)*. Cheshire, CT: Graphics Pr.

Tufte, E. R. (2001). *The visual display of quantitative information. Visual Explanations, 194–95*. Cockeysville, MD: PR Graphics.

Tukey, J. W. (1977). *Exploratory data analysis*. Boston: Addison-Wesley.

Tukey, J. W. (1977). *Exploratory data analysis*. Reading, MA: Addison-Wesley.

Tullio, J., Dey, A. K., Chalecki, J., & Fogarty, J. (2007). How it works: A field study of non-technical users interacting with an intelligent system. In *Proceedings of the SIGCHI Conference on Human Factors in Computing Systems*, 31-40. San Jose, CA: ACM.

Turner, A. (2006). *Introduction to neogeography. Short Cuts*. Sebasapol, CA: O'Reilly Media.

Turner, T. C., Smith, M. A., Fisher, D., & Welser, H. T. (2005). Picturing usenet: Mapping computer-mediated collective action. *Journal of Computer Mediated Communication,10*(4).

Tversky, B. (2004). Narratives of space, time, and life. *Mind & Language, 19*(4), 380–392. doi:10.1111/j.0268-1064.2004.00264.x.

Tversky, B., Bauer, J., Betrancourt, M., De Europe, A., & St-Martin, M. (2002). Animation: Can it facilitate? *International Journal of Human-Computer Studies, 57*(4), 247–262. doi:10.1006/ijhc.2002.1017.

Tzoumakas, V., & Theodoulidis, B. (2005). Force based visualizations for instructor support. In *Proceedings of the Fifth IEEE International Conference on Advanced Learning Technologies* (ICALT), 452-456. Washington, DC: IEEE Press.

UCLA. (2011). Retrieved from http://www.cens.ucla.edu/pub/ParticipatoryOpenMhealth-Apple-DE080711.pdf.

Ullman, J. D. (1982). *Principles of database systems* (2nd ed.). Washington, DC: Computer Science Press.

United Nations. (2000). *Handbook on geographic information systems and digital mapping*. New York, Series F No. 79. Retrieved http://unstats.un.org/unsd/publication/SeriesF/SeriesF_79E.pdf.

Usability Professionals' Association UPA. (n.d.). Glossary. *Usability Body of Knowledge*. Retrieved from http://www.usabilitybok.org/glossary.

USDA. (2011). Welcome to the USDA national nutrient database for standard reference. *National Agriculture Library*. Retrieved from http://ndb.nal.usda.gov/.

USGS. (2002). Using maps in genealogy: Fact sheet 099-02. *USGS Science for a Changing World*. Retrieved from http://egsc.usgs.gov/isb/pubs/factsheets/fs09902.html.

Van Ham, F., Schulz, H., & Dimicco, J. M. (2009). Honeycomb: Visual analysis of large scale social networks. In *Proceedings of the 12th IFIP TC 13 International Conference on Human-Computer Interaction: Part II,*429–442. Uppsala, Sweden: Springer.

van Reimersdahl, T., Bley, F., Kuhlen, T., & Bischof, C. H. (2003). Haptic rendering techniques for the interactive exploration of CFD datasets in virtual environments. In *Proceedings of the Workshop on Virtual Environments, 39*, 241-246. New Brunswick, NJ: IEEE Press.

Vanacken, L., Raymaekers, C., & Coninx, K. (2006). Evaluating the influence of multimodal feedback on egocentric selection metaphors in virtual environments. In *Proceedings of First International Workshop on Haptic and Audio Interaction Design,* 12-23. HAID Press.

Vanacken, L., Grossman, T., & Coninx, K. (2009). Multimodal selection techniques for dense and occluded 3D virtual environments. *International Journal of Human-Computer Studies, 67*(3), 237–255. doi:10.1016/j.ijhcs.2008.09.001.

Vande Moere, A., & Purchase, H. (2011). On the role of design in information visualization. *Information Visualization, 10*(4), 356–371. doi:10.1177/1473871611415996.

Vandenberg, S. G., & Kuse, A. R. (1978). Mental rotations, A group test of three-dimensional spatial visualizations. *Perceptual and Motor Skills, 47*(2), 599–604. doi:10.2466/pms.1978.47.2.599 PMID:724398.

Vasiliev, I. R. (1997). Mapping time: Discussion of historical attempts to define time, and integration of time information into diagrams of geographic data. *Cartographica, 34*(2), 1–44. doi:10.3138/D357-234G-2M62-4373.

Vassileva, J., & Sun, L. (2007). Using community visualization to stimulate participation in online communities. *E-Service Journal, 6*(1), 3–39. doi:10.2979/ESJ.2007.6.1.3.

Vézien, J.-M., Ménélas, B., Nelson, J., Picinali, L., Bourdot, P., & Lusseyran, F. et al. (2009). Multisensory VR exploration for computer fluid dynamics in the CoRSAIRe project. *Virtual Reality (Waltham Cross), 13*(4), 257–271. doi:10.1007/s10055-009-0134-1.

Viégas, F. B., & Donath, J. (2004). Social network visualization: Can we go beyond the graph. In *Proceedings of Workshop on Social Networks, 4*, 6–10. Chicago: ACM Press.

Viégas, F. B., & Smith, M. (2004). Newsgroup crowds and authorlines: Visualizing the activity of individuals in conversational cyberspaces. In *Proceedings of the 37th Hawaii International Conference on System Sciences.* Washington, DC: IEEE Press.

Viégas, F. B., Boyd, D., Nguyen, D. H., Potter, J., & Donath, J. (2004). Digital artifacts for remembering and storytelling: Posthistory and social network fragments. In *Proceedings of the 37th Annual Hawaii International Conference on System Sciences*, 109–118. Washington, DC: IEEE Press.

Viégas, F. B., Wattenberg, M., & Dave, K. (2004). Studying cooperation and conflict between authors with history flow visualizations. In *Proceedings of the SIGCHI Conference on Human Factors in Computing Systems*, 575–582. Vienna, Austria: ACM Press.

Viégas, F. B., Wattenberg, M., Kriss, J., & Ham, F. V. (2007). Talk before you type: Coordination in wikipedia. In *Proceedings of the 40th Annual Hawaii International Conference on System Sciences* (78). Hawaii: IEEE Press.

Viewzi. (2010). *Viewzi, inc.* Retrieved from http://www.viewzi.com/.

Villarroel, M. (2006). Visualizing shared highlighting annotations. *HCI Related Papers of Interaction,* (195).

Visblock™ . (2012). Retrieved from http://www.visbox.com/visblock.html.

von der Heyde, M., & Hager-Ross, C. (1998). Psychophysical experiments in a complex virtual environment. In *Proceedings of the Third PHANTOM Users Group Workshop.* Cambridge, MA: MIT.

Von Hippel, E. (1994). Sticky information and the locus of problem solving: Implications for innovation. *Management Science*, 40(4), 429–439. doi:10.1287/mnsc.40.4.429.

Waern, Y. (1990). *Cognitive aspects of computer supported tasks*. New York, NY: John Wiley & Sons, Inc..

Wagner, C., Rowe, M., Strohmaier, M., & Alani, H. (2012). Ignorance isn't bliss: An empirical analysis of attention patterns in online communities. In *Proceedings of IEEE International Conference on Social Computing*. Amsterdam: IEEE Press.

Wall, S. A., Paynter, K., Shillito, A. M., Wright, M., & Scali, S. (2002). The effect of haptic feedback and stereo graphics in a 3D target acquisition. In *Proceedings of Eurohaptics*,23-29. Edinburgh, UK: IEEE Press.

Walpole, R. E., & Myers, R. H. (1993). *Probability and statistics for engineers and scientists* (5th ed.). Englewood Cliffs, NJ: Prentice Hall.

Walsum, T. V., Post, F. H., Silver, D., & Post, F. J. (1996). Feature extraction and iconic visualization. *IEEE Transactions on Visualization and Computer Graphics*, 2(2), 111–119. doi:10.1109/2945.506223.

Wang, W., Wang, H., Dai, G., & Wang, H. (2006). Visualization of large hierarchical data by circle packing. In *Proceedings of the SIGCHI Conference on Human Factors in computing Systems-CHI '06*, 517–520. New York: ACM Press.

Ware, C. (2000). *Information visualization: Perception for design (interactive technologies)*. New York: Morgan Kaufmann.

Ware, C. (2000). *Information visualization: Perception for design*. San Francisco: Morgan Kaufmann Publishers Inc..

Ware, C. (2004). *Information visualization: Perception for design* (2nd ed.). New York: Morgan Kaufmann.

Ware, C., & Bobrow, R. (2004). Motion to support rapid interactive queries on node-link diagrams. *ACM Transactions on Applied Perception*, 1(1), 3–18. doi:10.1145/1008722.1008724.

Ware, C., & Bobrow, R. (2005). Supporting visual queries on medium-sized node-link diagrams. *Information Visualization*, 4(1), 49–58. doi:10.1057/palgrave.ivs.9500090.

Ware, C., & Gilman, A. (2008). *Visual thinking with an interactive diagram*. Berlin: Springer.

Washington D.C. Interactive Map. (n.d.). Retrieved from http://www.cs.umd.edu/class/fall2002/cmsc838s/tichi/fisheye.html.

Wattenberg, M., Viégas, F., & Hollenbach, K. (2007). Visualizing activity on wikipedia with chromograms. In *Proceedings of the 11th IFIP TC 13 International Conference on Human-Computer Interaction-Volume Part II*, 272–287. Rio de Janeiro: Springer.

Wattenberg, M., & Kriss, J. (2006). Designing for social data analysis. *IEEE Transactions on Visualization and Computer Graphics*, 12(4), 549–557. doi:10.1109/TVCG.2006.65 PMID:16805263.

Weather Underground. (2007). *An example URL of daily weather data of london heathrow airport in 2007*. Retrieved from http://www.wunderground.com/history/airport/EGLL/2007/1/1/CustomHistory.html?dayend=31&monthend=12&yearend=2007&format=1.

Weather Underground. (2013). Welcome to weather underground! *Weather Forecasts & Reports*. Retrieved from http://www.wunderground.com.

WebCrawler. (2012). *Infospace, inc*. Retrieved from http://www.webcrawler.com/.

Wegman, E. J. (1990). Hyperdimensional data analysis using parallel coordinates. *Journal of the American Statistical Association*, 85(411), 664–675. doi:10.1080/01621459.1990.10474926.

Welch, R. B., & Warren, D. H. (1980). Immediate perceptual response to intersensory discrepancy. *Psychological Bulletin*, 88(3), 638–667. doi:10.1037/0033-2909.88.3.638 PMID:7003641.

Welser, H., Cosley, D., Kossinets, G., & Lin, A. (2011). Finding social roles in wikipedia. In *Proceedings of the 2011 iConference*, 122–129. Seattle, WA: JALT.

Welser, H. T., Gleave, E., Fisher, D., & Smith, M. (2008). Visualizing the signatures of social roles in online discussion groups. Journal of Social Structure, 8.

Whittaker, S. (2012). Socio-technical lifelogging: Deriving design principles for a future proof digital past. *Human-Computer Interaction*, 27, 37–62.

Whorf, B. L. (1940). Science and linguistics. *Technology Review, 42*(6), 229–231, 247–248.

Wilkinson, L. (2005). *The grammar of graphics* (2nd ed.). Berlin: Springer.

Wilkinson, L., Anand, A., & Grossman, R. (2006). High-dimensional visual analytics: Interactive exploration guided by pairwise views of point distributions. *IEEE Transactions on Visualization and Computer Graphics, 12*(6), 1366–1372. doi:10.1109/TVCG.2006.94 PMID:17073361.

Willems, N., Wetering, H. V. D., & Wijk, J. J. V. (2009). Visualization of vessel movements. *Computer Graphics Forum, 28*(3), 959–966. doi:10.1111/j.1467-8659.2009.01440.x.

Willett, W., Heer, J., & Agrawala, M. (2007). Scented widgets: Improving navigation cues with embedded visualizations. *IEEE Transactions on Visualization and Computer Graphics, 13*(6), 1129–1136. doi:10.1109/TVCG.2007.70589 PMID:17968056.

Williamson, C., & Shneiderman, B. (1992). The dynamic homefinder: Evaluating dynamic queries in a real-estate information exploration system. In *Proceedings of ACM SIGIR'92 Conference*, 338-346. Copenhagen, Denmark: ACM Press.

Withings scales. (2012). Retrieved from http://www.withings.com/.

Wittenbrink, C., Pang, A., & Lodha, S. (1996). Glyphs for visualizing uncertainty in vector fields. *IEEE Transactions on Visualization and Computer Graphics, 2*(3), 266–279. doi:10.1109/2945.537309.

Wojtkowski, W., & Wojtkowski, W. G. (2002). Storytelling: Its role in information visualization. In *Proceedings of European Systems Science Congress*. New Brunswick, NJ: IEEE Press.

Wolf, G. (2008). *Genomic openness*. Retrieved from http://quantifiedself.com/2008/01/genomic-openness/.

Wolf, G. (2010). *Ted talk*. Retrieved from http://www.ted.com/talks/gary_wolf_the_quantified_self.html.

Wolfram Demonstrations Project. (n.d.). Retrieved from http://demonstrations.wolfram.com.

Wong, P. C., & Bergeron, R. D. (1997). 30 years of multidimensional multivariate visualization. In Nielson, , Müller, , & Hagen, (Eds.) *Scientific Visualization-Overviews, Methodologies, and Techniques*, (3-33). New Brunswick, NJ: IEEE Computer Society Press.

Wright, A. (2007). *Glut: Mastering information through the ages*. Washington, DC: Joseph Henry P..

Wu, K., & Zhang, S. (2013). A contour tree based visualization for exploring data with uncertainty. *International Journal for Uncertainty Quantification, 3*(3), 203–223. doi:10.1615/Int.J.UncertaintyQuantification.2012003956.

Xie, B., & Pearson, G. (2010). Usability testing by older americans of a prototype google map web site to select nursing homes. In *Proceedings of the 43rd Hawaii International Conference on System Sciences*. Hawaii: IEEE Press.

Xiong, R., & Donath, J. (1999). PeopleGarden: Creating data portraits for users. In *Proceedings of the 12th Annual ACM Symposium on User Interface Software and Technology*, 37–44. Asheville, NC: ACM Press.

Xu, J. J., & Chen, H. (2005). CrimeNet explorer: A framework for criminal network knowledge discovery. *ACM Transactions on Information Systems, 23*(2), 201–226. doi:10.1145/1059981.1059984.

Yahoo. (2012). *Yahoo! inc*. Retrieved from http://www.yahoo.com/.

Yakowenko, J., & Matange, S. (2004). Computer-implemented system and method for handling node-link representations. *U. S. Patent No. 7587409*. Retrieved from http://www.patents.com/us-7587409.html.

Yang, X., Asur, S., Parthasarathy, S., & Mehta, S. (2008). A visual-analytic toolkit for dynamic interaction graphs. In *Proceeding of the 14th ACM SIGKDD International Conference on Knowledge Discovery and Data Mining*. Las Vegas, NV: ACM Press. doi:10.1145/1401890.1402011.

Yannier, N., Basdogan, C., Tasiran, S., & Sen, O. (2008). Using haptics to convey cause-and-effect relations in climate visualization. *IEEE Transaction on Haptics*, *1*(2), 130–141. doi:10.1109/TOH.2008.16.

Yates, I. A. (1966). *The Art of memory*. Chicago: University of Chicago Press.

Yau, N., & Hansen, M. (2010). your.flowingdata: Personal data collection via twitter. In *Proceedings of CHI 2010 Workshop-Know Thyself: Monitoring and Reflecting on Facets of One's Life*. New York: ACM Press.

Yi, J. S., Kang, Y., Stasko, J., & Jacko, J. (2008). Understanding and characterizing insights: How do people gain insights using information visualization? In *Proceedings of ACM BELIV '08*. Florence, Italy: ACM Press.

Yi, J. S., ah Kang, Y, Stasko, J, & Jacko, J. (2007). Toward a deeper understanding of the role of interaction in information visualization. *IEEE Transactions on Visualization and Computer Graphics*, *13*(6), 1224–1231. doi:10.1109/TVCG.2007.70515 PMID:17968068.

Yin, R. K. (2009). Applied social research methods series: *Vol. 5. Case study research: Design and methods* (4th ed.). Thousand Oaks, CA: SAGE.

Young, R. M. (1981). The machine inside the machine: Users' models of pocket calculators. *International Journal of Man-Machine Studies*, *15*(1), 51–85. doi:10.1016/S0020-7373(81)80023-5.

Your.flowingdata . (2012). Retrieved from http://your.flowingdata.com/.

Yu, Y., & Liu, Z. (2010). *Improving the performance and usability for visual menu interface on mobile computers*. In *Proceedings of AVI*. New York: ACM Press.

Zeller, A. (2005). *Why programs fail: A guide to systematic debugging*. Boston: Morgan Kaufmann.

Zeng, T. Q., & Zhou, Q. (2001). Optimal spatial decision-making using GIS: A prototype of a real-estate geographical information system (REGIS). *International Journal of Geographical Information Science*, *15*(4), 307–321. doi:10.1080/136588101300304034.

Zeo . (2012). Retrieved from http://www.myzeo.com/sleep/.

Zhang, J. (2009). UWB systems for wireless sensor networks. *Proceedings of the IEEE*, *97*(2), 313–331. doi:10.1109/JPROC.2008.2008786.

Zhang, Y. (2008). The influence of mental models on undergraduate students' searching behavior on the web. *Information Processing & Management*, *44*(3), 1330–1345. doi:10.1016/j.ipm.2007.09.002.

Zhou, M., & Feiner, S. (1998). IMPROVISE: Automated generation of animated graphics for coordinated multimedia presentations. In *Proceedings of Second International Conference on Cooperative Multimodal Communication*, 43-63. New York: ACM Press.

Zhu, B., & Chen, H. (2008). Communication-garden system: Visualizing a computer-mediated communication process. *Decision Support Systems*, *45*(4), 778–794. doi:10.1016/j.dss.2008.02.004.

Zhu, B., & Chen, H. (2008). *Information visualization for decision making. Handbook on Decision Support Systems*. Heidelber, Germany: Springer-Verlag.

Ziemkiewicz, C., & Kosara, R. (2008). The shaping of information by visual metaphors. *IEEE Transactions on Visualization and Computer Graphics*, *14*(6), 1269–1276. doi:10.1109/TVCG.2008.171 PMID:18988973.

ZigBee Alliance . (2012). Retrieved from http://www.zigbee.org.

Zimmermann, T., & Zeller, A. (2002) Visualizing memory graphs. InDiehl, S (Ed), *Software Visualization* (191-204). New York: Springer. doi:10.1007/3-540-45875-1_15.

Zudilova-Seinstra, E., Adriaansen, T., & Liere, R. v. (2008). *Trends in Interactive visualization: State-of-the-art survey*. New York: Springer Publishing Inc..

Zue, V., & Glass, J. R. (2000a). Conversational interfaces: Advances and challenges. In *Proceedings of the IEEE*, 1166-1180. New Brunswick, NJ: IEEE Press.

Zue, V., Seneff, S., Glass, J. R., Polifroni, J., Pao, C., Hazen, T. J., & Hetherington, L. (2000b). JUPITER: A telephone-based conversational interface for weather information. *IEEE Transactions on Speech and Audio Processing*, *8*(1), 85–96. doi:10.1109/89.817460.

About the Contributors

Mao Lin Huang is Associate Professor and Director of Visualization Lab, at the Faculty of Engineering & IT, University of Technology, Sydney, Australia. His current research interests include information visualization, visual analytics, graph drawing, visual user interface, web navigation, and software engineering; and he has published over 120 papers in these areas.

Weidong Huang is a researcher with CSIRO, Australia. His research interests include HCI, CSCW, Human Factors, and Visualization. He has published a number of papers in these areas.

* * *

Olga Buchel has a Ph.D. in Library and Information Science from the Faculty of Information and Media Studies. Currently she works as a lecturer at Western University. Her research centers on map-based visualizations of document collections and the ways these visualizations can support higher-order cognitive activities such as decision making, sensemaking, visual analytics, knowledge discovery, and serendipitous discoveries. In the past she worked at the Alexandria Digital Library at the University of California which was the forerunner of Google Maps.

Luis Carli is a postgraduate researcher at the University of São Paulo, his research is about how programming helps in the graphic design process of information visualization. He was a visiting researcher in the Interface Culture department of the Kunstuniversität of Linz in 2011, he has presented works on the International Architecture Biennial of São Paulo in 2009, and on the International Festival of Electronic Language (FILE) in 2009, 2010, and 2011. In his current research study, he focuses on how programming helps develop and prototype graphic design structures for information visualization.

Marco Carnesecchi graduated in Human Computer Interaction in a joint programme between the University of Siena and Florence in May 2012. His thesis regarded the bridge between Information Visualization and studies on Thinking & Reasoning. During his Ph.D. he has been involved in several projects of Interaction Design supported by companies and public institutions regarding the design of user interfaces. He is currently Research Assistant at the University of Valle d'Aosta and he is part of the organizing committee of the Annual Conference of the Italian Cognitive Science association. His research interest concerns also assistive technologies, and studies related to play as a learning tool for children with disabilities.

Barbara Di Eugenio is Associate Professor in the Department of Computer Science at the University of Illinois, Chicago campus. There she leads the NLP laboratory (http://nlp.cs.uic.edu/). She obtained her PhD in Computer Science in 1993, from the University of Pennsylvania. She is an NSF CAREER awardee and a past treasurer of the North American Chapter of the Association for Computational Linguistics. She is one of the founding and managing editors of the Journal of Discourse and Dialogue Research. She was program co-chair of INLG 2012, and she is program-co-chair of SigDIAL 2013. Her research has been supported by NSF, ONR, Motorola, Yahoo!, and the Qatar Research Foundation.

Pat Fitzpatrick is an associate research professor at the Geosystems Research Institute (GRI) at Mississippi State University (MSU). Research activities involve hurricane research; data assimilation; numerical modeling; weather forecasting; storm surge; and wetland research. Prior to GRI, he was an assistant professor of meteorology at Jackson State University. Fitzpatrick earned a B.S. in meteorology at Texas A&M University in 1988, followed by a M.S. in 1992 with a thesis on numerical modeling of hurricane genesis. His doctorate work was performed at Colorado State University from 1992-1995 under Dr. Bill Gray, with a dissertation on satellite applications to predicting hurricane intensity.

Celmar Guimarães da Silva completed his Doctoral degree in Computer Sciences in 2006, at the Institute of Computing, University of Campinas (Unicamp). He is a faculty member with the School of Technology, also at the University of Campinas, since 2008. He coordinates the Technologist Degree in System Analysis and Development course in this university since 2011. His research interest is related to the Information Visualization area. He is a member of the Brazilian Computer Society.

Cathal Gurrin is the SFI Stokes lecturer at the School of Computing at Dublin City University, Ireland and a visiting researcher at the University of Tromso, Norway. Cathal is the director of the Human Media Archives research group at Dublin City University and a collaborating investigator in the CLARITY Centre for Sensor Web Technologies. His research interests focus on Information Access to Personal Life Archives, Multimodal Human Computer Interaction, and Information Retrieval in general. He has been an active lifelogger since mid-2006 and has amassed a large archive of over ten million Sensecam images and is actively developing search and organization technologies for Personal Life Archives. He is the author of more than 100 academic publications and is an experienced researcher in the field of Lifelogging.

Helena Haapio (LL.M, MQ) is a doctoral researcher at the University of Vaasa, Department of Business Law and Economics, where she teaches strategic business law. She works as contract coach with Lexpert Ltd, Helsinki, Finland, helping companies use contracts proactively to achieve better business results and prevent problems. Before founding Lexpert she served several years as in-house legal counsel. She also works as arbitrator. Helena is a long-time pioneer of research and education crossing the boundaries of traditional law. Her recent publications include *A Short Guide to Contract Risk* (Gower, 2013) and *Proactive Law for Managers: A Hidden Source of Competitive Advantage* (Gower 2011), co-authored with Professor George J. Siedel. For Helena, contracts are too important to be left to the lawyers alone. Through visualization, she seeks to revolutionize the way contracts are designed, communicated, and perceived.

T. J. Jankun-Kelly is an Associate Professor of computer science and engineering within the James Worth Bagley College of Engineering, Mississippi State University. His research lies at the intersection of scientific and information visualization. Specifically, he seeks to better understand the foundations of these disciplines to increase their effectiveness. He also applies visualization to problems in bioinformatics, computer security, social networks, and other domains. Jankun-Kelly received his Ph.D. from the University of California, Davis, in 2003 and is a member of IEEE and the ACM.

Heekyoung Jung is an Assistant Professor in the School of Design at University of Cincinnati. She holds her PhD in Informatics from Indiana University with her BS and MS degrees in Industrial Design from Korean Advanced Institute of Science and Technology (KAIST). She specializes in Human-Computer Interaction (HCI) that involves both user research and design of interactive information applications. She has worked on many research and consulting projects on information organization, representation, and navigation with focus on usability and aesthetics of user interface. Currently she teaches interaction design studio courses with focus on scenario-based design, rapid prototyping, and interface design for various screen-based digital media (i.e., laptop, tablet, mobile devices). Her recent research area is data visualization that supports exploratory navigation of a large amount of data in simple and engaging visual forms.

Tanyoung Kim is a Ph.D. Candidate in Digital Media Program at School of Literature, Media, and Communication, at Georgia Institute of Technology. Her research interest in the domain of digital media studies is the aesthetics and social/political impacts of information visualization. She approaches this interest with the methods from design research, for which her explores modern graphic design history and principles, rhetoric, and new media theories. She is also an active practitioner who makes interactive visualizations with various data. She has worked at Nokia Research Center and NHN corporation where she lead and participated in various projects spanning data visualization, user research, interaction design, information architect for web, application and online games. She holds BS and MS in Industrial Design from KAIST, Korea.

Nikos Koutsopoulos holds an MSc from the Department of Computer Science, University of Crete (2011), and is currently a PhD student. His research interests fall in the domain of programmer-centric interactive visualization and process improvement tools.

Andrew Johnson received his Ph.D. in Computer Science from Wayne State University, Detroit, MI, in 1994. He joined the Electronic Visualization Laboratory at the University of Illinois at Chicago in 1995, and joined the Department of Computer Science in 1997 where he is currently an Associate Professor. His research and teaching focus on interaction and collaboration using advanced visualization displays and the application of those displays to enhance discovery and learning. His work focused on projection¨Cbased virtual reality displays in the 1990s, and large tiled high-resolution flat panel displays in the 2000s. His current work focuses on the combination of these modalities in hybrid high-resolution virtual reality environments such as cave 2.

Wei Lai received his PhD from the University of Newcastle Australia. He is now a senior lecturer in Faculty of Information and Communication Technologies, Swinburne University of Technology, Australia. His research interests are information visualization, diagram layout, image processing, and pattern recognition.

Jason Leigh is a Professor of Computer Science and Director of the Electronic Visualization Laboratory and the Software Technologies Research Center at the University of Illinois at Chicago. Currently he is also a Fellow of the Institute for Health Research and Policy. Prior projects and research for which he is best known include, the OptIPuter, GeoWall, CoreWall, LambdaVision, Tele-Immersion, and Reliable Blast UDP. His research for the past ten years focused on Cyber-Commons-ultra-resolution display-rich collaboration environments amplified by high performance computing and networking. His newest area of research is called Human Augmentics-technologies for expanding the capabilities and characteristics of humans. His work in lifelike avatars has been featured on the Popular Science's Future Of, and he has been profiled on Nova ScienceNow. Leigh also teaches classes in Software Design and Video Game Design.

David Lewis gained his B.Sc. in Electronic Engineering from the University of Southampton in 1987, before working as a electronic design engineer for two years and then undertaking a M.Sc. in Computer Science at University College London (UCL). He worked as a research fellow at UCL between 1990 and 2002, investigating integrated, multi-domain network and service management. In this period he also completed a Ph.D. and worked part time for a network management technology start up. In 2002 he moved to the Knowledge and Data Engineering Group (KDEG) in TCD working in management of pervasive computing systems, knowledge-based networking and autonomic communication systems. He is currently involved in the *Centre for Next Generation Localisation* (CNGL) researching service integration and service management in integration of language technologies, web content and localisation workflows, with a focus on the role of community management. He is currently co-chair of the MultiLingualWeb-Language Technology Working Group at the W3C.

Jie Liang is a PhD candidate of software engineering at the University of Technology Sydney, Australia. She was awarded a university medal with first class honors. Her research focuses on financial data visualization, hierarchical information visualization and evaluation of visual analytics.

Alessandro Marcengo has a bachelor's degree in Psychology (with a major in Human Factors from the University of Torino, Italy, 1998). In 2001 he received his Master's Degree in Cognitive Ergonomics from COREP/Turin Polytechnic. Since 1999 he has worked on human factors and cognitive ergonomics area. Over the years he developed an extensive background on user experience designing and testing advanced user interfaces for mobile services and devices, Internet services and applications, Internet appliances, voice interaction services, etc. Lately he has been conducting in-depth studies on the usage of complex contents on different platforms and devices and the related communication pattern. He teaches several postgraduate courses on human factors and cognitive ergonomics. He has been involved with different roles in several EU projects. At present he's deepening perceptive, cognitive, and affective aspects in data visualization and quantified self.

Bob-Antoine Jerry Menelas is an assistant professor of Computer Science, at University of Quebec at Chicoutimi, Canada. He holds a M. Sc. (2006) from University of Angers, France and a Ph.D. (2010) from University of Paris Sud XI, France in computer science. Before joining University of Quebec at Chicoutimi in 2011, Menelas was a postdoctoral fellow at University of Calgary, Canada. His research interests include Virtual Reality, Haptics, visualization and serious games.

John McAuley is a PhD Student in the Centre for Next Generation Localisation at Trinity College Dublin. Before joining Trinity College, he received his master's degree from Dublin Institute Technology. He is currently completing his PhD thesis on the strategic management of peer-production communities. Although his main research area is on the development and maintenance of online communities, he maintains a keen interest on the effective design of visual analytic applications that can be used by non-expert users in domain specific areas. This incorporates an understanding of the principles of design and interaction coupled with an understanding of the principles of effective information visualisation.

Alexander O'Connor is a Post-doctoral Researcher in Digital Content Management for the Centre for Next Generation Localisation at Trinity College, Dublin. Alex's main areas of research are in the future of the Semantic Web, Personalisation and Global Intelligent Content. Alex holds a PhD in Computer Science, which focused on creating richer, more effective links between structured knowledge representations. He has co-authored approximately 20 papers, and has participated in the proposal and operation of several EU and Irish-government-funded projects. In addition to his research work, Alex is a co-founder of Emizar, a CNGL spin-out company which creates high-quality tailored, personalised customer support solutions that draw from enterprise, social and community support content.

Stefania Passera (MA) is a doctoral researcher at Aalto University School of Science, Department of Industrial Engineering and Management, where she is part of the multidisciplinary MIND Research Group. She has a background in graphic design, with a strong interest in information design, layout and typography. The leitmotiv of her work is to explore how design and designers can contribute to new multidisciplinary endeavors and what value their way of thinking and doing bring to the mix. Her current challenge and research topic is how to introduce visualization to a very word-dominated domain: contracts. The idea is to make contracts clearer, easier and user-friendlier through visualization that can help the readers make sense of complex information. Stefania has been working with private and public organizations in Finland on the development of user-centered visual contract documents, combining research and practice.

Amon Rapp earned a degree in Communication Sciences from the University of Torino, Italy. Since 2006 he's been working in the Research and Trends department in Telecom Italia as a User Experience Researcher. In 2007 and 2009 he won a research scholarship "Progetto Lagrange" in HCI Complex Systems sponsored by Telecom Italia, the Department of Computer Science at University of Torino and Fondazione C.R.T. At present he works as a User Experience Researcher in the Interdepartmental Research Center on Multimedia and Audiovisual of the University of Torino. He's also attending a PhD Program in Sciences of Language and Communication at the Computer Science Department at University of Torino. His main research areas are about the use of game design elements in Interactive Systems, User Experience Research Methodologies and Systems of Data Visualization.

Maria Riveiro is a Senior Lecturer of Computer Science at the Informatics Research Centre at University of Skövde, Sweden. Riveiro holds a M.Sc. in Telecommunication Engineering and a PhD in Computer Science from Örebro University, Sweden. Since 2005, she has been a member of the Skövde Artificial Intelligence Lab and the Information Fusion Research Program at the University of Skövde. Her research has spanned a range of topics including data mining, artificial intelligence, information visualization, visual analytics, information fusion and uncertainty management. Riveiro's current work focuses on finding optimal combinations of data mining and interactive visualization for the analysis of large data sets with uncertainty associated.

Antonio Rizzo is Full Professor of Cognitive Science and Technology at the University of Siena (2001-present). He was Director of the Academy of Digital Arts and Science–ArsNova in Siena (2004-2010) and chair of the European Association of Cognitive Ergonomics (2000-2006). From 1996 to 1999 he led the Human Factors Division of the Italian Railways constituted for introducing Human Factor Engineering principles in work processes. Research activities concern both theoretical and pragmatical aspects of artefacts in human psychological life.

J. Alfredo Sanchez is a professor at Universidad de las Americas Puebla (UDLAP), where he leads the Laboratory of Interactive and Cooperative Technologies (ICT, http://ict.udlap.mx). He earned MSc and PhD degrees in computer science at Texas A & M University, and a BEng degree in Computer Systems at UDLAP. His research and teaching interests lie in the areas of Human-Computer Interaction (HCI), Digital Libraries (DLs) and Knowledge Technologies. He has been visiting professor at the University of Waikato (New Zealand), and visiting scholar at the Center for Bioinformatics of the Missouri Botanical Garden. He has coordinated the Mexican Internet 2 communities on DLs and HCI and has been President of the Mexican Computer Science Society. He is a co-founder of the Mexican Association of Human-Computer Interaction (AMexIHC) and coordinator of the Human-Computer Interaction Research Line of the Thematic Network of Information and Communication Technologies (RedTIC) of CONACYT.

Anthony Savidis holds a Phd in Electronic Engineering from the University of Kent, UK (1999) is an Associate Professor (since 2007) of the Department of Computer Science, University of Crete and is an affiliated researcher at the Institute of Computer Science, FORTH (since 1999). His research interests are in the broader area of Programming Languages, Software Engineering and Applications: 1.) integrated design and implementation of novel programming languages: language, compiler, virtual machine, standard libraries, tools, debugger, integrated development environment; and 2.) software engineering methods, tools and applications: adaptive, automatically generated and distributed interactive systems; design tools and environments; defensive programming and fault tolerance.

Kamran Sedig is an Associate Professor in the Department of Computer Science and the Faculty of Information and Media Studies at Western University, Canada. He holds a Ph.D. in Computer Science from the University of British Columbia. He has been doing research in the area of human-centered interactive visualizations since 1993. He is interested in the design of computer-based computational tools that help people perform information-intensive complex cognitive activities, such as sense making, decision making, data analysis, and learning. As such, his research and publications span a range of topics such as information visualization, visual analytics, human-information interaction design, information interface design, health informatics, digital cognitive games, and cognitive and learning technologies. In the past few years, he has been working on the development of comprehensive frameworks that make the design and evaluation of visualizations and interactions more scientific.

Chad A. Steed is a Visual Analytics Researcher in the Computational Data Analytics Group at the Oak Ridge National Laboratory (ORNL). He holds a Ph.D. (2008) degree in computer science from Mississippi State University, where he studied visualization and computer graphics. Steed's research has spanned a range of topics including visual analytics, scientific and information visualization, data mining, intelligent user interfaces, database design, geoscientific data processing, and web application development. His current focus is on the formulation and practical application of unique visual analytics techniques that combine inferential, automated analytics with interactive visualizations to enhance cognition and decision support for extreme scale data set analysis.

Yiwen Sun received her Ph.D. in computer science from the University of Illinois at Chicago in 2012, where she conducted research on interactive visualization and visual analytics. More specifically, her Ph.D. focused on developing a methodology for automatically translating natural language into visualizations. She currently works at Microsoft Corporation.

J. Edward Swan II is a Professor of Computer Science and Engineering and an Adjunct Professor of Psychology, at Mississippi State University. He holds a B.S. (1988) degree in computer science from Auburn University and M.S. (1992) and Ph.D. (1997) degrees in computer science from Ohio State University, where he studied computer graphics and human-computer interaction. Before joining Mississippi State University in 2004, Swan spent seven years as a scientist at the Naval Research Laboratory in Washington, D.C. Currently, Swan is studying perception in augmented and virtual reality, including depth and layout perception and depth presentation methods, as well as empirical techniques for evaluating and validating visualizations. His research has been funded by the National Science Foundation, the National Aeronautics and Space Administration, the Naval Research Laboratory, and the Office of Naval Research. Swan is a member of ACM, IEEE, the IEEE Computer Society, and ASEE.

Masahiro Takatsuka is an Associate Professor at the School of InformationTechnologies, the University of Sydney, where he chairs the Research Committee and heads the ViSLAB (Visualization Research Group). His current research interests include the use of manifold surfaces to multidimensional scaling and Information Visualization, Advanced Collaboration Technologies, in particular, the use of Service Oriented Remote Collaboration, and Network Centric Computer Graphics. Takatsuka obtained his Ph.D. in Electrical and Computer Engineering from the Monash University. He is a Member of the IEEE and ACM.

Keqin Wu is a postdoctoral associate in the Department of Computer Science and Electrical Engineering, University of Maryland Baltimore County. She received the B.E. and M.E. degrees in computer engineering from the Ocean University of China in 2001 and 2004, and the Ph.D. degree in computer engineering from Mississippi State University in 2012. Her research interest includes scientific visualization, medical imaging, and user interface. She is a member of IEEE.

Yang Yang is a postgraduate researcher at Human Media Archives research group, Dublin City University. She worked on a wide range of projects including multimedia information retrieval, digital libraries, natural language processing, web search engine, adaptive computer interfaces, etc., and creates novel application scenarios and interaction concepts. Her current main area of interest is on information visualization for large-scale collection of personal lifelogging archives using human centered design approach. In her research study, she aims to create effective visualization and interaction strategy that allows users' browsing and searching on large amount of lifelogs for self-knowledge discovery through various emerging wearable sensor technologies.

Moonyati Yatid received a degree in Design and Information Sciences Engineering from Wakayama University, Japan in 2009. In the same year she began her Ph.D. studies majoring in Human-Computer Interactions in University of Sydney, Australia. Her research focuses on the areas of human factors and cognitive ergonomics related to collaboration technologies. This includes the design and evaluations of hardware and software tools to support better user experience (UX).

Liese Zahabi is an Assistant Professor of Visual Communication at Weber State University in Ogden, Utah. She received her Master of Graphic Design from North Carolina State University in 2010, and has worked as a graphic and interactive designer for over ten years. Her research interests focus on HCI and cognition, information-triage and online search, and metaphor.

Song Zhang is an Associate Professor of Computer Science and Engineering at Mississippi State University. He received the B.S. degree in computer science from Nankai University, China, in 1996, and the Ph.D. degree in computer science from Brown University in 2006. His research interests include scientific visualization, medical imaging, and computer graphics. He is a member of IEEE.

Angela M. Zoss joined Duke University in 2012 as Data Visualization Coordinator. She is a doctoral candidate at the Indiana University School of Library and Information Science, where she also worked as an Adjunct Instructor and a Research Assistant in the Cyberinfrastructure for Network Science Center, directed by Dr. Katy Börner. She holds a B.A. in Cognitive Science and Communication & Culture from Indiana University and a M.S. in Communication from Cornell University. Her research focuses on scientometric descriptions and evaluations of scholarly communication and the use of knowledge domain visualizations for navigation and information-seeking tasks. Additional research interests include visual literacy and differences in interpretation strategies across academic disciplines.

Index